HEALTH CARE
& THE LAW

HEAD OFFICE: 100 Harris Street PYRMONT NSW 2009
Tel: (02) 8587 7000 Fax: (02) 8587 7100
For all sales inquiries please ring 1800 650 522
(for calls within Australia only)

INTERNATIONAL AGENTS & DISTRIBUTORS

NORTH, CENTRAL & SOUTH AMERICA,
CARIBBEAN
Carswell Co
Ontario, Canada

HONG KONG
Sweet & Maxwell Asia
Hysan Avenue, Causeway Bay
Hong Kong

MALAYSIA
Sweet & Maxwell Asia
Petaling Jaya, Selangor

NEW ZEALAND, PACIFIC ISLANDS
Brooker's Ltd
Wellington

SINGAPORE
Sweet & Maxwell Asia
Battery Road

EUROPE, MIDDLE EAST AND AFRICA
ISM Europe, Middle East & Africa
Sweet & Maxwell Ltd
Andover, Hampshire

AUSTRALIA, PAPUA NEW GUINEA
Thomson Legal & Regulatory Ltd
Pyrmont, Sydney

JAPAN, KOREA, TAIWAN
ISM Asia Operations
Thomson Legal & Regulatory
Pyrmont, Sydney

Health Care & the Law

Fourth Edition

Janine McIlwraith
BMed RadSci (R/T), LLB (Hons), GDLP, LLM (Syd)

Bill Madden
BA LLB (Hons) (Macq); Accredited Specialist (Personal Injury)(NSW)

Lawbook Co. 2006

Published in Sydney by

Lawbook Co.
  100 Harris Street, Pyrmont, NSW

First edition (M Wallace) 1991
Second edition (M Wallace)...1995
Third edition (M Wallace) 2001
National Library of Australia
  Cataloguing-in-Publication entry

McIlwraith, Janine F. (Janine Flora), 1972- .
  Health care and the law.

    4th ed.
    Includes index.
    ISBN 0 455 22261 4 (pbk).

    1. Malpractice - Australia. 2. Medical care - Law and
    legislation - Australia. 3. Medical personnel -
    Malpractice - Australia. I. Madden, William J. (William James), 1957- .
    II. Title.

    344.94041

This edition is up to date as of June 2006.

Editor: Lara Weeks

Typeset in Rotis Semi Sans, 10 on 12 point, by Midland Typesetters, Australia

Printed by Ligare Pty Ltd, Riverwood, NSW

Foreword

Sir Laurence Street AC, KCMG, QC
Former Chief Justice of New South Wales

As our political leaders across Australia are constantly reminded by the media, the public expects—indeed demands—high quality, accessible health care. We are wonderfully well served by the dedication, commitment and skills of our health professionals—the fine body of women and men who fill the myriad roles across the spectrum from ambulance teams through hands-on practitioners (doctors, nurses and others) on to research scientists of world renown. But they do not function in a vacuum; they are bonded together within an administrative and legal environment in which standards of their profession are prescribed and where necessary enforced.

It is in this socio-legal context that our health system functions. And, if the system is to achieve maximum quality, our society—both providers and users of health services as well as administrators and legal advisers—needs to have, or at least to have access to, authoritative guidance on the textured relationship between health care and the law. This is the province addressed by the author of the first three editions of this work and by the authors of this Fourth Edition. It is a kaleidoscopic dynamic province, presenting to an author an almost unachievable task of analyzing and of marshalling a mass of material, medical and legal, into a single volume that is both comprehensive and user-friendly. But achieve it they have.

The conceptual scope of the book is at the same time all-embracing and capable of meaningful refinement to single topics and specific instances. The authors have brought to bear wisdom derived from many years professional experience across the multiple facets of the Health Care system. The result is a lucid, authoritative treatise that is both practically oriented and reader friendly.

This book will have a place on the shelves of teachers and students both in law and in health as well as on the shelves of practitioners and administrators.

I salute the authors for this valuable addition to the literature of *Health Care and the Law*.

8 August 2006

Preface

Health care is fundamentally about birth, life and death. Perhaps, therefore, we should not be surprised at the seemingly endless stream of ethical and legal issues it generates, challenging the minds of health carers, lawyers and governments in Australia and across the world.

The first edition of *Health Care and the Law* was written by Meg Wallace in 1991, with her second and third editions following in relatively quick succession.

This fourth edition has been extensively re-written to bring the law up to date as at May 2006. Changes in the five years since the third edition have been many, including those flowing from:

- the *Review of the Law of Negligence* and consequent civil liability legislation;
- the Commonwealth, State and Territory privacy regimes;
- further developments in case law on end-of-life decision-making; and
- the Australian Government *WorkChoices* legislation.

Whilst the law stated has become distinctively Australian, the issues are not.

The authors are indebted to Mark, Elizabeth and Ben for their patience and support during the writing process, to Ms Wallace for her earlier work and to Peter Berman SC DCJ (NSW), Tina Cockburn, Phillip Gleeson, Judy Gray, Phillip Pasfield and Dr Alison Radvan for their generous and helpful assistance in the preparation of this book.

The authors also express their gratitude to the editor of this text Lara Weeks; for her helpful suggestions, care and patience.

Referred to at the end of each chapter are a number of books and articles which have been of great assistance to us, and are suggested as further reading. While every care has been taken to establish and acknowledge copyright, the authors offer their apologies for any accidental infringement.

Any errors are of course the authors, and leaving those aside, we can adopt the adage *"the only constant in life is change"*. That certainly applies to the law regarding health care and enhances this area of study; but accordingly some of what we have written today will have inevitably developed further tomorrow, as it should.

JANINE MCILWRAITH
BILL MADDEN

August 2006

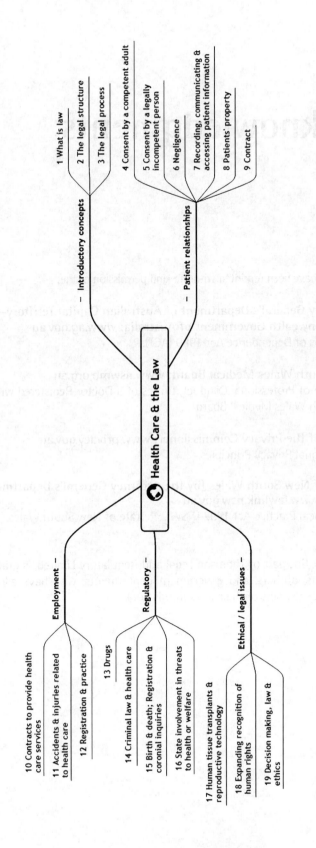

Health Care & the Law

Introductory concepts
1 What is law
2 The legal structure
3 The legal process

Patient relationships
4 Consent by a competent adult
5 Consent by a legally incompetent person
6 Negligence
7 Recording, communicating & accessing patient information
8 Patients' property
9 Contract

Employment
10 Contracts to provide health care services
11 Accidents & injuries related to health care
12 Registration & practice
13 Drugs

Regulatory
14 Criminal law & health care
15 Birth & death; Registration & coronial inquiries
16 State involvement in threats to health or welfare

Ethical / legal issues
17 Human tissue transplants & reproductive technology
18 Expanding recognition of human rights
19 Decision making, law & ethics

Acknowledgments

Extracts have been reprinted with the kind permission of the: -

**Attorney General's Department of Australian Capital Territory—
Commonwealth Government of Australia: www.ag.gov.au**
- Drugs of Dependence Act 1989 (ACT).

New South Wales Medical Board: www.nswmb.org.au
- Code of Professional Conduct: Duties of a Doctor Registered with the New South Wales Medical Board

Office of the Privacy Commissioner: www.privacy.gov.au
- National Privacy Principles.

State of New South Wales (by the Attorney General's Department of NSW): www.lawlink.nsw.gov.au
- Medical Practice Act 1992 (NSW). © State of New South Wales.

Lawbook Co., part of Thomson Legal and Regulatory Limited, is grateful to the publishers, authors, and government departments, who have allowed us to reproduce extracts of their work in this book.

Table of Contents

Part 1: Introductory Concepts

Part II: Patient Relationships

Part III: Employment

Part IV: Regulatory

Part V: Ethical/Legal Issues

Appendices

Table of Cases

Table of Statutes

AUSTRALIAN CAPITAL TERRITORY

QUEENSLAND

TASMANIA

VICTORIA

WESTERN AUSTRALIA

I

Introductory Concepts

1

1 What is Law

- Introduction

- Understanding Law

- Legal systems

- Sources of Australian Law

- Basic Principles

chapter 1

What is Law?

Introduction

[1.05] People obey ethical and moral rules because these are based on what ought to be done according to accepted social and cultural values, and a person's own conscience. Breaking these rules invites a feeling of guilt, shame or embarrassment, and the disapproval of others. People also obey the demands of the law because a breach of the law invites more tangible consequences, such as imprisonment or a court order to pay compensation or to carry out some act.

Law is the embodiment of what is considered desirable for social good, in the form of enforceable rules. Rules may be desirable because they are considered the morally or socially "right" thing to do, or best for the good government of the country, or simply a means of benefiting some members of society. Although all laws may be considered to be ethically based (this is sometimes debatable), not all ethical principles are covered by the law; for example, people may feel morally obliged to help someone they come across in the street who is injured, but they are rarely required by law to do so (see Chapter 6). There may be conflict between the law and actions which some believe to be morally acceptable, for example, the law allowing abortion in certain circumstances, the prohibition on euthanasia and the use of certain drugs, and the law's limited regulation of some newer technologies such as in vitro fertilisation.

There are many ways in which the law affects health carers, either by creating obligations or by conferring rights. Some examples follow, but the list is not exhaustive:

Table 1.1: Some ways in which health carers can be found responsible at law

Category	Examples
negligence	• failing to provide adequate information for a patient's informed consent (Chapter 4) • failing to adequately monitor a patient and respond accordingly (Chapter 6) • giving a patient the wrong drug (Chapter 6)
assault/battery	• giving care without consent • threatening a patient • forcing a patient to ambulate without her or his consent • restraining a patient for convenience of staff (Chapter 4)
defamation	• telling others harmful details about a patient (Chapter 7)
crime	• wrongly handling drugs • falsifying documents • unlawfully causing death (Chapter 14)
other offences	• failure to report child abuse (in some jurisdictions) • failure to report infectious disease (Chapter 16) • unauthorised collection, use or disclosure of a patient's health or personal information (Chapter 7)
other liability	• mishandling of patients' property (Chapter 8) • failure to carry out an employer's instructions (Chapter 10) • failure to obtain registration (Chapter 12) • discrimination against patients in some cases (Chapter 18)

Table 1.2: Some rights conferred on health carers by law

Right	Chapter where discussed
to question an employer's instructions	10
to receive compensation for work-related accidents	11
to a fair hearing before any adverse action is taken	1, 10, 14
not to be discriminated against on the grounds of race or sex (and other grounds in some jurisdictions)	18

Understanding Law

[1.10] Law can be studied at two levels. It can be seen in its broadest sense, as a means of creating some order in our society by the evolution of rules, mores and customs. The study at this level considers the nature of society, of "right", "justice", and "common good". This study, involving philosophical and sociological perceptions, is called *jurisprudence*. The other level of study is that in which lawyers are mainly involved and is the dominant concern of this book: the actual content of our laws (*substantive law*), and the mechanics of making and enforcing them (*procedural law*) (see below [1.15], Figure 1.1).

Classifications of law

[1.15] There are two main branches of law and there are sub-categories under each of those branches. The first branch is substantive law, or that part of the law which tells us what we can do, must do, or must not do, as well as the interpretation of the law, setting out rights and obligations, etc. Substantive law is divided into two sub-branches: civil law and criminal law. Civil law in turn has many sub-branches such as constitutional law, commercial law, contract law, bankruptcy law, administrative law and family law. The second branch is procedural law. This tells us how to go about putting the law into action. It includes such sub-branches as the law of evidence and court rules.

Figure 1.1: Classification of law

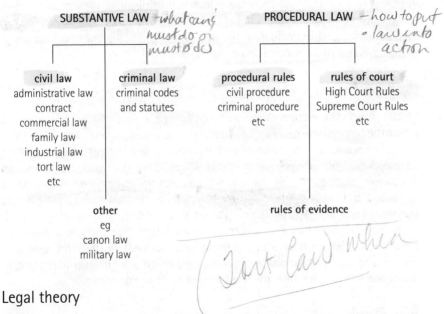

SUBSTANTIVE LAW		PROCEDURAL LAW	
civil law	criminal law	procedural rules	rules of court
administrative law	criminal codes	civil procedure	High Court Rules
contract	and statutes	criminal procedure	Supreme Court Rules
commercial law		etc	etc
family law			
industrial law			
tort law			
etc			

other
eg
canon law
military law

rules of evidence

Legal theory

[1.20] Straddling these two levels of study is an approach to understanding law which considers both the content and process of law in our society. It studies the effects of laws and their ability to fulfil the purposes and goals for which they were created. For example, one might consider what is the purpose of laws prohibiting the use of certain drugs, and is it effective? Could it be improved? Are the stated aims realistic, appropriate, acceptable and worthwhile? Versions of this approach to law have been variously called "critical legal theory", the "realist school of legal theory", or "sociological legal theory".

Legal Systems

[1.23] Throughout the world there are several broad categories of legal systems. Some of the main ones are briefly listed below.

Common law

[1.25] This originated and developed in England. It was created by elevating laws common to the many communal systems operating throughout the country to a national level. The system was extended to the various colonies and is therefore the basis of the Australian, New Zealand, United States and Canadian legal systems, among others. It is explained more fully below (see [1.75]). The term "common law" is now more commonly used to differentiate:

- judge-made law from statutory law (see [1.50]); and
- common law from equity (see [1.80]).

It is thus important to determine the context in which the term is used.

The common law system is based on the adversarial approach to resolving disputes. This means that the parties involved in disputes present their cases and argue the merits before a judge and/or jury. The judge and/or jury do not take an active part in instigating the acquisition of knowledge about the case, or determining what information is put before them.

Civil law

[1.30] This is the system of law in those European countries which inherited either the French or Roman cultural influence. It is based mainly on a code (that is, the law is almost entirely enshrined in statutes), and the approach to dispute resolution is inquisitorial rather than adversarial. The judiciary takes the initiative in seeking the facts and is not confined to dealing only with what is put before it. The judge's role is investigatory (the role assigned in our common law system to lawyers and police (Easton et al (1985))—the lawyers for each party play the role of an assistant to the judge rather than the role of advocate for the party, which they adopt in the adversarial system. The term "civil law" may also be used in Australia to differentiate a civil matter from criminal one, so again, the context in which the term is used must be considered.

Other systems

[1.35] Other systems of law include socialist law, Islamic law, and Asian legal systems.

Customary law

[1.40] Customary law, as its name implies, is a system of rules generated by the customs of a society. They have not been established by governmental processes similar to those recognised today as law-making. Two forms of customary law that affect the Australian legal system are international customary law and Indigenous (that is, Aboriginal and Torres Strait Islander) customary law. The former affects our international relationships and will not be discussed here. Indigenous customary law is discussed at [1.100] below.

Sources of Australian Law

[1.45] Australian law is, as mentioned, based on the common law system. An understanding of our law is probably best gained by considering the nature and development of our sources of law.

There are three main sources of law in Australia: legislation, judge-made law and indigenous customary law.

Laws made by a recognised authority—legislation

[1.50] These are documents setting out obligations and rights, penalties and procedures. The bodies which make these laws are the federal Parliament, and the Parliaments of the States, the Australian Capital Territory, the Northern Territory and Norfolk Island. These bodies pass laws in the form of *statutes* (otherwise called Acts of Parliament) which are then binding on all citizens, or on a particular class of citizens nominated in the legislation. Copies of all legislation can be purchased from the relevant government publisher, and most can also be accessed online at www.comlaw.gov.au.

Statutes can delegate the right to make further, more detailed legislation to other designated bodies or people (for example, a Minister of a government or a statutory body). Such legislation is in the form of rules and regulations, and is referred to as *delegated legislation*.

Statutes (made by Parliament) and rules and regulations (made by Parliament or a designated person or body) can all be equally binding on people. However, if rules or regulations have provisions which contradict provisions of a statute in the same State or Territory, the provisions of the rules or regulations are invalid insofar as they contradict the statute. If State legislation contradicts federal legislation, then the federal legislation prevails (see **[1.55]**).

Figure 1.2: Inter-relationship of different levels of legislation

Federal Parliament
makes

↓

LEGISLATION
which can allow for

↓

DELEGATED LEGISLATION
(regulations, rules)
which override

↓

State legislation
on the same subject
which may allow for

↓

STATE DELEGATED LEGISLATION
(regulations, rules)

Because Australia was originally a colony of Britain, all laws in force in England applied in the Australian colonies so far as was practicable, with pronouncements by the colonial governors on the advice of the Legislative Council in England on matters of doubt. Interestingly though, some aspects of the common law were applied differently by courts in Australia than those in Britain, such as laws restricting the rights of convicted persons. All legislation which applied in Australia was first enacted in the British Parliament.

Self-governing colonies, such as New South Wales, Queensland, South Australia, Tasmania, Victoria and Western Australia (although not necessarily as we know them today) were later established. The first Legislative Council was created under the *New South Wales Act*, a statute of the British Parliament, in 1823. This Act also established the Supreme Court of New South Wales. As Spigelman CJ pointed out in a speech given in 1999 to mark the 175th anniversary of the New South Wales Supreme Court, few nations have such established judicial institutions as this. In 1865 the *Colonial Laws Validity Act* was passed by the British Parliament giving the colonies power to make their own laws for their "peace, order and good government", while reserving some powers for the Imperial Parliament of England.

The *Commonwealth of Australia Constitution Act 1901* (Imp) was enacted by the British Parliament in 1901. Section 9 of that Act states "The Constitution of the Commonwealth shall be as follows" and thereafter sets out the provisions forming Australia's Constitution. When we refer to the Constitution, it is to s 9 of the Act that we refer to. The Constitution as we know it today remains largely unchanged from that which was enacted in 1901, although minor amendments have been made on eight occasions since then. The Constitution provided for Federation the same year, established a federal Parliament, and defined the legal relationship between the federal government and the States. Under the Constitution, the English monarch remained the head of state of Australia, represented here by the Governor-General, a situation that continues today.

The Constitution provided the federal and State Parliaments the power to legislate for their respective areas. However, the Constitution differentiates between matters on which the federal government can legislate (for example, regulation of currency, overseas trade, family law) and matters on which State Parliaments can legislate (for example, education, roads, criminal law). This division of legislative power was based upon the belief that the Commonwealth could better manage matters where a common policy and practice was desirable throughout the country.

The Australian Constitution

[1.55] The State governments' powers to make whatever laws are deemed fit is limited only by the narrowly defined powers of the federal government as set out in the Constitution. Section 107 of the Constitution provides that every power the State governments had prior to Federation was to remain vested in them unless "it is by this Constitution exclusively vested in the Parliament of the Commonwealth or withdrawn from the Parliament of the State".

To determine whether the federal government has the power to make legislation on any matter turn first to the Constitution, where the matters on which the federal government can legislate are listed, especially in s 51. States can legislate on any other matter. If a State refers one of its powers to the federal government, then the federal government can legislate on that matter.

Powers vested in the federal government include matters dealing with the seat of government and other Commonwealth places (s 52); customs and excise duties (ss 51(2), (3) and 90-93); the Commonwealth Public Service (ss 52, 67); Commonwealth Territories (ss 111, 122) and initiating constitutional referenda (s 128).

Some other powers are granted to the Commonwealth, but are not stated to be exclusive. These are known as *concurrent* powers, and are set out in s 51. There are 39 placita (decrees) in that section. These include such matters as trade and commerce with other countries (pl i); external affairs (pl xxix); nationalisation and aliens (pl xix); quarantine (pl ix); taxation (pl ii); census and statistics (pl xi); bills of exchange and promissory notes (pl xvi); marriage (pl xxi); and divorce and matrimonial causes (pl xxii).

Because these powers are concurrent, the States may make laws in these areas as well as the Commonwealth. The potential existence of both federal and State laws on a certain issue introduces the possibility of conflict between the law as stated by each piece of legislation. To address this issue, s 109 of the Constitution provides that where both federal and State legislation exists, and there is inconsistency between the laws, Commonwealth law applies, and the State law is rendered invalid: "When a law of a State is inconsistent with a [valid] law of the Commonwealth, the latter shall prevail, and the former shall, to the extent of the inconsistency, be invalid".

Referral of powers: States may formally *refer* a power which they have to the Commonwealth, thus permitting the federal government to legislate on the matter involved. This has occurred, for example, on the matter of ex-nuptial children, originally a matter not included among those on which the federal government can legislate. Recognition of the value of allowing the Family Court to deal with custody and access issues relating to ex-nuptial children (as well as those born within a marriage) has led to most of the States referring their power to make laws relating to custody of, and access to, such children. This means that these powers are now included in the *Family Law Act 1975* (Cth).

Statutory interpretation

[1.60] There arises the problem of just how the Constitution and, for example, the powers it vests in the federal government, are to be interpreted. The law as written may be ambiguous or unclear, and language is never so clear and absolute that its meaning is not open to debate. The issue of statutory interpretation, whether it involves the Constitution or any other written legislation, gives rise to a basic task for lawyers and is discussed below (see Chapter 3). Interpretation of statutes is also a major function of the courts, the High Court being the court which has the jurisdiction (power) to interpret the Constitution.

An example of the need for the High Court to interpret the Constitution occurred in the *Tasmanian Dam Case* (*Commonwealth v Tasmania* (1983) 158 CLR 1). The issue arose because the federal government legislated to prohibit the Tasmanian government from building a dam on the Gordon River, in order to protect the surrounding forest from destruction. Normally the federal government could not do this, but it invoked the fact that Australia is a signatory to the *UNESCO Convention Concerning the Protection of the World Cultural and Natural Heritage*. This, it argued, gave it the right to legislate on the matter as it came under the foreign affairs power.

The High Court was approached for interpretation of the meaning of "foreign affairs". It was argued by the Tasmanian government that the power only authorised the federal government to legislate about a matter which was inherently international in nature (that is, involving our relationship with another nation). This has been called the "narrow interpretation". The federal government argued that the power was wider because it had signed an international treaty (including a convention) which required it to put the terms of that treaty into effect domestically. These two views are very different in their nature and effect.

The High Court held that the wider view was the better legal view. The narrow view could have been what the founders of the nation had in mind, before the days of international conventions and agreements and, of course, such bodies as the United Nations. The wider view also accords with the plain meaning of the words (see **[3.60]**) as interpretation of the Constitution takes into account current legal practice and political processes, the Court decided that the wider meaning was more appropriate.

Legislating for the Territories

[1.65] The Australian Capital Territory, the Northern Territory and Norfolk Island are self-governing territories under the Constitution. That means they have legislative assemblies and can make their own laws similar to the States. However they do not have the same independence as the States. Section 122 of the Constitution states that the Commonwealth can legislate for the territories. This means that the Commonwealth Parliament can legislate on any matter for the territories, thus overriding Territory legislation and potentially depriving them of the right to make their own laws on that matter. This happened in 1998 when the Commonwealth Government passed the *Euthanasia Laws Act 1997*, overturning the Northern Territory's *Rights of the Terminally Ill Act 1995* which had provided for voluntary euthanasia (see **[14.275]**).

Changing the Constitution

[1.70] The Constitution is entrenched: that is, it cannot be *amended* (changed) or *repealed* (cancelled) unless there is a national referendum in which all citizens must take part. There must be an overall majority of voters in a majority of States to approve the change or repeal. The most recent referendum was in 1999 and concerned the issue of whether or not Australia should become a republic. The referendum failed, so no changes were made to the Constitution and Australia remains a monarchy. A look at past referenda suggests that people tend to be conservative and reject proposed changes to the Constitution, with the majority of referenda failing.

In 1946, however, one referendum succeeded in giving the federal government new powers in the medical area. Placitum (xxiiiA) of s 51 of the Constitution (inserted as a result of that referendum) adds the power for the Commonwealth to legislate for "pharmaceutical sickness and hospital benefits, medical and dental services (but not so as to authorise any form of civil conscription)".

Placitum (xxiiiA) has been interpreted by the High Court to mean that the federal government can regulate medical and dental services on a national basis where federal funds are concerned. Thus, although States can organise the provision of services themselves without federal government interference, if they accept federal funding they must agree to comply with federal government directives: the Commonwealth has wide powers to raise revenue and grant funding to the States (see *General Practitioners Society v The Commonwealth* (1980) 145 CLR 532).

Legislation other than the Constitution may be repealed or amended by later legislation. Repeal or amendment may be *express* (spelt out by the wording of the new Act) or *implied* (a natural consequence of it). There are also State Constitutions setting out the powers of State Parliaments, courts and bodies, as well as individuals. However such State Constitutions are in the nature of ordinary statutes, so usually can be amended by the State without a referendum process.

Laws developed by the courts—Common law

[1.75] Common law has its origins in feudal era England. Feudalism was fundamentally a system of land tenure, with personal service owed by many to an overlord who had immense powers including the exercise of customary law, based on local customs. The very completeness of its application made feudalism a potent force for law and order.

England was a rural society, and later overlordship carried with it as a further principle the right of every lord to hold a court for his tenants. There was very little legislation, but the lord enforced obedience to an existing and settled custom when disputes were to be resolved. This custom involved settling disputes by such methods as trial by oath, trial by battle and trial by ordeal. Where one person had caused another physical harm or loss of property, he or she was said to have an action in the law of "wrongs" (or to use the ancient Latin—French term, imported into our legal system and still used today, the law of "torts").

Initially, wrongs were seen as personal disputes, but as the central government began to grow and towns and cities developed (and the king wished to extend his power), some "wrongs" were increasingly seen as breaches of the king's peace. The "king's peace" grew and flourished with the extension and consolidation of the power of the king, until it covered the whole of England. When this had come to pass no person committed violence without being liable to a fine at the suit of the king: a precursor of modern criminal law. However, until the time of Henry II, the enforcement of law, even penal law, remained in private hands. Today, we still have the offence of "breach of the peace", with which a person who causes a serious disturbance to the peaceful activities of those around them may be charged.

Henry II instituted some dramatic changes. He set apart certain wrongs as matters for the interference of the Crown. Others were peculiarly the concern of the private citizen. This was the beginning of the crime/tort dichotomy ("public"/"private" law). Several crimes, such as robbery with violence, were established, which attracted physical punishment, but private vengeance resulted in mostly monetary compensation. Justice became the business of the monarch, not the lords.

In order to seek the aid of royal justice, it was usual to purchase a writ from the King's Chancery. This writ was a royal command based upon the king's royal authority. It specified the injury complained of, and directed that whoever had caused the harm should right the wrong or show cause before the king's justices why they should not.

It became obvious that a lot of actions would be comparatively similar in nature, if not in detail, and so common wording was used. Writs became standard in form, adapted for the particular category of action involved, for example trespass, personal injury, robbery. In the course of time, each category tended to develop its own peculiarities, for example, the method of proof for supporting or rebutting the claim in any particular category of case would differ from others. If the writ itself did not follow a common form, it was not incorporated in the Clerk's Register of Writs, and so no action would lie for that particular set of events.

In this way, then, a common law became increasingly prevalent, and this was aided particularly by a lawyer, Blackstone, who wrote a many-volumed *Commentary* on the law of England, bringing together the common principles he found in the law as practised throughout the land. His *Commentary* became the main authority for later decisions by the courts.

What has all this to do with today's law? The answer lies in the fact that the authority of a law is based on the idea of acceptance of a principle (or rule, or standard of behaviour) by a court, from another court higher in the same hierarchy in that jurisdiction. By the establishment of a "common law", then, principles derived from sources with accepted authority were set down as a guide for future decision-making to be changed only by courts with higher authority than the original court. This laid the foundations for one of the fundamental aspects of our legal system, *stare decisis* (meaning, roughly, "the decision binds"), the requirement that a court is bound by legal principles established by courts with higher standing than it has (see **[1.90]**ff).

Equity

[1.80] Common law could be very harsh, and somewhat rigid. One example of this is the common law principle that the person whose name is on a title deed to land is the person who owns it at law, and can therefore sell it at will and have sole rights to the proceeds of sale. This can cause hardship where someone else, whose name is not on the title deed, has made a contribution to the acquisition of the property by contributing to its purchase price, or enhanced its value by improving or renovating it. Over time a set of alternative approaches developed in some of the specialised courts, such as the Court of Chancery, which were based more on principles aimed at prevention of unjust enrichment at another's expense. The principles that developed were called "principles of equity". Thus, where at common law a person in the situation described above would not be able to reap the reward of her or his contribution to the property, in equity the fact that that person had contributed to its value could lead to a claim on its value in proportion to the contribution.

The principles of equity have since been incorporated into the jurisdiction of the common law courts. This means that the courts can consider both the common law *and* equitable remedies for which a person may be eligible. Generally, one or the other will be applicable, but where there is a conflict between the rules of equity and the common law, equity is to prevail.

The term "common law" is used in several, potentially confusing ways. It may refer to:

- common law principles exclusive of the principles of equity where the writer is drawing a distinction between common law principles, strictly speaking, and principles of equity; or
- both traditional common law and equity, to differentiate these from statutory law.

The meaning is to be deduced from the context of the use of the term.

Inter-relationship between statutory law and common law (including equity)

[1.85] Parliament creates an enormous amount of law each year, however, it is impossible for statutory law to cover every possible scenario. Therefore, where a gap exists in statutory law, judges and lawyers turn to the common law, as discovered through cases decided by the courts, in an attempt to find enlightenment there.

If a judge is faced with a matter where:

- there is no statutory provision governing the issue; or
- the issue has not been the subject of a previous judicial decision,

then he or she will look at cases with the most similar fact situations that can be found, and, using the principles used in those cases, develop principles for the matter now before the court. New law is thus developed for future reference.

Precedent

[1.90] Precedent is the word used to describe the system by which the common law is passed on to influence later decisions. Courts are arranged in a hierarchy, from the lowest courts (courts of petty sessions, local courts or magistrates' courts), to the highest courts (in Australia—the High Court; in England—the House of Lords). This hierarchy will be considered in more detail in Chapter 2. Decisions made in the higher courts have precedence over decisions made in the lower courts. This means that under some circumstances, when one has received a judgment of a lower court, one can appeal to a higher court to have the lower court's judgment quashed, and either a different judgment may be made or a new hearing may be granted. The decision of the higher court then applies, and it, and the reason for its decision, is binding on all courts lower in the same hierarchy in that jurisdiction.

It is important for lawyers to know which court a decision comes from, for a decision is only binding on a lower court in the same hierarchy. Decisions from a court in another hierarchy are of *persuasive precedent* only, that is, not binding on the court, but, depending upon the status of the court from which it comes, worth considering to the extent that a judge would feel obliged to justify not following it. For example, a higher New South Wales court decision is persuasive precedent in South Australia. As its name implies, persuasive precedent is not binding on a judge and can only be used if no binding precedent can be found. The decisions of the Australian High Court are binding on all Australian courts, unless they are specifically applied only to a particular State or Territory.

What this means for practical purposes is that when considering their judgment in a case, judges will look to the decisions of the higher courts. If a precedent can be found (or adduced from analogous situations), then the court is absolutely bound by that earlier decision. Thus a sort of rigidity is established, which gives some certainty to the law.

New law

[1.95] If there is no legislation on a particular matter, and also no precedent, then the law on that matter is uncertain, and cannot be known until the matter is taken to court and a ruling is made. Sometimes, to establish the law on an issue which is becoming a frequent matter of confusion and concern, a "test case" will be brought: when lawyers see a good opportunity, and funds are available, a case is taken to court, not merely because the particular parties want to settle the matter, but also to establish the law for future reference.

Indigenous customary law

[1.100] Indigenous customary law has developed over the thousands of years of occupation of Australia by Aboriginal and Islander peoples of Australia. Specific groups have spiritual and physical connections with particular areas of land, which gave rise to rules governing their relationships within the group and between groups and strangers. While customary law has most likely changed over time, there are still groups which operate according to customary law.

Some features of Indigenous customary law are:

- no abstract rules separating law from religion or other modes of conduct;
- different people know different laws, which are passed on orally;
- many laws are secret;
- it evolves from custom, or comes from spirits or the Dreaming;

- people are judged by relatives, ceremonial leaders and elders or the whole tribe;
- it is enforced mostly by relatives or the tribe;
- there is no concept of individual ownership; and
- the tribe is responsible for the care of the land.

Two principles apply in relation to Indigenous people and the British/Australian law introduced at the time of colonisation:

1. Indigenous people are subject to that law in the same way as non-Indigenous people. They are not a free and independent people who are entitled to any rights or interests other than those created or recognised by the laws of the Commonwealth, States or Territories or by the common law (*Walker v New South Wales* (1994) 182 CLR 45; citing *Mabo v Queensland (No 2)* (1992) 175 CLR 1), however,
2. there is provision for some recognition by courts of Indigenous customary law (Law Reform Commission of Australia, *The Recognition of Aboriginal Customary Laws* (AGPS, Canberra 1986)). This has occurred in the criminal law, particularly when courts are sentencing. For example, where an Indigenous person has been convicted of an offence which is also a tribal offence subject to tribal punishment, courts may in some cases take the tribal punishment into account. Other aspects of customary law have also been given statutory recognition. These include traditional interests in land, items of cultural heritage, traditional marriages for certain purposes and traditional hunting, fishing and gathering rights.

How does the law change?

[1.105] There is scope for change in the common law, despite *stare decisis*, as well of course, as the ability of Parliament to change statutes and introduce new ones. In order for a case to be cited by a lawyer as being applicable to a particular situation it must be analogous to the case being decided. As there are an infinite number of possible variations of any situation, and as times change and statutes are introduced to cover more and more activities, often similar situations are considered by judges to be different enough in the circumstances to warrant distinguishing the cited case from the matter currently before them. If one can distinguish the cases, then the legal principle(s) established in the cited case do not bind the court. This results in a gradual and slow development of the law to adapt to a changing society. There is further discussion on the way common law changes below (see **[3.125]**ff).

Some Basic Principles of Our Legal System

[1.110] There are several fundamental principles and presumptions which underlie all specific legislation and common law.

Principles of natural justice

[1.115] These were identified in early times by the Greek philosophers, and sought to vest some authority beyond the state, in the very nature of our humanity (if not in a god). There are two main principles: first, that no one may be deprived of their liberty, livelihood or goods without being given timely notice of the reasons for so doing, and without being given the opportunity to be heard in their own defence, and secondly, that no one may sit in judgment of another who has a vested interest in the outcome of the judgment. It was later recognised that these principles should apply to all citizens regardless of their individual characteristics (see Chapter 18).

Rule of law

[1.120] This body of principles establishes two things. First, it says, a person can only be found guilty of a criminal offence that existed at the time it was allegedly committed: that is, the state cannot create an offence after it has been committed. Secondly, it states that the executive branch of the government is subject to the law just the same as a citizen is, so that the citizen is protected from arbitrary action by public officials and members of Parliament.

Presumption of innocence

[1.125] This presumption requires the law to treat any accused person as innocent until they have been proven guilty (see Chapter 14).

References and Further Reading

Chisholm, R and Nettheim, G, *Understanding Law* (3rd ed, Law Book Co, Sydney, 1988)

Darvall, I, *Medicine Law and Social Change* (Darmouth Publishing Co, UK, 1993)

Davies, M, *Asking the Law Question* (Law Book Co, Sydney, 2002)

Derham, D P, Maher, F K H and Waller, P L, *An Introduction to Law* (8th ed, LBC, Sydney, 2000)

Enright, C, *Studying Law* (Macarthur Press, Sydney, 1991)

Freckelton, I and Petersen, K, *Controversies in Health Law* (The Federation Press, Sydney, 1999)

Harris, J W, *Legal Philosophies* (Butterworths, London, 1980), esp chs 2, 4, 8, 11

Heilbronn, G, Kovacs, D, Latimer, P, Nielsen, J and Pagone, T, *Introducing the Law* (5th ed, CCH, Sydney, 1996)

Hunter, R, Ingleby, R and Johnstone, R, *Thinking about Law* (Allen & Unwin, Sydney, 1995)

Johnstone, M, *Bioethics: A Nursing Perspective* (3rd ed, W B Saunders/Bailliere Tindall, Sydney, 1999)

Kercher, B, *Debt, Seduction and Other Disasters: The Birth of Civil Law in Convict New South Wales* (Federation Press, Sydney, 1996)

Kuhse, H, *Caring: Nurses, Women and Ethics* (Blackwell, Oxford, 1997)

McLean, S, "Law Ethics and Medical Progress: Allies or Adversaries?" (1999) 7 *Journal of Law and Medicine* 25

Spigelman, CJ, "175th Anniversary of the Supreme Court of New South Wales", speech given on 17 May 1999, accessed in May 2006 at www.lawlink.nsw.gov.au/lawlink/supreme_court/ll_sc.nsf/pages/SCO_speeches

2 The Legal Structure

Courts

Tribunals

The English Courts

Decisions from other countries

Law Reporting

chapter 2

The Legal Structure

Introduction

[2.05] In the Australian legal system, there is a division between the federal courts (those courts which deal with interpretation and application of the federal Constitution and laws made by the federal Parliament), and the State courts (which deal with State Constitutions and State law). The system is outlined in the following paragraphs.

Courts

What is a court?

[2.10] A court is an assembly, presided over by a judge or other person invested with judicial power, which follows the rules of procedure prescribed for that court, and is in some cases assisted by a jury. Courts are different from tribunals and other dispute resolution bodies (see **[2.95]**ff) in that they are independent from the executive government, and judges and magistrates who preside over them have tenure. The judge, or where there is a jury, the judge and jury, exercising different responsibilities as outlined in Chapter 3, determine such matters as:

- whether certain facts have been established;
- whether a person is guilty or not guilty of an offence;
- whether a person is liable or not for harming another;
- where required, the legal obligations and rights of a party or parties;
- the punishment appropriate for criminal or other offences; and
- the interpretation of statutory provisions, the provisions of a will, or of a contract.

A court may make orders, for example, requiring a person to do something, not to do specified things, pay fines, be detained and/or medically assessed, and treated.

Jurisdiction

[2.15] The concept of jurisdiction is central to the court system. It can apply to:

1. *geographical jurisdiction*, that is, the geographical district or limits within which the judgment of a court or orders of a court can be enforced or executed. This may be State, Territory or federal jurisdiction; or
2. *scope of jurisdiction*, that is, the authority of a court or judge to consider an action, petition or other proceeding; often lower courts have a monetary maximum; (see **[2.40]**); or
3. *type of jurisdiction*, that is, whether it is original jurisdiction (initial hearing) or appellate jurisdiction (see **[2.60]–[2.65]**).

Geographical jurisdiction

[2.20] Australia is divided into nine jurisdictions: federal jurisdiction (covering the whole of Australia), the six States, which have sovereign jurisdiction over State matters, and three Territories (the Australian Capital Territory, the Northern Territory and Norfolk Island), which have a more limited form of self-governance. State and Territory courts can generally only deal with people who live within, or events that take place within, their boundaries, and orders made by the court will normally be limited to those boundaries.

Where a State wishes to execute a criminal prosecution against a person who has allegedly committed a crime against the State, but is at the time of prosecution present in another State, the court in the State wishing to prosecute can apply to the courts of the other State for extradition of the accused (power to remove the person from the State in which they are currently residing and bring that person before a court in the State in which they allegedly committed the offence). The State applying for extradition has to prove it has a *prima facie* case against the person, that is, it must be able to demonstrate that "on the face" of it, there is sufficient evidence to suggest that the accused person may have committed the crime alleged. Extradition of a person from one country to another for the purposes of facing trial can also be granted, but this is dependent upon the existence of an extradition treaty between the countries concerned.

Federal jurisdiction

[2.25] Laws made by the federal government are administered by the federal courts and those State courts invested with federal jurisdiction. Section 71 of the Constitution establishes the High Court as the supreme court of the Commonwealth, and invests federal jurisdiction in such other courts as determined by the federal Parliament. The Federal Court was established in 1976 to relieve the workload of the High Court. More minor federal matters were dealt with by State magistrates courts however. The Federal Magistrates' Court was established in 1999 to deal with these.

Another federal court system is the Family Court (see **[2.85]**ff), established by the *Family Law Act 1975* (Cth). This is a special court with its own rules and Court of Appeal. Family law matters may originate in the State or federal magistrates courts, or the Family Court, depending on their nature.

Figure 2.1: The federal court system of Australia

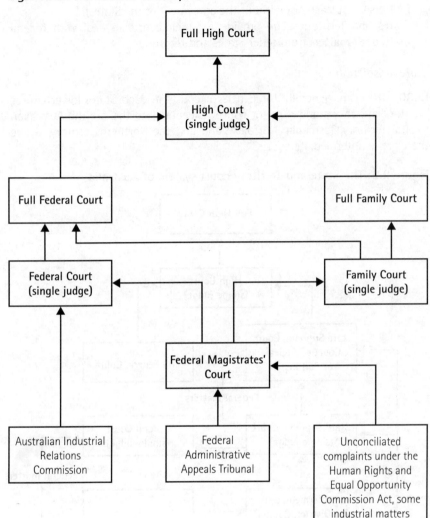

Federal matters may be heard in State courts, starting with the Magistrates' Court in some instances. To simplify complex matters that may come before the courts, and to prevent the need for expensive repetition of actions if they are found to have been commenced in the wrong court, in 1988 the Commonwealth and the States enacted legislation "cross-vesting" jurisdiction in some circumstances. This means a State court may hear a federal matter and vice versa, (applying the appropriate law) where it would be either impractical or unjust to refer the matter directly to the correct court. However, the High Court case of *Re Wakim; Ex parte McNally* (1999) 198 CLR 511 held that cross-vesting is invalid to the extent that it purports to confer State jurisdiction on a federal court. The Constitution, s 77, limits the matters on which the Commonwealth can confer power on the federal court, and thus the Court concluded:

(a) the federal government *cannot* provide for federal courts to deal with State matters (or at least, not without the agreement of the States);

(b) States and Territories *can* provide for their courts to deal with federal matters, or matters from other States and Territories.

State jurisdiction

[2.30] There are generally three tiers of courts in each State: lower courts, intermediate courts and superior courts. Exceptions to this are the Australian Capital Territory, Tasmania, Norfolk Island and the Northern Territory, where there are no intermediate courts.

Figure 2.2: The State and Territory court system of Australia

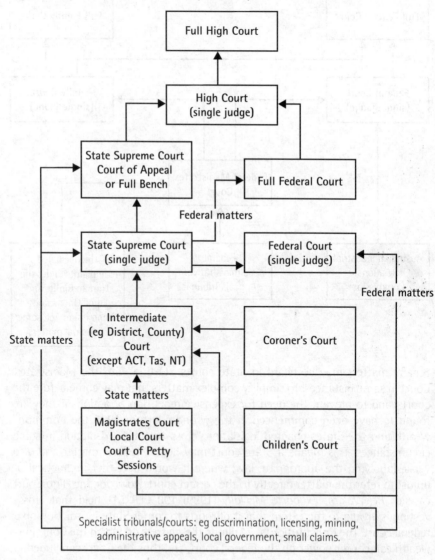

Lower courts

Magistrates courts

[2.35] These courts deal with less serious matters. The titles of these courts vary across the States:

- in the Australian Capital Territory, Queensland, South Australia and Victoria they are called Magistrates Courts and they deal with both civil and criminal cases;
- in New South Wales they are called Local Courts and they deal with both civil and criminal cases. In certain circumstances appeals in relation to criminal matters may be made to the District Court or Supreme Court; in civil matters, appeals may be made to the Supreme Court (see *Local Courts Act 1982* (NSW));
- in the Northern Territory civil cases are dealt with by Courts of Summary Jurisdiction, while Local Courts deal with minor criminal cases;
- in Tasmania, Local Courts deal with civil cases, and Courts of Petty Sessions deal with criminal cases; and
- in Western Australia Local Courts deal with civil cases, while Courts of Petty Sessions deal with both civil and criminal cases.

Matters dealt with at this level are:

- minor criminal offences, traffic offences and failure to pay fines;
- civil actions below a stipulated sum;
- children who are charged with crime, or are neglected (Children's Court); and
- investigation of a person's death or fires (Coroner's Court) (see Chapter 15).

These courts are presided over by a stipendiary (paid) magistrate, or, in some jurisdictions where there is no available magistrate, two justices of the peace.

An important feature of magistrates courts is that most decisions therein are summary, that is, they are made without a jury, after both parties involved have made their representations to the magistrate. The decision is usually made at the time of the hearing. There is provision in New South Wales for a jury in some coronial hearings (see *Coroners Act 1980* (NSW), s 18).

People charged with an indictable offence (usually a serious charge), have a right to a trial before a jury if they plead not guilty. However, they must first appear before a magistrate, at a committal hearing. The magistrate decides whether there is a case to answer, that is, whether the evidence against the person is such that a jury *could* (not would) find them guilty of the offence. This is called the finding of a prima facie case. The committal hearing is not a trial, in that there is no determination of guilt. If there is a finding of a prima facie case, the accused is committed for trial in a higher court. If the finding is that there is no prima facie case, the charge is dismissed and the accused goes free.

If a person pleads guilty to an indictable offence at the committal proceeding, and the magistrate is satisfied that the plea is genuine, the accused is committed to the appropriate superior court for sentencing. In the Northern

Territory and Australian Capital Territory there may still be a trial where the charge is one punishable by imprisonment for life, to ensure that there is indeed proof of the offence (see *Justices Act 1928* (NT), s 134; *Magistrates Act 1930* (ACT), s 90A).

Intermediate courts

[2.40] In New South Wales, Queensland, South Australia and Western Australia, these courts are called District Courts; in Victoria they are called County Courts. These courts hear matters involving more serious crimes, and civil claims involving larger amounts of money than those dealt with by the Magistrates Courts. The limit to the amount of money differs across jurisdictions, and in some instances may be varied by the consent of the parties (*District Court Act 1973* (NSW)—unlimited in cases of motor accident personal injury, $750,000 otherwise; *District Court Act of Queensland 1967* (Qld)— $250,000; *District Court Act of Western Australia 1969* (WA)—$250,000; *County Court Act 1958* (Vic)—unlimited in cases of personal injury, $200,000 otherwise).

Trials in these courts are presided over by a judge, and sometimes also a jury. Where the matter is an appeal from a magistrates court, or where the law precludes a jury (as it does in most non-criminal claims) a judge will sit alone. Appeals may be made from this court to the next highest court in the hierarchy—the Supreme Court, in its appellate jurisdiction, generally referred to as the Court of Appeal or Full Court of the Supreme Court, depending on the jurisdiction in question.

Superior courts

The Supreme Court

[2.45] As its name suggests, this court is the highest court in each State. The most serious crimes (such as murder, rape, serious assault, armed robbery) are dealt with here, after a committal hearing. In addition, civil matters involving unlimited sums of money are heard. A jury may hear the case, depending on the action being brought before the court.

The Supreme Courts are generally divided into divisions to deal with different kinds of matters, in particular the courts have separate trial divisions and appeal divisions (for example, in New South Wales, s 38 of the *Supreme Court Act 1970* provides that the Supreme Court be divided into three divisions: the Court of Appeal; the Common Law Division; and the Equity Division). Appeals from the lower courts and from the findings of Supreme Court trial divisions are heard by the "Court of Appeal" or Full Bench of the Supreme Court. In most instances, three Supreme Court judges, specially nominated, constitute the Court of Appeal or Full Bench. In limited circumstances appeals may be heard by only two judges (see, for example, *Supreme Court Act 1986* (Vic), s 11).

As mentioned at **[2.25]**, under some circumstances State courts are empowered to hear cases coming under federal law. Appeals in such instances will generally go to the State Court of Appeal or Full Bench, however, in some circumstances the appeal goes to the Federal Court (see *Jurisdiction of Courts (Cross-Vesting) Act 1987*, s 7 in each jurisdiction).

The High Court

[2.50] This is the highest court in Australia. It is primarily based in Canberra, but the judges still go on circuit in some circumstances. Almost all of the High Court's work is hearing appeals from the lower courts of the different States, which have worked their way up the hierarchy of courts, sometimes (rarely) all the way from a magistrate's court.

To limit the workload of the High Court, the *Judiciary Amendment Act (No 2)* was enacted in 1984. This Act gave expression to the principle that, in the interests of finality and manageability, an appeal to the High Court following an appeal to a State Court of Appeal should only occur where special leave is granted by the High Court. This occurs where:

* the appeal involves a question of law of public importance; or
* there are differences of opinion between courts as to the law, and it is in the interests of justice that the High Court hears the matter.

The other part of the High Court's work is to hear at first instance cases involving the Constitution (this is the High Court's exclusive jurisdiction), and other federal matters as established by Parliament, for example, matters involving the Commonwealth or an officer of the Commonwealth, and matters where the State governments are the litigants. A jury is not involved (except in very rare cases, for example, treason), and a "Full Bench" consists of seven judges. In many cases only five are required, and in limited circumstances a single judge may sit.

Scope of jurisdiction

[2.55] When a court goes beyond its power by, for example, making an order it is not empowered to make, an aggrieved party can seek an order from a higher court to remedy this situation. Such an order may be one of *mandamus* (an order to do something), *certiorari* (a declaration in relation to the wrong) or *prohibition* (an order restraining the lower court from taking specified action).

Type of jurisdiction

Original jurisdiction

[2.60] This is exercised when a case first comes to court, and the basic facts and legal issues are determined. It is sometimes called "trial jurisdiction" or "first instance" jurisdiction. Matters are heard for the first time with witnesses being called and exhibits presented. Based on the information put forward, a decision as to the facts and the legal position of those involved is made, with any appropriate order being issued by the judge, magistrate or other person presiding.

Appellate jurisdiction

[2.65] If a decision by the court in its original jurisdiction can be challenged, an appeal from that decision might be made to either a higher court, or to the original court exercising its appellate jurisdiction. For example, the Supreme Court of a State may hear a criminal trial in its original jurisdiction. This would be before one judge and a jury: see the explanation of criminal procedures below. If an appeal is made it will most likely be to the same court, now functioning as the Court of Appeal or Full Bench. In most cases, the matter on appeal will be heard by three judges (without the original judge or a jury).

Appeal courts do *not* generally hear a matter all over again. They do *not* re-examine the witnesses, although they may look at exhibits contained in the parties' appeal books. Because findings of fact may depend to some extent on the credibility of the witness, appeals courts are generally reluctant to review findings of fact. The court is, however, empowered to undertake review of findings of fact upon which a decision is based. Parties cannot appeal solely on the basis that the decision was against their interests. Appeals can only be brought on specified grounds, for example:

- the court did not have jurisdiction to hear the case;
- the judge in the trial hearing erred as to what the law is;
- the rules of evidence were not properly followed and evidence was wrongly admitted or withheld;
- the finding of fact by the trial judge was not reasonably available on the evidence;
- given the facts that were established, no one could reasonably have come to the decision arrived at by the judge or jury; and
- in some rare cases, fresh evidence has come to light, which was not available at the time of trial, and its absence has most likely caused a miscarriage of justice.

The appeal court may order a *retrial* (for example, where evidence was wrongly admitted), or quash the verdict or finding (for example, where it considers that the trial judge erred in law and the result is thus wrong at law, or a reasonable judge or jury could not have come to the decision arrived at, given the facts).

Rules of the courts

[2.70] Each court in the hierarchy has its own set of rules, which govern its procedure. A number of Australian jurisdictions are moving towards uniform civil procedure rules in order to eliminate unnecessary differences in procedure between their various court levels (see, for example: *Uniform Civil Procedure Rules 2005* (NSW); *Uniform Civil Procedure Rules 1999* (Qld)).

Specialist courts

[2.75] As well as the mainstream system of courts, there are special courts, bodies and tribunals for some areas of law. Some examples are set out below:

New South Wales Drug Court

[2.80] Drug dependent persons charged with criminal offences which would normally attract a prison sentence can be diverted from a Local or District Court into the Drug Court where they are given an opportunity to undertake a drug rehabilitation program.

Family Court

[2.85] A federal specialist court administers the *Family Law Act* 1975 (Cth), dealing with matters such as dissolution of marriage, parenting orders, and the division of matrimonial property. The court also has jurisdiction in some matters under other legislation such as the *Marriage Act 1961* (Cth) and child support legislation. The jurisdiction and the administration of the Court has changed over time as a result of changes to the *Family Law Act*, in response to recommendations of reviews both internal and external, and the creation of the Federal Magistrates' Court.

In keeping with its basic philosophy, the Family Court has less formal procedures than other courts. The judge and lawyers are not robed and the courtrooms are more informal. More importantly, in many matters the Court is given the power to make whatever orders it thinks fit, rather than orders based on strict legal requirements or precedent. This does not mean that no consideration is given to precedent, but that, where the judge or judges think justice or the interests of the parties (with the welfare of the children given paramount consideration) requires it, precedent will not be rigidly followed.

The Federal Magistrates' Court

[2.90] The jurisdiction of the Federal Magistrates' Court includes family law, consumer protection law, administrative law, bankruptcy and discrimination law. It is intended to be even more informal than the Family Court, and to provide a more accessible alternative to the higher courts.

Tribunals

[2.95] Tribunals are other decision-making and dispute-resolution bodies whose decisions are enforceable at law. They exercise jurisdiction within the administrative law system as administrative decision-makers at first instance, or appeal bodies from such decisions. Tribunals also provide a forum where citizens have an opportunity to challenge decisions which administrators have made, and have them reviewed for fairness and proper procedure.

It is difficult to generalise about the nature and work of tribunals, as each is a creature of statute, with a specified jurisdiction and powers. Some bodies exercise the function of tribunals while not being named as such, for example, health professionals' disciplinary boards, and health complaints commissions. However, some features are common to most tribunals. Like courts, they resolve conflicts, make decisions and review them. Despite their name, they may consist of one or more members.

Tribunals differ from courts in the following ways:

- they may not be permanent (that is, they may be established to deal with a particular matter);
- they need not be presided over by the judiciary, but the president at least is usually a judge, magistrate or legal practitioner;
- other members may be lay persons and specialists, their area of specialty depending on the matter before the tribunal;
- they generally are not bound by the rules of evidence;
- the parties may represent themselves, and the tendency is to exclude lawyers unless necessary in the circumstances; and
- precedent is not necessarily followed by all tribunals though most will do so for the sake of convenience and justice.

Jurisdiction of tribunals

[2.100] Tribunals may have a general jurisdiction, that is, deal with a wide variety of matters. Apart from Commonwealth and State Ombudsmen, there are also tribunals of general jurisdiction in some States and Territories, namely:

- the Commonwealth (Administrative Appeals Tribunal);
- Australian Capital Territory (Administrative Appeals Tribunal);
- New South Wales (Administrative Decisions Tribunal); and
- Victoria (Victorian Civil and Administrative Tribunal).

The New South Wales and Victorian tribunals have specialist Divisions (for example, the Equal Opportunity Division). Most States also have free-standing specialist tribunals (for example, the Discrimination, Mental Health, Guardianship, and Management of Property Tribunals in the Australian Capital Territory). See further discussion below.

Types of tribunals

[2.105] Three are three main types of tribunals; they are adjudicative tribunals, investigative tribunals and review tribunals.

Adjudicative tribunals

[2.110] These make primary decisions allocating services, providing law enforcement or regulatory functions. Examples are health professionals' disciplinary boards and Mental Health Tribunals/Boards.

Investigative tribunals

[2.115] These tribunals include ombudsmen, royal commissions and law enforcement agencies. Examples are the Independent Commission Against Corruption (NSW), National Crimes Authority, Commissioner for Taxation (Cth) and State Directors of Public Prosecutions, and regulatory agencies (for example, the Broadcasting Tribunal). Although, like adjudicative tribunals, they

make decisions relating to individuals, they may also have extensive investigative powers and capacity to make decisions with a larger element of policy
affecting a wider range of individuals.

Review tribunals

[2.120] These tribunals review decisions made in an administrative capacity
either by bodies or individuals. These may be decisions relating to social
security, licensing of builders, architects etc, which are specified as being
reviewable by that particular tribunal. These tribunals are "merits review"
bodies, that is, they consider not only whether a decision is consistent with
the law but also whether the decision is appropriate in the particular circumstances.

Generally, a merits review body can take into account facts which it has
before it at the time of review. Where facts arise that were not known to the
original decision-maker, the review body will generally refer the matter back to
the original decision-maker, to review its decision in the light of the new facts,
rather than making a substitute decision. An exception occurs where more
efficient and speedy resolution can occur if the review body makes a decision
and both parties agree.

Commissions

[2.125] These generally have a wider mandate than other tribunals and may
include among their activities the carrying out of research, education programs,
conciliation and arbitration of disputes, and scrutiny of legislation and
government policy. Examples include the Health Care Complaint Commissions,
the Human Rights and Equal Opportunity Commission (described in more
detail in Chapter 18) and the Australian Industrial Relations Commission
(explained in more detail in Chapter 10).

The English Courts

[2.130] The Privy Council sits in England and advises the Monarch. One of its
functions is to deal with appeals from the Commonwealth countries. Judges from
the House of Lords are appointed to this duty. In the past this was a further higher
step one could take either from the High Court of Australia on a federal matter, or
the State Courts of Appeal on a State matter, and was thus the highest court in
the Australian legal system. Its decisions bound the High Court and the State
courts. However, the Privy Council has gradually been removed from the
Australian court system. Appeals to the Privy Council from all Australian courts on
Commonwealth law were abolished by the *Privy Council (Limitation of Appeals)
Act 1968* (Cth). Appeals to the Privy Council from State courts were abolished by
the *Australia Act 1986* (Cth). As a result, decisions of the Privy Council are no
longer binding on Australian courts, but they are of persuasive precedent.

The House of Lords is the ultimate English law-making body, presided over
by judges who are members of the House of Lords. Australian courts were

bound by its decisions failing a decision of the Privy Council until appeals to the Privy Council were abolished. Its decisions are of persuasive precedent only. Another important court in England is the English Court of Appeal, a court directly inferior to the House of Lords.

These courts are mentioned because much of the law regarding health carers, particularly negligence law, has been developed through these courts, although, at least since the decision in *Rogers v Whitaker* (1992) 175 CLR 479 (discussed at **[4.295]**) there are now differences between the law in England and that in Australia.

Judicial Decisions From Other Countries

[2.135] The court systems of the United States, Canada, New Zealand and other common law countries are too complex to outline here. They have a court hierarchy similar to ours which is the source of many decisions on medical matters. These decisions may also be offered as persuasive arguments before our courts where the matter has not been decided in Australia.

Law Reporting

[2.140] As precedent is so important in the legal system, reporting of cases accurately and easy reference to them are crucial. Traditionally, official reports of appeal cases are reported by recognised bodies (which may include law book publishers), and series of reports covering each court level in each jurisdiction are published. Cases are cited in such law reporters by giving, after the name of a case, the year of volume (square brackets) or volume number (round brackets), the report series and the page number. A list of the most commonly cited series of reports is given in Appendix 1.

More recently, the increase in the number of cases available electronically has sparked a move towards medium-neutral citation. Such citation does not refer to any law reporter but rather lists: the name of the case; the year of the decision; the abbreviated title of the court in which the matter was heard; and the decision number.

Australia

Federal courts

[2.145] Cases from the High Court, and formerly the Privy Council, deciding matters from Australia are reported in the *Commonwealth Law Reports* (CLR), and another series called the *Australian Law Reports* (ALR). Thus the important High Court case on consent to medical treatment of *Rogers v Whitaker* which is to be found in volume 175 of the *Commonwealth Law Reports* at page 479, and was reported in the year 1992, is cited *Rogers v Whitaker* (1992) 175 CLR 479 (see **[4.295]**). Decisions from the federal courts are reported in the *Federal Law*

Reports (FLR) and the *Federal Court Reports* (FCR) and are similarly cited. The neutral citation for the case is *Rogers v Whitaker* [1992] HCA 58.

State courts

[2.150] Reports of State cases appear in series named for the State: see Appendix 1. For example, New South Wales Court of Appeal cases are reported as the NSWLR (*New South Wales Law Reports*). As these reports are bound by the year of the report, the identifier of the volume is the year, and this appears in square brackets. Thus, the case of *Albrighton v Royal Prince Alfred Hospital*, which deals with medical negligence, the judgment of which is reported in the second of the 1980 volumes of the *New South Wales Law Reports* at page 542, is cited as *Albrighton v Royal Prince Alfred Hospital* [1980] 2 NSWLR 542. This case is discussed at **[6.115]**.

The primary electronic resource for Australian court decisions is www.austlii.edu.au.

References and Further Reading

Ardagh, A, *Administrative Law* (5th ed, Butterworths student companions series, Butterworths, Sydney, 2004)

Derham, D P, Maher, F K H and Waller, P L, *An Introduction to Law* (8th ed, LBC, Sydney, 2000)

Flick, G, *Federal Administrative Law* (Law Book Co, Sydney, 1983)

Flick, G, *Natural Justice* (2nd ed, Butterworths, Sydney, 1984)

Heilbronn, G, Kovacs, D, Latimer, P, Nielsen, J and Pagone, T, *Introducing the Law* (5th ed, CCH, Sydney, 1996)

Morris, G, Cook, C, Creyke, R, Geddes, R, *Laying Down the Law* (3rd ed, Butterworths, Sydney, 1992)

Osborn's Concise Law Dictionary (10th ed, Sweet & Maxwell, London, 2005)

Streets, S, *Administrative Law* (2nd ed, Butterworths casebook companions series, Butterworths, Sydney, 2000)

Federal Magistrates' Court of Australia Website accessed at www.fmc.gov.au/

3 The Legal Process

Dispute resolution

Legal reasoning

Common law

Expert evidence

chapter 3

The Legal Process

Introduction

[3.05] The legal system is concerned with two main processes:

1. resolving disputes and prosecuting offences; and
2. establishing a person's status or rights and obligations.

Dispute Resolution

Civil, criminal or disciplinary action?

[3.10] Disputes at law arise when a person claims that another has done them a wrong. Criminal actions are instigated by the Crown (in the guise of the State, through the police) claiming a person has committed a wrong against it by committing a crime. A civil action is instigated by a person who claims that another person has wronged them, either physically, mentally or economically, or is likely to cause such harm by their proposed actions. Disciplinary proceedings are, strictly speaking, neither criminal nor civil proceedings. Disciplinary proceedings generally arise where a professional body believes a person's right to practise should be revoked or restricted.

Criminal cases are generally prosecuted by the State. However, in rare circumstances, a prosecution may be commenced by someone other than a police officer. Such actions are referred to as private prosecutions. Criminal cases are officially designated, for example, *R v Bloggs* (pronounced "the Queen and Bloggs"). If the prosecution is successful, the convicted person is punished. The aim of criminal proceedings is the punishment of the offender, not the compensation of the victim.

Actions against a professional, regarding their conduct in the course of their profession, are generally prosecuted by the relevant professional registration board before a specialised tribunal. For example, disciplinary action against a nurse in New South Wales would be brought by the Nurses and Midwives Board (NSW) and would be heard by the Nurses and Midwives Tribunal. Such cases are designated, for example, *The Nurses and Midwives Board of NSW v Jones*. The primary purpose of disciplinary proceedings is to maintain the standards of the profession and to protect the public. Medical practitioners in New South Wales, facing serious disciplinary action, are prosecuted by the Health Care Complaints Commissioner in the Medical Tribunal of New South Wales. Such actions are brought under the *Medical Practice Act 1992* (NSW) and are designated, for example, *Re the Medical Practice Act 1992 and Dr Smith*.

Civil cases, on the other hand, are brought about by a person claiming damage has been wrongfully inflicted on them by another person, and consequently, they are seeking compensation from the alleged wrongdoer. In this type of case the person claiming they have been wronged is said to be suing (not prosecuting) the alleged wrongdoer. The person suing is called the *plaintiff*, the person being sued is called the *defendant* (sometimes *applicant/ respondent*).

(The term "person" in law includes the plural, and refers to individuals, male or female, so long as they are born alive, and also to corporations and statutory bodies. Often the word "party" is used to refer to someone involved in a legal action.)

Civil cases are designated, for example, *Smith v Jones* (pronounced "Smith and Jones"), with the name of the plaintiff or applicant first, followed by that of the defendant or respondent. In appeal cases, the name of the person appealing (the appellant) is listed first and the name of the defendant (who is then called the respondent) second. For example, if the defendants in the hypothetical case cited above appealed, they would become the appellant, and the plaintiff would become the respondent (*Jones v Smith*).

There are many reasons why parties to a dispute may attempt to resolve the matter before an approach to the courts is made. Such reasons include:

* the expense of a court hearing;
* the stress associated with going to court;
* the uncertainty of the outcome;
* the often lengthy period of time before a matter receives a hearing date; and
* privacy (court hearings are generally open to the public).

Such negotiations are usually classified as "without prejudice", meaning that one party to the dispute will not be able to rely on what is discussed during negotiations should the parties fail to reach an agreement and the matter proceeds to court. Both parties will have in mind the possible outcome if the matter does go to court.

It is generally accepted that most civil cases are resolved out of court, that is, cases are generally filed with the court but are resolved either before the hearing is commenced or before judgment is delivered. Some claims are abandoned after they are commenced. In addition, some possible actions are never commenced.

Proof

The burden of proof

[3.15] In most circumstances, the party bringing an action has the burden of proving their case. That is, in order to succeed in their action, they must convince the judge or jury of the veracity of the allegations put forward. The level of proof required to satisfy this burden is referred to as the standard of proof.

The standard of proof

[3.20] In criminal cases the prosecution must convince the judge or jury *beyond a reasonable doubt* that the accused is guilty. This means that unless the prosecution has left no reasonable doubt in the jury's mind as to the accused's guilt, they must acquit. In a civil case the burden on the plaintiff or applicant is *on the balance of probabilities*. The court must find a defendant not liable unless the plaintiff has proved that it is more likely than not that the harm of which they complain was caused by the defendant. This is not as difficult a test as the standard of proof in a criminal case. In disciplinary cases the standard of proof is as for civil actions, that is, on the balance of probabilities. However, where the consequences of a decision for a defendant may be grave, the strength of the evidence required to satisfy the burden may be higher (*Briginshaw v Briginshaw & Anor* (1938) 60 CLR 336; restated in *Rejfek v McElroy* (1965) 112 CLR 517 and *Neat Holdings Pty Ltd v Karajan Holdings Pty Ltd & Ors* FC 92/053 [1992] HCA 66).

Outline of a criminal action

[3.25] The following main steps of a criminal and civil action are necessarily general. They are intended only to provide a basic insight into the legal process in a typical case.

Step 1   Alleged criminal behaviour takes place.

Step 2   It is reported to the police if they are not present at the scene.

Step 3   The police arrest the suspect (after obtaining a warrant from a magistrate where that is required). The various Australian jurisdictions vary on how much evidence the police must have. Some Australian jurisdictions require that they have enough evidence to reasonably believe the person committed the crime. Others allow arrest for a limited amount of time before police are prepared to lay charges. Once arrested a person is referred to as "the accused".

Step 4   The accused may be released on bail, which is an agreement or "recognisance" to appear in court when required, or may be remanded in custody, in which case he or she must be brought before a magistrate as soon as practicable. The magistrate may allow bail in the latter case. Where bail is allowed a surety may be required and conditions may be placed on the accused to ensure he or she will turn up for trial. A surety is a sum of money pledged on failure to appear for trial, or a person who undertakes the appearance in court of another (on pain of forfeiture of a sum of money).

Summary offence

[3.30] Summary offences are generally minor offences (such as petty theft, drunkenness or not paying a fine), and are tried by a magistrate without a jury. Summary offences are defined by legislation.

Step 5   The accused (now also called the defendant) appears in a magistrate's court and pleads either guilty or not guilty. If the plea is guilty, sentence is passed and the matter concluded. If the plea is not guilty—

Step 6   The prosecution presents evidence. Each witness for the prosecution is:
- "examined" by the prosecution (that is, led through their evidence);
- cross-examined by the defence to test their evidence;
- re-examined by the prosecution to reinforce their contribution to the case and repair any "damage" done to their testimony by cross-examination.

Step 7   The defence presents its evidence in a similar way.

Step 8   The magistrate makes a decision as to a verdict—guilty or not guilty. If not guilty, the accused is released and the matter concluded; if guilty, he or she is the subject of some form of penalty in the light of the maximum penalty set by law and any submissions made to the magistrate on that matter by either party.

Step 9   In some circumstances, an appeal may be made to a higher court by either party.

Indictable offence

[3.35] Indictable offences are generally serious offences (such as serious assault, murder or sexual assault), and the accused is entitled to trial by judge and jury, although in some circumstances he or she may elect to have a trial without a jury if the Crown consents. Indictable offences are defined by legislation.

Step 5   The accused appears in a magistrate's court for committal hearing, and pleads guilty or not guilty. If the plea is guilty, the accused is committed to the appropriate court for sentencing.

Step 6   If the plea is not guilty, the prosecution presents its evidence as above.

Step 7   The defence is not required to present any evidence at this stage.

Step 8   The magistrate decides whether there is enough evidence on which a jury could find the defendant guilty (a *prima facie* case). If not, the case is dismissed and the defendant goes free. If the magistrate does find a prima facie case, the defendant is committed for trial by judge and, usually, a jury.

Step 9   The accused appears before judge and jury for trial and pleads. If the plea is guilty, and the judge is satisfied that the defendant is genuine and mentally competent to so plead, sentence is passed, and the case concluded. If the plea is one of not guilty both prosecution and defence cases are presented by examination of witnesses and exhibits as before, only this time usually before a jury who are guided in matters of law by a judge, and who must decide on the facts presented whether the offence the accused is charged with amounted to a crime or not. The jury bring in their verdict of guilty or not guilty which must be accepted by the judge, whose task then is to either release the accused, if not guilty, or to pronounce sentence. The maximum punishment for any particular offence is set by legislation, but the judge has some discretion within that limit to impose anything from a token punishment (suspended sentence) to the maximum provided by the legislation. In making this decision the judge considers arguments on behalf of the parties as to what the sentence should be.

Step 10   In some circumstances, an appeal may be made to a higher court by either party.

Outline of a civil action

[3.40]   A civil action is similar to a criminal one in many ways, but has some significant differences.

Step 1   Harm occurs to a person (the plaintiff) or that person's property.

Step 2   The plaintiff may send the other party a letter of demand, stating the party's case and demands. If the claim is not met by the other person, or a settlement not negotiated, the plaintiff usually then sends a letter stating that if there is no resolution within a set time, the matter will be taken to court.

Step 3   The plaintiff files the necessary documents to commence an action with the appropriate court and then has those documents served on the defendant.

Step 4   The defendant has a set period of time to file a statement of defence with the court and serve that document on the plaintiff. The defendant may make a counter-claim, alleging that he or she has been harmed by the plaintiff; this must be duly answered by the plaintiff in a similar way.

Step 5   Depending on the type of action and in which court the case is to be heard, either party may seek further information through processes such as "further and better particulars", "discovery", "interrogatories", and/or the issue of subpoena.

At any stage the parties may resolve the matter through negotiation and discontinue or obtain consent judgment in the court proceedings. In many jurisdictions the courts now require that the parties have made some attempt at resolving the matter before the court will issue a hearing date. Mediation is often utilised in medical negligence cases in an attempt to reach a resolution to a matter without a court hearing.

Step 6   If both parties intend to proceed, they notify the court when they are ready and set a date for the hearing. In most jurisdictions matters are managed by the courts to ensure parties are prepared for hearing in a timely manner.

Step 7   Legislation has provided that juries are rarely used in civil cases, so that the case is usually before a judge alone.

Step 8   Evidence is presented in a similar way as that described for criminal trials, though expert evidence may be by way of written reports, without the need for the witness to attend court and give oral evidence. A decision is made and an award of compensation is ordered if the plaintiff's case is successful. An order will usually be made requiring the unsuccessful party to pay part of the successful party's legal costs.

Step 9   In some circumstances, an appeal may be made by either party to a higher court.

(Disciplinary proceedings are considered further at Chapter 12.)

Applications

[3.45] At common law, and under some statutes, a person may apply to the appropriate court for a ruling on particular matters. Some examples of applications are:

- for dissolution of marriage, custody of children, property distribution on dissolution and declaration of property interests etc, under the *Family Law Act 1975* (Cth).
- to have a guardian appointed for certain people under State legislation (see **[5.225]**ff).
- for an injunction, which is an order of a court by which a party to an action is required either to refrain from doing an act (restrictive injunction), or to carry out an act (mandatory injunction).

A person can apply for a declaration in some circumstances. A declaration is:

- a formal statement by a court intending to create, assert, preserve or testify to a right of a person; or
- a finding on a question of law.

An example of an application for a declaration is s 78 of the *Family Law Act 1975* (Cth), where a party to a marriage can seek a declaration from the Family Court in relation to their property rights.

Legal Reasoning

[3.50] Where there is a dispute as to the meaning of the law, or how it is to be applied, the courts use legal reasoning to come to an answer. It is important to remember that:

- legal reasoning is not the same as common sense, although common sense is invoked as the approach to use in some circumstances.
- legal reasoning does not necessarily aim at what we would consider morally just or fair.

How, then, do courts reason? The answer is, by applying principles of statutory interpretation and the use of precedent, as discussed below.

Statutory interpretation

[3.55] As mentioned earlier (at **[1.60]**ff), statutory provisions are subject to the same problems as all language: they are not always absolutely clear. Words may be unclear, vague or ambiguous. One provision of an Act may appear to contradict another, or, despite clear language, appear ambiguous in its overall construction.

Courts, in interpreting statutes, are guided by rules which have been developed by statute or common law. Thus we have Acts Interpretation Acts (both State and Federal) setting out some rules as to how to interpret certain words. We also have some common law principles which apply to terms in general, or specific terms in specific statutes. For recent examples of how the courts apply statutory interpretation principles see *Stingel v Clark* [2006] HCA 37 and *State of NSW v Ibbett* [2005] NSWCA 445 per Spigelman CJ at [2]-[23].

Rule: The literal rule

[3.60] A time-honoured rule is that, in the absence of specific provision to the contrary, words are to be given their ordinary everyday meaning, even if the result is inconvenient or improbable (*Amalgamated Society of Engineers v Adelaide Steamship Co Ltd* (1920) 28 CLR 129). This applies unless they are specific legal terms, when they must be given their legal meaning, for example, the word "negligence" has a common meaning which is much more restrictive in its legal sense (see Chapter 6).

Rule: Serve the object and purpose of the Act

[3.65] If the literal meaning is clear, the statute makes sense, and by giving that interpretation the purpose of the statute is fulfilled, one looks no further. If the purpose of the Act is not fulfilled by giving a word its ordinary and popular meaning, another meaning must be sought under the "purpose" rule. The purpose rule dominates, and the meaning that Parliament intended the word to have must be used, as far as is practicable, to give effect to the purpose of the Act.

The various Australian jurisdiction's Interpretation Acts state that the court must, in determining the meaning of a word, consider the purpose of the Act (see *Acts Interpretation Act 1901* (Cth), ss 15AA, 15AB; *Interpretation Act 1987* (NSW), ss 33, 34; *Acts Interpretation Act 1915* (SA), s 22; *Interpretation of Legislation Act 1984* (Vic), s 35; *Interpretation Act 1984* (WA), ss 18, 19; *Acts Interpretation Act 1931* (Tas), ss 8A, 8B; *Interpretation Act* (NT), ss 62A, 62B; *Acts Interpretation Act 1954* (Qld), ss 14A, 14B).

The purpose of an Act is the purpose Parliament had in bringing about the Act, and is generally discernible in the Second Reading Speech given by the Minister who introduces the Act into Parliament (but not always, see for example *McCracken v Melbourne Storm Rugby League Football Club & 2 Ors* [2005] NSWSC 107), but may also require consideration of other sources, such as documentation of Parliamentary debates, Parliamentary Committee reports, or Law Reform Commission reports. It is up to the discretion of the court as to what materials (given they are not prohibited from consulting them) they will use.

In determining the purpose of the Act it is important to consider the Act in the context in which it exists. In *Rush v Commissioner of Police* [2006] FCA 12 Finn J stated that:

> "It is now well accepted that the modern approach to statutory interpretation requires that 'context' be considered at the first instance, not merely at some later stage when ambiguity might be thought to arise. 'Context' here is used in a wide sense and includes legal and historical context: see *CIC Insurance Ltd v Bankstown Football Club Ltd* (1997) 187 CLR 384 at 408; *Braverus Maritime Inc v Port Kembla Coal Terminal Ltd* [2005] FCAFC 256 at [36]".

There is also a common law rule, the "mischief" rule, from which it can be said the purpose rule developed. The "mischief rule" is derived from *Heydon's Case* (1584) 3 Co Rep 7; 76 ER 637 and simply stated, seeks to determine what mischief the Act was intended to rectify. The Court stated that when interpreting a statutory provision, the following should be considered:

1. what the common law was before the Act was passed;
2. what the mischief or defect was for which the common law did not provide;
3. what remedy Parliament resolved was required; and
4. the "true reason" for the remedy.

An exception to this rule occurs where the words used are specifically defined, either in the applicable Interpretation Act, or in the specific Act itself. Most Acts have an interpretation section at the beginning, or a "dictionary" at the end, where key words are defined specifically for that Act. This, of course, is the first place to look in determining a word's meaning.

There may be further problems in determining the meaning of a statutory provision. Other maxims have been developed which courts may use to help with interpretation. They do not have any particular order and should be considered in the light of the purpose rule.

Rule: Words to be given their ordinary meaning

[3.70] The ordinary meaning must be given to a word unless that would lead to absurdity or some repugnancy or inconsistency with the rest of the Act, in which case the grammatical and ordinary sense of the word may be modified to avoid absurdity and inconsistency (*Grey v Pearson* (1857) 6 HLC 61). In more recent Australian cases it has been stated that departure from the ordinary meaning of word cannot be restricted to cases of absurdity, emphasising that a construction consistent with the legislative intention is essential (see *Cooper Brookes (Wollongong) Pty Ltd v Federal Commissioner of Taxation* (1981) 147 CLR 297).

Rule: Statute to be read as a whole

[3.75] A further basic principle is that, in determining the purport of a word or a provision, the whole statute must be considered to give meaning to its general intention. This principle is associated with the *noscitur a sociis* (the "birds of a feather") rule, described below.

Presumptions of interpretation of words

[3.80] There are several presumptions that courts bring to the interpretation of the words of statutes. The main ones are:

Noscitur a sociis ("birds of a feather stick together", or "one is known by one's associates") rule

[3.85] This rule is applied where a general term is interpreted according to its more restrictive neighbours. In the case of *Prior v Sherwood* (1906) 3 CLR 1054, the court held that a prohibition on bookmaking in any "house, office, room or place" did not include a public lane. The word "place" was to be interpreted in the light of the other words, and thus limited to indoors.

Ejusdem generis ("of the same kind") rule

[3.90] This is similar in its effect, but refers to things of the same class. It has been suggested, for example, that where a ferry is prohibited from carrying horses, cows, sheep and other animals, it is not prohibited from carrying tigers, as the list of animals, being only domestic ones, indicates the intention only of prohibiting domestic animals. That would be a decision to be made in the light of the intention of the Act, derived from other means, as outlined. If the intention of the Act is clearly to keep ferries completely animal-free, then the lack in the wording can be remedied by the wider interpretation.

Expressio unius exclusio alterius ("naming one thing excludes others") rule

[3.95] If specific reference is made to a particular member of a class, then, unless it causes absurdity, injustice or does not carry out the intention of the Act, all other members of that class are excluded. For example, a statute which makes it an offence for any person to sell intoxicating liquor to a minor or for any person to purchase intoxicating liquor intended for consumption by a minor, will catch only the seller of such liquor, not someone who gives it to a minor. Also it excludes the manufacturer who produces the liquor, even if it is intended for minors, so long as they do not actually sell it to a minor.

Presumptions of interpretation of statutes

Some statutes are to be interpreted in favour of the citizen

[3.100] When the question of the meaning of a statutory provision in, for example, criminal statutes and tax statutes, involves a decision either in favour of or against a citizen, and there is no reason for favouring one meaning rather than the other, courts have adopted the approach of applying the meaning that will favour the citizen rather than the State.

The *Human Rights Act 2004* (ACT), s 30 can be seen to reflect and expand this rule. The Act provides that in working out the meaning of a Territory law, an interpretation that is consistent with human rights is, as far as possible, to be preferred subject only to the purpose rule.

Common law should not be altered

[3.105] There is a presumption that, all being equal and in the absence of any clear indication otherwise, statutory provisions do not intend to alter the common law.

Statutes should not be retrospective

[3.110] In the absence of clear intention to the contrary in a statute's provisions, courts will not construe a statute to take effect before it was passed by Parliament.

The court's interpretation of a statute becomes common law, and is precedent for the future interpretation of that statute. The precedent only applies to the statute interpreted. So when deciding on the meaning of a word or provision, a lawyer will look for any case law involving interpretation of the statute. There are special publications which "annotate" statutes, pointing to cases where particular provisions have been interpreted by the courts, and there is also a publication, *Words and Phrases Judicially Considered*, which is regularly updated.

Useful publications for researching the meaning of words are: *Subject Index to the Acts and Regulations of the Commonwealth of Australia*, now continued as *Wicks Subject Index to Commonwealth Legislation* (Lawbook Co.) (giving an alphabetical list of topics and the relevant legislation on that topic), the *Commonwealth Statutes Annotations* (Lawbook Co.) and *Annotations to the Acts and Regulations of the Australian Parliament* (LexisNexis), which contain references to case law on specific sections of federal legislation. These are updated regularly. Similar publications exist for New South Wales (for example, *New South Wales Statutes Annotations* (LexisNexis)); Queensland (for example, *Statutes of Queensland Annotations* (LexisNexis)); and Victoria (for example, *Victorian Statutes Annotations* (LexisNexis)). There is the *Australian Digest* (Lawbook Co.), which provides a brief summary and index of case law by topic. It is supplemented annually. There is also the *Australian Legal Monthly Digest* (Lawbook Co.), a looseleaf service, which gives developments in statute law, case law, delegated legislation and legal publications by the month. The Digests can be consulted by topic name to get an updated summary of the law.

Checklist
INTERPRETATION OF STATUTES
✓ Is the word defined in the Act itself, or in a relevant Acts Interpretation Act? If so, use that definition.
✓ Has this particular provision been the subject of judicial interpretation? Is that decision binding?
✓ If not, what is the purpose of the Act, and what meaning would give effect to it?
✓ Is that meaning the ordinary meaning of the word (or the legal meaning if it is a legal term)?
✓ If not, is the purpose of the Act so clear as to warrant this unusual meaning of the word?
✓ Is the purpose of the Act clear enough to override any of the rules and presumptions mentioned above? If not, they should be applied in a way to give effect to the purpose of the Act.

Common Law

Determining the reason for a decision

[3.115] When declaring a decision in a case a judge explains the legal principle or principles which have been applied when coming to the decision. This is part of the official reason for the decision, or *ratio decidendi* (or if there is more than one reason, *rationes decidendi*); often called "ratio". It is this ratio that establishes precedent. Precedent is binding on all courts lower in the hierarchy.

A judgment may contain more than the reason for the decision, such as observations and general comments. These are known as *obiter dicta* often called "obiter"—"said by the way"—and are not binding on any court, although they may be followed anyway.

Where more than one judge gives judgment, there may be disagreement as to the decision which should be made. The majority decision is the one which is binding. There may be dissension, however, among these judges as to *why* they have come to that decision. The lawyer's task is to determine whether there are similar reasons given by the majority judges. These may not constitute a ratio decidendi, as there may not be a majority who have used the same reasons for their decision, but they have the qualified authority of obiter dicta. If there is a majority decision as to the verdict, but no common reason for it, the case is said to have no ratio, and is thus of limited use as precedent for other cases.

Distinguishing cases

[3.120] Because law is established by precedent, parties may attempt to differentiate between cases based on discrepancies in the facts of the cases. In the event that a party can demonstrate that the facts of their case are significantly different from a previous case, any principle of law established in the earlier case will be considered inapplicable in the current case.

The process of legal reasoning is complex. The apparently simple theory of considering the facts, determining the relevant law, applying it to them, and then declaring judgment, is not what it seems. Thus, when asked for advice on a particular issue, lawyers can, by going through the process, and considering arguments for both sides, only provide an educated opinion as to which party may have a better legal argument. No result can be guaranteed

☑ Checklist
APPLYING PRECEDENT
✓ Establish the importance of the case being applied. Is it binding or persuasive precedent?
ANALYSING EACH CASE
✓ What seem to be the important facts in the case under consideration?
✓ What other cases deal with similar facts?
✓ In those cases what was the decision and what order was made by the court?
✓ What propositions of law were relied on by the judge(s) as essential to the decision which was reached? (The answers to this question and that following identify the *ratio* of the case.)
✓ What facts were essential in linking those legal propositions to the decision?
✓ What propositions put forward in the judgment were *not* essential to the decision? (The answer to this question identifies the *obiter dicta*.)
ESTABLISHING ANY DISTINCTIONS BETWEEN THE PRECEDENT CASES
✓ In arriving at an overall statement on what the law is, are there any differences between the facts of the precedent cases?

What do judges do where there is no legislation or precedent?

[3.125] Sometimes there are situations before the court in which the facts are so novel there is no precedent case in which the facts are analogous. Such a case is called *res integra*, or a case of first impression.

In the absence of binding precedent, a judge is free to choose which of three approaches to take:

1. arguing from analogy—taking binding precedent cases with similar but distinguishable facts, extracting broad principles from them, and adapting the principles to the fact situation currently before the court;
2. following persuasive precedent—cases from other jurisdictions are considered and applied. Often English or United States cases are cited in judgments on issues not previously litigated in Australian courts; or
3. considering public policy—in the absence of clear legal directives, judges are to dispense justice as recognised by the society in which they are operating.

Checklist
LEGAL REASONING WHERE THERE IS NO CLEAR LAW
✓ Is there binding precedent on a different but similar fact situation which established a broad enough principle to apply to this situation?
✓ If not, is there persuasive precedent on this issue?
✓ If not, using public policy what is the most just decision?

Expert evidence

[3.130] The nature and scope of expert evidence is an enormous topic in itself; all that can be attempted here is a brief overview of some issues drawn substantially from the excellent comprehensive text by Freckelton and Selby (2005), to which readers are referred for more information.

In making decisions regarding health care, the courts will almost always need to rely upon "expert evidence". For example, a court hearing a negligence claim against a medical practitioner may be called upon to decide whether a drug dosage was excessive, or an MRI film properly read and reported. In order to reach a conclusion the court will require opinion evidence on those matters, from an "expert"—in other words, a medical practitioner sufficiently skilled in the relevant field. One should not necessarily equate "expert" with an esteemed "specialist" as the term is used in the health professions, for the court may require expert opinion evidence on the conduct of a general practitioner, a nurse, a chiropractor or the like and in those circumstances a suitable expert will generally be another practitioner from the same group.

An expert is permitted to offer opinions to the court regarding conclusions to be drawn from other evidence of a factual nature. The special role of the expert arose under the common law many years ago, and more recently has been reinforced by provisions in the Evidence Acts in the various Australian jurisdictions.

Rules for expert evidence

[3.135] Freckelton and Selby (2005) describe five common law rules for expert evidence, though some have been modified by Evidence Acts:

1. Does the witness have sufficient knowledge and expertise?
2. Is the opinion really one on which the court requires expert assistance, or can the court rely on common knowledge?
3. Is the claimed expertise recognised as credible by others?
4. Will the expert opinion seek to supplant the role of the court, in determining the ultimate issue?
5. Is the opinion based on matters directly within the experts' own observations?

Independence

[3.140] Much valid debate arises around the need for experts to be impartial and independent, rather than an advocate for one party or another to the litigation. When considering expert evidence, in order to decide whether to rely upon it or not, courts are concerned to ensure that an expert is clearly impartial and independent, failing which their evidence may not be accepted in whole or in part. For this reason, parties ought be careful in their selection of expert witnesses.

[3.145] Case: *Sherry v Australasian Conference Association (trading as Sydney Adventist Hospital) & Ors* [2006] NSWSC 75

[The facts of this case are set out at **[6.430]**. At this point, the decision is mentioned simply to highlight the concerns expressed by the trial judge, in relation to a medical practitioner called as an expert. The court said (extracting from the judgment at paragraphs 352–353)]:

In the opening to his report, Dr Harris acknowledged that he had "some previous knowledge" of all three doctor defendants by reason of their common engagement at the (a hospital). .... It was not put to Dr Harris, and it was not put against him in submissions, that he had consciously or deliberately tailored his evidence in order to accommodate any respect or admiration for, or dependence upon, either Dr Marshman or Dr W. The most that was put in submissions is that Dr Harris may have been unconsciously affected in his approach to the task he was asked to perform. This strikes me as another curious aspect of the reliance upon Dr Harris. It is strange that the doctor defendants would rely, as an expert commenting specifically upon his treatment, on the subordinate of one of them.

Seniority

[3.150] It is perhaps unsurprising that in matters which find their way to court, the parties each call experts who present conflicting views, perhaps because of assumptions made or perhaps because of differing opinions on proper practice. In such circumstances, a court cannot simply accept the evidence of the expert with greater seniority.

[3.155] Case: *CSR Ltd v Della Maddalena* [2006] HCA 1

[DM had the misfortune to have worked at the Wittenoom asbestos mill in the 1960s and was some 20 years later told he had evidence of asbestosis. He saw his brother die a slow and painful death from mesothelioma, and some 20 friends including all but four of the 13 people who had come from his home village in Italy to work in the same place. Although DM had not developed mesothelioma, he brought a claim based on a psychiatric disorder involving severe depression as a person who had been exposed to asbestos dust and at special risk of later developing asbestos-caused cancers. There was conflicting evidence given by medical practitioners called on behalf of DM and on behalf of CSR. His own doctors gave opinion evidence that he did have a psychiatric disorder. The forensic psychiatric opinion for CSR said he did not. The trial judge found in favour of CSR, however the Full Court overturned that conclusion and made comment about the relative seniority of the experts. Regarding the psychiatrist for DM]:

> "Professor German is well known to the Court as an eminent psychiatrist of over 40 years' standing. That is not to say he is infallible. However, a diagnosis and prognosis given by Professor German undoubtedly carries considerable weight."

In relation to the psychiatrist retained for CSR:

> "In contrast to Professor German and Dr Skerritt, Dr Febbo was a much less experienced psychiatrist. I say that without intending the slightest disrespect to Dr Febbo but simply to record the fact that as at the trial, he had been a specialist in that field for three years, albeit a psychiatric registrar for some years previously."

The majority of the High Court said that the reliance on some witnesses being "well known to the Court" constituted a breach of procedural fairness. A new trial was ordered. The High Court did not say that it was necessarily inappropriate for a decision to be based upon the greater level of experience of one expert compared to another. It seems clear however that if a court wishes to use that criterion to choose between competing expert opinions, the issue must be the subject of appropriate evidence on expertise and submissions during trial.

Expert witness codes of conduct

[3.160] In an effort to address concerns and any uncertainty regarding the duties of experts, courts in various Australian jurisdictions have introduced a "Code of Conduct". The Code is intended for provision to persons who are to give oral or written opinion evidence to courts, so as to explain their fundamental role and duties. The Code utilised by the New South Wales Supreme Court is reproduced below, as an example.

Uniform Civil Procedure Rules 2005
Schedule 7: Expert witness code of conduct
(Rules 31.17 and 31.28)

1   Application of code

This code of conduct applies to any expert engaged:

   (a) to provide a report as to his or her opinion for use as
       evidence in proceedings or proposed proceedings, or
   (b) to give opinion evidence in proceedings or proposed
       proceedings.

2   General duty to the court

   (1) An expert witness has an overriding duty to assist the
   court impartially on matters relevant to the expert's area of
   expertise.

   (2) An expert witness's paramount duty is to the court and
   not to the person retaining the expert.

   (3) An expert witness is not an advocate for a party.

3   The form of expert reports

   (1) A report by an expert witness must (in the body of the
   report or in an annexure) specify the following:

   (a) the person's qualifications as an expert,
   (b) the facts, matters and assumptions on which the
       opinions in the report are based (a letter of instruc-
       tions may be annexed),
   (c) reasons for each opinion expressed,
   (d) if applicable, that a particular question or issue falls
       outside his or her field of expertise,
   (e) any literature or other materials utilised in support of
       the opinions,
   (f) any examinations, tests or other investigations on
       which he or she has relied, including details of the
       qualifications of the person who carried them out.

   (2) If an expert witness who prepares a report believes that it
   may be incomplete or inaccurate without some qualification,
   that qualification must be stated in the report.

   (3) If an expert witness considers that his or her opinion is
   not a concluded opinion because of insufficient research or
   insufficient data or for any other reason, this must be stated
   when the opinion is expressed.

   (4) An expert witness who, after communicating an opinion
   to the party engaging him or her (or that party's legal representative), changes his or her opinion on a material matter
   must forthwith provide the engaging party (or that party's
   legal representative) with a supplementary report to that
   effect containing such of the information referred to in
   subclause (1) (b), (c), (d), (e) and (f) as is appropriate.

   (5) If an expert witness is appointed by the court, subclause
   (4) applies as if the court were the engaging party.

4   Experts' conference
(1) An expert witness must abide by any direction of the court:
(a) to confer with any other expert witness, and
(b) to endeavour to reach agreement on material matters for expert opinion, and
(c) to provide the court with a joint report, specifying matters agreed and matters not agreed and the reasons for any failure to reach agreement.
(2) An expert witness must exercise his or her independent, professional judgment in relation to such a conference and joint report, and must not act on any instruction or request to withhold or avoid agreement.

Immunity of experts

[3.165] For reasons of public policy, it has traditionally been accepted that expert witnesses are themselves immune from being sued, even if they give evidence which is itself negligent and so results in some harm or loss to a party to litigation. Although some commentators such as Freckelton & Selby (2005 at page 649ff) point to some shift from the generous past judicial attitude towards expert witnesses, they conclude that the likely outcome will be preservation of the expert witness immunity. The position as regards expert evidence and breach of professional standards or criminal penalty is even more complex, and remains controversial.

References and Further Reading

Introductory texts on law and some books on health care and the law should provide some guidance. They include:

Disney, J, et al (eds), *Lawyers* (2nd ed, Law Book Co, Sydney, 1986)
Enright, C, *Studying Law* (Macarthur Press, Sydney, 1991)
Frazer, S A, *How to Study Law* (Law Book Co, Sydney, 1993)
Freckelton, I and Selby, H, *Expert Evidence: Law, Practice, Procedure and Advocacy* (Lawbook Co., Sydney, 2005)
Gillies, P, et al, *The Law in Action* (3rd ed, CCH, Sydney, 1990)
Heilbronn, G, Kovacs, D, Latimer, P, Nielsen, J and Pagone, T, *Introducing the Law* (5th ed, CCH, Sydney, 1996)
Madden, B, "Medical experts and the courts", *Australian Health Law Bulletin* 14 (6)
O'Sullivan, J, *Law for Nurses* (Law Book Co, Sydney, 1983), chs 2, 14, 18
Pearce, D C, and Geddes, R, *Statutory Interpretation in Australia* (4th ed, Butterworths, Sydney, 1996)
Sawer, G, *The Australian and the Law* (Pelican, Sydney, 1972)
Wallace, J and Pagone, T (eds), *Civil and Legal Rights Handbook* (Collins Dove, Melbourne, 1983)
Also texts listed at the end of Chapters 6 and 14 should be useful.

Patient
Relationships

4 Consent to Health Care - Competent Adult

Trespass to the person

Elements of consent

Defences to Battery

Information & consent

Specific situations

Unlawful restraint / imprisonment

chapter 4

Consent to Health Care by a Competent Adult

Autonomy and Consent

[4.05] Historically, medical practice centred around the principles of beneficence and paternalism. Today, however, the situation is different:

> "Changes in societal values, the changing relationship between doctor and patient, abuse of position and misconduct on the part of practitioners, the great importance accorded to individual freedom of action and personal autonomy, along with advances in medical techniques which provided a greater range of patient choice, brought about a shift from paternalism to personal autonomy." [Mason (2000), p 13].

This focus on autonomy has led to the development in law of the principle that health care must not be given without the patient's consent. The words of Cardozo J, a most articulate American judge, are quoted in *Schloendorff v Society of New York Hospital* (1914) 211 NY 125 at 126 as the classic expression of the principle of medical autonomy:

> "Every human being of adult years and sound mind has a right to determine what shall be done with his own body; and a surgeon who performs an operation without his patient's consent, commits an assault."

The ongoing support for that principle in Australia was highlighted and clarified in the *Review of the Law of Negligence* (often referred to as the "Ipp Report") at paragraphs 3.35-3.36:

> "People have the right to decide for themselves whether or not they will undergo medical treatment. Originally, consent to medical treatment was seen as relevant only to the question of whether a medical practitioner administering the treatment could be sued for trespass to the person (battery), for interfering with the patient's bodily integrity. In this context, the law only required the medical practitioner to tell the patient, in general terms, about the nature of the proposed treatment. Under current law, however, the giving of information by the medical practitioner, and the

53

giving of consent by the patient, are seen as relevant to the issue of whether the medical practitioner has exercised reasonable care in relation to the patient. More importantly, it is now thought that medical practitioners must provide the patient with sufficient information to enable the patient to give 'informed consent.' This obligation is commonly (although inaccurately) referred to as the 'duty to warn.'"

These legal principles of course echo ethical principles, such as have been recently outlined in the *Code of Professional Conduct* published by the New South Wales Medical Board by reference to s 99A of the *Medical Practice Act 1992* (NSW); gradually being adopted in much the same form throughout Australia (see Appendix 5 for the full version of the Code). Standard 2.3 provides that to establish and maintain that trust medical practitioners should:

- give patients full information about their condition and treatment, outlining the risks and benefits, and prognosis. You should provide this information to the parent, guardian or person responsible where patients lack the maturity or ability to understand etc.
- give information to patients, parent, guardian or person responsible in a way they can understand;
- wherever possible, check that the patient, parent, guardian or person responsible has understood the information given and the course of action proposed, and that they consent to it, before you provide treatment or investigate a patient's condition;
- respect the right of patients to be fully involved in all decisions about their care;
- respect the right of patients to decline treatment or decline to take part in teaching or research.

Autonomy is recognised as a basic legal and human right of all competent adults. It has been the basis of many judicial decisions. Cases in Australia, England and the United States have demonstrated the conflict between the perspectives of patient autonomy and medical paternalism. Autonomy is based on the principle of the right of the patient to knowingly make decisions regarding medical treatment, no matter how unwise others may consider them, or how disastrous the effects on the person. There is no legal duty to provide medical care to a competent person who does not want that care. This means that legally, when there is a conflict between autonomy and beneficence, beneficence should always yield to the right of a competent person to consent to, or refuse, health care.

Summary of the Law of Consent

[4.10] A brief summary of the law on consent is presented here, and explained more fully below.

In law, there are two possible actions that can be taken against a health carer where consent to health care was absent: *trespass to the person* (including assault and/or battery or unlawful detention) or *negligence*.

To avoid an action in trespass to the person the health carer must take reasonable steps to ensure that the patient understands the broad nature and effects of the proposed procedure or intervention, and consents to it (here called "*general consent*") (*Rogers v Whitaker* (1992) 175 CLR 479; [1992] HCA 58).

To avoid an action in negligence the health carer must ensure that the patient is provided with sufficient information to make an informed decision with regards to the proposed procedure (here called "*informed consent*") (*Rogers v Whitaker* (1992) 175 CLR 479; [1992] HCA 58).

It can be seen that both elements should be present for lawful consent. In both cases, the patient must be capable of understanding the information.

What constitutes understanding?

[4.15] A patient must understand the nature of the treatment and be able to weigh up the risks and benefits (*F v West Berkshire Health Authority* [1989] 2 All ER 545). A patient's ability to understand will be determined by their competence. It is plausible that the level of understanding required will vary with the nature of the decision to be made.

What constitutes "broad nature and effects"?

[4.20] Briefly, this involves a description of the physical intervention proposed and its intended outcome (for example, how it is intended to benefit the patient, and its overall effects on the patient).

What are "material risks"?

[4.25] A risk is material if the health carer knows or should know that:

- a person in this patient's situation; or
- this particular patient,

would be likely to attach significance to it.

Trespass to the Person

[4.30] It is part of a health carer's work to touch a patient and to carry out procedures on her or him, be it washing, giving medication, open heart surgery, resuscitation or sustenance. According to the law no such action whatsoever may be taken without the patient's consent to it, other than in limited circumstances (as are discussed at **[4.165]**ff).

The common law has, for hundreds of years, maintained that any unwanted interference with a person's body, or creation of fear of such interference, is an actionable wrong at law, and the remedy is based on the law of trespass: in this case, trespass to the person.

It has been established in the courts that a competent person has an absolute right to withhold consent to medical treatment for any reason, rational or otherwise, or for no reason at all, even where that decision may lead to his or her own death (*Re MB* [1997] 8 Med LR 21). This includes medical procedures, whether therapeutic or experimental. This results in the hospital's concern to gain patients' consent before medical procedures are undertaken. However, the action in trespass covers all activity affecting another's physical integrity, so it applies to all health carers, as well as the public in general. There are several grounds for an action in trespass to the person: assault, battery and false imprisonment are the main ones.

Assault

[4.35] The term "assault" is often colloquially used to mean the "beating up" of a person. Strictly speaking, assault is carried out simply by intentionally creating in the mind of another the apprehension of unwanted physical contact. This does not have to be harmful contact. If a health carer, for example, threatens a patient with medication, loss of privileges or restraint if the patient does not behave (unless there is a real risk of harm from their actions (see **[4.245]**ff)), this can constitute assault. The threat does not have to be explicit, it need only be inferred from the carer's words or actions. Any fear of unwanted contact placed in the mind of a patient through the carer's actions may constitute assault.

Whether or not an assault has occurred is determined by what a reasonable person with the patient's characteristics would make of the situation. That is, the defendant need not intend to carry out the threat so long as the patient is made to believe that they will be touched against their will, and:

- the means for such touching are reasonably available; or
- the defendant ought to have foreseen that the patient would be likely to believe this (see *Macpherson v Beath* (1975) 12 SASR 174 per Bray CJ at 177).

Battery

[4.40] When the threat is carried out, that is the patient is touched against their will, that may constitute battery.

Damage need not be caused

[4.45] While assault and battery are criminal offences they may also form the basis of a civil action, for which the aggrieved person may claim damages. To sustain an action alleging assault and/or battery, the plaintiff need not show that any harm was suffered. Our society places such a premium on the personal integrity of the individual, that one is liable to compensate for the breach of that integrity, even where one has caused no physical or mental harm to someone (see *Weir v Tomkinson* [2001] WASCA 77 at [108]). The situation is quite different if the claim is brought in negligence (see **[4.280]**).

Battery may occur even where the intent is to benefit

[4.50] In the ancient case of *Cole v Turner* (1704) 6 Mod 149, it was held that "the least touching of another in anger is battery". However, later courts have held that it has never been the common law that anger is necessary (*Boughey v The Queen* (1986) 161 CLR 10). The intent may be to assist the person, even save life (see, for example, *Malette v Shulman* below **[4.190]**). The invasion to the person's autonomy itself is harm enough.

[4.55] Case: *Candutti v ACT Health and Community Care* [2003] ACTSC 95

C sued alleging that she went into hospital to undergo laparoscopic tubal ligation and instead of that procedure a laparotomy with tubal ligation was performed, a more invasive procedure to which she did not consent. C asserted that she consented to laparotomy only in the event of an emergency during surgery. It was the hospital's case that C consented to the laparotomy in the event that the laparoscopic procedure was unable to be performed. As C's abdomen was unable to be inflated with gas, and thus the laparoscopic procedure could not be performed, the surgeon proceeded with the laparotomy. The Court held that the laparotomy procedure was performed without consent and there was no life-threatening emergency which justified it. Thus, in the circumstances, the performance of the laparotomy amounted to trespass.

The patient need not be aware of battery

[4.60] Battery may take place when a patient is asleep, comatose or anaesthetised. The patient does not have to know that the unwanted act is taking place, nor does he or she have to have specifically stated an objection to it. If no permission for the act has taken place, and there is no necessity for the action to preserve or save the person's life or limb, then he or she has the right to sue the perpetrator of the act in battery. It is quite clear that any act that is not consented to and that is unnecessary is unlawful. Examples include the pelvic examination by students of anaesthetised patients, or practice in the insertion and removal of inter-uterine devices on them.

Implications for health carers

[4.65] Consent issues do not simply apply to the medical profession: all health carers are required to ensure they do not deal with people without their consent.

Health carers should keep in mind that there may be all sorts of reasons, unknown to them, that might cause a patient to come to a decision they might believe improbable. In that case they can attempt to persuade, but they cannot impose their views on a reluctant patient or pressure a patient into a particular decision. Health carers also need to be cautious that they do not become agents in the administration of treatment without the patient's consent.

> **[4.70] Case:** *Hart v Herron* [1984] Aust Torts Rep
> ¶80-201 (SC NSW)
>
>
>
> The plaintiff argued that on arrival at hospital, he expressed
> concern about the procedure he was to receive and asked to see
> his doctor. He said he was offered medication to "calm him down"
> and was subsequently given "deep sleep treatment" and electro-
> convulsive therapy. He sued in battery, as he alleged he had not
> consented to treatment. The defence argued, among other things,
> that the fact that he presented himself at the hospital and did not
> leave when he expressed concern about the treatment was an
> indication of his consent to it.

[4.75] The case at first instance was heard before a judge and jury. The jury
found that the plaintiff had not consented to the treatment and that the doctor
was liable in battery. The hospital, through its staff, was found not liable in
battery as the plaintiff had not made out his case against it. The Court rejected
the argument that attendance at a hospital is necessarily consent to
subsequent treatment, and the hospital was found liable for false imprisonment. A distinction was drawn between "genuine" consent (negated by trickery
or fraud) and consent, which may be "genuine" consent, but which is based on
inadequate information regarding the procedure, and was thus rather a matter
of negligence (see discussion at **[4.280]**ff). In determining whether the consent
was "genuine" the Court considered the evidence of one of the nurses who
testified that the general nature of the procedures that were carried out on
Mr Hart had been explained to, and accepted by, him. The plaintiff appealed,
seeking a new trial on damages against the doctor. The appeal was denied.

In circumstances where consent has not in fact been given health carers
who know consent has not been given may be responsible for their part in
battery, and cannot point to the fact that they have been told to act this way.
Staff are not required to follow unlawful orders of their employer (see Ch 11),
and may be individually responsible for acts of battery they carry out. Where a
health carer is expected to assist in a procedure to which the patient has not
consented, before refusing to assist he or she must consider whether to refuse
would result in harm to the patient.

It should not be presumed that because someone has entered hospital or
some other health facility they have given a blanket consent to whatever might
be done to them. They have the right to refuse any treatment at any time, and
indeed to leave the institution at any time. Consent, however, may be implied
from a person's words or actions. For example, if a patient waits in line for
treatment or rolls up her sleeve when she sees a nurse approach with an
injection, the nurse can presume consent (*O'Brien v Cunard SS Co* 28 NE 266
(1891)). Outward behaviour, not inner thought, is what is taken into account by
the courts, so that, if a patient indicates consent by some action, and the person
carrying out the procedure has no reason to doubt that they are knowingly
doing so, consent may be presumed. However, one should take care to ensure
that that is the case, and that the patient understands the nature and effect of

the procedure (including drugs to be given) to avoid an action in trespass, and any risk that is involved in the health care, to avoid an action in negligence.

[4.80] Case: *Shulman v Lerner* 141 NW 2d 348 (1966) (Michigan CA United States)

A dentist with an infected eyelid attended his doctor's surgery. Previously the condition had been dealt with non-surgically, but on this occasion the doctor removed the gland surgically, presuming the dentist's consent. The dentist sued in battery.

The doctor argued that consent could be implied by the fact that the dentist was familiar with surgical technique and would have understood by the preparation of instruments and draping of the eye that some sort of surgical procedure was to follow. The Court rejected this argument, stating that the dentist had been fully conscious, the procedure was neither life-saving nor urgent, and the opportunity for obtaining consent was available. The dentist was awarded $12,500.

[4.85] This case has a most important message for health carers. It indicates that the presumption should be that a person does not want treatment unless they specifically agree to it, not that they want it unless they specifically decline it. Passivity is not necessarily consent, and the onus is on the health carer to actively determine that the patient consents, not on the patient to express her or his refusal.

Elements of Consent

[4.90] It is important that there must be effective consent to health care procedures, and that that consent must be "real" in the eyes of the law. Simply having a signed consent form is not necessarily enough. Consent must have at least three elements:

- it must be *voluntary and freely given* (consent given under threat or duress, or the effect of stupefying drugs is not valid) and the patient must understand that it can be withdrawn at any time;
- it must be *specific* (the act carried out must be the act consented to); and
- it must come from a *competent person*, in other words the patient must be capable of understanding the nature and effect of the proposed care, and of making a choice in relation to having the care.

Consent must be voluntary

[4.95] Consent must be given without undue influence, or coercion. There must be no misrepresentation (whether deliberate or mistaken) as to the nature or necessity of a procedure, nor must there be threats, bribes, or other attempts to get the desired results (*Re T (Adult; Refusal of Medical Treatment)* [1993] FAM 95).

Misrepresentation will vitiate consent to treatment

Misrepresentation as to need for treatment

[4.100] Where a dentist induced patients to agree to extensive procedures, including fillings and root canal treatment which were not necessary, he was held liable in battery. The dentist deliberately withheld information in bad faith as he knew the patients would not consent if they understood the work was unnecessary (*Appleton & Ors v Garrett* (1997) 8 Med LR 75; see also *Re T* at **[4.205]**).

Medication and consent

[4.105] The question of the validity of consent to treatment arises in situations where a patient's consent to a procedure is sought whilst they are under the effect of medications prescribed to them.

> **[4.110] Case:** *Beausoleil v La Communitie des Soeurs de la Providence* (1964) 53 DLR 65 (CA Quebec)
>
> A patient asked to have a general anaesthetic rather than a spinal anaesthetic for a surgical procedure, as her mother had had serious adverse effects from a spinal anaesthetic. After she received her pre-medication, she was pressured into having a spinal anaesthetic by medical staff. As a result she became a paraplegic. She sued, claiming that her apparent consent had not been valid, as it had not been voluntary.

[4.115] The Court agreed that as she had been given the pre-medication, its potentially sedative effects meant that legally the plaintiff was not in a condition to agree voluntarily to the procedure. This principle indicates that any consent given after or during the giving of medication which affects a person's ability to receive and understand information, may not be valid.

The same principle casts doubt on the validity of a decision if a person who is under the influence of medication refuses treatment after having previously consented to it. Where the treatment is not urgent, health carers have the options of going ahead and carrying out the procedure, or postponing the treatment until the person is no longer affected by the drugs and can express his or her wishes. Where they go ahead, there is the risk that the person will bring an action in battery. It could be argued in defence that the health carers were of the honest and reasonable belief that the person was, at that time, not competent to make the decision to refuse the treatment, and that they acted in the best interests of the patient. However, given the non-urgent nature of the procedure, it is unlikely that this would be considered sufficient. Health carers may be better advised to postpone the procedure until the patient is restored to a state of competence.

Consent does not have to be in writing

[4.120] Legally recognised consent is the valid agreement of the patient to the treatment, however conveyed. Consent may thus be given by implication, by some kind of clear indication, verbally, or in written form. Evidence of consent may also be provided by witnesses (a written consent is preferable of course, signed by the patient and witnessed). Nonetheless, a consent form is merely *evidence* of consent (see **[4.435]**). Where a patient refuses consent to treatment, this should also be evidenced in writing or by witnesses.

Legal "competence"

[4.125] At law, every adult is to be presumed to be competent to make decisions unless there is clear evidence or knowledge that they are not. A competent adult is one who is capable of understanding the nature, consequence and risks of a proposed procedure and the consequences of refusing treatment.

The question of just what is required for someone to be held to have the capacity to consent to treatment was first addressed in detail by Thorpe J in *Re C (Adult; Refusal of Medical Treatment)* [1994] 1 WLR 290. In that case, C, a man who suffered from schizophrenia, refused to agree to a clinically indicated amputation of the leg. The judge stated that he found helpful the suggestion that the decision-making process follows three stages:

- comprehending and retaining treatment information;
- believing it (that is, they must not be "impervious to reason, divorced from reality or incapable of judgment after reflection" (*B v Croydon District Health Authority* [1955] All ER 683)); and
- weighing it in the balance to arrive at a choice.

Buchanan and Brock ((1989), p 19) propose the view that the necessary degree of understanding depends on the nature of the treatment and thus decision-making tasks vary substantially in the capacities they require of the decision-maker. They believe that some will demand a higher level of competence and higher level of understanding. The crucial question is how defective a person's capacity and skill to make a particular decision must be in order for that individual to be deemed to lack the capacity to make that particular decision.

This view is supported by the following comments of Lord Donaldson MR in *Re T* [1992] 4 All ER 649 (see further at **[4.205]** below):

"it may not be a case of capacity or no capacity. It may be a case of reduced capacity. What matters is whether at that time the patient's capacity was reduced below the level needed in the case of a refusal of that importance, for refusals can vary in importance. Some may involve a risk to life or of irreparable damage to health. Others may not."

Fluctuating and reversible loss of competence

[4.130] Whilst there has been no judicial ruling directly on the point where a person's lack of competence is episodic, fluctuating, limited or reversible, there is an obligation to take reasonable measures to remove any barriers to their gaining adequate capacity to make decisions about their bodily integrity and health. In a Report, *Assessment of Mental Capacity: Guidance for Doctors and Lawyers*, published by the British Medical Association in 1996, principle 12.7 states that "Doctors should be aware both that medical disabilities can fluctuate and that there are many factors extraneous to a person's disorder which may adversely influence capacity. It is the duty of the assessing doctor to maximise capacity." Ways in which capacity can be enhanced are set out below, and include:

- treating any condition which may be affecting capacity;
- waiting for a period of lucidity where capacity fluctuates;
- assisting the condition (such as short-term memory) through therapy where appropriate;
- ensuring that the difficulty is not one of *communication*;
- eliminating factors that may make capacity difficult, such as stress, anxiety, insecurity;
- sensitivity in approach and presentation of issues;
- ensuring adequate education, explanation and sufficient time for understanding; and
- ensuring the presence of a third party where that would help, and absence of a person where their presence causes stress.

What must a person understand?

[4.135] It has been held that a patient must understand the nature of the treatment, and be able to weigh up the risks and benefits (*F v West Berkshire Health Authority* [1989] 2 All ER 545). This is where it is most important to be clear that for the purposes of consent to health care (that is, to avoid an action in battery) the person need only understand "in broad terms, the nature of any procedure proposed to be performed upon them" (*Rogers v Whitaker* (1992) 175 CLR 479: [1992] HCA 58; see **[4.295]**).

[4.140] Case: *Chatterton v Gerson* [1981] 1 QB 432

A woman suffering from pain from a post-operative scar underwent an unsuccessful intrathecal block, with the result that the pain became almost unbearable. The procedure was competently performed, but the woman sued the specialist in battery and negligence. As to the battery allegation, she argued that because she had not been informed of the risks of the procedure, she had not given a valid consent to the surgery.

[4.145] The Court rejected C's claim in battery, stating that once a person has been informed in broad terms of the nature of the procedure that is sufficient for their agreement to the procedure to be consent. Any allegation that he or she should have been given information about risks of the health care is a question of negligence, not battery.

[4.150] Case: *Sidaway v Governors of Bethlem Royal Hospital* [1985] 1 All ER 643 (House of Lords (England))

Mrs Sidaway was an elderly patient who underwent an operation on her cervical vertebrae. There was a one to two percent risk of paralysis occurring inherent in this operation, but she was not informed of this. Unfortunately she did suffer some paralysis, and sued, alleging that it was the surgeon's duty to inform her of the risk.

[4.155] The House of Lords rejected this claim, re-affirming the decision of the case of *Bolam v Friern Hospital Management Committee* [1957] 1 WLR 582, which gave medical staff the discretion to decide what disclosure is proper and in the patient's interest. But, while the Court kept for itself the right to review such a decision, it would only do so where the discretion has fallen patently below what is deemed to be reasonable in the circumstances. Thus, the issue of informed consent comes under the category of negligence rather than trespass. In the Australian case of *Battersby v Tottman* (see **[5.245]**), the Court endorsed this approach strongly. At that time it held that courts should not doubt the judgment of doctors, nor refuse them the right to make decisions, unless convinced they are wrong. *Bolam's* case was further restricted by the Australian High Court in *Rogers v Whitaker* (see **[4.295]**).

The *Bolam* test, as stated by McNair J, states that a defendant will not be guilty of negligence:

"if he acted in accordance with a practice accepted as proper by a responsible body of medical men skilled in that particular art".

The *Bolam* test has since been modified in England, most notably in *Bolitho v City and Hackney Health* [1998] Lloyd's Rep Med 26 where Lord Browne-Wilkinson stated that, at least in cases of diagnosis and treatment, there will be cases where a defendant may be found liable in negligence despite evidence that there is a body of professional opinion that sanctions his conduct. This may occur in circumstances where a judge is not satisfied that the opinion relied upon is capable of withstanding logical analysis and thus the opinion is not "reasonable and responsible". (In relation to informed consent cases, see **[4.280]** ff.)

The unsatisfactory nature of the *Bolam* test in its original form was noted in the *Review of the Law of Negligence* at paragraph 3.11:

"... the *Bolam* rule, when strictly applied, can give rise to results that would be unacceptable to the community. They show the main weakness of the

Bolam rule to be that it allows small pockets of medical opinion to be arbiters of the requisite standard of medical treatment, even in instances where a substantial majority of medical opinion would take a different view. It is well-established that in many aspects of medical practice, different views will be held by bodies of practitioners of varying size and in different locations. This can result in the development of localised practices that are not regarded with approval widely throughout the profession. Thus, the *Bolam* rule is not a reliable guide to acceptable medical practice."

Consent must be specific

[4.160] Consent for surgery or other procedures will not be of any value unless the precise form of surgery or procedure is determined. Written documents should specify the treatment, for example, "left tympanoplasty". That procedure is all that the surgeon is allowed to perform (see *Candutti v ACT Health & Community Care* at **[4.55]** above). Courts have held, for example, that consent to an operation on the uterus is not consent to sterilisation (see at **[4.175]**; *Levi v Regional Health Authority* (1980) 7 *Current Law* 44). Consent may also specify who is to carry out the procedure.

Defences to an Action in Battery

[4.165] It is a defence to a claim of assault and battery that:

* any apparent threat or physical contact was unintended or an accident;
* the situation was an emergency, and measures used were to save life or health;
* the action taken was in self-defence when faced with imminent danger, by the use of no more force than was necessary to prevent that danger (self-defence);
* the action taken was for the protection of another (including the victim) from danger, again using no more than reasonably necessary force;
* the action taken was for the protection of property, with no more than reasonably necessary force (given the relative value of the welfare of those involved, compared with the value of the property); and
* there was statutory power to do so.

Emergencies

[4.170] As indicated above, presumption of consent allows health carers to carry out treatment in an emergency. "Emergency" has not been defined by the courts, but it has been described variously as being:

* a situation where a medical or surgical procedure is immediately necessary to save the life of a person: "Such would require the patient to be in grave danger, with death imminent in the sense of hours or days as against weeks or months" (Dix et al (1988), p 102);

- a situation requiring treatment necessary in order to save a person's life or to prevent serious injury to their health (*Australian Health and Medical Law Reporter* at ¶17.150).

When consent is an issue neither of the above definitions may be entirely satisfactory. Rather, the question of whether an emergency exists in relation to consent, for a person who is unable to do so, is based on whether serious harm would occur if attempts were made to seek consent from whomever is authorised to give it. That is, the word "immediate" should be applied literally. Any treatment which is simply thought to be desirable, or which may preserve life later, cannot be considered as necessary for the purposes of acting without consent. The action contemplated must be action to save life at the time of making the decision.

In addition to common law protections, some Australian jurisdictions provide legislative endorsement of the doctrine of emergency (see *Emergency Medical Operations Act* (NT), s 3; *Consent to Medical Treatment and Palliative Care Act 1995* (SA), s 13). However, such statutory references mention "emergency" but do not define it in uniform or precise terms.

[4.175] Case: *Murray v McMurchy* [1949] 2 DLR 442
(SC British Columbia)

A surgeon carrying out a caesarean section noted that the woman had a number of uterine fibroids, which were capable of causing harm to the woman, foetus, or both in a later pregnancy. He carried out a hysterectomy to prevent such an occurrence.

[4.180] The Court held that as the harm was avoidable and not imminent, his performance of a tubal ligation was battery.

Refusal of emergency treatment

[4.185] Where adults of apparently sound mind require emergency treatment, and are conscious, they can refuse it.

[4.190] Case: *Malette v Shulman* (1991) 2 Med LR 162
(CA Ontario)

M was seriously injured in a car accident and taken to hospital unconscious. She was carrying a card, unsigned and unwitnessed, which stated that she was a Jehovah's Witness and refused any blood transfusions. She deteriorated and was bleeding profusely from severe facial injuries, severed nose and internal bleeding. Dr S gave her a blood transfusion. She sued him, and he argued that as she had been unconscious he had been unable to inform her properly for her "informed refusal" and he was thus under a legal and ethical duty to give emergency treatment. The trial Court found in the plaintiff's favour and the doctor appealed.

[4.195] The Ontario Court of Appeal denied the appeal, stating that the card did impose a valid restriction on the treatment that could be given. The plaintiff did foresee this sort of situation, the Court said, and that was the very reason for her carrying it. The Court went on to state that it recognised the dilemma in which the doctor was placed, however he would not have violated his legal duty, or his professional responsibility if he respected the plaintiff's right to control over her body. He had no right to judge the rationality of her decision, so long as the instructions were valid. It was her responsibility if harmful consequences arise from her decision. It is important to note that M received what, in terms of today's figures, could only be considered to be nominal damages, and also had to pay her own legal costs. This is an indication of the legal approach to cases where a doctor may have technically breached the patient's legal right to autonomy, but has nevertheless acted in what he or she believed to be the interests of the patient. Readers should contrast this case with *Qumsieh v Pilgrim* (see **[5.285]**).

Uncertainty about refusal of emergency treatment

[4.200] Where there is uncertainty as to the validity of a patient's refusal of emergency treatment, health carers may be justified in presuming that the person consents to life-saving treatment. However, it should not be presumed that an emergency by its very nature automatically renders a person unable to make health care decisions. In less urgent situations, health carers should seek assistance to ensure their actions are lawful. This may require application to the appropriate court or tribunal for emergency guardianship or reference to a person responsible (see Chapter 5). The Supreme Court has an inherent jurisdiction, called "*parens patriae*" jurisdiction, to make any ruling affecting the well being of any child or incompetent adult citizen who is in need. Decisions can be made urgently, with consequent legal protection of medical personnel in carrying out the court's ruling.

[4.205] Case: *Re T (Adult: Refusal of Treatment)* [1992] 4 All ER 649

T, who was 34 weeks pregnant, was involved in a car accident and doctors told her she would require a caesarean section. After a conversation with her mother, who was a Jehovah's Witness (T was ambivalent in her views, but still did not believe in transfusions) T told the doctors that she did not want a blood transfusion. She was assured that a caesarean could be performed without blood transfusion, so she signed a form refusing transfusions in the process of giving birth. She was not told that a transfusion could be required for other reasons. A caesarean section was performed without a transfusion, but T later required one for haemorrhage. The doctor would have given it except for the purported refusal, and instead T was put on life-support. T's father and partner applied to the court for assistance.

[4.210] The Court authorised a blood transfusion, holding that T had neither consented to, nor refused, a blood transfusion, and that it was therefore lawful to go ahead and give her life-saving treatment. There was also doubt as to whether T's refusal was voluntary, or the result of undue influence of her mother.

A further example of resort to the Supreme Court is the case of *K v Minister for Youth and Community Services* [1982] 1 NSWLR 311, which involved differences of opinion over whether a minor should have an abortion (see below, Chapter 5). Corresponding jurisdiction for children other than those in State care now also vests in the Family Court (see **[5.40]-[5.50]**).

Emergency services

[4.215] Paramedics, ambulance officers, rescuers and fire fighters are subject to the law as outlined above. A competent person may refuse care even in an emergency. It is often the case that such refusal is considered not competent, and emergency workers may consider that they can ignore refusals. This could leave them open to action for assault and battery. However, where their work involves sudden accidents and catastrophes, it could well be that both emergency workers and victims are not in a state to assess or know:

- the true gravity of the person's injuries;
- the precise nature of any health care (as this may change from moment to moment); and
- given the circumstances of the event, the risks involved in any procedure undertaken.

In the face of this uncertainty, emergency workers may act in the interests of preserving life and health.

Some jurisdictions provide legislative endorsement of the extension of the common law doctrine of emergency to health care professionals outside of the hospital setting. The *Health Services Act 1997* (NSW), s 67I, provides that an ambulance officer is not liable for any injury caused in the carrying out, in good faith, of their duty in providing ambulance services. However, this section does not relieve the officer's employer of their vicarious liability.

In addition, some Australian jurisdictions have statutory provisions protecting from personal liability "good samaritans", who in good faith and without expectation of reward, provide assistance to an injured person in an emergency (see, for example, *Civil Liability Act 2002* (NSW), ss 55-58). Such legislation may not protect emergency services personnel or health care workers who are on duty at the time they provide assistance because of the paid nature of their services.

Suicide

[4.220] Where people have attempted suicide, the overwhelming practice in Australia has been to provide emergency treatment to preserve their lives, in the face of evidence that they do not want this. No one in Australia who has been "rescued" from a suicide attempt has successfully sued his or her "saviours" in battery to the authors' knowledge. The state is said to have an interest in preserving life, thus the law, when in doubt, opts for life rather than no life, and treatment rather than no treatment. This is also reflected in the fact that some Australian jurisdictions have provided in their Crimes Acts that it is not assault or battery at criminal law to restrain or attempt to stop a person from committing suicide (see *Crimes Act 1900* (ACT), s 18; *Crimes Act 1900* (NSW), s 574B; *Criminal Law Consolidation Act 1935* (SA), s 13(a); *Crimes Act 1958* (Vic), s 463B).

[4.225] **Case:** *Re Kinney* (Unreported, Supreme Court of Victoria, Fullagar J, 23 December 1998)

A terminally ill man apparently unsuccessfully attempted suicide by overdose causing him to lapse into coma. The man's wife sought an injunction to prevent doctors from providing him with surgery, the need for which had arisen following the insertion of an artificial airway. The wife alleged that the man had written a suicide note, although this was not produced to the Court. Fullagar J refused to grant the injunction on the basis that the wife did not have the authority to refuse consent, allowing the Public Advocate to consent to the treatment. Fullagar J also commented that the court could be seen to be assisting the suicide if he was to grant the injunction and he declined to do so, invoking the state's interest in preserving life in support of his decision.

[4.230] **Case:** *Bouvia v County of Riverside* (unreported, 16 December 1983, SC Riverside County Cal, No 159780); *Bouvia v Supreme Court*, 179 Cal App 3d 1127; 225 Cal Rptr 297 (1986)

The trial court refused B an injunction ordering the Riverside Hospital to cease force-feeding her to prevent her carrying out her wish to be allowed to die. The court agreed with the hospital that the injunction would require it to assist suicide, against ethical and professional standards, and also that it had the right to decide how to treat patients "taking up its space". On appeal the Superior Court of California held that the patient's motives for refusing treatment were not relevant. It considered relevant her dependency on the hospital and lack of alternative health care institutions that would care for her as she wished. The court concluded: "It is not illegal or immoral to prefer a natural albeit sooner death than a drugged life attached to a mechanical device ... [having accepted her the hospital] may not deny her relief from pain and suffering merely because she has chosen her fundamental right to protect what little privacy remains to her." It overturned the lower Court's decision.

[4.235] More recently it was held by the House of Lords that those who accede to a person's refusal of treatment are not aiding and abetting suicide (*Airedale NHS Trust v Bland*; see **[14.295]**).

Necessity

[4.240] There has developed, in criminal law, the defence of "necessity". It is used to argue that the defendant was justified in breaching the law as the action was taken to avert a harm which was much more severe. The defence has two elements:

- the defendant must have had a reasonable and honest belief in the need to act in this way to avert the harm (and that there is no better means of doing it);
- the harm to be avoided must be proportionately more severe than that which is caused.

Necessity was considered by the Supreme Court of Queensland in the case of *State of Qld v Nolan & Anor* [2002] 1 Qd R 454. The case involved conjoined twins, Alyssa and Bethany, whose condition was such that surgery to separate them was the only hope of saving Alyssa's life, but the same surgery would without doubt lead to Bethany's death. The twins' parents consented to the surgery, however, the State of Queensland approached the Court to confirm that the proposed surgery was in the best interests of both girls and to obtain the Court's opinion as to whether performing the surgery, which would lead to Bethany's death, would be an unlawful act.

In regards to the best interests of the children, Chesterman J referred with approval to a decision of the English Court of Appeal the preceding year in which a similar situation arose (*Re A (Children) (Conjoined Twins: Surgical Separation)* [2001] 2 WLR 480, see also **[4.425]**) and concluded that as the operation was not to be performed with the intention of causing Bethany's death, the fact that her death was the inevitable outcome did not prevent the surgery being considered in the best interests of both girls. Two justices of the English Court invoked the doctrine of necessity to conclude that the surgery would not amount to unlawful conduct at common law. Chesterman J did not think that doctrine of necessity had a counterpart in the Queensland Criminal Code and instead adopted the approach of Ward LJ in *Re A*, that carrying out the operation represented the "lesser of two evils" as the operation was compelled by law to save Alyssa's life and thus justified, although it would in Bethany's demise.

The issue in this case, therefore, was not so much whether necessity could be used to justify providing treatment without consent and provide a defence in any civil action that may arise, but rather whether it would establish a defence to otherwise unlawful conduct constituting a criminal act.

There is uncertainty whether a distinct defence of necessity exists in relation to medical treatment in the absence of consent. The High Court in *Rogers v Whitaker* referred to cases of emergency or necessity, suggesting that necessity does exist as a defence in its own right. There is little authority as to what the defence may entail. It was referred to *Re F (mental patient; sterilisation)* [1990] 2 AC 1, *Re W (a minor; consent to medical treatment)* [1993] 1 FLR 381 and *R v Bournewood Community and Mental Health NHS Trust* [1999] 1 AC 458. In *Airedale National Health Service Trust v Bland* [1993] AC 789, Lord Keith of Kinkel stated that where a person is unable to give or withhold consent "it is lawful, under the principle of necessity, for medical men to apply such treatment as in their informed opinion is in the best interests of the unconscious patient". Thus, even if Australian courts were to accept that a defence of necessity should be available in cases of medical treatment in the absence of consent, it is likely only to apply where the patient is incompetent. Given that there are specific laws in Australia relating to the care of those who are not competent (see Chapter 5) and as a clear definition of "necessity" has not been accepted for civil cases to date, it should be approached with caution (see Mason, p 9).

Self-defence

[4.245] Action may be taken which is necessary for self-protection, the protection of others, or the protection of property, even where this results in harm to the person. An individual's protection from civil liability in such circumstances is reinforced by the self-defence provisions in civil liability statutes of some Australian jurisdictions (see, for example, *Civil Liability Act 2002* (NSW), s 52).

[4.250] Case: *Fontin v Katapodis* (1962) 108 CLR 177; [1962] HCA 63 (High Court of Australia)

Katapodis (K) sued Fontin (F), a hardware shop assistant, in battery. K had purchased goods at the shop and some days later returned. F accused him of failing to pay for the goods. K produced a receipt after some argument and the manager apologised. Not F however; the argument between him and K continued and K seized a wooden T-Square, hitting F with it twice. F threw a piece of glass at K, who dropped the T-Square and raised his hand to protect his face. He suffered serious and permanent damage as a result of severance of the ulnar nerve at the base of the thumb. F claimed, on the basis of these facts, that his action was self-defence under the attack of K.

[4.255] The Court agreed that K had assaulted F, and that F was entitled to protect himself. However, it was decided by the Court that F's action was in excess of that necessary to so do. A piece of glass can do a lot of harm, the Court said, and aimed at the face, it is a very dangerous weapon—far more dangerous than that used by K. The Court stated that while K might have caused more harm if F did not prevent him from doing so, F's action in throwing a piece of glass was out of all proportion to the danger confronting him. He could easily have moved away.

Health carers may take measures, even severe ones, to protect themselves from harm from others, for example, disoriented or aggressive patients. Avoidance of contact (backing off) should be the first consideration of anyone in the face of an attack, seeking help the second. If it is not feasible to evade contact, choosing a weapon, striking blows or immobilising someone involves a consideration of what would stop the *attack* rather than what would stop the *person*—unless, of course, stopping the person is the only way to protect oneself or others, which leads to the next defence.

Defence of another and defence of property

[4.260] A similar principle applies where action is required to prevent someone from harming a third person. The amount of force used must be reasonably proportional to the degree of injury to be expected from the assault upon the stranger. As Crawford J said in *Goss v Nicholas* [1960] Tas SR 133 at 144:

> "The time factor must also be taken into account, and if it is possible gently to restrain the would-be assailant, then this should be the manner of dealing with him."

Of course, it is recognised that such situations may occur in an atmosphere of stress and emergency. A genuine and honest mistake as to the gravity of a situation may occur. If this is the case one court has held that it would be unjust to penalise someone who acted according to that mistaken belief; for example, that a gun is loaded when it is not, or that a person is armed when that is not so (*R v Fennell* [1971] 1 QB 428 (English Court of Appeal)). Section 52 of the *Civil Liability Act 2002* (NSW) also recognises this by stating that the conduct must be a "reasonable response in the circumstances as he or she perceives them".

Where defence of property is at issue, measures taken to protect it may involve force against another. Reasonable steps in this sort of situation would be calculated on the balancing of harm to a person against harm to property. Obviously one would draw the line in such a situation long before one would when human life and well being are involved. Section 52 of the *Civil Liability Act 2002* (NSW) also recognises this by indicating that the section does not apply if the person uses force that involves the intentional or reckless infliction of death only to protect property, or to prevent criminal trespass or to remove a person committing criminal trespass.

Statutory power to use force

[4.265] This can only occur when the patient comes under criteria set out by a court order, statutory requirement, mental health legislation (Chapter 5), child welfare or other legislation (Chapters 5 and 16).

Information and Consent

[4.270] It has been stated above that a certain amount of understanding is required before a person can be said to have given "competent" consent to treatment. However, there is general consensus at law that a person who has agreed to health care when they have not been adequately informed as to the nature and consequences of the procedure, and substantial risks (including side effects) should have a remedy at law.

English and Australian courts have considered lack of full information as being a matter of negligence rather than a lack of consent, so long as the patient knew the general nature of the procedure. This was established in the English case of *Sidaway v Governors of the Bethlem Royal Hospital* [1985] 1 All ER 643 (House of Lords). The decision was followed in Australia in *Battersby v Tottman* (1985) 37 SASR 524.

Lack of information as a ground for negligence

[4.275] In English and Australian law, where a person makes a decision based on unreasonably inadequate information, they may sue the person responsible in negligence. The action in negligence is outlined in Chapter 6, but, in relation to information, requires that the patient show that:

- the health carer had a duty of care to provide the information;
- that duty was breached by the failure to provide the information;
- the patient would not have agreed to the health care if adequate information had been given; and
- as a result, the patient suffered harm.

What information should be given?

[4.280] The court will consider what a reasonable doctor should have told the patient under the circumstances. It is the doctor's duty to take reasonable care to provide a patient with the information that patient would consider necessary to make an informed decision regarding the proposed procedure. The House of Lords has decided that the courts and not the medical profession will determine what is reasonable information in any particular case (*Gillick's* case [1985] 3 All ER 402, see Chapter 5). The High Court of Australia endorsed this principle in *Rogers v Whitaker* (see [4.295]). This is also reinforced by comments in *The Review of the Law of Negligence* and is reflected in various statutes of the Australian jurisdictions that enacted the recommendations of that report, such as s 5P of the *Civil Liability Act 2002* (NSW).

The *Review of the Law of Negligence* provides a helpful analysis of the type of information a doctor is required to provide his or her patients. The *Review* identifies two aspects to the duty to inform, a *proactive duty* and a *reactive duty*. The proactive duty relates to information a doctor must provide a patient, even where the patient does not communicate a desire to be given it. It requires a doctor to inform a patient of the material risks inherent in the proposed treatment. The reactive duty relates to information that a doctor knows or ought to know that a particular patient would be likely to attach significance to. It requires a doctor to provide information in response to a patient's questions or concerns or that he or she otherwise knows or ought to know the patient desires.

It is instructive to note that in a survey of 1,158 doctors published in May 1993, the year after *Rogers v Whitaker* was decided by the High Court, 84 percent of respondents said there were circumstances in which they would be justified in withholding information from patients. Of these 41 percent said they would withhold information because the patient might refuse the treatment, 53 percent because they considered the patient a poor decision maker. A significant number also based their decision on judgment as to the patient's anxiety (77 percent), illness (85 percent), or lack of interest in knowing (65 percent). On the other hand, other studies have shown that patients want doctors to give them information, even if it is unfavourable (94-96 percent), even when they do not ask for it (Hancock, L, *Defensive Medicine and Informed Consent* (Review of Professional Indemnity Arrangement for Health Care Professionals) (AGPS, Canberra, 1993)).

There are ethical guidelines relating to the giving of information. Courts may consider such guidelines in determining whether a doctor has taken reasonable care, however, the guidelines are not legally binding, and will not be conclusive of whether or not a doctor has fulfilled his legal duty to inform.

Some Australian jurisdictions have set out what is "informed consent" for specific purposes, such as for those who have a mental illness (see for example *Mental Health Act 1986* (Vic), s 53B; *Mental Health Act 1990* (NSW), s 183).

In situations not covered by legislation, there is a duty to disclose material or substantial risks; determination of what these are will depend on the circumstances of individual cases.

[4.285] Case: *Young v Northern Territory and Others*
(1992) 107 FLR 264

The plaintiff, who had a history of mild pelvic inflammatory disease (PID), made a six-weekly post-natal visit to Darwin Hospital. There she was advised that the oral contraception which she was taking would be inappropriate under the circumstances and that she should have an intra-uterine contraceptive device (IUCD) inserted. There was some question in the evidence as to whether the plaintiff's uterus had fully returned to its normal size, but it was accepted by the Court that the notation in the plaintiff's notes that it was "6 weeks" meant that it had not. The plaintiff said she did not want the IUCD, as a previous IUCD had caused her severe pain and excessive bleeding, and resulted in a laparoscopy and scarring. She finally agreed to the insertion, however, with resulting perforation of the uterus and lodgement of the IUCD in the eploicacae of the sigmoid. The IUCD had to be removed by laparoscopy, and curettage performed. As a result, she suffered from amenorrhoea, dyspareunia, uterine fibrosis, a diseased uterus and bilateral tubal disease.

[4.290] It was accepted by the Court, that, given the patient's recent delivery, her history in relation to the IUCD and PID, and the notation by the doctor that her uterus was still enlarged to some degree, there was an increased risk of perforation of the uterus. The Court held that the plaintiff should have been told of the risk of perforation, and of alternative forms of contraception. The Court went on to accept the plaintiff's assertion that she would not have had the IUCD inserted if she had been told of the risk of perforation (see however **[4.320]**ff, regarding hindsight bias). Thus, the Court found in favour of the plaintiff.

A more comprehensive consideration of what information should be given was undertaken by the High Court of Australia in the same year.

[4.295] Case: *Rogers v Whitaker* (1992) 175 CLF 479; [1992] HCA 58

W was almost totally blind in her right eye as the result of a penetrating injury in her childhood. Despite her injury, W led a "substantially normal life: completing her schooling, entering the workforce, marrying and raising a family". Nearly 40 years after the initial accident, W sought a referral to an ophthalmic surgeon for review, in preparation for her return to the workforce after an absence of some years. She was subsequently referred to Dr R who advised her that an operation on the right eye would improve the cosmetic appearance of the eye and probably restore significant sight to that eye. W ultimately agreed to the surgery.

Subsequent to surgery, complications developed in the right eye, spreading to the left eye and resulting in almost total blindness. This is known as "sympathetic ophthalmia", and is a recognised risk of eye surgery. At no stage was W warned of the probability of this occurring. W sued in negligence on several grounds, including failure of Dr R to warn her of the risk of sympathetic ophthalmia.

[4.300] The defence relied on the principle enunciated in *Bolam*. In that case the Court held that the decision of what to tell a person is one which the doctor can make, based on medical judgment. That would make a doctor not negligent if he or she acted in accordance with a practice of disclosure or non-disclosure accepted at the time as proper practice by a responsible body of medical opinion, even if some doctors adopt a different practice. Dr R produced evidence from a group of specialists who supported his actions. He also relied on the fact that the risk of sympathetic ophthalmia was considered to be 1 in 14,000, and therefore too remote to mention to the patient. The judge at trial ruled that the failure to warn of the risk of sympathetic ophthalmia amounted to negligence. He considered the following facts:

- W had expressed a keen interest in avoiding harm to her good eye, and Dr R was aware of this;
- she repeatedly asked about risks;
- Dr R was aware at the time of the risk, although it was remote;
- the failure to warn of the risk was not contemplated for therapeutic reasons; and
- had W been advised of the risk, she would not have had the surgery.

The appeal went first to the New South Wales Court of Appeal where it was dismissed, and then to the High Court of Australia. The High Court held that the principle in *Bolam* was no longer applicable in Australia in determining whether a medical practitioner had given adequate information about a medical procedure to a patient. Instead the Court followed the judgment of King J in *F v R* (1983) 33 SASR 189 in which he stated that although the Court will consider evidence by medical specialists of what is considered proper medical practice, it is ultimately for the Court to determine what the appropriate standard of care is, and that the paramount consideration is to be that a person is entitled to make her or his own decisions about her or his life. The Court went on to say that the more drastic the proposed procedure, such as major surgery, the more necessary it is to keep the patient informed about the risks.

The High Court drew a distinction between *diagnosis and treatment* on the one hand, and *provision of information*, on the other. The former was held to be determined by medical judgment and practice, whereas the provision of adequate information is a *right*. Information is a right. This right is not based on medical judgment, but on legal principles, and it is for the court to decide whether a person's right to be adequately informed about a procedure has been breached or not. This may be based on consideration of the medical profession as to what is considered appropriate practice, but in the final analysis it will be a matter for the court to determine, given the paramount consideration that people are entitled to make their own decisions about their lives.

The ultimate question, however, is not whether the defendant's conduct accords with the practices of his profession or some part of it, but whether it conforms to the standard of reasonable care demanded by the law. That is a question for the court and the duty of deciding it cannot be delegated to any profession or group in the community (*F v R* (1983) 33 SASR 189 per King CJ at 194: quoted with approval by the High Court in *Rogers v Whitaker*; see also *Ellis v Wallsend District Hospital* [1989] Aust Torts Reports ¶80-259; *H v Royal Alexandra Hospital for Children & Ors* [1990] Aust Torts Reports ¶81-000). The *Review of the Law of Negligence* reiterates that the court is the ultimate arbiter of the standard of care in regard to the provision of information by a doctor to his patient. The principle is now enshrined in legislation such as s 5P of the *Civil Liability Act 2002* (NSW).

Patient should be told of "material risks"

[4.305] The High Court stated that the patient should be told of any material risk inherent in the treatment. A risk is material if:

> "... in the circumstances of a particular case, a reasonable person in the patient's position, if warned of the risk, would be likely to attach significance to it or if the medical practitioner is or should reasonably be aware that the particular patient, if warned of the risk, would be likely to attach significance to it." (*Rogers v Whitaker* (1992) 175 CLR 479; [1992] HCA 58).

Thus, a material risk is one:

- to which a reasonable person in the patient's condition would be likely to attach significance;
- to which the health carer knows (or ought to know) the particular patient would be likely to attach significance; or
- about which questions asked by the patient reveal her or his concern.

The Court also established that the fact that a person does not insist on information being provided does not reduce the health carer's duty (or patient's right) that it be provided. This means that health carers must be careful to take account of factors associated with the special needs of patients, "be they wishes, anxieties or beliefs" (Kerridge and Mitchell, (1994), p 241). Justice Gaudron stated that where no specific inquiry is made, the duty is to provide the information that would reasonably be required by a person in the position of the patient. This requires the health carer to consider what they ought to anticipate as this particular patient's needs, wishes etc. For example, where the patient is a professional singer or speaker, one could argue that the health carer ought to anticipate that he or she would have a particular interest in any risk of harm to the vocal chords.

It was accepted that W may not have asked the right question to elicit information about sympathetic ophthalmia, but she made clear her concern that nothing should happen to her good eye.

[4.310] Case: *Rosenberg v Percival* (2001) 205 CLR 434; [2001] HCA 18

P had an underdeveloped jaw, and it was recommended that she undergo a sagittal split osteotomy. Postoperatively, she suffered excessive pain and further procedures were undertaken, resulting in "excruciating pain" on attempting to open her mouth. Yet further procedures were undertaken with the result that she had difficulty opening her mouth, eating and speaking. She claimed she lost her university lecturing position, and enjoyment of life. It was established that she had signs of a pre-existing temporo-mandibular joint (TMJ) disorder, a condition which evidence suggested may be linked to a small risk of increased TMJ problems after sagittal split osteotomy. The trial judge found in favour of the Dr R. P appealed to the Supreme Court, which reversed the decision. Dr R then appealed to the High Court.

[4.315] The High Court held that the two main issues arising from the case were, firstly, whether Dr R was in breach of his duty of care to P by failing to bring to her notice the risk of the harm that eventuated and secondly, if there had been such a breach of duty whether it was causally related to her injuries. That in turn involved the question whether, if she had been made aware of the risk, P would have decided not to undergo the surgery. The Court was not convinced that she would have forgone the surgery, and so it became unnecessary to determine the answers to the first two questions.

The Court, however, undertook a thorough consideration of the law in relation to information.

The Court reiterated the *Rogers v Whitaker* ruling that there are two alternative tests of materiality in determining what are "material risks": the objective test of what risks a reasonable person in the patient's circumstances would consider significant, and the subjective test of those risks the particular patient actually considers to be significant. As P had not expressed any particular concerns (except to have the operation), the Court held that, unlike *Rogers v Whitaker*, the issue was one of whether the objective criterion had been met, and determined that it had. It also agreed with precedent that a risk is real and foreseeable if it is not far-fetched and fanciful.

Other principles reinforced by the Court were that:

- the law demands no more than what was reasonable under the circumstances, and that "reasonable" is the operative word;
- matters such as the severity and likely eventuation of the risk must be weighed up against the need for the surgery and availability of alternative treatment;
- one should not be too quick to discard consideration of the subjective criterion simply because the patient asked no questions.

The Court pointed out that there is a danger in hindsight influencing a person's perception of whether a risk was foreseeable at the time information was given, as the fact that the risk did materialise can convince one it is foreseeable. The word "reasonable" when applied to foreseeability, means that foreseeability is limited to what would have been reasonable for the health carer, with the knowledge of an ordinarily skilled practitioner, to have foreseen as a material risk. Justice Kirby also considered the many reasons given for not setting out all foreseeable risks, such as time, the ability or willingness of the patient to understand the details and practicality. He recognised that these factors do affect the communication process, but pointed to the principles laid down by *Rogers v Whitaker*, which have not been changed over time, and which, he said, serve the purpose of "nagging" and "prodding" health carers as to best practice in communication and legal insurance against liability.

Hindsight bias

[4.320] The courts and legislature are cognisant of the effect of hindsight on a plaintiff's assertions that had they been warned of a particular risk, they would not have proceeded with the proposed treatment. McHugh J stated in *Chappel* *v Hart* that "given that most plaintiffs will genuinely believe that they would have taken another option, if presented to them, the reliability of their evidence can only be determined by reference to objective factors".

The possibility of hindsight influencing a plaintiff's assertions that they would not have had the procedure if warned of the risk is also dealt with in the *Review of the Law of Negligence*. The report recommended, "the question of what information the reasonable person in the patient's position would have wanted to be given is to be answered by reference to the time at which the relevant decision was made and not at a later time" (para 3.55). The intention of such a provision was stated to require the issue of hindsight to be explicitly addressed.

Such concerns about the reliability of the plaintiff's evidence are reflected in the *Civil Liability Act 2002* (NSW), s 5D(3)(b) which prevents a plaintiff giving evidence of what they would have done if they had been told of the risk which eventuated.

Prior to the introduction of the civil liability legislation, the courts (in cases such as *Rosenberg v Percival, Rogers v Whitaker*, and *Chappel and Hart*) weighed the plaintiff's testimony against objective factors such as:

- the remoteness or otherwise of a risk;
- whether there was a suitable alternative treatment available;
- the magnitude of the risk;
- whether the procedure was elective, including whether the procedure could reasonably have been delayed;
- the experience and skill level of the practitioner concerned.

Insight into the approach the courts are likely to adopt was provided by Kirby J in the High Court decision of *Hoyts v Burns* (2003) 201 ALR 470; [2003] HCA 61. See also *Elbourne v Gibbs* [2006] NSWCA 127.

[4.325] Case: *Hoyts v Burns* (2003) 201 ALR 470; [2003]HCA 61

This case involved a claim for compensation by a woman who suffered injury in a cinema. Her seat had been constructed in such a way that the seat base lifted up when a person was not sitting upon it. It had lifted up when she left the seat temporarily and in attempting to sit down again fell to the ground, injuring herself on the underlying seat structure. The case was originally also presented on the basis of inappropriate design of the seat but ultimately proceeded based on a failure to warn of the risk of the injury occurring in such circumstances.

[4.330] Justice Kirby delivered a separate judgment which expressly considered the evidence given by Ms Burns as to what she would have done if a warning sign had been displayed:

"...trial counsel for the Appellant protested that the 'evidence' about what would have been done if a sign had been displayed was a matter of 'speculation'. So indeed it was. Whether or not, strictly, such evidence is admissible, it is commonly received in Australian courts. Presumably, this practice emerged once it was established that the relevant test of causation applicable in Australia was a subjective one. Nevertheless, the evidence of what a Claimant would have done if a non-existent warning had been given by a hypothetical sign is so hypothetical, self-serving and speculative as to deserve little (if any) weight, at least in most circumstances."

Helpfully, Justice Kirby went on to foreshadow how the Court might proceed in circumstances where such evidence is excluded.

"The evaluation of what the Respondent would have done, if a sign of the kind devised by the Court of Appeal had been displayed is truly a matter of hypothesis based upon an evaluation of circumstances that did not in fact occur rather than an assessment of whether the Respondent was telling the truth about her postulated belief in what she said in the additional evidence that the Judge allowed."

Accordingly, that would appear to be the approach required of a court under s 5D(3)(b)—the establishment of an hypothesis based upon the evaluation of circumstances, rather than an assessment of whether the injured person was telling the truth about his or her belief. This seems to be the approach later taken by Hoeben J in *Richards & Ors v Rahilly & Anor* (at 256-257) when he said:

"The evidence of Mr Richards was that had the treatment options been explained to him, he would have chosen Vigabatrin.
    The evidence of Mr Richards to which I have referred is of little value. He understood how important that answer was to Rhiannon's case. Although his evidence on this question may well have been truthful, it suffers from the problem identified by McHugh J in *Chappel v Hart* .... and restated in *Rosenberg v Percival* .... The reliability of such evidence needs to be assessed by reference to other evidence."

Implications for Health Carers

[4.335] The case law has developed in the past few years to become more specific in its outline of what information should be given to patients. Provided that a procedure or medication involves a risk which is known or ought to be known to the health carer, then this should be disclosed to the patient if the patient, or a reasonable person in the patient's position, would be likely to attach significance to that information.

 Checklist
 WHEN IS "INFORMED CONSENT" REQUIRED?
   ✓ All health carers owe a duty of care to patients to consider the need
     for "informed consent" when any proposed procedure involves:

✓ a recognised risk of side-effects or adverse effects;
✓ any side-effects or adverse effects that the proposed patient would consider significant;
✓ alternative procedures that are reasonably available that the health carer can offer; and
✓ effects on the patient of not having the procedure.

A recognised risk can be established by considering:

✓ texts, articles and courses to which the health carer has or ought to have access;
✓ required knowledge;
✓ accepted and widespread practice; and
✓ codes of health care practice.

"Therapeutic privilege"

[4.340] There is a view that information may be withheld on the basis of "therapeutic privilege", which was referred to by the Court in *Rogers v Whitaker* (1992) 175 CLR 479; [1992] HCA 58 (majority judgment at para 16). "Therapeutic privilege" has not been clearly defined by the courts, and although the majority of judges did not discuss in detail to what extent therapeutic privilege applies, they did describe it as "an opportunity afforded to the doctor to prove that he or she reasonably believed that disclosure of a risk would prove damaging to the patient" (majority judgment at para 9) (see also *Canterbury v Spence* (1972) 464 F 2d 772 at 789; *Sidaway v Governors of the Bethlem Royal Hospital* [1985] 1 All ER 643 per Lord Scarman; *Battersby v Tottman* (1985) 37 SASR 524 at 527-528, 534-535; Mason (2000), p 7). Gaudron J did make some specific statements (at para 8 of her judgment) which indicated that therapeutic privilege should be very limited. She stated that:

> "I see no basis for any exception [from the need to inform the patient] or 'therapeutic privilege' which is not based in *medical emergency* or in *considerations of the patient's ability to receive, understand or properly evaluate the significance of the information* that would ordinarily be required with respect to his or her condition or the treatment proposed." (Emphasis added)

The question of just what circumstances, if any, justify withholding information on the basis of therapeutic privilege is thus unanswered by judicial decisions, but it is suggested that it is based on whether the provision of information will actually exacerbate the health problems of particularly at-risk patients (for example, those with a mental illness), or enhance their decision-making capacity by withholding information that would impair it, rather than making the expression of consent to a proposed procedure difficult (Freckelton (1999), p 119; Schwartz and Grubb (1985), p 19).

Emergency and necessity

[4.345] All the judges in *Rogers v Whitaker* referred to emergency and necessity as being circumstances which presented exceptions to the provision of information. However, as these circumstances were not relevant to the case at hand, they did not consider what actually amounted to circumstances of emergency or necessity. Emergency and necessity are dealt with at **[4.170]** and **[4.240]** respectively.

Effect of Rogers v Whitaker

[4.350] *Rogers v Whitaker* was a landmark case in that it established two main principles:

1) the patient has a legal right to adequate information about the nature of any proposed procedure, and the material risks associated with the procedure; and
2) that two broad perspectives are used in deciding how to judge the adequacy of information: the doctor-centred perspective (that is, usual practice adopted by the profession) and the patient-centred perspective (what is of importance and use to the patient). Whilst the doctor-centred perspective may be considered in evidence, the patient-centred perspective is paramount.

[4.355] **Case:** *Chappel v Hart* (1998) 195 CLR 232; [1998] HCA 55

The plaintiff, H, was advised by the defendant, Dr C, that she required surgery for removal of a pharyngal pouch in her oesophagus (Endoscopic Zenker's Diverticulotomy). The condition was one that was relentlessly progressive, and while she did not have to have the operation at this time, H accepted that it would be necessary at some time in the future. She was assured by Dr C that it was a "common operation". He also mentioned the risk of perforation of the larynx as a recognised complication. H, whose occupation required a degree of public speaking, expressed concern at the possible effect to her voice (she stated that she did not want to end up sounding like Neville Wran—a former New South Wales Premier who had surgery which resulted in his speaking with a rasp). Despite this, Dr C did not warn her of the possibility of perforation of the oesophagus, with resulting contraction of mediastinitis, which could lead to damage to the vocal chords. It was accepted that perforation could occur in between one in 20 and one in 40 procedures, and that consequent infection and damage to vocal chords was very rare. One expert witness testified that he had carried out between 100 and 150 such operations without the occurrence of perforation of the oesophagus. The trial Court also accepted evidence that the more experience the surgeon had, the less likely that complications such as these would occur. H argued successfully that as the operation was not urgent, had she known of the potential result, she would have sought a more experienced surgeon. Dr C appealed to the High Court.

[4.360] The High Court upheld the finding, concluding that Dr C was negligent in not providing the information to H. Given her questions about the possible effect on her voice, the Court held, he should have been more forthcoming. Having been put on notice of her concerns, he should have known that such a risk was a material one to her, and provided her with adequate and appropriate information for decision making.

H's argument was that if she had been made aware of the risk to her vocal chords, she would have undergone the operation later, after finding someone least likely to cause the harm which in fact resulted. While the facts of the case did not require the Court to consider precisely what information, if any, should have been given to H with regard to whether another surgeon may be able to perform the surgery with less risk, some of the justices did touch upon the issue. Justice Gaudron stated that "[i]f the foreseeable risk to Mrs Hart was the loss of opportunity to undergo surgery at the hands of a more experienced surgeon, the duty would have been to inform her that there were more experienced surgeons practising in the field". However, in this case the risk was physical injury and the duty was to inform her of that risk. In addition, McHugh J commented that the evidence did not suggest that "any other surgeon was so superior in skill to the defendant that an operation by that person carried with it a statistically significant lesser risk of perforation than an operation by the defendant".

Thus, whether there may exist a duty on health carers to provide patients with information related to their competence and skills is yet to be definitively answered by the courts. The decision of the High Court in *Chappel v Hart* may be considered the high water mark in support of the proposition that a practitioner's skill level should form part of the information required to be given to patients. It may be that a court would be reluctant to find a breach of duty other than in circumstances where the risk is markedly variant or as McHugh J suggested "statistically significant".

Answering a patient's questions

[4.365] As discussed at **[4.295]**ff, it was clearly established in *Rogers v Whitaker* that a person's questions should be taken as indicating that he or she may have particular concerns that will require special attention by health carers. This principle is expressed in the *Review of the Law of Negligence* as the *reactive* duty to inform. It is important to realise that in Australia, the test for determining whether or not a doctor has fulfilled his duty to inform a patient is ultimately a subjective test. That is, in determining whether a patient would have undertaken a procedure, if warned of a risk of harm involved in that procedure, a court asks whether this patient would have undertaken the procedure (see *Rosenberg v Percival* (2001) 205 CLR 434; [2001] HCA 18 per McHugh J at [24]).

What information should be given?

[4.370] The following case is instructive as to how the courts consider what information should be given.

[4.375] Case: *Gover v South Australia* (1985) 39 SASR
543 (SC SA)

A patient who suffered from thyroid eye disease underwent blepharoplasty and canthoplasty. She had not been told what was involved in the operations, or the risks or dangers of it. She had expected only the left eye to be operated on, and so was surprised when the surgeon told her that he did not know which one it was "so we done [sic] both". These procedures involved some degree of risk of blindness, entropion or trichiasis. In fact the patient did develop trichiasis and entropion. The Court had to consider whether the doctor was negligent in failing to warn her of the risks.

[4.380] Cox J held that the duty of care owed by a doctor includes "the whole of the professional relationship" including the provision of information. The next question involved what information should have been given. The judge said that professionals should keep abreast of developments. Thus the professional should be reasonably knowledgeable and up-to-date. Further, it was held that even where a risk may be small, if its effect is likely to be devastating (as blindness would be) then this should be told to the patient. In *Battersby's* case Cox J quotes the Chief Justice as saying in an earlier case:

> "The more drastic the proposed intervention in the patient's physical make-up, the more necessary it is to keep him fully informed as to the likely risks and likely consequences of the intervention [*F v R* (1983) 33 SASR 189 at 192-194]."

The following case focuses on the width of the information which ought be given to the patient about alternative treatment options.

[4.385] Case: *Richards & Ors v Rahilly & Anor* [2005]
NSWSC 352

R was six years old at the time of the appeal. She suffered long-term developmental retardation and brain dysfunction. She was diagnosed with epilepsy in the first two years of her life. It was her case that had she been diagnosed and treated with a specific drug earlier than actually occurred, the extent of her disabilities would have been reduced. She alleged negligence against Dr R on the basis that there was excessive delay in diagnosing the epilepsy. She alleged negligence against Royal Alexandra Hospital for Children on two bases. Firstly, that the drug Vigabatrin should have been used sooner in her treatment. Secondly, that there was a failure to advise the parents adequately or at all concerning the benefits and risks of Vigabatrin. It is this last point that is of interest here. R's parents alleged that they should have been advised of the possibility of treating R with Vigabatrin as a legitimate treatment option and alternative to that recommended by the medical practitioners. It was their case that had they been aware of that treatment option they would have chosen to utilise Vigabatrin in R's treatment.

[4.390] Hoeben J made the following statements with regard to the duty of doctors to identify possible treatment options (at 234-237):

"In such circumstances it seems to me that a doctor is not only entitled but bound to recommend to patients (in this case the parents) that treatment which the doctor considers most appropriate in the circumstances. It is not a question of that choice involving the personal preference of the doctor but rather the doctor performing the fundamental duty for which he or she has been retained, ie to diagnose and treat. Once the doctor has recommended a treatment then it is incumbent upon him or her to explain fully to the patient the risks involved in that treatment.

...It would impose an impossible burden on the medical profession if a doctor was bound to offer a patient every 'legitimate' treatment option that 'could work' and discuss the advantages and disadvantages of each option with the patient and then allow the patient to choose his or her option.

...An obligation to warn of a 'material' risk inherent in a proposed treatment is a significantly different obligation to one requiring the provision of full information concerning a number of treatment options preparatory to the patient choosing his or her treatment.

In my opinion there was no obligation on the part of the Hospital to explain the various treatment options to Rhiannon's parents, or either of them, including the option of being treated with Vigabatrin so as to enable them to choose which treatment option they preferred."

In the following case, the issue was whether the doctor's duty to inform extended to advising patients of a statutory requirement for consent to disclosure of certain test results.

[4.395] **Case:** *Harvey & Chen v PD* (2004) 59 NSWLR 639

PD and FH attended a joint consultation with Dr Harvey for the purpose of having blood tests to ensure neither of them had any sexually transmitted diseases, including HIV, preparatory to their marriage and engaging in unprotected sex. PD later telephoned the doctors' surgery and was advised by a receptionist that her HIV test was negative but that she was not entitled to receive FH's results. FH subsequently deceived PD into believing he was not HIV positive, when he was. PD later acquired HIV. The plaintiff sued the doctors in the medical centre for inadequate counselling, including the failure to advise her of the statutory requirement for consent to disclosure. The plaintiff succeeded at first instance and the defendant doctors appealed.

[4.400] The Court of Appeal dismissed the appeal, although all three judges founded their decisions on slightly different reasoning. The judges were however agreed that, as Spigelman CJ states, "the subject matter of the initial consultation and the fact that it was a joint consultation for the stipulated purposes meant that it was incumbent upon Dr Harvey, in the light of his knowledge of ethical requirements, patient confidentiality and s 17(2) of the *Public Health Act 1991*, to advise FH and PD of the need for each to consent to the supply of their results to the other".

The following case looks at whether a doctor has a duty to inform a patient of an error having been made in their treatment. (This case is also discussed at **[6.440]** and **[9.170]**.)

[4.405] Case: *Wighton v Arnot* [2005] NSWSC 637

W developed a lump on the right side of her neck and was referred to the defendant for treatment. She subsequently underwent three operations at the hands of the defendant. W alleged that on the third occasion Dr A severed the right spinal accessory nerve and was thereafter negligent in failing to inform her of his suspicion that he had severed the nerve, failing to confirm that he had severed the nerve, and failing to refer her to an appropriate specialist for timely remedial surgery.

[4.410] Studdert J held that Dr A was negligent in failing to:

(a) carry out sufficient post-operative testing to determine whether the nerve had been severed;
(b) advise W prior to her discharge from hospital of the suspected severance;
(c) advise W of the need for surgical repair of the nerve.

Studdert J stated (at 38):

> "What the exercise of due care required of the defendant was that he take reasonable steps to determine whether it was the accessory nerve which had been severed, and that he alert the plaintiff as to what had occurred."

Thus a duty to disclose may arise in circumstances where the knowledge is of relevance to the patient's medical outcome and is a necessary part of reasonable post-surgery care. The duty can be said to extend to an obligation to make investigations where an adverse outcome is suspected. To what extent a more general duty to disclose might exist remains unclear.

Causation: Plaintiff must prove that ignorance affected decision

[4.415] In the *Gover case* (see **[4.375]**) the plaintiff was not able to convince the Court that had she been given the information she would not have had the operation. Thus although she should have been told of the risks, she was unsuccessful in her suit because this critical element was missing.

Implications for Health Carers

[4.420] Because application of the law relies on present evidence of past facts, verification of conversations is best afforded by a written record made contemporaneously or as soon after the event as possible. Where verbal agreement to treatment is given and even where a written consent form is completed, a more comprehensive record of the conversation between health carer and patient is advisable.

Checklist
GUIDELINES FOR GIVING INFORMATION FOR PATIENT DECISION-MAKING
Giving information
✓ There should be no coercion, patients should be encouraged to be frank, ask questions, and make up their own minds. Provide independent interpreters and repeat information if required, and look for responses that indicate that information has not been understood.
✓ It is prudent, where possible, to provide the patient with a written document concerning the advice given and a written record of the conversation should be made.
✓ Where possible, give the patient adequate time to make a decision, ask more questions, talk to others, think about the matter, etc.
✓ Advise the patient that he or she can get another medical opinion, and assist the patient to seek it if it is requested.
✓ Ensure that the patient understands:
   – the diagnosis, including the degree of uncertainty in this;
   – the prognosis, and any degree of uncertainty in this;
   – the anticipated effects of not undergoing the proposed treatment;
   – the nature of the intervention, for example, how invasive it is, whether it will be painful, how long it will take, how they will feel before, during and after it;
   – any significant long and short term physical, emotional, mental, social, sexual, or other outcome which may be associated with the proposed treatment;
   – the time involved in the treatment;
   – the costs involved in the treatment; and
   – the availability of alternative treatments, the above information about them, and why they are not recommended.
This involves consideration of the patient's personality, beliefs, fears, values and cultural background.

Withholding information
The withholding of information may be justifiable in limited circumstances:
✓ the patient's physical or mental health might be seriously harmed (this involving more than the patient being disconcerted or dismayed, or the health carer's discomfiture at giving the information);

✓ the patient refuses information, and requests the health carer to make the decisions. This does not relieve the health carer from giving basic information, or from first encouraging the patient that, on the basis that the patient's body is the object of the treatment, he or she should also be the decision maker, may be better able to co-operate with the treatment if he or she is better informed, and that the decision should not be made by someone else; and

✓ it is an emergency and not practicable to give the information.

This checklist is based on guidelines produced in pamphlet form by the National Health and Medical Research Council in 1993. The guidelines were re-endorsed in 2004. At the same time, an additional document was published to supplement the guidelines entitled *Communicating with Patients: Advice for Medical Practitioners*. Both publications can be accessed at www.nhmrc.gov.au.

An important caveat should be made about these guidelines. They require more than has been demanded by law. However, in a somewhat circular fashion, as they have been established as a "reasonable standard" of care by the medical profession, they may be adopted by the courts as the *legal* standard of care to be demanded of health carers, as such guidelines are considered by the courts when determining that standard of care.

What if the patient does not want to know?

[4.425] Some patients will state that they do not want to be burdened with a whole lot of information, and leave the treatment decision to the health carer. The law does not have much to say on this matter. In the case of *F v R* (1983) 33 SASR 189 King CJ stated that the doctor is not required to inflict unwanted information on a patient, but the decision that the patient does not wish to be informed should not be made lightly. The Victorian Law Reform Commission ("Informed Decisions about Medical Procedures" (1989), p 18) suggested that, firstly, the patient should be sufficiently informed to decide that he or she does not want the information, secondly, that the doctor should determine *why* the patient does not want to be informed. It might be because he or she understands broadly what is involved, or is unable to deal with the matter (for example, through fear, or a feeling that he or she is not able to even consider the matter). If the latter is the case, the Commission says, the doctor should ensure the patient understands at least broadly what is involved.

Consent forms

[4.430] Much of the contact health carers have with patients will involve verbal or implied consent only. Where medical procedures are major, most health care workers ensure that they have written consent forms, which are signed by the patient. However, written consent may be revoked verbally, and at any time prior to the care. What are health carers' responsibilities when they are seeking to obtain a signed consent form for a procedure to be carried out by someone else?

The legal implications of consent forms

[4.435] First, the nature of consent forms should be understood. At law, a signed document is a contemporaneous record of a person's agreement, intentions or understanding. When one signs a contract, one is bound by its contents, but the law has recognised that evidence of the conditions under which one signs something may be potential evidence that credence should not be given to the document. See, for example, the section on setting aside contracts in Chapter 10. If, for example, one is affected by drugs, then, whatever is said in the document, despite one's signature, is suspect. Similarly, one may sign a form giving permission to others to carry out a procedure without fully understanding what the procedure is. The form is only *evidence* of the consent, not consent itself, and it is poor evidence of the patient knowing adequately what is being consented to if there is also no record of proper advice having been given at, or before, the time of signing.

In *Chatterton v Gerson* [1981] 1 QB 432 Lord Bristow stated that getting the patient to sign a pro forma expressing consent to undergo an operation should be a valuable reminder to everyone of the need for explanation and consent. But it would be no defence to an action in trespass to the person if no explanation had in fact been given. The consent would be expressed in form only, not in reality. Similarly, a signed consent form stating that all material risks had been explained is prima facie evidence only.

Health carers can legally witness someone signing a consent form, where the care is to be given by someone else. However, the person providing the care remains responsible for ensuring the patient has been adequately informed. Health carers should be wary of accepting the responsibility of providing such information in such circumstances. The written record should indicate who informed the patient. It should be borne in mind that what is said to the patient by a health carer may influence consent to treatment, and this influence may be misleading. A court could ignore such a document as not indicating proper consent. It is best for health carers to be very careful in discussing the nature and effects of treatment others are going to give and it may be prudent to suggest that the patient discuss it with the provider, and assist in facilitating this.

The *Review of the Law of Negligence* recommended that the duty to inform should be legislatively stated to apply only to medical professionals. The *Review* did, however, go on to comment on the interdisciplinary nature of modern medicine and stated that whilst in most cases the duty to inform will be owed by the treating medical practitioner, that will not always be the case. The *Review* states (at [3.42]):

> "In many instances of modern medical practice, the treatment of a patient, while under the direction of what (in common practice) is known as the 'attending medical officer', is shared by several health care providers. For example, in the course of pre-operative treatment, the operation itself and

post-operative treatment, the patient might be attended by the general practitioner, a physician, a radiologist, a principal surgeon and an assisting surgeon, a registrar, an intern, an anaesthetist, theatre nurses and ward nurses. Each one of these persons may administer treatment to the patient. It is unlikely that each will incur an obligation to inform the patient about the treatment administered, but it is quite possible that more than one of these persons will incur such an obligation.

The law is undeveloped in regard to determining precisely when a duty to inform will arise and on whom it will be imposed."

Whilst there have been no clear legal rulings as yet, it is likely that, with the emergence of allied health care specialities, where, for example, nurses and para-medics are providing care and advice, and technicians are involved in sophisticated diagnostic procedures, the person directly responsible for the provision of the health care service will bear the responsibility of adequately informing the patient and obtaining their consent.

Both the provider of health care, who neglects to undertake the responsibility of gaining the knowledgeable consent of a patient and a health carer, who takes on the task of informing the patient on behalf of someone else run legal risks, the former in trespass or negligence, the latter in negligence for negligent misstatement. Although it may be tempting to reassure the anxious patient who needs information and cannot seem to get it, health carers are advised under such circumstances to treat consent as not given, and attempt to get the provider concerned to see the patient.

Consent forms should be specific to the procedures involved. "Blanket" or standard forms signed on entry to a hospital or clinic covering any or all (or "appropriate" or "desirable") treatment to be given may be held to be too vague and general to be valid at law. Emergency treatment is covered by the presumption that the patient would wish to have treatment to save life and limb (unless otherwise clearly stated by the patient). It may be specifically added to the form, but is redundant, so general consent forms are inappropriate.

The following checklist is an example of what could be included in a consent form.

 Checklist
ELEMENTS OF A CONSENT FORM
- ✓ name and full identification of patient;
- ✓ name (and brief description*) of procedure agreed to;
- ✓ name of place for carrying out of the procedure;
- ✓ consent to specified associated treatments (these should have been discussed as part of the procedure);
- ✓ *acknowledgement of, and consent to, possible need for emergency treatment (this is presumed at law anyway, but it is good to remind both provider and patient of the possibility of such a contingency);
- ✓ *statement of what information had been given, for example, what the procedure involves, why it is required, why it is recommended in preference to alternatives;

> ✓ list of specific risks and advantages which have been discussed;
> ✓ name of person who will carry out the procedure, or, if not appropriate, acknowledgement that no specific person will carry it out; and
> ✓ agreement to another person carrying out the procedure, or any other necessary procedure, if circumstances require this.
>
> * Optional items are preferred items.

Some institutions and practitioners may wish to have additional statements to the effect that the patient assumes all risks and acknowledges that benefits are not guaranteed or certain. This does not necessarily protect health carers from potential liability in negligence, as the procedure must still be carried out with reasonable care and skill. In addition, common law and statute can operate to imply into the terms of a contract that the practitioner will perform their services with reasonable care and skill (for a discussion of implied terms at common law see *Breen v Williams* (1995) 186 CLR 71; [1995] HCA 63; for examples of statutory provisions see s 74 of the *Trade Practices Act 1974* (Cth) and s 40S of the *Fair Trading Act 1987* (NSW)).

Specific Situations

Blood transfusions

[4.440] As has been stated above, competent adults can validly refuse blood transfusions, even if their lives are in danger. Where a child's life is in danger, and parents refuse a transfusion, legislation in most Australian jurisdictions provides that where a child is likely to die without the transfusion, the treating doctor may, if a second doctor's opinion is secured, go ahead with the transfusion in the absence of a parent's or guardian's permission (see *Human Tissue & Transplant Act 1982* (WA), s 21; *Transplantation & Anatomy Act 1979* (Qld), s 20; *Human Tissue Act 1985* (Tas), s 21; *Human Tissue Act 1982* (Vic), s 24; *Transplantation & Anatomy Act 1978* (ACT), s 23; *Emergency Medical Operations Act* (NT), ss 2, 3; *Consent to Medical Treatment & Palliative Care Act 1995* (SA), s 13). See further Chapters 5 and 16.

Pregnant woman and consent

[4.445] The development of modern technology allowing examination of the foetus before birth can be said to "personify" the foetus. Thus where a woman refuses treatment that may have a detrimental impact on her foetus the issue arises as to whether the therapeutic interests of another being, the foetus, should be considered. McLean S and Petersen K ((1996), p 230) argue that what has often developed into a "maternal/foetal conflict" is based on several false assumptions: that the woman is a "mother" in relation to the foetus, when in fact she has not yet become one, and that this is a conflict between "persons" (who are equal). In law there is only one person, the woman; the foetus is a potential person only.

It is quite clear from legal precedent that a woman retains her right to autonomy when she becomes pregnant (see, for example, Seymour (1995)). The common law has established that the foetus has contingent legal interests but has no rights at law until born (*Paton v BPAS Trustees* [1979] 1 QB 276). In *Lynch v Lynch (by her tutor Lynch)* (1991) 25 NSWLR 411 Clarke JA, with whom Gleeson CJ and Hope AJA agreed, affirmed the decision in *X and Y (by her tutor X) v Pal* (1991) 23 NSWLR 26 that legal rights accrue only if and when a person is born, stating:

> "in this case once the respondent was born she attained the legal capacity to sue in respect of the breach of her legal rights notwithstanding that she had not been born when she suffered her injuries".

In terms of criminal law, in *R v King* (2003) 139 A Crim R 132 the court considered whether the death of a foetus could constitute grievous bodily harm to the mother and answered in the affirmative. The decision was codified by an amendment to s 4 of the *Crimes Act 1900* (NSW) in 2005 so that the definition of grievous bodily harm extends to the destruction of a foetus of a pregnant woman (other than in the course of a medical procedure).

[4.450] Case: *St George's Healthcare NHS Trust v S; R v Collins and Ors, ex parte S* [1997] 3 All ER 673 (English Court of Appeal)

S was 36 weeks pregnant and diagnosed with pre-eclampsia. She was advised that she needed to be admitted to hospital for an induced delivery. S fully understood the potential risks but rejected the advice as she wanted her baby to be born naturally. After extensive consultation with doctors and a social worker she was admitted to a mental hospital for assessment on the social worker's application. Subsequently she was transferred to another hospital which applied *ex parte* for the Court for a declaration dispensing with her consent. This was granted, and S was delivered of a baby girl by caesarean section. S was returned to the psychiatric hospital, where her detention under mental health legislation was terminated, and she discharged herself.

S later appealed against the grant of declaration dispensing with her consent, and applied for judicial review of her detention under mental health law, her detention and treatment at the second hospital, and her return to the psychiatric hospital.

[4.455] The Court re-iterated the right of an individual to autonomy, and to refuse treatment even when his or her life depended on receiving that treatment. It said that in the case of a pregnant woman, that right is not diminished merely because her right to do so may be morally repugnant. The removal of the child from her body amounted to trespass.

It also stated that the making of the order had occurred without S's knowledge or attempt to inform her or her solicitor of the application, and without any evidence or provision for her to apply to vary or discharge the order.

The Court went on to say that the mental health legislation cannot be invoked because a person's thinking process is unusual or bizarre and irrational, and contrary to the views of the overwhelming majority of the community at large. The legislation is only to apply if the case falls within the prescribed conditions. Moreover, people detained under the Act for mental disorder cannot be forced into a medical procedure unconnected with their mental condition unless their mental capacity to consent to such treatment is diminished. In the circumstances, then, S's treatment and transfer were unlawful.

The Court repeated and expanded on advice given in *Re MB* [1997] 2 FLR 426. Judge LJ at 703 stated that where a competent patient refuses treatment the advice given to the patient should be recorded. This record should include unequivocal assurance from the patient that the refusal represents an informed decision: that is, that she understands the nature of, and reasons for, the proposed treatment, and the risks and likely prognosis involved in the decision to refuse or accept it. If the patient is unwilling to sign a written indication of the refusal, this too should be part of a written record. It should be noted that this is merely a record for evidential purposes. It is not a disclaimer of liability, that is, it is still possible for the patient to prove that in fact the decision was not properly "informed".

The Court further stated that while pregnancy increases the personal responsibilities of a woman it does not diminish her entitlement to decide whether or not to undergo medical treatment. Although human, and protected by the law in a number of different ways, an unborn child is not a separate person from its mother:

> "Its need for medical assistance does not prevail over her rights. She is entitled not to be forced to submit to an invasion of her body against her will, whether her own life or that of her unborn child depends on it. Her right is not reduced or diminished merely because of her decision to exercise it may appear morally repugnant" [at 682].

Butler Schloss LJ stated in *Re MB* [1997] 2 FCR 541 at 561 (albeit obiter dicta):

> "The foetus up to the moment of birth does not have any separate interests capable of being taken into account when a court has to consider an application for a declaration in respect of a caesarean section operation. The court does not have the jurisdiction to declare that such medical intervention is lawful to protect the interests of the unborn child even at the point of birth".

This approach is supported by the case of *Re F (in utero)* [1988] 2 All ER 193 at 200, where refusing an application that a foetus should be made a ward of the court, Balcombe LJ observed:

"There is no jurisdiction to make an unborn child a ward of court. Since an unborn child has, ex hypothesi, no existence independent of its mother, the only purpose of extending the jurisdiction to include the foetus is to enable the mother's actions to be controlled."

Consent and research

[4.460] So far the discussion has been restricted to therapeutic treatment, that is, treatment of someone who is ill, with the intention of effecting either cure or relief from the condition. Research, of course, is done with the intention of gathering information. It should be kept in mind that the role of the carer–patient relationship changes; with research the roles become that of researcher–subject. The interest of the carer is consistent with the patient in the therapeutic relationship; presumably both want the patient to benefit. However, the interest of the researcher is not necessarily similar to that of the patient— rather than being solely interested in the benefit of the patient, the researcher's priority is to gather information.

When research is undertaken, patients should be told this (that is, there should not be the belief that they are undergoing proven therapeutic health care). No research project should be undertaken unless it has been carefully scrutinised by an independent ethics review committee, which considers, among other things, what information the subjects will be given, and how consent is to be obtained. Some research projects may be reliant upon the person being either misinformed or uninformed. In these cases the committee must give careful consideration to the reasons for the research and its necessity, the risks involved, why alternative methods of seeking the information are not suitable, and to the value of the research to society in general. These reasons must demonstrate clearly that the research cannot be effectively carried out in any other way, that it carries little risk, and is important and valuable enough to warrant the invasion of the physical or mental integrity of the subjects, and/or the use of misinformation. These guidelines are applicable to all health carers.

Unlawful Restraint or Imprisonment

[4.465] Allied to the action of battery, the action of "false imprisonment" covers situations where a person is unlawfully restrained from leaving a place against their will. This action is a relevant matter of concern to health carers because it covers two main types of situations:

- refusing to allow a person to leave a premises, or preventing them from doing so, where there is no lawful authority to keep them; and
- placing physical, chemical or mental restraints on a person, and thereby preventing them from freedom of movement (restraint).

The only time a person may be restrained against her or his will is:

- where there is a legal right to restrain (for example, under mental health, infectious diseases, quarantine or crimes legislation where they may be subject to powers of detention); and
- where a person is likely to harm herself or himself or someone else, or is likely to cause damage to property.

Detention

[4.470] People are falsely imprisoned when they perceive that they are confined to a particular place and believe there is no way of escape, or there will be reprisals if they leave. The confinement or absence of escape need not be fact—it is the person's own perception of the situation which is relevant. Thus a person who is led to believe that he or she cannot leave a hospital until payment for care is made would be falsely imprisoned.

[4.475] Case: *Symes v Mahon* [1922] SASR 447 (SC SA)

The defendant, a police officer in a country town, told the plaintiff that there was a warrant for his arrest for failing to maintain his child and that he should "come to town [Adelaide] to have matters cleared up". He was asked to undertake to be at the police station the next morning and responded "I suppose I'll have to". He did turn up at the station, and accompanied the police officer in the train to Adelaide. He was not arrested at any stage, the police officer maintaining that he was "taking Mahon up for questioning". In Adelaide he was allowed to leave on two occasions, only after seeking and being granted permission to do so. It turned out that Mahon was not the person who was the subject of the warrant, but a Mr McMahon.

[4.480] The Court held that although Mahon had never been in legal custody, and had at all times the freedom to leave, he submitted himself to the defendant's power reasonably thinking that he had no way of escape which could reasonably be taken by him.

This case establishes some important principles. First, giving patients to believe that they have no alternative but to remain in a particular place or submit to the control of others is unlawful and can result in an action for false imprisonment, even though they have the physical means of leaving. A second principle is that police cannot require someone to accompany them anywhere simply for questioning, unless the law specifically allows this.

Where there is no power to detain a person, even where it is thought to be for their own good, it may be false imprisonment. For example, in wards where some patients are involuntarily detained but others are voluntary patients, health carers should be very careful to ensure that if doors are locked, those who are voluntary patients are not only permitted freedom of movement, but are made to feel that no restraint is being placed on their freedom of movement, and that they are perfectly free to leave if they wish.

[4.485] Case: *Watson v Marshall* (1971) 24 CLR 621; [1971] HCA 33

The defendant was a police officer who asked the plaintiff to accompany him to the psychiatric hospital. The plaintiff believed (justifiably, the Court held) that if he did not go voluntarily he would be forced into going.

[4.490] The Court held that it was the plaintiff's belief that he had no choice which was relevant, not any objective assessment of the law and the situation. It is thus not legally acceptable to use subterfuge or to trick a person into remaining in a particular place or in the control of someone else, unless one can plead a defence as outlined above.

People are also unlawfully detained when they are physically confined to a particular place whether they are aware of this or not.

[4.495] Case: *Meering v Grahame-White Aviation Co Ltd* (1919) 122 LT 44 (House of Lords)

The plaintiff attended the defendant's office to give evidence relating to some stolen goods. Unbeknown to the plaintiff three detectives were stationed outside the office to prevent his leaving.

[4.500] The House of Lords held that this was false imprisonment. It follows that the unconscious or mentally unaware patient who is detained in a hospital without their consent may be the subject of false imprisonment.

[4.505] Case: *Hart v Herron* [1984] Aust Torts Reports ¶80-201 (NSWSC)

The plaintiff had been detained and given treatment to which he claimed he had not consented (including electroconvulsive treatment and deep sleep therapy).

[4.510] The Court held that even though he had no recollection of the imprisonment the fact did not prevent him from succeeding in his claim.

Restraint must be intentional and complete. Where there is a reasonable way out, even if it is unconventional (for example, windows) there is no "imprisonment". However, what is considered a reasonable way out in a medical setting may differ from other situations, such that, for example, a window might not be considered a reasonable means of exit.

[4.515] Case: *Balmain New Ferry Co Ltd v Robertson*
(1906) 4 CLR 379; [1906] HCA 83

A man bought a ticket for a ferry to Balmain. The sign over the wharf from which it left said that any person entering or leaving the wharf had to pay a penny whether or not they used the ferry. He entered through the turnstile (paying his penny) and found he had missed the ferry and would have to pay another penny to leave the wharf. Employees prevented him leaving by a small opening beside the turnstile. He sued the company for false imprisonment.

[4.520] The Court took into account the fact that the plaintiff had agreed to the terms of entry clearly established, that egress would cost him one penny. He had placed himself in such a position that he could not complain of a certain restraint of liberty. However he was not being denied exit under the terms on which he had entered. Only if he had been denied exit under any circumstances would he have been imprisoned.

[4.525] Case: *Sayers v Harlow Urban District Council*
[1958] 2 All ER 342 (CA UK)

A tourist visited the public toilets and found that, due to a faulty lock she was trapped in the cubicle. She failed to attract attention, and so proceeded to stand on the toilet roll holder to climb over the door. She slipped on the holder, injuring herself. Later she brought an action against the Council in false imprisonment and negligence.

[4.530] The Court dismissed Ms Sayers' claim of false imprisonment because there had been no intention to confine her. It upheld her claim in negligence because of the faulty lock, but reduced the damages because of her contributory negligence in standing on the toilet roll holder.

A health carer cannot argue that it is simply for the patient's own good that restraint be used but should have reasonable grounds to believe in the lawfulness of such action. If a patient wishes to leave a hospital or another health-care institution and the exceptions (above, **[4.225]**) do not apply, they should be allowed to go. Staff should attempt to get a signed statement from the patient, stating that despite advice to the contrary, the patient is leaving of her or his own free will. A witness should sign as well, if possible.

It is advisable for health carers to carefully warn the patient of the consequences of such a decision, to determine that the person understands what they are doing, and to get, in writing if possible, and witnessed by someone else, a statement signed or acknowledged by the patient to the effect that he or she has been fully informed of the consequences of the decision, and is making the decision voluntarily. Under these circumstances it is unlikely the courts would find health carers liable for *not* giving the treatment.

Restraint

[4.535] There are many situations in which it is considered necessary to restrain a patient who is violent, disruptive, difficult to care for or who may be mentally dysfunctional and in danger of self-harm.

There is a wide variety of *restraining behaviour*. This includes such activity as:

- yelling or haranguing to restrict movement by fear;
- the use of drugs to restrict movement;
- threats to physically restrict movement;
- threats to use seclusion to restrict movement and influence behaviour;
- actual use of physical or chemical restraint; and
- actual seclusion.

Actual restraint has been described as the application of devices such as belts, harnesses, manacles, sheets and straps on the person's body to restrict movement (but do not include the use of cot sides and chairs with tables fitted on their arms). Actual seclusion has been described as the sole confinement of a person at any hour of the day or night in a room of which the doors and windows are locked from the outside (*Mental Health Act 1986* (Vic), s 82).

As with an action of assault or battery, a person need not suffer damage, nor need they even be aware of the restraint (for example, a door locked without their knowledge). Restriction of patients, or refusal to allow them to leave hospital, where they are:

- competent;
- do not consent; and
- there is no legal justification,

are examples of false imprisonment. Legal justification to restrain a person would include, for example, self-defence, power under the mental health legislation, infectious diseases legislation, and child welfare legislation.

It should thus be clear that it is not enough to restrain a person simply for his or her own good. Health carers should have reasonable grounds to believe in the lawfulness of such action. Restraint should be limited to what is required for protection of the patient or others where there is no reasonable alternative: it must not be used as a management aid.

Freedom to leave hospital

[4.540] Patients who wish to leave a hospital or another health care institution where the exceptions described above do not apply should be allowed to go. Health carers have a duty of care to:

- warn them of the consequences of such a decision; and
- take reasonable steps to determine that they understand what they are doing.

In addition, it may be prudent to attempt to get a signed statement from the patient, stating that despite advice to the contrary, they are leaving, that he or she has been fully informed of the consequences of the decision, and is making the decision voluntarily.

A witness should sign as well, if possible. If the person is considered unable to understand what he or she is doing, and harm is likely to result, he or she may be appropriately dealt with as a non-competent person in need of care. If it is not an emergency, this may involve an application to a court or tribunal under the mental health or guardianship legislation.

Where a patient leaves hospital, the general duty of care on the part of health carers requires them to consider what will happen to him or her, and to take reasonable steps to ensure that any necessary care to which the person consents is undertaken. It would seem that they should at least provide the patient with information as to what further care he or she will need, and where and how this can be obtained. This was specifically addressed in *Niles v City of San Rafael* 42 Cal App 3d 230 (1974). The authors are not aware of any Australian ruling directly on this matter, however it is considered that such information would be part of the duty of care under general negligence principles (for example, *Kite v Malycha & Anor* Supreme Court of South Australia, Judgment No S6702 (10 June 1998); *Wang v Central Sydney Area Health Service* [2000] Aust Torts Reports 64,079).

Restraint and seclusion should be least restrictive

[4.545] Restraint and seclusion should be the least restrictive compatible with the care of the patient under the circumstances. There is no legislative guidance or standards as to procedures to be adopted in respect of restraint or seclusion, except in relation to the mentally ill (see **[4.550]** below) although facilities may have protocols for dealing with restraint. The potential for instilling fear and coercing behaviour by improper use of seclusion was raised by the Human Rights and Equal Opportunity Report, "Human Rights and Mental Illness" ((1993), p 271).

"Chemical" restraint

[4.550] The administration of drugs has been used for the purpose of restraining patients and keeping them quiet, especially those who suffer from mental illness or dementia. This method of restraint is potentially more devastating and harmful than physical methods. It is important to note that restraint by drugs may also amount to battery or false imprisonment where the restraint is for the convenience of health carers rather than the protection of the patient, staff or others. MacFarlane ((2000), p 106) states that:

> "The necessity to protect staff or other residents would be difficult to argue where the restraint (without consent) was due to the fact that the resident was being a nuisance or because the restraint was considered desirable in order to speed up recovery from some illness.

The situation is complex because of the need to balance the rights of the individual patient with those of others. Nevertheless it remains unlawful to chemically or physically restrain a person without just cause."

Restraint must be based on the principle of protection for the patient and/or others only (see **[4.545]**), and not carried out just for the convenience of health carers. Health care facilities may assist their staff by adopting a policy in relation to this issue which clearly sets out circumstances under which restraint may and may not be used.

Health carers should assess each case individually as to the benefits and harms of physical restraint, accept the views and values of individual patients, be able to justify the use or non-application of physical restraint, and be supported by a philosophy of care in their work place that advocates justice for staff and residents (Koch, S, "Ethical issues in restraint use", in RMIT Faculty of Nursing, *Nursing Law and Ethics, "Meeting the Challenge of Patient's Rights—Issues for the 1990s"* Proceedings of the Conference, November 1992 (Faculty of Nursing, RMIT, Melbourne), p 12).

 Checklist
CONSIDERATIONS FOR POLICY ON RESTRAINT
✓ All health carers of the patient should be consulted to see if alternative treatment can be adopted to alleviate the patient's need for restraint.
✓ Family should be consulted, as they may be able to offer assistance and ideas in relation to controlling the patient's behaviour (see *Spivey's* case at **[6.270]**).
✓ Any restraint should be the least restrictive measure to protect the patient—the aim should be to stop the harm, not the patient. Materials used should be such as to cause the least injury to the patient compatible with this aim.
✓ Authorisation from a person with appropriate authority (for example, a nursing manager, doctor) should be required.
✓ Management should be notified of the circumstances of any restraint of a patient.
✓ Family should be notified of any restraint of the patient, if not already consulted.
✓ Regular assessment of the patient and the reason for restraint should be carried out.
✓ Full and accurate documentation of the circumstances and type of restraint, as well as the other matters listed here should be made in the clinical notes.

Victoria has comprehensive legislation on restraint and seclusion, although this is limited to those who are mentally ill. The provisions of the legislation set out what could be considered guidelines for all patients, particularly residents of nursing homes and hostels for those with a disability (ss 81and 82 of the *Mental Health Act 1995* (Vic)). Other jurisdictions also have legislation concerning restraint and seclusion of the mentally ill (see, for example, *Mental Health Act 2000* (Qld); *Mental Health (Treatment and Care) Act 1994* (ACT); *Mental Health Act 1996* (Tas); *Mental Health Act 1996* (WA)).

References and Further Reading

Annas, G, "When Suicide Prevention Becomes Brutality: The Case of Elizabeth Bouvia" (1988), *Judging Medicine* (Havana Press, New Jersey), p 290

Australian Health and Medical Law Reporter (CCH, Sydney, 1991), (CCH, Sydney, 1983)

Betsas, A and Forrester, K, "Consent: Implications for Health Care Practitioners" (1995) 2 *Journal of Law and Medicine* 317

Bochner, S, "Doctors, Patients and their Cultures" (1988) in Hasler, J (ed), *Doctor and Patient Communication* (Academic Press, London)

Brazier, M, *Protecting the Vulnerable: Autonomy and Consent in Health Care* (Routledge, London, 1991)

Brody, H, *Ethical Decisions in Medicine* (Little, Brown & Co, Boston, 1981)

Brody, H, "Transparency: Informed Consent in Primary Care", 19 Hastings Center Report No 5, pp 5-9 (Sep/Oct 1989)

Bromberger, B and Fife-Yeomans, J, *Deep Sleep: Harry Bailey and the Scandal of Chelmsford* (Simon & Schuster, Sydney, 1991)

Buchannan, A and Brock, D, *Deciding for Others: The Ethics of Surrogate Decision Making* (CUP, Cambridge, 1989)

Bunney, L, "A Right to Die—Has Patient Autonomy Gone too Far?" (1993) 2 *Health Law Bulletin* 29

Clarke, S and Oakley, J, "Informed Consent and Surgeons' Performance" (2004) 29 (1) *Journal of Medicine and Philosophy* 11-35

Clarke, S and Oakley, J, "Informed Consent and the Surgeon's Performance" *Australian Health Law Bulletin* 13 (5)

Clarke, S and Oakley, J, "Informed Consent and the Surgeon's Performance – Part 2: objections considered" *Australian Health Law Bulletin* 13 (7)

Cockburn, T and Madden, W, "Intentional Torts Claims in Medical Cases" (2006) 13(3) *Journal of Law and Medicine*

Coney, S, *The Unfortunate Experiment* (Penguin, 1988)

Evans, S, "Autonomy of a pregnant patient v best interests of an unborn child" *Australian Health Law Bulletin* 14 (1)

Faden, R and Beauchamp, T, *A History and Theory of Informed Consent* (Oxford University Press, New York, 1986)

Faulder, C, *Whose Body is it?* (Virago, London, 1985)

Freckelton, I and Petersen, K, *Controversies in Health Law* (The Federation Press, Sydney, 1999), p 119

Gutman, J, "The Right Not to Know: Patient Autonomy or Medical Paternity" (2000) 7 *Journal of Law and Medicine* 286

Human Rights and Equal Opportunity Commission, *Human Rights and Mental Illness* (AGPS, Canberra, 1993)

Johnstone, M, *Bioethics: A Nursing Perspective* (W B Saunders/Bailliere Tindall, Sydney, 1989)

Kerridge, I H and Mitchell, K R, "Missing the Point: Rogers v Whitaker" (1994) 1 *Journal of Law and Medicine* 239

Kirby, M, "Patients' Rights—Have We Gone Too Far?" (1993) 2 *Health Law Bulletin* 13 and (1993) 2 *Health Law Bulletin* 38

Keeling, S, "Duty to warn of genetic harm in breach of patient confidentiality" *Australian Health Law Bulletin* 12 (2)

Kushe, H, *Caring: Nurses, Women and Ethics* (Blackwell Publishers, Oxford, 1997)

Langslow, A, "Witness to Battery" (1993) *Australian Nurses Journal*, August, 35-37

Lanham, D, *Taming Death by Law* (Longman Professional, Melbourne, 1993)

Law Reform Commission of Victoria, *Medicine, Science and the Law: Informed Consent*, Symposia 1986 (Globe Press, Melbourne, 1987)

Law Reform Commission of Victoria, *Informed Decisions about Medical Procedures* (1989)

Law Reform Commissions of New South Wales and Victoria, *Informed Consent to Medical Treatment* (NSW Government Printer, Sydney, 1988)

Lidz, C, et al, *Informed Consent: a Study of Decision Making in Psychiatry* (The Guildford Press, New York, 1984)

Luntz, H, Hambly, A and Hayes, R, *Torts: Cases and Commentary* (Butterworths, Sydney, 1985)

Madden, B, and Cockburn, T, "Duty to Disclose Medical Error in Australia" *Australian Health Law Bulletin* 14 (2)

Mason, J and McCall Smith, R, *Law and Medical Ethics* (Butterworths, London, 1994)

McFarlane, P, in McCullough, S, *Older Residents' Legal Rights* (Federation Press, Sydney 1992)

McHale, J, Fox, M and Murphy, J, *Health Care and the Law—Text, Cases and Materials* (Sweet & Maxwell, London, 1997)

McLean, S and Petersen, K, "Patient Status: the Foetus and the Pregnant Woman" 2 *Australian Journal of Human Rights* (2) 229

Milstein, B, "Informed Consent: the Envelope Expands (again)" (1997) 5 *Health Law Bulletin* 65

Mion, L, Minnick, A, Palmer, R, et al, "Physical Restraint Use in the Hospital Setting: Unresolved Issues and Directions for Research" (1996) *The Milbank Quarterly* Blackwell, Cambridge MA & Oxford UK

Mulheron, R, "The defence of therapeutic privilege in Australia" *Australian Health Law Bulletin* 11 (2)

Murchison, I A and Nichols, T, *Legal Foundations of Nursing Practice* (Macmillan, New York, 1970)

Pappworth, M, *Human Guinea Pigs* (Routledge & Keegan Paul, London, 1967)

President's Commission for the Study of Ethical Problems in Medicine and Biomedical and Behavioural Research, *Making Health Care Decisions* (Government Printing Office, Washington DC, United States, 1982)

Review of the Law of Negligence Final Report September 2002 accessed at http://revofneg.treasury.gov.au/content/home.asp

Rozovsky, F, *Consent to Treatment: A Practical Guide* (Little, Brown & Co, Boston, 1984)

Scott, R, "Duty to Disclose Risks of Treatment and Procedures" (1993) 2 *Health Law Bulletin* 1

Seymour, J, *Foetal Welfare and the Law* (1995) Report of the Enquiry commissioned by the Australian Medical Association

Skene, L, *Law and Medical Practice: Rights, Duties, Claims and Defences* (2nd ed, Butterworths, Sydney, 2004)

Stewart, C, "Advance Directives, the Right to Die and the Common Law: Recent Problems with Blood Transfusions" (1999) 23 *Melbourne University Law Review* 161

Sullivan, A and Large, A, "Alternative Treatment Options – When is a Risk/Benefit Discussion Required" *Australian Health Law Bulletin* 14 (3)

Sutherland, H, Lockwood, G and Till, J, "Are we Getting Informed Consent from Patients with Cancer?" (1992) 11(2) *Bioethics News* 5

Schwartz, R and Grubb, A, "Why Britain Can't Afford Informed Consent" 15 *Hastings Centre* Report No 4 (August 1985), p 19

Thampapillai, D, "Court Ordered Obstetrical Intervention and the Rights of a Pregnant Woman" *Australian Health Law Bulletin* 12 (4)

Victorian Law Reform Commission, *Informed Decisions About Medical Procedures*, Report No 24 (VGPS, 1989)

Young, P, *The Law of Consent* (Law Book Co, Sydney, 1986)

Wallace, M, "Restraint and the Law" Paper presented at the Royal College of Nursing Australia conference, *Restraint: Exploring the Pathway between Risks and Rights* (National Conference Centre, Canberra 1997)

Way, B and Banks, S, "Use of Seclusion and Restraint in Public Psychiatric Hospitals: Patient Characteristics and Facility Effects" *Hospital and Community Psychiatry* 41:1 (Jan 1990)

5 Consent by the Legally Incompetent

Incomptence by reason of age

The common law principle

Emergencies

Mature minors

Adults legally incapable of consenting to health care

Role of the court

Temporary incapacity

Chronic incapacity

Guardianhip

Advance directives & medical agents

Mental illness & involuntary patients

Special medical treatment

chapter 5

Consent to Health Care by a Legally Incompetent Person

Introduction

[5.05] This chapter continues the discussion of consent, looking at the rights of those who are considered at law not to be competent to give their consent to treatment, either by reason of their age, mental capacity at the time, or their status under other legislation. Such persons are called "incompetent" at law.

"Incompetence" by Reason of Age

"The common law principle"

[5.10] A basic principle in law is that a child cannot consent to medical treatment (but see Chapter 9 for a more detailed discussion of minors and contracts). Generally a person is a minor or "child" at law for most purposes until the age of 18 unless he or she marries (*Age of Majority Act 1974* (ACT), s 5; *Minors (Property and Contracts) Act 1970* (NSW), s 9; *Age of Majority Act* (NT), s 4; *Law Reform Act 1995* (Qld), s 17; *Age of Majority Act 1973* (Tas), s 3; *Age of Majority Act 1977* (Vic), s 3; *Age of Majority Act 1972* (WA), s 5; *Age of Majority (Reduction) Act 1970* (SA), s 3). However s 49(2) of the *Minors (Property and Contracts) Act 1970* (NSW) sets the age at which a child can consent to medical treatment at 14 years and s 6 of the *Consent to Medical Treatment and Palliative Care Act 1995* (SA) sets it at 16 years. In all the other jurisdictions the right to consent is traditionally vested in:

- a parent of the child, or person in whose favour a parenting order has been made under the *Family Law Act 1975* (Cth);
- a person to whom the parent has given the authority to make such a decision;
- a legally appointed guardian of the child (for example, child welfare officer, foster parent); and

- a court with the jurisdiction to make such a decision for the child (that is, the Family Court or the Supreme Court, exercising *parens patriae* jurisdiction).

"Mature" minors

[5.15] The High Court has ruled that a child can consent to treatment if he or she is capable of understanding the nature and consequences of that treatment ("mature minor") (see *Department of Health and Community Services (NT) v JWB and SMB (Marion's case)* (1992) 175 CLR 218; [1992] HCA 15 (discussed at **[5.30]**) in which the majority of the Court followed the decision in *Gillick v West Norfolk* and *Wisbech Area Health Authority* [1986] AC 112). The New South Wales legislation does not cancel a parent's right to consent to or refuse medical treatment on their child's behalf, but rather it is meant to prevent a child arguing that due to his or her minority, consent to treatment he or she may have given was invalid, and that the medical staff is liable in battery (see *K v Minister for Youth and Community Services* [1982] 1 NSWLR 311). The decision in *Gillick* suggests that once a child achieves sufficient understanding and intelligence to enable him or her to fully understand the proposed medical treatment, their parents' right to consent on their behalf ceases. In *Marion's case* the High Court confirmed that there is a diminishing of parental control as the child matures (see **[5.30]**).

Exceptions to the common law principle: Emergencies

[5.20] In emergencies, similar principles apply to children as for adults (see **[4.170]**ff, necessity at **[4.240]**ff, transplants at Chapter 17). In other circumstances, where a child is not mature enough, or otherwise not competent to decide, parents or legal guardians are at law authorised to make decisions for them. Statutory provisions also allow the State welfare authorities to take action to protect the safety and well being of a child (Chapter 17). In addition, all jurisdictions have statutory provisions providing doctors the authority to provide life-saving blood transfusions to children regardless of the presence or absence of parental consent (see **[4.440]**).

Statutory exceptions

[5.25] Several jurisdictions have legislation in relation to non-urgent treatment.

In New South Wales the *Minors (Property and Contracts) Act 1970* (NSW), provides that a medical or dental practitioner who provides treatment to a child of less than 16 years with the prior consent of a parent or guardian is protected from liability for assault or battery. Those who give treatment to a child over 14 years with the consent of the child only are also protected from liability. The law requires that some treatments, called "special medical treatment" must have the consent of the Guardianship Tribunal (*Children and Young Persons (Care and Protection) Act 1998* (NSW), s 175; *Children and Young Persons (Care and Protection) Regulations 2000* (NSW), r 15). For children under 16, special medial treatment includes:

- treatment that is intended or is reasonably likely to result in permanent infertility (not being treatment that is intended to remediate a life-threatening condition);
- drugs of addiction;
- certain experimental procedures; and
- vasectomy or tubal occlusion.

The list of special treatments is slightly different in relation to children aged 16 or over who are incapable of giving consent. For example, long-acting injecting contraception is not considered a special treatment, however termination of pregnancy is (see further *Guardianship Act 1987* (NSW), s 33 and *Guardianship Regulation 2005* (NSW), r 8).

In South Australia, the *Consent to Medical Treatment and Palliative Care Act 1995* (SA) permits children of 16 years or more to consent to medical or dental treatment as if they were an adult. Further, the common law principle is set out that a child under 16 may consent to treatment if the person treating them believes they are able to understand the nature, effects and risks of the treatment, and that the treatment is in the best interest of the child's health and well being. This opinion must be supported in writing by a second medical practitioner who has personally examined the patient (s 12). A person over 16 years may refuse emergency medical treatment (s 13).

The following case dealt with sterilisation, but also with the legal capacity of a child to consent to medical treatment. It is a comprehensive review of the law in relation to children, incapacity and consent to treatment:

[5.30] Case: *Secretary, Department of Health and Community Services v JWB and SMB (Marion's Case)*
(1992) 175 CLR 218; [1992] HCA 15

"Marion" was, at the time, a 14-year-old girl suffering from intellectual disability, deafness, epilepsy and behavioural problems. Her parents and doctors agreed on a hysterectomy to prevent pregnancy and menstruation as these were considered to have adverse psychological and behavioural consequences. Her parents applied to the Family Court of Australia for an order authorising the procedure. Questions arose as to (1) whether parents can legally authorise the sterilisation of their child; (2) whether the Family Court has jurisdiction to authorise the operation; and (3) whether Family Court authorisation is required by law in the Northern Territory. These matters were taken to the High Court.

[5.35] The High Court stated that except where sterilisation is an incidental result of surgery performed to cure a disease or correct a malfunction (that is, carried out for therapeutic reasons) parents do not have the power to authorise the operation. The Court importantly also held that parental power diminishes gradually as the child's capacity and maturity grows. A minor can give informed consent when he or she achieves a sufficient understanding and intelligence to comprehend fully what is proposed. It is irrelevant that the child may have an intellectual disability, so long as she or he understands the nature and effects of the proposed treatment. It went on to say that the Family Court does have the jurisdiction to authorise a "non-therapeutic" sterilisation. In such cases the Court's function is to decide whether, in the circumstances of the case, it is in the best interests of the child. Indeed, the jurisdiction of the Family Court is similar to the *parens patriae* jurisdiction of State and Territory Supreme Courts.

In *Marion's Case* at [39] the Court quoted Lord Brandon in *Re F* [1990] 2 AC at 70-71 in setting out the reasons for treating sterilisation as a special case:

- the operation is not reversible;
- it deprives a woman of a fundamental right to bear children;
- moral and emotional considerations mean that this right has great importance;
- if a court is not involved, there is a greater risk of the matter being decided wrongly;
- it may be carried out for improper reasons; or
- there is a need to protect those involved from legal action.

When parents do not have the power to consent to a medical procedure

[5.40] It is thus established that there are certain medical procedures to which a parent cannot consent, particularly parents do not have the legal authority to consent to a procedure for the primary purpose of sterilisation of a child. What other procedures may be considered at common law to require the Court's authorisation has not been the subject of judicial elaboration to date. In *Re Alex: Hormonal Treatment for Gender Identity Dysphoria* (2004) 180 FLR 89; FamCA 297, Nicholson CJ stated that he could see no reason why the principles established in *Marion's Case* should be confined to surgical procedures, but rather could apply equally to other interventions of similarly irreversible effect, such as the use of radiation or pharmaceuticals.

[5.45] Case: *Re GWW and CMW* (1997) 136 FLR 421; FLC ¶92-748 (Family Court of Australia)

The parents of a child of 10, B, applied for an order authorising the collection of bone marrow or peripheral blood stem cells for donation to his aunt, who suffered from leukaemia. The aunt was expected to die within 12 months without the transplant, and B had expressed a strong wish to donate the tissue. It was accepted that whilst B had an understanding of the nature of the procedure, his understanding was not adequate for him to provide informed consent. The questions for the Court were whether the parents could lawfully authorise the procedures, and if not, whether it was in B's best interests for the Court to intervene and exercise its welfare jurisdiction to authorise the procedures.

[5.50] Hannon J held that the Family Court did have jurisdiction to hear the application pursuant to its welfare jurisdiction. This was a special case outside the scope of parental power to consent. Hannon J stated that passages in the judgment of *Marion's Case* indicated that the approach taken in that case did not only apply to sterilisation, but extended to other "non-therapeutic" procedures, including "the donation of healthy organs such as a kidney from one sibling to another". He stated that while the procedure proposed here was not irreversible (in that the stem cells can regenerate and blood re-infused into the donor) it was nevertheless an invasive procedure requiring general anaesthetic that was not for the benefit of the child. The paramount consideration was the welfare of the child, and whether the procedure would be in his interests. The close relationship with his aunt, and the value of the continuation of that relationship to the child who wanted to assist her, were factors that outweighed the risk or discomfort of a surgical procedure. It is interesting to note that in weighing up the benefits and disadvantages, the judge also took into account psychological evidence that refusal of the application could be detrimental to B because he would be puzzled by the Court not allowing him to help his aunt. This, the Court was told, could lead to a lack of respect for authority and especially the court system.

The Family Court has jurisdiction to make orders where a child's welfare is at risk. State Supreme Courts are still the courts with jurisdiction in all States where a child comes under State welfare law (for example, is a ward of the State or otherwise under the control of State authorities).

[5.60] Case: *P v P* (1994) 181 CLR 583; [1994] HCA 20
(High Court of Australia)

This case involved a child who had a mental disability. Her parents believed that it was in her interests to be sterilised. They wanted court authorisation to do this, and decided that, as the New South Wales Guardianship Board requires that such a procedure would have to be either life-saving or for the prevention of serious damage to health (and this case did not fit those criteria) they would apply to the Family Court for authorisation of the procedure. The case went to the High Court as a case stated by the Chief Justice on the application by the Attorney-General of New South Wales.

[5.65] The majority of the High Court stated that the child welfare jurisdiction of the Family Court corresponds with the traditional *parens patriae* jurisdiction of the State Supreme Courts. They pointed out that the Family Court welfare jurisdiction adopted in 1988 (see **[1.55]**) does not extinguish that of the State Courts, but encompasses the substance of it, freed from the preliminary requirement of a wardship order. The intent of Parliament was that both jurisdictions should exist concurrently. The *Guardianship Act 1987* (NSW) prohibits sterilisation unless it is necessary to save life or prevent serious harm to health.

The *Family Law Act 1975* (Cth) and approach of the Family Court are much wider in their scope. In the case of a conflict between orders made by the Family Court and those of a State Supreme Court, the Family Court orders would necessarily prevail, as per s 109 of the Constitution (see **[1.55]**).

When can a child consent to treatment?

[5.70] The English House of Lords has established the legal category of "mature minor" for those seeking contraceptive advice or contraceptive measures.

[5.75] Case: *Gillick v West Norfolk and Wisbech Area Health Authority* [1985] 3 All ER 402 House of Lords (England)

A mother sought to have the Court rule that parents and guardians have a right to make decisions on behalf of children as to contraceptive advice or treatment. Her children, along with others, had been receiving information about contraception through the family planning clinic without the prior knowledge and consent of their parents. These children were under the age of 16.

[5.80] The majority of the House of Lords held, first, that children may authorise medical treatment when they are old enough and mature enough to decide for themselves. It would be arbitrary and unreal, the Court held, to draw a line between childhood and maturity at a certain number of years, disregarding human development and social change:

"Provided the patient, whether a boy or a girl, is capable of understanding what is proposed, and of expressing his or her own wishes, I see no good reason for holding that he or she lacks the capacity to express them validly and effectively to make the examination and give the treatment that [the doctor] advises" [per Lord Fraser at 409].

Secondly, the Court held that the rights of parents to control their child are for the child's benefit, and are recognised only so long as they are needed for the protection of the child. Absolute dominion over their child by parents is now a thing of the past and parental rights dwindle proportionately with the child's maturity. Accordingly, there may be occasions when the child's interest indicates that a parent's rights be disregarded. The principle of *Gillick* was adopted by the Australian High Court in *Marion's Case* (above at **[5.30]**).

Lord Fraser (at 413) made the following useful suggestion, with which Lord Scarman and Lord Bridge expressly agreed:

"[where a girl] refuses either to tell the parents herself or permit the doctor to do so ... the doctor will, in my opinion, be justified in proceeding without the parents' consent or even their knowledge provided he is satisfied on the following matters: (1) that the girl ... will understand his advice; (2) that he cannot persuade her [that parents should be informed]; (3) that she is very likely to begin or to continue having sexual intercourse with or without contraceptive treatment; (4) that unless she receives contraceptive advice or treatment her physical or mental health or both are likely to suffer; (5) that her best interests require ... advice, treatment or both without the parental consent."

Lord Scarman expanded on what might constitute sufficient understanding, stating:

"when applying these conclusions to contraceptive advice and treatment it has to be borne in mind that there is much to be understood by a girl under the age of 16 if she is to have legal capacity to consent to such treatment. It is not enough that she should understand the nature of the advice which is being given; she must also have a sufficient maturity to understand what is involved. There are moral and family questions, especially her relationship with her parents; long term problems associated with the emotional impact of pregnancy and its termination; and there are risks to health of sexual intercourse at her age, risks which contraception may diminish but cannot eliminate. It follows that a doctor will have to satisfy himself that she is able to appraise these factors before he can safely proceed upon the basis that she has at law capacity to contraceptive treatment".

It is important to note that the comments of Lords Scarman and Fraser, referred to above, did not form part of the ratio of the case, as there were differences of opinion on these points. However, in 2004, the UK Department of Health published the *Best Practice Guidance for Doctors and Other Health Professionals on the Provision of Advice and Treatment to Young People Under 16 on Contraception, Sexual and Reproductive Health* in which the criteria elucidated by Lord Fraser were reiterated and acknowledged as good practice to be followed by health professionals.

[5.85] Case: *Axon, R (on the application of) v Secretary of State for Health* [2006] EWHC 37 (Admin)

This was an application by Sue Axon (a mother) for two declarations:
(1) that a doctor is under no obligation to keep confidential advice and treatment which he proposes to provide to a person under the age of 16 years in regard to contraception, sexual health and abortion and must therefore not provide such information without the parents' knowledge, unless to do so might prejudice the child's health; and
(2) that the *Best Practice Guidance for Doctors and Other Health Professionals on the Provision of Advice and Treatment to Young People Under 16 on Contraception, Sexual and Reproductive Health* is unlawful.
In effect, the Court was asked whether the principles enunciated by Lord Fraser in *Gillick* accurately represented the law.

[5.90] Silbers J held that the guidelines enunciated by Lord Fraser in *Gillick* together with the comments of Lord Scarman [at 188C] regarding what would constitute sufficient understanding, should be adapted and applied to more complex issues than contraception, such as abortion. He went on to conclude that the Guidelines were not unlawful and stated:

> "the medical professional is entitled to provide medical advice and treatment on sexual matters without the parents knowledge or consent provided he or she is satisfied of the following matters
>
> (1) that the young person although under 16 years of age understands *all* aspects of the advice [In the light of Lord Scarman's comments in *Gillick* .... he or she must "have sufficient maturity to understand what is involved" that understanding includes all relevant matters and it is not limited to family and moral aspects as well as all possible adverse consequences which might follow from the advice];
>
> (2) that the medical professional cannot persuade the young person to inform his or her parents or to allow the medical professional to inform the parents that their child is seeking advice and/or treatment on sexual matters [as stated in the 2004 Guidance, where the young person cannot be persuaded to involve a parent, every effort should be made to persuade the young person to help find another adult (such as another family member or a specialist youth worker) to provide support to the young person];
>
> (3) that (in any case in which the issue is whether the medical professional should advise on or treat in respect of contraception and sexually transmissible illnesses) the young person is very likely to begin or to continue to have sexual intercourse with or without contraceptive treatment or treatment for a sexually transmissible illness;
>
> (4) that unless the young person receives advice and treatment on the relevant sexual matters, his or her physical or mental health or both are likely to suffer [In considering this requirement, the medical professional must take into account all aspects of the young person's health]; and
>
> (5) that the best interests of the young person require him or her to receive advice and treatment on sexual matters without parental consent or notification."

Silbers J emphasised that the guidelines must be strictly observed and are not "a license for doctor's to disregard the wishes of parents".

When can a child refuse health care?

[5.95] The statutory provisions considered earlier with regard to a child's right to consent to medical treatment do not expressly consider whether that right extends to include a right to refuse medical treatment. As such, that matter remains governed by common law. To date, the courts have been reluctant to give a "mature minor" the right to *refuse* health care.

[5.100] Case: *Re W (a minor) (medical treatment)* [1992] 4 All ER 627 (CA England)

A teenager suffering from anorexia nervosa who understood her condition but who wished to seek treatment in her own time, refused treatment for her condition. The local authority applied to the Court for an order for her treatment. The judge held that although she had sufficient understanding to make an informed decision, he had inherent power under his *parens patriae* jurisdiction to order the treatment be given. W appealed.

[5.105] By the time of the appeal, W was deteriorating to the point where medical opinion estimated her reproductive capacity could be lost within a week, and her life a short time later. The Court of Appeal made an emergency order that W be removed to a specialist unit for treatment, on the basis that her wishes were outweighed by the threat of irreparable damage to her health. The Court made it clear that it was not considering the importance of a child's views generally, nor the weight it would have given her view earlier on, when she was not so ill. However it later said at a full hearing, that its inherent jurisdiction over children meant that it could override the wishes of a person under 18 years. It also pointed out that although children can agree to treatment they understand (in the UK this is provided for in the *Family Law Reform Act 1969* (UK)), this does not mean an absolute right of *refusal* of treatment. It simply means that where parents have refused treatment and a child consents to it, then the health carer is protected from a suit in battery.

Thus it would appear that a *Gillick*-competent child's refusal of treatment may be overridden by either an effective consent to the treatment provided by the child's parents, or a court order.

In *DoCS v Y* [1999] NSWSC 644 (30 June 1999) the Supreme Court considered the question of whether the court can make an order, based on the best interests of a child, even where that child is a "mature minor" and has refused treatment (see also Eades (2000), p 54).

[5.110] Case: *DoCS v Y* [1999] NSWSC 644

X, a teenage girl was diagnosed as suffering from anorexia nervosa. Both X and her parents Y and Z believed the diagnosis to be wrong and were non-compliant with recommended treatment, which included forced feeding because of her dangerously low body weight. She was considered in danger of death or serious future physical and metal deterioration without this treatment. The attitude and behaviour of both the girl and her parents made voluntary treatment impossible. The Director General, New South Wales Department of Community Services applied for an order for her treatment. The judge considered whether recent legislation granting the Family Court *parens patriae* jurisdiction (that is, the right to make orders for the welfare of those requiring care), meant that State Supreme Courts were thus stripped of this jurisdiction, as the Family Court, acting under federal law, has precedence over State Courts dealing with similar matters.

[5.115] The judge held that the "complex web of provisions" of the *Family Law Act 1975* (Cth) did not extinguish the *parens patriae* jurisdiction of the Supreme Courts of the States and Territories. The judge made X a ward of the Court and placed her in the custody of the New Children's Hospital at Westmead. He also authorised the staff at the hospital to detain her, using reasonable force if necessary, and to treat her. The orders excluded the parents Y and Z from any say in the medical treatment of their daughter X, and countermanded X's own wishes as to her treatment. However, the judge noted that the Court's power to override the wishes of the child should be exercised "sparingly", and that in this case he had considered the wishes of both the girl and her parents carefully before reaching the conclusion that her wishes were affected by her medical condition, which appeared to prevent her from understanding the seriousness of her medical condition and from taking proper account of the expert medical advice which was available to her. He went on to say that:

> "The justification for overriding her wishes is that on the evidence, her long term health and even her survival were seriously at risk unless steps were taken to give her the medical treatment she needed."

[5.120] Case: *R v M* (unreported, 15 July 1999, Royal Courts of Justice, Family Division, UK)

A girl, M, 15 and a half years old, suffered sudden onset of heart failure. It was considered that the only treatment available to save her life was a heart transplant. Her mother consented, but M did not. Despite extensive counselling and explanation M remained steadfast, and the hospital applied to the Court for authorisation to operate. Time was limited to a few days if M was to benefit from the surgery. The solicitor appointed to represent M, submitted that M was intelligent and understood her circumstances but was overwhelmed by her situation, and recommended to the judge that he authorise the transplant.

[5.125] The Court found that it was in M's best interests to have the transplant. The judge authorised the transplant stating that whilst a child's wishes should be considered seriously, the exercise of the Court's overriding power is justified where refusal of treatment would lead to death. He recognised that M would have to live with the effects of his decision, and could well resent it for the rest of her life. Gutman (2000), p 114 concludes that the Court failed to give adequate weight to the far-reaching consequences of the decisions, and its serious and life-long consequences, and indeed potential lack of compliance with treatment required of M because of her feelings about the procedure.

Consideration of a child's wishes

[5.130] This does not mean that a child's wishes should not be taken into account. The court in *Re W* (see **[5.100]**) made a strong statement to the effect that the refusal of treatment by a child, although not automatically legally actionable, is nevertheless of great importance for health carers in making clinical judgments, and should reasonably be considered. Lord Balcombe said, at 643:

"In a sense [consideration of the child's wishes] is merely one aspect of the test that the welfare of the child is the paramount consideration. It will normally be in the best interests of a child of sufficient age and understanding to make an informed decision that the court should respect [her or his] integrity as a human being and not lightly override [her or his] decisions on such a personal matter as medical treatment, all the more so if the treatment is invasive."

Thus it seems a court may override a child's wishes where their refusal of treatment is considered not in their best interests and may lead to death or serious injury or where the court considers the child lacks the capacity to appreciate the consequences of the refusal.

"Mature minor"—Disagreement with parents

[5.135] The Australian High Court in *Re Marion* (see **[5.30]**) noted and endorsed the majority view in *Gillick*, and stated (at 237) that:

"parental power to consent to medical treatment on behalf of a child diminishes gradually as the child's capacities and maturity grow and that this rate of development depends on the individual child."

Thus, it would appear that where a *Gillick*-competent child consents to treatment, that will be sufficient for a health professional to proceed, even if the parents object. The situation is likely to be different where a child refuses medical treatment, as discussed above at **[5.130]**.

Where there is a difference between a child and their parents, and the health carer believes the treatment is necessary for the child's welfare, she or he has the option of approaching the appropriate body for an order in relation to the child.

When a parent refuses care considered necessary by the child's medical professionals

[5.140] Where a parent's refusal of treatment is considered by the child's doctor or health carer to be other than in the best interests of the child, the medical professional may make an application to either the Children's Court or

Supreme Court in their State, or to the Family Court for an order authorising the proposed procedure. The power of the court in exercising its *parens patriae* jurisdiction exceeds that of parents, enabling the Court to override a parent's refusal of treatment where the Court considers the refusal is not in the best interests of the child.

[5.145] Case: *Re Michael* (1994) 17 Fam LR 584; FLC 92-471 *Re Michael (No 2)* (1994) 18 Fam LR 27; FLC 92-486 (Family Court of Australia)

The parents refused consent for surgery upon their son, aged 11, who suffered a congenital heart abnormality. The refusal was not an outright refusal, rather the surgeons wished to perform major surgery whereas the parents wished a minor temporary procedure to be carried out. The Public Advocate made application on behalf of the child, and was in the first matter held entitled to do so under the *Guardianship and Administration Act 1986* (Vic). In the second matter the Public Advocate made application for orders permitting him to consent to the major surgery on the child's behalf. The matter was resolved on undertakings.

Child under care of third parties

[5.150] A child may be in the care of someone other than a parent, for example, a guardian, institution, teacher, baby sitter, relatives or neighbours.

Where a child in such a person's care requires emergency treatment there is no doubt that this can be given and no other consent is necessary (see **[4.170]**).

Minor treatment and first aid can be consented to by the child who understands this.

Given that the third person is acting *in loco parentis*, delegated authority to consent is vested in them. There is no established limit to such authority, but it is suggested that authority would only apply to consent to treatment which is necessary for the continued good health of the child and which would be impractical to delay until a parent or guardian could be contacted. See Figure 5:1.

Child who is the subject of abuse or neglect

[5.155] When it is suspected that a child is the subject of abuse, some jurisdictions require certain classes of people, such as doctors, nurses, teachers and social workers, to report this to the authorities (see Chapter 16).

Child welfare legislation may be invoked, permitting welfare officers to take custody of the child and to organise treatment for her or him (*Children and Young People Act 1999* (ACT); *Children (Care and Protection) Act 1987* (NSW); *Child Protection Act 1999* (Qld), *Health Act 1937* (Qld); *Community Welfare Act* (NT); *Children's Protection Act 1993* (SA); *Children, Young Persons and Their Families Act 1997* (Tas); *Children and Young Person's Act 1989* (Vic); *Child*

Figure 5.1: Consent to health care for a Child

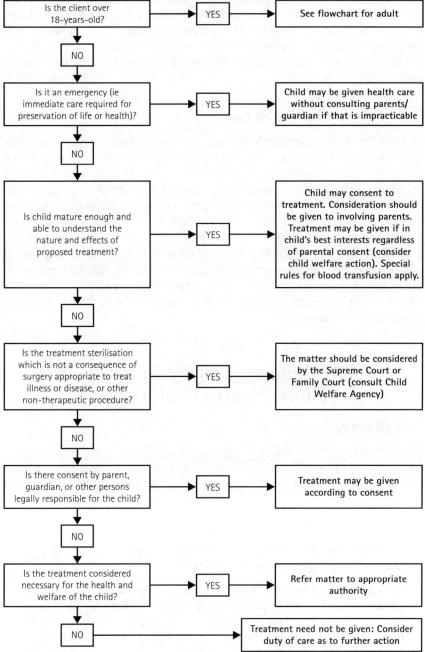

Note:

Where major treatment is being proposed, it is advisable that the capacity of the child is determined by a specialist (for example, in intellectual disability, child development or psychology). It is also advisable to refer to a specialist for determination of the need for major treatment.

Welfare Act 1947 (WA)). Also, some jurisdictions give medical personnel power to detain a child in a hospital, examine and administer treatment necessary for the child's welfare pending further legal action. Health carers should know what can be done, and who to notify when they suspect that a child in their care has been subject to abuse, or is being—or is likely to be—neglected. If in doubt, the State or Territory child welfare authorities can be contacted for assistance.

Children in need of health care

[5.160] The child protection legislation, mentioned above, provides extensive provision in all Australian jurisdictions providing for welfare officers to take action to remove, detain and arrange for the treatment of children in need of care. Definitions of what is meant by "in need of care" differ (see Chapter 16), but generally this includes abuse and neglect, either physical or emotional. The authority for consent to care is established by the relevant jurisdiction's legislation, and that person is the guardian for the child at the time care is authorised. This may be the Minister or Director of Child Welfare. For practical purposes it is the authorised officer who can direct that the care be given on his or her behalf. It should be noted that if a child requires a special examination (vaginal, anal or penile), there are special requirements in relation to those whose consent is required.

Adults Who are Legally Incapable of Consenting to Health Care

Role of the court

[5.165] The court that has *parens patriae* jurisdiction over adults who are not competent is the State or Territory Supreme Court. The following case dealt with such a person, and also illustrates the urgency with which the Court can act.

[5.170] Case: *Northridge v Central Sydney Area Health Service* (2000) 50 NSWLR 549; NSW SC 1241

At 2.56pm on a Sunday the duty judge at the Supreme Court was contacted at home by phone by a security officer at the Court, who advised that Mrs Northridge had rung seeking an order preventing the administration of a hospital from withdrawing treatment from her brother, a patient at the hospital who was suffering from brain damage and who she claimed would die if not treated. The judge formulated some questions for the purpose of elucidating the facts from Mrs Northridge, and by 3.25pm these were answered by phone. The judge immediately rang the relevant hospital registrar, who advised that the decisions to discontinue treatment of the patient had been made on the basis of neurological examination, which disclosed only some basic brain activity after an overdose of drugs. The patient was considered to be in a persistent vegetative state, and had been taken off all treatment, and was "not for resuscitation". The judge indicated that unless some accommodation could be reached with the treating medical officers in relation to continuation of treatment, a hearing would be required that evening. The matter was tentatively listed for hearing the following day, and arrangements were made for legal representation of the parties. Mrs Northridge was appointed as "tutor" for her brother (that is, the person acting for him). As a result of this action the doctors agreed to reinstate antibiotics and lift the "not for resuscitation" order.

[5.175] To ensure the continued care and rehabilitation of the patient, and that no order against resuscitation be made, the judge finally made an order that the patient remain in a hospital or other institution within the area and under the care of the defendant, be provided with necessary and appropriate medical treatment to preserve life and promote his good health, and that no "not for resuscitation" order be made in respect of the patient. In fact the patient recovered a substantial degree of cognitive ability, and was transferred to a nursing home under a rehabilitation program.

The judge held that one of the prerogatives of the Crown is the right to take care of the person, and property, of those who through disability are unable to do so for themselves. This is part of the *parens patriae* jurisdiction of the Supreme Court. He pointed to *Marion's Case* (see **[5.30]**) where Brennan J stated that:

> "The law will protect equally the dignity of the [hale] and hearty and the dignity of the weak and lame: of the frail baby and of the frail aged; of the intellectually able and the intellectually disabled ... our law admits of no discrimination against the weak and disadvantaged in their human dignity."

It was also pointed out by the judge that not only should hospitals have a clear resuscitation policy, doctors and hospital staff must comply with the policy. It may not be unlawful for doctors to withhold futile treatment from patients, but failure to adequately consult with families may well result in an order from the court to continue treatment.

The law relating to persistent vegetative state and not for resuscitation orders is considered further in Chapter 14.

In considering who can consent on behalf of adults with impaired decision-making capacity, this section deals with those suffering from:

- temporary decision-making incapacity (for example someone who is affected by medication, is suffering from sudden and severe emotional shock or fluctuating dementia, or who is unconscious);

- permanent decision-making incapacity (for example those suffering from intellectual disability, chronic dementia); and
- those suffering from a mental illness.

Temporary decision-making incapacity

[5.180] Where someone is temporarily unable to give permission for treatment, and the treatment proposed is not urgent, health carers should wait until the patient has regained the capacity to consent where this is feasible. Where the patient's state of lucidity is unstable, health carers should, both legally and ethically, take the effort to determine what level of understanding prevails at the particular time, or wait until the person is lucid. Blanket labelling of such a person as "incompetent" is a potential denial of their legal and human rights.

These rights are enshrined in the *Human Rights and Equal Opportunity Commission Act 1986* (Cth), based on international covenants which give those with some kind of mental impairment the same rights as other human beings "to the maximum degree of feasibility" (*United Nations Declaration on the Rights of Mentally Retarded Persons*), and in anti-discrimination legislation in all jurisdictions in Australia (see below, Chapter 18). The common law also provides that any person who is competent enough may exercise rights to own property, marry, enter into contracts, and consent to (and refuse) health care.

Impairment caused by drugs

[5.185] Consideration should be given to the effect of medication on patients' decision-making capacity, particularly drugs that may not be specifically given for neuroleptic and mind-altering purposes, such as pain relief, hormones, sedatives etc. A common situation that may arise occurs where the patient is asked to sign a consent form for an operation after the pre-medication is given, or after preparations for a procedure have commenced. Any consent purported to be given in such a situation would most likely be rejected by a court where it was considered that the person was incapacitated by drugs, felt some pressure to sign, or did not feel free to receive, question and consider the information necessary.

[5.190] Case: *Demers v Gerety* 515 P 2d 645 (1973) (New Mexico Court of Appeal United States)

The plaintiff, who did not speak much English, had made it clear he did not want surgery for repair of a ventral hernia if it would affect his ileostomy. Told he could have his wish, he signed a consent form for the hernia repair only. After sedation, with no explanation, and in the dark (he had to be guided as to where to

> sign, and could not read the form) he signed a form which happened to be a second consent form, permitting revision of ileostomy and repair of hydrocele.

[5.195] The Court rejected the argument that it was a valid consent. Obviously several factors were present to make this "consent" invalid; as well as being temporarily incompetent, the patient did not voluntarily give consent to the procedure, although he voluntarily signed his name. It would seem that staff were less than frank in giving him information as to the nature of the procedure, and why they thought he should have it. The Court referred to the "ritual of the consent form"; the relentless determination to have the document signed, regardless of how that is done. Courts will discount consent forms where they are not convinced the patient gave consent at least knowing the nature of the procedure, and freely consenting to it.

Chronic decision-making incapacity

[5.200] "Intellectual disability" is the term generally used to describe those who have a permanent or long-term intellectual deficit which renders them to some extent unable to lead a normal life without some degree of assistance. Their impairment may be mild or severe, but although they may improve with care, their condition is not expected to be rectified with treatment. Those who have an intellectual disability are divided into persons who are capable of understanding the particular medical procedure proposed, despite their handicap, and those who cannot. If they are so capable, they have the same rights as those without an intellectual disability. The first consideration is whether a person is capable of giving consent, as the law presumes that people can consent for themselves, and that presumption is only discarded when it is clear that they are unable to do so.

Others in this category are those suffering from chronic dementia and Alzheimer's disease. Their condition is generally progressive, again with no real prospect of cure or significant improvement with treatment.

Who can consent for a person with decision-making impairment?

[5.205] Where a person suffers from the inability to consent to treatment, health care cannot generally be given legally without with the consent of a substitute decision-maker who is authorised by law to act on their behalf. This person is determined by legislation (which differs across jurisdictions) as outlined below. There is no common law authority that allows relatives to consent to treatment on behalf of an incompetent adult.

The following flowchart provides a quick guide to determining who can consent to health care for an adult who is unable to do so. It is explained in more detail below.

Figure 5.2: Consent to health care for an adult with impaired decision-making capacity

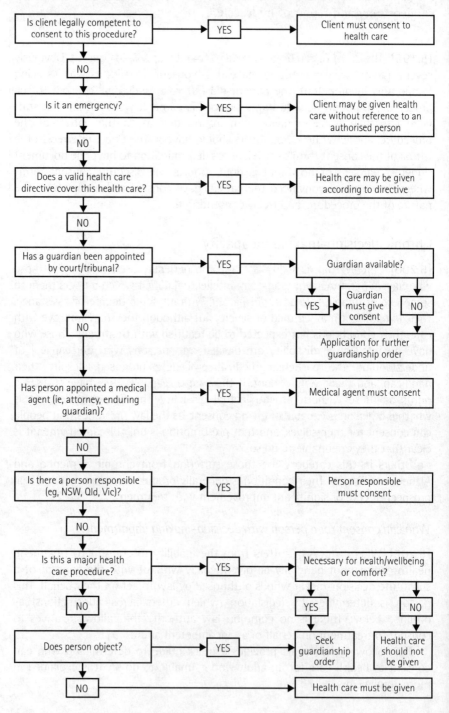

Notes:
1 A "prescribed" or non-therapeutic procedure requires the authorisation of a court or tribunal.
2 Where the person has made a directive and there is a guardian or person responsible etc, consent must be given according to the directive.
3 Some jurisdictions provide that where a person responsible is not available, the next person on the prescribed hierarchy may be eligible to give consent. If so, and there is no person left in the hierarchy, there is no person responsible. (see **[5.215ff]** below)

Where non-urgent treatment is proposed for a person who is not competent, consent must be given by a person who is authorised under law to do so. This may be a medical agent appointed by the person when competent to do so, or a guardian appointed by the person themselves or a court or tribunal. In most jurisdictions, providing that no person has formally been appointed as a substitute decision-maker, consent may be given by a spouse, relative or carer.

Consent by spouse or relatives

[5.210] It is often the policy of hospitals to obtain the consent of a spouse or relatives to health care when consent cannot be given by the patient. There is a basic legal principle that no one can legally give or withdraw consent to treatment for another legally incompetent adult without a court order, or, where provided for, an enduring power of attorney. Otherwise such consent has no legal standing. The medical staff can only act on implied consent for life-saving measures on the part of the patient; consulting relatives is simply a matter of courtesy.

This also means that any belief that a spouse must give consent to, for example, sterilisation or a legal abortion is incorrect. In *Attorney-General (Qld) (Ex rel Kerr) v T* (1983) 46 ALR 275 the Court refused the putative father of a foetus the right to prevent the mother from having an abortion, and in *F v F* (1989) FLC ¶92-031 the Family Court refused to recognise the right of a husband to restrain his wife from having an abortion. This follows a similar finding by the English Court in *Paton v BPAS Trustees* [1979] 1 QB 276.

Exceptions

[5.215] However, legislation regulating reproductive technology in Victoria, South Australia and Western Australia requires a spouse's consent in some circumstances (see **[17.140]**ff).

Most jurisdictions now have legislation providing that spouses, relatives and carers can consent to treatment under some circumstances (*Guardianship Act 1987* (NSW); *Powers of Attorney Act 1998* (Qld), *Guardianship and Administration Act 2000* (Qld); *Guardianship and Administration Act 1993* (SA); *Guardianship and Administration Act 1995* (Tas); *Guardianship and Administration Act 1986* (Vic); *Guardianship and Administration Act 1990* (WA)).

In New South Wales the *Guardianship Act 1987* (NSW) provides that the "person responsible" for an adult who is not capable of consenting to treatment may consent to major and minor medical and dental treatment. There is a hierarchy of persons from whom the "person responsible" is to be ascertained. That hierarchy is, in descending order:

- a legally appointed guardian, if that person has authority pertaining to medical decisions;
- a spouse with whom the person has a close and continuing relationship;
- a carer; or
- a close friend or relative.

The act defines circumstances in which a person has the care of another and the meaning of close friend or relative.

A doctor or dentist may also administer minor medical or dental treatment where there is no "person responsible" or that person is not contactable, the patient does not object, and the treatment is necessary for her or his health and well being. This was expected to reduce significantly the need for medical guardians, "lead to fewer guardianship orders and less need for state bodies like the Guardianship Board or the Public Guardian to come to the assistance of those with disabilities and their families" (Guardianship Board NSW, *The Guardianship Board Report 1993* (NSW Guardianship Board, Sydney, 1993), p 56).

In Queensland ss 62 and 63 of the *Powers of Attorney Act 1998* (Qld) provide for a "statutory health attorney" to make decisions about an incapable person's health care. A person's statutory health attorney is the first in the listed order of the following people who is "readily available and culturally appropriate" to provide consent:

- the person's spouse (where the relationship is close and continuing);
- the person's adult carer (excluding a paid carer); and
- a close friend or relative.

If there is no-one listed available there is an "adult guardian"—a statutory authority who has power to consent to treatment on behalf of an incompetent person appointed under the *Guardianship and Administration Act 2000* (Qld) which complements the *Powers of Attorney Act 1998* (Qld). Under the guardianship legislation, if there is disagreement as to what health care should be given, the adult guardian has the power to make the final decision. Health care that is "minor and uncontroversial", but necessary to promote the health and well being of the person can be given without consent where the health carer does not know and cannot reasonably be expected to know of any objection previously made by the person themselves or from any sufficiently interested persons.

Section 66 provides that the determination of consent may only be made with the first of the following situations to apply:

1. the patient's advance health directive;
2. a tribunal appointed guardian or in accordance with a tribunal order;
3. an enduring power of attorney appointed by the patient; or
4. the statutory health attorney.

In South Australia s 59 of the *Guardianship and Administration Act 1993* (SA) provides that the "appropriate authority" may consent to treatment on behalf of an incompetent person. The appropriate authority is a guardian if one has been appointed and has the power to make medical decisions, or a relative of the person or the Guardianship Board. Relative is defined by the Act.

In Tasmania s 39 of the *Guardianship and Administration Act 1995* (Tas) provides that a "person responsible" may consent to medical or dental treatment on a person incapable of giving consent, with the exception of special medical procedures, where they believe the treatment is in the best interests of the person concerned. A "person responsible" means one of the following, in order of priority:

(i) her or his guardian;
(ii) her or his spouse;
(iii) the person having the care of the person;
(iv) a close friend or relative of the person.

The circumstances under which a person may be considered to have the care of a person or be a close friend or relative of the person are set out in the Act.

In Victoria s 39 of the *Guardianship and Administration Act 1986* (Vic) provides that a "person responsible" may consent to treatment for someone who is not competent to make decisions. A "person responsible" is the first person from a list who is willing and able to make a decision. Those on the list, in order of precedence, are:

- an agent appointed under s 5A of the *Medical Treatment Act 1988* (Vic);
- a person appointed for the purpose by the Civil and Administrative Tribunal;
- a guardian appointed by the Tribunal;
- an "enduring guardian";
- a person appointed in writing by the person before they became incapable of making decisions to make decisions for the patient;
- the patient's spouse or domestic partner;
- the patient's primary carer; and
- the patient's nearest relative (again a list noting the precedence of relatives is set out in the Act).

In Western Australia s 119 of the *Guardianship and Administration Act 1990* (WA) provides that where a person cannot provide consent, the person who may consent to medical and dental treatment on their behalf is the first in order of priority of the following persons:

1. the guardian;
2. the spouse or de facto partner;
3. a person who regularly arranges or provides domestic services to the person on an unpaid basis;
4. the nearest relative who maintains a close relationship with the person;
5. any other person who maintains a close relationship with the person.

"Special" medical procedures

[5.220] Most jurisdictions provide that only a court or tribunal can agree to the administration of certain procedures to a person who is not competent to consent to them. These procedures are generally:

- removal of tissue for donation (again there are some exceptions);
- sterilisation or long-acting contraception and abortion;
- psychiatric care for psychiatric illness; and
- withdrawal of life-sustaining measures.

These are discussed more fully below at **[5.445]**.

Guardianship

[5.225] It can be seen that the law requires that those with some sort of cognitive impairment be given the same fundamental rights as everyone else, and this includes the right to self-determination (see Chapter 18 for a discussion of these rights). Where it is considered that an adult is not capable of understanding what is involved, in an emergency the ordinary considerations regarding emergencies apply (see **[4.170]**ff). Where there is no emergency and it is believed that a person is unable to understand the nature of proposed treatment because of their lack of competence, those proposing the treatment should seek the consent of the appropriate person as set out in that jurisdiction's legislation.

The appropriate person may be a guardian designated by law. If there is no other person who is legally authorised to make decisions for the patient, an application for a guardianship order should be made to the appropriate court or tribunal for a guardianship order. Each Australian jurisdiction has legislation for the appointment and conduct of guardians. Someone simply exercising factual (but not legal) control over the person is not in a position to give or withhold consent. The law simply refuses to recognise that one adult may control the life of another, no matter how retarded, without express statutory or court authority (*Kirby v Leather* [1965] 2 All ER 441, discussed in Hayes (1985), p 58).

Figure 5.3: Grounds for Guardianship/Management Orders

STATE	GROUNDS FOR GUARDIANSHIP ORDER*	GROUNDS FOR MANAGEMENT ORDER†
ACT	Guardianship and Management of Property Tribunal: Person has impaired decision-making ability in relation to a matter relating to their health or welfare; there is likely to be a need for a decision in relation to such a matter; or the person is likely to do something which is likely to involve unreasonable risk to their health, welfare or property; and if a guardian is not appointed their needs will not be met or will be adversely affected. *Guardianship and Management of Property Act 1991* (ACT)	Guardianship and Management of Property Tribunal: Same as for guardianship but where the person's impairment is in relation to decisions regarding financial matters affecting their property. *Guardianship and Management of Property Act 1991* (ACT)

STATE	GROUNDS FOR GUARDIANSHIP ORDER*	GROUNDS FOR MANAGEMENT ORDER†
NSW	**Guardianship Tribunal/Supreme Court**: Person has a disability and, by virtue of that disability, is totally or partially incapable of managing his or her person. *Guardianship Act 1987* (NSW)	**Supreme Court/Magistrates Court**: Person is incapable of managing his/her affairs. *Mental Health Act 1990* (NSW), s 51; *Protected Estates Act 1983* (NSW), s 16(1), *Guardianship Act 1987* (NSW), s 25E
NT	**Local Court**: Person is under an intellectual disability by reason of which the person appears to be unable to make reasonable judgments or informed decisions relevant to daily living and is in need of a guardian. *Adult Guardianship Act* (NT)	**Local Court/Supreme Court**: Person is under an intellectual disability by reason of which the person appears to be unable to make reasonable judgments or informed decisions relevant to daily living and is in need of a guardian (*Adult Guardianship Act* (NT), s 16). Person is, by reason of age, disease, illness or mental or physical infirmity, in a position which renders it necessary in the interests of that person, or in the interests of those dependent upon that person, that the person's estate be protected. *Aged and Infirm Persons' Property Act* (NT)
Qld	**Guardianship and Administration Tribunal**: Person has impaired capacity for a personal matter, and there is a need for a decision in relation to that matter, or the person is likely to cause unreasonable risk to her/his health welfare or property and without appointment the person's needs or interests will not be met or adequately protected. *Guardianship and Administration Act 2000* (Qld)	Same as for guardianship.
SA	**Guardianship Board**: Person is unable to look after her or his own health, safety or well being as a result of mental incapacitation and does not have an enduring guardian and a guardian should be appointed. *Guardianship and Administration Act 1993* (SA)	Same as for Guardianship, but in relation to where the person is unable, wholly or partially, to manage her or his affairs.

STATE	GROUNDS FOR GUARDIANSHIP ORDER*	GROUNDS FOR MANAGEMENT ORDER†
Tas	**Guardianship and Administration Board**: Person has disability, by reason of which they are unable to make reasonable judgments in respect of all or any matters relating to his or her person or circumstances and is in need of a guardian. *Guardianship and Administration Act 1995* (Tas)	**Guardianship and Administration Board**: Disability renders the person unable to make reasonable judgments in respect of matters relating to all or any part of her or his estate and is in need of an administrator of her or his estate. *Guardianship and Administration Act 1995* (Tas)
Vic	**Victorian Civil and Administrative Tribunal**: Person has a disability, by reason of which they are unable to make reasonable judgments in respect of all or any of the matters relating to her or hiss person or circumstances and who is in need of a guardian. *Guardianship and Administration Act 1986* (Vic)	**Victorian Civil and Administrative Tribunal**: Disability renders the person unable to make reasonable judgments in respect of matters relating to all or any part of her or his estate and is in need of an administrator of his or her estate. *Guardianship and Administration Act 1986* (Vic)
WA	**Guardianship and Administration Board**: Person is: (1) incapable of looking after his or her own health and safety; (2) unable to make reasonable judgments in matters regarding his or her person; (3) in need of oversight, care or control in the interest of his or her own safety or for the protection of others; and (4) in need of a guardian. *Guardianship and Administration Act 1990* (WA)	**Guardianship and Administration Board**: Person unable, by reason of mental disability, to make reasonable judgments in respect of matters relating to all or any part of that person's estate and is in need of an administrator. *Guardianship and Administration Act 1990* (WA)

* This is an order nominating a person to manage the represented person's day-to-day living arrangements and medical care.
† This is an order (very often made in favour of the Public Trustee) for management of the person's estate and financial affairs.

Guardians may be given full (or "plenary") powers, which means they can make decisions covering all aspects of the person's life—for example, where they live, education, lifestyle and medical treatment. They may be given limited or conditional powers, with the limits on the matters about which decisions can be made by the guardian set by legislation, and conditions under which the guardian can make decisions specified by the court's or tribunal's order. An order may also be temporary, specifying the period of time or events which determine the existence of the guardianship. A guardian may apply to the Board for directions where guidance is sought as to her or his rights and responsibilities.

A guardian must act according to the known wishes of a person and in her or his interests, but cannot consent to a "special medical procedure" (see **[5.220]**, **[5.445]**), which can only be authorised by a court or tribunal. In most cases parents, friends, or "interested persons" are eligible to apply to be a guardian. When necessary an emergency appointment can be made. This raises the question of who is best able to make decisions on behalf of the person concerned.

In practice, health care decisions are often made primarily by health care workers in consultation with the family, with no specific guardian appointed at law. Minor health care is often given without even consulting the family. It is very easy to overlook the rights of such people because they are unable to complain, and they may be difficult to deal with. All health carers are potentially legally liable for administering care without proper consent. Apart from being unlawful, such action is unethical as it undermines a person's right to self-determination.

The parents or family may not always be best able to decide impartially, and/or according to the person's wishes (see the *Qumsieh* case at **[5.285]**). In such situations someone involved in the person's care may believe that the arrangement is not optimal and challenge the person's authority to make decisions in the circumstances.

Guardianship orders

[5.230] The purpose of Guardianship Boards and Tribunals is to apply varied expertise to the issues of guardianship, to make orders which best suit the needs of the person and the specific circumstances, and allow for as much autonomy as possible. The Board or Tribunal is to give consideration to the wishes of the person where these are ascertainable when appointing a guardian, as must guardians when they are making decisions on behalf of the person. However, the legislation also provides that the person's welfare and interests should be given consideration in decision-making. Whether these considerations may in some circumstances conflict, and if so, how that conflict is to be resolved remains to be seen. In the case of *Re MC* [2003] QGAAT 13 the Tribunal stated that, in relation to the Queensland legislation, the crucial test was whether the treatment option was the least restrictive of the patient's rights and whether it was in their best interests. Thus the guardian's view and values regarding what is in the patient's best interests may potentially lead to the making of a decision contrary to the wishes of the person. (For further discussion of this issue see *White and Willmott* [2004].)

Where guardian and patient disagree

[5.235] It is important to note that while guardians can consent to treatment or withhold their consent it is questionable whether they can *order* involuntary treatment against a person's will, and whether health carers can force treatment on an unwilling person without further authorisation from a court or tribunal. Obviously it is best practice to avoid distress and alienation through enforced treatment, to ensure both the comfort, dignity and well being of the patient, and his or her co-operation with the care for optimum effect. Alternatively, more acceptable care should be considered if at all practicable. It is suggested that where the patient objects to health care:

- which is considered necessary for his or her well being;
- to which there is no reasonable acceptable alternative; and
- to which the guardian or the patient objects,

application to the appropriate court or tribunal should be considered. In the case of *K v Minister for Youth and Community Services* [1982] 1 NSWLR 311, the Supreme Court of New South Wales was dealing with an application by a social worker to override the refusal of permission for abortion by the guardian of a child who was a ward of the State. The guardian was, therefore, the Minister for Youth and Community Services. However, the Court ruled that it could override his decision as guardian, and did so. In the famous United States case of Karen Quinlan (*Re Quinlan* 355 A 2d 647 (1976)), Karen was a 21-year-old who was in a permanent vegetative state and there was a dispute between her parents, who wished to cease artificial ventilation, and the hospital administration, which wanted it maintained. Karen's father sought, and was granted, guardianship *ad litem* of her, which gave him the right to decide whether artificial ventilation should be continued or not.

Other legal obligations towards those with an intellectual disability

[5.240] All Australian jurisdictions have legislation which promotes the autonomy of those with an intellectual disability in as much as it allows for the health and well being of the person (*Disability Services Act 1986* (Cth); *Disability Services Act 1991* (ACT); *Disability Services Act 1993* (NSW); *Disability Services Act* (NT); *Disability Services Act 1992* (Qld); *Disability Services Act 1993* (SA); *Disability Services Act 1992* (Tas); *Intellectually Disabled Persons Services Act 1986* (Vic), *Disability Services Act 1991* (Vic); *Disability Services Act 1993* (WA)).

The lack of what the law calls a "sound mind" may be diagnosed by physicians, but must ultimately be decided by a court when the diagnosis is questioned. Legislative provisions in each Australian jurisdiction set out the procedure for appointment of guardians. Bodies have been established by all jurisdictions for this purpose (Figure 5.3). Some Australian jurisdictions have a statutory public advocate who, among other functions, can offer information, advice and assistance to those with an intellectual disability, intervene on behalf of a person who lacks capacity, investigate complaints, and apply for guardianship over them (see further **[5.435]**).

Health carers should always explore the possibility of such a patient's capacity to consent before giving treatment. It may in fact take longer, and involve much more careful counselling and explanation, but nevertheless is required by law.

[5.245] Case: *Battersby v Tottman* (1985) 37 SASR 524 (CA)

The plaintiff suffered a serious mental illness involving acute depression and suicidal tendencies and was potentially homicidal, according to evidence. She was given very heavy doses of the drug Melleril (which belongs to a group of medicines known as the phenothiazine antipsychotics, having as its active ingredient thioridazine) over a prolonged period of time, and as a result suffered serious and permanent damage to her eyes: a recognised risk of the medication. She sued the doctor in negligence, as he failed to inform her of the risk of serious and permanent eye damage, and failed to arrange monitoring of her eyes, believing that such information would have an adverse effect on her. Thus, she claimed, he failed to obtain her valid consent.

[5.250] Both at the trial and the appeal, the courts held that her condition was such that she would not have been able to have adequately weighed up the relative risks and benefits of the treatment.

King CJ said (at 527), referring to his own statement in an earlier case *F v R* (1983) 33 SASR 189:

"I adhere to what I said [there] at 193: 'Even where all other considerations indicate full disclosure of risks, a doctor is justified in withholding information, and in particular refraining from volunteering information, when he judges, on reasonable grounds, that the patient's health, physical or mental, might be seriously harmed by the information. Justification may also exist for not imparting information when the doctor reasonably judges that a patient's temperament or emotional state is such that he would be unable to make the information a basis for a rational decision.'"

This approach, called "therapeutic privilege" is also dealt with at **[4.340]**. It appears to apply to patients of either "sound" or "unsound" mind, and can severely limit the legal right of a patient to be fully informed. It is important to note that *Battersby v Tottman*, described by some commentators as having a number of unfortunate aspects, (see *Kerridge* at 166) was decided some 20 years ago; a different outcome may have arisen today.

Ensuring autonomy during future decision-making incapacity

[5.255] There is a way that people can attempt to retain their autonomy even when they are unable to make decisions about their health care. This is by making an advance directive. An advance directive (sometimes, erroneously called a "living will") is a document written in anticipation of the possibility of the writer being in a state of incapacity. The directive is to have effect if, and only if, that person actually becomes incapacitated. This means that the requirements for giving consent apply to the author of a directive at the time it is made. An example of an advance directive is a statement, written by a person who is competent that, should illness or accident in the future reduce him or her to a permanent vegetative state, he or she does not wish to receive artificial ventilation or other life-preserving treatment. Another common request of those who are terminally ill and approaching the end of their life, is that resuscitation not be given when it is otherwise required for survival.

As has been stated, and is dealt with in more detail below, when a person is unable to decide on treatment, decisions will be made for them. These will be based on the person's interests (the "best interest" principle) and welfare (the "substituted judgment" principle); and, to the extent they are known, their wishes. However they will not necessarily reflect the views of the person. In an advance directive, the person's intentions and values can be set out so that these can be known to guide the decision-maker. It is particularly useful where there is no family to consult as to their wishes, or the family's understanding of their wishes is divided or unclear.

Common law

[5.260] The question arises as to just what legal force directives have. There have been several decisions in the United Kingdom and Canada which have upheld the validity of advance directives, including the refusal of life-saving treatment (see, for example *Mallette v Shulman*, see [4.190], and *Re T*, see [4.205]). These cases suggest that an advance directive will be binding, provided that:

1. the patient was competent to consent at the time the directive was made;
2. the patient intended and anticipated their decision to apply to the situation that ultimately arose;
3. no undue influence was exerted on the patient in making the directive.

There is no Australian judicial consideration of the issue, although these decisions are likely to carry some weight as precedent. Thus it would appear that a health carer cannot administer treatment if they are aware of a valid advance directive refusing consent. Whilst an advance directive need not at common law be in writing to be valid, an oral statement alone may be difficult to verify.

Consideration of whether the person envisaged the type of situation that has arisen, or may have changed their mind since the directive was given may invalidate a directive. On the other hand, where the directive is clear and unequivocal, it is likely to carry the same legal force as a contemporaneous competent decision. Some of the difficulties with legal recognition of a person's wishes expressed in advance are discussed in relation to *Qumsieh* (see [5.285]; see also Stewart, (2000)).

What is the "triggering event"?

[5.265] Advance directives may be drafted for use in any health care situation in which people anticipate they will lack capacity to make decisions for themselves. This raises the question of what constitutes the "triggering event", that is, when the directive comes into effect, and this would depend on the nature of the directive. A "general" advance directive is one that anticipates any situation where the person is unable to express his or her choice. It would seem that a general advance directive comes into effect when the person is declared to be incompetent by a prescribed person (or persons). If, however the directive was to apply only to a current condition (see below) or a terminal condition (a "specific" advance directive) then one would have to satisfy the particular requirements set out.

Jurisdictions giving legislative effect to advance directives

[5.270] South Australia was the first State to legislate on this matter. The *Consent to Medical Treatment and Palliative Care Act 1995* (SA) permits a person to give directions while of sound mind, for when he or she may be in the terminal phase of a terminal illness or is in a persistent vegetative state. "Terminal illness" means any illness or condition that is likely to result in death. The "terminal phase" of a terminal illness is defined as having been reached when there is no real prospect of recovery or remission of symptoms, on either a temporary or permanent basis. The direction must be in the form prescribed by the regulations and must be witnessed by either:

(a) a justice of the peace; or
(b) a commissioner for taking affidavits in the Supreme Court; or
(c) a member of the clergy; or
(d) a registered pharmacist.

In addition, the Act provides that health carers who comply with a patient's direction are protected from criminal and civil liability in relation to that compliance where they act in good faith, in accordance with professional standards and in order to preserve or improve the quality of life.

In the Northern Territory the *Natural Death Act* (NT) provides that a person of sound mind who does not wish to be subjected to extraordinary measures in the event of his or her suffering a terminal illness, may make a direction in the prescribed form. "Extraordinary measures" are defined as medical or surgical measures that prolong life, or are intended to prolong life by supplanting or maintaining the operation of bodily functions that are temporarily or permanently incapable of independent operation. The direction must be witnessed by two witnesses. The legislation states that non-application of extraordinary measures does not constitute a cause of death.

In Victoria the *Medical Treatment Act 1988* (Vic) allows for a person to execute a refusal of treatment certificate. To do so, a registered medical practitioner and another person must be satisfied that:

• the person has clearly expressed a decision to refuse treatment generally, or treatment of a particular kind, for a *current condition*; and
• the decision was made voluntarily; and
• the person had adequate information to make the decision and understood it; and
• the person was of sound mind and over 18.

A refusal of treatment certificate must be witnessed by the registered medical practitioner and other person and must be in the form prescribed by the legislation.

The treatment refused may be any operation or administration of drug or any other medical procedure, but does not include palliative care (relief of pain, suffering or discomfort, or reasonable provision of food and water). The person does not have to be terminally ill. The Act establishes the offence of medical trespass for a medical officer who provides treatment knowing a refusal of treatment certificate applies. It also provides immunity from civil or criminal action for medical staff that act in good faith and in reliance on a refusal certificate.

In Queensland, s 35 of the *Powers of Attorney Act 1998* (Qld) provides that an adult person may give directions about health matters and special health matters, for her or his future health care and give information about her or his directions. These may be a consent, in the circumstances specified, to particular future health care of the person when necessary and despite objection by the person when the health care is provided. It may also require, in the circumstances specified, particular life-sustaining measures to be withheld or withdrawn.

The legislation provides that people can also appoint one or more attorneys to exercise power for a health matter on their behalf in the event the directions prove inadequate, and provide terms or information about how to go about exercising that power. A direction in an advance health directive operates only while the person has impaired capacity for the matter covered by the direction; and is as effective as if he or she was competent and making the decision when the treatment was being given. The person cannot make a direction to withhold or withdraw a life-sustaining treatment except under certain circumstances.

In the Australian Capital Territory, s 6 of the *Medical Treatment Act 1994* (ACT) provides that a person of sound mind may make a direction in writing, orally or in any other way in which the person can communicate to refuse, or for the withdrawal of, medical treatment, either generally or of a particular kind. To be valid, a written direction must be:

(i)   in accordance with the prescribed form; and
(ii)   signed by the maker or another person in the presence of and at the direction of the maker; and
(iii) witnessed by 2 persons in the presence of each other and the maker.

A direction not in written form is not valid unless witnessed by 2 health carers present at the same time, one of which must be a medical practitioner. The Act also provides immunity from civil or criminal action for medical staff that act in good faith and in reliance on a refusal certificate.

New South Wales lacks such specific legislation as the other jurisdictions mentioned here. However, s 33(3) of the *Guardianship Act 1987* (NSW) appears to endorse the validity of an advance directive to some extent in stating that "a person shall be taken to object to the carrying out of medical or dental treatment . . . (b) if the person (i) has previously indicated, in similar circumstances, that he or she did not want the treatment to be carried out, and (ii) has not subsequently indicated to the contrary".

In June 2004, the New South Wales Department of Health released a document entitled "Using Advance Care Directives (NSW)". The document states that an advance care directive that demonstrates specificity, currency and competence should be considered legally binding, based on common law principles.

Western Australia and Tasmania do not have legislation on this issue.

Patient refusal of treatment agreed to in an advance directive

[5.275] It may be the case that a person has agreed to treatment in an advance directive then refuses violently to accept it when incapacitated. This may be, for example, a person who has agreed to specific treatment, having a particular person care for them, or to being moved into a particular nursing home. There is no legal precedent for such a case to the authors' knowledge, however, it is suggested that in such cases, unless a less distressing and more acceptable form of care can be used, and the care is considered necessary for the person's health and well being, application should be made to the appropriate body for authorisation to carry out the care. It is recommended that no person (no matter what their mental capacity) should be treated in a way to which they seriously object without an order from a court or tribunal.

Psychiatric treatment is not covered by advance directives

[5.280] Mental health legislation in the various Australian jurisdictions seems to suggest that where a person has a mental illness, any advance directive may not be effective, particularly in relation to psychiatric health care to a non-competent person (see for example, s 8(1) of the *Mental Health Act 1986* (Vic)).

Difficulties that arise in relation to advance directives

Qumsieh's Case

[5.285] *Q v Guardianship & Administration Board & Pilgrim* (1998) 14 VAR 46; VSCA 45

This case highlights the difficulties faced by the judiciary in Australia in assessing purported refusals of life-saving treatment by competent adults. In that case, Mrs Qumsieh was a Jehovah's Witness and thus did not believe in blood transfusion. During her first pregnancy she created an advance directive stating her desire to refuse blood transfusion in any circumstances. When she was admitted to hospital for the delivery of her baby she signed a consent form for operative treatment and the administration of anaesthetic. She also made a hand-written note on the consent form that she did not wish to be administered blood or blood products. Following the birth she suffered post-partum haemorrhage. The hospital continued to withhold transfusion and her condition slowly worsened. Her husband sought to have the Public Guardian appointed to override his wife's refusal.

The matter came before the Guardianship and Administration Board in an urgent hearing. Mr Qumsieh and the hospital were represented; no separate representation was provided for Mrs Qumsieh. The Board was satisfied that Mrs Qumsieh fulfilled the requirements of the *Guardianship and Administration Act 1986* (Vic) in order that a guardian may be appointed to her. The Board was shown the consent form Mrs Qumsieh had signed but found that it was limited to procedures being conducted under anaesthetic. The Board was not shown the advance directive, nor was the Board told Mrs Qumsieh's reason for refusing blood transfusion.

The Board appointed the Public Trustee as guardian and then made further orders appointing the husband as guardian. The husband subsequently provided the hospital consent to transfusion allowing his unconscious wife to receive a blood transfusion. On recovery, the wife sought a review of the Board's order by the Supreme Court under the *Administrative Law Act 1978* (Vic).

[5.288] The judge in the Supreme Court refused the application on the grounds that there was no matter of substantial importance involved. He stated that "the order was made to save her life and no court would contemplate exercising its discretion to grant a remedy". This judgment was appealed in the Victorian Court of Appeal.

The Court of Appeal also dismissed the appeal, holding that the Board was entitled to act on evidence before it, and did not have to "look over its shoulder" to ensure that all the evidence was before it. The judge had been correct in his decision, it held, because of the circumstances of the case, given:

- the large number and variety of grounds for the appeal;
- the large number of respondents the appellant wanted to make party to her claims;
- the fact that the challenged order was now exhausted (that is, it had had its effect and could not be reversed); and
- it would "bring the appellant into disrepute with her husband".

Sufficient basis existed for the judge's conclusion that he should exercise discretion under s 4 of the *Administrative Law Act 1978* (Vic), to refuse application for order for review, since it considered that no matter of substantial importance was involved.

The appellant applied for leave to appeal to the High Court of Australia, arguing that she should have a right to raise a controversy *ex post facto*, as a declaration of invalidity which the *Administrative Law Act* indicates she is entitled to seek, would assist her in any future decisions in relation to whether or not she would take the matter further, and that while the Board's order was exhausted the matter was one of public importance (that is, the right to refuse treatment). However the High Court also dismissed the case stating that the facts of the case and the fact that the events were in the past militated against the grant of special leave to have the appeal heard.

Recording of, and access to, advance directives

[5.290] There are no uniform provisions for recording of, or access to, advance directives. Section 14 of the *Consent to Medical Treatment and Palliative Care Act 1995* (SA) creates a register for directions and medical powers of attorney. In Victoria, s 5E of the *Medical Treatment Act 1988* requires that the Board of a hospital or nursing home take reasonable steps to ensure that a copy of any refusal of treatment certificate be: (i) kept on the patient's record, (ii) given to the CEO of the hospital, and (iii) a given to the principal registrar of the Tribunal within 7 days of completion. The *Medical Treatment Act 1994* (ACT), s 20 requires a health carer who is aware a patient has made a direction to notify the superintendent. In turn, the superintendent is required to take all reasonable steps to ensure that a copy of the direction is placed with the patient's file. The remaining Australian jurisdictions lack any provisions relating to the recording of advance directives. Thus ensuring a person's health carers are aware of any advance directive may be difficult in some circumstances. A person who has multiple or a serious illness may be being cared for by a large number of health carers. They may or may not be in a health care facility, and may be transferred between facilities or discrete treatment areas within the same facility. There is a need to ensure that health carers are at any time aware of the existence of an advance directive. Health carers should treat an advance directive in the same way as they would treat a consent form and ensure its existence is communi-cated to, or available for, all who may be involved in a person's care.

Appointment of a medical agent (power of attorney)

Ordinary power of attorney

[5.295] The idea of an enduring power of attorney arises out of the legal concept of an ordinary power of attorney. An ordinary power of attorney is a document whereby a person (the donor of the power: for the purposes of this discussion referred to as the "patient") gives someone else (their "attorney") the power to act on his or her behalf for certain purposes which then binds the patient at law. The power of the attorney commences at a time stated by the patient, and ceases to have effect when he or she:

- loses the capacity to understand the effect of the power which has been given;
- dies; or
- revokes the power.

Enduring power of attorney ("medical attorney", "enduring guardian", "medical agent")

[5.300] A person may appoint an agent to make decisions on his or her behalf when he or she is not able to do so through some form of mental or physical impairment. An enduring power of attorney (EPA) differs from an ordinary power of attorney in that it only operates when the patient is no longer competent. In all jurisdictions except the Northern Territory, a person can appoint an enduring attorney or enduring guardian to make decisions in relation to health care. This power does not come into effect until the patient is declared incompetent. Both a medical attorney and an enduring guardian will be called a "medical agent". The agent is required to act according to his or her understanding of the wishes of the patient, and, where a valid consent (or refusal) is given by the attorney, it has the same effect as if it were made by the patient.

The advantage of appointing a medical agent is that it is an inexpensive and simple way for a person to choose who will make decisions about health care when he or she is unable to do so. The person who acts as attorney may be any adult who is trusted in that capacity by the patient. It obviates the need for the appointment of a guardian by a court or tribunal, and can be changed or revoked at any time.

An enduring power of attorney generally permits a person to authorise the attorney to:

- consent to medical treatment;
- refuse medical treatment; or
- consent to the donation of an organ, blood or tissue on their behalf,

if they are unable to do so themselves. The patient may nominate specific treatments which may or may not be consented to, and conditions under which this may occur.

Some jurisdictions allow for an enduring guardian to make day-to-day decisions about such matters as residence, education, work, etc.

In the Australian Capital Territory a competent adult can appoint a person to consent to, or refuse medical treatment under the *Powers of Attorney Act 1956* (ACT). The *Medical Treatment Act 1994* (ACT) provides for the appointment of a person to *refuse* medical treatment only.

In New South Wales the *Guardianship Act 1987* (NSW) provides for a competent adult to appoint an enduring guardian. The enduring guardian can make general lifestyle decisions for the person, as well as decisions about health care, when they cannot do so for themselves.

In Queensland the *Powers of Attorney Act 1998* (Qld) provides that competent adults may appoint an "enduring attorney" to make health care decisions on their behalf on loss of competence. If there is no enduring attorney, a statutory health attorney is authorised to make decisions.

If a statutory guardian is not available, the "adult guardian", a statutory authority, becomes the relevant authority for making decisions on the person's behalf. There is provision for reviewing a decision by a statutory guardian, but not one by the adult guardian.

An attorney cannot consent to "special medical treatment" (see below **[5.445]**ff). Application for this must be made to the Supreme Court.

In South Australia under the *Consent to Medical Treatment and Palliative Care Act 1995* (SA) a competent adult can appoint an "agent" to make decisions about health care on his or her behalf. He or she can also appoint an enduring guardian under the *Guardianship and Administration Board Act 1993* (SA) to undertake the personal care and welfare (including health care) of the person. An agent is not authorised to refuse:

- the natural provision or natural administration of food or water; or
- the administration of drugs to relieve pain or distress; or
- medical treatment intended to assist the person gain capacity, unless he or she is in the terminal stage of a terminal disease.

In Tasmania under the *Guardianship and Administration Act 1995* (Tas) a competent adult can appoint an enduring guardian with all the powers of a guardian appointed at law. These include the power to make health care decisions when the person is not competent to do so.

In Victoria the *Medical Treatment Act 1988* (Vic) provides that a competent adult can appoint an agent under an enduring power of attorney to refuse medical treatment on the person's behalf in the event of incapacity. The *Guardianship and Administration Act 1986* (Vic) allows for the appointment of an enduring guardian, who may consent to treatment if "and only to the extent that" the person becomes unable to make these decisions. An enduring guardian cannot consent to a special procedure.

In Western Australia the *Guardianship and Administration Act 1990* (WA) provides for the appointment of an enduring power of attorney for decision-making in relation to health care.

The legislation differs in detail across jurisdictions and generally lacks a requirement that a person be given specific medical or legal information before appointing a medical agent (which is desirable). Those appointing a medical agent would be well advised to record whether he or she has received independent medical and legal advice, to prevent the validity of an EPA or its terms being brought into question.

Who may witness the appointment of a medical agent/enduring guardian?

[5.305] Each Australian jurisdiction differs as to the requirements for witnesses to the appointment of an agent, although all require them to be over 18 years of age. Most jurisdictions require at least one witness to be authorised at law to take a declaration (for each State's requirements see: *Guardianship and Administration Act 1990* (WA), s 104; *Guardianship and Administration Act 1986* (Vic), s 35A; *Guardianship and Administration Act 1995* (Tas), s 32; *Guardianship and Administration Act 1993* (SA), s 25; *Powers of Attorney Act 1998* (Qld), s 44; *Guardianship Act 1987* (NSW), s 6C). Finding such a person may make the document harder to execute, however given the seriousness of the power being conferred, it may be considered that such a requirement should be universal. Relatives of the patient and the agent are also generally prohibited from witnessing the appointment. Most jurisdictions also require use of a specified form in order for the conferral of power to be valid.

Role of witnesses

[5.310] Jurisdictions differ in the requirements placed on witnesses to the appointment of a medical agent, for example, Queensland and South Australia require witnesses to indicate that the patient appeared to understand the effect of the document they were signing. It is thus necessary for witnesses to be aware of their obligations. It is recommended that a person who approaches health carers to be witnesses to the appointment of a medical agent be referred for legal advice to ensure the validity of the document.

Obligations and powers of person acting as medical agent

[5.315] The law is generally quite clear in relation to the obligations of medical agents in all jurisdictions. They are entitled to consent to, or refuse, treatment according to the terms of their appointment as attorney even if health carers believe the decision is not in the best interests of the patient. Most jurisdictions specifically state that in exercising powers under an enduring power of attorney while the patient is incapacitated, the medical agent shall act, as far as possible, and that can be ascertained, as the patient would have acted if the patient were not incapacitated. In doing so, he or she must take into account the need for preventing the patient from becoming destitute, and the desirability of maintaining, so far as is possible, the patient's style of life as it was before the incapacity. Where the patient's views on a particular issue are not known the attorney must act in the patient's best interests.

Transitory incapacity

[5.320] The question arises as to what happens when the patient regains capacity either permanently or transiently. While presumably the power of the medical agent would no longer be effective (until any further incapacity occurs) there is no clear provision for this in the legislation. Variations in the depth of incapacity may also occur. Victoria requires that an agent's powers are to be exercised, "if, and only to the extent that", the appointor becomes incapacitated. Issues relating to the question of capacity are dealt with in Chapter 4.

Role of health carers

[5.325] Questions also arise as to the role of health carers in dealing with consent to, or refusal of, treatment by an attorney. For example, there may be uncertainty as to how a health carer is to satisfy him or herself that the power of attorney is made in compliance with legislation. This is not uniformly dealt with in legislation and so it can only be presumed that where a health carer reasonably believes a document to be a valid appointment of a medical agent, he or she can act on it. Victoria provides that a registered medical practitioner or dentist who, in good faith carries out medical or dental treatment on a person in compliance with the legislation, is not guilty of assault, battery or professional misconduct or liable in a civil action for assault or battery. In contrast, the Australian Capital Territory expresses the protection to cover "health professionals" and in Queensland the legislation refers to "health providers". Where the protection pertains solely to medical and dental practitioners and medical and dental treatment, other health carers and other health care may not be covered.

Revocation of appointment of a medical agent

[5.330] Provision is made in most Australian jurisdictions for the revocation of an appointment of a medical agent (see *Guardianship and Administration Act 1986* (Vic), s 35C; *Guardianship and Administration Act 1995* (Tas), s 33; *Guardianship and Administration Act 1993* (SA), s 26 and *Consent to Medical Treatment and Palliative Care Act 1995* (SA), s 8(9); *Powers of Attorney Act 1998* (Qld), Part 5; *Guardianship Act 1987* (NSW), s 6H; *Medical Treatment Act 1994* (ACT), s 5). Generally speaking in order to revoke an appointment the person must be competent and specifically revoke the appointment in writing.

Those suffering from a mental illness

[5.335] The Australian Government participated in the development of the United Nations' Principles for the Protection of Persons with Mental Illness and for the Improvement of Mental Health Care (1991) and these principles were included in the National Mental Health Plan (1992) (NMHP). The Principles state, among other things, that:

- a mentally ill person is to have all the rights of any other person, and is to be free from discrimination;
- the determination that a person has a mental illness shall be made in accordance with internationally accepted principles;
- a person is to be able to live and work within the community to the extent of her or his capabilities;
- treatment is to be based on the principle of the "least restrictive alternative", to be individualised, discussed with the patient and reviewed regularly;
- patients are to be protected from exploitation, abuse and degrading treatment;
- a person is not to be detained involuntarily unless this is necessary for the safety of the person or others, or to prevent serious deterioration in the person's condition;
- where necessary for the above reasons detention may be for a short period pending review; and
- detention should involve the least restrictive measures for the least necessary time, and follow legislatively established procedures.

In 1993 the Human Rights and Equal Opportunity Commission was critical of legislation in every jurisdiction of Australia for its inconsistency with these principles, and as a consequence most Australian jurisdictions reviewed their mental health legislation (*Report of the National Inquiry into the Human Rights of People with Mental Illness*, 1993). A second NMHP was released in 1997 consolidating the reform initiatives and focusing on promotion and prevention aspects of mental health care. A third NMHP has now been released to cover the period 2003-2008. This plan has service, quality care and sustainability amongst its primary themes. It is theoretically based on the Australian National Health Strategy document entitled 'Promotion, Prevention and Early Intervention for Mental Health' published in 2000.

On 28 April 2006 the Commonwealth Government released a report entitled *A National Approach to Mental Health – From Crisis to Community*. The report was the second and final report of the Senate Select Committee on Mental Health, complementing the first report of the same title released on 30 March 2006. The introduction of the second report describes the role of the reports in facilitating change in relation to mental health as follows:

> "As the committee's inquiry progressed, the urgent need for reform in the area of mental health gathered momentum in the eyes of the public and among governments. In February 2006 the Council of Australian Governments (CoAG) agreed to initiate a rapid process of discussion and policy development on mental health, with an action plan to be developed by June 2006. The committee was committed to ensuring that its inquiry and findings had a significant influence on this important reform process. It therefore decided to divide its report into two parts. The first report, *A national approach to mental health – from crisis to community*, was tabled in the Senate on 30 March 2006. That report, representing the bulk of the committee's work, provided a wide-ranging review of many aspects of mental health care in Australia and delivered a set of important, unanimous recommendations that the committee believes should be addressed in the CoAG reform process.
>
> This second, and final, report sets out further detailed recommendations that arise from the committee's inquiry and findings in particular areas of concern. These recommendations are no less important than those set out in the first report."

The reports make recommendations in relation to:

- funding for mental health services;
- reform of the National Mental Health Strategy (NMHS) to guarantee the right of access to services;
- strengthening consumer advocacy;
- harmonisation of Mental Health Acts in relation to involuntary treatment; and
- increasing community health and treatment facilities.

The reports are available at www.aph.gov.au/senate/committee/mentalhealth_ ctte/ (accessed in May 2006).

Involuntary detention and treatment is a legal act, subject to the rule of law, with those seeking to deprive a person of their liberty being answerable on legal rather than medical grounds. Thus, while there are often medical arguments about whether a person actually suffers from a mental illness, mental disorder or otherwise, legislation is more concerned with establishing criteria that warrant the detention and treatment of a person against their will.

Definition of "mental illness"

[5.340] The definition of "mental illness" varies slightly in each Australian jurisdiction (*Mental Health (Treatment and Care) Act 1994* (ACT), Dictionary; *Mental Health Act 1990* (NSW), Schedule 1; *Mental Health and Related Services Act* (NT), s 6; *Mental Health Act 2000* (Qld), s 12; *Mental Health Act 1993* (SA), s 3; *Mental Health Act 1996* (Tas), s 4; *Mental Health Act 1986* (Vic), s 8; *Mental Health Act 1996* (WA), s 4). The Australian Capital Territory, New South Wales and Northern Territory Acts use similar terms, and define mental illness as:

> "a condition which seriously impairs, either temporarily or permanently, the mental functioning of a person and is characterised by the presence in the person of any one or more of the following symptoms:
> (a) delusions;
> (b) hallucinations;
> (c) serious disorder of thought form;
> (d) a severe disturbance of mood;
> (e) sustained or repeated irrational behaviour indicating the presence of any one or more of the symptoms referred to in paragraphs (a)-(d)."

Queensland and Victoria also utilise similar wording defining mental illness as a condition characterised by significant "disturbance of thought, mood, perception and memory".

The Australian Capital Territory (s 5), New South Wales (s 11), Victoria (s 8(2)), Queensland (s 12), the Northern Territory (s 6) and Western Australia (s 4(2)) provide a list of behaviour which does *not* constitute mental illness. This includes:

- religious, political and philosophical beliefs and practices;
- sexual orientation, preference or promiscuity;
- immoral, illegal or anti social behaviour;
- drug or alcohol ingestion; and
- developmental disability of mind.

In Tasmania (s 4) a diagnosis of mental illness may not be based solely on:

- antisocial behaviour; or
- intellectual or behavioural nonconformity; or
- intellectual disability; or
- intoxication by reason of alcohol or drugs.

Certification of a person as mentally ill is a very serious responsibility for the medical profession. A proper understanding of what constitutes mental illness in the particular jurisdiction of practice is required, along with the requisite diagnostic skills.

Mental illness or mental disability?

[5.345] It seems generally accepted by the medical profession that mental illness is a condition which is potentially treatable, with impaired function either reducible or temporary, whereas mental disability is a permanent condition, with no reasonable prospect of recovery. It is also clear from legislation that the law is concerned with drawing a distinction between:

- people who are mentally ill and no actual or potential danger to themselves or others, either because of the nature of the illness or the fact that they are willingly undergoing treatment which allows them to live safely in the community; and
- people who are mentally ill and are an actual or potential danger to themselves or others; and
- people who are not mentally ill, but who are, nevertheless, an actual or potential danger to themselves and others. There is some difference of opinion in the various jurisdictions as to how to deal with these people.

When the law will order treatment

[5.350] The law is not concerned with restricting the freedom of the first category of people. It is only when the mentally ill become part of the second and third categories that they attract this concern. Thus, for legal purposes, most legislation requires something more than simply the presence of mental illness, however defined, for detention. Law makers are more concerned with the danger people pose to themselves or others, than they are with the presence or nature of any mental illness. Thus the legal focus is on behavioural outcomes of mental impairment such as a threat of serious physical harm to themselves or others, rather than the precise nature of the mental impairment itself.

Health carers should be aware that because a person is diagnosed as having a mental illness, he or she is not necessarily unable to give or withhold consent to health care at law. Those with a mental illness may sue in battery where they have been given non-urgent treatment to which they are capable of consenting, but did not consent. Such people have the right to be treated in the same way as a person who is not mentally ill in all matters except those which relate to an order by a court (see below, Chapter 18).

Because each Australian jurisdiction has its own legislation, and this can become somewhat complicated, a detailed description of statutory provisions in each jurisdiction will not be set out here. However, some main aspects of the law and mental illness will be considered. Carers who are dealing with patients who are considered not competent to make decisions should be familiar with the relevant jurisdiction's law regarding their powers and responsibilities towards those patients.

Voluntary patients

[5.355] Some jurisdictions provide legislative provisions governing a person's voluntary admission to a psychiatric treatment facility. In South Australia the legislation specifically states that a person may be admitted to an approved treatment centre at his or her own request (s 11). In the Northern Territory a person may be admitted as a voluntary patient where the medical practitioner is satisfied that the person is likely to benefit from admission (s 25(8)). Where admission is refused, the person has a right of appeal (s 25(9)). In New South Wales a person may be admitted to hospital as an informal patient at his or her request (s 12), however, the medical officer may refuse admission where they are not satisfied that the person is likely to benefit from care or treatment as an informal patient (s 17). Where a person is refused admission by a medical officer they may apply to the medical superintendent for review of that decision (s 19). In Tasmania a person refused voluntary admission is to be advised of the right to seek a second opinion (s 20).

At common law voluntary patients in an institution should be treated like any other member of the community, and with the same dignity and respect. They may consent to or refuse treatment as they wish, as they are legally entitled to be considered competent enough to do so. Their property should not be confiscated, nor should they be denied information, services or freedom of movement to a greater extent than any other competent person. This has been endorsed by the Australian High Court in *Marion's Case* (see **[5.30]**). It is only when voluntary patients fulfil the requirements for involuntary treatment that their refusal to consent to treatment can be overridden.

Voluntary patients should be free to walk around hospital grounds and even leave the hospital if they so wish. There is a distinction between a person leaving hospital and a person being discharged, the latter involving an undertaking by the hospital that their condition is satisfactory for leaving. In Western Australia, a voluntary patient seeking to be discharged is to be referred to be examined by a psychiatrist, and may be detained for up to six hours for this purpose (ss 29, 30). A voluntary patient (in any jurisdiction) who leaves without being discharged cannot automatically be apprehended and returned. They must fulfil the emergency apprehension provisions described below. They should not be detained in the facility unless legal authority to do so is obtained through the proper legal process.

Involuntary patients

Emergency detention and treatment

[5.360] At common law a person who has been wrongfully detained can apply for a writ of *habeas corpus*, by which a court requires the person to be brought before it, and the reason for detention considered. There is, however, provision for the lawful detention of those apparently suffering from some sort of mental disorder. These laws are very complex, and it is not possible to give other than a general outline here. Carers of those who are suffering from mental illness should be familiar with the law in their jurisdiction as the question of whether they can insist on a patient submitting to restraint and treatment, which may be a critical aspect of the patient's treatment, may vary from case to case. Subject to variations, most Australian jurisdictions provide for the apprehension, detention, conveyance to a health facility, examination and treatment of a person who is considered to fulfil prescribed criteria. These generally require that not only is the person considered to have a mental illness in the broad medical sense, in the opinion of those apprehending her or him, but that their continued freedom must be considered to be likely to result in some harm either to themselves or to others. Relatives or friends in some jurisdictions may request the apprehension of someone they believe to be in such a condition. This may involve a magistrate issuing a summons, or an authorised person (for example, a police officer or doctor) taking the person into custody.

A doctor may also issue a certificate which allows police or ambulance officers, etc, to detain a person and bring him or her to a hospital. There is generally a deadline set (from four to 24 hours) within which the person must be examined, and in most jurisdictions the person may be kept for up to 72 hours for observation and assessment. The person must then either be released, or further detention maintained under certain circumstances. These are summarised below.

The Australian Capital Territory (Part 5 of the *Mental Health (Treatment and Care) Act 1994* (ACT)) allows a person who is believed to be suffering from mental illness, and there is a danger of self-harm or harm to others, to be apprehended by the police and taken to an approved health facility. The person must be examined by a doctor within four hours. The person may be detained for 72 hours, after which time an application must be brought in the Mental Health Tribunal for a treatment order. The Act requires the Tribunal to be satisfied that the person is suffering from a mental illness, is likely to do serious harm to herself, himself or others, psychiatric treatment is likely to reduce the likelihood of such harm resulting, and the treatment cannot be adequately provided by less restrictive means. The *Mental Health (Treatment and Care) Act* provides that the minimum necessary treatment and restraint is to be given for the patient's and the community's safety and well being.

In New South Wales, Chapter 4, Part 2 of the *Mental Health Act 1900* (NSW) provides that where a doctor or accredited person certifies that a person is mentally ill or disordered, the person may be detained if that is considered necessary and there is no other care of a less restrictive kind is appropriate and reasonably available. They must be examined within 12 hours of arrival at the hospital by the medical superintendent, and a further opinion obtained as soon as possible thereafter. If there is agreement that detention is required, the person is detained pending application before a magistrate for a treatment order. If they are considered mentally disordered they may be kept no longer than 72 hours. Pending the appearance before the magistrate, they may be treated as the medical superintendent thinks fit, but due regard must be given to the effects of medication on their ability to communicate adequately with a representative at the inquiry.

The Northern Territory (in Parts 3 and 6 of the *Mental Health and Related Services Act* (NT)) sets out the following criteria for involuntary admission on the grounds of mental illness:

* the person has a mental illness;
* by reason of mental illness they require treatment;

- they are likely to cause harm to himself, herself, or another person; or
- are likely to suffer serious mental or physical deterioration; and
- they are not capable of giving informed consent or have unreasonably refused treatment; and
- there is no less restrictive means of ensuring treatment is received.

A person admitted as an involuntary patient on the grounds of mental illness may be detained for up to 24 hours or up to seven days, if the person making the recommendation is an authorised psychiatric practitioner. Treatment must not be administered to an involuntary patient without authorisation from the Tribunal unless the treatment is necessary to prevent imminent harm or further physical or mental deterioration, or to relieve acute symptomatology.

In Queensland the *Mental Health Act 2000* (Qld) provides that a police officer or ambulance officer must take a person to an authorised mental health service where the officer reasonably believes the person has a mental illness and because of that illness there is an imminent risk of significant harm to the person or someone else. Where an examination order exists a person may be detained for not longer than six hours in order to undergo examination. A person may be detained for involuntary assessment for an initial period of 24 hours; this may be extended by a period of a further 24 hours but must not exceed 72 hours. A request for assessment may be made by any adult who reasonably believes the person has a mental illness requiring involuntary assessment if they have observed that person within the preceding three days. A recommendation for assessment may only be made by a doctor or an authorised mental health practitioner who has seen the person within the preceding three days.

In South Australia, Part 3 of the *Mental Health Act 1993* (SA) states that a patient may be detained initially for up to three days on the recommendation of a doctor, and examined by a psychiatrist as soon as possible after admission, within 24 hours if practicable. He or she may then be detained for a period of a further 21 days where detention is "justified", such an order for further detention may not be made more than twice. The opinion of two psychiatrists is required for a second extension to be ordered. The Guardianship Board may order a person be detained for a period not exceeding 12 months where the Board is satisfied that a person who is being detained in an approved treatment centre has a mental illness that requires treatment and detention is in his or her interests or for the protection of others. On application by the patient, a relative, guardian, doctor or the Public Advocate the Guardianship Board may revoke such an order.

In Tasmania the *Mental Health Act 1996* (Tas) states that if a police officer or authorised officer considers on reasonable grounds that a person has a mental illness and as a result of that illness a serious risk of harm to the person or others exists, the officer may take the person into protective custody and as soon as possible thereafter must take them to an assessment centre. An application for an order for involuntary admission may be made by an authorised officer or the person responsible. A person admitted as an involuntary patient must be examined by an approved medical practitioner within 24 hours of admission. A continuing care order may be made for a person where the criteria for involuntary admission are met for a period not exceeding six months.

In Victoria, Part 3 of the *Mental Health Act 1986* (Vic) states that a medical practitioner may recommend detention of a person considered mentally ill and in need of treatment. The person must be examined by a psychiatrist within 24 hours of an involuntary treatment order being made. As a result of this examination the person may be detained further. Continued detention may be authorised by the chief psychiatrist for a period not exceeding three months. Further detention may be authorised by a committee of three psychiatrists for a further period not exceeding three months. There is no limit to the number of times the continued detention of a person may be renewed. Provision is made for notification to the Secretary of the Department of Human Services and for three-monthly reviews of the detention. The Mental Health Review Board must hear appeals against detention without delay and must conduct an initial review of the order within eight weeks after the order is made and periodic reviews at intervals of not more than 12 months.

In Western Australia, the *Mental Health Act 1996* (WA) provides that an authorised mental health practitioner (psychologist, nurse or occupational therapist with at least three years experience in the management of persons with a mental illness) or a medical practitioner who suspects on reasonable grounds that a person should be made an involuntary patient may refer the person to a psychiatrist for examination at an authorised hospital. The person can be detained for up to 24 hours to be examined by a psychiatrist. The psychiatrist may order that the person be detained for no longer than 28 days, with a further determination for detention up to six months.

For those who, because of mental illness, are unable to exercise the understanding and insight required for autonomous decision-making, the principle applies that they can be given emergency health care or restrained where they place themselves or others in danger without their having consented to it. Under mental health legislation courts and tribunals can go further, and authorise the treatment of a person against his or her will, by force if necessary. Thus in all jurisdictions there is an eventual time limit at the end of which the person must be released, or a court or tribunal order for compulsory treatment sought. Detention periods stated are maximum periods, and the person may be detained for shorter periods, or released at any time by the relevant authorised person or body. The person may appeal the detention to a nominated body, such as the Guardianship Board, Mental Health Tribunal or Court. There must be periodic reviews of a detained person and that person's situation. The person may be entitled to have a nominated representative who is notified of all legal action and who may advise and act for the patient, and represent them at a hearing. Other safeguards may also be established, such as the right to communicate to those outside the institution, to be informed about all treatment, and to seek legal review of the involuntary detention at any time. The institution must then justify detaining the person.

[5.365] Case: *Hunter Area Health Service & Anor v Presland* (2005) 63 NSWLR 22; NSWCA 33

The respondent killed Ms Laws, his brother's fiancée. He was subsequently charged with and tried for murder. A special verdict of not guilty on the grounds of mental illness was entered. He was detained in a psychiatric hospital as a forensic patient until released by due process of law. The day before the respondent killed Ms Laws, he had been taken by police to a public hospital following an episode of bizarre and violent behaviour. Later that evening he was transferred to a psychiatric hospital for assessment and was admitted as a voluntary patient. After his assessment the following morning he was discharged into the care of his brother and killed Ms Laws approximately six hours later.

[5.370] The respondent's case was that it was negligent of the hospital and the psychiatrist who discharged him not to have detained him as an involuntary patient under the *Mental Health Act 1990* (NSW). The trial judge accepted that the plaintiff manifested a psychotic state and had threatened to kill people in the incident prior to his arrest. The judge held that the respondent was inadequately assessed by the psychiatrist concerned resulting in his discharge, subsequently finding in favour of the plaintiff. The defendant appealed on numerous grounds, however, the substantive issues (and the ones of most interest here) were first, the nature and content of the duty of care owed to patients presented for psychiatric treatment both at common law and under the *Mental Health Act 1990*, and secondly, whether the respondent's unlawful acts disentitled him to recover damages.

The New South Wales Court of Appeal, by a 2/1 majority, upheld the appeal and the verdict for the plaintiff was set aside. All three judges agreed that the psychiatrist and hospital owed the respondent a general duty of care to exercise reasonable care and skill in the provision of professional advice and treatment and that this duty extended to the exercise of the statutory powers in ss 18 and 21 of the *Mental Health Act 1990*. It was generally accepted that the duty of care owed to the respondent was breached. The judges differed however on their opinions as to whether the respondent should be entitled to recover damages in the circumstances.

Sheller JA stated that public policy must loom large in a court's consideration of whether a person should be compensated for harm suffered as a consequence of killing. With regard to the statutory scheme he opined [at 296]:

> "the MHA is directed to enabling detention only as a last resort. I doubt that the policy behind the statutory provisions contemplates or permits a party to recover damages because a medical superintendent has refused to admit the claimant to a hospital as an informal patient albeit that the decision to refuse was a negligent decision. This 'would have the tendency to discourage the due performance' by the statutory authority and medical superintendents of their statutory duties; *X (Minors) v Bedfordshire County Council*."

Sheller JA went on to consider the responsibility of one person to another for harm done to that person by a third party. He quoted with approval a passage from *Smith v Leurs* (1945) 70 CLR 256; [1945] HCA 27 where Dixon J [at 262] stated that "the general rule is that one man is under no duty of controlling another man to prevent his doing damage to a third". Sheller JA went on to comment that in the case at hand, the nature of the harm suffered by the respondent pointed "as a matter of commonsense" against the existence of legal responsibility for that harm in the appellants.

Santow JA was of the opinion that the duty owed did not extend so as to permit any recovery for non-physical injury suffered by the respondent. He went on to state that no such extended duty could be derived from the *Mental Health Act 1990* and would be inappropriate by reason of the purpose and scope of the statutory scheme, distorting the impartiality of the exercise of discretion under the Act, by promoting a bias towards detention. He expressly stated his decision to be based not on the maxim of *ex turpi causa non actio* or the moral culpability of the respondent, but rather on what he conceived legal policy, based on community values, would consider just.

Spigelman CJ dissented on the grounds that the factors which are entitled to weight in determining the scope of the duty owed to the respondent are control and vulnerability. In his opinion, the authorities establish that, where a person has been held not criminally responsible for his actions on the grounds of insanity, the common law should not deny the person a right to a remedy and the acts which would otherwise constitute a crime do not break the causal chain.

(This case is also discussed at **[6.150]**).

Subsequent to the decision in *Hunter Area Health Service & Anor v Presland*, amendments were made to the *Civil Liability Act 2002* (NSW) and related legislation. By ss 54A-54D, restrictions are placed on claims that arise at the time of, or following conduct of the person that on the balance of probabilities would have constituted a serious offence if the person had not been suffering from a mental illness at the time of the conduct.

Orders for treatment

[5.375] As stated in Chapter 4, it is erroneous to characterise the principles of autonomy and beneficence as "rights" which can compete in certain circumstances. The first is a right, the second an ethical directive, which must be subject to the first. However, when dealing with those who are unable to appreciate their own position, or their need for care, several rights come into conflict: the right of a person to care and protection, their right to dignity and self-determination; their right to freedom from unnecessary detention and the right of the community to protection from harm. These are all legitimate rights (see discussion of rights in Chapter 18; Hundert (1990)). Consequently, legislation attempts to strike a balance between these rights.

The precise criteria for authorising involuntary health care vary between jurisdictions, but generally the person must be suffering from a psychiatric illness to be the subject of psychiatric treatment. Others who are mentally disordered or dysfunctional and a danger to themselves or others may be the subject of treatment and care orders, which involve other kinds of treatment and care. They may be detained, or allowed to live in the community (or other specified place) where they receive that care and support. A difficulty arises from the fact that "care" may cover much more than the administration of psychiatric medication.

Mental illness or dysfunction must be established

[5.380] It is important to establish some form of mental illness or dysfunction before an order can be made. The following case was decided before amendments to the legislation in the Australian Capital Territory but the principle remains relevant.

[5.385] Case: *Burnett v Mental Health Tribunal & Ors*
(unreported, SC ACT, No 84 of 1997)

B had been diagnosed as having a mild psychiatric disorder, and had had a series of disputes with neighbours, behaving aggressively towards them on occasions, which led to her being hospitalised. An order for her involuntary treatment was made by the Tribunal, without explaining its reasons. Her psychiatrist's view was that although B had acted in an irrational and distressing way, her illness could not be described as severe in a clinical sense. B questioned whether there was evidence of psychiatric illness, and showed that she was able to care for herself and generally manage her own affairs, including her financial affairs.

[5.390] The judge held that there was no evidence in the Tribunal's transcript that B was experiencing any of the symptoms referred to in the Act's definition of "psychiatric illness" such as delusions, hallucinations etc. It stated that the Tribunal should not act on unsubstantiated allegations, but should look for clear evidence of mental dysfunction and danger of harm if the order is not made. There must be "clear and persuasive" evidence demonstrating the need for an order, and the person involved should be given an opportunity to be heard, if this is possible. The judge concluded that even if he had been convinced that B suffered from a psychiatric illness as defined in the Act, he would not have been convinced that a detention order was necessary to protect B, the neighbours or the community.

Procedural fairness (or "natural justice") is also required (see **[1.115]**; see also *EO v Mental Health Review Board* [2000] WASC 203 (SC WA)).

Community care

[5.395] Where a person is suffering from a mental illness, in all jurisdictions except South Australia, an order for community care may be made for those who are considered a danger to themselves or to others, but can continue to function in the community with the assistance of medication or care (see *Mental Health (Treatment and Care) Act 1994* (ACT), Part 4, Div 4.5; *Mental Health Act 1990* (NSW), Chapter 6, Part 3; *Mental Health and Related Services Act* (NT), Part 7; *Mental Health Act 2000* (Qld), Chapter 4, Part 2, Div 2; *Mental Health Act 1996* (Tas), Part 7; *Mental Health Act 1986* (Vic), s 14; *Mental Health Act 1996* (WA), s 66). Where a person breaches such an order, by, for example not turning up for depot medication or at other required appointments or failing to take medication, action can be taken to carry out the treatment, or the person may be brought into hospital for review. Whilst there is reluctance to visit the heavy hand of force on these people, the order does make them the subject of accountability to the court or tribunal. Such orders generally have a maximum time limit ranging from three to 12 months, however the person may be discharged earlier if it is considered appropriate to do so. As with orders involving detention, the court or tribunal can set a time within the life of the order for review of the person's condition.

Community care orders are often used for someone who is suffering from either a psychiatric illness or a mental disorder which responds well to medication, but who lacks insight into the illness and/or is likely not to comply with medication requirements, with the danger of consequently becoming ill. This can lead to the "revolving door syndrome" with its cycles of well being and illness, and resulting in frequent crises and admissions to hospital. In such cases all the person may need is the regular medication to remain well enough to function satisfactorily in the community, and a community order may facilitate this by ensuring medication is administered regularly (see *Harry v The Mental Health Review Tribunal & Anor* (1994) 33 NSWLR 315).

Rights of those with a mental illness

Period of involuntary treatment or detention is set

[5.400] An involuntary treatment order must set limits on the period for which it operates; as noted above the maximum periods vary between jurisdictions. It is most important that this period is clearly recorded and followed, as it becomes unlawful to continue the treatment after an order has expired. Sometimes the court or tribunal will require that an order be reviewed before it expires, so that there is adequate provision to extend it if this is warranted, and there is not a gap in treatment. The terms of an order should also be made clear in a patient's notes and followed carefully.

Care should be the least restrictive practicable

[5.405] Whilst courts and tribunals can order detention and care, and overall restrictions of movement or residence, the specific nature of that care (for example, the nature and dosage of medication, day-to-day physical and behavioural restrictions) cannot be determined by a court or tribunal: it can only authorise health carers to determine and administer appropriate care. Some Australian jurisdictions specifically provide that treatment must be the least restrictive practicable, and the most appropriate under the circumstances. However, it can be seen that the day-to-day decisions as to the nature of treatment and other aspects of the person's life come to be dependent on those who are caring for the person.

This is particularly critical for all health carers. The hospital or other facility for those who are mentally ill is their home for the duration. They are deprived of privacy, and must live in a communal environment with limited scope for individual and sexual expression. Health carers have an inordinate amount of power and control over every aspect of their lives. This can include what they eat, wear and do, how their possessions are dealt with, what movement they have, who they can communicate with and whether they will be isolated from others or not. Health carers can decide whether to meet their needs, big or small, to "punish" inappropriate behaviour, to confiscate possessions, to search persons and rooms. Issues of consent permeate all these activities, and the principles cited at the beginning of this section must be applied.

Health consumers' rights are dealt with generally in Chapter 18, but it is worth emphasising that according to common law principles health carers should afford those with a mental illness, including involuntary patients, their rights to their property, privacy and autonomy to the extent that this does not interfere with their specifically ordered treatment. Unless restricted by legislation or a treatment order, they should be allowed to exercise their autonomy in matters other than specifically ordered treatment, to the full extent of their abilities, with the onus on those who propose to restrict that autonomy to show that they are unable to do so. Proper accounting for money and other patient property is required. In the past, there have been findings of abuse and exploitation of patients in several psychiatric institutions, the best-known ones being:

- the Royal Commission into events at Chelmsford Hospital New South Wales in 1990 (negligence in deep-sleep treatment, lack of consent to treatment, ignoring of drug and electroconvulsive therapy regulations);
- the Commission of Inquiry into events at Ward 10B, Townsville Hospital in 1991 (negligent and non-autonomous so-called group therapy, lack of confidentiality, chemical restraint); and
- the task force into allegations of abuse and neglect of residents of Aradale Psychiatric Hospital, Victoria (ill-treatment, stealing of food and misappropriation of patients' money).

A National inquiry carried out by Mr Brian Burdekin (*Human Rights and Mental Illness* (Canberra AGPS 1993)—the "Burdekin Report") found that there was widespread lack of information given to consumers about processes and medication, discrimination against those with a mental illness, assaults and abuse and lack of privacy.

Electroconvulsive therapy and psychiatric surgery

[5.410] Special provisions are made for consent where electroconvulsive therapy and psychiatric surgery are concerned in all jurisdictions except South

Australia and Tasmania. Each jurisdiction sets out a definition of "informed consent" or requirements for the explanation to be given for the purposes of these procedures. This includes information about the nature of the proposed treatment, its risks and alternatives, and why this treatment is recommended (the New South Wales description of informed consent is set out in s 183 of the *Mental Health Act 1990* (NSW)). The requirements aim at ensuring the person is able to understand these matters, and weigh the benefits and risks of the treatment, and are similar to those contained in the guidelines set out for informed consent by the National Health and Medical Research Council (see Checklist at **[4.420]**).

Electroconvulsive therapy

[5.415] Jurisdictions impose limitations on electroconvulsive therapy as follows.

In the Australian Capital Territory (Part 7, Divisions 1 and 2 of the *Mental Health (Treatment and Care) Act 1994* (ACT)) "informed consent" as defined in the legislation is required before ECT can be given. Where informed consent is not possible, application must be made to the Mental Health Tribunal by the Chief Psychiatrist or a doctor, and must be supported by another psychiatrist. The Tribunal can only make an order for ECT if it is likely to benefit the patient, all other reasonably available treatments have been tried unsuccessfully, and it is the most appropriate form of treatment reasonably available.

New South Wales (in Chapter 7, Part 2 of the *Mental Health Act 1990* (NSW)) limits the use of ECT to specific hospitals or facilities. A patient other than an involuntary patient must give "informed consent" as prescribed by the Act, and two doctors must be present, one the doctor performing the ECT and the other an anaesthesiologist. The treatment must be considered necessary in the face of no adequate alternative. The Mental Health Review Tribunal may agree to treatment for involuntary patients, after being satisfied the person is unable to consent, and the medical superintendent has done all such things as are reasonably practicable to notify the person's nearest relative, guardian (if any) and up to two personal friends (unless the person objects) of the intention to seek consent for the procedure from the Tribunal. The treatment must be considered reasonable and proper, and necessary for the safety or welfare of the person.

In the Northern Territory, Part 9, Division 2 of the *Mental Health and Related Services Act* provides that ECT must not be performed without the person's informed consent. The Tribunal may authorise ECT where the person is unable to give consent and the Tribunal is furnished with a report from two authorised psychiatric practitioners that it is reasonable and proper to administer ECT and without the treatment the person is likely to suffer serious mental or physical deterioration. In addition, all reasonable steps must have been taken to consult the person's primary care provider. ECT may be performed on an involuntary patient where two authorised psychiatric practitioners are satisfied that it is immediately necessary to save the person's life, prevent serious mental or physical deterioration or relieve severe distress. Where treatment is administered in such circumstances, report must be made as soon as practicable to the Tribunal of the therapy that is performed.

In Queensland the *Mental Health Act 2000* provides that ECT may be administered where the person has provided informed consent or the Tribunal has approved the use of the treatment. In order for a psychiatrist to make an application to the Tribunal for approval to administer ECT they must be satisfied that it is the most clinically appropriate treatment alternative. ECT may be performed without consent on an involuntary patient where a psychiatrist and the medical superintendent certify in writing that ECT is necessary to save the patient's life or prevent the patient from suffering irreparable harm.

South Australia (s 22 of the *Mental Health Act 1993* (SA)) provides that informed consent (not defined) must be obtained in writing prior to the administration of ECT. Where the person is incapable of giving consent, consent may be given by the person's medical agent or by the Guardianship Board. Consent is not required for an episode of ECT where administration of that episode is urgently needed for the protection of the patient or other persons and it is not practicable to obtain consent in the circumstances.

The law in Victoria (Part 5 Divisions 1AA and 2 of the *Mental Health Act 1986* (Vic)) also requires informed consent similar to New South Wales. Exceptions to this occur where the patient is incapable of this, in which case it must be authorised by a psychiatrist who is satisfied that:

- it is necessary to prevent deterioration in the person's condition;
- alternatives have been considered;
- the treatment has clinical merit;
- the treatment is appropriate; and
- all reasonable efforts have been made to notify the patient's primary caregiver or guardian of the proposed performance of ECT.

Tasmania (*Mental Health Act 1996*) does not have specific provisions in relation to ECT.

In Western Australia (Part 5, Division 5 of the *Mental Health Act 1996* (WA)) ECT cannot be given without a patient's "informed consent" where this is possible. Otherwise it must be recommended by the treating psychiatrist and approved by a second psychiatrist. Approval must not be given unless the treatment is considered to have clinical merit and to be appropriate in the circumstances. If no approval is given, the treating psychiatrist may apply to the Mental Health Review Board, which cannot substitute the second psychiatrist's withholding of approval, but can recommend an alternative treatment, transfer the person to another psychiatrist, or order that the person is no longer an involuntary patient.

Psychiatric surgery

[5.420] While Tasmania places no special restrictions on psychiatric surgery, safeguards are placed on the carrying out of psychiatric surgery in other jurisdictions.

The Australian Capital Territory (Part 7, Divisions 1 and 3 of the *Mental Health (Treatment and Care) Act 1994* (ACT)) requires that before a person can receive psychiatric surgery, the doctor proposing the treatment must apply to the Chief Psychiatrist. The application must be accompanied by a copy of the consent form showing that the patient consented, or an order from the Supreme Court permitting the surgery to be carried out. The Chief Psychiatrist then forwards the application to a committee which determines whether the Chief Psychiatrist should approve the surgery. The committee must be satisfied that there are reasonable grounds for believing that the surgery will provide a substantial benefit to the person and that all reasonable alternatives have failed or are likely to fail. The neurosurgeon and psychiatrist on the committee must support the recommendation. Where the patient has neither granted nor refused consent, an application may be made to the Supreme Court for authorisation of the surgery.

In New South Wales (Chapter 7, Part 1 of the *Mental Health Act 1900* (NSW)) a person must give "informed consent" as defined by the Act, and a Psychosurgery Review Board must hear the matter at a public hearing (unless the person objects) at which the person may be represented by a legal practitioner. In order to consent to an application, the Board must be satisfied that the patient is capable of giving informed consent and has given informed consent, the surgery has clinical merit and all other reasonable treatments have been adequately administered without sufficient benefit to the patient. Where the person does not consent but the surgery is still considered necessary, the matter must be taken to the Supreme Court for a decision as to whether the person can consent, and if not, whether the surgery should be given.

South Australia (s 22 of the *Mental Health Act 1993* (SA)) has informed consent requirements for psychosurgery for those who are capable of giving effective written consent. In addition, the surgery must be authorised by two independent psychiatrists as well as the surgeon.

Victoria (Part 5, Division 1 of the *Mental Health Act 1986* (Vic)) requires a person to provide informed consent (as defined by the Act) to psychosurgery. A psychiatrist who seeks to arrange for a neurosurgeon to perform psychosurgery must apply to the Psychosurgery Review Board for consent. The Board may give consent for the surgery where it is satisfied that the person has the capacity and has in fact consented, the proposed surgery has clinical merit, and all other reasonable treatments have been adequately administered without sufficient and lasting benefit.

Western Australia (Part 5 Division 4 of the *Mental Health Act 1996* (WA)) requires an application for authorisation of psychosurgery to be made to the Mental Health Review Board. The Board must be satisfied that the person has given informed consent, the treatment has clinical merit, is appropriate in the circumstances and every available alternative has been satisfactorily given without a sufficient and lasting benefit.

In the Northern Territory the *Mental Health and Related Services Act*, Part 9, Div 1 provides that no person may perform psychosurgery on another person. In Queensland, s 161 of the *Mental Health Act 2000* provides that a doctor may perform psychosurgery on a person if the person has given consent or the tribunal has given approval.

Consent to non-psychiatric care by psychiatric patient

[5.425] According to common law, those with a mental illness can exercise their capacity to determine general health care in the same way as anybody else (*Secretary, Department of Health and Community Services v JWB and SMB (Marion's Case*) (1992) 175 CLR 218; [1992] HCA 15; see **[5.30]**). However, some jurisdictions provide for substituted decision making for "medical treatment" for those with a mental disability in some circumstances. The restriction of legal principles to "medical treatment" leaves in limbo other aspects of health care, and in the case of the mentally ill and involuntary care, their daily living activities. A source of guidance is thus the statement of rights at **[5.335]**.

Legislation addressing consent to non-psychiatric care is set out below. As with the previous outlines of legislation in the various Australian jurisdictions, the following should be considered a rough guide only. Those caring for people with a mental disability should familiarise themselves with the detail of the law in their jurisdiction.

In New South Wales (Chapter 7, Part 2 of the *Mental Health Act 1900* (NSW)) there are a number of complicated provisions:

- *Urgent treatment:* a prescribed person may consent to urgent surgery on an involuntary patient whether or not they are capable of consenting. This is in contrast to the basic principle of common law which allows a competent person to refuse such care.
- *Non-urgent treatment:* "Special medical treatment" (treatment likely to result in permanent infertility or other procedures prescribed by the Regulations) must not be given without the consent of the Mental Health Review Tribunal. The Tribunal must be satisfied that the treatment is necessary to save the patient's life or prevent serious damage to their health. Such consent cannot be given for someone under 16 years. Presumably, such consent is required by the Supreme Court or the Family Court. For surgical procedures, a medical superintendent must notify a patient's "nearest relative" that he or she proposes surgical treatment for either an involuntary or voluntary patient. If after 14 days the nearest relative gives written consent, the medical superintendent may apply to an authorised officer for consent to the operation. If no consent is forthcoming from the nearest relative, the superintendent may apply to the Mental Health Review Tribunal. The authorisation of treatment by a nearest relative (a spouse, parent or carer) is, where the person is competent, in contrast to the principle of autonomy, and, where the person is incompetent, to the common law principle that relatives *per se* cannot consent (see **[5.210]**). It differs from the concept of "person responsible" in relation to guardianship (see **[5.215]**ff).

In Victoria (Part 5, Division 4 of the *Mental Health Act 1986* (Vic)) informed consent (as defined by the Act) must be obtained for major non-psychiatric treatment. Other non-psychiatric treatment may be consented to by the patient, or where the patient is incapable of providing consent by the first of the following people able to make that decision: medical agent, guardian, or an authorised psychiatrist,

In Western Australia (Part 5, Division 6 of the *Mental Health Act 1996* (WA)) the Chief Psychiatrist may consent to non-psychiatric treatment for an involuntary patient. This power is expressed to not limit a power conferred by any other written law by which a person may consent to the medical treatment of another person. Presumably the common law would apply to voluntary patients.

Seclusion or restraint of mentally ill patients

[5.430] Restraint of patients generally has been dealt with above (see **[4.465]**). Most jurisdictions regulate restraint and seclusion, New South Wales and South Australia being the exceptions. A brief description of the contents of the legislation is provided below.

Victoria (ss 81, 82 of the *Mental Health Act 1986* (Vic)) has provisions for restraint and seclusion. Mechanical restraint or seclusion must only be used for the purpose of treatment of the person, or to prevent injury to the person, others, or to property. It must be approved by an authorised psychiatrist or, in an emergency the senior nurse on duty and notified to a medical practitioner without delay. The person must be under continuous observation by a registered nurse or doctor, reviewed at least every 15 minutes by a registered nurse, and provided with adequate basic facilities such as food, clothing and toilet arrangements. The person must be examined at least every four hours or when determined by the psychiatrist.

Western Australia (Part 5, Divisions 8 and 9 of the *Mental Health Act 1996* (WA)) provides specifically for seclusion and mechanical bodily restraint. Seclusion or physical restraint must only be carried out at a legally recognised facility, and authorised by a medical practitioner, or, in an emergency, a senior mental health practitioner (nurse or other person appointed as such), in which case a medical practitioner should be notified as soon as practicable. A person is not to be secluded unless it is necessary for the protection, safety or well being of the person or others. A person is not to be mechanically restrained unless it is necessary for the treatment, protection, safety or well being of the person or others or to prevent the patient persistently destroying property. The authorisation for seclusion or restraint must have a set time limit. Seclusion is subject to conditions such as proper facilities being available for basic physical needs, regular monitoring, and reporting to the Mental Health Review Board. The use of mechanical bodily restraint must also be reported to the Board.

Tasmania (*Mental Health Act 1996*, Part 6, Division 1) requires that an involuntary patient be placed under restraint only where it is necessary for medical treatment of the patient, or to prevent injury to the person or others, or to prevent persistent destruction of property. It must be authorised by a medical practitioner or an approved psychiatric nurse and must not exceed a period of four hours. An involuntary patient may be placed under seclusion where it is necessary for the protection of the patient or others and is authorised by a medical practitioner or an approved psychiatric nurse. Where a patient is kept in seclusion they must be visited by a member of the nursing staff at intervals of not more than 15 minutes and be examined at intervals of not more than four hours by a medical practitioner. They must be provided with adequate bedding, clothing, food, drink and toilet arrangements.

In Queensland (Chapter 4, Part 3 of the *Mental Health Act 2000*) a doctor may authorise the mechanical restraint of a person only where they are satisfied it is the most appropriate way of preventing injury to the patient or someone else. The senior registered nurse on duty must ensure the person's reasonable needs are met, they may also direct the removal of restraint where they are satisfied the person can be safely treated without restraint. Seclusion may be authorised by a doctor, or, in urgent circumstances, by the senior registered nurse on duty (in such cases, seclusion must be reported to a doctor immediately). Seclusion may be authorised where it is necessary to protect the patient or others from imminent physical harm and there is no less restrictive way of ensuring the safety of the person and others. The senior registered nurse must ensure the person is continuously observed or observed at intervals (not exceeding 15 minutes) as stipulated by the doctor. The senior registered nurse may authorise the person's release from or return to seclusion in some circumstances.

In the Northern Territory (*Mental Health and Related Services Act*, ss 61, 62) provisions for mechanical restraint or seclusion of persons are substantially the same as those described in Victoria. In addition, the person-in-charge of an approved treatment facility must ensure that a record is kept of the details of the person's seclusion and this record must be made available to the principal community visitor at intervals not longer than six months.

In the Australian Capital Territory (*Mental Health (Treatment and Care) Act 1994*, s 35) the chief psychiatrist may subject a person to confinement or restraint that is necessary and reasonable to prevent the person causing harm to himself, herself or others or to ensure they remain in custody. In doing so the chief psychiatrist must have regard to the objectives of the Act and provisions regarding the maintenance of freedom, dignity and self-respect. If the Chief Psychiatrist subjects a person to involuntary restraint or seclusion, the Chief Psychiatrist must:

(a) enter in the person's record the fact of and the reasons for the involuntary restraint or seclusion; and

(b) tell the public advocate in writing within 24 hours after the person is subjected to the involuntary restraint or seclusion; and

(c) keep a register of the involuntary restraint or seclusion.

Guardianship and protection of mentally ill persons

[5.435] All jurisdictions have established special bodies or agents which act as a further means of protection of mental health patients. These may be, for example:

• guardianship boards or courts with the power to appoint guardians and managers of property, which may give orders regarding the general upbringing, education and training and care of the mentally ill, as well as their day-to-day affairs;

- community visitors (Northern Territory), who regularly inspect mental health institutions and act on behalf of patients;
- welfare officers (New South Wales), who visit patients on leave;
- the public advocate (Victoria), who assists and advises people with serious complaints about mental health services and treatment; and
- the Community Advocate (Australian Capital Territory), who visits people detained on an involuntary basis and periodically reviews seclusion orders.

Health carers and the mentally ill

[5.440] Health carers should be aware of the status of admission of any psychiatric patient, what orders, if any, have been made, and of the need to inform the patient of what treatment he or she is receiving, and to encourage his or her co-operation and informed decision-making whenever they can.

Health carers should thus be aware of:

- the rights of the patient, including rights to privacy, the facility's resources, communication with outsiders, and access to, and use of, money and possessions;
- the rights of the relatives to communicate and visit;
- the right to complain, and access to facilities for complaint; and
- the rights and obligations of the institution and its staff in the care of the person.

This includes an understanding of:

- powers of detention and treatment in their jurisdiction generally;
- the specific powers and permissible treatment for any particular patient in their care;
- the requirements for review of detention and treatment;
- rights and procedures of appeal by those involved; and
- the rights of patients generally.

Special medical treatment

Adults and children

[5.445] All jurisdictions have provisions covering specifically designated medical treatment, such as drugs of addiction, experimental treatment, and sterilisation for those who are unable to exercise the ability to make decisions. Legislation provides that guardians for adults cannot consent to "special procedures". These are considered by the Guardianship Board or Tribunal. The treatment must be for the promotion or maintenance of the health or well being of the person, and not the administrative convenience of carers. In the Northern Territory the local court has initial jurisdiction over the matter. The matter may be taken to the Supreme Court for a ruling in all jurisdictions. For children, both the State Supreme Courts and the Family Court have jurisdiction, with the Family Court taking precedence where there is a conflict of decisions (see P v P at [5.60]).

In *Marion's Case* (see **[5.30]**) the Australian High Court held that a decision to authorise the sterilisation of an intellectually disabled child should not come within the ordinary scope of parental power to consent to medical treatment. The Court's authorisation is necessary because:

- this surgery affects the fundamental right to a person's inviolability;
- there is a significant risk of making a wrong decision, which is complicated by the potentially conflicting interests of the child (to reproductive integrity) and the carers (to the improved facility and effectiveness of caring for the child); and,
- the gravity of the consequences of wrongly authorising a sterilisation, flowing from the permanency of the effects of the surgery, and the effect of surgery against one's wishes.

The Court concluded that the Family Court has the jurisdiction to hear cases involving sterilisation of mentally impaired children. Its welfare jurisdiction is very wide, subject only to constitutional limitations, and overrides State and Territory laws to the contrary. Section 45(2) of the *Guardianship Act 1987* (NSW) also provides that treatment involving sterilisation can only be carried out to save someone's life or prevent serious damage to their health ("therapeutic sterilisation"). However Part VII of the *Family Law Act 1975* (Cth) gives power to the Family Court to make orders in relation to the health care of a child where it is necessary in the child's interests.

[5.450] Case: *R-B (A Patient) v Official Solicitor* [2000] Lloyd's Law Reports (Medical) 87 (CA UK)

A was a 28-year old with Down's Syndrome, lacking capacity to give or withhold consent to treatment. His mother applied to the High Court, under its inherent *parens patriae* jurisdiction for a declaration that sterilisation was in his best interests, despite A not wanting it. She was concerned that should he need to enter residential care in the future, he could form a relationship with another resident. One consultant psychiatrist testified that the sterilisation would give A more freedom and would result in the need for less supervision. Another disagreed, stating that A was unlikely to engage in sexual intercourse and that the operation was not in his best interests. Whilst A was not likely to engage in frequent sexual intercourse, the operation would not free him from the possibility of disease, or the problems that might arise from a close relationship with another person. The Official Solicitor argued also that the fact that A did not want the operation should be taken into account, as should the right, conferred by the *European Convention on Human Rights* (to which England is a party) to privacy and to found a family (a right also enshrined in the *Declaration of Human Rights*, to which Australia is a signatory).

[5.455] The Court refused to authorise the sterilisation. It held that the best interests of the patient included medical, emotional, and all other welfare issues. Doctors not only have to act according to responsible and competent professional opinion, but also in the interests of a mentally incapacitated person. The judge, not the doctor, decides what is in the person's best interests. In A's case he would not be any more free from supervision, as he could still be subject to exploitation and the emotional implications of a close relationship. If A were to later be in a situation, such as residential care, where he was in danger of the disadvantages mentioned, a fresh consideration of the situation could be undertaken.

[5.460]   Case: *JLS v JES* (unreported, SC NSW Equity Division, No 1871/1996 available online at www.austlii. edu.au/au/cases/nsw/supreme_ct/96001871.html)

JES was severely intellectually disabled. Her mother applied to the New South Wales Supreme Court for the Court's consent to an abdominal hysterectomy which would render her permanently infertile. At the time, s 20B of the *Children (Care and Protection) Act 1987* (NSW) provided that a court could only authorise such an operation if satisfied that it was necessary to prevent serious injury to the child's health. The Court had previously authorised the administration of DepoProvera for the purposes of contraception. However, JES suffered from the side-effects of the drug, and still had intermittent bleeding at the sight of which she was terrified. Doctors decided that surgical intervention was necessary to control her symptoms. They argued that hysterectomy would prevent serious damage to her health by eliminating haemorrhage and preventing psychological distress. It would enhance the quality of life and prevent pregnancy.

[5.465] The Court gave its consent pursuant to the then s 20B of the Act that a hysterectomy be carried out on the child. It held that:

- the effects of menstruation constituted serious damage to the health of JES;
- it was necessary to carry out the operation because alternative therapy was ineffective;
- JES's intellectual disability and neurological disorders were such that she could never exercise a right to have children with any understanding of what was happening; and
- the proposed surgery would improve her mother's ability to continue to care for her.

Given the courts' reasoning in other cases, it appears that the last criterion should only be applied when the former ones are present.

Sandor (1999) argues that sterilisation should be a procedure of last resort, but that "Even government estimates suggest that medical assaults through sterilisation procedures on children are undetected and undeterred" (p 21). The figures are stark: whilst courts and tribunals had authorised 17 sterilisations of girls between 1992 and 1997, data collected by the Health Insurance Commission showed that "at least" 1045 girls had been sterilised during that period (p 17, quoting Brady and Grover (1997)). He concludes that "informed adherence to the law" is required of those involved in a special medical procedure on a child:

> "If neither money nor morality is an incentive to the redress of medical assaults by sterilisation, and the representative body for medical practitioners wants past violations shielded from scrutiny, then people with disabilities and those who care for their integrity have every right to wonder which period in history they are living in (Sandor, p 21)."

Important Reminder for Health Carers

[5.470] This chapter sets out the law in a general fashion. Health carers should become familiar with the law in their jurisdiction, and be clear as to the distinction between legal requirements and guidelines.

References and Further Reading

See also Further Reading list for Chapter 4.

Australian Health and Medical Law Reporter (CCH, Sydney, 1991)

Batholomew, T and Carvalho, T, "General Practitioners' Competence and Confidentiality Determinations with a Minor who Requests the Oral Contraceptive Pill" *Australian Health Law Bulletin* 13 (2)

Carney, T, *Law at the Margins* (OUP, Melbourne, 1991)

Dickey, A, *Family Law* (2nd ed, Law Book Co, Sydney, 1990)

Eades, J, "Parens Patriae Jurisdiction of the Supreme Court is Alive and Kicking" *Law Society Journal* (February 2000), 53

Foukas, T, "Psychiatric Advance Directives—Part 1" 8 *Australian Health Law Bulletin* 1; "Part II", 8 *Australian Health Law Bulletin* 13

Freckelton, I and Petersen, K, *Controversies in Health Law* (The Federation Press, Sydney, 1999)

Gleeson, P, "Axon, R (on the application of) v Secretary of State for Health" *Australian Health Law Bulletin* 14 (5), 53

Gutman, J, "Comment, R v M" 7 *Journal of Law and Medicine* 113

Hayes, S and Hayes, R, *Mental Retardation: Law Policy and Administration* (Law Book Co, Sydney, 1982)

Human Rights and Equal Opportunity Commission, *Human Rights and Mental Illness: Report of the National Inquiry into the Human Rights of People with Mental Illness* (Australian Government Publishing Service, Canberra, 1993)

Hundert, E, "Competing Medical and Legal Ethical Values" in Rosner and Weinstock (see below) (1990), p 53

Kee, P, "Refusal to Consent to Treatment on Religious Grounds" *E Law Murdoch University Electronic Law Journal* Vol 2, No 2 (July 1995)

Kennedy, I, "Commentary Re H (mental patient) [1993] 1 FLR 28" (1993) 1 Med Law Rev 237

Kerridge, I, et al, "Advance Directives" in Freckelton, I and Petersen, K, *Controversies in Health Law* (The Federation Press, Sydney, 1999), p 302

Kerridge, I, Lowe, M and McPhee, J, *Ethics and Law for the Health Professions* (2nd Edition, The Federation Press, Sydney, 2005)

Kloczko, A, "Court Order Authorises Blood Transfusion Against Young Person's Will" *Australian Health Law Bulletin* 13 (8)

Law Reform Commission of New South Wales, *Issues Paper 24 (2004) – Minors' Consent to Medical Treatment,* accessed at www.lawlink.nsw.gov.au/lrc.nsf/pages/ip24

Leo, N, "Advance Directives: The Legal Issues", Discussion paper prepared for the Office of the Public Advocate, January 2004, available at www.publicadvocate.vic.gov.au/CA256A76007E8265/Home?OpenPage

McFarlane, P, *Health Law: Commentary and Materials* (The Federation Press, Sydney, 2000)

Mason, A, "The Year 2000: Psychiatric Lecture" presented at the Hyatt Hotel, Canberra, ACT, on 15 November 2000

Morgan, J, "Minors and Consent to Medical Treatment: Reflecting on Gillick", Law Reform Commission of Victoria, Symposia 1986 (Globe Press, Melbourne, 1987)

Mulheron, R, "The defence of therapeutic privilege in Australia" *Australian Health Law Bulletin* 11 (2)

New South Wales Department of Health, *Using Advance Care Directives (NSW),* June 2004, accessible at www.nsw.gov.au

O'Sullivan, J, *Law for Nurses* (Law Book Co, Sydney, 1983)

Pyra, K, "Administration of Blood Products: A Recent Case" *Australian Health Law Bulletin* 14 (7)

Rosner, R and Weinstock, R, *Ethical Practice in Psychiatry and the Law* (Plenum Press, New York, 1990)

Roth, M and Bluglass, R, *Psychiatry, Human Rights and the Law* (Cambridge University Press, Cambridge, 1985)

Sandor, D, "Sterilisation and Special Medical Procedures on Children and Young People: Blunt Instrument? Bad Medicine?" in Freckelton, I and Petersen, K, *Controversies in Health Law* (The Federation Press, Sydney, 1999)

Scott, R, "Liability of Psychiatrists and Mental Health Services for Failing to Admit or Detain Patients with Mental Illness: Hunter Area Health Service v Presland" *Australian Health Law Bulletin* 14 (3)

Stewart, C, "Qumsieh's Case, Civil Liability and the Right to Refuse Medical Treatment" 8 *Journal of Law and Medicine* Vol 7 (August 2000), 56

Stewart, C, "Advanced Directives, the Right to Die and the Common Law: Recent Problems with Blood Transfusions" (1999) *Melbourne University Law Review* 161

Skene, L, *Law and Medical Practice Right Duties Claims and Defences* (2nd ed, Butterworths, Sydney, 2004)

White, B and Willmott, L "Will You Do As I Ask? Compliance With Instructions About Health Care In Queensland" (2004) 4 (1) QUT Law and Justice Journal 77

6 Negligence

Duty of care

Standard of care

Special situations

Damages

Causation

chapter 6

Negligence

Introduction

[6.05] Once patients have given consent to their care, health carers have a recognised legal relationship with a patient which requires proper professional care for that patient. Failure to provide this leaves them open to being sued by an aggrieved patient for negligence, for breach of contract, and/or (rarely) for breach of statutory duty, through which the patient seeks damages for harm suffered as a result. The law of contract is dealt with in Chapter 9.

Professional Negligence, Clinical Negligence or Malpractice

[6.10] Professional negligence, more commonly called clinical negligence in England or malpractice in the United States of America, is perhaps the area of greatest legal importance for health care workers, as it provides the most common reason for legal action against them. It is the most common way to seek compensation for harm wrongfully suffered at the hands of the health care profession. Negligence is called a "tort" (French for "wrong") at law. As its name implies, action can only be taken for harm that should not have occurred in the normal course of events, so a health carer is not liable for harm that occurs despite care which is reasonable in the circumstances. Thus, the fact of harm or injury does not of itself necessarily mean that someone was negligent (see, for example *Roe v Minister of Health* at **[6.295]**).

Negligence law until quite recently was derived almost entirely from decisions of various courts, with some occasional statutory adjustments on minor aspects. However following the *Review of the Law of Negligence* report released on 2 October 2002, various "civil liability" statutes have been enacted in Australian jurisdictions. Unfortunately despite the first recommendation of the *Review of the Law of Negligence* for uniform legislation throughout Australia, that has not occurred. We are therefore left with a matrix of common law and slightly differing legislation in each jurisdiction. Perhaps so far as the substantive law regarding professional negligence is concerned the outcome in any one case will vary little, however readers should take care to consider the legislation as it applies in the relevant jurisdiction. In this chapter, the *Civil Liability Act 2002* (NSW) is referred to, with a table of comparable legislation appearing at Appendix 2.

A finding that a health carer is liable for an isolated act of negligence is different from a finding that he or she is incompetent (*Professional Indemnity Review* (1995), p 169; Nisselle (1999), p 135). Even the best of practitioners may make an error of judgment leading to a finding of technical legal negligence. This is clearly recognised by the courts, for example, as Simpson J observed in *Sherry v Australasian Conference Association (trading as Sydney Adventist Hospital) & 3 Ors* [2006] NSWSC 75 when she said at [553]:

> "...What I have found is that SAH, Dr Walsh and Dr Marshman in their own ways did not, on this occasion, achieve the level of service our high standards of medical practice demand. This involves no judgment of moral culpability, and no judgment as to the general competence or attention to detail of any of the participants. This was a singular occurrence and should not be taken as typical of the standard of work of any of them. In each case the finding of breach of duty is at what may be termed a relatively low level. The degree of breach of duty is not quantitatively related to its consequences. Just as a momentary lapse of attention by the driver of a motor vehicle might have disastrous consequences, so also might—and has—a short term lapse of attention by doctors and nurses. In this case the consequences are tragically disproportionate to the level of breaches of duty I have found. Compensation is, however, not measured by the degree of the breach of duty, but by consequences. The tragic outcome should not overshadow an appreciation of what it was that went wrong."

In contrast, the medical Registration Boards investigate allegations of incompetence, often now analysed as unsatisfactory professional conduct or professional misconduct (see Chapter 12).

Preventable adverse events

[6.15] A nationwide study, the *Australian Hospital Care Study,* commissioned by the then Minister for Human Services and Health, found that in the year 1992, 230,000 public and private hospital admissions involved an adverse event which was preventable. Of these, between 25,000 and 30,000 people were estimated as suffering some degree of permanent disability, and between 10,000 and 14,000 people to have died. Those aged over 60 were found to have a greater chance of experiencing an adverse event while in hospital. There was no variation according to sex, marital status, insurance status or racial background. The total hospital bed days as a result of the adverse effects in 1992 was estimated at about 3.2 million, with half of these relating to preventable adverse events. The cost of these bed-days was estimated at about 650 million dollars.

A task force on Quality in Australian Health Care (QAHC) was established as a result of this study. This became known as the Quality in Australian Health Care Study, or QAHCS. The QAHCS issued an interim report of its analysis of adverse events in hospital patients. Here are some of the findings:

- Falls are among the most frequent incidents reported in hospitals. Sometimes these are unpreventable, but the task force did find that matters such as lack of identification of those at risk, lack of control of external factors such as poor lighting, slippery floors and inappropriate footwear often contribute to falls.
- Another problem was the treatment of children with respiratory disease in emergency centres at night. Early discharge was a frequent cause of later complications. The treating doctor was often a very junior medical officer. There was inadequate planning of ongoing medical treatment, or continuity of care.
- Deep vein thrombosis and pulmonary embolism occurred in 30 of every 100 rate risk following an operation of 45 minutes duration in those patients who have cardiovascular conditions. There is a greater risk for longer operations, especially those involving the pelvis, legs or brain.
- The role doctors, nurses and other health carers have in assuring quality care is not only developing good care practices, but also in thorough incident monitoring. It involves not only identifying and improving areas of clinical practice but also establishing ways of preventing adverse incidents which might lead to legal action (see *Professional Indemnity Review* (1995), p 20).

The *Professional Indemnity Review* was a wide-ranging one, but it too endorsed both a comprehensive incident monitoring scheme which could preferably be national in its scope under the National Health Outcomes Program, and other quality initiatives with the goal of improving patient safety across all disciplines. The Review also endorsed pro-active risk management in terms of identifying and anticipating those situations which might lead to adverse incidents. One area of potential error identified by the Review was long hours of work which lead to fatigue. The established practice of requiring doctors to work long hours, and increasing pressure on nursing and other staff to double up on shifts or work extended hours, increases the likelihood of negligence occurring in health care facilities. Maximum safe working hours should be set and minimum rest periods allowed for all health professionals and institutions. Requiring health carers to work long hours as a tradition rather than a necessity could constitute negligence; in the same way was the tradition of understaffing a hospital unit, as might be implied from the comment of Simpson J in the *Sherry* decision (see **[6.10]** above) at [466]:

> "...I note in passing that Dr Walsh had been on duty in excess of 14 hours. He agreed in cross-examination that he may, by 10.15 pm, have been tired. Little was made of this, and, in the absence of more detailed evidence and argument, it should not be given too much weight."

Safety and quality in health care has remained a significant focus. Australian Health Ministers recently agreed for an *Australian Commission on Safety and*

Quality in Health Care to commence operation from 1 January 2006. The Commission will succeed the *Australian Council for Safety and Quality in Health Care*, which was established in January 2000 for a five-year term, and ceased on 31 December 2005.

Safety and quality work is of course not limited to Australia; for example, the World Health Organisation (WHO) in October 2004, launched the *World Alliance for Patient Safety* in response to a World Health Assembly Resolution (2002) urging WHO and Member States to pay the closest possible attention to the problem of patient safety. The Alliance raises awareness and political commitment to improve the safety of care and facilitates the development of patient safety policy and practice in all WHO Member States. Each year, the Alliance delivers a number of programmes covering systemic and technical aspects to improve patient safety around the world. More information on the Alliance can be obtained from their website: www.who.int/patientsafety/en/ (accessed in May 2006).

Incidence of medical litigation

[6.20] With the benefit of studies on the extent of adverse events, it has long been recognised that only a small percentage of patients who suffer from an adverse incident actually sue in negligence (Nisselle (1999), p 130; Studdert "Medical Malpractice" (2004) *New England Journal of Medicine* 350-353). However until recently, there was little reliable data publicly available on the level of medical negligence litigation in Australia and any changes in that level. In the private sector, two reports have been published thus far by a group known as the Medical Indemnity Insurers Association of Australia (MIIAA); see www.miiaa.com.au/. In the public sector, the Australian Institute of Health and Welfare has begun to publish data: see www.aihw.gov.au/ safequalityhealth/index.cfm.

Communication and adverse incidents

[6.25] Not only is good communication essential for adequate consent to treatment, it has an important role to play in risk management, in the view of commentators, including Nisselle (1999) and the *Professional Indemnity Review* (1995). According to a survey nearly one-third of those taking legal action in 1994 were doing so to obtain more and better information. This, according to Nisselle, indicates "the perception of a 'conspiracy of silence' within the medical profession". He points out (at p 133) that the giving of full and frank information has the valuable effect of preventing legal action in the long run, while it may involve some short-term costs:

> "The scientific 'Find it—Fix it' model of medicine ignores the other half of medicine, namely, the humanist skills by which rapport is established and maintained and the patient motivated to accept the doctor's advice. More effective communication is not just a risk management tool."

He quotes Meryn (1988) who states that studies have found significant positive association between doctors' communication skills and patient satisfaction.

Legal advice was traditionally to admit nothing when an adverse incident has occurred, with a view to defending any legal claim that may arise from it. Increasingly, however, commentators such as those above argue that it is important that patients are advised promptly and fully when something has gone wrong. Attempts to "cover up" whether real or perceived, are both fruitless and likely to inflame an already difficult situation and result in the strengthening of the resolve of a patient for compensation. In some circumstances it may be wiser to admit fault and pay reasonable compensation than to create a situation where litigation is protracted, costly and hostile. The trend towards an honest expression of regret after an adverse event has been recognised and supported by the *Civil Liability Act 2002* (NSW) apology protection provisions at ss 67-69, such that in specified circumstances an apology made by or on behalf of a person does not constitute an express or implied admission of fault or liability by the person and is not relevant to the determination of fault or liability.

As shall be seen, like the principles underlying the law on consent to health care, those underlying the law of negligence permeate every possible activity a carer may engage in, either on or off-duty.

What is Negligence?

[6.30] There are three main elements that constitute what is called a "negligence action" in law. A person, A, to succeed in proving negligence on the part of another, B, must show that B:

- owed a duty of care to A;
- has breached that duty of care, through some act or omission by B;
- has, by this act or omission, caused A physical or financial harm (It is important to note that this third element has two parts—the causative link, and the physical or financial harm, usually called the "damage").

All three elements must be proved to the satisfaction of the court before negligence is made out, and it is up to the injured person (the plaintiff) to prove these elements, not the other party to disprove them. This means that:

A the plaintiff must prove all the elements of the action (in law this is called having the "burden of proof"); and

B the defendant need only throw enough doubt on A's argument to convince the decision-maker (either a judge or, more rarely, a jury) that any one of the elements above was not present (see *Barnett v Chelsea Hospital* below **[6.695]**).

Duty of Care

[6.35] Due to the dependence upon the health carer for the physical and mental care, and well being of the patient, the law has established that the health carer owes what it calls a "duty of care" to the patient. This is based on the principle that a person must take reasonable care to avoid acts or omissions which would be likely to harm any person they ought reasonably foresee as being so harmed (their legal "neighbour"). If they fail to do this, they may be subject to the civil action of negligence. Where the health carer's act has been so grossly negligent as to have been deliberately reckless of life and limb it may be prosecuted by the criminal courts as criminal negligence or manslaughter. The patient may also then be entitled to aggravated and/or exemplary (punitive) damages. This chapter deals with the civil action for negligence. Criminal negligence is dealt with in Chapter 14.

To understand duty of care, let us consider a little history.

[6.40] Case: *Donoghue v Stevenson* (the "snail in the ginger beer bottle" case) [1932] AC 562 (House of Lords England)

A woman's companion bought her a bottle of ginger beer and poured it out for her. The ginger beer contained what appeared to be the decomposing remains of a snail, which caused the woman both physical and mental harm, severe enough for her to sue the manufacturer of the drink.

[6.45] This was a landmark case in establishing the modern definition of duty of care. The woman issued a writ alleging negligence against the manufacturers, but they responded with a demurrer (a claim that the facts did not give rise to any action in law). This was because, at the time, one only had a legal duty of care in certain specific relationships, such as master and servant, parent and child, carrier of goods or people. A manufacturer had no personal obligation to someone who bought its goods unless there was one of these special relationships, or a contract between the manufacturer and the purchaser: here no such relationship existed, and there was no such contract—any contract had been between the manufacturer and the retailer in the first instance, and the retailer and the companion who bought the drink in the second. As so many people had been harmed by faulty goods that they had purchased and there was no redress at law, it was widely believed within the legal profession that it was time to change the law. The *Donoghue* case was, in fact, very important in this respect.

The trial judge ruled that there was no case to answer, so the woman (described as a "pauper", but no doubt generously supported by lawyers who saw the need for change) appealed to a higher court. Ultimately the case was taken, after further appeal, to the House of Lords, who in their ruling made a strong legal statement which changed the course of the law, and is influential even today. This ruling set out a new principle of negligence. The Law Lords established that the manufacturer of ginger beer had a duty of care to all foreseeable users of its goods, whether they personally bought the goods from the manufacturer or not. But the case had much more far-reaching consequences than that. One of the judges, Lord Atkin, in his judgment (at 580) stated what has become known as the "neighbour test":

"The rule that you are to love your neighbour becomes in law, you must not injure your neighbour; and the lawyer's question, Who is my neighbour? receives a restricted reply. You must take reasonable care to avoid acts or omissions which you can reasonably foresee would be likely to injure your neighbour. Who, then, in law is my neighbour? The answer seems to be persons who are so closely and directly affected by my act that I ought reasonably to have them in contemplation as being so affected when I am directing my mind to the acts or omissions which are called in question."

This test was not the ratio of the case, so the case stood for a much narrower principle. However, judges adopted it formally in the English courts in the ratio of a later decision.

[6.50] Case: *Dorset Yacht Co v Home Office* [1970] AC 1004 (House of Lords England)

Some young Borstal inmates who escaped from a camp damaged vessels from a nearby yacht club in their attempt to get away. The yacht club sued the Home Office, which was responsible for the Borstal. The Home Office argued that, among other things, one cannot be held responsible for the acts of another who is of full age and capacity, and who is not one's servant or acting on one's behalf.

[6.55] The Court (again the House of Lords) rejected this. It held that it was not the action of the boys which was the negligence in question, but the failure of the officers to supervise them adequately. The issue was not the foreseeability of the harm resulting from a third person's acts, but the foreseeability of the consequences of one's own acts or omissions. The Home Office was found negligent. Lord Reid (at 1026-1027), expressed the Court's view of the "neighbour test" thus:

"[Lately] ... there has been a steady trend towards regarding the law of negligence as depending on principle so that, when a new point emerges, one should ask not whether it is covered by authority but whether recognised principles apply to it. *Donoghue v Stevenson* may be regarded as a milestone, and the well-known passage in Lord Atkin's speech should I think be regarded as a statement of principle. It is not to be treated as if it were a statutory definition. It will require qualification in new circumstances. But I think that the time has come when we can and should say that it ought to apply unless there is some justification or valid explanation for its exclusion."

This has been endorsed by the Australian High Court.

A "qualification" has been made by the courts, that there must be a relationship of "proximity" between the plaintiff and defendant. This was elaborated in the case of *Jaensch v Coffey* (see below **[6.190]**). There, it was held that the relationship of proximity is to be determined by considering the existence of:

- *physical proximity* (that is, closeness in space and time between the plaintiff and the defendant);
- *circumstantial proximity* (for example, the relationship between the plaintiff and the defendant); and
- *causal proximity* (for example, the closeness or directness of the relationship between the particular act or omission and the injury sustained), *Jaensch v Coffey* has been described by some authors (Walmsley (2002), p 23) as establishing a two-stage test, foreseeability and proximity.

Later in *Pyrenees Shire Council v Day* (1998) 192 CLR 330; [1998] HCA 3 a three-stage test was promoted, involving an additional consideration of whether it is fair, just and reasonable that the law should impose a duty of care in the particular circumstances. *McGlone* (2005, p 123) observes that in *Sullivan v Moody* (2001) 207 CLR 562; [2001] HCA 59 the High Court rejected both the two- and three-stage test in favour of consideration of a range of factors, perhaps better described as a single test of reasonableness in the circumstances, according to community standards. (See Kerridge (2005), p 141; and for a detailed consideration see McGlone (2005), pp 111-126.)

These somewhat esoteric considerations will, in most practical circumstances, not impact on health carers, as the law has long recognised the existence of a duty of care between health carer and patient. Health carers will almost certainly have a duty of care to another who is directly in their care, leading to responsibility for their actions towards that person, and in some circumstances a duty to a person who has not formally become a patient as yet, such as when a person approaches a medical receptionist with a view to a consultation. (See *Alexander v Heise* [2001] NSWCA 422 discussed further at **[6.105]**). A health carer may also be deemed to have a duty of care to people of whose specific existence they may not even be aware, but whose existence they ought to foresee as probable such as the sexual partner of an HIV positive patient or the partner of a patient undergoing a sterilisation procedure: *BT v Oei* [1999] NSWSC 1082; *McDonald v Sydney South West Area Health Service* [2005] NSWSC 924 (see **[6.125]**). Thus they may be responsible for the harm caused to third persons by someone in their care (see **[6.765]**ff).

Reasonable foreseeability

[6.60] It is important to note that the harm foreseen must be probable, not merely possible. No doubt one can imagine no end of cataclysmic possibilities bedevilling the simplest procedures. There is a recorded case of a person who regularly took a short-cut through a graveyard being killed by a tombstone which after many years, happened to fall on him just as he was passing beneath it. But, as mere mortals, we are expected by law only to anticipate the probable—something which has a significant probability factor. It is not easy to put a figure on this, however, as the courts are not, at this stage, in favour of approaching such mathematical specificity as the *Wagon Mound* case (discussed below) indicates. Some courts have looked with favour on a formula of "more probable than not" or, "more than 50 per cent probability", or that the occurrence of the event is "not far-fetched or fanciful" (the latter being the test accepted in *Wyong Shire Council v Shirt* (1980) 146 CLR 40; [1980] HCA 12 but rejected in the *Review of the Law of Negligence* in favour of the term "not insignificant" now found in *Civil Liability Act 2002* (NSW), s 5B(1)).

[6.65] Case: *Overseas Tankship (UK) Ltd v The Miller Steamship Co Pty Ltd ("The Wagon Mound") (No 2)* [1967] 1 AC 617 (Privy Council England)

A ship spilled bunkering oil into Sydney Harbour. Workmen at a nearby dock were carrying out welding, which caused sparks to fall into the water. The ship's engineer believed (correctly) that bunkering oil is very hard to ignite when spread on water. However, a nearby dock and ships berthed there were destroyed by fire when cotton waste in the water, saturated with oil, caught fire from molten metal from the dockside welding activities. The owners of the damaged ships sued the owner of the engineer's ship.

[6.70] One of the questions which the Privy Council (which at that time heard appeals from Australian courts, **[2.130]**), had to consider was the reasonability of the ship's engineer failing to act on the fact that the oil could burn, albeit in rare circumstances. A little more history may help the reader to follow its reasoning.

Until the 1950s the law recognised two types of situation:

- A situation which, if contemplated, would be considered either impossible, or, so fantastic or far-fetched that no reasonable person would have paid attention to it; or
- A situation where there was a real and substantial risk of the harm occurring, and which a reasonable person would take necessary steps to prevent.

A third type of situation, however, had been first recognised in a case involving a cricket ball which, as the result of a terrific hit, soared over the 17-foot high fence of a cricket pitch in a little town, and hit a passer-by, injuring her (*Bolton v Stone* [1951] AC 850). Such a hit had occurred, it was revealed, about six times in 28 years, no one having been hit before. It was also established that the cost of building a suitable fence to prevent its occurrence would be difficult for the cricket club to meet. This sort of situation was identified as one where the harm is plainly foreseeable and possible, but the probability is very remote. The House of Lords held in the cricket ball case that the risk was so small, that a reasonable person would be justified in disregarding it. The Court held, however, that in such a situation a reasonable person would not always disregard the risk. He or she would only disregard it if it were reasonably justifiable to do so, for example, the benefits outweigh the risk, or the cost of averting the risk is disproportion-ately high.

The judges believed that both those factors were present in the cricket case, but those sitting on the *Wagon Mound* case decided there was no justification for ignoring the risk of fire, despite its low level of probability. The horrendous damage that can (and did) result from fire, and the easy means of preventing the spread of oil which were available, made the failure to prevent the risk, even though considered unlikely, negligent at law. One must balance the various factors, the Court said: on the one hand how serious and immediate the foreseeable harm might be, and on the other hand the likely benefits of the planned activity.

It is not enough that the event should be such as can reasonably be foreseen; the further result that injury is likely to follow must also be such as a reasonable man would contemplate, before he can be held negligent. Nor is the remote possibility of injury occurring enough; there must be sufficient probability to lead a reasonable man to anticipate it.

[6.75] Case: *Goode v Nash* (1979) 21 SASR 419

A doctor was participating in a program for screening people for glaucoma. This involved placing a tonometer on the eye. To prevent cross infection, the tonometer was sterilised over an open flame. The plaintiff suffered serious and permanent injury to his eye when the tonometer was placed on the eye before it had properly cooled down.

[6.80] The Court held that the doctor was liable even though this had never happened to him before. The activity was so potentially dangerous and the consequences of negligence so grave, he ought to have taken precautions to prevent its happening.

All the approaches mentioned above have been accepted at one time or another, and the reasonable health carer should use cautious common sense when considering whether a risk is worth avoiding under the particular circum-stances that exist at the time. It must be remembered that health carers are recognised by law as being involved in busy schedules, emotionally and physically tiring work, and should, both because of that and despite it, act in the most effective, efficient and harmless way that they reasonably can under the circumstances.

These difficulties in formulation of foreseeability remained at the time of the *Review of the Law of Negligence* and led to a specific recommendation (Recommendation 28) resulting in s 5B(1) of the *Civil Liability Act 2002* (NSW). Section 5B(1) provides that a person is not negligent in failing to take precautions against a risk of harm unless the risk was foreseeable (that is, it is a risk of which the person knew or ought to have known), the risk was not insignificant, and in the circumstances, a reasonable person in the person's position would have taken those precautions. Section 5B(2) goes on to direct that in determining whether a reasonable person would have taken precautions against a risk of harm, the court is to consider the probability that the harm would occur if care were not taken, the likely seriousness of the harm, the burden of taking precautions to avoid the risk of harm, and the social utility of the activity that creates the risk of harm.

Precise nature or amount of harm need not be foreseen

[6.83] Case: *Vacwell Engineering Co v BDH Chemicals* [1971] 1 QB 111 (CA England)

Chemical manufacturers were aware that one of their products had explosive qualities, but were unaware that it was highly explosive on contact with water. A scientist, using the chemical, but improperly warned of its volatility, was killed when it exploded on contact with water. His employers sued the manufacturers in negligence for not properly warning them.

[6.85] The Court held that the manufacturers had been negligent in not properly warning users of the chemical's nature, for although they knew it provided a risk of violent reaction and possible explosion they had not adequately warned of this. The fact that they did not know the likely magnitude of the explosion and the extent of the danger was no excuse. See also *Richards v State of Victoria* [1969] VR 136 where a blow to the temple in a classroom fight led to a ruptured cerebral artery, resulting in spastic paralysis. The Court held that it was foreseeable that such a blow might cause injury to the brain, and the defendant could not complain if the injury was greater than expected.

Duty of care is a question of law

[6.90] As indicated, the difference between the tort of negligence and other nominate torts, such as assault, nuisance or defamation, is that the types of action for which a negligence action can be brought are limitless and undefined: they cover the full spectrum of human behaviour. By allowing compensation for anyone who suffers harm from another's actions, we would certainly stifle initiative and suppress our avowed social policy of individualistic private enterprise. People would be either too frightened to do anything, or required to pay compensation for any and every harm they caused. So in recent times a primary concern of the courts dealing with negligence actions has actually been to limit claims; containing them within reasonable levels.

Establishing whether or not a duty of care exists is all-important, it is the threshold for establishing negligence. If no duty of care between the parties to an action can be established, there is no case to answer (as seen in *Donoghue v Stevenson* at **[6.40]**).

"Reasonable foreseeability'" as policy

[6.95] If the test of reasonable foresight were simply applied in determining whether a duty of care existed in a given situation, it would be no more than the test applied in determining whether the defendant breached her or his duty of care by acting unreasonably in the situation being considered. In fact, it has been established that there is a need for the judge to also consider public policy, an approach which was acknowledged by Lord Diplock as the basis for deciding when to exclude the "neighbour test" (see [6.45]), and has been elaborated in later cases. Katter ((1999), pp 14ff) notes that the very word "reasonable" is value-laden, and that determining what is "reasonably foreseeable" involves injecting a subjective value judgment into objective factual issues of duty and standard of care. Policy considerations are often used to determine proximity, writes Katter ((1999), p 93), and thus may be disguised as legal principle. At p 58 he quotes Fleming ((1953), p 486) who describes the use of proximity as:

"an ingenious exploitation of the inherent indeterminacy of the foreseeability concept in the interest of furthering a specific policy demanded by contemporary social opinion."

This public policy aspect gained attention in the *Review of the Law of Negligence* (at para 7.28) in the context of what was described as the social utility of the risk-creating activity:

"Some activities are more worth taking risks for than others—a plaintiff may be required to submit to a risk for the sake of some greater good that they would not be expected to accept if some lesser interest were at stake. A common situation in which precautions that would normally be thought reasonable need not be taken is where an emergency vehicle is speeding an injured or sick person to hospital. As Denning LJ said in *Watt v Hertfordshire County Council* [1954] 2 All ER 368, 371 it is one thing to take risks when driving for some commercial purpose with no emergency, but quite another to take risks for life and limb."

These considerations formed part of *Review of the Law of Negligence* Recommendation 28 and led to the *Civil Liability Act 2002* (NSW), s 5B(2) direction that in determining whether a reasonable person would have taken precautions against a risk of harm, the court is to consider amongst other things the social utility of the activity that creates the risk of harm.

Policy considerations involving many factors, such as history, morals, justice, convenience and social practice have influenced judicial decisions with regard to the presence of duty of care. Examples of policy can be found in the cases below, particularly those establishing a duty of care (see especially *Chapman v Hearse* at [6.175]). One might be confused when reading the judgment of a case, for, while it may seem that the reasonable person could have foreseen harm occurring as a result of his or her actions, he or she may be found not to have had a duty of care (or vice-versa). It is thus useful to consider whether the judge has resorted to public policy to come to what is considered a just decision in the case.

There is no absolutely sure way, then, to predict what activities will be covered by duty of care and what activities will not. As Katter points out, use of value charged precepts such as reasonable foreseeability means that there is more than one possible result for each individual case as they are not verifiable by objective empirical observation (Katter, p 14). However, there is adequate case law to give some strong indications as to when one assumes a duty of care.

When does one assume a duty of care?

[6.100] Given the above, it can be said that a duty of care will probably arise either when the reasonable person becomes aware (or ought to be aware) of potential harm to another from her or his activities or omissions, or when one accepts the care of another, whichever applies to the situation at hand. However, there is no question that a duty of care arises between a health carer and a person who has been accepted as her or his patient. There may be an issue as to whether that actually happens in some circumstances.

[6.105] Case: *Alexander v Heise* [2001] NSWCA 422

This claim pursuant to the *Compensation to Relatives Act 1897* (NSW), arose out of the death of A's husband, due to a cerebral haemorrhage. A had attended at H's surgery, he being a GP, and had organised an appointment for her husband. The receptionist arranged an appointment for a full medical check up for the following week. The day before the appointment, however, A found her husband unconscious and twelve days later he died of a grade V berry aneurism. A argued that had her husband seen a doctor before he suffered the aneurism, his death could have been avoided.

[6.110] The Court held that both the doctor and the receptionist owed a duty to the prospective patient (who had not attended the surgery before), but as the duty was not breached in the circumstances the precise scope and content of the duty did not need to be determined. The receptionist was attempting to ascertain the duration and severity of the problem and assess its degree of seriousness. She was exercising her judgment. On the information provided by A it was understandable that she would not conclude that it was an urgent problem or that she needed to refer it immediately to H. Accordingly there was no breach of duty on the part of the receptionist and it followed that there was no breach of duty by H.

[6.115] Case: *Albrighton v Royal Prince Alfred Hospital* [1980] 2 NSWLR 542 (CA NSW)

The patient suffered from kypho-scoliosis and spina bifida from birth, and had a large hairy naevus on her lower back. She was admitted to hospital at age 15 for corrective surgery on her spine, and for possible halo-pelvic traction for straightening and lengthening it. Because of the hairy naevus, there was a recognised danger of "tethering" of the spinal cord (adherence to surrounding tissue) and consequent damage to the cord resulting in paraplegia from the traction. In fact traction was applied and paraplegia resulted. She sued in negligence, but the question was, who was liable? Involved in the case was a neurosurgeon, who had been asked to see the patient to advise on traction, but who had not done so by the time the damage occurred.

[6.120] There was not much evidence of what had happened to cause this unfortunate result, but the medical records showed that the orthopaedic surgeon had written a consultation request to the neurosurgeon, who had received it and written in the patient's medical notes: "As she has had (just) [sic] traction I will see her next week." (In fact traction did not occur until two days later). The Court held that the neurosurgeon both knew of the potential danger, and had accepted the patient into his care, although he had not seen her, and thus a duty of care existed. One does not have to be in direct contact with someone to owe them a duty of care, and as *Donoghue v Stevenson* indicates (see **[6.40]**), one need not even be aware of a specific individual at all. Thus, where a reasonable health carer would be aware of potential harm from her or his actions to foreseeable but unknown people in general, there is a duty of care (for example, a duty of care to visitors to a hospital; see **[11.250]**ff).

Duty of care to third persons

[6.125] The above principle means that a duty of care is owed not only to patients but to others whose personal well being and property may be harmed by failure to take reasonable care of a patient.

Thus, for example, potentially dangerous individuals must be properly supervised and cared for to prevent them from harming others, and not carelessly allowed to leave an institution if they show a tendency to violence (*Holgate v Lancashire Mental Hospital Board* [1937] 4 All ER 19). In this case the hospital made no proper inquiry as to the circumstances after discharge of the patient. (See also *Godfrey v NSW (No 2)* [2003] NSWSC 275.)

[6.130] Case: *BT v Oei* [1999] NSWSC 1082

A man was the patient of a medical practitioner. He suffered Hepatitis B yet was not (the Court found) advised by the medical practitioner to undergo an HIV test. Later the man formed a relationship with a woman who was not a patient of the medical practitioner. She acquired HIV by transmission from the man, and succeeded in a claim against the medical practitioner who was held to owe a duty to the male patients later sexual partners.

[6.135] Case: *McDonald v Sydney South West Area Health Service* [2005] NSWSC 924

Mr McDonald was the father of a child born after the mother, Ms Foster, had a sterilisation procedure which failed as a result of negligent technique—the Filshie clip on the left fallopian tube was not applied so as to completely occlude the tube. The father sued to recover the costs of raising his child and succeeded in his claim. The Court held that the medical practitioner knew or ought to have known that if he did not perform the tubal ligation properly Ms Foster and her partner may suffer the financial detriment of having to raise an additional child. Further, as an existing partner of Ms Foster, the relationship between the plaintiff and the defendant was so close or special that a duty of care did arise.

[6.140] The Court distinguished this case from *Goodwill v British Pregnancy Advisory Service* [1996] 2 All ER 161 where the plaintiff's boyfriend had undergone a vasectomy before the couple met. Subsequently the plaintiff conceived a child and brought proceedings seeking damages for the expenses associated with her daughter's birth and the costs of raising her. The Court found that the defendants were not in a sufficiently proximate or special relationship with the plaintiff such as to give rise to a duty of care. Emphasis was placed on the circumstance that the plaintiff was not Mr McKinlay's sexual partner at the time the defendants advised him. At the time that the advice was given to the father of the child, the defendants had no knowledge of the plaintiff. She was not an existing partner of his, but was to be a future sexual partner.

Care should also be taken with an individual who shows a tendency to harm herself or himself.

[6.145] Case: *Pallister v Waikato Hospital Board* [1975] 2 NZLR 725 (CA New Zealand)

A patient being treated for suicidal tendencies was confined in a room. The door was left open for ventilation and in the hope the patient would learn to cope with freedom of movement. He left the room and jumped from a window, killing himself. His widow sued the hospital in negligence. The Court held that the hospital had breached its duty of care; staff were on notice that the patient would be likely to harm himself, and so the duty to act accordingly was clear. This raises the question of what should happen when a person threatens, or talks about, suicide. Where the person is a patient, then particular consideration should be given to appropriate action.

[6.150] An unusual set of facts arose in the appeal *Hunter Area Health Service & Anor v Presland* (2005) 63 NSWLR 22; NSWCA 33. Mr Presland was discharged by a psychiatrist from a psychiatric hospital, in circumstances where he was at risk to himself and others as a consequence of a mental illness. Six hours after he was released from the psychiatric hospital, he killed his brother's fiancée. Presland was acquitted of the murder on the grounds of mental illness and sued for damages in respect of the consequences for him. Although successful at the initial trial, the verdict was overturned on appeal. The majority held with regard to public policy or the normative aspects of causation, it would be unjust to render the hospital and doctor legally responsible for a non-physical injury traced back to unlawful but not criminal conduct. Subsequent to this decision, the *Civil Liability Act 2002* (NSW) was amended by insertion of s 54A—damages limitations if a loss results from a serious offence committed by a mentally ill person.

Is there a duty to rescue a stranger from harm?

[6.155] It has been stated that at common law there is no duty to assist a person who is in danger, where no relationship of care has been established. (See *Capital & Counties PLC v Hampshire County Council* [1997] QB 1004.) Thus there is no legal obligation to stop at the scene of an accident to provide care, or go to the aid of a stranger in trouble. The *Medical Practitioners' Act 1958* (NSW) (later replaced by the *Medical Practice Act 1992* (NSW)) provides that a doctor who does not respond to an urgent call for assistance may be guilty of professional misconduct. However, that is a different matter to being sued in a court of law and being held negligent for not assisting. An exception to the common law principle was made in the following case.

> **[6.160] Case:** *Lowns v Woods* [1996] Aust Torts Reports ¶81-376 (CA NSW)
>
> A 10-year-old boy, P, who had a history of epilepsy was on holiday on the northern New South Wales coast. One day his mother found him suffering a serious and prolonged epileptic fit. She immediately sent her son to a nearby ambulance station, and her daughter to a nearby doctor's surgery, knowing that P required intravenous valium. The daughter gave evidence that she arrived at the doctor's surgery and told Dr L that her brother was having the fit. He told her to bring him to the surgery, and she replied that this was impossible. He then said to get an ambulance, which she said had been done, and insisted that the doctor was needed. He refused to go. The ambulance officers had to take P to a local medical centre before he could receive the IV valium, however it was not successful in stopping the fit, and he had to be taken to Gosford Hospital for treatment. As a result P was seriously brain-damaged. P, through his parents, sued Dr L in

negligence for failing to attend to, and treat him. The trial judge found, for the first time in an Australian court, that Dr L's refusal to treat P when asked to do so was negligent. Dr L appealed against this finding to the Court of Appeal.

[6.165] The Court of Appeal upheld the trial judge's ruling. The three judges acknowledged that the decision was at odds with the general common law position that there is no duty to rescue or assist someone who is in danger, even where it can be foreseen that such a failure might cause harm. However, two of the judges held that in this case a duty of care did arise, as proximity existed between Dr L and P. One of the judges, Cole JA, expressed the reasoning by stating that proximity existed in all four possible ways:

- there was *proximity of relationship* because Dr L foresaw that his refusal could cause harm to P;
- there was *physical proximity* because he was not far away;
- there was *circumstantial proximity* as there were no barriers to his attending and assisting P; and
- there was *causal proximity* because the administration of IV valium could have prevented the brain damage.

This was the basis for establishing a duty of care. Kirby P was also swayed by the special duty of the "noble" medical profession, which is subject to higher standards than is the ordinary citizen. He also determined that s 27(2) of the *Medical Practitioner's Act 1958* (NSW) was relevant. This section made failure to assist a person in an emergency unprofessional conduct.

The Court thus applied the proximity test of *Jaensch v Coffey* (see **[6.190]**), but Cole JA based the test of relational proximity on the foreseeability of harm, tying together the tests for both the presence of a duty of care and the standard of care to be applied. By doing this the Court was able to establish a duty of care to go to the aid of a "stranger" (one to whom a relationship of care has not been otherwise established), at least where the test of proximity has been met. In his minority judgment, Mahoney J, questioned where the limits to the duty would be set, and stated that he believed the obligation to assist strangers in an emergency should not be imposed through tort law.

Queensland enacted protection for medical practitioners and nurses who "render medical care, aid or assistance to an injured person in circumstances of emergency", both at the scene and during transport to a place for medical treatment, where that act or omission is done in good faith without gross negligence and performed without fee or reward (*Law Reform Act 1995* (Qld), s 16). Later, despite the reservations expressed in the *Review of the Law of Negligence* at para 7.20-7.24, "Good Samaritan" protections were included in the *Civil Liability Act 2002* (NSW) as ss 55-58, such that a Good Samaritan does not incur any personal civil liability in respect of any act or omission done or made by the Good Samaritan in an emergency when assisting a person who is apparently injured or at risk of being injured. The sections do not affect the vicarious liability of any other person for the acts or omissions of the Good

Samaritan, defined as a person who, in good faith and without expectation of payment or other reward, comes to the assistance of a person who is apparently injured or at risk of being injured.

Whilst health care providers may not have a duty of care to go to the aid of those injured in an accident, if they do, by their actions they *establish* a duty of care towards those they assist. That duty may still be relevant despite the Good Samaritan protections referred to above, where there is expectation of payment or for a vicariously liable employer and given the limited nature of the protection provided. Courts will give every consideration to factors such as shock to all concerned at the accident, the speed with which decisions have to be made, and the difficult circumstances in which aid has to be rendered.

Duty of care owed to rescuers

[6.170] The courts have considered the situation where person A negligently causes harm to another, person B, and person C is harmed in trying to rescue person B. A may be liable for the harm caused to the rescuer.

[6.175] Case: *Chapman v Hearse* (1961) 106 CLR 112; [1961] HCA 46 (High Court of Australia)

C, driving in bad weather conditions, negligently negotiated a right-hand turn at an intersection. This resulted in a pile-up of cars on the road, with C being thrown onto the road, unconscious. A passer-by, Dr C, went to his aid, and was kneeling on the road administering assistance to C. They were on the right side of the road. An oncoming car, also driven negligently, hit and killed Dr C. His widow sued the driver of that car, H, and H claimed contribution to the damages from C, arguing that his negligence in the first place also contributed to Dr C's death, as he would not have been hit if it weren't for C's need of care, to which Dr C was responding. C argued that, negligent as he was, he did not have a duty of care to his rescuer, Dr C, as he could not have foreseen that he would come to his aid.

[6.180] The High Court of Australia disagreed with this argument. The judges held that C should have foreseen that if he drove negligently he might not only harm another, or himself, but be the author of harm to a third person who came to his aid. The Court approved of a United States case, *Wagner v International Railway Co*, 232 NY Rep 176 (1921) at 180, where Cardozo J said of this sort of situation:

> "The risk of rescue, if only it be not wanton, is born of the occasion. The emergency begets the man. The wrongdoer may not have foreseen the coming of a deliverer. He is accountable as if he had."

Liability for mental harm

[6.185] There is also a duty of care to those who might be psychologically harmed by the horror of the damage one may have caused.

[6.190] Case: *Jaensch v Coffey* (1984) 155 CLR 549; [1984] HCA 52

A policeman was seriously injured by the negligent driving of J. The policeman's wife was witness to the events at the hospital to which she was called. These involved several critical returns to theatre to repair internal injuries, and seeing her husband in considerable pain. She was told his condition was poor and was urgently recalled later to intensive care as his condition had deteriorated further. At this time she was told he had damaged kidneys and liver. She saw him with "all these tubes coming out of him". She feared her husband would die, and continued to do so for three to four weeks. As a result she suffered severe anxiety and depression, which led to gynaecological problems and a hysterectomy.

[6.195] In the lower court the judge held that J could foresee that his causing of harm to another could result in a wife having to go to the hospital, having to wait anxiously for her husband's recovery, and suffering mental harm as a result. The appeal by J was disallowed in the Court of Appeal of South Australia, so he appealed to the High Court. There the original decision was upheld. The implications of such a finding are clear: where one can reasonably foresee harm to another, one will be held by the courts to also foresee psychological harm that close relatives may suffer as a result of such harm. It has also been held that those who witness a horrific accident, and rescue workers at the site of an accident, are also in the class of people to whom a duty of care is owed.

[6.200] Case: *Tame v NSW; Annetts v Australian Stations Pty Limited* (2002) 211 CLR 317; [2002] HCA 35 (High Court of Australia)

These two cases were dealt with together by the High Court. In *Tame*, T suffered a psychiatric illness as a reaction to an erroneous statement by a police officer in a traffic accident report, which recorded that she was driving whilst affected by alcohol. Although T initially succeeded, the High Court said the defendant was not liable as it was not reasonably foreseeable that a person of normal fortitude would develop a psychiatric reaction to an error of that kind. *Annetts* was a claim by the parents of a teenage boy who died in circumstances for which the defendant was held

> liable. The boy's body was not found for some months which led
> to an argument, ultimately unsuccessful, that the defendant
> should not be liable as the parents' illnesses were caused by the
> slow accumulation of stress, rather than the result of a shock. (See
> McGlone (2005) at page 183).

[6.205] The area of liability for mental harm was another considered in the *Review of the Law of Negligence*. At para 9.28, the *Review* proposed (Recommendation 34) a legislative statement of what was perceived to be the current state of the law, embodying the following principles:

a) There can be no liability for pure mental harm (that is, mental harm that is not a consequence of physical harm suffered by the mentally harmed person) unless the mental harm consists of a recognised psychiatric illness.

b) A person (the defendant) does not owe another (the plaintiff) a duty to take care not to cause the plaintiff pure mental harm unless the defendant ought to have foreseen that a person of normal fortitude might, in the circumstances, suffer a recognised psychiatric illness if reasonable care was not taken.

c) For the purposes of (b), the circumstances of the case include matters such as:
   - whether or not the mental harm was suffered as the result of a sudden shock;
   - whether the plaintiff was at the scene of shocking events, or witnessed them or their aftermath;
   - whether the plaintiff witnessed the events or their aftermath with his or her own unaided senses;
   - whether or not there was a pre-existing relationship between the plaintiff and the defendant; and
   - the nature of the relationship between the plaintiff and any person killed, injured or put in peril.

The approach taken by the *Civil Liability Act 2002* (NSW) can be found in Part 3, ss 27-33.

Duty of care to the unborn

[6.210] It has been held by the courts that a duty of care is owed to a foetus, although it is not a person at law, and therefore cannot bring an action in law until it is born (see *Hawkins v Clayton* (1988) 164 CLR 539; [1988] HCA 15 per Deane J). Thus, although the harm has been caused before the foetus is a person at law, the right to sue for harm caused before birth becomes exercisable once the foetus does become a person. A health carer for a pregnant woman owes a duty of care to her and to the foetus.

[6.215] Case: *Watt v Rama* [1972] VR 353 (SC Vic)

A pregnant woman was involved in a car accident in which the other driver was at fault. The child, when born, had obviously suffered some harm from the accident. The child sued the driver in negligence through a representative.

The issue was whether the negligent driver owed a duty of care to the foetus. The Court held that as there are a significant number of pregnant women in the community, and pregnancy can be reasonably foreseen by others in the general community, so not only do drivers have a duty of care to other drivers and passengers, but also to a potential child who may be harmed. This approach was approved in a medical context in a later English case.

[6.220] Case: *B v Islington Health Authority* [1991] 1 All ER 825 (Queen's Bench Division England)

The plaintiff's mother had undergone a dilatation and curettage. At the time, unknown to her, she was pregnant. She later gave birth to B, a baby girl, who suffered numerous physical abnormalities, which affected her relationships with men and impaired her earning capacity.

B sued the health authority in negligence alleging that her injuries had been caused by the surgery on her mother, and that the staff should have ascertained whether her mother had been pregnant at the time of the operation. The hospital argued that they had no duty of care to the B as she was, at the time the injuries were caused, an embryo, which under English law lacks legal personality. Thus no duty of care could be owed to her, nor could it be said that she suffered injuries. The Court held that the three elements of negligence crystallise at the time of birth, and thus the three requirements of negligence were fulfilled.

[6.225] Case: *Lynch v Lynch and GIO* [1991] Aust Torts Reports ¶81-117

A child born with cerebral palsy suffered prenatal injury as the result of an accident in a car driven by her mother. The child sued the mother and the mother's insurer. The defendant argued that the child was not a person when the accident happened, and indeed there was unity of personality with the mother, and so the child could not sue her, as the mother could not have a duty of care to herself.

The Court followed *Watt v Rama* holding that once the child was born alive the right to sue crystallised. It also rejected the unity of personality argument, and stated that parents have a duty of care to their "unborn children", and should be liable for any injuries they negligently cause to them.

[6.230] A duty of care may be owed to someone, even before they are conceived, where a health care worker would be reasonably able to foresee harm occurring to a foetus through negligent care of the potential parent. The most common situations that would come under this category of events are the negligent cross-matching of blood leading to disorders of a child later conceived, the negligent giving of X-rays, and negligent genetic counselling.

[6.235] Case: *Kosky v Trustees of The Sisters of Charity* [1982] VR 961 (SC Vic)

The plaintiff, who was Rh-negative, had been negligently given Rh-positive blood after a car accident by the defendant hospital. There were no immediate effects, but eight years later she gave birth to a child suffering from complications due to Rh iso-immunisation and the prematurely induced birth which it required.

The Court said there was a duty of care to the future child, even though it was not conceived for many years after the initial action, which later caused the harm, had occurred.

[6.240] Further examples of the duty to an unborn child are *X v Pal* (1991) 23 NSWLR 26 (see **[6.875]**) and *Hughes v Sydney Day Nursery* [2002] NSWCA 11. (See discussion in Walmsley (2002), p 183.)

A particularly complex area of the law concerning unborn children is that known as "wrongful life". Wrongful life cases are not the same as the group of cases sometimes called "wrongful birth"; they are dealt with below at **[6.665]**. Wrongful life cases consider arguments whereby the children, once born, allege that the medical practitioner treating their mother ought to have advised the mother to terminate the pregnancy as the child would live a terrible existence with great attendant care costs. The earliest well-known English case in this area is summarised below.

[6.245] Case: *McKay v Essex Area Health Authority* [1982] 2 All ER 771 (CA England)

A pregnant woman had contracted rubella in the early months of pregnancy. However, this was not diagnosed, and the child was born severely disabled. The mother and the child sued the doctor, who failed to diagnose the illness, in negligence. The issue was whether the doctor owed a duty of care to the child to have advised abortion.

The Court considered the issue thus: first, the doctor had not caused the harm; the disease had. The duty of care involved preventing the effects of the disease as much as was reasonable, which involved advising the mother on the possibility of abortion. However, the duty of care did not extend to entitlement of the child to prevention from life itself as this is a principle repugnant to public policy. Therefore, compensation could be claimed by the mother for the cost and burden of providing care for the child. As the child's disability existed independently and prior to the doctor's action, she could not claim damages for the disability.

[6.250] A similar issue was recently argued before the High Court of Australia, in *Harriton v Stephens* [2006] HCA 15 and *Waller v James; Waller v Hoolahan* [2006] HCA 16, which were heard together. The High Court matters were on appeal from the New South Wales Court of Appeal decision in *Harriton v Stephens; Waller v James & Anor; Waller v Hoolahan* (2004) 59 NSWLR 694; NSWCA 93. The New South Wales Court of Appeal was divided on the issue, with a majority of two judges finding against the claimants and one judge finding for them. The High Court, by a 6-1 majority, dismissed each appeal. The broad question to be decided by the Court was stated by Kirby J (at 6 in *Harriton*) as:

"to decide whether a child, born with profound disabilities, whose mother would have elected to terminate her pregnancy had she been aware that there was a real risk of the child being born with such disabilities, is entitled to damages where a medical practitioner negligently failed to warn the mother of that risk."

More specifically, the questions for determination by the High Court were: "(1) whether a wrongful life action constitutes a valid cause of action; and, if so, (2) what heads of damage are recoverable" (Kirby J at 33 in *Harriton*).

The majority reasoning for dismissing the appeal centred on the notion that the alleged damage was not such as to be legally cognisable. As put by Crennan J (in *Waller*):

"The appellant's claimed damage in each of his appeals is his life with disabilities. This inevitably involves an assertion by the appellant that it would be preferable if he had not been born, irrespective of whether the conduct about which he complains occurred prior to, or during, his mother's pregnancy with him ... the appellant's life with disabilities is not legally cognisable damage in the sense required to found a duty of care towards him. This is so whether or not the proposed duty of care is formulated as a duty upon Dr James and Sydney IVF to him as a 'prospective child' of the parents, or a 'potential child', or a 'potential person', or as a duty of care upon Dr Hoolahan to him as a foetus. For those reasons, and the reasons set out in *Harriton v Stephens*, the appellant's damage in each of the appeals is not actionable."

In contrast, Kirby J, dissenting , opined (in *Waller*):

"In my view ... such actions are consistent with the general principles of negligence law. The established duty of care which health care providers owe to the unborn in respect of pre-natal injuries requires the exercise of reasonable care in investigating risks of disability that might afflict prospective children and warning those in relevant relationships with the provider of such risks. The heads of damages ordinarily available in personal injury cases are quantifiable and may be awarded. There are no convincing reasons of legal principle or policy to preclude recovery."

For a detailed review of the issues, see Kapterian, *Journal of Law and Medicine*, Vol 13(3), 336; and McGlone (2005), pp 126-127.

Occupier's duty of care to those on property

[6.255] A duty of care is owed to those who come on to property for which one is responsible. This is discussed in Chapter 11.

Standard of Care

[6.260] The tort of negligence extends over the whole range of human activity and is not confined to particular types of conduct or activity, as are most other torts. It is concerned with how activities are carried out, rather than with the activities themselves. It is difficult to separate the notions of duty of care and breach of that duty. In considering whether one has breached a duty of care, the courts look at the standard of care which would reasonably be expected from a person acting in the defendant's circumstances, in the capacity in which the defendant was acting (as for example, a physiotherapist, doctor, nurse). The discussion of duty of care and its breach thus necessarily revolves around the notion of reasonable care, notwithstanding that commentators may differ in attributing matters to the category of "duty", "breach" or "standard" of care.

One could say that the tort of negligence is the method by which our law lays down a standard of social behaviour. Just as the criminal law upholds, for example, the notion of private property, and the crime and tort of assault and battery enforce the idea of the right to personal autonomy, the action of negligence endorses the principle that a person cannot behave in a way that reason should warn is likely to harm those people he or she should consider. Kerridge (2005, p 139) notes the statement in *Cekan v Haines* (1990) 21 NSWLR 296:

"It exists both to compensate a person who has suffered a wrong and also to state the standards of the community in respect of wrongs."

Tort law differs from contract law in that tort law covers all people, whether they have had prior association with each other or not, and it sets a broad standard that is common to all. Contract, on the other hand, requires that the parties involved have already set their own standard of behaviour by agreement.

Lord Atkins' "neighbour principle" in *Donoghue v Stevenson* (see [6.40]) also sets out the standard of care owed by health carers: that is, one of reasonable care. Health carers do not have to be perfect, but have only to exercise the skill that a reasonable health carer professing the skills in question would be expected to exercise in the circumstances. This is what is called the "objective" test. The court does not look at, for example, the *actual* intelligence, experience or personality of the particular health carer on the particular day in question, but rather at a hypothetical "reasonable" carer in similar circumstances, and considers what he or she would do. To help them do this, other carers who are experienced in the field (called "expert witnesses") are called to give their opinion as to whether the actions in question were in fact reasonable under the circumstances.

The best way to understand is to consider past cases and examples. In the case of *Bolam v Friern Hospital Management Committee* [1957] 1 WLR 582 McNair J, in his address to the jury (at 586-587), described the test of the reasonable health carer in the following terms:

"... the test is the standard of the ordinary skilled man exercising and professing to have that special skill. A man need not possess the highest expert skill; it is well established law that it is sufficient if he exercises the ordinary skill of an ordinary competent man exercising that particular art."

Following the *Review of the Law of Negligence*, Australian jurisdictions have to varying degrees implemented a statutory definition of the standard of care. The *Civil Liability Act 2002* (NSW), s 50, provides:

"(1) A person practising a profession ('a professional') does not incur a liability in negligence arising from the provision of a professional service if it is established that the professional acted in a manner that (at the time the service was provided) was widely accepted in Australia by peer professional opinion as competent professional practice.

(2) However, peer professional opinion cannot be relied on for the purposes of this section if the court considers that the opinion is irrational.

(3) The fact that there are differing peer professional opinions widely accepted in Australia concerning a matter does not prevent any one or more (or all) of those opinions being relied on for the purposes of this section.

(4) Peer professional opinion does not have to be universally accepted to be considered widely accepted."

Standard of care depends on the circumstances

[6.265] It is impossible to predict what is a reasonable standard of care in every possible health care situation in one statement. No two situations are exactly the same and individual cases will be considered by the courts on their merits. Standards change over time with changes in medical knowledge and practice; *Cekan v Haines* (1990) 21 NSWLR 296:

"There is no doubt that those standards change over time. Economic and social change, community expectations and knowledge in relevant people affect those changing standards."

Some examples will be given in this chapter, but as the duty to practise a reasonable standard of care covers all health care activities, be it sponging patients, giving medication, writing reports or anything else, further chapters of the book will, where relevant, cover the standard of care for the particular health care activity dealt with there.

 Checklist
SUGGESTED CONSIDERATIONS IN IDENTIFYING A REASONABLE STANDARD OF CARE
✓ Is this the way I've been taught to proceed in these circumstances?
✓ Is this situation covered by official Hospital Procedure or instructions?
✓ Is this the way freely available textbooks or journals tell me to proceed?
✓ Is advice and/or assistance reasonably available and should I seek it?
✓ What do my colleagues and superiors say should be done in this sort of situation?

Factors determining "reasonable" care include:
✓ the circumstances (for example, urgency, resources);
✓ practice established by the profession;
✓ the condition of the patient (for example, see *Mahon v Osborne* at **[6.355]**); and
✓ the magnitude of any probable harm (for example, see *Bolton v Stone* at **[6.70]**).

Some important examples of the courts' approach to the standard of care for health carers follow.

[6.270] Case: *Spivey v St Thomas' Hospital*, 31 Tenn App 12 at 211; SW 2d 450 (1947) (CA Tennessee United States)

S was admitted to St Thomas' Hospital suffering pneumonia. He was febrile. His bed was on the first floor near a window. During the night, while he was delirious and unaware of his actions, S got out of the window, fell to the ground and as a result of head injuries caused by the fall, died the next day. The Court was presented with the following facts:

6 pm   On admission S was delirious, and trying to get out of bed; the window was two or three feet from his bed, and there was conflicting evidence as to whether it was locked or not.

8.30-9.30 pm S's brother and friend had been sitting with him and they were told to leave several times between 8.30 and 9.30 pm, despite their request to stay and prevent him getting out of bed.

1 am	He was restless and tossing. Side rails put on bed, sodium luminal imi given.
2.30 am	S was more restless, temp 105.8F, irrational. Ankle and wrist restraints and canvas sheet to prevent his getting out of bed. This required two "strong" orderlies and took half an hour. Ten minute visual checks through glass door panel.
3.20 am	He was apparently sleeping.
3.45 am	S was out of bed, "sitting there looking out in the hall". Assistance called, but by the time it arrived he had fallen out the window.

[6.275] When his relatives sued the hospital for negligently causing his death, the Court looked at whether the staff had been unreasonable in not taking more precautions against harm which they could foresee (at least in general terms). It concluded that the failure to secure the window and to keep a closer watch on the patient in view of his earlier violence was a breach of the nurses' duty of care to the patient. The care fell below the standard of care which a reasonable nurse would give.

Under the common law, although courts consider evidence from experts as to what is considered reasonable care, courts do not blindly follow what is the current practice. In *Albrighton v Royal Prince Alfred Hospital* [1979] 2 NSWLR 165 Reynolds J said that this would be:

"plainly wrong, because it is not the law that, if all or most of the medical practitioners in Sydney habitually fail to take an available precaution ... then none can be found guilty of negligence."

Courts thus reserved to themselves the right to determine that although the actions of a defendant might have been consistent with current practice within the profession, current practice may be unreasonable. This would include such practice as never questioning the instructions of a senior professional, or doing things the way he or she prefers, when probable harm is clearly foreseeable. Courts will, however, accept that some degree of experimentation is desirable in medicine (see discussion of *Roe v Minister of Health* below at **[6.295]**). Also, where there is a difference of professional opinion:

"a judge's 'preference' for one body of distinguished professional opinion to another also professionally distinguished is not sufficient to establish negligence in a practitioner whose actions have received the seal of approval of those whose opinions, truthfully expressed, honestly held, were not preferred" [*Maynard v West Midlands Regional Health Authority* [1984] 1 WLR 634].

In the case of *Bolam v Friern Hospital Management Committee* [1957] 1 WLR 582 McNair J said at 586: "there may be one or more perfectly proper standards [of care] and if [a doctor] conforms with one of those proper standards, then he is not negligent". There thus may be several acceptable standards of care, based on the views of experienced practitioners. As long as a method of care is accepted as reasonable by health carers who are experienced and recognised as well qualified in the profession, although some (even a majority) might personally prefer another method, it could be acceptable at law. This became known as the "*Bolam* test".

The tension between the courts power and what became known as the *Bolam* test was the subject of attention in the *Review of the Law of Negligence* and led to the introduction of what might be called the "modified *Bolam* test" in s 50 of the *Civil Liability Act 2002* (NSW) (see **[6.260]**). That is, a Court applying s 50 cannot find there has been a breach of the standard of care if the defendant medical practitioner was acting in a fashion *widely accepted* in *Australia* by *peer* professional opinion as *competent* professional practice. However the Court is left with power to find there has been a breach of the standard of care in the perhaps rare circumstance where a practice widely accepted in Australia by peer professional opinion as competent professional practice is nonetheless *irrational*. The term *irrational* is not defined in the *Civil Liability Act 2002* (NSW), but some interpretative guidance can be obtained from the commentary in the *Review of the Law of Negligence* at paras 3.17–3.20 and by reference to the decision in *Bolitho v City and Hackney Health Authority* [1998] AC 232.

It is debateable as to whether the statutory definition of the standard of care provided by *Civil Liability Act 2002* (NSW), s 50 differs from the approach taken by the Australian courts under the common law. If it does differ, the differences will not be apparent in the great majority of medical negligence cases. What is good health care, or competent professional practice, is often open to debate. One of the reasons for drawn-out and expensive court cases is the scope for argument as to what actually occurred in a particular situation and whether a particular activity was reasonable or not. When considering the reasonableness of an action, the court will take into account, among other things, the following factors.

Circumstances surrounding an event

[6.280] Those attending an emergency which occurs on a road or in a rehabilitation centre or small regional health care centre, for example, where experience, equipment and preparation are not geared for this, would not be expected to react with the same efficiency as those, say, in an accident and emergency or intensive care ward. Where staff are trained and prepared for emergencies, a higher standard of care is required. Where this is not the case, carers should at least be able to identify an emergency, and know how to get help in the area where they work. Industrial nurses, for example, should be prepared for reasonably foreseeable accidents, and have a plan of action prepared.

Health carers may in some cases be justified in carrying out procedures for which they are not trained, or which are normally only carried out by those with different or more specialised education, in emergencies, but if they do, they must act reasonably under the circumstances: they must not be wanton in their rescue attempts (see *Wagner's* case at **[6.180]**). Conversely, health carers must, where appropriate, refer on cases outside their field of competence.

It would seem, from the case law, that four main principles should be followed in relation to emergency treatment:

- health carers should be able to identify potential emergency situations and symptoms indicating the need for emergency care, and be familiar with appropriate procedures for dealing with them (such as services or people to contact). That is, they should continually ask themselves "what if...?" and know when to call for help;
- health carers should be familiar with appropriate procedures to be followed in reasonably foreseeable emergencies. Equipment should be checked and in readiness, and procedures rehearsed;
- records should be kept as carefully as is possible under the circumstances. This may involve some unorthodox measures (for example, recording the administration of drugs or application of tourniquet, on a patient's forehead when patients are evacuated to the hospital grounds during an earthquake);
- management have a responsibility to ensure that proper procedures for emergencies are developed and in place, that equipment is in readiness and staff are properly advised and trained. Health carers in industry and other non-hospital settings may need to educate management on the need to do this.

Statutory law

[6.285] Breach of statutory provisions is a *prima facie* (but not absolute), indication of unreasonable (and therefore negligent) practice. The most obvious example would be the statutory provisions for the administration of drugs (see Chapter 13). These are intended, among other things, to protect patients from harm (for example, provisions for the checking of, and signing for, those drugs which are given). In these provisions the legislation is setting out a general standard of reasonable practice. It is conceivable that breach of legislative provisions may not be negligent behaviour (for example, in an emergency or extraordinary situation) (see **[6.490]**ff), so other factors listed here may also be taken into account.

Procedure manuals, departmental directives, health and safety policies, protocols etc

[6.290] Courts will also consider these as evidence of recognised reasonable practice for those in the health care profession. Staff are expected to be aware of hospital procedure manuals, etc, and employers should make them available. In dispensing reasonable care, it is expected that staff would follow such advice, although there may be exceptional circumstances. Evidence that a carer acted contrary to the hospital procedure manual in carrying out post-operative care, for example, would be *prima facie* evidence of negligence, and would place a heavy burden on her or him to convince a court that the circumstances justified the deviation from established procedure.

General knowledge and practice of the profession

[6.295] Case: *Roe v Minister of Health* [1954] 2 QB 66 (CA England)

An anaesthetist adopted a practice, recently developed at that time (1947), which was intended to prevent the danger of infection when administering spinal anaesthesia. This practice was to soak ampoules of the anaesthesia in phenol, thereby rendering them sterile for use. On the day in question, he used two of these ampoules to provide two patients with spinal anaesthesia for knee surgery. Both men subsequently became paraplegic as a result of corrosion of the spinal cord from leaking of minute amounts of the antiseptic into the apparently intact ampoules which contaminated the drug. No one had been aware of the possibility of this happening.

[6.300] The Court found that no one in the doctor's position could have known of the possibility of the seepage, although of course by the time of the trial it was well and truly known. The Court held that the state of knowledge of those involved at the time of the event is what is considered by law and therefore the anaesthetist had not been negligent.

[6.305] Case: *Lowns & Anor v Woods & Anor* [1996] Aust Torts Reports ¶81-376 (CA NSW)

Some of the facts of this case are outlined above (see **[6.160]**). A second action in negligence relating to the unfortunate outcome of P's fit was brought on his behalf against the specialist (Dr P), who was his treating doctor at the time. The action against Dr P was based on his failure to advise P's parents about the administration of rectal valium to stop or ameliorate the effect of his fitting. Dr P gave evidence that there were questions about the safety and effectiveness of administering rectal valium at the time, and that only in a limited number of cases would he advise family to use it, one of these being where there was poor control of seizures by medication and the child was more than an hour away from medical care. Expert evidence overwhelmingly supported his decision not to advise its use for P. The trial judge, however, determined that it was reasonable to foresee that P could suffer *status epilepticus*, and that this could occur when he was more than an hour away from medical assistance. Given the relative risks of brain damage without the administration of valium and the effect on the respiratory system of administering it, the reasonable response would have been to have advised the parents in its administration. Dr P was thus found negligent. He appealed to the New South Wales Court of Appeal, which heard the case along with the action against Dr L.

[6.310] The New South Wales Court of Appeal upheld Dr P's appeal. The Court reviewed the evidence before the trial judge and determined that he had not taken enough notice of some of the reasons for the practice of not advising parents about rectal valium in cases such as P's. These included the absence anywhere in the world of such a practice, the risks of respiratory depression involved, the absence of such a practice in authoritative textbooks and publications, and the fact that valium was not licensed or produced in a form for rectal use in Australia.

On the issue of accepting the evidence of medical practice, Mahoney JA said that judges can substitute their own view of what a medical risk involves for that of a treating doctor, as set out in *Rogers v Whitaker* (see **[4.295]**). But he went on to say that:

> "the courts should be slow to intervene where what is involved is the weighing up of advantages and disadvantages, medical necessities and the like by the profession."

[6.315] Case: *John Edwin Caley v Northern Regional Health Board* [1997] Aust Torts Reports ¶81-429 (SC Tas)

C died two weeks after giving birth to her third child, suffering from a pulmonary embolism by a clot of blood formed elsewhere in the body. It was argued that an embolus had developed post-partum and that the respondent hospital was in breach of the duty of care it owed her in failing to take appropriate steps to avoid the risk that in fact eventuated.

The particulars of that breach were that the hospital:

* Failed to examine C sufficiently, competently or at all.
* Failed to take heed of the swelling in her right foot.
* Discharged her without any or any adequate discharge plan.
* Discharged her without advice as to what she should do if the swelling in the right foot persisted.
* Failed to warn her that a blood clot could develop which could be fatal.

The jury found for the respondent. The plaintiff appealed this finding. It was not disputed that the respondent owed C a duty of care, but that the trial judge erred in law in failing to put adequate directions to the jury in relation to determining whether the hospital breached that duty of care.

[6.320] The Appeal Court stated that, in relation to deciding whether the hospital's duty of care had been breached, that the jury had to be satisfied on the balance of probabilities that:

1) a reasonable hospital authority in the position of the respondent would have foreseen the risk of an embolism developing in the sense that such an "injury" or condition was not far fetched or fanciful; and
2) the respondent failed to do that which a reasonable hospital authority would have done in the circumstances to avoid that injury; and
3) the failure caused death.

The Court held that Step 1 was not an issue, as it was accepted by both parties that the risk of embolism was not "far-fetched or fanciful". However, in relation to Step 2, the Court said that the jury must be told that they should consider from the point of view of the reasonable hospital, "the magnitude of the risk and the degree of the probability of its occurrence, along with the expense, difficulty and inconvenience of taking alleviating action and any other conflicting responsibilities which the defendant may have" (*Wyong Shire Council v Shirt* (1980) 146 CLR 40; [1980] HCA 12 per Mason J).

In short, the jury had to consider not only whether the likelihood of risk was reasonably foreseeable, but also whether those responsible reasonably weighed:

- the likelihood of the risk becoming a reality;
- its probable effects; and
- other responsibilities they might have,

with the practicality of measures to avoid that foreseeable risk.

These elements are now reflected and expanded in the *Civil Liability Act 2002* (NSW) at s 5B, which provides:

"(1) A person is not negligent in failing to take precautions against a risk of harm unless:
  (a) the risk was foreseeable (that is, it is a risk of which the person knew or ought to have known), and
  (b) the risk was not insignificant, and
  (c) in the circumstances, a reasonable person in the person's position would have taken those precautions.
(2) In determining whether a reasonable person would have taken precautions against a risk of harm, the court is to consider the following (amongst other relevant things):
  (a) the probability that the harm would occur if care were not taken,
  (b) the likely seriousness of the harm,
  (c) the burden of taking precautions to avoid the risk of harm,
  (d) the social utility of the activity that creates the risk of harm."

Anticipating a patient's actions

[6.325] Case: *Wendover v State*, 313 NYS 2d 287 (1970)
(CA New York United States)

An obese, mentally deficient epileptic patient was admitted for her second stay as a result of a suicide attempt. She was in a private room, but under close supervision. Despite this, and the fact that she was extremely restless, repeatedly letting down the side rails, she managed to move the bed next to a radiator without staff's knowledge. As a result she was badly burned when she had an epileptic fit.

[6.330] In this case the Court was satisfied that the nurses could not have foreseen the patient moving her bed, and that there was no way the hospital could have prevented the accident. The Court would have considered the patient's past behaviour, her mental state, her medical condition, and the general nursing experience in this area, to evaluate the reasonableness of the nurses not keeping an even closer watch on her. Readers might like to compare this case with that of *Spivey* (see **[6.270]**). Part of legal reasoning is to analyse two similar cases, as these are, and attempt to determine some principle which will reconcile the different outcomes.

Different practices accepted within the profession

[6.335] Where there are different accepted practices within the profession, it is recognised by law that a reasonable practitioner may follow any one of them without attracting liability in negligence. As long as there is a responsible body of practitioners subscribing to the method used by the defendant in a case, and the method is applied according to that body of thought, then, despite the fact that some practitioners would not act in that way, it is open to the court to find the defendant not liable (as noted above at **[6.265]** and **[6.275]**, this principle is now reflected in the *Civil Liability Act 2002* (NSW) at s 50; see also *Bolam's* case **[6.275]**).

Departure from recognised practice may, as already stated, be indicative of negligence, although not necessarily so. In the case of *Hunter v Hanley* [1955] SC 200 it was expressed by Lord Clyde (at 206) that three things must be established to show negligence when the defendant has departed from recognised practice:

- there must be an established and usual practice;
- the defendant departed from that practice; and
- no reasonable practitioner would have departed from the practice if he or she had been acting with ordinary care.

[6.340] Case: *Chasney v Anderson* [1950] 4 DLR 223 (SC Canada)

A surgeon carrying out a tonsillectomy followed common practice in that hospital by not using sponges with tapes attached to them or having nursing staff carry out a sponge count. Sponges with tapes attached were available, as were nursing staff to carry out the count. The child suffocated to death because a sponge was left in situ. The issue was whether the hospital was negligent, and whether the doctor, by following the usual practice there, was also negligent.

[6.345] The Court held that the hospital was not negligent because it provided the means for reasonable precautions, while the surgeon was (but the employer is liable for knowingly allowing employees to act dangerously: see vicarious liability, **[6.765]**). He had departed from a recognised and available practice for no good reason, despite expert evidence that the practice he adopted was a general and approved one at the time. Where the defendant practitioner pleads common practice, the court will take evidence of this into account as prima facie pointing to reasonable practice, but maintains the right to rule that such practice was, at least in the situation being considered, negligent (see also *Sidaway v Governors of the Bethlem Royal Hospital* [1985] 1 All ER 643, discussed at **[4.150]**).

Other limiting factors

[6.350] The condition of the patient may cause one to act in ways which might otherwise be hazardous.

[6.355] Case: *Mahon v Osborne* [1939] 2 KB 14 (CA England)

A surgeon operated on a young man with a burst appendix under difficult circumstances: the patient was having respiratory difficulty, it was 4 am, and there was not the usual number of staff available. After carrying out the surgery, it was revealed that respiratory difficulty was increasing, and the surgeon decided to "close up" as quickly as possible. Before doing so he did, however ask the nurses whether the swab count was correct, they checked and told him it was. The patient was returned to the ward in a satisfactory condition but some days later became very ill as the result of a pack which had been left inside him. After emergency surgery to remove it he died. His family sued the surgeon and nurses in negligence (in those days a hospital was held to be not responsible for the actions of staff during surgery).

[6.360] The plaintiffs argued that, among other things, the nurses were negligent in their counting of the packs and swabs, and that the doctor was also negligent in this, as well as being the person responsible for the overall conduct of the surgery. The trial court found the doctor negligent (there is no explanation as to why the nurses were not) and he appealed, arguing, among other things, that the circumstances of the surgery as explained should have been taken into account in the trial, and that they had not. The appeal court agreed, stating that the difficult circumstances of the surgery may well have prevented the surgeon acting in what otherwise would have been a reasonable fashion, and remitted the case for retrial.

Probability of harm

[6.365] The same statements apply here as were made above at [6.60] regarding the foreseeability of harm. Here we are talking about harm that is foreseeable as likely to happen, but now looking at the question of how likely it is to happen (see *Bolton v Stone* at [6.70]). A 70 per cent chance of side effects may warrant more substantial precautions than a 10 or 15 per cent chance. This consideration is closely bound up with the following factors.

Person suffering from specific disability

[6.370] A person will be held liable for harm which occurred because the victim had a specific disability, of which the person was, or ought to have been, aware. The standard of care will depend on the facts of the situation. The following case may assist in explaining this.

[6.375] Case: *Haley v London Electricity Board* [1965] AC 778 (House of Lords England)

The plaintiff had been blind for many years. He conquered his disability to such an extent that he was employed by the London County Council. He routinely walked a short distance along the footpath, using a white stick to avoid obstacles, to a spot where he asked someone to assist him to cross the road to where he caught a bus to work. On the morning of the accident Electricity Board workmen had dug a trench in the footpath. To prevent harm to pedestrians they placed a punner, which was a stick attached to a weight, across the footpath. The punner was attached to a railing on the inside of the footpath, so it sloped across the footpath from ground level to a height of about two feet. This was not the normal type of barricade used by the Board. The walking stick used by the plaintiff to guide him did not detect the punner, and he tripped over it. As a result of his injuries he became deaf. He sued the Electricity Board in negligence.

[6.380] The House of Lords held that the Board should have foreseen that some people using the footpath could be visually impaired. The Board gave evidence that it did cater for blind people in the type of barricade normally used. The Court said that it could accept that the Board would not have to take extra precautions if it could not foresee that blind people would be using the footpath at that time, or that the probability was so remote the Board would be

justified in not taking extra precautions. In this case, however, these considerations did not exist, and the Board should have foreseen the possibility, and so
was liable. Consideration of the inability or disability of those who are immature
or feeble in mind or body is owed by those who know of, or ought to anticipate,
the presence of such persons within the scope of their own operations.

Those who deal with a section of the population which has a higher than
average number of those with a disability need to be particularly conscious of
anticipating their special needs. Where there is no clear indication of a person's
disability, however, one is not expected to foresee it.

Magnitude of harm

[6.385] If a danger is remote but potentially catastrophic if it occurs, more
care should be taken than if it were just as remote but not so serious (see *Bolton
v Stone* at **[6.70]**; *The Wagon Mound,* above at **[6.65]**). An example given by
the courts is that of a car approaching a hill on a little used country road. If the
car behind it overtakes while approaching the crest of the hill (the driver being
unable to see any approaching car), it may have only a remote chance of
meeting another car, but if it does the results could be disastrous. The driver's
decision not to overtake in this situation, would depend more on the magnitude
of the harm that would occur if he or she met an oncoming car than on the
(remote) likelihood of doing so. This has been expressed in the maxim that the
greater the magnitude of the foreseeable harm, the less the probability of its
occurring is required before preventative measures are taken. This principle has
now been reflected in the *Civil Liability Act 2002* (NSW), s 5B(2)(b).

Social utility of the activity

[6.390] A dangerous action but one necessary to bring about more good than
foreseeable harm may be accepted by the court. This is based on a similar
principle to that of necessity (see **[4.240]**). This principle has now been
reflected in the *Civil Liability Act 2002* (NSW), s 5B(2)(d).

[6.395] Case: *Daborn v Bath Tramways Motor Co Ltd*
[1946] 2 All ER 333 (CA England)

During the Second World War, when London was being bombed,
all ambulances which could be found were pressed into service as
they were needed to attend to the injured. Several old left-hand-
drive vehicles were used, and because of difficulties in seeing the
signalling driver, a bus collided with one of them, causing injury.

[6.400] The Court held that the plaintiff, the ambulance driver, was not guilty
of contributory negligence as the special need for ambulances outweighed the
need to have better equipped vehicles on the road. This defence would most
likely only arise where there is some disaster or catastrophe (for example, the

landslide at Thredbo where people were submerged in the rubble, rescue operations and emergency care may pose some risks to third parties).

Some Special Situations

Learners and the inexperienced

[6.405] Generally, the law will give no special consideration to beginners and learners. The beginner who takes on a particular health care role is just as responsible for providing a reasonable standard of care as are those who are more experienced in that role. Thus, a person taking on the role of a senior health professional should act as a reasonable senior health professional, a junior as a reasonable junior, and so on. Health care facilities, or those supervising students, are expected to provide an adequate standard of care to patients to prevent harm from negligence, and this involves adequate supervision and training of students. The student is also responsible for ensuring that he or she does not undertake care for which he or she is not prepared.

[6.410] Case: *Collins v Hertfordshire County Council*
[1947] KB 598 (High Court England)

A final year medical student was employed as a resident junior house surgeon despite not being so qualified, because of the demands of wartime. She was asked by the surgeon in charge by telephone to obtain procaine 1 per cent from the hospital pharmacy. She mistook the order to be for *cocaine* 1 per cent and ordered cocaine orally from the pharmacy. It was given to the patient, who died.

[6.415] The Court's finding in this case was in contrast to that of *Daborn* **[6.395]** in two apparent respects. In this case, it was held that the junior had opportunities to consider and correct her mistake, and that she should be held to the standard of a junior house surgeon, as that was the position the institution placed her in (although she was not so qualified). This is in accord with the legal principle that if one holds oneself out to have a certain level of skill, or holds a particular position requiring it, or claims that staff are adequately trained to provide that level of skill, one must operate as a reasonable person of the class of practitioners at that level. A medical officer would have known (and in fact the student did) what a lethal dose of cocaine was, and should have followed more stringent measures in executing the surgeon's orders.

[6.420] Case: *Wilsher v Essex Area Health Authority*
[1988] 1 All ER 871 (House of Lords England)

A neonate suffered almost total blindness after intensive care. He
had been born prematurely, and suffered from several serious
illnesses, one of which was oxygen deficiency. There was a low
probability that he would survive. During his treatment in the
neonatal intensive care ward, a catheter was inserted into a vein
rather than an artery by an inexperienced junior doctor. A
registrar was asked to check this, failed to notice the mistake and
made the same mistake himself several hours later. The neonate
was given excess amounts of oxygen and suffered from near
blindness, and, through his representatives, sued the hospital in
negligence. There were two issues involved in this case, one was
the standard of care owed to the child, the other was whether the
doctor's actions actually caused the harm. The latter issue known
as "causation" is discussed below (see **[6.690]**). The lower court
found that the standard of care owed by the doctors was only that
reasonably required of doctors having the same formal qualifications and experience as those involved, and so there had been no
breach of the standard of care. The plaintiff appealed and the case
finally went to the House of Lords.

[6.425] The House of Lords considered three possible standards of care:

1) a "team" standard, that is, that each of the members of a unit held
   themselves out to be able to offer the specialised procedures the unit set out
   to perform;
2) a standard of care that can actually be offered by an individual, based on his
   or her personal experience and qualifications; and
3) a standard of care based not on the individual, but the *post* that he or she
   occupies.

The "team" standard was rejected, as it would mean that, for example an intern
or student nurse would be required to possess the skill and experience of a
consultant medical specialist. The standard of care based on the individual was
rejected as being tailored to the actor, and not the action, and to tie the
patient's right to complain to the chance skill of the person who happens at
the time to be caring for him or her, rather than the standard of care given
by the hospital. It was held to have no place in tort law.

The third standard was accepted as the correct standard. The Court rejected
the view that the standard of care to meet is what a reasonable person of the
carer's qualifications and experience would do. Rather that of the ordinary
person exercising and professing a special skill, is the correct test, and thus, as
Lord Glidewell put it:

"the law requires the trainee or learner to be judged by the same standard as
his more experienced colleagues. If it did not, inexperience would frequently
be urged as a defence to an action for professional negligence."

It thus may be that an employer will be found negligent for requiring or allowing a person to practice at a level at which he or she is manifestly not adequately trained or competent. Where the desired level of skill cannot be offered, this should be made quite clear to patients, so that they can determine if they want to assume some of the risk of harm or go elsewhere. (See *Tzaidas v Child & 3 Ors* (2004) 208 ALR 651; NSWCA 252, which considered in part whether the hospital, though a community hospital, was equipped to deal with anticipatable consequences of a mother being carrier of haemophilia B.) Otherwise, patients can expect a reasonable standard of professional care, with adequately trained staff, proper allocation of resources and responsibilities, and supervision of care. This is a part of the function of an employer offering services to the public. This issue is considered more fully below at **[6.765]**, as part of vicarious liability, and at **[6.770]**, as part of non-delegable duty. The following case considered the liability of a hospital for the inadequate staffing of an ICU.

[6.430] Case: *Sherry v Australasian Conference Association (trading as Sydney Adventist Hospital) & Ors* [2006] NSWSC 75

S had been admitted to SAH for heart surgery known as minimally invasive direct coronary arterial bypass (MIDCAB) in which heart surgery is performed through a small surgical incision in the chest wall (thoracotomy). Postoperatively S was transferred to SAH ICU and came under the care of the intensivist and career medical officer. Late the following day S suffered an increase in chest pain arising from what was later determined to be haemothorax, a collection of blood in the pleural cavity. Before drains could be inserted S suffered cardiac arrest and died despite resuscitation attempts. The direct cause of death was later established by a pathologist's report for the Coroner as massive intrathoracic haemorrhage.

[6.435] The case against SAH (brought by S's wife and family) was put in two ways. First, it was said in the usual way that nursing and other staff acted negligently, or negligently omitted to act, and SAH was vicariously liable (see **[6.765]**). Secondly, it was put that SAH was directly liable because it failed to provide the ICU with adequate staffing levels in that the medical "cover" afforded to the ICU was inadequate. On that second issue there was argument as to certain Guidelines which identified different grades of ICU. The Court held that the Guidelines relevant to a Level 3 ICU were applicable. But, even if the ICU were to be classified as a Level 2 facility, both the Minimum Standards and the Guidelines suggested that the ICU ought to have had dedicated medical coverage. The Court observed that whist standards are not absolute they do give guidance in the assessment of what is a reasonable level of medical cover. Whilst departure from the Minimum Standards or Guidelines did not necessarily entail a conclusion that the standard of care provided was inadequate, that conclusion could not be escaped merely on the basis of evidence led by the defendants that other hospitals operated at a standard the same as or similar to that of SAH.

Failure to provide proper and adequate information can be the basis of a negligence action at law. This is dealt with in Chapter 4 as part of the consideration of consent.

However, such failure may in some circumstances be relevant after the event.

[6.440] Case: *Wighton v Arnot* [2005] NSWSC 637

W developed a lump on the right side of her neck and was referred to A for surgical excision. W alleged that during surgery A severed the right spinal accessory nerve; that was not disputed and was a recognised risk of the procedure. However, the Court held that A was negligent in failing to carry out sufficient post-operative testing to determine whether the nerve had been severed, failing to advise W prior to her discharge from hospital of the suspected severance and failing to advise W of the need for surgical repair of the nerve. The Court stated [at 38]:

> "What the exercise of due care required of the defendant was that he take reasonable steps to determine whether it was the accessory nerve which had been severed, and that he alert the plaintiff as to what had occurred."

What if a person disagrees with instructions?

[6.445] The duty of care owed to patients by health carers includes the obligation to question the directions of those superior to them which they reasonably believe are likely to result in harm to a patient. The unusual medication order, for example, should be checked with the medical officer concerned (see Chapter 13). Health carers should not adopt the attitude that they are "only carrying out orders", but should use their knowledge and experience in rendering reasonable care to those who depend on them. This requires that they discuss any direction about which they are concerned with the person giving it. If they are not comfortable with the result, the matter should be taken further.

[6.450] Case: *Darling v Charlston Community Memorial Hospital*, 211 NE 2d 253 (1965) (SC Illinois United States)

D was a young man who broke his leg while playing football. He had a comminuted fracture of the right tibia and fibula. The attendant surgeon at the well-equipped and staffed hospital brought the bones into proper alignment and applied a plaster cast without underlying stockinette or padding. D was admitted to a ward of the hospital, where, over a two-week period, the leg deteriorated, until his family moved him to another hospital where the leg had to be amputated due to infection. The family sued the hospital and treating surgeon in negligence.

Nurses' notes contained repeated notations of increasingly oedematous, darkening and insensitive toes, and of increasing pain and ineffectiveness of the analgesia which was ordered. The surgeon visited D frequently at the request of the nurses, but did not call an orthopaedic specialist because, in his opinion, the situation was satisfactory. He cut back the plaster cast and removed a section of it to relieve pressure, but inadvertently cut D's skin exacerbating the development of infection.

The doctor admitted liability and settled out of court, so the case proceeded against the hospital. The jury found the hospital liable, because of the lack of action on the part of the nurses. The hospital appealed, stating that it was not liable for the nurses' conduct because they were under the instructions of the doctor.

[6.455] The appeal court dismissed the appeal. It held that the duty of care of nurses extends further than bringing to the attention of the responsible doctor the deteriorating condition of a patient, and so broke new ground. The duty of care of nurses, the court held, includes informing the hospital administration of any departure from normal or proper care that puts a patient's life or health in danger. The nurses could not say simply: "Well, we told the doctor and reported all unusual developments, we could not do any more.'" The Court disagreed. As well as some neglect in their observations and reporting, it held, they were negligent in not taking the matter further, until they got satisfaction on behalf of D by reporting it to the next appropriate person on the hospital staff who could take action, and so on up the line of authority. When the nurses were aware that there was a dangerous impairment to the circulation in D's leg, which would become irreversible in a matter of hours, it became the nurses' duty to inform the attending physician, and if he failed to act, to advise the hospital authorities so that appropriate action might be taken (at 258).

Whistleblowers

[6.460] Unfortunately, nurses have often been considered the servants of the medical profession, and where they have questioned it they have been considered to have stepped outside of their role and warranted dismissal, or subjection to harassment and even assault. Johnstone ((1994), Ch 6) gives a detailed study of cases in which nurses have questioned the medical treatment of their patients. This is dealt with further in Chapter 10. Over time, parliaments have recognised the benefits of statutory protections, not limited to nurses or health care professionals, for whistleblowers who have knowledge about conduct or practices within public sector organisations which warrant public scrutiny. Kerridge (2005, pp 171-172) summarises the basic protection of whistleblower legislation as being to protect the whistleblower, who in good faith and in the public interest discloses information, so as to ensure that the person to whom the disclosure is made takes appropriate action, and to facilitate the making of such disclosures. The approaches adopted throughout Australia are different. The Northern Territory, at the time of writing, has not enacted legislation, but has issued a *Public Interest Disclosure Bill 2005* (Draft). Relevant legislation elsewhere is as follows: *Protected Disclosures Act 1994* (NSW), *Whistleblowers Protection Act 2001* (Vic), *Whistleblowers Protection Act 1994* (Qld), *Whistleblowers Protection Act 1993* (SA), *Public Interest Disclosure Act 2003* (WA) and *Public Interest Disclosure Act 1994* (ACT).

The checklist below lists recommended steps, according to legal and ethical principles, for questioning either instructions that have been given, or a particular situation, such as a problem with staffing or resources. It is recognised that health carers may be unwilling to follow them because of the possibility of reprisals by those who could make their working life difficult. Crispin Hull points out, for example, that in relation to the activities at Sydney's Chelmsford Hospital in the 1960s and 1970s, where deep-sleep therapy was used and many patients died, resulting in a Royal Commission:

> "Chelmsford nurses complained to authorities in the early 1970s. They and relatives of victims were threatened with defamation proceedings if they spoke out." (Hull, C, "Justice hides behind the law", *Canberra Times*, 2 April 1994, p C3.)

It is recognised that the checklist provides a guide as to the conventional approach to questioning instructions. The law is likely to become more demanding of health carers who are increasingly being recognised as professionals, although in the absence of a definition in the *Civil Liability Act 2002* (NSW) for professionals, the application of s 50 to any particular group must await clarification by the Courts. This developing recognition will hopefully lead to more mutual support of management and staff in asserting the right to question instructions which cause concern. Increasingly, at least in institutional settings, risk management systems and root cause analysis processes welcome reports by all health carers which highlight process errors as a means of reducing the chance of their recurrence.

 Checklist
PRINCIPLES FOR ACTION WHEN A SITUATION CAUSES CONCERN
(This applies to such matters as a treatment order, short staffing, inadequate resources, faulty equipment etc. It may also involve a patient demanding care under circumstances which would prevent reasonable care.)
✓ Discussion of the matter is most important in resolving such situations. First, attempts should be made to discuss it with those directly involved, or responsible for the situation. Only then, and if

the matter is serious enough, should one take it further, to management or, if not in a health facility, a relevant authority. This is an important procedure legally: it establishes concern at the standard of care on the part of the health carer, preserves confidentiality, and demonstrates his or her intention to remedy the situation.
✓ Care to the patient is a central concern (for example, emergency, surgery, dependent patient), and he or she should not be abandoned. Carers should consider continuing necessary care, with action to remedy the situation (or prevent an adverse situation arising) at the first opportunity.
✓ Employee health carers are required to follow reasonable and lawful instructions of the employer (see Chapter 10), they are also required to:
  - exercise a duty of care towards their patients; and
  - further the employer's operation, including its activities as a health care facility, or if in another area of enterprise, its legitimate activities (including employment and welfare of workers).
Thus if health carers feel that failure to act will endanger the health or wellbeing of a patient or colleagues, or is contrary to the good operation of the employer's activities, this is a matter for management, as it is ultimately responsible for the standard of care given to patients, and/or the proper operation of its activities.
✓ A record should be kept of the event, and action taken, for example, in the patient's notes, an incident report to management (see Chapter her behaviour, failure to co-operate, or demand for particular treatment, requiring the health carer to refuse to continue the relationship under those circumstances). Good contemporaneous notes may counteract a claim of negligence against the health carer, especially where he or she has continued to work under the circumstances complained of in the interests of the patient's welfare. Records can become lost or destroyed: it may be that independent records should be made and kept in secure circumstances.

One example of dealing with an unsatisfactory situation is where, in a busy ward, more nurses are considered necessary to give adequate care to patients. Request by the charge nurse for more staff is met by the response that this is not possible. The charge nurse may make a note of this through an incident report, as well as in patients' notes.

The following case involved a surgeon who did not consider himself competent in a particular specialty.

[6.465] Case: *Luck v Blamey & Associates* [2000]
VSC 77, 3 March 2000

A woman was referred to a general surgeon for treatment. After biopsies were performed, she was diagnosed as suffering from scleroderma. The surgeon wrote to the woman stating that, as he was not a specialist dermatologist, from whom she would require treatment, he did not wish to continue treating her. She sought an interlocutory injunction from the court compelling the surgeon to treat her, which was denied.

[6.470] The Court held that the doctor was entitled to refuse to carry out treatment which he considered was beyond his specialty. This case also involved the issue of specific performance of a contract for personal services (see Chapter 9).

Emergency care

[6.475] There is no specific statute which comprehensively sets out the role and duties of health carers or hospitals in relation to emergency treatment. This is subject to the common law principles set down by the courts, with some statutory overlays. There are some specific laws about drugs (see Chapter 13). Under the *Civil Liability Act 2002* (NSW), there are 'Good Samaritan' provisions as referred to above **[6.165]** however they relate to persons who act without expectation of payment or other reward, not to paid employees providing emergency care.

Emergency workers: Ambulance, rescue etc

[6.480] Emergency workers are under the same duty of care as other health carers. A duty of care could be said to arise wherever it becomes known to emergency workers that there is a need for services. Limited statutory provisions exist—for example, the *Health Services Act 1997* (NSW) provides at s 67I that a member of staff of the Ambulance Service of New South Wales or an honorary ambulance officer is not liable for any injury or damage caused by the member of staff or officer in the carrying out, in good faith, of any of the employees or officers duties relating to the provision of ambulance services, or the protection of persons from injury or death, whether or not those persons are or were sick or injured. The immunity applies to the individual officer, not to the Ambulance Service itself. (See **[6.505]** below.)

[6.485] Case: *Kent v Griffiths and Ors* [2000] EWCA 16 (3 February 2000)

K, an asthmatic, suffered an attack and was attended by her doctor. At 4.25 pm the doctor telephoned the London Ambulance Service (LAS) and asked for an ambulance to take her to casualty "immediately". Despite several further calls, the ambulance did not arrive for 35 minutes, which was held not to have been a reasonable time to travel the necessary 6.5 miles. In the process K suffered respiratory arrest. K sued several parties, one of the issues being breach of duty of care by the LAS. The trial judge found the LAS liable, but gave them permission to appeal the question as to whether there was a duty of care owed to the plaintiff by the LAS as it was a novel one. Earlier cases had held that the fire brigade and the police do not have a duty of care to individuals who seek their assistance, as their duty is to the community as a whole, and specific activity is discretionary, based on the wider duty (see, for example, *Capital & Counties Plc v Hampshire County Council* [1997] QB 1004 which held that a fire brigade did not have a duty of care to answer calls to fires or take reasonable care to do so; *Alexandrou v Oxford* [1993] 2 All ER 328 as to police when responding to an emergency call, and *OLL Ltd v Secretary of State for Transport* [1997] 3 All ER 897 in relation to coastguards when making a rescue at sea). The LAS thus argued that they did not have a duty of care to the plaintiff, and were therefore not liable.

[6.490] The Court of Appeal, in a case that drew heavily on public policy, held that the acceptance of the emergency call created the duty of care. It found a distinction between the services provided by the abovementioned services and the ambulance service. They owe a duty to the public at large, and responses to individual cases are subject to discretion in the operation of that overall responsibility. By contrast, once a call to the ambulance service has been accepted, the service is dealing with a named individual upon whom the duty becomes focused. Furthermore, once the call has been made and the ambulance service agrees to transport the patient, those caring for him or her are likely to refrain from further attempts to get the person to hospital. This was not a general reliance but a specific one, and it is foreseeable that a specific person would suffer if there were a delay. The Court stated ambulance transport was really an extension of the services offered by doctors and nurses at the hospital. The ambulance was an extension of the means provided by the public purse by which the plaintiff was to be treated by the hospital.

The Court went on to say that the requirements of proximity were fulfilled. Further, there were no circumstances which made it unfair or unreasonable or unjust that liability should exist. It finally pointed to its belief that the public would be greatly disturbed if they held that there was not a duty of care in this case.

[6.495] Case: *American National Bank & Trust Company, Special Administrator of the Estate of Renee Kazmierowski, v City of Chicago* (Cook County Circuit Court) (10 August 2000)

The administrator of the estate of a deceased person brought an action in negligence against the City of Chicago and two paramedics. After a call had been received from the deceased, who stated she was suffering an asthma attack and gave her address, the paramedics went to her apartment. There was no response to their knocking on the door, nor could a firefighter (also called), get a response at the back door. There was no sign of anyone being at the apartment, and after checking that they had the right address, the paramedics decided they were not needed and left. Later, in a response to another call, they returned and were let into the apartment where they found the person lying dead on the floor. The action cited negligence and wilful misconduct on the part of the paramedics in failing to enter the apartment (it was claimed the door was unlocked), and the operator in failing to keep the decedent on the phone while the paramedics responded. The question arose as to whether there was a duty of care. Legislation covering paramedics was held to provide that they were immune from action in negligence if they acted within the scope of their training, so long as their activity was not "wilful or wanton".

[6.500] The Court agreed that the defendants could not be held liable in negligence, unless their actions were "wilful and wanton". The Court considered the definition of "wilful and wanton" adopted by the Court in a previous case *Schneiderman v Interstate Transit Lines Inc* (1946) 394 Ill 569 at 583:

"A wilful or wanton injury must have been intentional or the act must have been committed under circumstances exhibiting a reckless disregard for the safety of others, such as failure, after knowledge of impending danger, to exercise ordinary care to prevent it or a failure to discover the danger through recklessness or carelessness when it could have been discovered by the exercise of ordinary care."

The operator had been told by the deceased "I think I'm going to die. Hurry". The operator did not attempt to keep her on the phone despite standards adopted by the service requiring dispatchers to do so. This, the court held, fulfilled the test set out for wilful and wanton misconduct, which also applied to the actions of the paramedics. The policy of "Try Before You Pry" which dictates that emergency workers try doors before using destructive measures to enter premises was also part of the training of paramedics. The fact that they confirmed the address, did not try the door or other means to determine if someone was inside amounted also to wanton and wilful misconduct.

[6.505] Case: *Worley v The Ambulance Service of NSW*
[2004] NSWSC 1269

W was a postman who rode a motor cycle along the footpaths of the suburbs, collecting mail and delivering it to letter boxes. He ran the risk, as an open-air worker, of insect bites and stings. The letter boxes into which W had to put the mail were often close to flowering shrubs which attracted insects. W had been stung on previous occasions and had proved allergic to bee venom. On the particular day relevant to the claim, W complained of having been stung by a bee and his colleague telephoned the Ambulance Service at 12.01pm. The ambulance left the base at 12.04pm and arrived at the Mail Delivery Centre at 12.17pm.

[6.510] In the proceedings, W alleged negligent treatment by the Ambulance Service, the detail of which is not presently relevant. The issue arose as to whether the Ambulance Service could be held liable at all, either in contract or in tort. Counsel for the Ambulance Service argued that there was no contract between the Ambulance Service and W. A work colleague had telephoned the Ambulance Service and requested that an ambulance attend. The Court regarded him as having made that request as agent for W. After the Ambulance Service had completed the job it sent W an account for its services. Those circumstances would ordinarily be taken as evidence of a contract and were so held. Counsel referred to the great number of demands placed on the Ambulance Service for its services throughout the whole of New South Wales, to the high number of ambulance officers who had to be recruited and trained and to the fact that it did not exist to make a profit. It was funded by the New South Wales Government and although it ordinarily charged for its services, it frequently did not do so, for example, for pensioners.

It was submitted that in the circumstances the law would not hold the Ambulance Service responsible for the consequences of the actions of its officers done in good faith in the course of their duties. The Court did not regard these circumstances as removing any actionable requirement for care in treating members of the public. Exactly the same things might be said about public hospitals of this. It was argued that the *Ambulance Services Act* (the relevant legislation at the time, although it has since been repealed) required only the provision of an adequate, not a reasonable, service. For present purposes the Court drew no distinction between the two words.

Reference was made to cases where statutory bodies had failed to act and had been found not to be liable, such as *Romeo v Conservation Commission of the Northern Territory* ((1998) 192 CLR 431; [1998] HCA 5), *Sullivan v Moody* ((2001) 207 CLR 562; [2001] HCA 59) and *Pyrenees Shire Council v Day* ((1998) 192 CLR 330; [1998] HCA 3). However this was not a case where the Ambulance Service failed to act. It was about the actual response of the Ambulance Service and about whether, as required by its Act, it protected W from injury and achieved adequate standards of ambulance services.

Notably absent from the *Ambulance Services Act* was any statement that no suit lies in contract or otherwise against the Ambulance Service. On the other hand, ambulance officers were personally protected by Section 26 of the Act. The *Ambulance Services Act* was consistent with the intention of the Parliament to make the Ambulance Service liable for the negligent acts of its employees carried out in the course of their duties. Nothing in the Act or at common law led the Court to grant the Ambulance Service relief of immunity from suit.

The Court held that the ambulance officer was negligent in administering adrenaline to W intravenously and the Ambulance Service was held vicariously liable. Whilst W was successful at first instance, the decision was overturned on appeal in *Ambulance Service of NSW v Worley* [2006] NSWCA 102. However, the issue discussed above was not among those pursued on appeal and received little consideration. The Court of Appeal was asked to determine primarily whether the ambulance officer was negligent in administering adrenaline when W was not close to death and whether the Ambulance Service was negligent in the preparation of the relevant protocol. The Court of Appeal did confirm (at 61-62) that, pursuant to s 26 of the *Ambulance Services Act 1900* (NSW), the ambulance officer could not be held personally liable for his own negligence, though the Ambulance Service could be vicariously liable for the tort committed by him. Thus, the discussion in the first instance decision in relation to the duty of care that is owed by individual officers and the Ambulance Service as a whole remains of relevance.

The *Civil Liability Act 2002* (NSW), Part 5 creates a further public policy overlay, dealing with the liability of public and other authorities. Section 42 specifies a series of principles which the Courts must apply in determining whether a public or other defined authority has a duty of care or has breached that duty of care. The specified principles include reference to financial and other resources reasonably available to the authority, the allocation of those resources, the broad range of activities of the authority and compliance with general procedures and standards. Further, by virtue of s 43, an act or omission of an authority will not constitute a breach of statutory duty unless the act or omission was in the circumstances so unreasonable that no authority having the functions of the authority in question could properly consider the act or omission to be a reasonable exercise of its functions.

It would seem that the standard of care that emergency workers owe is dependent upon those set as being reasonable for them. The *Civil Liability Act 2002* (NSW), s 50 may well apply, or if not the principles set out in s 50 are a good starting point for considering the common law position. In establishing what is reasonable action, courts will consider training programs, plans and protocols to deal with emergencies. Emergency carers should consider the Checklist above at **[6.460]** (reasonable standard of care).

Hospitals

[6.515] Where a hospital operates an emergency ward, it has a duty of care to all who pass through its doors, for, unless the contrary is made clear to the public, all comers are offered at least initial assessment there. Once a person's presence is made known to any of the medical staff, there is a duty to provide diagnosis and first aid of a reasonable nature, and to then take reasonable care in either referring the person on for further care (for example to a ward, or to another doctor) or of discharging the person with adequate information to protect her or him from danger. However as noted above (see **[6.510]**) where the hospital is a public authority or otherwise brought within the relevant part, the *Civil Liability Act 2002* (NSW) creates a further public policy overlay which may be relevant, depending upon the facts of a particular case.

The following cases could be held to set out principles that should apply to all those who hold themselves ready to provide emergency care. (See also *Alexander v Heise* discussed at **[6.105]** above.)

Proper assessment and diagnosis

[6.520] First, one could point to *Barnett v Chelsea and Kensington Hospital Management Committee* (see **[6.695]**), where the court held that "the duty of a casualty officer is in general to see and examine all patients who come to casualty". A doctor should not rely on the nurse's assessment although he or she may rely on the triage nurse as to the priority which patients should receive.

Triage nurses

[6.525] Triage nurses are specialist nurses in that they are required to exercise special skill. They must have the necessary knowledge and experience to adequately carry out the functions required, and share with the hospital the obligation to ensure that those coming to the accident and emergency department are properly assessed for their need of treatment, and that any doubt is referred to a medical officer. The nurse should know what signs and symptoms to look for, how to establish them and the various categories in which to place patients. Hospitals should have a clear set of categories, and a process for training staff and assessing their competence.

Where patients do not fit an established category, assistance should be sought in determining what care to give, and where a person is referred elsewhere, the patient should be given a clear indication of where to go, and assured that they can and should do this. They should also be informed of what to do if their condition worsens.

The consumption of alcohol or drugs may make diagnosis difficult.

[6.530] **Case:** *Methodist Hospital v Ball*, 362 SW 2d 475 (1961) (CA Tennessee United States)

A 16-year-old boy was admitted to casualty but was unattended for 45 minutes. He was then sent, without examination, to another hospital. The doctor did not examine him because he accepted the opinion of several laymen that the boy was drunk. The boy later died of a ruptured liver. Expert evidence was heard by the Court to the effect that he would have lived had he been diagnosed and treated promptly.

Reasonable care

[6.535] After diagnosis the patient should be offered reasonable first aid care.

[6.540] Case: *New Biloxi Hospital v Frazier*, 146 So 2d
882 (1962) (CA Mississippi United States)

The patient was admitted, bleeding heavily from gunshot wounds.
Two nurses took his observations and called a doctor, but made
no attempt to stop the bleeding. The doctor attended the man and
at that time there was a large pool of blood on the floor and his
vital signs were poor. He was transferred to another hospital and
died there soon after.

[6.545] The Court found the hospital liable in negligence for the failure of its
staff, including the nurses, to keep the patient there and to offer the care
necessary for his wellbeing.

Adequate follow-up on discharge

[6.550] There is a difference between a person leaving a health care facility of
their own volition and the formal discharge of a person from the facility. The
former is done at the person's own behest, whether or not they are considered
fit to leave, and the latter is done with the warrant of the facility that the
person is in a suitable condition to leave. Once the patient has been stabilised,
and treated in the emergency department, staff must provide for proper
reference to, or information about, after-care.

[6.555] Case: *Niles v City of San Rafael*, 42 Cal App 3d
230 (1974) (CA California United States)

A child who had suffered a blow to the head was examined, and
after a time allowed to leave. The hospital failed to admit the
child, or to give the father a card they had listing symptoms
which would indicate that he should return. The child already had
five of the seven symptoms listed on the card.

[6.560] The hospital was found negligent. The staff had not properly
considered the next step in the treatment programme. The Checklist at **[6.570]**
could really apply to all patients who leave a health care facility, but is particularly crucial for casualty patients.

The following case dealt with the care of a person who left the emergency
ward of his own volition, and other aspects of care in the emergency ward.

[6.565] Case: *Wang v Central Sydney Area Health*
Service [2000] NSWSC 515

W was a young man who was assaulted walking home from a
suburban train station, and possibly rendered unconscious for a
short period. He managed to walk home and two friends took

him to Royal Prince Alfred Hospital. There they told the receptionist he needed to see a doctor urgently. The receptionist
responded that they would have to wait. A triage nurse (the "first
triage nurse") examined W, and noted his pupils were even and
responding, his grip strong, and that he appeared conscious and
alert (although pale and in some distress). She put the plaintiff
second on the list, to be seen after a complex abdominal case.
In the interim she had W sit in the waiting room, where she
could watch him. W waited for attention for some time after
being seen by the triage nurse, who went off duty and was
replaced by a second triage nurse (the "second triage nurse")
while they were there. A further group of concerned friends
arrived to accompany W.

After some time (about one and a half to two hours after
arriving), and before W had been treated, W and friends left the
Emergency Department. The Court accepted evidence that one of
the group approached the second triage nurse and requested that
a doctor see W. They were told that this was not possible, and they
should wait. One of the group later asked her if they could go
elsewhere for treatment, such as a private hospital. She told him
they could do whatever they wanted to do. The group left and
went to the city Superclinic, there W was treated by a doctor, who
obtained a history of the event and noted the possibility of loss of
consciousness. He debrided a deep, eight centimetre cut on W's
head, and examined him carefully for brain injury. As he
concluded W had no abnormal neurological signs, the doctor told
W and friends he should really return to hospital for further
investigation and treatment, but in the face of their rejection of
that idea decided to advise them of what action to take if there
was any deterioration in his condition. He told them W should
not be left alone, and advised them to take him to a Chinese-
speaking doctor in the morning to arrange for an x-ray and any
necessary on-going care. It appeared from evidence in the court
that details of the doctor's advice, being passed through an
interpreter, may not have been fully comprehended by those who
were directly caring for the plaintiff. One fact that the Chinese
witnesses mentioned was that the W's (Chinese) speech was very
slow. The Court recognised that the triage nurse and the doctor at
the clinic may not have noticed this, being unfamiliar with the
language.

Some hours later W suffered from nausea, vomiting and then
a convulsion. His flatmates, new to the country, telephoned
friends and some time later W was taken back to the hospital by
ambulance. On examination it was found that his skull had been
fractured and he was suffering from an extra-dural haemorrhage.
Surgical intervention was unable to prevent irreversible brain
damage.

> W sued the Area Health Service, the hospital, the clinic doctor and the clinic. It was alleged that the first triage nurse's examination of the plaintiff was inadequate and alternatively that she should have consulted a doctor. Also the second triage nurse should have consulted a doctor before W left the hospital. Further it was alleged that the clinic doctor should have insisted W return to any hospital at all, or have kept W at the clinic for observation and necessary emergency action.

[6.570] The Court heard that W would most likely have made a full recovery if treatment had been given at the hospital. It made the following ruling.

Treatment by the hospital

- The primary duty of the hospital was to assign W his appropriate priority through the triage system and to observe him in the waiting area in case his condition deteriorated. No duty to provide him with medical services arose until he could be accommodated in the treatment area. Under the circumstances, he was allotted the appropriate priority.
- Examination by the first triage nurse is not expected to have been the same as that which would have been carried out if W had gone to the treatment area. The examination by the first triage nurse was adequate under the circumstances.
- Given the limited resources and demands on them, a triage nurse would need to notify a doctor of a patient's attendance only if the symptoms indicated the need for urgent treatment. The department was very busy at the time, and W did not appear to have such symptoms. The first triage nurse was not negligent in not notifying a doctor of the patient's presence.

Leaving the hospital

- The hospital also had a duty to furnish W with appropriate advice when it was intimated that he might leave the hospital. They did not do that. The judge was impressed by the practice of one hospital when patients indicated an intention to leave:
  - attempts are made to persuade them to stay, explaining why it is in their interests to do so;
  - if that fails, they are given the names of medical clinics in the area (they would be unlikely to want to go to another hospital and wait again);
  - staff consider such factors as the patient's condition, where they intend to go, the availability of resources both at the hospital and elsewhere, and the patient's capacity to deal with the situation.

Liability of the Clinic doctor and the Clinic

- The doctor at the clinic had a duty to insist W go back to a hospital, observe the capacity of his friends to care for him, enquire as to his domestic circumstances (such advice and enquiries are "embraced within the broad duty of care which a doctor owes to a patient under the *Rogers and Whitaker* ruling"). The doctor did see a return to the hospital as the best course of action, and offered to write a letter for them, but he could not persuade the group to accept this advice. The clinic did not have the resources to keep W there for observation, and he took what he considered to be the best option under the circumstances. As to determining the domestic arrangement and ability of friends to care for him, he had not made an adequate inquiry as to their relationship to him, who actually lived with him, and whether any of them would be sufficiently able to deal with his care if he deteriorated. However, it was clear from their concern and outrage at events that they were very good friends and really cared for him, and the doctor's failure to make these inquiries was not unreasonable under the circumstances. He, and consequently the clinic, were not liable in negligence.

 Checklist
CONSIDERATIONS WHEN PATIENTS LEAVE CARE
(whether or not they are formally discharged)
✓ Where are they going?
✓ What support or care will they need?
✓ Can this be given where they are going?
✓ Do they (or those they will be with) know how to care for them(selves)?
✓ Do they know what symptoms indicate the need for further medical attention?
✓ Do they know how to seek further attention?
✓ Do they know what other complications can occur?
✓ Do they know how to deal with any that do?
✓ Are they physically and mentally able to deal with any complications?

Accidents and other incidents surrounding an emergency

[6.575] Sometimes the person at the scene of an accident or coming into the casualty ward with the most apparent harm (for example, bleeding) may not be the most seriously injured. Where parents have been involved in the incident which injured their child but appear unharmed, they may be ignoring their own injuries or weakness in their concern for their child. Those accompanying a casualty at an emergency or in the emergency ward might suffer harm, faint or collapse as a result of their own minor injuries, shock, stress, or what they witness in casualty. Staff should be aware of this possibility and take as many precautions as they reasonably can. This might take the form of, for example, ensuring that if parents are with children receiving treatment such as stitches, they are seated, invited to leave for the duration, or encouraged to speak up if they feel faint. Although the possible incidents are infinite, the point must be kept in mind that:

1) health carers cannot be expected to anticipate everything, and need only act reasonably at the time; and
2) attention is given to those who appear to need the most urgent care, and staff would thus be expected to be concentrating on them.

Expanded health care practice

[6.580] Recently several State governments have been considering provision for nurses in nominated circumstances to be given primary care tasks for which doctors are traditionally responsible, including suturing wounds, plastering fractured limbs, pathology requests, prescribing drugs such as contraceptives, managing medication and conditions such as asthma, and urinary tract infection (see Chapter 12). Different State-based approaches are being considered, and the lack of a uniform approach, as well as the different views of the bodies involved, makes it impossible to set out standards of care with finality.

However, expanded nursing practice will require the establishment of new standards of nursing knowledge and skill, and those involved will need to ensure that they are able to give reasonable care in the new settings. This development may result in acknowledgment by both the nursing profession and health administrators of the need to more clearly establish those areas which are to be considered the province of nursing practice.

Overall, the expansion of nursing practice is not different in kind to the expansion of health care technologies. Both are served by the principles underlying the law of negligence, and will require consideration by those involved of what is reasonable care under the particular circumstances facing the health carer at the time. As noted above at **[6.265]**, standards change over time with changes in medical knowledge and practice; and the law recognises such changes. *Cekan v Haines* (1990) 21 NSWLR 296:

> "There is no doubt that those standards change over time. Economic and social change, community expectations and knowledge in relevant people affect those changing standards."

Those who adopt new technologies and practices before their probable consequences are properly understood are risking liability at law unless they follow protocols and guidelines that have been approved for the undertaking of research.

[6.585] Case: *Hall v Petros* [2004] WADC 87

H sued P in negligence. The claim whilst not for a breach of duty of care in the provision of treatment, but rather for a breach of duty of care in the provision of adequate information, highlights some issues in the adoption of new technologies and practices.

H consulted P with a complaint of incontinence and P carried out a surgical procedure on the plaintiff which included repair of an enterocele and intra vaginal sling plasty (IVS). The IVS was carried out with nylon tape and involved the use of a technique pioneered in Australia and in Sweden by P.

[6.590] Expert evidence on behalf of H indicated that there were no independent studies on the IVS technique to support it. It had not been extensively reported on and was not used by the majority of gynaecologists in Australia. The "gold standard" procedure at the time was the colpo-suspension. At the relevant time, the IVS procedure did not form part of the Royal Australian College of Gynaecologists examinations.

H was unaware of other mainstream procedures or of any risk of infection or other morbidity associated with tape rejection arising from the specific procedure performed, including the risk of an unusually severe reaction to tape rejection.

H succeeded on her claim for breach of duty of care in the provision of adequate information, hence the Court did not have to decide whether the surgery performed by P utilising the new technique was of itself negligent.

Damages

[6.595] A plaintiff must show that he or she suffered from harm, and that the harm was caused by the defendant's act or omission. Just as one can cause harm to another, but will not be liable at law if he or she was not negligent, a person can be negligent, but will not be liable at law if no damage has been caused. You can give the wrong drug, fail to record crucial medical information about a patient, or leave that person unattended when care is required, for example, causing them distress, worry, and discomfort. But if no harm in legal terms has been caused, they can do nothing to obtain compensation through suing in negligence for this (although disciplinary action for professional misconduct can be taken; see Chapter 12). Discussed below are compensatory damages, where a person is granted financial compensation by reference to what they have lost. In rare negligence cases the law also recognises two other forms of damages, known as aggravated damages and exemplary damages. Aggravated damages, the scope and availability of which have been the subject of recent debate, may be awarded in circumstances where a wrongdoer's reprehensible conduct aggravated the injury to the victim's dignity and feelings. Exemplary damages may be awarded to punish a wrongdoer in circumstances of contumelious disregard of a patient's rights (*Lamb v Cotogno* (1987) 164 CLR 1; [1987] HCA 47) and so are sometimes called punitive damages. The *Review of the Law of Negligence* recommended abolishing exemplary and aggravated damages (see for example *Civil Liability Act 2002* (NSW), s 21). Earlier cases of interest include *Backwell v AAA* [1997] 1 VLR 182, *B v Marinovich* [1999] NTSC 127 and *Tan v Benkovic* (2000) 51 NSWLR 292; NSWCA 295.

In law, the amount of compensation granted as the result of a successful negligence action is referred to as "damages". The harm caused may vary from being very minimal to death. The law will not award damages where harm has been *de minimus*, so slight or vague that it is considered a waste of the court's time to pursue the matter.

Following the *Review of the Law of Negligence*, some Australian jurisdictions have enacted legislation imposing "thresholds" such that general damages (for pain, suffering and emotional distress) will not be available to a person with minor or moderate injuries. Similarly, some have enacted legislation imposing "caps", a maximum figure, which a court may award for general damages. Such legislation varies greatly throughout Australia, hence it is beyond the scope of this book to do more than make the reader aware of the various approaches found in the various jurisdictions' civil liability legislation.

Previously, no damages were awarded for the death of a person, as only the person harmed could bring suit (the action dies with the plaintiff). The obvious hardship to a bereaved dependent family was mitigated in the last century in most Australian jurisdictions by legislation allowing particular close relatives to receive compensation where they can prove negligence, and that they have suffered pecuniary loss from the death of the victim. Payment incurred for medical treatment, funeral expenses, etc, may also be recovered by the deceased's estate. A widow or child may sue where the deceased provided them with maintenance or services, but death itself, and the grief it causes, has no value in the eyes of the law, except where it results in long-term and serious psychological harm known as "nervous shock" (see **[6.185]**). There are exceptions in South Australia and the Northern Territory, where a sum of money can be awarded for the grief and suffering caused by the death of a loved one ("solatium").

When claiming damages, one lists financial losses as either "special" or "general". More recently the language "economic" and "non-economic" has come into use. Damages may be for losses which are past, or anticipated in the future.

Types of damages

Special damages

[6.600] Special damages are those which can be accurately listed, item by item. They include such things as medical expenses, cost of appliances, or housing alterations for someone with a physical disability. They are expenses already incurred, or future expenses for which a quote can be produced.

General damages

[6.605] General damages are those which are not amenable to accurate assessment, such as pain and suffering. They are necessarily subjective, based on such things as:

* injuries and disabilities;
* the lifespan of the plaintiff; and
* the probable long-term progression of the plaintiff's condition.

The court, in assessing damages, will consider:

* payment, past and predicted, for medical care and rehabilitation;
* cost of amenities which may be required for both welfare and general living;
* loss of earnings which have been incurred, and will be incurred in future, including superannuation losses;
* requirements for care; and
* pain and suffering.

Most Australian jurisdictions have a system where a "once and for all" sum is calculated and awarded at the time of the trial. No change can be made in that sum, despite either the unexpected improvement, or the unexpected deterioration, of the plaintiff. "Structured settlements" may be entered into by agreement of the parties, whereby compensation is paid in increments (an annuity) and in a way that is more secure for the plaintiff than a lump sum. (See McGlone (2005), pp 277-278.)

Types of harm

[6.610] There are three types of harm recognised at law. They are physical, economic and psychological harm (commonly known as "nervous shock").

Physical harm

[6.615] This is self-explanatory. Harm to the body which can be objectively measured in terms of physical change to the body or to the use of it. Associated harm to mental faculties caused by physical injury comes under this category. Physical harm of the same magnitude may be of more serious consequence to one person than to another, for example, minor damage to the nerves of the left hand may not be of much importance to a right-handed academic, but may be a handicap of momentous proportions to a concert pianist, or even quite significant to a person who plays the piano for pleasure. See for example *Finch v Rogers* [2004] NSWSC 39 referred to further at **[6.735]**. A young man studying at the Canberra School of Music suffered permanent nerve damage to both ears encompassing high frequency hearing loss, tinnitus and hyperacusis. The plaintiff also suffered peripheral neuropathy with incomplete recovery and consequential depression. The court noted the disabling and isolating effects upon the plaintiff of tinnitus and hyperacusis, and the transformation of his life, which was described as profound. Ultimately, his disabilities were assessed at 70 per cent of the most extreme case hence $269,150.

Economic harm

[6.620] Loss of income, both past and future, is considered by the courts, as well as such things as expenses for medical treatment and replacement and acquisition of property which may be required due to the harm. Expenses, such as those incurred in giving the plaintiff holidays away from permanent hospitalisation to maintain morale, have been awarded by the courts. (See for example, *Sharman v Evans* (1977) 138 CLR 563; [1977] HCA 8 and *Diamond v Simpson (No 1)* [2003] NSWCA 67.)

Dependents of a person who has been physically harmed by negligence may sue where the injured person is no longer able to support them at all, or to the same degree, because of the harm. These may be, for example, a spouse, parents or children. The important thing is that the damages are quantified. Thus, as stated, the death of a person in itself is not recognised in compensation: it is only when those left behind can show that the death has resulted in an economic loss. As expressed by one judge:

"Sorrow does not sound in damages. A plaintiff in an action for negligence cannot recover damages for no more than an emotional response to a distressing experience, sudden, severe and saddening" (*Mount Isa Mines v Pusey* (1970) 125 CLR 383; [1970] HCA 60 per Windeyer J).

Psychological harm

[6.625] This, in law, is called "nervous shock". In restricted circumstances it is compensation for medically recognised, permanent and significant psychological harm resulting from someone's negligence. Traditionally, the only people eligible are those who directly experience or witness the harmful event, or relatives who suffer nervous shock as a result of learning of the harm. Also, the person claiming must be able to show that they were a person of normal fortitude in the first place, or if not, that the defendant knew or ought to have known that they were not, and failed to act accordingly (see *Miller's* case, **[6.630]** below, and Liability for Mental Harm at **[6.190 ff]** above). Most cases involving nervous shock flow from the plaintiff being present at the scene of a horrendous accident, or being a rescuer at such a scene (in *Mount Isa Mines v Pusey*, above, the plaintiff was present at a work accident where two colleagues died, one of whom he assisted), or being a spouse or parent of someone who suffers a sudden fatal accident (*Jaensch v Coffey* (1984) 155 CLR 549; [1984] HCA 52, *Petrie v Dowling* (1992) 1 Qd R 284). For an outline of the gradual acknowledgment of nervous shock by the courts and an assessment of the current state of the law see *McGlone* (2005, pp 181–184).

Three cases which involved different approaches to nurses and nervous shock suffered as the result of their actions are worth considering. Readers may also wish to refer to *Locke v Bova & Anor* [2004] NSWSC 534, which concerned a claim for nervous shock to a doctor witnessing trauma to his wife in hospital.

[6.630] Case: *Miller v Royal Derwent Hospital Board of Management* [1992] Aust Torts Reports ¶81-175 (SC Tas)

A nurse on night duty placed a six-year-old boy in a chair and secured him with a velcro strap for his protection. Unfortunately, after she went off duty, the boy slipped down in the chair and strangled on the strap. The issue in this case was not the negligence or otherwise of the boy's treatment, but rather the effect of the news of his death on the nurse, who was rung and told of the incident. She received no counselling after the incident, and her somewhat irresolute early attempts to talk about the matter to friends were unsuccessful. She suffered so extensively from the incident (including psychiatric illness) that she sued the hospital for damages.

[6.635] The Court held that the hospital had a duty of care to the nurse to provide her with emotional support consequent upon her being informed of the death of the boy. The provision of such support was commonly provided in other similar circumstances. Support was offered to the day staff, whilst "surprisingly" in the judge's view, no such support was offered to the plaintiff. "A moment's reflection" the Court held, would have made it clear that the plaintiff would suffer emotionally more than the other staff. However, what was required did not amount to offering or providing formal counselling. Evidence was accepted that in 1987 the provision of such counselling in like situations was not recognised as appropriate or suitable. Further, given the plaintiff's past history, her predisposition to such an outcome meant that the counselling would have been of doubtful assistance. The defendants exhibited "thoughtless indifference" to the plaintiff's well being in not taking interventionist steps which would have prevented the nervous shock, or at least would have minimised its injurious effect. However, she had not established that the injury was foreseeable in the circumstances, or that causation had been established. The standard of care aspects of this decision may well be decided differently today.

The second case was quite different.

[6.640] Case: *Millicent and District Hospital Inc v Kelly* (10 September 1996, SC SA, No SCGRG 2486 of 1995 S5798)

This case involved a woman of 19 years who was 10 to 12 weeks pregnant. She was admitted to hospital after abdominal pain and bleeding, and became distressed that she may have suffered a miscarriage. After undergoing dilation and curettage, she awoke and saw a clear plastic specimen bottle containing what she took to be a part of a limb. She turned away and asked a nurse to remove the container. A group of nurses who were in the room failed to remove the container, and one of them said that sometimes doctors do that to help the patient accept that they have had a miscarriage. The patient subsequently developed a mild post-traumatic stress disorder. She sued in negligence, and was awarded $20,000 in damages, and the hospital appealed, arguing that the cause of the patient's harm was seeing the specimen in an "emotionally charged, vulnerable and prescribed drug-induced state affecting her faculties", and not the failure of the nurses to remove it when it was obviously distressing her. The Court held that the respondent was "splitting hairs" and its argument was not relevant, and that causation was proved. It held that there was foreseeability of harm in that the defendant could and should have foreseen that the sight of the container with its contents would augment the distress of the miscarriage, and that it could, and should, have foreseen that that distress would descend into illness. By leaving the container in place, and in effect stating that this was to make her realise she had lost the child, the defendant was in breach of the duty it owed the plaintiff.

[6.645] While the second case found the nurses negligent, it is suggested that it is based on a more sound reasoning, given the more modern principles established above regarding duty of care and the standard of care to be applied, and that the purpose of the law of negligence is to ensure that care is taken not to harm those who one "ought to have in contemplation" as being reasonably likely to be harmed by one's actions. It also shows how careful health carers should be that their actions are not inconsiderate—for people can be very vulnerable, especially when ill, suffering mishaps in pregnancy, or under the influence of medication.

[6.650] Case: *Hunter Area Health Service v Marchlewski & Anor* [2000] NSWCA 294

Following shoulder dystocia, the plaintiffs' child Maria was born clinically dead suffering brain damage caused by cerebral hypoxia which was caused by asphyxia during the delivery. She was resuscitated and placed on a ventilator life support system. Based upon the history of asphyxia, a grossly abnormal EEG, epileptic seizures and other evidence of severe damage to Maria's brain, kidney and lungs, the neonatal specialists formed a firm opinion that her prognosis was extremely poor. After removal from ventilator life support Maria continued breathing. Without consultation with the parents, the hospital decided that the child should not be resuscitated when her heart failed. Maria had a respiratory arrest; she was not fully re-ventilated and she died.

[6.655] The hospital later admitted its original breach caused brain damage leading in turn to death and admitted breach of duty of care leading to the parents' nervous shock.

The Court of Appeal was required to consider only some aspects of the damages awarded to the parents.

Legislative provisions

[6.660] In the various Australian jurisdictions, statutes have altered the traditional common law approach to nervous shock. As noted above, the area of mental harm was another considered in the *Review of the Law of Negligence*. The approach taken by the *Civil Liability Act 2002* (NSW) can be found in Part 3, ss 27-33 (see **[6.205]**).

Wrongful birth

[6.665] "Wrongful life" cases were discussed above at **[6.140]**. Wrongful birth has been used to describe cases where a child is born with disabilities when, had the mother known of this likelihood, she would have terminated the pregnancy. Other examples include failed sterilisation or failed contraception due to negligence. In those cases, the mother or parents can sue for the effects of bearing and rearing the child, including the economic, emotional and physical burden. In the case of *Rand v East Dorset Health Authority* [2000] Ll Law Rep (Medical) 181 a baby was born with Down Syndrome as the result of negligent failure to identify the condition in time for the mother to have an abortion. The Court held that to pay the full cost of maintenance of the child as opposed to that in excess of the normal cost of raising a child, would entail comparison of existence to non-existence. Only the losses related to the disability were recoverable, such as losses to a business from having to give up work to care for the child.

A different approach was taken in the leading Australian case in this category, described below. Subsequent to that decision of the High Court, some Australian jurisdictions amended their civil liability legislation to limit the scope of future cases of similar type. For example, the *Civil Liability Act 2002* (NSW), s 71 provides that a court cannot award damages for economic loss for the costs associated with rearing or maintaining the child that the claimant has incurred or will incur in the future, or any loss of earnings by the claimant while the claimant rears or maintains the child. It is important to note however that the section does not preclude the recovery of any additional costs associated with rearing or maintaining a child who suffers from a disability that arise by reason of the disability.

[6.670] Case: *Cattanach v Melchior* (2003) 215 CLR 1; [2003] HCA 38

Dr C was found negligent in performing a tubal ligation upon M, who sued seeking compensation for the costs of raising the child. She initially succeeded and the matter was taken on appeal. Ultimately the High Court by a narrow majority confirmed that M was entitled to recover the past and future expenses of raising the child. (For a detailed consideration of the judgments and arguments for and against awarding the costs of raising a child, see *Skene* (2004, pp 356–362.)

Amount of damage

[6.675] Once it has been established that a defendant owed a duty of care to the plaintiff, he or she will be liable for harm that he or she has negligently caused. It is the *type* of harm that must be foreseen, not the extent of it. This may seem a contradiction in terms, but it matters not if the plaintiff suffered from a condition which made him or her abnormally susceptible to harm. This is called the "egg-shell skull" rule, and was established as long ago as 1901:

> "it is no answer to the sufferer's claim for damages that he would have suffered less injury or no injury at all, if he had not had an unusually thin skull or an unusually weak heart" (*Dulieu v White & Son* [1901] 2 KB 669 at 679).

Notwithstanding this relatively simple statement of principle, there remains considerable scope for argument as to the recoverability of certain types of damage. For example, until recently in New South Wales at least, it was possible for a mother to recover the cost for provision of commercial care for infant children, if the mother was unable to provide that care herself as a result of a tort. Such an entitlement had been confirmed by the New South Wales Court of Appeal in *Sullivan v Gordon* (1999) 47 NSWLR 319; NSWCA 338. However in *CSR Limited v Eddy* (2005) 222 ALR 1; [2005] HCA 64, the High Court overturned the effect of the New South Wales Court of Appeal decision, so that such damages are no longer available other than in Australian jurisdictions where the entitlement is established by statute.

Another factor in determining the amount of damage tends to bridge the concepts of damage, as discussed above, and causation, as discussed below. It is the concept of loss of a chance, whereby a patient has suffered damage as a result of breach of duty, but may have suffered the damage even in the absence of such a breach of duty.

[6.680] Case: *Rufo v Hosking* (2004) 61 NSWLR 678; NSWCA 391 (Court of Appeal NSW)

R was diagnosed to be suffering from systemic lupus erythematosus (lupus or SLE), a very serious inflammatory condition. In due course she came under the care of H, a paediatric immunologist. Only eight months later, R was admitted to hospital suffering from vertebral microfractures.

[6.685] It became common ground at the trial that the microfractures arose from osteoporosis caused by the corticosteroid dosages (dexamethasone) that R had been having over that short eight month period. It was held that in failing to introduce a steroid sparer Imuran to R's treatment regime sooner, H was in breach of his duty of care. However on the balance of probabilities, R would have developed osteoporosis and vertebral compression fractures from the administration of corticosteroids anyway, but nonetheless she was deprived of a chance of averting that outcome as a result of H's negligence.

On the all or nothing rule R would have received nothing. However the treatment did result in a material increase in that that risk which, if it did transpire, would be likely to have very serious consequences for her, as it did. The court remitted the matter for a further trial, to determine the value of the chance R lost.

(It is interesting to contrast the outcome in *Rufo v Hosking* with the different approach taken not long afterwards in England. See *Gregg v Scott* [2005] UKHL 2.)

Causation

Defendant must have actually caused the plaintiff's harm

[6.690] The determination of whether a particular course of action or an omission caused an event is not without problems in the law. To succeed in a claim, a plaintiff must prove that the breach of duty of care caused the relevant damage. Following another recommendation of the *Review of the Law of Negligence*, the *Civil Liability Act 2002* (NSW), s 5E confirms that the plaintiff always bears the onus of proving, on the balance of probabilities, any fact relevant to the issue of causation. Often the "chain of causation" is determined by what is called the "but for" test. That is the first step in determining legal causation, and is most appropriate where the facts are relatively simple. The "but for" test is satisfied if it can be shown that the damage would not have occurred "but for" the defendant's negligent act. This can best be illustrated by the following case.

> **[6.695] Case:** *Barnett v Chelsea and Kensington*
> *Hospital Management Committee* [1969] 1 QB 428
> (High Court England)
>
> B and his fellow workers were nightwatchmen. One New Year's Eve they felt very ill after drinking their tea. They went to the local hospital, where the nurse thought they were drunk, but she was pressed to call the doctor. Unfortunately he also felt sick and left instructions for them to contact their own doctor the next day. They left, but five hours later B died. It seems arsenic had been put into the tea. B's widow sued the hospital and the doctor, alleging that he had a duty of care to treat her husband and had failed to discharge this duty, causing his death.

[6.700] It might seem just that the doctor pay for neglecting the man, but in fact he was not held to be liable. Let us consider why. First, it would seem that he had a duty of care to B. Indeed he did. So he had an obligation to attend to him: the first requirement for proving negligence had been fulfilled. A reasonable doctor would have foreseen that failure to see him and treat him could result in the patient suffering from further harm. In fact he did not even attempt to diagnose B's illness. The second requirement for proving negligence had been met. However, the doctor escaped liability because even if the doctor had given B the best and most prompt treatment available, he still would have died. The doctor's failure to act was thus held not to be the cause of B's death. All three elements of the negligence action must be proved for it to succeed, and Mrs B had not been able to prove the element of causation.

Another important lesson from this case is that omissions, or failures to act, can be just as culpable in the eyes of the law as actions.

[6.705] Case: *Wilsher v Essex Area Health Authority*
[1988] 1 All ER 871 (House of Lords England)

(Different aspects of this case are considered at **[6.420]**).

W, a premature neonate suffered almost total blindness after intensive care. During that time a catheter was twice inserted into a vein rather than an artery, and in both cases he was given excess oxygen. W (through his representatives) sued the hospital in negligence.

[6.710] Both the trial judge and the Court of Appeal ruled in favour of W, and the hospital appealed to the House of Lords. There was no question that a duty of care had existed between W and the Health Authority, and that the duty of care had been breached. However, the House of Lords overturned the earlier decisions on the basis that causation had not been adequately proved. W could have developed the blindness from several conditions he had suffered, such as patent ductus arteriosus, hypercapnia, intraventricular haemorrhage, and apnoea. Expert witnesses had differed on what had caused the blindness, and the Court was not satisfied that W had proved, on the balance of probabilities that the blindness had been caused by the excessive oxygen. The Court held that where there are a number of possible causes of harm, one of which is the defendant's breach of duty of care, the combination of the breach of duty and the harm is not enough to make them liable. It was not up to the defendant to prove they did *not* cause the harm: the plaintiff must prove that they did. (Which is the same as noted above **[6.690]**, regarding s 5E of the *Civil Liability Act 2002* (NSW)). On this basis the Court could not find the defendant liable.

[6.715] Case: *Hotson v East Berkshire Area Health Authority* [1987] 2 All ER 909 (House of Lords England)

As the result of a fall, H developed avascular necrosis, but the employees of the health authority did not diagnose this for five days. H sued the Authority, stating that a failure to diagnose was the cause of the necrosis.

[6.720] The House of Lords heard expert evidence and decided that, had the diagnosis been made promptly, H would still have developed the necrosis. The cause was not the failure to diagnose or treat H's condition.

Remoteness of damage

[6.725] The "but for" test is an inclusive one, and, if taken to its extreme, could stretch back in time indefinitely (for example, but for your good grades at school, you wouldn't have studied medicine—but for your missing out a position at another hospital, you would not have been working at this one, but for your working at this hospital, you would not be treating cancer patients, and so on). To limit those factors which should be included in the legal causation of an event, the courts again turned to foreseeability, to limit liability to those events which are not too remote.

Common sense approach

[6.730] Subsequent to the "but for" test, the courts looked to "common sense" when determining cause. This approach was adopted in *Chappel v Hart* (see Chapter 4), but there was criticism of the court's approach, it being argued that, while the reasoning of some judges was based on the common sense reasoning that the higher the skill of the surgeon, the less the risk of harm, in fact the risk of harm was just the same, no matter who operated. The skill of the surgeon may have meant that statistically the harm would have been less likely, but it was not negligence on the part of the defendant who caused the harm. There was not proof that "but for" his actions the plaintiff would not have suffered harm: she may well have done even with a more skilled surgeon.

Necessary condition approach

[6.735] Most recently, partly through development of the common law and partly through changes following the *Review of the Law of Negligence*, the courts have grappled with an approach to causation analysis which some authors have called the "necessary condition" test (see McGlone (2005), pp 219-226.) That approach is a two-stage one, considering "factual" causation and "normative" causation. The *Civil Liability Act 2002* (NSW), s 5D expresses the test in the following way:

> "Section 5D
> (1) A determination that negligence caused particular harm comprises the following elements:
>   (a) that the negligence was a necessary condition of the occurrence of the harm ("factual causation"), and
>   (b) that it is appropriate for the scope of the negligent person's liability to extend to the harm so caused ("scope of liability").
> (2) In determining in an exceptional case, in accordance with established principles, whether negligence that cannot be established as a necessary condition of the occurrence of harm should be accepted as establishing factual causation, the court is to consider (amongst other relevant things) whether or not and why responsibility for the harm should be imposed on the negligent party."

As can be seen from s 5D, to label the test as the necessary condition test may not be entirely accurate, given that s 5D(2) envisages exceptional cases where factual causation may be established where negligence cannot be established as a necessary condition of the occurrence of harm.

The factual/normative test is perhaps more complex in abstract than in its practical application, as exemplified in *Finch v Rogers* [2004] NSWSC 39. Having been diagnosed with testicular cancer, F underwent surgery for removal of the affected testicle. No complaint was made concerning the operation, however it was alleged there was a failure by R to properly investigate and monitor F thereafter, so as to ascertain whether the tumour had metastasised. As a result of the delay, F required an additional cycle of chemotherapy. That additional cycle brought with it permanent tinnitus and peripheral neuropathy of particular significance to F given his musical background. (See the discussion above at **[6.615]**.) The claim was subject to the provisions of the *Civil Liability Act 2002* (NSW). Section 5D was expressly considered and the court held (at [147]):

> "Here I have determined, as a matter of probability, that Associate Professor Boyer would have treated the Plaintiff. Addressing the issue of factual causation, but for the breach, and the delay which was the consequence of the breach, the following can be said. First, that Mr Finch would probably have been given Indiana BEP chemotherapy on Monday, 30 December 1996 or at the latest, Monday, 6 January 1997. Second, that on either day, he would have been regarded as a good prognosis patient. Third, that given his response to chemotherapy (which was good) he would have needed only three cycles, not four; Fourth, that he would not have suffered the disabling consequences of ototoxicity and neurotoxicity which were evident after the fourth cycle."

The court went on to consider the factual and normative limbs (at [148]):

> "In short, I consider that the Defendant's negligence was a necessary condition of the harm that ensued [section 5D(1)(a)]. I further believe that it is appropriate that the scope of the Defendant's liability extend to the harm so caused [section 5D(1)(b)]. The consequences were in each case a foreseeable result of the breach."

[6.740] Case: *Metropolitan Health Service v King* [1999] WASCA 236 (Court of Appeal WA)

Shortly after K's discharge from the hospital after the third of a series of treatments there, he was diagnosed with thoracic osteomyelitis resulting from enterobacter cloacae infection. This required intensive treatment.

The trial judge found that the infection was contracted during the third period of hospitalisation and that it was caused by an unidentified nurse's handling of his intravenous (IV) infusion. The judge awarded the respondent $30,000 in damages.

An intravenous cannula had been inserted into a peripheral vein in the left arm. Hospital procedure required that once an IV infusion is inserted by a doctor, the nursing staff monitor it and change infusion bags or patient controlled analgesia syringes as required. The Court recognised that despite aseptic procedures, infection can occur without negligence.

K alleged that he was woken in the middle of the night of either 14 or 15 December 1995 and:

- his IV infusion bag was changed by a nurse whose name is unknown;
- whilst the nurse was attempting to unfasten the plastic tube from the cannula she dislodged the cannula and it slid partially out of K's left arm causing sharp pain and bleeding from the site;
- the nurse mopped up the blood with Kleenex tissues, changed the saline bag, mopped up some further blood and slid the cannula back into the plaintiff's arm; and
- the nurse did not wash her hands or swab the cannula site with antiseptic solution prior to sliding the cannula back into the plaintiff's arm.

Nursing notes showed no change of IV infusion during the night. They recorded that it was changed late the evening before, and early the next morning.

On 16 December, at about 10.30 am, records showed that the infusion was running into the surrounding tissues rather than the vein, and the cannula was removed.

Second siting of the IV infusion

Records showed that on 16 December, at about 8.45pm, a new Intravenous infusion was inserted in another site on the same arm. They also showed that on 18 December the second infusion site was found to be red, swollen and painful, and the patient hot and feverish.

The trial judge cited hospital requirements that nurses should not attempt to push back a dislodged cannula for fear of infection and/or damage. It should be removed, and a new cannula inserted elsewhere by a doctor using proper aseptic procedures. If the events described by the respondent did happen, he ruled, the nurse could be found negligent. Relying solely on K's evidence, despite the nurses' notes, he ruled that they did occur.

The next question was whether the "cannula incident" caused K's infection. Experts said the infection arose at the *second site*. If the "cannula incident" occurred before the drip was resited, it could not have caused the infection in question. The trial judge resolved this difficulty by simply declaring that the cannula incident must have happened later, *after* the resiting of the cannula to the second site in the left arm.

The hospital appealed, claiming that the verdict should have been in favour of it because the judge was not entitled to overcome the causal difficulty by making a finding, unsupported by any evaluation of the evidence as to when the incident

> occurred (K insisted the incident occurred in relation to the first
> site). No reason was given by the judge for the finding that he
> made.

[6.745] The hospital's arguments were accepted by the Court of Appeal. It found that there was no record of the presence of signs of infection at the first site, and infection was not the reason for removal of the drip from that site. The first recorded observation of a drip site infection was at the second site, two days after. There seems little doubt that this infection, the signs of which were inflammation and soreness, was at the second site. If, the "cannula incident" occurred at any time before removal from the first site, it could not have caused this infection. There was no suggestion that the infection at the second site was caused by negligent handling of the cannula at the first site, or that both sites became infected. It found that the infected site (unquestionably the second site), was the point of infection entry. Thus, there was no evidence that the "cannula incident" (if indeed it did occur) was the cause of the infection in question.

The Appeal Court concluded that on K's own evidence at trial, any mishandling of the cannula would have occurred at a time which exonerated the hospital from blame for the subsequent infection.

The following case is instructive regarding negligence: it also gives some good advice regarding seeking assistance where there is inadequate staff (not to mention tea breaks and care of post-operative patients).

> [6.750] Case: *Laidlaw v Lion's Gate Hospital* (1969) 70
> WWR 727 (SC British Columbia Canada)
>
> L was admitted to the post-operative room of the hospital after a
> routine cholecystectomy. There were eight stations in the room,
> and two nurses on duty at the time. When L arrived, nurse M had
> left for coffee, and so nurse S was alone with two patients, a
> third arriving in nurse M's absence before L and yet another
> patient (R). This last patient was accompanied by an anaesthetist
> and a nurse who then, it seems, left. Nurse S had interrupted her
> attentions to each patient as the next arrived, not finishing their
> observations. By this time a patient had left, so nurse S was
> caring for four patients. She left L's observations to administer
> an injection to R, and after this answered the telephone before
> returning to L who was in severe respiratory distress and
> required resuscitation. As a result she (L) sustained permanent,
> extensive brain damage.

[6.755] This case is very complex, and only some actions of the nurses will be considered here. The nurses acknowledged that normally it was the practice of the hospital, and their practice, for two nurses to be on duty at all times when the room was in use. However, coffee breaks are taken when things are quiet, and the remaining nurse can also call on extra help if she needs it. The nurses said they did not expect the patients to bunch up so rapidly. The Court responded that when five patients are scheduled for surgery, nurses should be ready to receive them at any time, thus nurse M should not have gone for coffee; or at least the nurses should have asked for someone to relieve her. Nurse S should have called for assistance, anyway, when things got busy (she could also have called on the staff entering the room). In giving their opinion with regard to the standard of care required, medical witnesses spoke in terms of constant and total care, with observation every minute or two, considering the particular vulnerability of post-operative patients.

These days a different situation may arise in post-operative care rooms. Modern science provides technology which automatically monitors vital signs such as blood pressure, pulse, temperature, etc, either constantly or at intervals, and sounds an alarm if these are abnormal. This means staff need not be physically at the bedside of patients so frequently and can concentrate on other matters. The legal issues may change as well. Important from the legal point of view may be what reliance one can place on the technology, which will be translated into such questions as how reasonable it is to trust the machines, and under what conditions and for how long it is reasonable to entrust a patient to them.

When One Does Not Feel Capable Of Reasonable Care

[6.760] There may be occasions where a health carer feels that because, for example, of lack of training, experience or resources, he or she cannot offer a reasonable standard of care. It is suggested that the Checklist at **[6.460]** regarding unsatisfactory situations should be followed. With proper notice, this shifts to the principal (that is, the employer or facility engaging the health carer as a visiting medical officer or otherwise, to carry out its enterprise) the legal responsibility of providing reasonable care to the patient.

This advice is based on the following reasoning:

- When negotiating a position as a health carer, prospective appointees should quite clearly confirm the area or areas in which they might be required to work. They and the principal should ensure that they will not be required in an area in which they are not suitably qualified, unless the intention is to provide necessary training and experience in that area.
- Where a principal may require an applicant for a position in, for example, employing a nurse to carry out any duties (such as "relieving" on the wards) as required from time to time, and the applicant may agree to do this, health carers should not undertake health care for which they are not competent, nor should the principal expect them to do this.

The respective responsibilities of employees and employers are set out in Figure 6.1.

Figure 6.1: Respective responsibilities of employers and employees

(That is, an employer or facility engaging them as a visiting medical officer or otherwise to carry out its enterprise).

Carer's duty to patient	To provide reasonable care (as outlined in this chapter).
Carer's duty to principal	To further the objectives of the principal by providing reasonably competent health care to patients. This would include discussion of her or his experience and competencies, so that he or she can be appropriately placed to provide services to patients (see Chapter 10 on the contract of employment).
Employer's duty to patient	To provide reasonable services, including adequate and competent staff (see also Chapter 10).
Employer's duty to carer	To provide adequate and safe facilities, staff training and support so that he or she can provide reasonable care to the patient (see also Chapter 10).

By informing the principal of one's lack of competence, one is invoking the principal's, as well as the health carer's, duty of care to the patient, and placing on the principal the responsibility of finding, if he or she believes it is necessary and reasonable, someone else to provide the care for patients. The carer has taken reasonable steps to ensure proper care if the principal has been adequately and initially informed of her or his qualifications or lack of them: it is then up to the principal. However, one should bear in mind the passing remarks of the court in *Sherry* (see **[6.430]** above) as to whether, in some circumstances, a health carer, knowing the deficiencies of a hospital, might need to refuse to provide services at the hospital or face personal liability.

Of course, that is of significance for an independent person such as a visiting medical officer and less so for an employee. If the employer is told that an employee does not feel competent to work in a particular area and does not change the situation, the employer has taken the risk of breach of duty of care. The employee's responsibility, in obeying the direction to work under these circumstances is:

1) to give the best care possible under the circumstances; and
2) to make sure that there is adequate evidence of the employer having been informed. The employee should make a written report of the situation (an incident report is one effective way, witnessed if possible). Some institutions have highly structured and quite limited incident report forms. This should not deter carers from filling them in as best they can, attaching further pages if necessary. Most systems involve regular formal review of such forms by safety committees, quality assurance review committees, etc, so matters such as frequent allocation of insufficiently experienced staff or under-staffing must be addressed at a management level if they are reported as "incidents". See the Checklist "Principles for Action when a Situation Causes Concern" at **[6.460]**.

Vicarious Liability

[6.765] Liability at law for negligence is personal: that is, it is sheeted home to the actual individual who caused the harm. There are, however, exceptions to this principle. Where a patient suffers harm as the result of negligence on the part of an employee, the patient may in fact sue the employer, not the individual health carer, as an employer is vicariously liable for the negligence of its employees. This can also apply to someone who is acting as the agent of another. This is not to be confused with independent contracting, such as agency nursing, where vicarious liability depends on the determination of "control"—see **[6.780]** and the discussion regarding borrowed employees by *McGlone* (2005, p 353)).

Vicarious liability is based on the principle that you are responsible for the actions of those you engage to do your work for you. It stems from the ancient common law principle of responsibility of a master for his servant. This means that despite the utmost effort on the part of the employer to ensure that the best care is given to its patients, and even the lack of knowledge on the part of the employer of the negligent activity, so long as the employee is carrying out activities which are part of the employer's enterprise, the employer is responsible for the patient's welfare.

Non-delegable duties

[6.770] The concept of non-delegable duty is similar to that of vicarious liability, and arises where an organisation has undertaken responsibility for a vulnerable person. Hospitals are therefore said to owe a non-delegable duty to their patients in many circumstances (see *Samos v Repatriation Commission* [1960] WAR 219) but not always (*Ellis v Wallsend District Hospital:* see **[6.783]**). To the extent that the non-delegable duty was anything more than to take reasonable care, following the release of the *Review of the Law of Negligence* we have provisions such as the *Civil Liability Act 2002* (NSW), s 5Q, which provide that the extent of liability in tort of a person for breach of a non-delegable duty is to be determined as if the liability were the vicarious liability of the defendant for the negligence of the person in connection with the performance of the work or task. (See the discussion by *McGlone* (2005), pp 359-363.)

Where a patient suffers harm from the actions of health care employees, that person can sue both the health care facility (for example, a hospital) and any staff he or she believes are responsible. (Often the employee will not be held personally liable to pay compensation though, due to statutory protections such as the *Employees Liability Act 1991* (NSW). See **[6.810]** below.) The hospital is the first in the line of possible defendants for three reasons. First, the hospital has a duty of care to those who come under its care, and has undertaken to have the resources to do so. Secondly, a contract exists between the patient and a hospital or other health care facility which obliges it to give reasonable care. Finally, the facility is more likely to be able to compensate the patient, because of its financial resources and insurance back-up. It is of little benefit suing someone who cannot pay. However, a patient may choose to sue either, or both, the health carer and the hospital, in which case the court may order respective damages payable by both parties, depending on their contribution to the harm caused.

The two questions involved in establishing the existence of vicarious liability are:

- whether the person involved was an employee or agent at the time he or she caused the harm; and
- whether the harm was caused by actions carried out in the course of employment.

Who is an employee?

[6.775] A person who works for another for pay may be either an employee or an independent contractor. This is another complex and confusing issue at law, but it is helpful to consider the case of *Stevens v Brodribb Sawmilling Co Pty Ltd* (1986) 160 CLR 16; [1986] HCA 1. In that case the High Court of Australia considered how to determine whether someone was an employee. The judges considered various tests that have been devised in the past and came to the conclusion that tests should be applied to a contract to do work for someone, to distinguish the employee whom one engages to work for one, from the independent contractor such as a plumber, whom one engages to carry out a specific job.

Tests used to determine employment

[6.780] With the development of complex outsourcing and other arrangements for bodies to carry out their functions, it may sometimes be hard to determine whether a person is an employee of a particular enterprise or not. The courts will approach the question of deciding who is an employee by using several tests, generally in the following order:

1) **Control test.** This test is the surest guide to whether a contract of employment or some other contract exists between the parties. The test considers how much control the alleged employer has over the work of the alleged employee: does it control the place of work, the facilities, the manner in which it is carried out, the tools of trade, hours of work, and so on? The more often one can answer "yes" to these questions, the more likely it is that the person is an employee.

   Where the person performing services is a professional or an artist, exercising skill, expertise or judgment beyond the capacity of the employer, the employer may not actually have much scope for controlling the employee's actions. However, there may be, in the conditions of employment, authority to command inasmuch as there is scope for it. A trapeze artist has been held to be an employee of a circus, because the circus management could direct times and places of performance, rehearsal times, pay and leave conditions, and supplementary duties. This was held to override any freedom the artist had in carrying out his art (*Zuijs v Wirth Bros Pty Ltd* (1955) 93 CLR 561; [1955] HCA 73).

2) The **organisation test** can be used to clarify the position. This test considers the extent to which a person's work contributes to the general enterprise of the apparent employer. If the person's work is integral to the organisation's activities (for example, delivering health care) it is more likely to be a contract of employment. If the work is peripheral to the organisation's activities (for example, development of a new wing of the hospital building) it is less likely to be a contract of employment. This test is also not a complete approach, and has been met with judicial criticism, for example in *Ellis v Wallsend District Hospital* below. In that case Mason J stated that the organisation test does no more than shift the focus to whether the person was part of the organisation's enterprise or not.

3) **Other tests**. The control test was found unsatisfactory on its own, and the organisation test was not widely used in Australia. The current approach of the courts has been described as a "multi-facet test", involving consideration of a range of factors. (See *McGlone* (2005, p 350); *Stevens v Brodribb Sawmilling Co Pty Limited* (1986) 160 CLR 16; [1986] HCA 1.) Conditions such as the right to dismiss, to set the conditions and hours of work, the right to the exclusive services of the person and the ownership and maintenance of equipment also indicate that a person is an employee rather than an independent contractor.

Courts have distinguished between health care professionals who have been selected by patients to treat them in a hospital or other institution or clinic, and those selected by the treating body itself. The case of *Albrighton v Royal Prince Alfred Hospital* [1980] 2 NSWLR 542 (see **[6.115]**) addressed this issue. There it was held that where the patient selects the treating health professional, the hospital is not responsible for the negligence of that professional; however, this principle must be qualified by the tests above, in that the court will consider the arrangements under which the professional works. If they are required to abide by hospital rules, standards and procedures, for example, thereby submitting to some extent to the hospital's control, they may become part of the organisation and the hospital may well be found liable for their negligence. In the *Albrighton* case the court considered that because the doctors accepted and complied with the hospital's forms and routines, and had abided by its by-laws they were employees. A lot depends on the nature of the action which caused the harm: whether it was solely based on the visiting doctor's professional judgment, over which the hospital may have had no control, or whether it was an action pursuant to hospital rules or standards by which the professional has agreed to be bound.

[6.783] Case: *Ellis v Wallsend District Hospital* (1989) 17 NSWLR 553

E agreed to undergo an excision of certain neck vertebrae and division of nerve roots. The surgeon was a visiting surgeon at the hospital. Consent was given in the belief that the procedure would probably relieve chronic neck pain, after considerable hesitation and several requests for assurances from the surgeon concerning the safety of the procedure. Although the surgeon told her the procedure was unusual, he did not mention that there was a risk of developing paraplegia and a low prospect of relieving pain. After the procedure E developed quadriplegia. She commenced action against the surgeon in negligence and against the hospital. The surgeon died and E settled her claim against his estate. She continued her action against the hospital. The question as to whether the hospital was vicariously liable was also considered by the Court.

[6.785] The Court held that the hospital was not vicariously responsible for the surgeon's negligence. The majority held that E had established a relationship with the surgeon before entering the hospital, which had in no sense chosen the surgeon for her. The majority approached the matter by asking the question, in treating E, was the surgeon acting on his own, or the hospital's behalf? He had an agreement with the hospital whereby he undertook to treat free of charge patients who came to the hospital for relief, in exchange for the use of facilities and nursing services for those of his own patients who he would book into the hospital. The patients he booked in would pay the hospital for its services. Honorary medical staff were subject to the control of the hospital in some degree, being required to adhere to directions for maintaining administrative efficiency and integrity. However, the majority held, these did not amount to such control as would render the hospital vicariously liable for their actions. Indeed they considered that the surgeon was an independent specialist working on his own account in the treatment of the hospital's patients. He was never an employee.

Kirby P dissented, stating that the hospital benefited by having honorary doctors among their officers, and the hospital "should not be allowed to escape responsibility for injury to patients happening on their premises as a result of the activities of health professionals, including honorary surgeons". He held that the employment relationship did exist between the hospital and the surgeon. The by-laws of the hospital were for mutual benefit, tied the surgeon inextricably into the organisation of the hospital, integrating him into the discipline and direction of the hospital. He held that this was substantiated by the consent form, which stated that no assurance has been given that the operation will be carried out by any particular surgeon.

In respect of direct duty of care to E, the Court held that where private patients do not have doctors allocated by the hospital but choose their own doctor, the hospital does not owe a duty of care for the doctor's negligent actions, but the hospital does owe a duty of care for those of its nursing staff and paramedical care.

An important case which clarifies the position and also deals with negligence in nursing care follows.

[6.790] Case: *John James Memorial Hospital Ltd v Keys*
[1999] FCA 678 (Federal Court of Australia)

K was 73-years-old and had led an active social and family life up to the time of her hospitalisation. However, she required the aid of a walking frame. In 1996 she consulted a general practitioner with severe sciatic pain and was referred to a consultant physician, Dr G. The pain became so intense that Dr G arranged her admission to the John James Memorial Hospital Ltd for pain relief and observation. She was put on a regime of Tegretol in conjunction with Pethidine. Voltaren, an anti-inflammatory analgesic was also given.

Whilst in hospital she suffered two falls, the first occurring on 23 April. Five nurses were on the day shift (the normal complement), caring for 24 patients in the ward, plus a charge nurse and desk nurse. K was one of about five patients whose care was allocated to registered nurse D. K had been given 200 mg of Tegretol at 6 am. Later that morning, K had been assisted to the bathroom by D, and told to ring the buzzer when ready so that D could assist her to shower.

Meanwhile, D, who was making K's bed, was called to another patient in another room, from which she was unable to hear the buzzer. She returned to K's room after not more than five minutes and resumed making the bed. K's husband arrived and on going to the bathroom to say good morning, found it obstructed by K lying on the floor. After some time (it was "within the hour") and instructing K to move her legs, D gained entry and found K lying on the bathroom floor covered in soap. She was showered and returned to bed.

The second fall occurred in the early hours of the next night. After hearing a loud thump in K's room, registered nurse A and another nurse found K lying on the floor. K told her she had fallen while on the way to the bathroom.

K sued the doctor and the hospital in negligence, for injuries suffered, including exacerbation of her original condition.

The trial judge had found that Nurse D had not been negligent:

- in being ignorant of the risk that K was so confused and disorientated that she needed especially close supervision; and
- in failing to realise that K was so heavily affected by her medication that she needed constant supervision.

He stated that a patient should not be allowed out of bed if such supervision was required, and no-one had considered that her condition required this. He concluded that D should have been made aware that the drugs she was taking would have the likely effect on K of disorientation and confusion and that she should have been more closely supervised. He found that there was a failure in the chain of communication from the doctor to the nursing staff.

The trial judge went on to consider that the hospital was vicariously liable for the acts and omissions of all those involved, including Dr G. He interpreted *Albrighton v Royal Prince Alfred Hospital* (above) as setting out the principle that a hospital is vicariously liable for the acts and omissions not only of its employed staff but "also those doctors whose patients the hospital admits for care and treatment under the doctors, whether the doctors are paid by the hospital or not". As he believed that the nursing staff on duty at the time had not been properly advised as to the probable effect of the drugs, the hospital was vicariously liable for the omission.

K was awarded $69,248 for the injuries she suffered in both falls. The matter was appealed by the defendant hospital.

[6.795] The Appeal Court held that before the trial judge could hold the hospital liable for the effect of a failure at an unidentified point in the chain of communication between Dr G and Nurse D, it was necessary to ensure that the hospital was liable for the acts and omissions of every participant in the chain.

It found that the trial judge had misstated the effect of *Albrighton*. That case only provides that a hospital *may* be liable for the acts and omissions of a treating, non-employed doctor. A hospital is vicariously liable where it functions as a place where a person in need of treatment goes to obtain treatment, but not, as in this case, where it functions merely as the provider of medical care facilities as an adjunct to the doctor's treatment of the patient. Consideration should be given to the circumstances of K's admission, the arrangements regarding control of the hospital over the doctor's work, matters of remuneration, and the doctor's obligation to work. In this case K selected Dr G through her general practitioner, not the hospital. Dr G chose the hospital, not the reverse. K was being treated as a private patient in a private hospital and Dr G was apparently remunerated by her insurer.

Dr G and Nurse D had both testified that they knew Tegretol could cause drowsiness and could possibly lead to confusion. Nurse D was not aware of it causing disorientation. K at the time of her first fall was in a "confused and disorientated state" and both Nurse D and Dr G testified that confusion and disorientation was foreseeable by any trained person who had knowledge of K's medication regime. Nurse D had conceded in her evidence that it was not necessary for her to be informed by a "chain of communication" stemming from Dr G, that K was likely to be experiencing drowsiness and possible confusion as a result of the medication.

The Appeal Court concluded that Nurse D:

• knew, or should have known, of the probability of confusion and disorientation as a result of the medication;
• knew that if she left K's bedroom she would not be able to hear the buzzer inside the toilet; and

- should have realised that, if she did not answer the buzzer, K might move without assistance and suffer a fall.

It was thus negligent of Nurse D to leave the bedroom, without warning K or checking on her. It was foreseeable that, during Nurse D's absence from the bedroom, K would, after forgetting or being unable to obtain assistance, undertake the risky step of moving without it.

The Court agreed that the nature and extent of the injuries sustained by K, and the effects of the accident upon her and her life, warranted a higher award of general damages than had been awarded by the trial judge. The Court increased the award to $30,000 for general damages. Judgment was entered for K in the sum of $82,448 plus costs.

Who is an agent?

[6.800] An agent is someone engaged to act in the principal's interest, to carry out a service one has undertaken to offer the patient. Honorary and visiting medical officers, anaesthetists, and others retained by an institution may be just as much the institution's responsibility in negligence as the employees. In the case of *Roe v Minister of Health* [1954] 2 QB 66 Lord Denning stated that a hospital is responsible for all its staff:

> "whether they are permanent or temporary, resident or visiting, whole time or part time ... even if they are not servants, they are the agents of the hospital to give the treatment. The only exception is the case of consultants or anaesthetists selected and employed by the patient himself."

The principles above apply to other health carers as well. In most cases the carer engaged by a patient directly, or through an agency, is an independent contractor, the agency not being an employer, but rather simply a source of finding work. As well as specialists who are approached by patients (or referred to them) and treated by them at a facility, nurses engaged directly by a patient or through a nursing agency to care for them in a hospital would be subjected by the courts to the above tests to determine whether they personally are liable to the patient, or whether the hospital should be found vicariously liable. Where the hospital engages nurses through an agency, there is more scope for the hospital's liability, for it becomes more closely responsible for the standard of the nurses' work and having this control over nurses' services, the hospital also fulfils the "organisation test".

If a health carer is not working under a contract of employment he or she is very strongly advised to acquire indemnity insurance, which provides cover for harm caused through negligence. Professional bodies can advise as to policies available.

What is considered to be "in the course of employment"?

[6.805] Activities which are directed or authorised by an employer, or those which are reasonably incidental to directed or authorised activities are considered to be within the course of employment. Not everything an employee does is specifically stipulated by an employer. In general health care many of the activities a carer will undertake are implied and many are carried out subject to professional judgment and decision-making. These are all carried out within the course of the employment as they are considered to be authorised by the employer. The administration of a drug, ordered by a physician would be covered, for example, even if that drug were to be given negligently, for the administration of drugs is authorised by the employer. However, for example, the prescribing of a drug of dependence by a nurse would not be covered, as such an action, being beyond the scope of nursing activities, would not be authorised by an employer. Another example is where one is travelling in an employer's motor vehicle, so long as one is either directly on route, or diverting for refreshment, one is within the course of employment (*Chaplin v Dunstan Ltd* [1938] SASR 245). Where the employer has prohibited giving lifts, to do so may take one out of the course of employment. However, compulsory third party insurance would enable those injured to claim against the insurance policy of the owner of the car so long as the driver was authorised to drive it; the question thus becoming academic. It may be crucial, however, where the employee is injured, in determining whether the employee is eligible for workers' compensation. This is discussed in Chapter 11.

Employers can also be liable for negligent work practices and activities which they permit or tolerate.

Indemnity and contribution

[6.810] Despite the vicarious liability of an employer, there is the corresponding right of the employer to turn to the negligent employee or agent and require them to contribute to compensation for the harm he or she may have caused.

All Australian jurisdictions have legislation providing for a defendant to claim a proportionate contribution from a third person who they can show contributed to the harm. For example, in *Diamond v Simpson* (No 3) [2003] NSWCA 373 the plaintiff was born under circumstances from which she has suffered lifelong cerebral palsy. In a lengthy trial she was awarded damages of $14 million, reduced on appeal to $11 million. The doctor admitted negligence and sued the hospital for contribution. (*Law Reform (Miscellaneous Provisions) Act 1955* (ACT); *Law Reform (Miscellaneous Provisions) Act 1944* (NSW); *Law Reform (Miscellaneous Provisions) Act* (NT); *Law Reform Act 1995* (Qld); *Law Reform (Contributory Negligence and Apportionment) Act 2001* (SA); *Tortfeasors' and Contributory Negligence Act 1954* (Tas); *Wrongs Act 1958* (Vic); *Law Reform (Contributory Negligence and Tortfeasors' Contribution) Act 1947* (WA).)

Where a patient has been harmed by an employee's negligence, and the employer found vicariously liable, the employer may, in some circumstances, in turn seek indemnity from the negligent employee. In New South Wales, the Northern Territory and South Australia legislation protects employees from being sued by the employer for indemnity (*Employees Liability Act 1991* (NSW);

Law Reform (Miscellaneous Provisions) Act (NT), s 22A(1); *Civil Liability Act 1936* (SA), s 59). In those jurisdictions without such legislation, action by employers against employees is very rare (perhaps because there is not much chance of the defendant being able to pay). Certainly it can, and is, more likely to be claimed where the employee is guilty of serious and wilful misconduct. (See for example, *State of NSW v Wayne Eade* [2006] NSWSC 84 where the State of New South Wales sued a former police officer, for recovery of monies awarded to a person the former police officer had corruptly falsely imprisoned.)

This depends, of course, on negligence being established on the part of the employee. Health carers are not completely immune from liability, and the belief that if you do anything wrong the hospital will stand behind you and take all responsibility should be treated with due scepticism. Certainly, where employees have no money, compensation cannot be extracted from them, but some contribution may be demanded from negligent staff, and the employer also has the options of disciplinary measures (see Chapter 12).

Defences to a Negligence Action

[6.815] When a person is the subject of a negligence action, there are several defences available.

Absolute defences

[6.820] These are so called because if they can be successfully invoked they release the person from further action absolutely: the case goes no further. Absolute defences are as follows.

Expiration of limitation period

[6.825] All jurisdictions have a limitation period beyond which an action cannot be brought. In some jurisdictions it was six years (the Australian Capital Territory, Victoria and Western Australia), others reduced the length of time to three years (New South Wales, the Northern Territory, Queensland and Tasmania). More recently, following the *Review of the Law of Negligence*, three years has become the common limitation period. Where the plaintiff was a minor when harmed, the limitation period did not start to run until the person had reached majority. That has also changed following the *Review of the Law of Negligence*. No matter how much harm is suffered, if the action is not brought within the limitation period, it will not be heard unless an extension of the limitation period is granted by the Court as described below: see *Kosky below*, **[6.830]**. The limitation period traditionally ran from when the accident happened, with extensions generally available (at least in some jurisdictions) from when the effects of the accident first manifested themselves. The *Review of the Law of Negligence* recommended a new test whereby the limitation period be calculated by reference to what became known as the date of discoverability. The text of the relevant recommendation is set out below. However it is important to note that the various Australian jurisdictions have not followed the recommendation consistently. A detailed analysis of the complex variations amongst the various Australian jurisdictions is beyond the scope of this book.

"*Review of the Law of Negligence*
Recommendation 24
The Proposed Act should embody the following principles:
(a) The limitation period commences on the date of discoverability.
(b) The date of discoverability is the date when the plaintiff knew or ought to have known that personal injury or death:
  (i)   had occurred; and
  (ii) was attributable to negligent conduct of the defendant; and
  (iii) in the case of personal injury, was sufficiently significant to warrant bringing proceedings.
(c) The limitation period is 3 years from the date of discoverability.
(d) Subject to (e), claims become statute-barred on the expiry of the earlier of:
  (i)   the limitation period; and
  (ii) a long-stop period of 12 years after the events on which the claim is based ("the long stop period").
(e) The court has a discretion at any time to extend the long-stop period to the expiry of a period of 3 years from the date of discoverability.
(f) In exercising its discretion, the court must have regard to the justice of the case, and in particular:
  (i)   whether the passage of time has prejudiced a fair trial of the claim.
  (ii) the nature and extent of the plaintiff's loss.
  (iii) the nature of the defendant's conduct."

[6.830] Case: *Kosky v Trustees of The Sisters of Charity*
[1982] VR 961

A pregnant woman had a routine blood test in 1975. This showed she had Rh iso-immunisation. Her son was born prematurely and with brain damage. She happened to read a newspaper report some eight years later about similar effects occurring after the administration of incompatible blood to another woman. She contacted the hospital where she had been treated after a car accident in 1967 to see if she had been given blood. That hospital reported that the wrong blood had been prepared for her, but not given. She persisted in her inquiries and found that this advice was a mistake. The Court was asked to extend the limitation period, which had expired, for bringing an action against the hospital.

[6.835] Because she did not have all the information, and could not reasonably have had it within the limitation period, she (and her son) were allowed to bring the action for an event that occurred 13 years earlier, and eight years before the son's conception (see Dix et al (1989), p 234).

No duty of care

[6.840] The defendant shows that the requirements for having a duty of care to the plaintiff did not exist. See, for example, the issues touched on in *McDonald v Sydney South West Area Health Service* [2005] NSWSC 924 and *Goodwill v British Pregnancy Advisory Service* [1996] 2 All ER 161 at **[6.140]** above.

No breach of duty

[6.845] The defendant admits there was a duty of care, but argues that there was no breach of that duty: all reasonable care was given under the circumstances.

[6.850] Case: *Whitehouse v Jordan* [1980] 1 All ER 650 (CA England)

An obstetrician applied forceps during a difficult delivery, and the child was born severely mentally handicapped. The plaintiff, the mother, claimed he had used undue force in delivering the child, and thus was negligent.

[6.855] The doctor was able to adduce evidence, through testimony of his colleagues, that he had not used force which was unreasonable. The Court accepted this.

[6.860] Case: *Hart v Herron* [1984] Aust Torts Reports ¶80-201 (SC NSW)

The plaintiff sued a psychiatrist in negligence, assault and battery. He had been given electroconvulsive therapy without his consent. He later became gravely ill with pneumonia.
He alleged negligence for the following reasons:

1) he did not require psychiatric treatment at all;
2) proper care was not taken to obtain his informed and valid consent;
3) proper precautions for deep sleep therapy were not taken; and
4) timely diagnosis of pneumonia was not made, and proper treatment for it not given.

The defendant conceded negligence according to (3) and (4). The question of negligence in relation to (2) was mentioned earlier (see **[4.70]**).

[6.865] The Court referred to *Whitehouse v Jordan* [1980] 1 All ER 650, and applied it to this case. It was thus held that although the defendant differed in his opinion from another medical practitioner this did not mean that he had been negligent (the *Bolam* test). However it was held that so far as (3) was concerned, the fact that Hart was sedated so deeply that he could not be aroused for exercise or use of toilet facilities was backed by evidence that it was a departure from professional practice.

No causation

[6.870] The defendant here argues that although there was a duty of care, and this was breached, the unreasonable behaviour did not cause the harm. See the case following and also *Barnett v Chelsea Hospital* at **[6.695]** above).

[6.875] Case: *X v Pal* (1991) 23 NSWLR 26 (Court of Appeal NSW)

A woman who had untreated syphilis gave birth to a child with multiple abnormalities including intellectual disability, epilepsy and dysmorphia. Two obstetricians and a paediatrician who were treating the mother at the time had failed to test her for syphilis despite her symptoms. Expert medical evidence indicated that the abnormalities could not have been caused by congenital syphilis, for although it is possible for it to result in intellectual disability, this does not normally become evident until much later in the child's development.

Other conditions, such as hepatosplenomegaly, skin rash, jaundice or periositis, which would have been pathognomic of syphilis were not present, and the abnormalities the child did have were more likely to be the result of intra-uterine developmental abnormality.

[6.880] The Court held that although the child was born with congenital syphilis, many of the abnormalities were not caused by that condition but from another unspecified cause. Damages were limited to the fact that the child was, as a result of the defendants' negligence, born with the disease, and did not cover those abnormalities which the plaintiff could not show were caused by it. The sum awarded was $15,000. See also *Hotson v East Berkshire Area Health Authority* [1987] 2 All ER 909 discussed at **[6.715]**, where it was held that avascular necrosis suffered by a man after a fall and a delay of five days for proper treatment after misdiagnosis was not caused by the delay but the original injury.

No cause because of intervening factor (novus actus interveniens)

[6.885] Sometimes a defendant will concede that he or she acted negligently, and perhaps even caused some harm. However, it is argued that after this negligent action someone else did something which exacerbated the damage to such an extent that the initial cause is no longer operative, and the defendant should thus not be considered liable for it. In this case, the defendant maintains, the result of her or his action would have been different if the second person had not come along and changed the course of events. Negligent medical care can be held to be an intervening factor, but it is considered that where someone has negligently caused harm which necessitates medical treatment, that treatment would have to be *grossly* negligent before a court would see it as breaking the chain of causation. A way of determining whether an action is an intervening factor, which breaks the chain of causation can be demonstrated by considering the following hypothetical situation:

> "Jack drives through a red light and injures Mary, who is driving carefully. Mary is taken to hospital and is on the road to recovery. She is given prophylactic antibiotics, to which she develops a reaction which includes severe diarrhoea, resulting in mild dehydration. To counteract this Mary is given parenteral fluids, but the nurse negligently administers fluids too quickly. Mary develops emphysema and dies (see *Jordan v The Queen* (1956) 40 Cr App R 152)."

In this situation, as Mary was on the path to recovery, one can argue that the original tortfeasor should not be liable for Mary's death—the original action was too remote from the resulting harm. This can be contrasted with the situation where, say:

> "after an original injury on a training exercise, a soldier is carried to the first aid centre. On the way he is dropped several times (causing further injury) and finally given the wrong treatment. He dies, and there is evidence that if he had received immediate and different treatment he would have survived. However the initial injury is still operative and a substantial cause of his death."

In this case the chain of causation has not been broken by the actions of those treating the soldier, as the original harm was still operative at the time of death (see *Smith v The Queen* [1959] 2 QB 35 and *Chapman v Hearse* (1961) 106 CLR 112; [1961] HCA 46 discussed at **[6.175]**). Whilst there are contributing factors that may mean others are also liable in a civil action, the original tortfeasor would be held substantially responsible for the event.

An intermediate situation can result where the court considers that the subsequent acts did not break the chain of events but were contributing factors to the final harm. Liability is shared according to the estimated degree of causation of each act.

[6.890] Case: *Bugden v Harbour View Hospital* [1947] DLR 338 (SC Canada)

The plaintiff was treated at the defendant hospital for an injury to his thumb. The doctor decided to set it and asked nurse B, an experienced graduate nurse, for some novocaine. Nurse B asked nurse S to get the novocaine. Nurse S handed nurse B a phial which was labelled, and, without looking at the label nurse B handed it to the doctor, who, also without checking the label, injected it into Bugden. The drug injected was in fact adrenalin, and Bugden died within an hour.

[6.895] Each person involved argued that the other was in fact liable, as an intervening factor, but the court argued that the nurses should share the liability. Each nurse owed a duty of care to the patient, and the subsequent breach of duty by another will not relieve one who has contributed to the harm. The more appropriate defence in this case would have been that of joint liability (see [6.930]).

Partial defences to a negligence action

[6.900] A partial defence is one where the defendant concedes some degree of liability for the harm, but argues that either the plaintiff or a third party should share the responsibility. If they are successful, they will be liable to pay a proportion of the compensation, in proportion to their degree of culpability. (See *Diamond v Simpson* at [6.810]; see also *Ballard v Cox & Anor* [2006] NSWSC 252.)

Voluntary assumption of risk

[6.905] This defence only applies to those cases where there has been some express or implied bargain between the parties to the effect that the plaintiff has expressly or impliedly given up his or her right to sue the defendant if he or she acts negligently. The plaintiff must have undergone the risk fully understanding the very kind of risk which has materialised. A classic example is accepting a ride from someone who is manifestly intoxicated. A person who agrees to undertake a course of action does not automatically waive his or her right to sue if an ordinary and inherent risk of that activity materialises. Such a waiver must be clearly entered into between the parties, that is, it must be shown that the plaintiff has expressly or impliedly agreed to bear the legal risk of injury and thus relieve the defendant of any liability arising from his or her duty of care. It thus does not apply to consent to medical treatment in normal circumstances. For a more detailed discussion, see McGlone (2005, pp 249-254 and 366ff) regarding multiple tortfeasors.

Contributory negligence

[6.910] The defendant argues that the plaintiff, by her or his behaviour, contributed to the harm. For a more detailed discussion, see McGlone (2005, pp 240-249 and 366ff) regarding multiple tortfeasors.

[6.915] Case: *Brockman v Harpole*, 444 P 2d (1968) (Supreme Court Oregon United States)

A registered nurse working in a doctor's surgery syringed a patient's ears. His eardrums were punctured, but the nurse was able to show that she was badgered considerably by the patient who did not want to wait.

[6.920] The Court in this case held that the nurse did not have to pay full compensation, because the patient had contributed substantially to his own harm. The outcome of this case had it been decided in more recent times may be suspect, as the nurse could arguably have simply refused to undertake the treatment.

[6.925] Case: *Kalokerinos v Burnett* (NSW Court of Appeal, Unreported, CA 40243/95)

B alleged breach of duty of care by Dr K in the diagnosis and treatment of B's cervical carcinoma. When seen by K, B's cancer could have been treated by hysterectomy in such a way as would have meant that B would not have suffered from the consequences of radiation therapy (from which did suffer) such as radiation fistula with consequent bowel and urine diversion.

However, B had failed to take any steps to seek medical attention for vaginal bleeding, a condition which she knew was potentially very dangerous, for a period of 4 months, even though she continued to suffer from serious bleeding and became ill. The Court held that constituted a failure to take reasonable care for her own safety and consequently deducted 20 per cent from the damages awarded to her, to reflect contributory negligence.

Joint liability

[6.930] The defendant is able to point to another person and show that, through their negligence, they are jointly liable, and should share the cost of compensation, as in *Bugden's* case (see **[6.890]**) and *Diamond v Simpson* (see **[6.810]**) and McGlone (2005, p 366ff) regarding multiple tortfeasors.

Further discussion on negligence appears in the following references:

References and Further Reading

There is a wealth of literature on negligence, but the following books are helpful.
Australian Health and Medical Law Reporter (CCH, Sydney, 1991)
Balkin, R and Davis, J, *Law of Torts* (Butterworths, Sydney, 1996)
Clarke, J, "Causation in Chappel v Hart: Common Sense or Coincidence?" (1999) 6 *Journal of Law and Medicine* 335
Dix, et al, *Law for the Medical Profession* (Butterworths, Sydney, 1988)
Dunford, L and Pickford, V, "Is there a Qualitative Difference between Physical and Psychiatric Harm in English Law?" (1999) 7 *Journal of Law and Medicine* 36
Fleming, J, *The Law of Torts* (9th ed, Law Book Co, Sydney, 1998)
Fleming, J, "Remoteness and Duty: The Control Devices in Liability for Negligence" (1953) 31 *Canadian Bar Review* 471
Gunson, J, "An Opening of Floodgates? The Loss of Chance Argument in Medico-Legal Litigation" Address to BLEC Conference (Melbourne, 31 March 2000)

Ipp J et al, *Review of the Law of Negligence* (Australian Government, Department of Treasury, 2002), available online at: http://revofneg.treasury.gov.au/content/reports.asp

Johnstone, M, *Nursing and the Injustices of the Law* (Saunders, Sydney, 1994)

Katter, N, *Duty of Care in Australia* (LBC Information Services, Sydney, 1999)

Kapterian, G, "Harriton, Waller and Australian Negligence Law: Is There a Place for Wrongful Life" (2006) 13(3) *Journal of Law and Medicine* 336

Kerridge I, Lowe, M and McPhee, J, "*Ethics and law for the health professions*" (2nd ed, The Federation Press, Sydney, 2005)

Langslow, A, "The Four Elements" (1981) 10(9) *Australian Nurses Journal* 20 at 21

Luntz, H and Hambly, D, *Torts: Cases and Commentary* (Butterworths, Sydney, 1995)

Madden, B, "South Eastern Sydney Area Health Service v King" (2006) 14(7) *Australian Health Law Bulletin* 83

Madden, B, "Sherry v Australasian Conference Association (t/as Sydney Adventist Hospital)" (2006) 14(7) *Australian Health Law Bulletin* 1

Mann, A, *Medical Negligence Litigation: Medical Assessment of Claims* (International Business Communications, Sydney, 1989)

McGlone, F and Stickley, A, *Australian Torts Law* (Lexis Nexis Butterworths, 2005)

Mason, K, "Fault, Causation and Responsibility: Is Tort Law just an Instrument of Corrective Justice?" (2000) 19 Aust Bar Rev 20

Meryn, S, "Improving Doctor—Patient Communication" (1998) 316 BMJ 1922

Murchison, I A and Nichols, T, *Legal Foundations of Nursing Practice* (Macmillan, London, 1970)

Nisselle, P, "Managing Risk in Medical Practice" (1999) 7 *Journal of Law and Medicine* 130

Phillips, A, *Medical Negligence Law: Seeking a Balance* (Dartmouth, Dartmouth Publishing Company, 1997)

Review of Professional Indemnity Arrangements for Health Care Professionals, *Compensation and Professional Indemnity in Health Care: A Final Report* (Australian Government Publishing Service, Canberra, 1995)

Rice, S, *Some Doctors Make You Sick* (Angus & Robertson, Sydney, 1988)

Scott, R, "Liability of Psychiatrists and Mental Health Services for Failing to Admit or Detain Patients with Mental Illness: Hunter Area Health Service v Presland" *Australian Health Law Bulletin* (14) 3

Skene, L, *Law & Medical Practice – Rights, Duties, Claims & Defences* (Lexis Nexis Butterworths 2004)

Staunton, P and Whyburn, R, *Nursing and the Law* (4th ed, Saunders, Sydney, 1997)

Studdert, D, "Medical Malpractice" (2004) *New England Journal of Medicine* 250

Tito, F, *Compensation and Professional Indemnity in Health Care* (AGPS, Canberra, 1995)

Villa, D, *Annotated Civil Liability Act 2002 (NSW)* (Thomson Lawbook Co, Sydney, 2004)

Walmsley, S et al, *Professional Liability in Australia* (Thomson Lawbook Co, Sydney, 2002)

Weir, M, *Complementary Medicine: Ethics and Law* (Prometheus Publications, Qld)

Whippy, W, "A Hospital's Personal and Non-Delegable Duty of Care for its Patients: A Novel Doctrine of Vicarious Liability Disguised?" (1989) 63 ALJR 182

7 Patient Information

Acquiring information

Communicating information & privacy

Defamation

Patient access

chapter 7

Recording, Communicating and Accessing Patient Information

Introduction

[7.05] Health carers necessarily obtain information about patients. Most of it must be recorded, much of it is confidential, and some of it can be accessed by different people at specified times, in various circumstances.

Acquiring the Information

Who owns medical records?

[7.10] Under the common law, medical records are owned by the maker of the records, that is, the government department or institution, the private hospital or practice, or the individual sole practitioner, as the case may be.

[7.15] Case: *Breen v Williams* (1995) 186 CLR 71; [1995] HCA 63 (High Court of Australia)

The appellant, B, sought access to her medical records for the purpose of participating in class action against manufacturers of breast implants in the United States. It was conceded she could apply for these records through discovery or by subpoena, however this action was based on her right, through contract and/or other common law principles, to access to the records. She argued that she had a proprietary interest in the record, as an implied term of contract (see below, and Chapter 9). Alternatively, she claimed a right to the records as a consequence of the finding in *Rogers v Whitaker* (see **[4.295]**), on the grounds that the

---

principles the Court upheld included the principle of autonomy and the patient's right to know about their health, and a rejection of paternalism and the right of the medical profession to determine a patient's interests. The defendant argued that the handwritten notes were prepared and maintained in the belief that they were private to him, and that such notes made by doctors could include commentary and musings that were not conclusive or what the doctor would consider appropriate for the patient to see, and could be confusing and cause anxiety without explanation. Such records also included administrative matters such as correspondence with lawyers and the medical defence union and thus did not relate to the patient's treatment and management.

[7.20] The High Court concluded that the doctor had a proprietary right to notes and records prepared by him or her. Where the health carer acts as an agent of the patient in providing services, documents brought into existence as a result of that function may be the property of the patient. Generally, however, the contract entered into by a patient and health carer involves the proper care and treatment of the patient, and does not include the ownership by the patient of records made in the process of doing this. The patient's "right to know" does not include the right to the documents.

This means that in Australia there is no common law right of patients to access to their medical records. However rights are established by legislation in each Australian jurisdiction. The public sector has for some time been covered by the Freedom of Information legislation, which requires the production of personal records, with some exceptions. The private sector has more recently been covered by ad hoc legislation and the federal and State privacy regimes.

The federal public sector is governed by the *Freedom of Information Act 1982* (Cth). Section 11 provides that subject to the Act, every person has a legally enforceable right to obtain access in accordance with the Act to a document of an agency, other than an exempt document; or an official document of a Minister, other than an exempt document. The Act provides definitions for exempt documents, provision for fees, a mechanism for application, time limits and a mechanism for review of decisions under it. The Attorney-General's Department site contains information about the *Freedom of Information Act* (FOI), information on how to apply, a list of federal FOI contact officers; State and Territory matters; links to other FOI sites, research aids and annual reports. (see www.ag.gov.au/foi). The State's public sectors are governed by State legislation, such as the *Freedom of Information Act 1989* (NSW), *Freedom of Information Act 1982* (Vic) and similarly named Acts elsewhere. The Federal Attorney-General's site referred to above has a helpful page linking to the various State and Territory FOI sites.

In addition to the various jurisdictions' FOI regimes, rights regarding collection of, and access to, information are created under specific State and Territory legislation (see [7.25]), legislation regarding "privacy" and other legislation dealing with access to health records). (See further discussion at [7.355].)

Functions of medical records

[7.25] A patient's records serve two broad functions:

1) They are a means by which members of the health team can provide good care for patients, they become a historical account of a patient's health care for future reference, and may, with the patient's consent, be a useful tool in medical research. It is obviously part of a reasonable standard of health care that records of a patient's treatment are kept in most circumstances. There is no single Commonwealth case law or legislation specifically requiring that medical records be kept for health care generally, however the Australian Medical Association Code of Ethics 2004 provides, at paragraph 1(f): "Maintain accurate contemporaneous clinical records". At a State or Territory level, legislation makes specific provision for records to be kept. For example, the *Medical Practice Act 1992* (NSW), s 126 provides that the regulations under that Act may make provision for or with respect to requiring registered medical practitioners and corporations engaged in the provision of medical services to make and keep specified records. The *Medical Practice Regulation 2003* (NSW), Part 3 then sets out requirements for records relating to patients, when records are to be made, how long records are to be kept, what should occur in the event of a disposal of a medical practice and in relation to storage. The *Code of Professional Conduct* (pursuant to s 99A of the *Medical Practice Act 1992* (NSW)) reflects the regulatory require-ments, noting at Standard 1.2 the obligation to keep clear, accurate and contemporaneous patient records (see further Appendix 5). Similar provisions exist in other Australian jurisdiction. Hospitals and health institu-tions may have drawn up guidelines, and there should also be procedure manuals available for guidance. Legally, many standards have been established to determine reasonable practice in making and dealing with records, as will be discussed below.

2) They are a contemporaneous record of events which have taken place They are therefore likely to be an accurate account of those events. Records are critical in negligence or other cases in establishing the facts of treatment.

Both of these purposes have legal implications. As a means of patient care, records can be used in court either to prove or to refute a claim of negligence on the part of health carers. As a contemporaneous record of events, medical records can be used to enlighten the court on what care was or was not given, and the condition of the patient at any particular time. Also, the lack of proper record-keeping can be used as evidence of a breach of the standard of care owed to the patient or in a disciplinary context. Carers should be aware of these uses by the law, and should adapt their report writing to these needs. It is suggested that health care can only be enhanced by keeping the above in mind.

For the purposes mentioned above, the following principles should be applied.

Writing reports: Notes for health carers' protection

Reports should be contemporaneous

[7.30] The sooner after the event that a report is made the more likely it is to be accurate, therefore a court is more inclined to accept it as a true and complete record of events. Also, prompt reporting shows efficiency and a greater likelihood of honesty and frankness. The following is an example of the acceptance of a contemporaneous report in preference to a witness's recollection of events.

[7.35] Case: *R v Adams*, The Times, 5 November 1981 (Original hearing, Central Criminal Court London)

Dr A was tried for the murder of his patient, M, who was being nursed at home. M had been given barbiturates and other drugs, including morphia and heroin (legally permissible). The prosecution argued that combinations of morphia, sedomid and heroin had been given over time in such quantities as to indicate that they had been given with the intent to kill the deceased rather than the intent to relieve pain. One of the nurses gave evidence that Dr A would visit M in the evenings about 11 o'clock. At these times Dr A would be alone with M, she said, and would administer drugs in addition to those given and recorded by the nurses, the nature of which they were unaware. The nurse said she could recall giving no drug other than morphia at night. This evidence was obviously damning to Dr A's case.

[7.40] Dr A's counsel procured a copy of the nurse's notes, and questioned the nurse mentioned above in great detail on her memory of the events. She did not know at that stage that the notes were available. She swore to the events she had outlined, and no one doubted her honesty or integrity. What counsel was able to show, however, was that her ability to recall accurately was less than perfect. She could recall giving injections, but not the actual doses. The nurse's notes showed that:

- she had indeed given drugs other than morphia to the deceased;
- all injections administered to M, on previous evenings, including those given by Dr A, were recorded;
- Dr A's visit on the night in question was recorded, as well as the drugs he had given;
- these were the same drugs and dosages as administered on at least one previous occasion; and
- M's condition had been recorded as "very low" a month before she died.

This evidence must have been crucial in the jury's decision to acquit Dr A, for as the doctor's counsel suggested, "mistakes of memory can be made", and the nurse would not have recorded the administration of the drugs, or the doctor's visits, unless these events had happened.

For this important reason, medical records may be used by a witness to refresh her or his memory, or, as in the case above, to challenge the accuracy of a witness's recollection. It is quite reasonable to assume that notes written at the time of the events would be more accurate than those written later, or the reliability of a witness's memory some months or years later at a trial.

This principle has another implication. Whenever a person is conscious of possible legal action over some event, he or she is advised to make a written account of what occurred, separately from the patient's medical record, which should be as accurate as possible. After making such a document, it should be placed in safekeeping in case of need at a later date.

Reports should be adequate and accurate

[7.45] While not including irrelevant material, reports should be carefully and fully made. As pointed out by one commentator: "Writing in a patient's chart should be taken as seriously as providing quality patient care" (Greenlaw (1982), p 125).

Failure to report matters adequately may be evidence of negligence, as it goes to the heart of the first purpose of records stated above: the assistance of good care of the patient. In *Whitree v New York*, 290 NYS 2d 486 (1968), the defendant doctor did not make notes in the hospital record. The Court said: "It is this careless administrative medical procedure that, in our opinion, militates against adequate medical care." Greenlaw ((1982), p 126), points out that charting is not simply a clerical responsibility but a clinical one. Ideally, all institutions should have a set of minimal requirements for reporting, and means of ascertaining that these are maintained. Adequate time should be allowed on each shift for the making and receiving of reports, as they constitute one of the most important aspects of patient care.

Reports should be objective

[7.50] Other than in the context of expert opinion, opinions are generally not accepted in courts, nor is hearsay. If a health carer did not directly see, hear, feel, smell or taste something, but wishes to report its occurrence, it is helpful to state the source of information in reporting it. An example is, "Mrs Jones claims she fell out of her bed"; "Mr Smith states he was attacked with a knife"; "James complaining of pain, says it has got worse". If a health carer thinks Mrs Jones is suffering from shock, the carer should not only say this but rather include signs and symptoms such as "Mrs Jones is pale, sweating, has a feeble pulse with a blood pressure of 90/40" and add, if you wish, "Query shock" to alert others to its possibility. Obviously such reports for patients as "usual day", "good night", etc, are of little use to a court, and may in fact indicate lack of attention to detail on the part of those reporting.

In discussing problems arising from record-keeping, health carers often state a fear that opinions and personal comments, such as stating a patient is "difficult" or their symptoms "imagined", may be used against them, as the basis of a claim in defamation or negligence. One should question why an opinion, other than an honest and reasonably determined diagnosis or preferred treatment, is necessary in medical records. Is it a record of what one has seen, heard, smelt or tasted? If not, is it clear that this is the writer's opinion? Is it a *clinical* opinion? Is it an opinion based on facts?

That is not to say that opinions should not be expressed. There will frequently be times when opinion is called for, for example, where problem-solving approaches to patient care are used. Nursing diagnoses, for example, may be involved, as well as identification of other problems which need to be addressed. These occasions will give rise to opinion, and it is valid and appropriate to record this. However, the adequacy of the opinion is something which cannot later be readily judged unless objective bases for the opinion are also recorded. Clinical data will therefore support the validity of the opinion. In these reports one should be aware of the need to record both objective data or clinical observations, as well as the opinions formed on the basis of this information. An indirect consequence of writing out the objective data first, is that the opinion is more likely to be an accurate one, as the need to justify it will ensure that it is well considered.

Reports should be legible and clear

[7.55] The need for clarity and legibility is obvious, but this rule is breached with frequency. Be cautious in the use of abbreviations and popular terms. These should be widely used and known in the profession. For example, the terms "prn" ("when required") and "ADL's" ("activities of daily living") etc.

Errors should not be obliterated

[7.60] Where a mistake has been made on a hand-written record, rule neatly through it and write the correction beside or above the erroneous words clearly and legibly. Unless the correction is made immediately, appearing beside the crossed out mistake and forming part of the original signed report (for example "Mr Smith was ~~awake~~ asleep at 6 am"), the correction should be signed or initialled and dated by the person making it, who should be the original report writer. If this is not done it could be alleged that changes have been added by someone else or made at a later time, with less than honourable motives. The original mistake should still be legible, and should not be obliterated. It could be a note in the margin where the mistake is corrected after further writing. If more room is required for the correction, it may be written on a sheet of paper and attached. This should, of course, be signed and dated. A marginal note should be made on the original that the addition has been made (for example, cross out the mistake and note in the margin "see attached correction", the attached correction also being initialled and dated is then affixed to the original.

The reason for this advice is to prevent alterations being made to reports after events have occurred when those events have become, or are likely to become, the subject of legal action. Obviously alterations should not be made for the purpose of falsifying a report, but any detection of an alteration which is not clearly and openly made, no matter how innocent its intention, may lead to suspicions that the writer intended to mislead. Clarity in establishing when and by whom the correction is made explains what precisely happened, and provides evidence of the standard of care given by those concerned.

Reports should not be rewritten

[7.65] It is very important to note that reports and charts should never be rewritten at a later date. Errors could be made in the process. The value of a patient's medical record is that it is made contemporaneously with the events it documents; the existence of a "rewrite" policy can call into question the accuracy of every patient record within an institution. If there is additional information which was forgotten at the time the entry was made, it should be included as an addendum. A "rewrite" policy reinforces the mistaken notion that charting is a clerical rather than a clinical responsibility (Greenlaw (1982), p 126). Thus the practice of redoing charts to make them look neater is clearly a dangerous one from the legal point of view.

Treatment orders should not be transcribed

[7.70] For the same reason, treatment orders should not be transcribed into a patient's notes from the original order. They might be erroneously transcribed, which is very possible if the order is difficult to read, and become the source of mistaken treatment. It is also possible, for example, that a doctor may verbally tell a nurse that he or she is going to order one medication, which is written in the patient's notes, and change her or his mind and write down another order, which may be given by another nurse. Refer the reader to the drug chart, where a doctor has written the order. One would write, for example, "seen by Doctor X: medication (or 'sedation', 'pain relief') ordered as per chart". Health carers should, at all times, refer to the original treatment order before carrying out the order; transcribed orders may encourage failure to do this. Similarly, it is better not to rewrite a report from a note which has been scribbled on a piece of paper: write it straight into the patient's notes. However, where health carers are busy, it is advisable to have a pocket notebook on hand to make notes contemporaneously with care, for reference and later inclusion in the patient's medical report. One has then an accurate contemporaneous record, rather than having to rely on memory (when tired and rushed at the end of the shift) as to the time and nature of specific care. Keep the notebook in case it is needed for future reference. Remember that every record of health care treatment is potential evidence in a court of law, be it a scrap of paper or bound volume.

Reports should not be written or signed on behalf of another health carer

[7.75] Reports should represent the knowledge of the person in whose name they are written. The best way of ensuring this is never to write on behalf of another. The person signing a report vouches for its truth and accuracy. Evidence that this was not the case, on even one occasion, will cast doubt on the whole report. Thus:

- the health carer who actually carried out a procedure or administers a drug should write it in the patient's record;

- if not, the person writing the report should check any entry of it on a drug/treatment record before stating that it was recorded as given at the particular time (or was given "according to chart");
- if charting is not required, the person writing the report should check with the person who administered the care, stating that it was "reported as given" at the particular time.

Medical records as evidence

[7.80] Generally, when asked to give evidence in court, or in a statement of facts, a person is required to give only an account of what was experienced by her or his own senses (see, however, **[3.130]** regarding expert evidence). Reciting of what one was told is hearsay evidence, and not usually admissible. Thus, if a person is told by Jack that Fred shot Bob, such a person's evidence would be inadmissible as evidence of the fact that Fred did shoot Bob. It could be admitted, however, as evidence, that the conversation between them took place. Carers should not use hearsay in their daily notes (this includes entries on charts and other reports), unless they identify it as such, because hearsay statements may not be accurate and nurses are protected from liability for negligence by alerting others to the possibility of inaccuracy.

As medical records are not first-hand evidence of what occurred at a particular time, they would normally come under the hearsay rule in a court of law. The court would normally require the writer to swear to their accuracy in fact. However, *Evidence Act* legislation in each Australian jurisdiction allows the court to admit business records as evidence. Medical records can also be subpoenaed by one of the parties. Medical records are described as any record of information, including books, plans, drawings and photographs, made by an owner or employee as part of the business of the enterprise. As they are written at the time of the activity to which they relate, they are taken to be the most accurate of records of what happened at the time. Courts have held that medical records are business records, and that all medical records are potentially admissible. It is up to the court to decide the usefulness of such records.

[7.85] Case: *Albrighton v Royal Prince Alfred Hospital* [1979] 2 NSWLR 165 (Appeal: [1980] 2 NSWLR 542)

The facts of this case are given at **[6.115]**.

In the trial hearing the judge prevented the plaintiff from tendering all the relevant records. It was argued that at least entries by junior medical staff and nursing staff should not be admitted as evidence. In addition it was argued that entries that were illegible, unintelligible, heavily abbreviated, equivocal or ambiguous should be excluded on the grounds that their weight would be too slight to justify admission.

[7.90] On appeal it was held that all available records, no matter by whom they were made are admissible unless the trial judge should rule that they were not relevant to the issue, namely to liability or damages for pain and suffering. Records of a hospital are kept for the information of health carers and treating doctors and are not therefore likely to be "repositories of the speculations of the inept". As to whether they were unintelligible etc, the Court held that they could still be admitted because defects could be overcome by oral evidence ("the unintelligible may be explained, the abbreviated may be expanded" (at 568)). If, at the end of the day, some of the text is unintelligible to the Court, it is either harmless and can be disregarded, or if not, it can be corrected in evidence or the summing up or addresses of counsel. The court (or judge in the absence of a jury) is to determine what weight to place on them.

Dying declarations

[7.95] An important common law exception to the hearsay rule is the dying declaration. This is a statement by a person who is in expectation of imminent death. Therefore if Bob, who is dying, tells someone that Fred shot him, that remark could be admitted and considered as strong evidence that Fred did indeed commit the crime. The rationale for this exception is that it is considered that a person would not lie when facing death as there would most likely be no benefit in doing so. It has happened that a man who was expected to die from gunshot wounds made accusatory statements. In fact he survived, but his accusations were still admitted as dying declarations, as they were made when he truly anticipated death. Many of the traditional rules regarding exceptions to hearsay and evidence generally have now been incorporated into legislation such as the *Evidence Act 1995* (Cth), *Evidence Act 1995* (NSW), *Evidence Act 1958* (Vic) and similarly named Acts in the other Australian jurisdictions.

Incident reports

[7.100] Most hospitals and other health care facilities have adopted the incident report as a means of advancing good quality patient care. Any accidents or other incidents which are unusual (that is, which should not occur in the normal course of events), are recorded and reviewed by the risk management team or administration. The subject matter of them is thus brought to the attention of the administration, and, from the legal point of view, where the reports indicate the need for it, the administration is subsequently obliged to take reasonable action, either to deal with any harm already caused, or to prevent future harm occurring. This becomes a matter of reasonable care in its administration of services to patients, and the provision of a safe and effective working environment for staff.

Incident reports have several uses:

- they identify practices and work environments which give rise to an unacceptable level of risk of harm to patients or health carers (for example, methods and equipment—or lack of it—for lifting patients);
- they monitor the effectiveness of particular practices or equipment (for example, new staffing arrangements or procedures);

- they assist in satisfactorily dealing with an unusual occurrence by the provision of information to those who need to know about it (for example, treatment of injuries, repair of faulty equipment); and
- they are a means of recording events and conditions (including the condition of an injured person) which can be used in the establishment of, or defence to, legal action (for example, identification of the cause of an accident, and standard of care given to the injured before and after it).

They are, therefore, potentially very important legal documents.

Incident reports may be used where health carers believe that their work conditions are unsafe, for example, to establish the extent and causation of back injuries or assaults by patients in an area where it is thought that these are too frequent. Under-staffing is another area of concern where the incident report may be a means of discharging one's duty of care when one feels that on any particular occasion one was expected to work to a standard which was not possible through lack of resources, or where under-staffing is a regular occurrence.

It can be seen that from the administration point of view the incident report is used at several levels:

- identification of existing or potential problems;
- provision of adequate remedies where these have occurred;
- monitoring of the effect of remedies;
- elimination of unsafe conditions or practices (industrial health and safety legislation requires employers to take specific measures for developing safe work environments, see further Chapter 11);
- consequent reduction of workers' compensation claims;
- consequent reduction of and/or protection in negligence claims.

Where there is the possibility of legal action, health carers and management should notify the insurance company covering them or the facility at the first practical opportunity. Where an incident involves staff injury, workers' compensation claim forms should be completed as soon as practicable (again to ensure that the report is contemporaneous and thus accurate).

Incident report as evidence

[7.105] Where an account of an unusual event is documented in an incident report it can be used, as can other medical records, to establish the facts for legal purposes. This means the report can provide protection for staff where it shows clearly that care was reasonable, and if the event was due to negligence, it can establish that reasonable steps were taken to remedy any harm caused, thus helping to lessen the damages for which anyone is liable. Honesty and accuracy are advisable, as detection of anything that could indicate attempts to cover up the facts could exacerbate the liability of those concerned.

Because incident reports are admissible in court, it is very important to keep in mind that they should not contain opinion statements, for example, the cause of the accident, or allocation of fault: opinions may indicate a less than reasonable approach on the part of health carers, especially if they are wrong, and the allocation of blame may be taken as a confession (even where the one confessing was not in fact negligent).

There is no limit to the uses of incident reports, despite the fact that forms may be drawn up in such a way that they limit the perceived methods for reporting, and the topics one can report. It is suggested that where an incident report form does not make allowances for a particular event, or give room for all the details to be included, carers should attach a sheet of paper and include these. Again, as with medical records, there should be a clear notation referring to the addition on the form, along the lines of "see Attachment A". The notation and the attachment should be signed and dated.

Incident reports are used by quality assurance committees to identify unsatisfactory aspects of the organisation's activities, to determine causes and rectify them. Reporting by quality assurance committees should follow specific guidelines in accordance with the hospital or organisation policy.

Checklist

INFORMATION TO INCLUDE IN INCIDENT REPORTS

- ✓ date and time of incident;
- ✓ place where the incident occurred;
- ✓ names and details of all parties concerned (written legibly);
- ✓ brief but full and accurate account of what the writer experienced (no hearsay unless identified as such, and no allocation of blame);
- ✓ if a person was harmed, their condition before the incident took place;
- ✓ any harm caused and to whom or what it was caused (objective observations, with any opinion or diagnosis identified as such);
- ✓ any action taken, and by whom it was taken (for example, doctor or relatives called, treatment given);
- ✓ any further treatment ordered and follow-up requirements (such as observations, check-ups);
- ✓ list of witnesses (legible); and
- ✓ where the report concerns faulty equipment, the equipment should be clearly identified: location and identifying number or name, and details of the sign which has been attached to the equipment warning of its fault should be recorded.

Reporting a serious incident

[7.110] Where a serious incident has occurred it is crucial that authorities are notified immediately, not only to provide care for anyone injured, but also to enable the hospital insurer and legal representatives to be contacted. This should be done within hours of the event, by phone at least. Health carers involved should consider legal advice as soon as possible for the following reasons:

- There is a difference between the incident report and any statement made to a lawyer. The latter may be protected by lawyer-client legal privilege, which means that it would be inadmissible as evidence against the carer in any hearing. Thus health carers are advised to avail themselves of legal advice if they are asked to make a statement, or wish to do so, and are in any way concerned that they may be legally implicated by what they say. A free legal consultation may be available at a Legal Aid Office, through the State or Territory Law Society, or one's union.

- If the carer is an independent contractor and insured, he or she can benefit by notifying the insurance company of the occurrence as soon as possible. Indemnity insurance covers negligent actions.

Health carers should, of course, resist improper attempts to get them to make statements which they do not believe are a true representation of the facts, or to alter their statement. This may be done to prevent unfavourable legal action being brought against the hospital staff.

Communicating Information

Privacy and confidentiality

[7.115] As noted by *Skene* (2nd ed, 2004, paras [9.1], [9.8]), privacy issues such as those described below are conceptually different to confidentiality issues. Privacy focuses on the collection of information, and confidentiality focuses on its communication. However, the two concepts usually overlap to a substantial extent and so are dealt with together. The terms are used interchangeably.

Privacy

[7.120] Health carers are in the position where they may be the repository of information which, in the circumstances, should be treated as confidential. Patients trust health professionals not to disclose all that they learn in their day-to-day caring for them. At common law there was no clearly defined legally enforceable patients' right to privacy, the relationships of health carer and patient nevertheless gave rise to privacy obligations, which are set out below.

What is confidential information?

[7.125] Disclosures made to another with the express condition that they are confidential are, obviously, the subject of confidentiality at law. However, the health professional gains a lot of information which is not expressly given with the proviso that it is confidential and not to be disclosed to anyone. Also, through dealings with the patient the health carer may have indirectly received information about other people, such as family members or a spouse. Unless there is a clear understanding to the contrary, all such information is by implication confidential due to the fact of the carer–patient relationship. This includes all information relating to the carer's professional relationship with the patient. Gossip during the tea-break can be a breach of that confidentiality, and carers should be careful what they say on such occasions.

It has been suggested that the purpose of the right to privacy is not merely the protection of the special nature of the relationship between health carers and their patients, nor the peace of mind and reputation of the patient, although these are certainly reasons for respecting patients' privacy. The most important reason, it is argued, is the need to ensure that a patient feels able to disclose those facts which may be embarrassing, but vital for her or his proper care and treatment. Modern technology has created the potential for inroads into any absolute concept of confidentiality, as the use of electronic recording, transfer and access to information, and ever-growing corporatisation of large groups of health carers (such as medical centres, which can include doctors, pathologists and other ancillary services) means that many people other than the health carers themselves (such as clerical and reception personnel) may have access to patient information in the course of their work. Health insurance and Medicare claims, drug prescriptions and referrals to rehabilitation workers, and secretarial services in the processing and filing of records involve the creation of further records and files or simply the sharing of facts about the patient.

Research, which is a growing area of academic development, particularly for nurses and health care academics, may mean that the patient's records become the province of even more people. Policies and practices may easily be rendered ineffective in protecting privacy, so continual vigilance should be maintained in practising this ethical and legal requirement of one's profession.

The extent of health carers' duty of confidentiality

[7.130] The precise nature of any common law obligation of confidence is uncertain, as it has grown in a rather haphazard fashion (Brazier (1992), p 46). In the case of *Seager v Copydex* [1967] 1 WLR 923 it was established by Lord Denning (at 931) that:

> "[A person who] has received information in confidence shall not take unfair advantage of it. He must not make use of it to the prejudice of him who gave it without obtaining his consent."

Just what this means in practical terms, however, is not clear.

Under common law, it would seem, the duty to maintain confidentiality applies to all those who come in contact with the confidential information as part of the health care process, including filing clerks and secretaries. The obligation does not cease when the professional relationship has ceased, nor with the death of the patient. It also applies to the patient of someone else. Unintended breach of confidence may be the subject of a negligence action by the patient.

The health carer–patient relationship is not "privileged"

[7.135] The relationship between doctor and patient is definitely *not* the same as that between lawyer and client; the latter being privileged and generally protected from disclosure in court (see, however, **[7.225]**). Where a judge directs a doctor or other health carer to disclose confidential information, failure to do so could result in contempt of court proceedings, and could possibly lead to imprisonment. In the case of *Hunter v Mann* [1974] 2 WLR 742, an English court convicted a doctor of contempt for refusing to disclose information about patients of his who were wanted in connection with a criminal offence.

Some Australian jurisdictions have, however, created statutory evidence protections of relevance to health carers. For example, New South Wales has amended its *Evidence Act 1995* (NSW) to create a category of "professional coincidental relationship privilege" (s 126Aff) and "sexual assault communication privilege" (s 126Gff). Communications made by a person to another who is acting in a professional capacity and under an obligation to maintain confidentiality and communications in relation to sexual assault (such as counselling) may be exempt from production in legal proceedings. Victoria has amended its *Evidence Act 1958* (Vic) (s 32Bff) to extend a similar privilege to communications made to a medical practitioner or counsellor by a person who has been sexually assaulted.

Statutory provisions for protection of privacy

[7.140] Privacy and confidentiality considerations now have the overlay of a statutory regime, which is of relatively recent origin and so still somewhat in a state of flux. The *Privacy Act 1988* (Cth) contains 11 Information Privacy Principles (IPPs) which apply to Commonwealth and Australian Capital Territory government agencies. It also has 10 National Privacy Principles (NPPs) which apply to parts of the private sector and to all health service providers. The Principles cover a range a self-explanatory areas, as follows:

Principle 1—Collection
Principle 2—Use and disclosure
Principle 3—Data quality
Principle 4—Data security
Principle 5—Openness
Principle 6—Access and correction
Principle 7—Identifiers
Principle 8—Anonymity
Principle 9—Transborder data flows
Principle 10—Sensitive information

The National Privacy Principles are further summarised in Appendix 3.

To assist health service providers in the private sector to understand their new obligations, the Office of the Privacy Commissioner has produced *Guidelines on Privacy in the Private Health Sector* and a *Short Guide for the Private Health Sector*. The Office has also produced tailored information specific to doctors and pharmacists in conjunction with the Medicare Australia. See **[7.150]** and the website of the Federal Privacy Commissioner for more information: www.privacy.gov.au/.

Privacy legislation at the State and Territory level

[7.145] The Federal Privacy Commissioner's website helpfully provides links to the equivalent State and Territory sites: www.privacy.gov.au/links/index.html#2

As often occurs in the Australian federal system, there are differences between the federal provisions and the provisions of the various other Australian jurisdictions. The following outline is drawn from the Federal Privacy Commissioner's helpful summary at www.privacy.gov.au/privacy_rights/laws/ index.html#5, where more detail is available.

Table 7.1: Summary of State legislative instruments regarding privacy

State	Statutory Provision
New South Wales	Privacy and Personal Information Protection Act 1998 Health Records and Information Privacy Act 2002 Freedom of Information Act 1989 State Records Act 1998 Criminal Records Act 1991 (Spent Convictions) Listening Devices Act 1984 Workplace Surveillance Act 2005 Telecommunications (Interception) (New South Wales) Act 1987 Access to Neighbouring Land Act 2000
Victoria	Information Privacy Act 2000 Health Records Act 2001 Freedom of Information Act 1982 Public Records Act 1973 Surveillance Devices Act 1999 Telecommunications (Interception) (State Provisions) Act 1988
Queensland	State Government Standards Nos 42 (Information Privacy, Sep 2001) and 42A (Information Privacy for the Qld Dept of Health, Sep 2001) (administrative standards); also see Parliamentary report (tabled April 1998) Freedom of Information Act 1992 Public Records Act 2002 Criminal Law (Rehabilitation of Offenders) Act 1986 (spent convictions) Invasion of Privacy Act 1971(listening devices, invasion of privacy of the home) Invasion of Privacy Regulations (1998) Whistleblowers Protection Act (1994) Police Powers and Responsibilities Act 2000 (Chapter 4 deals with Covert Evidence Gathering Powers)
Western Australia	Freedom of Information Act 1992 State Records Act 2000 Spent Convictions Act 1988 Surveillance Devices Act 1998 Telecommunications (Interception) Western Australia Act 1996

State	Statutory Provision
South Australia	Cabinet Administrative instruction to comply with Information Privacy Principles (originally issued in 1989, re-issued in 1992) Freedom of Information Act 1991 State Records Act 1997 Listening and Surveillance Devices Act 1972 Telecommunications (Interception) Act 1988
Tasmania	Personal Information Protection Act 2004 Freedom of Information Act 1991 Archives Act 1983 Annulled Convictions Act 2003 (spent convictions) Listening Devices Act 1991 Telecommunications (Interception) Tasmania Act 1999
Northern Territory	Information Act 2002 (privacy, FOI and public records) Criminal Records (Spent Convictions) Act 1992 Surveillance Devices Act 2000 Telecommunications (Interception) Northern Territory Act 2001
Australian Capital Territory	Health Records (Privacy and Access) Act 1997 Freedom of Information Act 1989 Territory Records Act 2002 (public records) Human Rights Act 2004 (right to privacy) Spent Convictions Act 2000 Listening Devices Act 1992

In New South Wales for example, there is specific legislation, the *Health Records and Information Privacy Act 2002* (NSW) governing the handling of health information in both the public and private sector in respect of health. This includes hospitals, whether public or private, doctors, and other health care organisations. It may include other organisations that have any type of health information—so for example, a law firm which obtains health information during a court case, a university that undertakes research, or a gymnasium that records information about a person's health and injuries.

The Acts in various jurisdictions differ, even in how many privacy principles they espouse. The New South Wales legislation for example, contains not 10 but 15 Health Privacy Principles (HPPs). Arguably however the *Health Records and Information Privacy Act 2002* (NSW) governs the handling of information in both the public and private sector. The New South Wales HPPs can be grouped into seven main headings:

* collection;
* storage;
* access & accuracy;
* use;
* disclosure;
* identifiers and anonymity; and
* transferrals and linkage.

See the website of the New South Wales Privacy Commissioner for more information: www.lawlink.nsw.gov.au/lawlink/privacynsw/ll_pnsw.nsf/pages/PNSW_index.

Guidelines for National Privacy Principles about health information for the private sector

[7.150] As mentioned at **[7.140]**, the Privacy Commissioner has produced certain publications and guidelines, made publicly available on the internet at www.privacy.gov.au/health/pubs/index.html#1. Those include:

- *My Health My Privacy My Choice*—a consumer's guide to privacy and health information
- *Health Information and the Privacy Act 1988: A Short Guide for the Private Health Sector* (December 2001)
- *Some Privacy Issues for Doctors* (December 2001)
- *Some Privacy Issues for Pharmacists* (December 2001)

There are also a series of information sheets available at: http://www.privacy.gov.au/business/infosh/index.html.

To comply with the privacy legislation, individuals and private organisations should review existing procedures and formulate and implement policies in relation to the collection, storage, disclosure and access to personal information. They must ensure that systems are in place and employee training is carried out, so that those dealing with personal information are aware of, and follow, the Privacy Principles.

State and Territory legislation

[7.155] There are specific statutory requirements in each Australian jurisdiction for the staff of government health authorities to respect the confidentiality of patients whom they treat, as well as general privacy legislation. For example, *Health Administration Act 1982* (NSW); *South Australian Health Commission Act 1976* (SA); *Tasmanian State Service Act 1984* (Tas); *Health Services Act 1988* (Vic). The *Privacy Act 1988* (Cth) provides that all Commonwealth officers have an obligation to keep records confidential. The requirements generally provide that it is unlawful for any person to disclose any information relating to patients except with their consent, when required by law, or to lessen a serious threat to the life and health of the individual. Health carers should be familiar with such provisions by finding out what legislation applies to them and the relevant provisions regarding confidentiality. These may also provide for those occasions when staff may be required to disclose certain matters to their employer.

There are also requirements in some Australian jurisdictions to report child abuse and in all jurisdictions, certain infectious diseases. This legislation is outlined in Chapter 16.

Ethical codes, guidelines and administrative instructions

[7.160] Codes of ethics for most established health care professional bodies, such as the Hippocratic Oath, the Australian Medical Association Code of Ethics, nursing codes of conduct and ethical codes for allied health care professionals set out provision for health carers to maintain the confidentiality of patient information.

In 2005, New South Wales introduced a *Code of Professional Conduct* under the *Medical Practice Act 1992* (NSW), which is reproduced on the New South Wales Medical Board website at www.nswmb.org.au/ and extracted at Appendix 5.

Legislation

[7.165] At the time of writing, most medical boards in the Australian jurisdictions have adopted, or are in the process of adopting, provisions in essentially the same terms as the New South Wales Code. However, as regards records, the Code tends to simply assert an obligation to keep clear, accurate and contemporaneous patient records in accordance with the requirements of the *Medical Practice Regulation 2003* (NSW), Schedule 2. It is that schedule which deals with the form and contents of medical records, under the following headings:

1. Information to be included in record
2. General requirements as to content
3. Form of records
4. Alteration and correction of records
5. Delegation

The New South Wales Regulation provides a good precedent for medical record content, even for those practising where it does not apply.

Breach of confidence

[7.170] Both common law and equity provide relief for breach of confidence. The law is not fully developed in these areas, but four actions at common law appear to be available:

*   breach of contract;
*   tort ("breach of confidence")
*   negligence; and
*   defamation.

To a limited extent, varying between jurisdictions, there can be said to exist a statutory protection, though the individual statutes may impose a penalty rather than giving rise to an entitlement to civil damages. Of course, a patient may argue that legislation gives rise to an implied contractual term. (See the discussion by Kerridge, p 245, referring by way of example to the *Health Administration Act 1982* (NSW), *Human Tissue Act 1983* (NSW), and *Public Health Act 1991* (NSW).)

As to whether there exists in Australia a general protection of privacy, after *Victoria Park Racing and Recreation Grounds Co Limited v Taylor* (1937) 58 CLR 479; [1937] HCA 45 it was long thought that no such remedy existed. However, *Australian Broadcasting Corporation v Lenah Game Meats Pty Ltd* (2001) 208 CLR 199; [2001] HCA 63 raises that possibility. (See also *Campbell v MGN Limited* [2004] UKHL 22 and the discussion by Kerridge, p 250.)

Breach of contract

[7.175] Patients enter a contractual relationship with their health carer, whether it is implied or specific (see Chapter 9). There may be a specific term of the agreement for treatment of a patient that information received by the professional is to be the subject of confidence. This would be rare. However, it has been argued that there is an implied term of the contract that the health carer will act in the "best interests" of the patient (*Sidaway's case* at **[4.150]**). But there is some degree of uncertainty as to whether this includes an implied contractual term of confidentiality. The High Court in *Breen v Williams* (see **[7.15]**) considered whether access to medical records by a patient is included in an implied term to act in the patient's interests. Gaudron J and McHugh J considered *Sidaway's case* and held that a doctor does not warrant that he or she would be liable for any act that objectively was not in the best interests of the patient. This would put too uncertain an obligation on the doctor, and thus be contrary to the principles of contract law. They questioned whether there is an implied term to act in the patient's interests in Australian law. They held that even if there is, the only relevant contractual term implied by law would be to provide reasonable care and skill in advice, diagnosis and treatment.

The patient may have contracted for treatment by a health care provider who is an employer (for example, a hospital). Dissemination of confidential information about the patient by the employee health carer would then raise the question of whether there was a breach of contract by the employer through its employees. Where a report involving information regarding a patient is required by a third party such as a prospective employer or insurance company, carers should make sure that they have the permission of the patient to release such information. Such consent should preferably be in the form of a written authority, signed by the patient. The fact of the request may indicate the patient's consent, but in any circumstances where it is possible or likely the request may be sent without the patient's consent, those holding the information should investigate further.

If information is lawfully passed on to a third person with the understanding that it is confidential, the relationship between the patient and the third person, given the principle of privity of contract (see Chapter 9), under the common law at least, is uncertain. Where A gives confidential information to a health carer, B, who passes it on to a third party, C, with A's knowledge and express or implied consent, for the purpose of rendering a service to A, the terms of the giving of information are subject to the same terms existing between A and B. It is thus B's responsibility to ensure C is aware of the confidential nature of the information, and for C to maintain the confidentiality. However, as indicated above, the privacy legislation will most probably still apply to C (see [7.145]). This would not be because of any contractual term, but rather because of other legal principles applying to confidentiality as outlined below.

The tort of breach of confidence

[7.180] There does not have to be a contract between people for an obligation to maintain the confidentiality of information. An action for breach of confidence can be brought where:

- the information is confidential in nature;
- it has been imparted in circumstances giving rise to an obligation of confidence; and
- it is used without authorisation to the detriment of the person who gave it.

A breach of confidence thus occurs in equity where confidential information is disclosed without authorisation. Whether the information given to health carers by a patient comes under the category of confidential information has not been specifically ruled on by the courts, but it would seem to have the necessary quality of confidence, particularly as it is intimate and personal, and because professional ethics have deemed it so.

Equitable remedy: Breach of confidence

[7.185] There is a remedy in equity (see [1.80]) for disclosure of confidential information which has been discovered through a relationship of trust, such as a marital relationship.

[7.190] Case: *Argyll v Argyll* [1967] Ch 302 (CA England)

The Duke of Argyll sought to sell information about the private life of his estranged wife, the Duchess of Argyll, to the newspapers. This information involved secrets disclosed to him during their marriage. The duchess applied to the court for an injunction preventing him from doing so.

[7.195] The Court held that within marriage, there is a duty for each spouse to maintain the confidence of the other. Note that this is an equitable principle, not a common law one, though there may in some circumstances be an entitlement to compensation (see *Stephens v Avery* [1988] 2 All ER 477; and generally the discussion regarding "personal confidences" (by Dal Pont and Cockburn (2005, paras [6.35]ff and [6.95]ff)) there is no allowance for damages for harm or hurt reputation or feelings. An application may be brought for an injunction preventing a person from disclosing information where disclosure is anticipated, or from continuing to do so if information has already been disclosed.

Tort law: Action in negligence

[7.200] Where confidential information is negligently disclosed, a person may claim that this has resulted in harm. He or she must show that:

- the health carer failed to exercise reasonable care by disclosing the information;
- it was reasonably foreseeable that disclosure could harm the patient; and
- the patient suffered harm as a result of the disclosure.

[7.205] Case: *Furniss v Fitchett* [1958] NZLR 396

A husband and wife were having marital difficulties. They both attended the same doctor, Dr Fitchett. At the husband's request, the doctor wrote a report stating that in his opinion Mrs F suffered from paranoia, and "An examination by a Psychiatrist would be needed to fully diagnose her case and its requirement". The doctor did not ask the purpose of the report, nor did he mark it "confidential". The document was kept secret by the husband for 12 months, then used by her husband's lawyer in proceedings for marital separation. As a result of being confronted by the document, Mrs F suffered psychological harm. It is of note that the doctor argued that his intention in writing the report was to ensure that Mrs F would not be committed to a psychiatric institution, without further examination by a specialist. He also conceded that he knew that the disclosure to his patient of his opinion of her mental condition would be harmful to her. The jury found the doctor liable, and he appealed.

[7.210] The Court held that:

- while the doctor did not have to foresee the precise manner in which the contents of his report would come to the knowledge of Mrs F, given the circumstances, he ought to have foreseen that the information could be expected to be used in some legal proceedings and thus come to her knowledge;
- he should have foreseen that in giving the document to the husband with no restrictions on its use it could come to the notice of the wife; and
- the doctor thus had a duty of care to Mrs F, that no expression of his opinion as to her mental condition should come to her knowledge.

Readers might like to question whether giving a written report to the husband at all, even with the motive claimed by Dr Fitchett, was justified. Unless exceptions outlined below apply, confidential patient information should only be given under the following circumstances:

- the recipient is someone who needs to know the information for the patient's welfare;

- it is limited to information necessary for that purpose; and
- it is disclosed in a way that is least harmful to the patient.

In passing, it is of interest to consider whether such an action would be maintainable in Australian jurisdictions with provisions such as *Civil Liability Act 2002* (NSW), s 32(1), which provides that a person does not owe a duty of care to another person to take care not to cause the plaintiff mental harm unless the defendant ought to have foreseen that a person of normal fortitude might, in the circumstances of the case, suffer a recognised psychiatric illness if reasonable care were not taken. The analysis may become somewhat confusing in circumstances such as applied in *Furniss v Fitchett*, where Mrs Furniss already suffered paranoia to some degree and perhaps was not of normal fortitude to begin with.

When confidential information may be disclosed

[7.215] Courts have held that confidential information about a patient should only be disclosed if:

- the patient agrees to the disclosure;
- disclosure is compelled by law;
- there is a duty to the public to disclose; and
- the interests of one of the parties is involved (for example, the patient's, carer's or hospital's).

Agreement to disclosure

[7.220] Even without the relevant privacy principles, health carers should consider all information they receive from, or about, a patient as confidential, unless the patient has specifically agreed to its disclosure or it is on the public record. However, a patient is presumed to have agreed to the disclosure of confidential information only where it is necessary for his or her welfare, in the normal course of administration of the medical practice or health facility, or where the information is required to obtain insurance payments or other benefits which are known to the patient to be part of the process of their care— and even then, with careful regard to privacy legislation.

Compulsion by law

[7.225] There is legislation which requires disclosure of certain information to the authorities, for example, infectious diseases and child abuse (more fully dealt with in Chapter 16). Health carers are also required to disclose any information which is required in the process of a court proceeding, or to produce records or other information in court proceedings. No action could be taken against a carer by the patient in these circumstances (see *Brown v Brooks*, below at **[7.255]**). However, caution must be exercised even in the context of court proceedings, as demonstrated by the following case.

> **[7.230] Case:** *Kadian v Richards* (2004) 61 NSWLR 222;
> NSWSC 382; *Richards v Kadian* [2005] NSWCA 328
>
> The plaintiff was a six-year-old boy, A, born with congenital
> heart disease and a defective right kidney. The first defendant was
> the paediatrician who had care of A during the first nine months
> of his life, and was sued concerning an alleged delay in diagnosis
> of the congenital heart disease. The second defendant was in
> effect the Auburn Hospital, where A's mother received some
> antenatal treatment, and where A was born. When A was nine
> months old, the first defendant referred him to Dr Gary Sholler, a
> paediatric cardiologist. A also saw a paediatric nephrologist Dr
> Deborah Lewis, who treated A from time to time throughout his
> life. The defendants' representatives wished to speak to Dr Sholler
> and Dr Lewis.

[7.235] The plaintiff's representatives refused. However, they did offer to
consider provision of consent for a written report, as follows: "In an attempt
to resolve this dispute before 1st November, please provide us with a list of
questions which the first defendant proposes to have Dr Sholler address, so that
we can consider whether to advise the plaintiffs to authorise Dr Sholler to
address such questions in writing. We suggest that the said list of questions
be provided to us by way of a proposed letter of instruction addressed to
Dr Sholler, requesting a formal report."

This offer was refused:

> "We do not propose to prepare a specific list of questions. It is not practicable
> to do so as the answers to set questions may necessitate other areas of
> inquiry ... We are prepared to provide you with a list of issues ... which we
> intend to discuss with Dr Sholler ... it may be necessary to proceed beyond
> the listed issues ...".

At the trial, the defendant failed in his application for a declaration that in
commencing these proceedings the first plaintiff has waived his right to confidentiality which arises from the doctor-patient relationship between the first
plaintiff and Dr Sholler and Dr Lewis, or an order that the proceedings be stayed
until the plaintiff provides a signed written authority permitting Dr Sholler and
Dr Lewis to discuss their management and treatment of the first plaintiff with
legal representatives of the first defendant.

The first defendant also failed on appeal to the New South Wales Court of
Appeal. The Court was required to consider whether by commencing litigation,
A had to some extent, impliedly waived certain of his rights of confidentiality.

The Court noted that A's act of commencing proceedings against the first
defendant was inconsistent with doctor-patient confidentiality continuing to
exist between A and the first defendant, concerning the matters which were the
subject of the litigation. A defendant must have a fair opportunity to defend
the case brought against them. If a defendant were bound by an obligation of
confidentiality concerning his treatment of a plaintiff, it would not be possible

for him to tell his own lawyers what happened concerning treatment, in order to defend himself. Neither could he tell expert witnesses what had happened.

But as the trial judge noted, even when a patient sues his own doctor, not all obligations of confidentiality between them are waived (see **[7.225]**).

It should be noted that there is no legally protected doctor–patient relationship, except through statute, as mentioned above at **[7.135]**. Lord Denning stated in *Attorney-General v Mulholland* [1963] 2 WLR 658 (at 665):

> "The only profession I know of which is given a privilege from disclosing information to a court of law is the legal profession, and then it is not the privilege of the lawyer but of his patient. Take the clergyman, the banker or the medical man. None of these is entitled to refuse to answer when directed to by a judge. ... The judge will respect the confidences which each member of these honourable professions receives in the course of it, and will not direct him to answer unless not only it is relevant but also it is a proper and, indeed, necessary question in the course of justice to be put and answered. A judge is the person ... to weigh these conflicting interests ... on the one hand the respect due to confidence in the profession and on the other hand the ultimate interest of the community in justice being done."

It is important to emphasise again however that this statement of common law principle must be considered subject to statutory provisions in the various Evidence Acts.

Disclosure in the public interest

[7.240] A health carer may also disclose information if it is in the public interest to do so. The public interest exception has been described by some commentators as the most problematic exemption, as it is difficult to specify with precision and mostly derived from case law, although there are some code and legislative recognitions as outlined below at **[7.265]** (see Skene (2004, para [9.39]ff)). An example could be where a health carer is aware of a patient's likelihood to kill or harm another person or other people. This could be because of psychiatric illness or physical disability where the welfare of others is dependent on physical integrity: for example, an airline pilot's weak heart. In a Californian case, *Tarasoff v Regents of the University of California* 551 P 2d 334 (1976), a patient told his psychologist that he intended to kill his girlfriend. The psychologist did not warn either the girlfriend or her family, and the man did indeed kill her. The court held that in failing to notify the girl or her family the psychologist breached a duty of care which he owed to the victim as a member of the public. The court stated that any duty the doctor owed to the patient was outweighed by the public interest in safety, which placed a duty on the doctor to warn of the potential harm.

The following case involving disclosure of confidential information and the duty of health carers to the public, as well as their patient, sets out some important issues.

[7.245] Case: *W v Edgell* [1990] 1 All ER 855 (CA England)

The plaintiff, W had been convicted of manslaughter after killing five people. He was diagnosed as suffering from paranoid schizophrenia, which involved delusion of persecution by his neighbours. W was detained under a mental health order in a secure psychiatric hospital, the order being for an indefinite period. Some years later a mental health review tribunal considered his case, and recommended that W be released to a less secure facility. This recommendation was based on a report by a Dr G, W's treating psychiatrist, that his condition was being controlled by medication and that he was suitable for transfer. The Home Secretary refused consent to the transfer, and W appealed to the tribunal for a review of the Home Secretary's decision. W's solicitor's sought an opinion from Dr Edgell an independent consultant. Dr Edgell's report was in fact unfavourable to W, and he sent it to the solicitors believing it would be presented to the tribunal. He was concerned, because he believed W was still dangerous, and his outstanding interest in explosives and guns had not been adequately explored in Dr G's report.

W's solicitors, not wanting Dr Edgell's report to be seen by the tribunal, withdrew W's application. Dr Edgell then sent a copy of his report to the hospital where W was detained, the Home Secretary and the Department of Health and Social Security.

W sought an injunction to refrain further communication of the report, return of copies and damages for breach of confidentiality.

[7.250] The Court dismissed W's application holding that Dr Edgell's duty to W to maintain confidentiality was overridden by his duty of care to bring his concerns to the proper authorities. However, the competing interests were really the public interest, firstly in the maintenance by the health care profession of the confidence and privacy of patients, and secondly in the protection of the public from danger. Whilst the general principle is that for disclosure in the public interest, the risk to others must be "real, immediate and serious", and W would not be released before further examination, the Court considered the circumstances of the case, and held that the number of killings by W were enough to give rise to "the gravest concern for the safety of the public" (per Sir Stephen Brown P at 846).

[7.255] Case: *Brown v Brooks* (18 August 1988, SC NSW) (discussed in *Australian Health and Medical Law Reporter* (1991) ¶27-770)

A man was charged with sexual assault of his stepdaughter. He underwent counselling by a clinical nurse specialist at his local public hospital, and in the course of the counselling discussed his relationship with the stepdaughter. These sessions were recorded in his medical records. After learning about these sessions, the police required a statement from the nurse in relation to what was said in the sessions. The man sought an injunction to prevent the hospital or the nurse giving information to the police.

[7.260] The Court refused the injunction, stating that it is contrary to public policy to give preference to the right to confidentiality when it would impede the investigation of a crime. While recognising the desirability of maintaining the confidentiality of consultations between patients and health service providers, the Court said that confidence could not be maintained where information was necessary for the prosecution of a serious crime.

Other examples of where disclosure to an appropriate authority has been held to be in the public interest are:

- disclosure of information about a blood donor where a blood recipient contracted HIV from a transfusion (*Australian Red Cross and Anor v BC* Supreme Court of Victoria (7 March 1991));
- disclosure to the authorities of a patient's proclivities for arson (CCH (1993) ¶27-770), or crime (Skene (2004, para [9.40]). The Australian Medical Association and the Medical Board of Victoria supported a call by police to all doctors in Victoria to come forward if they have any information in relation to the perpetrator of attacks on young girls, dubbed "Mr Cruel" (see Mendelson (1994); Morrell, S, "Dob in Mr Cruel, Docs told" *Herald Sun*, 21 May 1992); and
- where a patient suffers from HIV/AIDS and will not tell his or her partner (Royal Australasian College of Surgeons, *Infection Control in Surgery, Management of AIDS (HIV) and Hepatitis B*, p 3 cited from Skene (1998), p 206; but see **[7.275]** and **[7.300]** below, regarding legislation on this particular issue).

An example where disclosure was held not to be in the public interest is the following case.

[7.263] Case: *X v Y & Ors* [1988] 2 All ER 648 (Queen's Bench Division UK)

The plaintiffs, members of a health authority, sought an injunction to prevent publication by a newspaper of confidential information that two doctors in general practice suffered from AIDS. The newspaper had initially wanted to publish the names of the doctors, but agreed to publish non-identifying information. The question was whether disclosure was in the public interest, the newspaper arguing that the public was entitled to such information. They said that no harm would be caused to the plaintiff if no names were given. The plaintiffs said that publication would be a breach of confidentiality, and produced evidence that with proper counselling, the continuing practice of general practitioners who had AIDS did not present a danger to the public.

The Court held that while there was a public interest in allowing the press to keep the public informed, that public interest was outweighed by the public interest in confidentiality and trust in relation to AIDS patients' records.

[7.265] Generally, the various ethical codes, if comprehensive, recognise public interest exceptions to the confidentiality principle. For example, the New South Wales Medical Board, *Code of Professional Conduct* at 2.3 says "treat information about patients as confidential. There may be circumstances where the public interest requires that confidentiality be breached. You should seek appropriate advice in these circumstances."

Similarly there are various statutory provisions. The *Privacy Act 1988* (Cth), s 14 at Principle 10(1)(b) permits the use of personal information where the record-keeper believes on reasonable grounds that use of the information is necessary to prevent or lessen a serious and imminent threat to the life or health of the individual concerned or another person. Similar provisions exist at the State level—see for example the *Privacy and Personal Information Protection Act 1998* (NSW), s 17(c). However, it is important to note that there are on occasion over riding statutory provisions, as discussed further below at **[7.275]**.

Disclosure to relatives

[7.270] Because of dealings with the patient, health carers come in contact with family and other relatives. The patient's confidence should be respected here, and unnecessary information should not be given without permission. The fact that the patient is a child should make no difference to this principle when considering what one can tell relatives. It is important to remember that when disclosure is made to relatives without consent, it must only be those matters that are in the interest of one of the parties, and made only to those persons who are directly affected, or are directly responsible for further action. Health carers should consider the interest of the patient above any other person's unless this is clearly outweighed by the possibility of harm to that person.

Sometimes relatives ask that information be kept from the patient, whether it is in relation to their condition (for example, that the patient has cancer) or some other matter (for example, that a close family member is dead). Compliance with such a request should not be considered mandatory, and on such occasions health carers should consider a person's right to such information, and whether it is in this particular patient's interests to receive the information. It is appropriate to inform the relative(s) of one's view that the patient should be told, and give them the chance to provide the information themselves, or by other means.

The HIV-positive patient

[7.275] Issues regarding the competing public policy considerations of patient privacy and public protection are by no means of interest only for academic discourse. The patient with a dangerous transmissible disease is a good example. Where the health carer knows that a person is HIV-positive but their spouse or partner does not, and the patient does not wish to tell the partner, the question arises as to whether the carer should disclose this information. Some argue for the preservation of confidentiality, but others contend that the partner's welfare is too important: that the patient's right to privacy is overridden by their partner's right to know. The answer for certain diseases is prescribed by legislation, for example the *Public Health Act 1991* (NSW), under which such disclosure is prohibited in respect of Acquired Immune Deficiency Syndrome and/or Human Immunodeficiency Virus infection. Indeed, s 17(2) of that Act creates a criminal offence. The obligation is framed in terms of a positive obligation to take steps to prevent disclosure, rather than in terms of a negative obligation not to disclose. Further, it is not limited to revelation of results, but extends to disclosure of the fact that a test has been or will be conducted. See *Harvey & Anor v PD* (2004) 59 NSWLR 639; NSWCA 97 for an interesting discussion of these issues by the New South Wales Court of Appeal.

Medical staff should notify the State government of those who are HIV-positive (see Chapter 16).

[7.280] Case: *X v Sattler* (unreported, 31 May 1989, SC WA) (*Australian Health and Medical Law Reporter* (1991) ¶27-760)

X sought an injunction against the disclosure by the defendants, broadcasters of a radio program, that he was not only HIV-positive, but that he knowingly or otherwise infected others with the virus. He argued that the allegation of infecting others was untrue, and would seriously damage his reputation, career, health and relationships. He admitted he had had a relationship with a woman who was also HIV-positive, who was at the time of the hearing dead, but that he had had no other relationship in the past three years, and had no intention of infecting anyone else.

[7.285] The Court granted the injunction in the absence of evidence to support the allegations. The judge held that the imputations were clearly defamatory, and should not be broadcast.

[7.290] Case: *Royal Melbourne Hospital v Mathews* (*Australian Health and Medical Reporter* (1991) ¶27-770.42)

The Assistant Director of Medical Services at the Royal Melbourne Hospital refused to give police the medical records of a person who had attended the outpatients' department, and who was charged with knowingly infecting another person with HIV. The hospital sought an injunction restraining the police from searching the hospital and seizing medical records of the patient. The hospital also sought a declaration that the *Health Services Act* provision prohibiting disclosure of information relating to patients applied, or alternatively, a declaration to clarify whether the hospital was under any obligation to deliver up the records.

The judge held that a staff member of a health service is bound to hand over patient records to police who have a valid warrant for them, and would not be breaching patient confidentiality. He required the hospital to hand over the records.

[7.295] Case: *Royal Women's Hospital v Medical Practitioners Board of Victoria* [2006] VSCA 85

X, a 32 week pregnant woman attended the emergency department of the Royal Women's Hospital. X requested that her pregnancy be terminated as she had been informed, as a result of an ultrasound performed prior to her attendance at the Hospital's emergency department, that her foetus may have skeletal dysplasia, a condition commonly known as "dwarfism". The appellant referred Ms X for counselling and a further ultrasound was taken which confirmed the diagnosis of skeletal dysplasia. X became hysterical and suicidal and demanded that her pregnancy be terminated. She was referred to a psychiatrist for counselling and assessment and the psychiatrist some days later recommended termination of the pregnancy to preserve the psychiatric health and life of X. A termination procedure was performed.

[7.300] Later a Senator for the State of Victoria wrote to the Medical Practitioners Board of Victoria, making allegations regarding the treatment of X and the termination of her pregnancy at the Hospital. The Senator alleged that the diagnosis was a misdiagnosis and requested that the Board conduct an investigation into the professional conduct of the medical practitioners who performed the 32 week termination. A search warrant was issued to seize hospital and medical records. The hospital objected to production of documents seized and the matter ultimately came before the Victorian Court of Appeal, which was required to consider whether the hospital was entitled to claim public interest immunity on a class of documents, being X's records.

The Court of Appeal held that public interest immunity was not applicable on the circumstances, as it was limited to decision-making at highest governmental levels.

In New South Wales the Director General of the Health Department can inform a person who could contract HIV through sexual activity or needle-sharing with an infected person of the infected person's condition under the *Public Health Act*. In Tasmania under the *HIV/AIDS Preventative Measures Act 1993* (Tas) a medical practitioner who becomes aware that a patient who is HIV-positive is continuing to engage in conduct which has the potential to infect others may also disclose the HIV status of the person to the person at risk. Doctors and authorised health care workers may disclose this information where requested by the patient to do so. Other jurisdictions have legislation giving powers to the medical officer responsible for public health to detain persons or otherwise direct their movements where they are placing the public at risk (see Chapter 16).

Duties to third parties

[7.305] The *Review of the Law of Negligence* in Chapter 8 made passing reference to the scope of health care providers' duties to third parties, under the heading "Duties of Protection". The discussion there was admittedly in the context of the liability of occupiers of land to visitors rather than in the context of disclosure of information. At paragraph 8.36, the Panel said:

> "Duties of protection play a very important part in the law in safeguarding the interests of vulnerable members of society. We think that this area of the law is best left for development by the courts. We think that it is neither necessary nor desirable for us to make any general recommendation about the incidence of protective relationships."

Australian Law Reform Commission reference

[7.310] The tension between the privacy disclosure exceptions and prohibitions such as those in the *Public Health Act 1991* (NSW) have been the subject of ongoing debate. At the time of writing, the Federal Attorney General had made a reference to the Australian Law Reform Commission, for inquiry and report on matters relating to the extent to which the *Privacy Act 1988* and related laws continue to provide an effective framework for the protection of privacy in Australia. In performing its functions in relation to this reference, the Commission will consider amongst other things relevant existing and proposed Commonwealth, State and Territory laws and practices, other recent reviews of the *Privacy Act 1988*, current and emerging international law and obligations, developments and trends in other jurisdictions. The Commission is to report no later than 31 March 2008.

Defamation

[7.315] Defamation is the publication of something which wrongfully tends to lower someone in the estimation of others. Communication was traditionally analysed as either oral (slander), or in writing (libel). *McGlone* (2005) observes that defamation is closely linked with the tort of injurious falsehood (see pp 375 and 390ff). Unfortunately, as noted by the Federal Attorney-General, defamation law in Australia was constituted by a patchwork of common law and State and Territory statutes. As long ago as 1979, the Australian Law Reform Commission concluded in its report, *Unfair Publication: Defamation and Privacy*, that significant changes were needed in the substantive law governing rights of action and defence. Yet, it was only in 2005 that real steps were taken towards uniform defamation laws.

At the time of writing, some Australian jurisdictions have enacted legislation to promote uniform laws of defamation in Australia such as the *Defamation Act 2005* (NSW), *Defamation Act 2005* (Vic), *Defamation Act 2005* (Qld) and the like. Referring for example to the New South Wales Act, it is important to note that s 6 provides that the Act does not affect the operation of the general law in relation to the tort of defamation, except to the extent that the Act provides otherwise (whether expressly or by necessary implication). Some statutory alterations to the general law are obvious, such as s 7, by which the distinction at general law between slander and libel is abolished. This chapter refers to the general law unless otherwise stated, and therefore readers should take special care to consider the statutory overlay which may apply in the relevant jurisdiction. Different criteria apply to a defamation action from those for breach of contract or negligence, because the sole interest allegedly harmed in a defamation action is the reputation of the person. Therefore different elements will have to be proved, and different defences will apply. Defamation is generally a civil wrong, but in some circumstances, for example blasphemy, sedition or obscene libel, as well as defamation causing serious harm, it is covered by criminal law.

Examples of defamation may be an imputation that a colleague is incompetent, or gossip about a patient having venereal disease, or of someone having committed a crime. In the case of *Kitson v Playfair, The Times*, 23-28 March 1896, an obstetrician informed the "head of his patient's household" that in his opinion she had had a recent miscarriage. The result of this was that she was cut off from family inheritance. She successfully sued the doctor in defamation. One must, however, consider the circumstances of the case. The fact that what is said may be true is not always an excuse for telling everybody: on the other hand, not every defamatory statement is actionable, even when the statement is quite false. The points below should be referred to.

The law regarding defamation is not concerned with invasion of privacy or hurt feelings, other actions mentioned above may be more appropriate if harm is severe enough. It is also not possible to defame the dead, no matter what grief and distress may be caused to the relatives thereby. What must be considered is the reputation of the person involved. The purpose of the law of defamation is to strike a balance between freedom of speech and protection of one's reputation.

Subject of a defamatory statement

[7.320] Traditionally, any person or incorporated body may have been the subject of a defamatory statement. As well as an individual, a company, hospital or government department might be entitled to bring an action as a single legal individual where the body as a whole has allegedly been defamed. However this general statement should be treated with caution. In New South Wales for example, an elected local council is unable to sue in defamation (see *Ballina Shire Council v Ringland* (1994) 33 NSWLR 680) though as *McGlone* (2005, p 388) notes, an individual councillor may be able to. Certain corporations may be precluded from suing for defamation by statute, such as under s 9 of the *Defamation Act 2005* (NSW) which provides that a corporation has no cause of action for defamation in relation to the publication of defamatory matter about the corporation unless it was an excluded corporation at the time of the publication. A corporation is an excluded corporation under the Act if the objects for which it is formed do not include obtaining financial gain for its members or corporators, or it employs fewer than 10 persons and is not related to another corporation. Where more than one person alleges defamation, the statement would need to have been such that all those bringing the action could show that by imputation their reputation is besmirched, even though no specific assertion has been made against them individually. The statement may be contained in verbal comments or advice, medical reports, nurses' notes, patients' records or any other communication, whether as part of one's work or otherwise.

Elements of a defamation action

[7.325] The four elements of a defamation action are:

- there must be a statement of fact or opinion or implied fact or opinion;
- it must tend to harm a person's reputation by disparaging him or her, causing others to shun or avoid him or her, or subjecting him or her to hatred, ridicule or contempt;
- it must have been published; and
- it must refer to the person alleging the defamation.

The statement: There is no established form prescribed for a matter to be considered defamatory. So long as a statement of fact or opinion is made, or an implied statement of fact or opinion (for example, a satirical cartoon, song or play), which expresses or suggests the author's low esteem of someone, which by implication invites the receiver to share that view, it is potentially defamatory. Circumstances surrounding the statement will be important: when, where and how it is made will be crucial factors in the effects it may have. Hurt pride is not enough. In the case of *Tolley v Fry* [1930] 1 KB 467 at 479 the English Court of Appeal held that "To write or say of a man something that will disparage him in the eyes of a particular section of the community, but will not affect his reputation in the eyes of the right thinking man, is not actionable within the law of defamation."

Defamatory material: A defamatory statement must be shown to be one which the reasonable person would consider tends to bring the subject of it into contempt, ridicule, or diminished reputation. One can defame without intending to so do. For example, a newspaper article gave a fictional account of an English churchwarden's dallying with a woman of bad character in France, for whom the unusual name Artemus Jones was used, was the subject of a defamation action by a barrister from Wales, whose name happened to be Artemus Jones (*Hutton & Co v Jones* [1910] AC 20). A Victorian newspaper published details of allegations made against a certain constable of police named Lee, the paper mistakenly named the policeman as Detective Lee. There were two detectives named Lee in the police force, and they both successfully sued the newspaper (*Lee v Wilson* (1934) 51 CLR 276). Where the defamation is unintentional, an apology and retraction of the statement may satisfy the law.

Defamation may occur through the implication that a patient has a socially unacceptable disease or lifestyle, or that one's colleague or employer is incompetent or less than reasonable in her or his standard of care.

Publication: A statement must be made, or in legal parlance, "published". It does not have to be public. So long as one person has received the communication, there is potential defamation of the subject. Obviously, the more people who receive the material, the more harm is likely to occur.

Reference to the subject: One does not have to refer directly to a person to defame them in a statement. It is only necessary that the reasonable person would be likely to associate the material with a particular subject.

A person who successfully sues in defamation is entitled to compensation for damaged reputation.

Specific defences to an action in defamation

[7.330] As well as the exceptions to the disclosure of information set out above, there are several other specific defences to the dissemination of allegedly defamatory material.

Under the uniform legislation referred to above at **[7.315]** certain defences are recognised. For example, at ss 25-33, the *Defamation Act 2005* (NSW) recognises defences of justification, contextual truth, absolute privilege, publication of public documents, fair reporting of proceedings of public concern, qualified privilege for provision of certain information, honest opinion, innocent dissemination and triviality. The analysis below refers to general law principles.

Justification: The law of defamation presumes that defamatory material is false (that is, damages should not be awarded for injury to a character the plaintiff did not or ought not possess). Therefore one may be justified in disclosing something about a person as long as it is true. Truth must apply both in substance and in fact, that is not only are the facts disclosed true, but there is no suppression of facts which would alter the imputation.

Absolute privilege: This defence to an allegation of defamation applies to situations requiring unrestricted liberty of expression without fear of litigation. Such situations may vary from jurisdiction to jurisdiction, but generally involve:

- official communications between senior Ministers of the State, and between them and the Crown;
- statements made in the course of parliamentary proceedings and official reports of them, including *Hansard*, and broadcasts of Parliament (indirect reports made of these events are subject to qualified privilege: see below);
- statements made, including evidence given, in judicial and quasi-judicial proceedings (Royal Commissions and disciplinary tribunals have to be covered by special legislation to make them situations of absolute privilege);
- some communications between a solicitor and client which are for the purpose of litigation; and
- communications between husband and wife.

Qualified privilege: Qualified privilege applies to those occasions where:

"the person who makes a communication has an interest or a duty, legal, social or moral, to make it to the person to whom it is made, and the person to whom it is so made has a corresponding interest or duty to receive it. This reciprocity is essential" (*Adam v Ward* [1917] AC 309 at 339 per Lord Atkinson).

Situations where qualified privilege applies (again subject to variation in different jurisdictions), may be said to include:

- answers to police questions;
- communications between solicitor and client;
- evaluations of work performance;
- references written for job applications;
- a report required as part of one's employment;
- communication between employer and employee; and
- some newspaper reports which are made in the public interest, such as fair and accurate reports of those bodies mentioned above, or the revelation of facts where the duty described above exists.

One cannot say anything one likes in these situations, statements are governed by the principle that the public good requires that expression can be given to one's beliefs for good and proper reason. Lord Atkinson elaborated on this point in *Adam v Ward* [1917] AC 309 (at 318):

"[The] authorities, in my view, clearly establish that a person making a communication on a privileged occasion is not restricted to the use of such language merely as is reasonably necessary to protect the interest or discharge the duty which is the foundation of his privilege; but that, on the contrary, he will be protected, even though his language should be violent or excessively strong, if, having regard to all the circumstances of the case, he might have honestly and on reasonable grounds believed that what he wrote or said was true and necessary for the purpose of his vindication, though in fact it was not so."

Fair Comment: This defence is usually relied upon by journalists, and involves commentary on people and events in the public domain. One example, though in the context of an argument by the publisher regarding a defence under the *Defamation Act 1974* (NSW), regarding a report of court proceedings, follows.

[7.335] Case: *Rogers v Nationwide News Pty Limited*
(2003) 216 CLR 327; [2003] HCA 52

Rogers v Whitaker (1992) 175 CLR 479; [1992] HCA 58 was a famous case in the law of professional negligence. It received wide publicity in the legal and medical professions, and was extensively reported in the general press. (It is referred to throughout this book.)

Mrs Whitaker, who for many years had been almost totally blind in her right eye, consulted Dr Rogers, who advised surgery on that eye. After the operation, she lost the sight of her left eye, without any improvement to the right eye. This was not the result of any lack of care or skill in the performance of the operation. The procedure that was undertaken involved an inherent risk, a risk said to occur only once in approximately 14,000 such procedures, of a development of sympathetic ophthalmia. Dr Rogers had failed to warn Mrs Whitaker of that possibility. He argued that, in so doing, he was acting in accordance with the standards of the medical profession generally; but the High Court held that those standards were not determinative, that he should have warned the patient, and that he was liable to compensate her.

The newspaper publication complained of by Dr Rogers, following later litigation between Mrs Whitaker and the Australian Taxation Office, included a statement that said she was "blinded by a surgeon's negligence". The article also stated that she was "[b]linded during an eye operation", and that she "lost sight in both eyes after an operation involving corneal grafts performed by a prominent eye surgeon".

[7.340] In the defamation appeal, the High Court observed that the publication was a serious misrepresentation of the *Rogers v Whitaker* case, and it defamatory of Dr Rogers to say that his negligent surgery had blinded Mrs Whitaker. Dr Rogers was found liable to pay Mrs Whitaker damages because he had failed to warn her of a remote risk inherent in the surgical procedure he recommended and performed. There was no finding that he was negligent to recommend the procedure, or that he was negligent in the manner in which it was performed.

In the defamation claim it was not in dispute that the article conveyed the imputation that Dr Rogers had blinded Mrs Whitaker by negligently and carelessly carrying out an eye operation on her. The High Court said that plainly the imputation was defamatory. Apart from the quantum of damages, the only issue in the High Court was whether Nationwide News could make out a defence under the *Defamation Act 1974* (NSW).

The High Court held that the defences under *Defamation Act 1974* (NSW) were not available, and the award in favour of Dr Rogers of $250,000 was not disturbed.

Health carers and the giving of information

[7.345] The law in relation to confidentiality can be summarised as being based on two principles: first, a patient's medical record and general information about her or him should not be disclosed, and secondly, where there is some justification for disclosure, information that is not relevant to the situation (for example a patient's history of an abortion when the matter has to do with a recent industrial injury) should not be disclosed.

The following guideline may be of assistance:

Information requested by the patient herself or himself: The information should be made available, but this might helpfully be done through a responsible medical officer, who can assist the patient to understand the meaning and context of information.

Information requested by relatives: No information should be given without the competent patient's consent, unless there are compelling reasons (see the discussion above at **[7.270]**). Even the fact that a person is in the facility may be information that will be harmful to the patient (for example, an abusive partner), and based on the principle of autonomy, the patient has the right to decide who does or does not receive the information. Health carers should thus not presume that the patient's condition and details can be discussed with relatives, or even a spouse. Where the patient is not competent, his or her dignity and confidentiality should be the overriding consideration, and information should only be given on the basis of being necessary in the patient's interests. Where the patient is a child, parents and guardians may have an interest in receiving the information, but where a child is competent to consent to treatment, it would appear that his or her wishes as to the giving of information to parents should not be disregarded lightly. It is probably only where the welfare of the child requires notification of the parents that this would be justified. (For an interesting analysis of the contrasting rights of a parent and a child seeking advice concerning contraception and abortion, see Gleeson (2006) and *Axon, R (On the Application of) v The State Secretary for Health)* [2006] EWHC 37 (High Court, England & Wales)).

Information requested by other health professionals: As long as the patient consents to care and the information is relevant to that care, it can be passed on as necessary. Staff members of a facility do not have an automatic right to access patient information or pass it on. Information should thus not be given to professionals who are not legitimately involved with care to which the patient has consented. If a health carer wants advice, or just the opportunity to talk over treatment of her or his patient with a colleague who is not involved with the patient's care, identifying information should not be given.

Information requested by solicitors, insurance companies, compensation boards, etc: The patient's permission should be obtained before disclosure, and only information pertinent to the purpose of the request should be supplied.

Information requested by a court, Royal Commission or Commission of Inquiry: This is generally by subpoena (which is an order for someone to attend court, or to produce documents) and, of course, must be complied with (see **[7.295]**). Certified copies of the requested records (unless originals are specifically required) should be supplied in a sealed envelope. Anyone who is not a party to the case, whose records have been subpoenaed should be notified by those providing the records, with details of the hearing. Where medical records are sought as part of the process of "discovery" (preliminary examination by parties to a case), usually only copies of those documents relevant to the case should be released, but in such circumstances legal representatives will be involved and able to give evidence.

Information requested by the police: Generally, a police officer has no more right to confidential information than anyone else. Requests for information or to examine records should be referred to senior management of the facility where practicable. Information should only be passed on through a responsible health care official who is assured that the police officer is authorised to receive the information in the execution of his or her duty (for example, the investigation of a crime or traffic accident). The health carer may be required to give information where the police have a valid warrant or are pursuing an investigation for a criminal offence. The information given should be limited to the information specified by the warrant. If a carer is asked by the police to give information as to, for example, what the patient has said or done while in hospital, whether or not the matter is a coronial or criminal one, he or she ought to obtain legal advice regarding their legal obligation to answer such questions, and should politely decline to respond. Let police know you wish to be helpful, but would need to seek advice as to the patient's rights. In that situation health carers are witnesses, and should only become involved in a case after discussion with legal advisers. One must answer questions when under oath, and cannot be sued in defamation for any information given in a court proceeding. Records of deceased patients should not be handed to police without similar specific authorisation.

Information requested under statutory right: The authority of the person or body requesting the information should be carefully checked, ensuring that only material relevant to the statutory demand is released.

Information requested by researchers: Information should not be given directly to a researcher but requests should go through an ethics committee, which has ensured proper provision for the patient's consent or privacy regime exemption has been made.

Information requested by other institutions/health carers: Where the information is required for emergency treatment, the information should be given, but after verification of the requesting body or person. A note should be made of the information released, to whom it was released, and the reason for the request. Where the request is non-urgent, the patient's consent should be obtained before release. It should be borne in mind that discharge summaries are the release of confidential information, and if in doubt as to whether the patient is aware of the practice of issuing these, he or she should be informed. Also summaries or letters to agencies (for example, welfare agencies or rehabilitation agencies) should only be sent with the patient's consent or under some legal entitlement.

Information requested by the media: The patient's permission must be obtained before information is given. It should be remembered that information that may seem general and which does not seem to identify the patient may do so indirectly, and so health carers should be very careful in these circumstances. Management of the facility should take responsibility for the release of such information, either directly or indirectly through strict guidelines. It should be noted that filming or photographing part of the facility (which identifies where the person is) may be an infringement of his or her privacy.

Information requested by an employer: Consent of the person is required, and care should be taken to give only that information which is relevant to the employer's financial responsibility.

Health care workers need to take care when disclosing confidential information as part of allegations against others such as:

- the standards of treatment and care practised by their employer or other specific employees;
- reporting matters where the welfare of particular people, or the public in general, may be adversely influenced by the actions of someone else; and
- complaints about sexual harassment or other personal maltreatment by another.

Checklist
WHEN CONFIDENTIAL INFORMATION MAY BE DISCLOSED
The information is true (or reasonably believed to be so) and given in good faith, and
✓ it is necessary for treatment to which the patient has consented;
✓ the patient has consented to the disclosure;
✓ it is a necessary part of the employer's function of health care, and in the interests of the employer;
✓ it is disclosure to a government authority under statutory requirement (for example, reporting child abuse, the reporting of an infectious disease (Chapter 16));
✓ it is disclosure for the public good (for example, potential danger to the community);
✓ it is disclosure in response to legal requirement (for example, giving evidence in a trial);
✓ for the protection of a person or property, including the patient (see also qualified privilege); or
✓ to the police to aid their inquiries, although one is not obliged to answer police questions (see also qualified privilege).

Patient Access to Records

[7.350] The High Court of Australia has held that, at common law, medical records are owned by the maker of the records or their employer (*Breen v Williams* (1995) 186 CLR 71; [1995] HCA 63 (see **[7.15]** above) per Brennan CJ), except possibly reports such as X-Rays and pathology reports, for which the patient or their insurer pays (at 270 per Dawson and Toohey JJ). There is thus no legal right on the part of patients to access medical records that are created by a health carer to assist him or her in providing care, and it is, at common law, the right of the owner of medical records to refuse access to them to a patient. Where the health carer is an employee, ownership of the records vests in the employer. Medical staff generally resist patient access to records because there may be material contained in them which they would rather the patient not have. Some facts may be considered to be harmful to the patient, and candid comments could be the subject of defamation.

At common law, then, it would seem that the patient may have a right to X-rays and other reports for which he or she has paid (albeit through Medicare or private health insurance), but this has not been fully considered by the courts and is now unlikely to be considered given the statutory mechanisms for patient access to records which now exist.

The governments of each Australian jurisdiction have provided that people may have access to their medical records belonging to Commonwealth bodies by the Freedom of Information legislation described above at **[7.20]** and the privacy regimes described above at **[7.140]**. The legislation makes access to public sector medical records a legally enforceable right on the part of a person about whom it is written, or a recognised person on their behalf, such as a guardian or solicitor.

Information about a child may not be given to a guardian where there is a conflict of interest between the child and the guardian (for example, where a child's medical record reveals information given by the child indicating child abuse). This may also be the case where there would be unreasonable disclosure of a child's personal affairs, or the interests of the child would be prejudiced. For an interesting analysis of the contrasting rights of a parent and a child seeking advice concerning contraception and abortion, see Gleeson (2006) and *Axon, R (On the Application of) v The State Secretary for Health)* [2006] EWHC 37 (High Court, England & Wales).

Legislative moves towards a right to access records in private facilities

[7.355] There has been a trend in the various Australian jurisdictions to create a broad right for a patient to access medical records, not limited to records held in the public sector. The Australian Capital Territory has enacted the *Health Records (Privacy and Access) Act 1997* (ACT), which covers both the public and private sector. It establishes a right of access to her or his medical records, while containing a set of privacy principles to protect the records from being accessed by unauthorised persons. Parents and guardians share a right to access medical records of children, and guardians can access the records of adults who are not competent. However, the more recent trend is for such issues to be covered by legislation concerning privacy. At the federal level, the *Privacy Act 1988* (Cth) creates a regime which allows a patient to inspect records, but not an automatic right to simply request photocopies. There is, however, a trend towards provision of such rights at the State level, see for example the *Health Records and Information Privacy Act 2002* (NSW).

Where the record holder has reasonable grounds to believe that the provision of the records would create a significant risk to the life or health of the patient or any other person, then there are provisions whereby access can be denied to them, but a person can be nominated to access the records and present the information to the patient (see, for example, ss 29-30 of the *Health Records and Information Privacy Act 2002* (NSW)).

The area of privacy and access to information is a rapidly evolving one. A particularly fascinating aspect is in relation to genetic information, where there may be competing public and private interests in respect of not only access to information, but possibly rights not to know certain information.

The Australian Law Reform Commission has undertaken a major inquiry into the ethical, legal and social implications of the new and emerging genetic technologies entitled *Essentially Yours: The Protection of Human Genetic Information in Australia* (ALRC 96, 2003) available at www.austlii.edu.au/au/other/alrc/publications/reports/96/.

One of the main terms of reference of the Inquiry was to consider how best to protect privacy with respect to human genetic information. Thus, a large part of the Inquiry focused on the privacy and confidentiality issues related to the collection, storage, and use of human genetic information. (The report is discussed with regard to genetic testing and its impact on reproductive technology at **[17.190]**ff.)

The report recognises that human genetic information has a strong familial dimension—an individual's genetic information will usually reveal information about, and have implications for, his or her parents, grandparents, siblings, children, and generations to come. Thus, there may be circumstances in which an individual's presumptive right to privacy, and to confidentiality of the doctor-patient relationship, may be called into question by the competing needs of genetic relatives.

Chapter 21 of the report considers how patients, doctors and other health carers should collect and handle genetic information, with particular attention being paid to the potential for an individual's genetic information derived in the course of treatment or diagnosis to bear significance for relatives. The Inquiry considered that there may be exceptional circumstances where it should be permissible for health carers to disclose a patient's genetic information to relatives without the consent of that person.

The report points out that whilst genetic samples hold a wealth of personal information that may be revealed through testing and analysis, the samples themselves do not currently receive protection under the privacy legislation. The recommendations of the Inquiry relating to privacy and confidentiality included the following:

- Privacy legislation to be modified to extend its coverage to the handling of identifiable genetic samples;
- Privacy legislation to be amended to permit the disclosure of an individual's genetic information in circumstances where it is necessary to prevent a serious threat to a person's life or health, even where that risk is not "imminent";
- AHMAC develop nationally consistent rules governing the disclosure of genetic samples and information for law enforcement purposes;
- Employers should not be permitted to gather and use genetic information except in rare circumstances;
- Strategies should be put in place to ensure the insurance industry use of genetic information is restricted to use in a scientifically and actuarially sound manner;
- DNA parentage testing should be conducted only with the consent of the person sampled or pursuant to a court order.

References and Further Reading

Texts on tort law generally, as listed at the end of Chapter 6, deal with confidentiality and defamation.

Abadee, A, "The Medical Duty of Confidentiality and the Duty to Disclose: Can they Co-exist?" (1995) 3 *Journal of Law and Medicine* 75

Australian Health and Medical Law Reporter (CCH, Sydney, 1991)

Australian Law Reform Commission: *ALRC 96 Essentially Yours: The Protection of Human Genetic Information in Australia* (2003)

Brazier, M, *Medicine, Patients and the Law* (Penguin, London, 1992)

Dal Pont, G and Cockburn, T, *Equity and Trusts in Principle* (Lawbook Co, Sydney, 2005)

Devereaux, J, *Medical Law: Text, Cases and Materials* (Cavendish, Australia, 1997)

Dix, et al, *Law for the Medical Profession* (Butterworths, Sydney, 1988), ch 7

Downing, J, "Ownership of Medical Records and Duties of Confidentiality in Medical Practice" (2001) *Journal of Law and Medicine* 460

Gleeson, P, "Axon, R (On the Application of) v The State Secretary for Health)" (2006) 14(5) *Australian Health Law Bulletin* 53.

Greenlaw, J, "Documentation of Patient Care, An Often Underestimated Responsibility" (1982) 10 (3) *Law Medicine and Health Care* 125

Hamblin, J, "When Less is More: Should Health Information Always be Disclosed to the Individual Concerned" *Australian Health Law Bulletin* 14(6)

Intergovernmental Committee on AIDS, Privacy Working Party, *Report* (AGPS, Canberra, 1993)

Kerridge, I, Lowe, M and McPhee, J, *Ethics and Law for the Health Professions* (2nd ed, The Federation Press, Sydney, 2005)

Langslow, A, "High Drama Lay in Nurses' Notes" (1984) 13(7) *Australian Nurses' Journal* 29

Luntz, H, Hambly, A and Hayes, R, *Torts: Cases and Commentary* (Butterworths, Sydney, 1985), ch 15

McGlone, F and Stickley, A, *Australian Torts Law* (Lexis Nexis Butterworths 2005)

Mendelson, D, "Mr Cruel and the Medical Duty of Confidentiality" (1994) 1 *Journal of Law and Medicine* 120

Skene, L, *Law and Medical Practice – Rights, Duties, Claims & Defences* (Lexis Nexis Butterworths 2004)

Skene, L, *Law and Medical Practice* (Sydney, Butterworths, 1998)

Taylor, G and Wright, D, "Australian Broadcasting Corporation v Lenah Game Meats: Privacy, Injunctions And Possums: An Analysis Of The High Court's Decision" [2002] *Melbourne University Law Review* 36

8 Patients' property

Bailment

Suggested procedure for
health care facilities

Special considerations

chapter 8

Patients' Property

Introduction

[8.05] The legal right to goods is composed of two elements: ownership and possession. Ownership and possession may vest in different persons. Consider an example, where a patient entrusts her clothing to a hospital employee, to be given to her spouse. Ownership of the clothes vests in the patient. That means the patient has the right to the clothes against the whole world, and can do what she likes with them. Possession vests in the hospital, which has a right to possession of the clothes against the whole world except against the patient, who remains the owner, and the spouse, who has a greater right of possession than the hospital, as the hospital's right of possession is conditional on delivering them to the spouse. The spouse in turn has a right of possession against the whole world except for the patient, who remains the owner and can demand possession.

At law, the entrusting of one's property to another, for purposes such as dry cleaning, repair, safekeeping (including giving them to a hospital or another person when one is ill), or pawning one's goods, as well as the hiring of goods, is called bailment. The person who gives the goods to another's care is called the bailor, the person to whom the goods are given is called the bailee. Bailment involves temporarily divesting oneself, as owner, of the possession of one's goods, while retaining ownership of them.

A health care facility may find itself caring for a person's property as the result of:

- lodgment on, or during, admission (voluntary bailment);
- admission of a person in an emergency (involuntary bailment); or
- its being left behind by a person on leaving.

A person, hospital, nursing home or other institution having custody of a patient's property is legally bound to take reasonable care of that property. This duty extends to employees of the person, hospital, nursing home or other institution.

Bailment

[8.10] The law of bailment is mainly covered by common law and has generally been applied to cases involving commercial activities, but it does contain some important precepts for health care workers. The act of bailment involves principles of contract, but money is not always paid for bailment, and there is available to the bailor a remedy for negligence. Bailment does not require a specific agreement. For example, a person may find a lost chattel, and take it into his or her possession. He or she is under no obligation to do so, but having taken possession of it, has undertaken the obligations of a bailee. Reasonable efforts must be made to protect the chattel, find the owner and return it to him or her on demand (*Parker v British Airways Board* [1982] QB 1004 at 1018, per Donaldson LJ). It is thus useful to consider bailment as a special area of law. The core of bailment is possession; any person who knowingly and voluntarily possesses goods belonging to someone else will be considered a bailee (*The Pioneer Container* [1994] 2 AC 324).

Before considering the rules relating to bailment, it may be useful to remember that as health carers come into contact with patients' property both when it is given to them for safekeeping and when they have to handle it on other occasions, there are two types of situations in which the law is interested:

- the wrongful interference with a person's goods, for example, the taking of a person's possessions or using them without permission of the owner; and
- the careless or negligent treatment of a person's goods when they have been given for safekeeping.

Interference with goods

[8.15] This generally involves the wrongful handling of another's goods, and is divided in law into three kinds of activity:

- the wrongful taking of goods, out of the possession of another, for example, is called theft (called in tort law "trespass to goods");
- dealing with goods in a manner inconsistent with the rights of the owner, for example, buying or selling another's goods, "borrowing" another's goods without their permission, using goods in a way which is contrary to a person's wishes or instructions, or destroying them (called in law "conversion of goods");
- wrongfully refusing, after demand, to deliver goods to the person entitled to possession of them (whether that person is the owner or not). This would include the refusal of nursing staff to return clothes or other possessions when the patient asked for them (called in law "detinue").

It can be seen that these categories might overlap in any given situation. The common element is that someone is wrongfully deprived of their lawful exercise of ownership or possession of their goods, without their consent.

The negligent handling of goods

[8.20] Once possession of goods has been granted to a bailee, the goods must be kept secure and handled in a reasonable manner (*Gilchrist Watt and Sanderson Pty Ltd v York Products Pty Ltd* [1970] 3 All ER 825). What constitutes reasonable care depends of the circumstances of the case. Action can be brought by someone against a bailee, where goods have been stolen, or are returned damaged or altered because of negligent handling.

Where damage or loss occurs to an article in the bailee's possession, the bailee will bear the onus of proof to establish that either (a) the bailee took reasonable care of the possessions; or (b) the loss or damage was not the result of the bailee's failure to take reasonable care (*Custom Lease Pty Ltd v Simpson* (unrep, 14/7/1983, CA NSW, 12393 of 1979).

Categories of bailment

[8.25] The law classifies bailment into three kinds. The distinction between the various kinds of bailment may be relevant in determining the extent of the duties and liabilities of the parties in some cases.

Bailment for reward

[8.30] Here the bailee is paid for the bailment of the goods. Examples are the depositing of goods with someone for safekeeping in a bank, or in a railway station "left luggage" department; leaving clothes with a dry cleaner, or a car with a car repairer. It is accepted that the bailment undertaken when a person hands over money or valuables to a health care facility is a bailment for reward, as even where they do not pay directly for their care, they are paying indirectly for treatment through taxes or levies to the government or other body. In *Martin v London County Council* [1947] 1 All ER 783, where a patient had handed over her jewellery on admission to hospital, the Court held that the hospital was liable as a bailee for reward because the patient paid for care indirectly through taxes. In Australia, one could argue that Medicare contributors are similarly paying the facility indirectly for their care.

The bailee comes under a duty to take reasonable care of the property; to refrain from deviating from the bailment agreement; and to redeliver the goods in due course. The bailee's duty to take care of the property extends to taking reasonable care to protect goods in his or her possession against wrongdoing by a third party. The duty to redeliver is generally one to redeliver the exact goods bailed.

Gratuitous bailment

[8.35] This occurs when goods are "deposited" with the bailee, and the bailee voluntarily accepts them, but is not paid for this service. Once the goods are accepted the bailee becomes responsible for them, and remains so for as long as the goods remain in his or her possession. The goods must be returned on the demand of the owner.

The duty of care involved here is what is called the "ordinary" duty of care, based on the reasonable person, and requiring one to take whatever steps are reasonable to secure and preserve the possessions and return them.

Involuntary bailment

[8.40] One may also find oneself an involuntary bailee. This occurs when one finds oneself in possession of another's goods without prior notice or agreement. This can occur:

1) out of necessity (for example when one stops to help another and finds oneself in possession of his or her property). Here there is not a prior arrangement to bail the goods, nor is there any choice on the part of the bailee; and

2) accidentally (for example where one finds something which has fallen out of a person's pocket).

In these cases, no responsibility to take charge of it lies with the bailee. However if he or she does take charge of the goods, then an implied bailment comes into effect, and reasonable care is required to find the owner, care for the safety of the goods and return them to the owner.

The bailee is not under a general duty of care to protect the goods against damage, theft or loss. The person will be liable only for damage, loss or theft if it results from wilful or perhaps reckless conduct on their part.

Duty and standard of care

[8.45] While the duty of care imposed in each category of bailment may be the same, the standard of care required to meet that duty may differ. There have been numerous English judicial findings on point. Of note, Lord Salmon has stated that the difference in the standard of care required between a bailment for reward and a gratuitous bailment is "a very fine line, difficult to discern and impossible to define" (*Port Swettenham Authority v TW Wu & Co* (M) Sdn Bhd [1979] AC 580). Thus, it is "unlikely that a modern Australian court would distinguish between the duties owed by a gratuitous bailee and a bailee for reward" (*Halsbury's Laws of England* ¶40-120). Arguably, there may be a greater difference in the standard of care required between voluntary and involuntary bailments.

Suggested Procedure for Health Care Facilities

The best rule: Leave it at home!

[8.48] Patients should be encouraged not to bring unnecessary property to a health facility, or relatives should be requested to take the property elsewhere, if the patient is in agreement. However, this principle should be balanced with an appreciation of the emotional value possessions may have for patients who are staying for longer periods, such as nursing home residents and mental health patients. Reasonable accommodation should be made for those possessions which are of importance for the patient's comfort and wellbeing.

Careful recording of property received

[8.50] When a patient hands over property to a health carer, the nature and condition of that property should be carefully noted, as a record for both the patient and the hospital and as evidence of the transaction of handing over the property. Property should be stored in such a way that it is clearly identified as belonging to the patient, and will not be in unreasonable danger of damage or theft.

Care of valuables

[8.55] Special care should be taken with valuables. Ideally valuables should not be kept in a ward, but in a central office in a secure place such as locked cupboard or safe (less than this would not, in most cases, be considered by the courts as reasonable care). Health carers should be cautious of taking temporary custody of valuable or expensive possessions, moving them from place to place, or handing them over to anyone, without careful documentation and witnessing. (See **[8.70]** and **[8.75]** below.)

Witnessing by a third person

[8.60] Personal possessions, and a list of them, should be checked by a third person as well as the patient when the list is compiled. This list should be signed by all three people. If the patient is unable to check the list, then a relative or friend should be asked to sign as witness on the patient's behalf. Those taking custody of items should describe them accurately.

Handing of property to relatives

[8.65] Health carers should be conscious of the fact that it is unlawful to deal with another person's property as if they were the owner of that property. That is, if a carer hands it over to any person (other than, for example, hospital personnel for safekeeping), without the owner's permission, this is considered in law to be exercising a right in that property to which the carer may not be entitled. It is a general policy of many hospitals, that goods may be handed over to a person who is reasonably believed to be a relative or friend, or otherwise has entitlement to receive them. Where the goods are not valuable this may be considered acceptable, as the consent of the person could be presumed, and probably happens every day. However, it is technically unlawful handling of the person's property. Handing valuable property over to relatives or friends (or police without a warrant) could be dealing unlawfully with the property. If in doubt, it should not be handed over to anyone other than the patient. Management should deal with these matters and take steps to establish the validity of the claim. Whatever the circumstances, careful recording of the transaction should be made, with a description of the property, names of those who give and receive them, and the date and time. Both the person giving and the person receiving should sign for the goods. Wrongful delivery to a third person may constitute "conversion": *Glass v Hollander* (1935) 35 SR (NSW) 304.

Some Special Considerations

Valuable possessions

[8.70] Where the facilities exist, valuable possessions (such as jewellery) should be transferred as soon as possible after recording to the hospital management, who should have proper means for safekeeping. If there is no such provision, or it is not available after-hours, then the valuables should be kept under lock and key until they can be transferred somewhere safer. Where valuables are given to a relative or other representative of the patient, records should be carefully and fully kept regarding to whom they are being given and their particulars. This record should be signed by the person handing over the possessions, the person receiving them, and a witness.

Money

[8.75] Money may be deposited by the health care facility in a trust account, the amount deposited becoming a debt to the patient, payable on demand. The money is not the subject of bailment in this case, as the exact notes given to the facility are not demanded in return. Rather, the patient is a creditor, the facility a debtor, and the amount owing could be the subject of a suit for payment of a debt, or, where the money is deposited with the intention of benefit to a third person or body, the law of trust. The debt would apply absolutely, and the issue of negligence would be irrelevant in this case.

Emergency admissions

[8.80] Where, due to lack of time or facilities, a patient's possessions cannot be carefully checked and listed, it is suggested that they be quickly and carefully put in a bag or envelope, sealed and put somewhere as safe as circumstances will allow. If possible, someone should witness this, and jointly sign and date (including the time) the package across the seal.

Subject to time permitting, where valuable property is contained in a wallet, purse or other container and this is not opened by staff, a note should be made to that effect on the bag or envelope containing the goods. Where the container has been opened, staff may be liable for anything allegedly missing from it. If it was opened before coming into the possession of the staff, but there is a witnessed document stating that it was not opened by them, there is less likelihood that they will be held responsible. If it is opened, for example, a wallet is searched for identification, then the contents should be listed and witnessed again to establish what was there.

Possessions kept with the patient

[8.85] These are kept at the patient's bedside and at the patient's risk. Thus, a watch or radio which disappears from the patient's bedside is not the responsibility of the nursing staff unless the patient is unable to care for such goods, in which case if they are to remain there (which ideally should not occur), the staff must take reasonable measures to protect them (for example, encouraging the owner to have them locked away when not in use). Otherwise they should be put in safekeeping. If, for example, a perfectly competent patient is to undergo surgery, then arrangements should be made for care of valuables which have been kept at the bedside for the duration of the patient's incompetence.

Transfer of patient

[8.90] Care should be taken to adequately check possessions when patients are being transferred from one place to another. The list of possessions obtained on admission to a ward should again be checked against the possessions being transferred, and duly witnessed by the patient (or representative) where possible, and another staff member.

When a patient becomes incompetent

[8.95] Where an adult patient becomes incompetent, the health care facility should not hand over valuable property to anyone other than the person who has the right of management of the patient's property. If there is no such person, the facility should hold the property on trust until one is appointed by the courts or Guardianship Tribunal. The Public Trustee or Public Advocate or equivalent can be contacted, who can then make an application for an order to deal with the person's property. Where the patient is a child, parents are the legal guardians (unless there is clear evidence to the contrary), and are entitled to deal with the property of the child. A person's spouse is not the automatic owner of her or his property.

When a patient dies

[8.100] The law provides that when a person dies, all that person's property becomes the possession of the executor of the estate. The executor is nominated by the person in her or his will, or, where there is no will, it is usually necessary for the Supreme Court to approve an administrator. Relatives may thus have no right to possession of the deceased's belongings (if they are entitled under the will, that is for the executor to determine, and he or she must go through certain procedures, such as paying debts, before distribution). A relative may be nominated the executor under the will, but health carers are not required to solve this legal question. Carers should be wary of handing out the deceased's possessions to relatives and should refer requests for property of any value to the hospital administration, whose duty it is to hold such property in trust until they hand it to the person demonstrating that he or she is the executor of the deceased's estate.

Exemption 'No responsibility taken' clauses

[8.105] A health care facility may limit its liability for goods left with it by specifically providing that it will not be responsible for them. This would most likely be a clause in the contract of bailment (the form signed by the patient) to the appropriate effect. It is important to note:

- Such a limitation must be specifically brought to the patient's notice (signs in a foyer may or may not be enough) (*Mendelssohn v Normand* [1970] 1 QB 177), and it must be reasonable notice under the circumstances: for example, in a language the patient can understand. It must form part of the actual agreement made by the patient. Unless all reasonable measures to bring the limitation of liability to the patient's attention are taken, he or she may not be bound by it (*Thornton v Shoe Lane Parking* [1971] 2 WLR 585).
- The clause must be clear and unambiguous. General phrases such as "all care and no responsibility" will have no effect (*Paterson v Miller* [1923] VLR 36).

[8.110] Case: *Sydney Corporation v West* (1965) 114 CLR 481; [1965] HCA 68 (High Court of Australia)

W parked his car in a council car park. The ticket he received stated that the ticket must be presented for taking delivery of the car, and also that "the council does not accept any responsibility for the loss or damage to any vehicle or for any injury to any person however such loss, damage or injury may arise or be caused." An unauthorised person claimed the car, stating he had lost the ticket, and the attendant allowed him to take delivery of the car. W sued for the replacement value of the car.

[8.115] Despite the formidable exemption clause, the High Court held that although the council was relieved of liability for the consequences of negligence where it carried out acts which were authorised by the contract, the contract had specifically required that the ticket be produced for delivery of the car, and in this case the worker involved did not follow the authorised procedure. Thus, they concluded, the council was not covered by the exemption clause in this case, and was liable.

Courts will accept exemption clauses so long as they have been brought to the awareness of the contracting party, or are reasonably available for that party to see, but will also construe them literally against the party seeking exemption. Therefore, the person or institution holding goods under bailment must show that they meticulously adhered to the terms of the bailment.

[8.120] Case: *Thomas National Transport (Melbourne)* *Pty Ltd v May & Baker (Australia) Pty Ltd* (1966) 115 CLR 353; [1966] HCA 46 (High Court of Australia)

An interstate carrier regularly held M & B's goods in its warehouse overnight in Melbourne when storage was required, before sending them on to Sydney. They also used a sub-contractor to transport the goods from M & B's premises to the warehouse. Some goods were destroyed while they were stored overnight, not while they were at TNT's warehouse, but at the premises of the sub-contractor. The contract had an exemption clause that said that TNT was not liable for harm occurring to goods while they were in transit or storage.

[8.125] The Court said that TNT could rely on the exemption clause and so escape liability only if it was acting strictly according to the contract. The use of the sub-contractor was not stipulated in the contract, it was found, and this was a deviation from the contract significant enough to prevent TNT from relying on its exemption clause.

Unclaimed belongings

Common law

[8.130] At common law, if goods are not collected after bailment, the bailee does not have the right to dispose of them, unless it is necessary to do so to prevent harm to the bailee or in the interests of the owner, and the bailee has made reasonable attempts to contact the owner.

Statute law

[8.135] Most Australian jurisdictions have some legislation providing that unclaimed belongings become the property of the person or body who holds them, giving them the right to keep or dispose of them. Some Australian jurisdictions also have legislation in relation to uncollected moneys, requiring advertising for the owner and other procedures (see Table 8.1).

Table 8.1: Legislative provisions regarding unclaimed belongings

ACT	Limitation Act 1985, ss 43-45
	Uncollected Goods Act 1996
NSW	Limitation Act 1969, ss 65 & 68
	Health Services Act 1997, ss 132, 133 & 140
	Uncollected Goods Act 1995
	Unclaimed Money Act 1995
NT	Disposal of Uncollected Goods Act
QLD	Disposal of Uncollected Goods Act 1967
	Public Trustee Act 1978, Part 8;
SA	Unclaimed Goods Act 1987
	Unclaimed Moneys Act 1891
Tas	Disposal of Uncollected Goods Act 1968
	Unclaimed Moneys Act 1918
Vic	Disposal of Uncollected Goods Act 1961
	Unclaimed Moneys Act 1972
WA	Disposal of Uncollected Goods Act 1970
	Unclaimed Money Act 1990

New South Wales also has legislation specific to money and personal effects left at a public health organisation. Section 133 of the *Health Services Act 1997* (NSW) provides:

"(1) The following money and personal effects are taken to be the property of a public health organisation:
   (a) all money and personal effects (being choses in possession) that are:
      (i) left in its custody by any patient who dies in one of its hospitals or health institutions, and
      (ii) not claimed by the person lawfully entitled to them within a period of 12 months after the patient's death, and
   (b) all money and personal effects (being choses in possession) that are:
      (i) left in its custody by any patient discharged from one of its hospitals or health institutions, and
      (ii) not claimed by the patient or other person lawfully entitled to them within a period of 12 months after the date of discharge.
(2) All such money, and the proceeds of the realisation of any such personal effects, are to form a distinct and separate fund of the public health organisation to be called a Samaritan Fund."

Checklist
DEALING WITH PATIENT'S PROPERTY ON ADMISSION OR TRANSFER
References to "patient" includes reference to patient's representative where applicable.
Have I:
✓ Informed the patient about hospital policy?
✓ Listed each object by type and condition?
✓ Identified valuable property and separated it from other goods?
✓ Clearly identified the location of, or the person with custody of, all property?
✓ Secured the witness of at least one other health carer and the patient, if possible?
✓ Given the patient a copy of the list (receipt)?
✓ Made proper provision for the dispatch of property which is to go elsewhere in the hospital?
✓ Made proper provision for any goods which are to remain in the ward or under my supervision?
✓ Obtained a receipt on the handing-over of the goods to any person?

References and Further Reading

See references on tort law following Chapter 6.
Australian Health and Medical Law Reporter (CCH, Sydney, 1991)
O'Sullivan, J, *Law for Nurses* (Law Book Co, Sydney, 1983), ch 2
The Laws of Australia (Lawbook Co, Sydney), Chapter 8: Contracts: Specific, 8.5 Bailment; Chapter 20: Health and Guardianship, 20.3 Institutional and Professional Liability, Chapter 2: Liability of Institutions, Part G Patient's Property

9 Contract

What is a contract

Terms of the contract

Contracts for health care

Capacity to contract

When a contract is not
enforceable

Discharge of contracts

Remedies for breach

chapter 9

Contract

Introduction

[9.05] Where a patient enters hospital, makes an agreement for care with a health care facility, or sees a private practitioner (for example, a nurse or doctor), then a contract has been entered into between the patient and the care giver. The contract does not have to be *express* (that is "spelt out"): it is *implied* (*Breen v Williams* (1995) 186 CLR 71; [1995] HCA 63 at [26]). The patient undertakes to pay a fee, in return for which the facility or practitioner undertakes to provide the agreed treatment with reasonable skill and care. Where treatment is billed to Medicare or an insurance provider the patient is still considered as being the source of consideration as the health carer receives a benefit from the public purse (Staunton and Whyburn (1989), p 107; Walmsley (2002), para 2.250). In order to carry out their part of the bargain, health care facilities enter into specialised contracts of employment with staff, which are dealt with below (Chapter 10). The employee carer has a contract with the employer, but not with the patient. Poor health care is not only the basis of a potential negligence action, it is thus also a breach of that contract with the employer; as well as a potential breach of the employer's contract with the patient if the employer is at fault in not providing competent staff. If a health carer is directly engaged by a patient (for example, a home birth or private nurse) then there is a direct contract between the health carer and patient. It must be established that a contract exists between parties before one party can sue the other for breach of that contract. The requirements for a valid contract are set out below (see **[9.10]**).

Carers should be aware of the distinction between liability in contract and liability in negligence. The duty to act with reasonable skill and care in caring for patients always applies, whether or not a contract exists. Where there is a contract between a professional and a patient, principles applying to contracts operate in addition to those of tort law. Principles of contract law are different from those of negligence in some respects. However, where a contract for health care is implied, that standard and duty of care required will generally be the same as in tort law.

311

What is a Contract?

[9.10] A contract is an agreement between two or more people which, if it has certain features, will be legally binding. It need not be in writing—it can be verbal, or even implied from a person's actions. When, for example, people ask the local car mechanic to fix their car, or the dentist to fix their teeth, they are entering into a contractual relationship. Unless it is otherwise agreed, there is an implied condition that, in exchange for some form of *consideration* (most often in the form of payment of monies), the mechanic or dentist will give appropriate professional service. The law of contract is covered mainly by common law principles, therefore one must consult precedent to elucidate these. The following requirements have been established for the formation of a valid contract:

Checklist
REQUIREMENTS FOR A VALID CONTRACT
✓ intention to create a legal relationship;
✓ an identifiable offer and acceptance;
✓ clarity as to the parties between whom the legal relationship is created;
✓ consideration (something of value) exchanged between those involved, or agreement made under seal;
✓ genuine agreement on the part of each person involved;
✓ legal capacity on the part of each person making the agreement; and
✓ lawfulness of the activity involved.

Intention to create a legal relationship

[9.15] Intention to create a legal relationship is necessary in order to form a contract; "it is of the essence of contract...that there is a voluntary assumption of a legally enforceable duty" (*Australian Woollen Mills Pty Ltd v Commonwealth* (1954) 93 CLR 546; [1954] HCA 20). Intention is often presumed where there is consideration. However, several types of agreement are presumed of themselves not to be legally binding. For example, agreements made between husband and wife, such as agreements to pay money, carry out chores, arrangements over child care, etc, are generally not considered to involve an intention to create legal relations unless this is clearly expressed, or there is legislation which attaches legal obligations to agreements (for example the *Family Law Act 1975* (Cth) which attaches the obligation of mutual support to married couples).

The intentions of the parties may be express or implied. In determining whether the parties intended to create a legally binding agreement, the courts will generally apply an objective test. This was re-affirmed by the High Court in *Taylor v Johnson* (1983) 151 CLR 422; [1983] HCA 5 where the majority stated (at para 7 in the joint judgment):

> "[T]he law is concerned, not with the real intentions of the parties, but with the outward manifestations of those intentions."

A number of factors will be relevant to determining the parties' intentions including: the relationship between the parties; how the agreement came about; and the nature and subject of the agreement (*South Australia v Commonwealth* (1962) 108 CLR 130; [1962] HCA 10).

The legal approach can be ascertained by comparing two cases, and the reasoning of the courts in coming to different conclusions on somewhat similar facts.

[9.20] Case: *Balfour v Balfour* [1919] 2 KB 571
(CA England)

A married couple had to part because of the wife's ill-health after a holiday in their homeland, England, and the husband returned to Ceylon to work. The husband agreed to pay £30 per month maintenance to the wife while she was in England. At some later stage, the wife decided she would not return to the husband, and when the payments stopped, sued him for breach of contract.

[9.25] The judgment is discussed below (see **[9.35]**).

[9.30] Case: *McGregor v McGregor* (1888) 20 QBD 529
(CA England)

A husband and wife, after charging each other with assault, before the matter came to court agreed to drop charges and separate. The husband agreed to pay weekly maintenance, and the wife agreed to support herself and the children. The husband later refused to continue payments and the wife sued for breach of contract.

[9.35] The wife was unsuccessful in the first case, but in the second case, the wife succeeded. The reasoning of the courts revolves around the facts of the cases. In the first case, the Court said, the couple did not wish to affect their legal relations; the agreement was part of their ongoing marriage. In the second case, however, the couple intended to affect their legal relations. Whereas they were married and living together, now they were separated. The Court was considering not so much what the parties said (though that may come into consideration) as what they were intending to do.

[9.40] Case: *Jones v Padavatton* [1969] 2 All ER 616
(CA England)

The defendant P was a divorced woman living in Washington in 1962. She gave up a good job on J, her mother's, promise that if she went to London and read for the Bar there J would pay her a regular allowance. After P had been in London for two years, J bought a house there for her to live in. The house was big enough for tenants. P did not send any rents to J, who was paying off a large mortgage, and in 1965 P remarried. In 1967 J claimed possession of the house and the P counter-claimed for money she had spent on the house.

[9.45] The Court decided that they had meant to create legal relations. It looked at the circumstances of the negotiations of both mother and daughter, and decided that they both intended that the daughter should have a legal right to receive, and the mother a legal obligation to pay, the original allowance of $200 a month for a reasonable time for completion of Bar exams. The new arrangement was neither a variation of the original, nor (because of its vagueness) a new contract entitling the daughter to stay on in the house. The mother could have possession of the house, as the agreement did not allow for indefinite possession of it by the daughter.

In setting out the reasoning to be followed in such cases, Salmon LJ said (at 621):

"Did the parties intend the arrangement to be legally binding? This question has to be solved by applying what is sometimes ... called an objective test. The court has to consider what the parties said and wrote in the light of all the surrounding circumstances, and then decide whether the true inference is that the ordinary man and woman, speaking or writing thus in such circumstances, would have intended to create a legally binding agreement."

Agreement to oust law

[9.50] It may be specified that an agreement is not to be legally binding, or subject to legal enforcement. Many raffles, pools and competitions have, as a condition of entry, that they are not subject to legal enforcement.

[9.55] Case: *Appleson v H Littlewood Ltd* [1939] 1 All ER 464 (CA England)

A alleged he won some money (£4,335) in a football pool. The defendants showed that the conditions of entry had stated that the competition was not subject to legal enforcement, and did not give rise to any legal relationship, rights, duties or consequences. A was thus unable to claim the money, the Court holding that the arrangement was one of honour only, and that the plaintiff had accepted it with his eyes open (at 468).

Offer and acceptance

[9.60] Where a contract is in dispute and it is established that legal relations were intended, the court will consider whether an agreement was reached between the parties. The analysis of whether an agreement has been reached traditionally consisted of a clear offer of some benefit being made by one person (the offeror), and an acceptance of that particular offer being clearly and without qualification made on the part of someone else (the offeree). However,

> "[t]his doctrine, of the formation of contracts by offer and acceptance, encounters difficulties when sought to be applied, outside the realms of commerce and conveyancing, to the everyday contractual situations which are a feature of life in modern communities" (*MacRobertson Miller Airline Services v Commissioner of State Taxation (WA)* (1975) 133 CLR 125; [1975] HCA 55 per Stephen J at para 6).

Consequently, the court's application of the doctrine can appear somewhat contrived in some cases and, in addition, the development of equitable remedies (such as the doctrine of promissory estoppel) have modified the traditional rule of offer and acceptance in some cases. Statutes such as the *Trade Practices Act 1974* (Cth) have also affected the application of the traditional rule.

An objective test is applied to determine agreement.

Tickets as offers

[9.65] Under some circumstances a person need not be aware of all the details of the offer. The best example of this is where, after paying for goods or services, one is given a ticket or docket on which are written the conditions under which the goods or services are to be provided. So long as the conditions are reasonably available to be read, and the company giving the ticket could reasonably assume that people would know it contained conditions of the contract on it, then the purchaser is bound by the conditions even if informed of them after paying. If it is unreasonable to make that assumption, the company should notify each person receiving a ticket that the conditions are there (just printing such notice on the ticket may not be enough) and then, even if one is illiterate, one may be taken to know the conditions.

Withdrawal of offers

[9.70] An offer may be withdrawn, but this must occur before it has been accepted otherwise the withdrawal is ineffective. The offeror must communicate the revocation to the offeree.

The following principles apply to offers

[9.75] Contracts can be made orally, in writing, or by implication. An agreement need only be in writing where the law requires this: for example, for contracts involving real property (land and buildings). A contract may be oral, or implied. An example of an implied contract is where someone enters a hospital for emergency treatment. There is an implied offer by a hospital to give necessary life-saving treatment by the fact that the Emergency Department is open, and acceptance of the offer and conditions pertaining to it are implied by a person's actions.

The offer must be communicated to the offeree. A person cannot accept an offer about which he or she has no knowledge.

[9.80] Case: *R v Clarke* (1927) 40 CLR 227; [1927] HCA 47 (High Court)

The Western Australian government offered a reward for information leading to the arrest and conviction of the person or persons who committed the murder of two policemen, and stated the Governor would pardon any accomplice, not guilty of the murders, who first gave such information. C was arrested in connection with one of the murders. He gave police information which indeed did lead to the conviction of two men for the murder of one of the policemen. C gave evidence that although he was aware of the offer when giving the information, he had no intention of claiming the reward, and had not thought of it, but had given the information to prevent his own conviction. Nevertheless he later claimed the reward, and the government argued that they were not required to pay it.

[9.85] The case went to the High Court, where the government was reluctantly supported. The Court held that for the acceptance to be valid, the acceptor must act on the offer, and not for some other reason. A useful example provided was a situation where an offer of £100 to any person who should swim a hundred yards in the harbour, would be met by voluntarily performing the feat with reference to the offer, but not be satisfied by a person who was accidentally thrown overboard on that date and swam the distance simply to save his life, without any thought of the offer.

This principle would suggest that health care workers cannot demand payment for services which have been given and for which the patient did not agree to pay, for example, where an appendix is removed during a cholecystectomy when the removal is neither an emergency nor agreed to. Of course, such a scenario would also raise issues of trespass to the person (see **[4.10]**).

Bilateral contracts

[9.90] An example of a bilateral agreement is where a vendor offers to sell another person a boat for $2,000. The offer is clear: "Give me $2,000 and I'll give you the boat". The person may take up the offer or turn it down. As soon as he or she says "yes" the two people have entered into a contract: the money must be paid to obtain the boat and the boat must be given over to obtain the money.

Failure to honour the agreement, or the terms of it, may lead to an action in damages for breach of contract (see below **[9.335]**). There are situations where either party could get out of the contract. These are also described below.

This is the most common sort of contract. There is a widespread misconception that when goods are put on display in a shop, or advertised, the vendor is making an offer. In fact they are not "on offer" in the legal sense. They are "invitations to treat" and the shopkeeper is in fact made an offer by the customer when he or she asks for the goods. The shopkeeper then has the right to accept or refuse the customer's offer (with the proviso that under certain consumer legislation a vendor may be required to sell, and at the price on the goods as advertised).

Unilateral contracts

[9.95] An example of a unilateral contract is where a person offers a reward for the return of a lost cat. A person hearing of the offer or the finder of the cat are under no obligation to return it, and the owner's obligation to pay the reward only comes into being when the cat is returned.

Gratuitous offers

[9.100] Finally, one can make a gratuitous offer, for example, to give one's health carer a gift of $1,000. Such a promise is only enforceable if it is made under seal, that is, made in writing and with the formalities creating a deed (see **[9.140]**).

Conditions

[9.105] The test then, is whether the offeror took reasonable steps to ensure that the reasonable person would be aware of what conditions exist as to the offer. The courts have considered cases where an offeree reasonably thought that the piece of paper handed to her or him was merely a receipt and not a written contract, such as, where a deck chair was hired (*Chapelton v Barry Urban District Council* [1940] 1 KB 532), or where clothes were left at the dry cleaners (*Causer v Browne* [1952] VLR 1). Under the circumstances it was not reasonable to expect someone to be bound by the conditions set out in that document. If a document is signed, however, those signing it are generally held to have read and understood the contents of the document, whether they have or not, and whether the conditions in it are reasonable or not, and no matter how small the print is.

Offers must be specific

[9.110] An offer must be specific, that is, both parties must be quite clear on the benefits to be exchanged. For health care workers, this means that treatment to be given must be clearly explained to the patient, and only the treatment agreed upon must be given, except for any emergency treatment, where consent is implied (see Chapter 4).

Acceptance

[9.115] An acceptance must be in response to an offer and conveyed to the offeror. Nothing further must be left to be negotiated between the parties; they must be satisfied with all the conditions. It must be an unconditional assent to the terms of the offer. In the case of *Neale v Merrett* [1930] WN 189, Merrett offered his property to Neale at £280. Neale responded by post accepting and enclosed £80 as deposit, promising to pay the balance later. The court held that there was no contract as Neale's acceptance was not unconditional. There was no obligation on the part of Merrett to honour his offer. If the offeree wants to change the terms, he or she makes a counter offer, and in doing so becomes the offeror.

Time limit: Unless the time for acceptance is stipulated by the contract, it must occur within a reasonable time. The acceptance is not operative until it is conveyed to the offeror.

Privity of contract: Only those to whom the offer is made can accept it: third parties cannot oblige the offeror to act by accepting. If an offer is made to the whole world, anyone may accept it. If there can only be one acceptor of such an offer, authority seems to indicate that the first acceptor is entitled to performance of the offer (*Robinson v McEwan* (1865) 2 WW & A'B 65), however, this is not clear.

Revocation

[9.120] One can revoke an acceptance, but the revocation must reach the offeror before the acceptance. When it has been received, the person accepting cannot change an acceptance without the consent of the offeror: acceptance brings the contract into being. In a health care setting, this does not mean the person cannot refuse treatment to which they have previously agreed. It means that payment agreed to is legally owed, even though the treatment is not received. Where the health carer does not suffer any financial or other detriment (that is, through loss of time or expense in relation to equipment) there may be no liability on the part of the person revoking their consent).

Contracts by mail

[9.125] There are certain rules for contracts by mail, which may seem arbitrary, but have been adopted for convenience:

- An offer by mail is not effective until it reaches the offeree: the person must know of it. The same applies to the revocation of an offer. It takes effect when the offeree receives it. Those making an offer are advised to set a time limit on acceptance. Then they have a point in time beyond which any acceptance is not actionable, and they can follow up and ensure no acceptance is missed.
- An acceptance by mail is effective when it is posted. The offeror need not know of its existence to be bound by it. This is so even if the letter of acceptance is delayed or never reaches the offeror (*Household Fire*

Insurance Co v Grant (1879) 4 Ex D 216). The offeree should keep a record of having sent the letter, so that proof of this is available if required, otherwise the acceptance may not be provable. It is advisable to arrange for verification of the acceptance being received. In practice, many contract offers now specify a means for acceptance, to avoid communication errors.

Consideration

[9.130] Unless the contract is under seal (see **[9.140]**) it is called a simple contract, and must involve some form of consideration. Consideration must move from the promisee and must be a benefit to the promisor or a detriment to the promisee (*Beaton v McDivitt* (1987) 13 NSWLR 162 (CA) per Mchugh JA at 181). This means that something of value is to be conferred by the promisee on another, be it money, property, services or information, etc. Consideration may be adequate even though of nominal value. Most contracts involve promise of a mutual exchange of benefit, for example, one party undertakes to work for, or to provide health care of, the other for a sum of money. When considering whether a valid contract exists the court is not concerned with whether the consideration is adequate or not, so long as it is sufficient to indicate the parties were serious about the deal.

Past consideration, privity

[9.135] There are two more points about consideration that should be made: past consideration, that is, something done or paid for in the past cannot hold someone to a promise to which the thing or money did not then relate. If a grateful patient, on leaving a dentist's care promises a gift of $600, that is not an enforceable promise, as the care was given with no expectation of the money. Secondly, only the person who has given consideration may enforce the contract: if a health carer is engaged to care for Mr Jones, that does not create an obligation to attend to a relative of Mrs Jones.

Deeds

[9.140] Contracts under seal are called deeds. These are in writing, and are "signed, sealed and delivered". This procedure has been simplified by legislation and court decisions. More recently, parties' signatures need only be attested to by a witness who is not a party to the deed, and the document be expressed to be a deed. Although they may be used to sanctify mutual promises, deeds apply to promises of gifts. They will be enforced in the absence of consideration, and they take effect on the moment of delivery (physical delivery is not necessary, intention to deliver is enough). Neither knowledge on the part of the promisee, nor acceptance of the offer (as with simple contracts) is required.

Deeds last longer, that is, one can sue for breach of contract based on a deed for up to 15 years (Victoria), or 12 years (other States), after the deed has been made, whereas with a simple contract the limitation period is six years. Where one is suing for breach of contract resulting in personal injury, the limitation period is shorter.

The importance of writing

[9.145] As already stated, simple contracts need not be in writing. There are exceptions to this principle through legislation, for example:

- bills of exchange including cheques;
- transfers of shares or title to land;
- assignment of copyright; and
- in some Australian jurisdictions, credit purchase agreements, and some details of door-to-door sales.

Legislation may also require certain contracts to be evidenced in writing, such as:

- sale of land agreements in all jurisdictions;
- contracts of guarantee;
- hire purchase agreements;
- agreements not to be performed within one year; and
- sales of over $20 in some jurisdictions, unless the buyer has accepted and actually received at least some of the goods, or has paid a deposit.

Terms of the Contract

[9.148] The rights and obligations of the parties are defined by the terms, which may be express or implied.

The benefit of contracts in writing

[9.150] Where terms of the contract are in writing, and there is no reason not to believe the parties meant the writing to constitute the whole of the agreement, the courts will generally consider what is written down to be final and complete. The words will be scrutinised for their meaning, the terms for their provisions, and no party will be able to argue that they did not mean what the reasonable reader would take them to mean. Only if a person can convince the court that the words on paper are not the complete or accurate agreement will it consider other evidence (such as oral undertakings also made at the time) as to what the parties arranged.

Most readers will be familiar with being handed a document which has a large amount of small print, being shown a spot and told "just sign here". That small print constitutes the terms or conditions of the contract, and any warranty on the part of the offeror as to the nature and condition of any goods, or the quality of performance of the contract. The use of standard form contracts has led the courts in some cases to impose an evidentiary burden on the party seeking to rely on particularly onerous or unusual terms contained in such contracts (see *Baltic Shipping Co v Dillon (The Mikhail Lermontov)* (1991) 22 NSWLR 1). The burden will be discharged where it is shown that reasonable steps were taken to draw the relevant term to the other party's attention at the time of signing.

Implied terms

[9.155] Sometimes not all the terms of a contract are contained in it. This might be for three main reasons:

- the parties may not have thought of all the contingencies that would arise or for some reason it is necessary to read into the contract certain terms to make it work;
- the very nature of the contract indicates that the parties would have accepted that the terms in question would apply, also perhaps in this category are terms implied by reason of custom, usage or course of dealing; and
- there may be legislation that imposes on particular courses of behaviour certain terms and conditions (the classic example of this is the contract of employment, which by statute contains many conditions in relation to sick leave, holiday leave, minimum rates of pay, etc—see Chapter 10).

Conditions necessary for the courts to find implied terms in a contract were summarised in *BP Refinery (Westernport) Pty Ltd v Hastings Shire Council* (1977) 280 CLR 266; [1977] HCA 40 at [40] of the majority judgment (High Court of Australia/Privy Council). These are that the proposed term must be:

- reasonable and equitable;
- necessary to give business efficacy to the contract, so that no condition will be implied if the contract can be carried out effectively without it;
- so obvious that it "goes without saying";
- capable of clear expression; and
- able to operate without contradicting any express term of the contract.

In a more recent case the High Court considered these criteria and accepted that they were best applied where there was a written, formal contract. Where there is no formal contract, as may be the case in most health care agreements, the actual terms of the contract must be ascertained before implied terms can be considered. In other words, the intention of the parties must be identified and what they actually agreed upon be established, before any question of what should be implied arises. The Court accepted the finding of Deane J in *Hawkins v Clayton* (1988) 164 CLR 539; [1988] HCA 15 at [5], that the Court should refer to the imputed intention of the parties, "if and only if, it can be seen that the implication of the particular term is necessary for reasonable or effective operation of a contract of that nature in the circumstances of the case" (*Byrne v Australian Airlines Ltd* (1995) 185 CLR 410; [1995] HCA 24 at [12] of the majority judgment).

Contracts for Health Care

[9.160] Cases establishing the law in relation to contracts with health carers deal with doctors and their patients, but are arguably applicable to all those who undertake to provide health care to another.

In *Breen v Williams* (see facts at **[7.15]**) the High Court of Australia established that in the absence of a specific contract between a doctor and patient the consideration on the part of the patient is "either a payment, promise of payment, of reward or submission by the patient, or an undertaking by the patient to submit, to the treatment proposed" (per Brennan CJ at para 3). The payment need not come from the patient, but from another source, such as an insurer, or Medicare (per Gummow at [26]). Most health care contracts are verbal or implied and most health care patients are unaware that they are entering a contract. The use of an action for breach of contract only as a means of compensation for unsatisfactory treatment is very rare, as it is often considered more appropriate to bring an action in negligence or to frame the claim in both negligence and contract. However, the law will recognise the patient's right to receive what was implied or verbally agreed upon in the way of treatment, and an implied term of that agreement is that treatment will be provided with reasonable skill and care. There have been rare cases where it was argued that the doctor contracted to provide a particular result, such as the success of a vasectomy—see *Thake v Maurice* [1986] QB 644. Negligence may be easier to prove, as the implied terms of the contract may be in doubt (as discussed below). Compensation is not granted for such things as pain and suffering, and loss of quality of life, as can be the case in negligence. Civil liability legislation (as discussed in Chapters 4 and 6) now operates to limit damages available to a plaintiff in personal injury actions, whether the claim is brought in negligence or contract—see for example, *Civil Liability Act 2002* (NSW), s 5A.

Terms of the health care contract

[9.165] Case: *Breen v Williams* (1995) 186 CLR 71; [1995] HCA 63

The facts of this case are set out at **[7.15]**. The appellant argued, among other things, that she had a contract with her doctor, an implied term of which was provision of access to medical records.

[9.170] The Court found that there was no formal contract between the parties. However, as indicated above, there was a contract in effect. The principles in relation to implied terms as set out above were endorsed, the provision of information being tied to the undertaking to advise and treat the patient with reasonable skill and care. This implied term for provision of health care is similar to that in tort, being based on a standard reasonable under the circumstances. Thus, Brennan CJ held (at 79), that the doctor has a contractual duty to provide information or advice when requested and:

- not to give it might prejudice the general health of the patient;
- the request is reasonable in the circumstances; and
- reasonable reward for the disclosure is offered or given.

Wighton v Arnot [2005] NSWSC 637 at [68] (discussed at **[6.440]** and **[4.405]**) appears to adopt a similar approach.

The Court limited the doctor's implied duty under a contract to advising and treating the patient with reasonable skill and care. However, this may involve follow-up or contacting a patient after the provision of care has ended. An example of this may be the provision of information about the history or condition or treatment of the patient on an earlier occasion where failure to provide this would prejudice the patient's "future medical treatment or physical or mental well being". New information about the effects of treatment given to patients in the past (for example, the development of Creutzfeld-Jacob Disease from human growth hormone derived from corpses) could be such a situation where a contractual obligation exists to advise those patients (Skene (1998), p 42).

The provision of adequate information, to provide an effective consent, may be implied as a term in a contract for health care. This can be derived from the requirement under contract law that the parties are agreed on actions each is to undertake, and from the requirement to provide care that will not prejudice the patient's physical or mental well being. Part of that well being comes from being properly informed when making decisions about one's health. However, this argument may have practical difficulties and so arguments in relation to consent are customarily in the context of trespass or negligence.

In Australian law it was uncertain as to whether there is a specific implied contractual duty to maintain patient confidentiality. It may be that confidentiality is another manifestation of the overall implied requirement of advising and treating the patient with reasonable skill and care (again, it is necessary to show that the contract would not work if the implied term did not operate). There is some indication in English case law that confidentiality is a term of the contract between health care provider and patient (see for example *Parry-Jones v Law Society* [1969] 1 Ch 1; *Argyll v Argyll* [1967] Ch 302). However, given the privacy regime described in Chapter 7, this is of little ongoing practical application.

Capacity to Contract

Who can make a contract?

[9.175] Someone will only be obliged to fulfil a contract if that person has the capacity to agree to it. At common law this means the person must be 18 years of age and mentally able to agree. Thus minors (those under 18) and those of unsound mind may be held not to have the capacity to enter into contracts. The categories of those unable to contract will be considered more fully below.

Minors generally cannot contract

[9.180] At common law, a minor, can repudiate a contract entered into by her or him before majority, or, if the minor intends to be bound by it, ratify it immediately on attaining majority. This generally involves lasting property rights (for example, as owner or lessee of land). Although this means the minor is under no obligation under the agreement until then, the adult with whom it is made may, nevertheless, still be obliged to carry it out. The law, apart from being quite clear on the point that a contract made by a minor is not absolutely void (that is, not a contract at all), but rather voidable (that is, valid from inception until whoever may be entitled to repudiate it does so), what the position of the other party is in terms of its obligation is left to the consideration of the court in the individual case.

When a minor may be bound by contract

[9.185] It has generally been held that minors should be protected from unwise transactions through youthful exuberance and indiscretion. There are, however, two important exceptions to this principle.

A minor may be bound by a contract for necessaries. Note the word used is not "necessities". Necessaries does not mean the necessities of life, although these are included. It means goods and services fit to maintain one in the lifestyle to which one is accustomed (*Dale v Copping* (1610) 1 Bulst 39; 80 ER 743) and necessary for this at the time of contract. The social position, means, along with the age and occupation of the minor, will be considered whether he or she was adequately supplied with similar goods already. The case of *Chapple v Cooper* (1844) 153 ER 105, a nineteenth century case that is still relevant, held that "necessaries" can include food, raiment, lodging, instructions in art or trade, or intellectual, moral and religious information, attendance of others. As "class" is a part of society, the court held, the subject matter and extent of the contract may vary according the "station he is to fulfil":

> "But in all cases it must first be made out that the class itself is one in which the things furnished are essential to the existence and reasonable advantage and comfort of the infant contractor. Thus, articles of mere luxury are always excluded, though luxurious articles of utility are in some cases allowed" (at 107).

Statute also defines necessary goods (*Sale of Goods Act 1954* (ACT), s 7; *Sale of Goods Act 1923* (NSW), s 7; *Sale of Goods Act* (NT), s 7; *Sale of Goods Act 1896* (Qld), s 5; *Sale of Goods Act 1895* (SA), s 2; *Sale of Goods Act 1896* (Tas), s 7; *Goods Act 1958* (Vic), s 7; *The Sale of Goods Act 1895* (WA), s 2). Whilst there are minor variations in the definitions contained in the statutes, necessary goods are generally considered to be those goods suitable to the condition of life of the minor and his or her requirements at the time of sale and delivery.

The imprecise nature of what constitute "necessaries" means that there are many court cases determining the issue. Changing social and moral values and differing circumstances may provide a variety of answers.

A minor may also be bound by a beneficial contract of service, such as contracts for education, training, medical treatment and transportation. In the absence of harsh and oppressive terms such a contract will generally be considered beneficial.

If a minor is seeking medical treatment, does an agreement to give this treatment mean a contract exists? What is the consideration involved? If parents are paying, is the contract with the parents or with the child? What if the parents agree to pay for what they believe is treatment for a sore throat and the minor is in fact receiving contraception?

There has been little case law in relation to the contract for health care in relation to children. It can only be inferred that a health carer may have a contract with a minor for health care services where the minor is paying for those services on his or her own behalf or the services are funded through Medicare. The child would be bound by the contract to pay for services, presuming the health care is considered beneficial.

However if the child's parents are paying for the health care, then the contract may well be with the parent. There would have to be an agreement by the parent, either specifically given or implied, that they will pay. The contract is then with the parent, with a duty on the part of the health carer to provide the care to the child as a service to the parent, not the child, the parent being required to pay. Other duties flowing from the health carer to the child would result from the professional relationship between them, not any contract.

Legislation in New South Wales & South Australia altering the common law position

[9.190] In New South Wales, the *Minors (Property and Contracts) Act 1970* provides that minors may make binding contracts. Minors are presumed to have contractual capacity for most purposes to the extant that they are capable. Unless the minor, by reason of his or her youth, lacks the understanding necessary for his or her participation in the contract, the contract will be binding. The Act also provides an alternative means for minors to contract by official sanction.

In South Australia, the *Minors Contracts (Miscellaneous Provisions) Act 1979* provides for minors who wish to enter specific contracts with official sanction. Court approval is required before the contract is entered into; once it is entered it is binding. In addition, a court may appoint an agent to transact on behalf of a minor.

Persons of "unsound mind"

[9.195] Who is legally of "unsound mind"? There are two categories of persons of unsound mind: those who have been certified as such under State legislation and those otherwise recognised as being of unsound mind (see above, Chapter 5). Those who have been officially recognised by the law through certification as being of unsound mind generally have no contractual capacity. Others who are recognised as having some degree of mental incapacity may be bound by a contract. If such a person wishes to rescind a contract on the ground of incapacity, he or she must plead and prove that:

(i) he or she was unable to understand the contract at the time of formation due to mental incapacity; and

(ii) the other person knew, or ought to have known, of the incapacity. Thus a contract entered into by a person with some degree of mental incapacity is not void but may be voidable (see **[9.180]**). Contracts for necessaries supplied to a person lacking mental capacity are binding in the same way they are for minors.

Intoxication. Intoxication is considered at law in the same manner as mental incapacity. A person who is intoxicated at the time of entering a contract may only rescind that contract where they are able to show that their intoxication rendered them unable to understand the nature of the contract they entered into and the other party to the contract knew, or ought to have known, they were intoxicated to that extent at the time (*Blomley v Ryan* (1954) 99 CLR 362; [1954] HCA 79).

When the mentally incapacitated person presents for treatment. It would seem that individuals not certified as being of unsound mind, but who are incapacitated to some extent could be bound by contract to the extent that they knew what they were contracting for when they contracted: for example, such a person may be held to an agreement to pay for health care services; the very fact that a person presents for treatment may indicate not only the knowledge that he or she is ill, but also the understanding that treatment is needed, as well as the nature of such treatment. (Note, a distinction must be made between the contract and informed consent point of view (see above, Chapter 5).)

Unincorporated bodies

[9.200] What are they? Unincorporated bodies are groups of people, such as practitioners acting together as one, who are not a registered company. Most commonly this is a partnership. As these groups of people are separate entities in law and not a legal "person" as is a corporation, such a body cannot be a party to a contract. Each person separately must be a party if it is to be binding, either personally or through an agent (partners are each other's agents and so may bind each other). A group of practitioners may call themselves a "company" without being incorporated under appropriate companies incorporation legislation, and a group of people may register a business name under the business names legislation. In both cases those involved are still separate individuals under the law.

When a Contract is Not an Enforceable Agreement

[9.205] Those making a contract must, under law, be *ad idem*, that is, regarding both the terms of the agreement and their consent thereto, they must be of one mind and freely consent to all the terms of the contract. A contract may be set aside where there is:

- misrepresentation of essential facts;
- mistake as to essential facts or terms in limited circumstances;

- duress by one of the parties to the contract;
- undue influence exerted by one of the parties to the contract; or
- fraud perpetrated by one or more parties.

Misrepresentation

[9.210] A misrepresentation is an undertaking that something exists which does not accord with the true situation, generally made in order to induce a person to enter a contract. It must be innocently made, as such an undertaking made deliberately is classified as fraud.

Where there is an innocent misrepresentation of fact by one party to a contract, and this is relied on by the other party at least in part inducing them to enter the contract, the contract may be rescinded. Misrepresentations of fact must be distinguished from advice, promises, predictions and expressions of opinion.

It is worth mentioning here that some contracts, mainly insurance agreements, rely on the utmost good faith of the party applying for insurance to answer all questions which they are asked truthfully, and also to volunteer any other information that may be relevant to the risk being taken by the insurer. Failure to do so may enable the insurer to rescind the contract.

Fraudulent or negligent misrepresentation may lead to further action, either in criminal law or tort.

Mistake

[9.215] Courts are reluctant to hold that a contract is unenforceable because of a mistake made by one of the parties. One must distinguish mistake at law from error of judgment or mistake in personal assessment of facts. Take, for example, the person who looks at a car for sale and decides it is worth $5,000. That person cannot complain if he or she later discovers it is worth $500. There is a maxim at law *caveat emptor*—"let the buyer beware". Only a few mistakes will be allowed in law. They are:

- mistake as to the nature of contract;
- mutual mistake as to a fact; and
- mistake as to the party one is contracting with.

Mistake as to the nature of the contract

[9.220] This is not to be confused with mistake as to the law regarding the contract, but rather, it is a mistake regarding what type of document one is signing. The test is whether the mistaken party's signature evidences her or his agreement to the terms set out in the document (*Gibbons v Wright* (1954) 91 CLR 423; [1954] HCA 17). A person seeking to prove that their signature does not evidence agreement (described in law as *non est factum*, that is "it is not my deed") to the terms must be able to demonstrate that, at the time of signing the document, he or she was reasonably mistaken as to the nature or extent of the obligations created by it (*Saunders v Anglia Building Society* [1971] AC 1004).

Where the claim is proven, the contract will be void. However, individuals of full capacity will rarely be able to succeed in such a claim (*Saunders v Anglia Building Society* [1971] AC 1004).

Mutual mistake as to a fact

[9.225] Where both parties are mistaken as to one or more facts, and they base the contract on this mistake, the contract can be held to be void only if the existence of the agreement depends on the reality of the mistaken facts. The contract will be void only where the mutual mistake concerns an essential term of the contract (*Goldsbrough, Mort & Co Ltd v Quinn* (1910) 10 CLR 674; [1910] HCA 20). For example, where a painting was sold, both parties mistakenly believing it was painted by the artist Constable, the Court held that the contract was not void, as both parties were agreed on the sale of the same subject matter, the painting itself (*Leaf v International Galleries* [1950] 2 KB 86).

Mistake as to the party one is contracting with

[9.230] In order for a contract to be void on the basis of mistaken identity, one of the parties must be mistaken as to the real identity of the other and be able to show that the contract was conditional on the identity of that person (*Porter v Latec Finance (Qld) Pty Ltd* (1964) 111 CLR 177; [1964] HCA 49).

Examples in health care would include the engaging of dentist Y to give care and advice to a patient who believes she is a registered dentist. If she is, in fact, a registered dentist but her name is Z, and if she gives adequate dental care as agreed, the contract would most likely be enforceable: the patient would have to pay. If dentist Y was the dentist's real name, but she is not a registered dentist, that mistaken identity could be said to go to the heart of the contract, even if the dental care is reasonable. The patient would most likely have to show that he or she would not have agreed to be cared for by Y if he or she had known the truth. However, unless that can be proved, Y is most likely entitled to be paid for services rendered.

Duress

[9.235] The use of undue pressure to acquire a benefit is called duress. Common law has restricted duress to acts or threats of violence to the person, of deprivation of liberty, and the unlawful detention of goods. Recent law has extended beyond tangible property and includes the concept of economic duress, that is, the illegitimate threat of economic harm if one does not sign the contract. Where there is duress in the formation of contract, the agreement may be rescinded.

Undue influence

[9.240] If the situation falls short of the common law definition of duress, one may be able to invoke the law of equity (see **[9.345]**ff), which has developed remedies where one party holds an unfair advantage over the other, through superior power or status. Where there has been such pressure or an abuse of influence in the formation of a contract, that contract may be set aside.

The very existence of certain relationships between the parties to a contract may give rise to the presumption of undue influence. The basis for the presumption is that certain types of relationships inherently contain influence or ascendency of one party over the other. Such relationships have been traditionally held to be solicitor and client, trustee (person entrusted with one's money or finances, for example, a bank) and beneficiary (person who has a claim on them, for example, account owner or person nominated to benefit), doctor and patient, parent and child, teacher and child, religious adviser and disciple. Where these relationships existed at the time consent was given, there is a presumption that there will have been undue influence unless the party with superior knowledge and resources can prove that there was no such influence, and that the transaction was entered into freely and voluntarily. The court will consider whether full disclosure of the facts was made to the inferior party by the superior party, whether independent advice was given (that is, advice by a third impartial person with relevant knowledge), and the actual circumstances of the consent. Examples include the cases below.

[9.245] Case: *Lloyd's Bank Ltd v Bundy* [1974] 3 WLR 501

A bank secured a guarantee by a farmer of his son's overdraft. The court found that the farmer was elderly and stood to lose everything he had.

[9.250] The Court found that the bank, as trustee of his money and finances stood in the role of fiduciary, had to show that it recommended independent advice. As the bank hadn't done this, it was held to have had undue influence and the contract was declared void.

[9.255] Case: *Tasker v Algar* [1928] NZLR 529

A mentally ill man made gifts of money to friends who cared for him. On his death the administrator sought to have the gifts set aside, on the ground of undue influence.

[9.260] The Court found that a fiduciary relationship existed between the man and his friends and that the friends therefore had to show that there was no undue influence.

Where there is no special relationship, the person claiming undue influence will have the burden of proving that fact.

It is not hard to imagine that undue influence may affect the relationship between health carer and patient in some instances. Health carers and others must be careful not to dominate patients to such a degree that their advice amounts to undue influence, but must allow the patient to be free to decide, based on a fair and impartial disclosure of facts. (Note also the ethical duties in this regard, for example Standard 4.1 of the New South Wales Medical Board, *Code of Professional Conduct* which states: "avoid financial involvement such as loans and investment schemes with patients".)

Fraud

[9.265] Fraud exists where one of the parties has intentionally misrepresented a crucial fact (not opinion or law), and:

- it was made knowingly, or with reckless indifference to its truth;
- it was made with the intention of inducing the other party to act upon it; and
- it must have actually misled the aggrieved party.

In such a case the aggrieved person may rescind the contract, and sue for any damages suffered as a result of the fraud.

Unconscionable contracts

[9.270] A further development in equity has been a willingness on the part of judges to set aside contracts which impose harsh terms on one party due to an inequality of bargaining power. "Unconscionable conduct" has been defined as "serious misconduct or something clearly unfair or unreasonable" (see *Hurley v McDonald's Australia Pty Ltd* [1999] FCA 1497 cited with approval in *Australian Competition & Consumer Commission v Lux Pty Ltd* [2004] FCA 926).

[9.275] Case: *Commercial Bank of Australia Ltd v Amadio* (1983) 151 CLR 447; [1983] HCA 14 (High Court of Australia)

Vincenzo Amadio (A) was managing director of a failing company which had a very large overdraft at the plaintiff bank. To prevent closure of the account, a deed of mortgage on property owned by A's parents was executed by them. They were old and spoke little English, had been given incorrect information by A, and although this had been corrected by the bank manager, they received no independent advice at all. When the company went into liquidation and the bank demanded $240,000 from the couple, they sued for release from the deed. They lost, but the Supreme Court (South Australia) granted an appeal. The matter went to the High Court.

[9.280] By 3-2 majority, the High Court held that the contract was unconscionable. This was not because of any dishonesty or moral obliquity on the part of the bank manager, but rather because the couple had not received proper advice as to the effect of the document they signed, or had its contents properly explained to them by their son (it was worded in very complicated legal writing). When the couple questioned the facts which (they were later to learn) had been wrongly represented to them by their son, and which the bank manager had to correct, the Court said, he should have been put on notice that steps should be taken to ensure they were properly informed. Thus the couple's disability through ignorance and the inequality between them and the bank should have been evident, and it was unfair and unconscionable of the bank to proceed to procure their signature.

Relief such as this against unconscionable dealing is a purely equitable remedy (see **[9.345]**ff). However, there are now statutory provisions in some jurisdictions allowing the court, where it finds a contract or a provision of a contract to be unjust, to refuse to enforce part or the whole of the contract, declare part or the whole of the contract void, or make an order varying part or all of the contract (see for example, the *Contracts Review Act 1980* (NSW)).

This form of action has not been used widely in the medical arena, although there may be some scope for patients to bring an action in the courts alleging that they have been manipulated into agreeing to procedures when they did not fully understand what was going on.

Contracts which are illegal or against public policy

[9.285] An agreement may be validly made, but may be void or prohibited by statute or common law because it involves activities which are either illegal, prohibited, immoral or otherwise against public policy.

Historically, at common law, those contracts which involve illegal, or what has been considered immoral, behaviour have been held to be void *ab initio* (that is, "from the beginning"). Such contracts involve subject matter such as commission of a crime (for example, an illegal abortion), a tort or a fraud on a third party, acts which are prejudicial to public safety, acts which are prejudicial to the administration of justice or which lead to corruption in public life, and contracts to defraud revenue.

While prohibited activity can be fairly easily identified, activity which is immoral and/or against public policy will depend on current opinion. As recently as 1973 in *Andrews v Parker* [1973] Qd R 93 the Queensland Supreme Court said: "The law shall not enforce an immoral promise such as a man and a woman to live together without being married." Similarly, other activities deemed immoral in the past may no longer be so considered.

Contracts to bear a child for another (surrogacy contracts)

[9.290] In recent years there has been much ethical and legal debate concerning surrogacy agreements. The Federal government and most State governments have issued reports declaring that these agreements are against public policy, and thus should at least be discouraged. (Family Law Council, *Creating Children: A Uniform Approach to the Law and Practice of Reproductive Technology in Australia* (Canberra, AGPS, 1985); Australian Capital Territory,

Attorney General's Department, *Discussion Paper: Surrogacy in the ACT* (Canberra, Australian Capital Territory Government Printer, 1993); New South Wales Law Reform Commission, *Artificial Conception: Surrogate Motherhood Report* (Sydney, 1988); Special Committee Appointed by the Queensland Government to Inquire into the Laws Relating to Artificial Insemination, In Vitro Fertilisation and Other Related Matters (*Report*, 1984); Select Committee of the South Australian Legislative Council, *Report on Artificial Insemination by Donor In Vitro Fertilisation and Embryo Transfer Procedures and Related Matters in South Australia* (South Australian Government Printer, 1987); Tasmanian Committee of Inquiry to Investigate Artificial Conception and Related Matters in Tasmania (*Final Report*, 1985); Victorian Committee to Consider the Social, Ethical and Legal Issues Arising from In Vitro Fertilisation, *Report on the Disposition of Embryos Produced by In Vitro Fertilisation* (1984); Western Australian Committee of Inquiry, *Report of the Committee Appointed by the Western Australian Government to Inquire into the Social and Legal and Ethical Issues Relating to In Vitro Fertilisation and its Supervision* (1986)).

Most Australian jurisdictions now have legislation concerning this issue. Queensland and South Australia have legislated to make the entering into a surrogacy contract illegal per se, in Queensland doing so attracts a penalty (*Surrogate Parenthood Act 1988* (Qld); *Family Relationships Act 1975* (SA), Pt IIB). The legislation in Victoria and Tasmania (*Infertility Treatment Act 1995* (Vic), Pt 6; *Surrogacy Contracts Act 1993* (Tas)) declares surrogacy contracts null and void, that is, those entering a contract will not be penalised, but they cannot enforce any of the terms of the agreement: it is as if it did not exist, so the woman bearing the child cannot sue for any money promised to her or force anyone to take the child, nor can she be made to give up the child as she had promised. Most jurisdictions' legislation distinguishes between paid and unpaid surrogacy arrangements also referred to as commercial and altruistic arrangements, respectively. Commercial arrangements attract penalties in Victoria, the Australian Capital Territory (*Parentage Act 2004* (ACT), Pt 4) and Tasmania. New South Wales has no legislation specifically designed to regulate surrogacy agreements, as such they are neither prohibited nor encouraged. Similarly, Western Australia lacks legislation specifically dealing with surrogacy arrangements. Child welfare laws, and custody and guardianship laws would, of course, apply if they were relevant to such a situation.

[9.295] Case: *Matter of Baby M*, 537 A 2d 1227 NJ
(1988) (CA New Jersey United States)

This case involved the agreement of a woman, W to bear a child, the result of artificial insemination with the sperm of a Mr S, and to relinquish the child to him and his wife on its birth. She was to be paid $10,000 for a live birth, and less if the child was stillborn. After the birth W refused to relinquish the child, and Mr S sued for breach of contract, demanding custody of the child (who was seized for them by the police).

[9.300] The trial judge ruled in favour of Mr S, invoking the contract. However the Court of Appeal (at 1248) reversed this decision. It held that the contract entered into was null and void as it was against public policy. The agreement was in effect the sale of a child, and this was not sanctioned by the law: "In surrogacy, the highest bidders will presumably become the adoptive parents regardless of suitability, so long as payment of money is permitted."

Any decision as to who should have custody of the child should be made on the basis of the child's best interest, the Court continued, not on who had agreed to be the parent of the child. So although the Court eventually gave custody to Mr S, it made it clear that this was not because of the contract, but because Mr S was the father, and under the circumstances it was in the child's best interest to live with him and his wife. English precedent on this topic supports the view that surrogacy agreements (which are prohibited as commercial enterprises) will be taken into account by the court in deciding the right of any person to adopt a child, but that the court must give priority to the welfare of children (*Brooks v Blount* [1923] 1 KB 237; *Re C (A Minor) (Wardship: Surrogacy)* [1985] FLR 846).

In Australia, the case of *Re Evelyn* (1988) FLC ¶92-807 dealt with the enforcement of a surrogacy agreement. That case involved a child born as a result of a surrogacy agreement, where the birth parents did not want to give her up. The Family Court held that the agreement could not be enforced where a case involves the custody of a child, the paramount consideration is the welfare of the child, thus considerations of immorality become irrelevant. For further discussion about the law regarding surrogacy see **[17.155]**ff.

Discharge of Contracts

[9.305] A contract comes to an end, that is, is discharged, on one of the following events:

- performance;
- agreement;
- frustration;
- election upon breach; or
- the occurrence of a specified event or condition.

Performance

[9.310] Where parties have performed their promises fully and precisely, according to the terms of their agreement, the contract is discharged. Unless a specific time for the carrying out of one's obligations is stipulated (making time of the essence), these should be carried out within a reasonable time. Where activities are to be performed for a stated period of time, the contract is discharged at the end of that time. When a party has discharged her or his obligations under a contract, that party may demand discharge (often by payment) from the other(s).

Agreement

[9.315] Where a contract has not been fully discharged the parties may agree to consider it discharged. This is a further contract and all elements, including consideration, must be present. Where no one has completed her or his part of the agreement, then consideration is no problem: each party simply agrees to release their rights under the original contract in consideration for a similar release by the other. Where one party has discharged some or all obligations required under the contract but the other has not, then some further consideration is required for the agreement to be legally enforceable.

Frustration

[9.320] Normally contracts are based on at least a presumption that those involved will carry out their promise as long as they remain able to do so: and that only ill-health, unexpected events, accident, war, non-occurrence of a foreseen event, etc, which renders it impossible or unreasonably difficult for them to act will excuse them from their obligation. In that case each party must fulfil those obligations which fell due before the frustrating event occurred: the contract is not void from the beginning. If the frustration is self-induced the above does not apply.

Election upon breach

[9.325] Where one party has breached a term of the contract, the other party may elect either to discharge the contract or to seek a remedy as outlined below, depending on the nature of the breach. The party may be able to claim for any damages suffered, but cannot thereafter seek specific performance of the contract (see **[9.350]**).

Occurrence of a specified event or condition

[9.330] This is self-explanatory: where it is specified that if something happens or some stipulated condition occurs the contract will be deemed discharged.

Remedies for Breach of Contract

[9.335] There are three main actions that can be brought where the terms of an agreement have been breached.

Common law remedy

Damages

[9.340] Breach of contract is actionable *per se* (*Hawkins v Clayton* (1988) 164 CLR 539; [1988] HCA 15). A person need not prove loss or damage to sue for breach of contract, although where no such loss or damage exists, damages will be nominal only as the purpose of an award of damages for breach of contract is to put the party in the position they would have been had the contract been performed (*Butler v Egg & Egg Pulp Marketing Board* (1966) 114 CLR 185; [1966] HCA 38). An award of damages is generally an appropriate sum of money as compensation for loss of goods, business or other value that has resulted from the breach, or the cost of remedying the effects of the contract not having been fulfilled. The court considers the terms of the contract (written, oral or implied), and what could fairly be contemplated as a reasonable sum, which the parties would have had in mind at the time of making the contract. The plaintiff must be able to demonstrate that the loss or damage is a result of the breach of contract.

Equitable remedies

[9.345] Equitable remedies are flexible and discretionary, that is, equitable relief is moulded to meet the justice of the particular case. This does not mean, however, that the court's order is based upon idiosyncratic notions of fairness and justice, but rather the consistent application of equitable principles. Equitable remedies may be personal or proprietary. Equitable proprietary remedies include constructive trusts and tracing. Equitable personal remedies include specific performance, injunctions, declarations, monetary remedies (account of profits, equitable damages and equitable compensation), rescission, rectification, and restitution. Two of the most common equitable remedies which are awarded in contract cases, specific performance and injunctions, are discussed further below.

Specific performance

[9.350] Specific performance is a court order which requires a party to perform her or his contractual obligations. Assuming that the contract is valid, binding and for valuable consideration, the court will only award specific performance where:

- An award of monetary damages would be an inadequate remedy. This is because equitable relief will not generally be awarded where there is an adequate remedy at law. For example, common law damages will be inadequate where the subject matter of the contract is not freely available on the open market due to its unique, rare or unusual nature, such as a contract for the sale of a painting; and
- It would not be unjust to order specific performance by the defaulting party; that is, there is no equitable defence or discretionary consideration which would preclude relief. For example, a court will generally refuse to specifically enforce a contract for personal services or which involves continual supervision, or where the plaintiff has unreasonably delayed in commencing proceedings.

Injunction

[9.355] An injunction is an order by a court that either forbids a person to do an act or thing (prohibitory injunction), or requires a person to do something (mandatory injunction). An injunction may be awarded when there is a contract where someone has promised to refrain from some activity, and the other person has reason to believe the person will go ahead and do it (*quia timet* injunction), or it can be an interim measure where a further, more detailed court hearing is to be held. Whereas failure to pay damages after they have been ordered by the court can lead to seizure of property or garnishment of wages to claim the ordered amount of money, where an order for specific performance or an injunction is ignored the person involved may be imprisoned for contempt of court.

References and Further Reading

Bowden, G and Morris, A, *An Introduction to the Law of Contracts and Tort* (The Estates Gazette Ltd, London, 1978)

Carter, J, *Outline of Contract Law in Australia* (Butterworths, Sydney, 1986)

Carter, J and Harland, D, *Contract Law in Australia* (3rd ed, Butterworths, Sydney, 1998)

Dix, et al, *Law for the Medical Profession* (Butterworths, Sydney, 1988)

Goold, I, "Surrogacy: Is there a case for legal prohibition" *Australian Health Law Bulletin* 12 (2)

Graw, S, *An Introduction to the Law of Contract* (5th ed, Lawbook Co, Sydney, 2004)

Khoury, D and Yamouni, Y, *Understanding Contract Law* (3rd ed, Butterworths, Sydney, 1992)

Lindgren, K, Carter, J and Harland, D, *Cases and Materials on Contract Law in Australia* (Butterworths, Sydney, 1998)

Lindgren, K, Carter, J and Harland, D, *Contract Law in Australia* (2nd ed, Butterworths, Sydney, 1992)

Staunton, P and Whyburn, R, *Nursing and the Law* (4th ed, Saunders, Sydney, 1988)

The Laws of Australia (Lawbook Co, Sydney, 1994), Vol 7, Contract

Vermeesch, R and Lindgren, K, *Business Law in Australia* (10th ed, Butterworths, Sydney, 2001)

Walmsley, S et al, *Professional Liability in Australia* (Lawbook Co., Sydney, 2002)

III

Employment

10

10 Contracts to provide health care services

Employee or independant contractor

Implied terms: common law

Implied terms: Statutes, enterprise agreements & industrial instruments

Federal & State industrial legislation

chapter 10

Contracts to Provide Health Care Services

Introduction

[10.05] The basis of a health carer's relationship with an employer is that of contract. A contract of employment is usually entered into where wages or a salary are paid for work done. This is also called a "contract of service". However, a person may do work for another through a "contract for services". This makes one not an employee, but an independent contractor (see *Marshall v Whittaker's Building Supply Co* (1963) 109 CLR 210; [1963] HCA 26).

It can become important to establish whether a person is an employee or not as the relationship of employee and employer can give rise to:

- contractual and tortious rights and duties (including vicarious responsibilities);
- statutory duties and rights;
- duties to persons outside the employment relationship.

(*Laws of Australia*, 26. Labour Law/26.1 Individual Employment, Chapter 2, Part A, para 6).

Employee or Independent Contractor

Determining the Difference

[10.10] At law, there is no hard-and-fast rule to distinguish the two types of contract. Where a contract is called into question the court will consider all the facts involved. There are number of indicia of employment, such as whether the worker was part of the employer's organisation (*Marshall v Whittaker's Building Supply Co* (1963) 109 CLR 210; [1963] HCA 26) or whether the worker was engaged to produce a specific result (see *Performing Rights Society Ltd v Mitchell & Booker (Palais de Danse) Ltd* [1924] 1 KB 762). However, none of these issues is determinative in isolation. The foremost factor for establishing whether a contract is one of employment is called the "control test": the amount of control by the employer over the conditions, workplace and tools of the employee are considered. The control test is satisfied when an employer has the power to direct the manner in which a worker performs work (*Stevens v Brodribb Sawmilling Co Pty Ltd* (1986) 160 CLR 16; [1986] HCA 1). The courts have recognised that other factors must also be considered, such as, mode of remuneration, provision and maintenance of equipment, the obligation to work, provision of holidays, deduction of income tax, and delegation of work by the putative employee (*Stevens v Brodribb Sawmilling Co Pty Ltd* (1986) 160 CLR 16; [1986] HCA 1; *Hollis v Vabu Pty Ltd* (2001) 207 CLR 21; [2001] HCA 44).

A contract of employment generally has the following features:

- one person determines the work that is to be done, as they require it, and the other makes herself or himself available by the hour;
- the first-mentioned person also controls the premises and equipment, and how they are to be used;
- the first-mentioned person has the power to hire and fire at their discretion; and,
- the person rendering the service is paid regularly, and is entitled to recreation leave and other benefits.

On the other hand, when an independent contractor is engaged:

- the contractor is asked to carry out a specific task, the completion of which brings the contract to an end;
- the contractor generally owns the equipment (and perhaps the premises) and determines how it is to be used;
- dissatisfaction with the work is remedied by suing for breach of contract (see Chapter 9), or negligence (see above, Chapter 6), otherwise the contractor must be paid for the whole job; and
- the contractor has no claim for payment (unless special arrangements are made) until the work is completed.

Sometimes a person may be designated in a written contract as an independent contractor, despite their position, in fact, being closely controlled by the employer. This could be a way of attempting to avoid liability for such things as workers' compensation or holiday pay. In these circumstances one considers the facts of the situation, to determine which category most accurately describes those involved:

> "the court should look at the substance of the transaction and not treat a written agreement, which was designed to disguise its real nature, as succeeding in doing so if it amounted merely to a cloud of words and, without really altering the substantial relations between the parties, described them ... in terms appropriate to some other relation. In other words, the court is prepared to look beyond the express terms of the contract to examine the accuracy of the purported categorisation of the relationship" (*Cam & Sons Pty Ltd v Sargent* (1940) 14 ALJ 162).

On the other hand, a person who is ostensibly under a significant degree of control may be an independent contractor. See for example, the following case.

[10.15] Case: *Vabu v Federal Commissioner of Taxation*
(1996) 33 ATR 537

Vabu Pty Ltd operated a business called Crisis Couriers, which engaged couriers using a variety of vehicles for delivering parcels and other items. Vabu paid bicycle couriers a flag-fall payment for each contract of carriage, and other motorised vehicle couriers a flag-fall and per-kilometre fee. Couriers were required to wear uniforms, appear neat and tidy, replace vehicles when required by the company, observe a starting time and work a prescribed number of hours. They were to accept work assigned to them, deliver goods in the manner directed, accept re-routing and take no more leave than permitted. However, they were also required to supply their own vehicle, pay for petrol, insurance and registration of vehicles, provide their own street directories, blankets, ropes etc, and received payment per delivery rather than a wage or salary.

[10.20] The Court held that the couriers were in fact independent contractors. It did not give the control test the priority it had had in the past, but considered it equally with other tests.

The tests devised by the courts are a guide only: a contract may have a mixture of features from both categories. Where there is a conflict over the nature of the relationship of the parties the court will take all these factors into account and weigh them up to decide into which category the contract falls:

> "The law, as I see it, is this: if the true relationship of the parties is that of master and servant under a contract of service, the parties cannot alter the truth of that relationship by putting a different label on it. ... On the other hand, if their relationship is ambiguous and is capable of being one or the other [that is, either service or agency], then the parties can remove that ambiguity, by the very agreement itself which they make with one another. The agreement itself then becomes the best material from which to gather the true legal relationship between them" (*Massey v Crown Life Insurance Co* [1978] 2 All ER 576 at 579 per Denning MR).

The contract itself may or may not be carefully scrutinised and relied upon according to the circumstances of the individual case. It is important to note that where there is a written contract of employment a court will be restricted to considering the terms which are expressly or impliedly contained in the written document. The court cannot go into the manner in which the parties went about putting the contract into practice, unless this can be shown to amount to an agreement which adds to, or changes the terms of, the original contract (something the parties are quite entitled to do). Such addition or change would be subject to the requirements for any contract: for example, there would have to be mutual agreement. As well as making a written document irrelevant if it is at odds with the actual agreed behaviour of the parties, there may be a change in an otherwise unambiguous document and relationship. An example would be where the original contract was for a nurse to work in the paediatric section of a hospital, but, after formal consultation with the employer, or on a regular basis when asked on specific occasions, he or she agreed to be available to work in the general intensive care unit.

When is a health carer an independent contractor?

[10.25] It follows from the above discussion that those who work in a health care establishment are most likely to be employees, except for visiting medical officers and others on contract. Those who work independently (for example, an agency nurse engaged to care for a patient at home, a home birth nurse, a general practitioner) are in most cases independent contractors. Where a hospital engages someone through an agency to fill a staffing shortage the status of the person is not so clear. There would appear to be enough control in the latter case by both the agency and the hospital to make both employers in relation to different aspects of the work. Matters such as pay and allocation of hours and location are areas that would be the province of the agency, matters such as the nature of the work and workers' compensation would be that of the hospital. However, the concept of joint employment, although recognised in overseas jurisdictions such as the United States of America, is not clearly established in Australia in the absence of express contractual terms. An aggrieved patient could argue that the hospital bears the responsibility for all whom it engages to carry out its obligations to its patients, notwithstanding that their contract may be different from others it clearly employs (for example, see *Ramsey v Larsen* (1964) 111 CLR 16; [1964] HCA 40 and, regarding non-delegable duties of care, *Albrighton v Royal Prince Alfred Hospital* [1980] 2 NSWLR 542).

Other relationships

[10.30] There are other relationships in which one person may do work for another. Two which may be of particular interest to health carers are:

• principal and agent; and
• partnership.

Principal and agent

[10.35] An agent is one who is authorised to act for another, and has power to create and effect legal relationships between her or his principal and third parties. An agent must act with the principal's approval, and in so doing may bind the principal by contract to the third party. Examples are real estate agents and commercial travellers. However, a specific contract of agency need not exist: simply by placing another in a position where, "according to ... law or ... the ordinary usages of mankind [a person] is understood to represent and act for the person who has so placed him; but in every case it is only by the will of the employer that an agency can be created" (*Pole v Leask* (1863) 33 LJ (Ch) 155 at 161-162). One difficulty in establishing agency as opposed to employment is that many employees are, by the very nature of their work, agents of their employer. They may, in fact, be both.

The court must examine the terms of employment, and consider the nature of the agreement. Health carers may be exercising the powers of agency when they commit their employer to some service for a patient, for example, community nurses signing up patients for treatment or rehabilitation services. Power of attorney is a form of agency, where a person authorises another to act on their behalf.

Partnership

[10.40] This occurs where two or more people agree to combine for some object, such as providing a service. Health carers in private practice may decide to do this. A partnership is not a company. A company is a legal "person" separate from the individuals who constitute it. Those individuals are generally not personally liable for the debts of the company, and it can purchase goods, employ people, sue and be sued as if it was a single individual. In a partnership the members act as separate individuals, and liability for debts and negligence is shared jointly and severally by the individuals involved. One partner is not an employee of the partnership unless he or she specifically and separately enters such a relationship by contract. Partners are principals in their own right, and any work they do is not subject to the regime of industrial regulation which protects employees.

Implied Terms of Employment: Common Law

[10.45] Terms may be included in an employment agreement, but there are also terms which are implied by the law: they exist just as if they were specifically agreed upon by the parties, and in fact no agreement can be made that contradicts some of them. This is because employment attracts common law and statutory duties and privileges for both the employer and employee. There are four possible sources of implied conditions for employment contracts: common law, statutory law, collective agreements and industrial awards. Some common law implied conditions in the employment contract, which presumably cannot be ruled out and which set out the employee's duties, are as follows.

Implied undertakings by the employee

To carry out any lawful and reasonable direction of the employer

[10.50] Control or the right to control is still the single most important characteristic by which the employer employee relationship is identified. And there is no better indicator of control than the existence in one party of the right to give directions as to what is to be done and how it is to be done by the other party. The right of the employer to give, and the obligation of the employee to obey directions is, in the eyes of the law, foremost among the terms of the contract of employment, even though it is often an implied term, the parties having said nothing about it (Macken et al (2002), p 90).

A health care employee should clarify with a prospective employer just what duties are to be involved, and whether duties are limited to certain areas of care or are more general. The duty statement is a critical document in doing this, and should be carefully developed by the employer and studied by the prospective employee. If an employee is not prepared to carry out all instructions that the employer might give (for example, he or she feels inexperienced or untrained in certain areas of care), this should be the subject of discussion when the employment is being negotiated. There is a responsibility on the part of a health care provider to its patients, to provide adequately trained and experienced staff. Employing adequately educated and experienced staff or providing additional necessary training is a crucial part of carrying out this obligation.

The range of duties an employee may be expected to perform, where the detail of duties is absent from a contract, is limited to those duties that "properly appertain" to his or her position (*Commissioner for Government Transport v Royall* (1966) 116 CLR 314; [1966] HCA 80). The requirement of obedience involves only lawful and reasonable directions (*R v Darling Island Stevedoring & Lighterage Co Ltd; Ex p Halliday; Ex p Sullivan* (1938) 60 CLR 601; [1938] HCA 44). Orders which endanger an employee's life, health, or safety or which he or she reasonably believes would endanger her or his life, health or safety are not lawful orders, and there is no obligation to obey them (*Re Dismissal of Fitters by BHP* [1969] AR (NSW) 399). Presumably this would apply to directions which it is believed would endanger the life and health of patients or others. This raises the possibility of conflicting legal duties, with possible liability for breaching either of them. The health carer must choose as to which one to follow.

Refusing to work

[10.55] Failure to carry out the service contracted for will free the employer from the obligation to pay the employee, because service is that for which the wages are being paid. Alternatively, the refusal of duty may constitute serious and wilful misconduct justifying summary dismissal.

The employer is entitled to require an employee to carry out any lawful order, that is, any order reasonably related to the rendering of services contracted for. This is why it is important to let an employer know of anything one is unable or unwilling to do which could otherwise be expected of someone in the category under which one is employed. Unless otherwise stipulated, a health carer, for example, a physiotherapist, is employed to carry out any of the duties which it is reasonable to expect of someone with the training and experience he or she claims to have. A first-year doctor should not be expected to carry out the responsibilities and care expected of a specialist (or even registrar) except perhaps in an emergency. Similarly, a general nurse should not be required to carry out the duties which only a specialist nurse would be trained to carry out.

Under common law, a refusal to carry out lawful and reasonable directions may be grounds for summary dismissal, at least where it amounts to an intention to repudiate or renounce the employment contract (*Adami v Maison De Luxe Ltd* (1924) 35 CLR 143; [1924] HCA 45. Where the refusal occurs because the employee believes he or she cannot properly carry out a particular service, or should not carry it out under the circumstances, but expresses willingness to carry out any other orders, it seems the employer is liable for wages for any service accepted.

Where one does not feel competent the primary consideration is health carers' responsibility to provide reasonable care to the patient. Here, the issue is their responsibility to the employer, and the requirement that directions be followed. A health carer may be lawfully obliged by his or her contract of employment to care for someone, but feel that he or she cannot reasonably do so, lacking competence or resources. There is a conflict of duties here, and no clear legal answer, as there is no priority of legal duties: whatever choice is made, there is a potential legal sanction; threat of action in negligence, or in breach of contract (with loss of pay, or job). One may consider that the best solution under the circumstances, is to:

- consider the ethical ramifications of the issue and take the least morally culpable course (see Chapter 19); and
- remember to make a written record of this (see Chapter 7).

There is a further consideration from the employer's point of view. Given the knowledge that particular staff may not be competent in certain areas of care, the employer has a duty to consider alternative staffing to fulfil its duty of reasonable care to the patient or provide the necessary training to existing staff.

To carry out orders with reasonable care

[10.60] An employer can expect staff to carry out their duties with reasonable care. This is the same as, but separate from, the duty of reasonable care demanded by the law of torts. Here, the duty is to the employer, there it is to the patient. Harm to a patient is not required for action to be taken against an employee for not carrying out duties reasonably carefully, as it is in tort law. Instead of damages, the employer can call the employment contract into question and either dismiss or discipline the employee who so acts.

Where a patient has been harmed by an employee's negligence, and the employer is found vicariously liable, the employer may, in some circumstances, in turn seek indemnity from the negligent employee. In New South Wales, the Northern Territory and South Australia legislation protects employees from being sued by the employer for indemnity (*Employees Liability Act 1991* (NSW); *Law Reform (Miscellaneous Provisions) Act* (NT), s 22A(1); *Civil Liability Act 1936* (SA), s 59). See also **[6.765]**ff on vicarious liability. Generally an employer is insured, and insurance policies may provide that action will not be taken against a negligent employee. In addition, the *Insurance Contracts Act 1984*

(Cth), s 66 further reduces the likelihood of an employee being required to indemnify an employer by providing that an insurer has limited rights to be subrogated to the rights of an insured employer against the employee.

To serve the employer faithfully

[10.65] It is difficult to state specifically what is required in terms of serving an employer faithfully, as situations vary, but as a generalisation it would involve the duty to not knowingly injure the employer, or do anything contrary to the employer's interests. Such actions could be:

Denigrating the standard of medical treatment given by the employer. This could be done by actions or words which undermine patients' or prospective patients' confidence in the standard of medical care offered by the employer or are otherwise adverse to the employer. It may involve only one patient, or be a public communication or action, or participation in debate. Where one is convinced of the poor standard of care offered by one's employer, one discloses this at the risk of action by the employer for breach of contract based on a breach of duty of good faith (see *Lane v Fasciale* [1993] AILR ¶339 (SC Vic)). The principle is based on the premise that confidential and discreet communication with the employer will resolve the issue, otherwise one moves on, to find another position elsewhere with a more satisfactory employer. In the public sector, the exposure of an employee to action may be limited by "whistle-blower" protection legislation as discussed at **[6.460]**ff.

Disclosure of any information received by a health carer in furthering the employer's interest. There are two sorts of knowledge one acquires in a job: general knowledge necessarily acquired in carrying out one's duties, and knowledge gained through special access to documents, plans, procedures, and scientific knowledge which is specific to the employer. It is hard to distinguish between the two in many cases, but generally it can be said that the first is experience one can take and use elsewhere, the second is specific confidential information and trade secrets and research results which would not normally be used elsewhere. However, contractual terms may specify further information which is not to be disclosed.

Disclosure of confidential information which would normally be protected may be justified when made to those other than the employer if it is done in the public interest. Australian courts have limited the justifiable circumstances to where disclosure reveals "iniquity" (see for example *Corrs Pavey Whiting & Byrne v Collector of Customs (Vic)* (1987) 14 FCR 434). Again, in the public sector, the exposure of an employee to action for disclosure of confidential information may be limited by "whistleblower" protection legislation as discussed at **[6.460]**ff.

Disclosure also may be made where an employee is in charge of her or his employer's documents or files, and is subpoenaed to produce them in court.

To take reasonable care for the employer's property

[10.70] An employee has a duty to take reasonable care to protect an employer's property (*Bolton Gems Pty Ltd v Gregoire* [1996] AILR ¶ 5-063).

Disclosure of information to the employer

[10.75] There is an obligation at common law to inform the employer of any information which an employee gains during the course of their employment that is of value to the employer (*Associated Dominions Assurance Pty Ltd v Andrew* (1949) 49 SR (NSW) 351). The extent to which incompetence or wrongdoing on the part of other staff should be disclosed, if it is in the employer's interest to know of this, is not settled. The obligation may depend on the individual's position, such that those in managerial positions may be so obliged but general employees not (*Swain v West (Butchers) Ltd* [1936] 3 All ER 261 (CA)).

Employees' role in safety

[10.80] Staff should be conscious of the need to ensure that safety is maintained in the workplace. This includes the maintenance of equipment and its proper use, for instance, equipment should not be too high or too low and it should be easily accessible. An employee's obligations arising under occupational health and safety legislation are discussed in Chapter 11.

Workers' compensation, for which employers are insured, provides for most injuries that occur at work, but where employers are held to have been negligent, in some cases they can be sued (see further Chapter 11).

Implied undertakings by the employer

[10.85] Implied conditions of the contract which concern the employer are:

• payment of wages; and
• ensuring reasonable care for safety of employees is taken.

Payment of wages

[10.90] An employer is obligated to pay wages in exchange for an employee's work. The employer is also required to fulfil conditions set out by common law, statutory law and industrial instruments relating to holidays, sick leave etc. Standing by ready to work, and being available for emergencies will, if part of one's duties, most likely be considered service, and the basis for pay (see *Electricity Commission (NSW) v Federated Engine Drivers & Firemen's Association of Australasia (NSW)* [1975] AR (NSW) 504). Payment of wages is conditional upon performance by the employee of the full range of work assigned, or possibly, at least, a readiness and willingness to do so (*Csomore v Public Service Board (NSW)* (1987) 10 NSWLR 587 at 595).

Duty to ensure reasonable care for safety of employees taken

[10.95] An employer is under a common law duty to take reasonable care for the safety of employees. The duty is substantial (see *Kondis v State Transport Authority* (1984) 154 CLR 672; [1984] HCA 61) and non-delegable (*Wilsons &*

Clyde Coal Co Ltd v English [1938] AC 57). The duty includes the provision of a safe place of work, safe systems of work, and competent fellow employees (*Wilsons & Clyde Coal Co Ltd v English* [1938] AC 57). The duty requires that an employer take reasonable care to carry out operations in a manner that will not subject his employees to unnecessary risk (*Wilson v Tyneside Window Cleaning Co* [1958] 2 QB 110). The duty is not absolute; the employer must ensure reasonable care for safety is taken but is not required to ensure safety (see *Wood v Cliff Robe River Iron Associates* (unreported 01/08/1983, SCWA). Occupational health and safety legislation also creates duties with regard to workplace safety (see Chapter 11).

[10.100] Case: *Latimer v AEC* [1953] AC 643 (House of Lords England)

A particularly heavy rainstorm caused oil to spread onto the floor of a factory, making it slippery. The plaintiff slipped on the floor, and sued the employer, arguing that the factory should have been closed down until it was safer.

[10.105] On appeal from a finding in favour of the plaintiff, the House of Lords argued that there was not enough evidence that the risk of harm was great enough to warrant closing down the whole operation. They reversed the original order, finding for the defendant. The Court stated that provision of a safe workplace is a duty which is non-delegable and personal. That is, responsibility cannot be delegated to any other person (although performance of tasks necessary to provide the safe workplace may), and the duty is owed to each worker personally.

[10.110] Case: *Sroka v Ridge Park Private Hospital* (1981) 28 SASR 15 (Supreme Court)

A nurse's aide injured her back when she assisted a difficult, elderly, hemiplegic patient who was attempting to move from a commode to a chair without waiting for assistance. The aide broke the patient's fall, and after the patient was on the floor attempted to move her into a chair. The aide sued the employer hospital, arguing that it had not provided adequate assistance or equipment for the lifting and care of patients which would also provide for the prevention of back injuries. The hospital responded that in her attempts to drag the patient to a chair, the aide was contributorily negligent in not seeking assistance from other staff, and thus they were not liable.

[10.115] The Court held that the employer was negligent in that it could foresee that patients would provide occasional emergencies, and that nurses would be called upon to act quickly, with little time for reflection. Given this possibility, the employer should have made appropriate provision for a safe system for lifting patients. This may include adequate staffing and equipment, and nurses should not have to search for assistance when it is needed. The court did accept the argument that the nurse had acted carelessly in attempting to move the patient after she was on the floor, but only to the extent of 20 per cent of the damages.

The circumstances of the individual employee must be taken into account where these ought to have been known by the employer, for example, where the employee suffers from a disability. Special precautions should be taken to prevent harm to the employee. *Paris v Stepney Borough Council* [1951] AC 367, was a case involving such a situation. A maintenance worker who was known to be blind in one eye was blinded completely when he struck a rusty bolt with a steel hammer and a chip from the bolt pierced his good eye. Lord Morton of the House of Lords stated:

> "I think that the more serious the damage which will happen if an accident occurs, the more thorough are the precautions which an employer must take ... I think it follows logically that if A and B, who are engaged on the same work, run precisely the same risk of an accident happening, but if the results of an accident will be more serious to A than to B, precautions which are adequate in the case of B may not be adequate in the case of A, and it is a duty of the employer to take such additional precautions for the safety of A as may be reasonable ..."

Discipline of employees

[10.120] Employers have a common law right to discipline employees, qualified by legislation and industrial instruments (see below). This power was quite extensive in the past. The case of *R v Keite* (1697) 1 Ld Raym 138; 91 ER 989 held that "if a master gives correction to a servant it ought to be with a proper instrument, as a cudgel, etc. And then if by accident a blow give death, this would be but manslaughter" (quoted from Creighton et al (1983), p 116). Today, of course, corporal punishment would be a criminal activity, and discipline of employees is now much more constrained! Generally, the principles to be applied to disciplinary actions are as follows:

- any power to discipline is ultimately subject to the terms of the contract, which may include award conditions and statutory rules;
- any sanction which does not derogate from these contractual rights of the employee (and the general law of the land) may be lawfully imposed;
- any sanction which does derogate from the employees' contractual rights is a breach of contract;
- any sanction which is expressly or impliedly authorised by the contract of employment is prima facie lawful;
- disciplinary action may not involve payment of wages for work done which is less than the agreed/required rate, but may involve withdrawal of bonuses in some circumstances. If, for example, a bonus entitlement is expressed as

being the entitlement of all employees and attached to something like company profits, these could probably not be reduced as a disciplinary measure. If they were conditional on employees' work (for example, attached to good conduct, or maintenance of good work practices), they could be reduced (Macken et al (2002), p 117).

Disciplinary action may involve withholding bonuses subject to the principles above, demotion, transfer to other duties or areas of work, refusal of promotion and dismissal as the ultimate sanction. There is very little law on this topic, so little further guidance can be given in a text such as this.

The following case, whilst brought pursuant to Industrial Relations legislation and therefore using the terminology "harsh, unjust or unreasonable", nonetheless considers some of the broader issues that may also be subject of a claim at common law, such as breach of confidentiality.

[10.125]　Case: *Howden v City of Whittlesea* (1990) 32 AILR 392 (6 September 1990, Industrial Relations Commission of Victoria)

A nurse who suspected that a child she was attending was the subject of abuse reported her concerns to Community Services Victoria as she felt this was a matter beyond her expertise. When the mother discovered that she was under investigation she made a formal complaint to the Manager of the Family and Children's Services Branch. The nurse was summoned to a meeting with the Manager and the Director of Human Services. She was read the letter of complaint but was not given a copy or allowed to read it for herself. She was then asked to resign, but as she did not, she was dismissed for professional misconduct for breaching confidentiality. The Australian Nurses Federation took her case to the Victorian Industrial Relations Commission, arguing that the nurse had been denied procedural and natural justice, and that her dismissal was harsh, unjust and unreasonable.

[10.130] The Commission held that the nurse's dismissal had been harsh, unjust or unreasonable because she was not guilty of misconduct. She had also been denied procedural justice as she was given no opportunity to answer the allegations and no time to consider her position when she was asked to resign, nor was she given a copy of the letter which contained the allegations about her. In relation to the allegation of misconduct for breach of confidentiality, the Commission pointed out that her actions were not misconduct, as nurses cannot be expected to keep all information confidential because if they did, they could not function well in the best interests of their patients and the community (see Chapter 7). It also pointed out that the *Community Welfare Services Act 1970* (Vic) permits notification of suspected child abuse (see Chapter 16).

Implied Terms of Employment: Statutes, Enterprise Agreements and Industrial Instruments

[10.135] There are State and Commonwealth statutes setting out basic conditions of employment, which become terms of the employment contract along with those specifically agreed upon by the parties. Such provisions may deal with recreation leave, hours of employment, frequency of wage payments, etc. Public hospitals and statutory health facilities will have rather extensive legislation setting out work conditions. However an enterprise agreement or industrial award (see below) may in fact be more generous to the employee than the legislation. Terms and conditions provided for in industrial instruments are not automatically incorporated into a contract for employment, unless that is the intention of the parties (*Byrne & Anor v Australian Airlines Ltd* (1995) 185 CLR 410; [1995] HCA 24). Where an agreement or award is more generous than the corresponding legislation the former will generally take precedence. Health carers can find out about legislation and awards from the federal, State or Territory Departments of Industrial Relations (the title may differ), or the appropriate union or employees' association office.

Industrial relations generally

[10.140] Statutory law regarding industrial relations provides mechanisms for establishing and registering awards, conducting industrial relations in such matters as union–employer negotiation, and handling disputes through conciliation and arbitration. The federal government has, to date, derived its jurisdiction to legislate on industrial and workplace matters primarily through s 51(xxxv) of the Constitution, the conciliation and arbitration power. However, other sections of the Constitution have been used by the Federal Government in this regard including s 51(i)—the trade and commerce power, s 51(xx)—the corporations power, and s 52(ii)—the public service power. State facilities exist under various State Acts (Australian Capital Territory and Northern Territory are covered by the the Commonwealth Act; *Industrial Relations Act 1996* (NSW); *Industrial Relations Act 1999* (Qld); *Fair Work Act 1994* (SA); *Industrial Relations Act 1984* (Tas); *Commonwealth Powers (Industrial Relations) Act 1996* (Vic); *Industrial Relations Act 1979* (WA)). Other legislation, both for federal bodies and private employers, as well as State Governments themselves, are set out in different Acts, covering the particular categories of employers and employees concerned.

Examples of important issues covered by industrial legislation are the payment of wages, payment of sick leave, provision of holiday leave, and the power of the appropriate tribunal or court to make void in whole or in part, contracts, or provisions in them that are harsh, unfair or unconscionable, against public interest, provide for less payment than allowed by law, or are designed to avoid a statute or an award.

Subsequent conduct of parties changes nature of contract

[10.145] Legislation may provide that an employment contract that was fair at the time it was entered into may be declared unfair by the Industrial Commission because of the subsequent conduct of the parties or variation of the contract (see, for example, *Industrial Relations Act 1996* (NSW), s 106; *Reich v Client Server Professionals of Australia Pty Ltd* [1999] NSWIRComm 416). This is consistent with the principle that the terms of a contract of employment may be considered to change according to changing conditions and behaviour, despite the original written or verbal agreement.

General principles of industrial relations law

[10.150] Whilst jurisdictions differ in the details of their industrial relations legislation, there are some generalisations that can be made about industrial relations.

Development of industrial relations mechanisms

[10.155] All contracts may involve a degree of bargaining, and in recognition of the inequality that generally exists between the employer and employee, a system of industrial relations has arisen to give strength to the bargaining position of workers and to decrease the potential for industrial unrest. The Commonwealth Court of Conciliation and Arbitration was established under the *Conciliation and Arbitration Act 1904* (Cth). The Court was empowered to create new rights and obligations for employees and employers by the making of awards and to determine existing rights through award interpretation. That body has been replaced at various points in time over the ensuing years such that today, the Australian Industrial Relations Commission (AIRC), established by the *Workplace Relations Act 1996* (Cth), is the country's foremost industrial relations body.

A new law introducing substantial change to Australia's workplace relations system came into effect in early 2006. Under the *Workplace Relations Amendment (Work Choices) Act 2005*, the role of the AIRC changed but its role in conciliation remains and where the parties to a dispute empower it to do so it may arbitrate. The work of the AIRC now includes:

- assisting employers and employees in resolving industrial disputes;
- handling certain termination of employment claims;
- rationalising and simplifying awards;
- dealing with applications about industrial action.

AIRC is no longer responsible for certifying collective agreements. Increases in minimum rates and a number of other key conditions are now primarily the responsibility of a new body, the Australian Fair Pay Commission.

To assist users of AIRC services in understanding the changes introduced, a series of fact sheets and procedural guides are available through the AIRC web site at www.airc.gov.au/.

Federal and State Industrial Legislation

[10.160] Every Australian jurisdiction has a "basic" industrial relations Act, and other legislation providing for specific conditions (such as long service leave, superannuation etc). The *Workplace Relations Amendment (Work Choices) Act 2005* introduces substantial amendments to the *Workplace Relations Act*. It introduces a new system of industrial relations to provide a single, national set of rules for minimum terms, conditions, awards and agreements. At the time of writing, this legislation is being challenged by the States in the High Court as going beyond the Commonwealth's legislative power. If the legislation survives, it will involve radical change to Australia's industrial relations system.

A detailed examination of the new Commonwealth legislation and its effect on the State legislation that preceded it is beyond the scope of this book and with the situation currently in such a state of flux, any attempt to provide a summary would no doubt be obsolete by the time the book is published. As a result, the following discussion provides a brief outline of the States' industrial relations systems only, as they were prior to the introduction of the controversial Work Choices legislation.

Industrial relations in each State and Territory

[10.165] In New South Wales the *Industrial Relations Act 1996* (NSW) accords a more prominent role to awards than any other jurisdiction and provides for Enterprise Agreements (EAs). The Industrial Relations Commission of New South Wales can approve an EA which has been entered into by an employer and an employee, union, or a committee representing the employees, where at least 65 per cent of employees of an enterprise support the agreement (see *Review of the Principles for Approval of Enterprise Agreements 2002, Re* [2002] NSWIRComm 342). The EA will have no effect until the Commission approves it. The Industrial Registrar keeps a register of all approved EAs. The Industrial Relations Commission may declare an agreement void on the basis that it is unfair. The Commission has jurisdiction to deal with a broad range of matters to do with industrial matters, including:

- making, interpretation, application, breaches, and enforcement, of conditions of an award or agreement;
- unfair contracts;
- industrial action; and
- employer and employee organisations.

An Industrial Committee may be established with a member of the Commission presiding, and representatives from an industry, or part of an industry to exercise the functions of the Commission for that industry or portion of it. Industrial magistrates may hear matters that the legislation refers to a Magistrates' Court. The judicial members of the Commission can sit as a court, the Industrial Court of New South Wales, and make binding rulings on the parties. Dispute resolution includes procedures for employee and union consultation, and the Commission has a general jurisdiction to conciliate and arbitrate disputes. The Commission must attempt conciliation, and may require conferences between the parties.

Minimal conditions are set out in the legislation setting hours of work and leave. Other legislation sets out enterprise-specific conditions, such as conditions for work in mines and with hazardous materials. Some of these affect health care workers who deal with, for example, radiation and X-rays.

An employee may lodge a complaint with the Commission where there is an alleged, actual or threatened harsh, unreasonable or unjust dismissal. The application must be made within 21 days. The Commission may order reinstatement, re-employment, remuneration or compensation. Discrimination against employees or prospective employees is prohibited by the *Anti-Discrimination Act 1977* (NSW).

In 1996 Victoria referred most of its industrial relations legislation powers to the Commonwealth. As a result:

* the *Workplace Relations Act* covers matters in the Victorian private sector such as industrial disputes, and workplace agreements;
* the Commonwealth AIRC is the sole industrial tribunal for Victorian workers;
* the Commonwealth Parliament has the power to make legislation in relation to:
  - employment agreements;
  - conciliation and arbitration of industrial disputes;
  - minimum terms and conditions; and
  - termination of employment.

Excluded are such employees as public servants, Victorian parliamentarians, ministerial assistants, parliamentary officers and judicial officers.

Between 1997 and 1999, Queensland had a "clone" of the *Workplace Relations Act*, with awards reduced to 20 allowable matters, and individual agreements "Queensland Workplace Agreements" or QWAs. However, with the accession of a Labor Government in 1998 the law was changed to more closely resemble the New South Wales legislation. A comprehensive review of Queensland's industrial relations legislation followed, leading to the introduction of the *Industrial Relations Act 1999* (Qld). The Act establishes an Industrial Relations Commission similar in structure and function to that of New South Wales, but with some differences. A modified version of QWAs was retained, and the Act also provides for certified agreements. The Act also provides for the filing of QWAs.

A contract of employment that is unfair may be declared void, or varied, by the Commission, and application may be made to the Commission where dismissal is considered harsh, unjust or unreasonable.

The *Fair Work Act 1994* (SA) establishes the Industrial Relations Commission and the Industrial Court of South Australia. Enterprise Agreements must be approved by the Commission and the Commission may also make awards. Both instruments have in-built protections similar to those of the other Australian jurisdictions. There is an Industrial Relations Advisory Committee, that assists the Minister in relation to policy and legislative proposals, and an Employee Ombudsman—an independent body that advises employees on their rights and obligations, scrutinises awards and agreements that are before the Commission, investigates claims of coercion in the negotiation of agreements, investigates the conditions of outworkers, represents employees in proceedings in certain circumstances and provides advice to employees on occupational health and safety matters.

The *Industrial Relations Act 1979* (WA) and the *Minimum Conditions of Employment Act 1993* (WA) are the primary pieces of State legislation governing industrial relations in Western Australia. The *Industrial Relations Act* provides for the making of Employer-Employee Agreements (EEAs), which may be registered by lodging the EEA with the Registrar of the Western Australian Industrial Relations Commission. EEAs may be made whether or not an award applies, but may not be made if an industrial agreement applies. EEAs override any relevant award, are subject to safeguards, and may be cancelled at any time with the agreement of the parties or by the Commission. The Act also provides for the making and registration of industrial agreements.

The *Industrial Relations Act 1984* (Tas) provides for the Tasmanian Industrial Commission to make awards and approve agreements, under similar conditions to those in other Australian jurisdictions. The provisions with relation to EAs are similar to those of New South Wales, but Tasmania requires only 60 per cent agreement by the workplace for acceptance of an enterprise agreement. A Commissioner may approve an EA after determining that the process of bargaining was satisfactory, the agreement is fair, and minimum conditions have been met.

The Australian Capital and Northern Territories are both subject to the Commonwealth legislation.

References and Further Reading

Anderman, S, *Labour Law: Management Decisions and Workers' Rights* (2nd ed, Butterworths, London, 1993)

Australian and New Zealand Equal Opportunity Law and Practice (CCH, Sydney, Looseleaf Service)

Australian Council of Trade Unions, *Changes in Industrial Relations: Summary of the Workplace Relations Act 1996* (Australian Council of Trade Unions, Melbourne)

Australian Employment Law Guide (CCH, Sydney, Looseleaf Service)

Australian Enterprise Bargaining Manual (CCH, Sydney, Looseleaf Service)

Australian Industrial Relations Commission website at www.airc.gov.au

Australian Labour Law Reporter (CCH, Sydney, Looseleaf Service)

Baragwanath, M, *Workplace Relations Act in Practice: The Essential Cases* (NSW Newsletter Information Services, Manly, 1998)

Boland, R and Anderson, N, *Handbook on Employment Law and Practice* (Allen and Unwin, Sydney, 1997)

Creighton, B and Stewart, A, *Labour Law: An Introduction* (Federation Press, Sydney, 2000)

Cripps, Y, "Protection from Adverse Treatment by Employers: A Review of the
Position of Employees who Disclose Information in the Belief the Disclosure is in
the Public Interest" (1985) 101 LQR 506

Deery, S, Plowman, D and Walsh, J, *Industrial Relations: A Contemporary Analysis*
(McGraw-Hill, Sydney, 2000)

Federal Industrial Law (Butterworths, Sydney, Looseleaf Service)

Industrial Law New South Wales (Butterworths, Sydney, Looseleaf Service)

Johnstone, M, *Nursing and the Injustices of the Law* (W B Saunders/Baillie Tindall,
Sydney, 1994)

Laws of Australia (Lawbook Co., Sydney) Chapter 8 Contracts: Specific; Chapter 26
Labour Law

Leo Cusson Institute, *Employment Law and Industrial Relations* (Leo Cusson
Institute, Melbourne, 1999)

Luntz, H, Hambly, A D and Hayes, R, *Torts: Cases and Commentary* (Butterworths,
Sydney, 1985)

Macken, J, McCarry, G and Sappideen, C, *The Law of Employment* (4th ed, Lawbook
Co, Sydney, 2002)

McKenna, D, *The Labor Council's Easy Guide to Your Rights at Work* (Pluto Press,
Sydney, 1993)

Nolan, D, *The Australasian Labour Law Reforms* (Federation Press, Sydney, 2000)

NSW Department of Industrial Relations, *Enterprise Bargaining: Enhancing Productivity Innovations and Equity* (NSW Department of Industrial Relations, Sydney,
1997)

NSW Department of Industrial Relations, Sydney, *Enterprise Bargaining: Enhancing
Productivity Innovations and Equity* (1997)

Recruitment and Termination Guide (CCH, Sydney, Looseleaf Service)

Walmsley, S et al, *Professional Liability in Australia* (Thomson LBC, Sydney, 2002)

11

11 Accidents & injuries related to health care

Injuries to patients

Injuries to health carers

Occupational health & safety

Workers compensation

Liability of occupiers

chapter 11

Accidents and Injuries Related to Health Care

Injuries to Patients

[11.05] Whilst accidents and injuries may be the fault of no-one, action may be taken by patients where they have suffered harm from an accident that is the result of:

- negligence of the management of a health facility;
- negligence of the staff of a health facility;
- negligence of a self-employed health carer; or
- negligence on the part of the "occupier" of the premises (see **[11.250]**ff).

The law in relation to negligence is covered in Chapter 6.

Where there is an accident involving a patient, it should be recorded and reported as soon as possible, no matter what the cause. "Accident" here includes wrong treatment. From the legal point of view, apart from the need to avoid allegations of negligence, there is an issue of veracity in prompt reporting. Delay or lack of full and frank disclosure of events can give rise to the suspicion that facts have been hidden. Also, the sooner after the event the report is given, the more likely it is, in the court's eyes, to be an accurate account of what happened, as memories fade with time (see **[7.30]**ff). Some details may not be so important for the patient's immediate health, but may be vital to later establish what happened. Note should be made of the day, time and place of the event, the details of the accident and its cause, if known. Finally, the names of witnesses to the accident, or the whereabouts of the nearest people should be recorded. If one is at all concerned about an event and thinks that it may give rise to legal action, a written account, apart from any official incident report, can be made and kept for future use.

Advising the insurer of a health facility as soon as possible is also prudent, in anticipation of likely legal actions. Early notification of an adverse event may be required, otherwise an insurer may decline a claim.

Injuries to Health Carers

Safe working environment

Common law

[11.10] Employers and those hiring independent contractors both have a contractual duty to provide safe premises and a safe system of work. There is also a duty of care under tort law to prevent foreseeable harm to those who, it could reasonably be foreseen, could be harmed from their actions or omissions. Under common law, a worker must also take reasonable care for his or her own safety and protection, and that of co-workers. Some actions under tort law are restricted by workers' compensation legislation (see below). Codes of practice for health care facilities establish standards for safe working environments, safe working practices and for both medical and other workplace emergencies.

[11.15] Case: *State of NSW v Seedsman* [2000] NSWCA 119 (CA NSW) (described in *Australian Torts Reporter* ¶35-110)

A woman who served with the New South Wales Police Service was exposed to crimes against children. Her duties required her to interview 200-300 victims of physical, sexual and emotional child abuse when she was new to the Service and untrained in this work. Scenes she confronted included children with fractures, burns, brain-damage, retinal detachment, and dead and mutilated bodies of children. She developed insomnia, nightmares, tearfulness and flashbacks, and became subject to a constant fear that her own son could become a victim of abuse. After being diagnosed with post-traumatic stress disorder, she applied for discharge on medical grounds, and instituted proceedings against the State of New South Wales claiming damages for her psychiatric injury.

The trial judge found that the New South Wales Police Service had failed to provide the woman with a safe system of work. Attempts had not been made to protect her from mental injury that could result from exposure to the type of human tragedies with which she was required to deal. It determined that the State of New South Wales had the requisite knowledge that stress in the workplace of this type could lead to psychiatric disorders. The State of New South Wales appealed to the New South Wales Court of Appeal, arguing that it was not foreseeable, at the relevant time, that a police officer could suffer recognisable psychiatric injury (as distinct from stress) as a result of the work the respondent was required to do. Specifically, it was submitted that post-traumatic stress disorder in the workplace was unknown until the 1990s.

[11.20] The Court determined that the possibility of mental disturbance was foreseeable, given the extensive exposure by a young, new recruit without special training or preparation. It could not be argued that the foreseeability in this case had to be related to police work, for negligence is concerned with human beings and not specific occupations. The case was unique in that it involved a very young police officer without adequate training dealing with exceptional human depravity, a significant number of occasions of death and intense suffering of young children, and the frequent observation of dead and mutilated children. The Court further held that the fact of the employment rela-tionship imports a non-delegable duty to ensure the health and safety of employees. In a case like this where a person of ordinary fortitude would be likely to have been affected similarly, a claim for injury in the absence of physical injury is allowed (see also *Mt Isa Mines v Pusey* (1970) 125 CLR 383; [1970] HCA 60; *Tame v New South Wales; Annetts v Australian Stations Pty Limited* (2002) 211 CLR 317; [2002] HCA 35 and discussion at **[6.195]–[6.200]**).

Statute law

[11.25] The right to a safe workplace has been underscored by policy and legislation in every Australian jurisdiction. That addresses:

- prevention of injury and the provision of a safe working environment, which is dealt with by the development of "occupational health and safety" legislation, policy and practices (*Occupational Health and Safety (Common-wealth Employment) Act 1991* (Cth); *Occupational Health and Safety Act 1989* (ACT); *Occupational Health and Safety Act 2000* (NSW), *Occupational Health and Safety Regulation 2001* (NSW); *Work Health Act* (NT); *Workplace Health and Safety Act 1995* (Qld); *Occupational Health, Safety and Welfare Act 1986* (SA); *Workplace Health and Safety Act 1995* (Tas), *Workplace Health and Safety Regulations 1998* (Tas); *Occupational Health and Safety Act 2004* (Vic) (and various occupational health and safety regulations); *Occupational Safety and Health Act 1984* (WA)); and
- compensation when injuries, accidents and illnesses occur which arise out of, or occur in the course of, work, or activities incidental to work (*Safety Rehabilitation and Compensation Act 1988* (Cth); *Workers' Compensation Act 1951* (ACT); *Workers' Compensation Act 1987* (NSW), *Workplace Injury Management and Workers Compensation Act 1998* (NSW); *Work Health Act* (NT); *Workers' Compensation and Rehabilitation Act 2003* (Qld); *Workers' Rehabilitation and Compensation Act 1986* (SA), *WorkCover Corporation Act 1994* (SA); *Workers Rehabilitation and Compensation Act 1988* (Tas); *Accident Compensation Act 1985* (Vic), *Accident Compensation (WorkCover Insurance) Act 1993* (Vic), *Accident Compensation (Occupational Health and Safety) Act 1996*; *Workers' Compensation and Rehabilitation Act 1981* (WA)).

Both these issues will be considered below.

Occupational Health and Safety

[11.30] Formerly, legislation subjected specific machinery or work sites (which were recognised as being harmful) to safety regulations and required such measures as fencing, protective shields for machinery, and protective equipment for workers. More recently, health and safety legislation has put more responsibility on both employers and employees to create and maintain an overall safe environment for all workers. This means that all situations and personnel may be the subject of a general consideration for optimal conditions, rather than some specific situations being subject to minimal specific standards.

This raises the question of what constitutes a safe workplace. As well as harm from physical dangers such as faulty equipment, substandard infection control and structural dangers, health carers can be subject to physical or sexual assault or harassment, verbal abuse from patients or colleagues, and stress resulting from such events as patient death, lack of communication or co-operation among team members and events affecting the provision of quality care (Michael and Jenkins (2001)).

Employers

[11.35] Most responsibility for ensuring a safe workplace lies on the employer (through management). In all jurisdictions, legislation imposes on employers a duty to take reasonable care for the health, safety and welfare of employees whilst they are at work, although the duty is expressed in slightly different terms in each legislative instrument. The duty extends to independent contractors, those present at the workplace (including visitors, patients and trespassers), and (except in New South Wales) those outside the workplace but affected by operations at the workplace. Self-employed people owe a duty to those who may be affected by their operations. To the extent that they may have control over premises used as a workplace, owners and others in control of premises or (in some jurisdictions) plant and machinery, must take care for the safety of persons who work there subject to variations across jurisdictions.

There is some difference in approach as to what is practicable or reasonably practicable in relation to a safe working environment. This includes assessment of health and safety problems, ensuring the workplace is safe, providing training and supervision to staff, providing adequate facilities for the welfare of employees, and providing a safe means of access to, and egress from the workplace. In addition, others such as the manufacturers of equipment and substances for use at work also have an obligation to ensure these are of a satisfactory standard, and that any hazards are clearly indicated to those concerned.

The Commonwealth, Australian Capital Territory and South Australia require that all, and the Northern Territory requires that some, employers develop a written health and safety plan (*Occupational Health and Safety (Commonwealth Employment) Act 1991* (Cth), s 16(2)(d); *Occupational Health and Safety Act 1989* (ACT), s 3(2)(e); *Occupational Health, Safety and Welfare Act 1986* (SA), s 20; *Work Health Act* (NT), s 29(3)(e)).

All jurisdictions have established bodies that develop codes of practice to provide employers and the self-employed with guidance for providing safe workplaces (Cth: Safety, Rehabilitation and Compensation Commission; ACT: Occupational Health and Safety Council; NSW: WorkCover Authority; NT: Work Health Authority; Qld: the Minister; SA: SafeWork SA Advisory Committee; Tas: WorkCover Tasmania; Vic: WorkCover Authority; WA: WorkSafe Western Australia Commission). Failure to follow the guidelines can be used as evidence of failure to provide a safe working environment or system.

Workers

[11.40] Among those with health and safety responsibilities are workers themselves. Although provisions vary across jurisdictions, workers are generally required to:

- take reasonable care to ensure their own safety, as well as the safety of other workers. What is reasonable depends not only on the totality of the circumstances that exist, but also on an assessment of difficulties to be surmounted and the available staff and resources (for example, *Inspector Callaghan v De Sandre* [1989-92] Australian Industrial Safety, Health and Welfare Cases 48,966 (¶52-864); *Inspector Callaghan v Longley* [1989-92] Australian Industrial Safety, Health and Welfare Cases 48,967 (¶52-865));
- co-operate, so far as is reasonable, with instructions (such as safety rules or infection control instructions) given by the employer for promoting the health and safety of employees;
- ensure the proper use of equipment which is provided in the interests of the health and safety of employees.

Australian Safety and Compensation Council

[11.45] The Australian Safety and Compensation Council (ASCC), is established under the *Australian Workplace Safety Standards Act 2005* (Cth) and forms part of the Commonwealth Department of Employment and Workplace Relations. The main role of the ASCC is to provide leadership and facilitate national efforts to prevent workplace death, injury and illness through the establishment of codes of practice and national standards (although these instruments are of an advisory nature only). The ASCC comprises of representatives from the Commonwealth and each jurisdiction's government, together with representatives from employee organizations and employer groups. The first meeting of the ASCC was in October 2005. More information about its operations can be found on its website: www.nohsc.gov.au/AboutNohsc/

Health and safety representatives

[11.50] In most circumstances, employees have the right to elect a health and safety representative (except in the Northern Territory). Those representatives have rights, such as the right to:

- time away from work for training;
- access to certain categories of information;
- inspect the workplace;
- inquire into accidents;
- accompany official inspectors;
- require an employer to establish a health and safety committee in some circumstances; and
- be present at interviews between an inspector and an employee on health and safety matters.

(See *Occupational Health and Safety (Commonwealth Employment) Act 1991* (Cth), Part 3 Div 1; *Occupational Health and Safety Act 1989* (ACT), Part 5 Div 5.1; *Occupational Health and Safety Act 2000* (NSW), ss 17-18; *Workplace Health and Safety Act 1995* (Qld), Part 7 Div 3; *Occupational Health, Safety and Welfare Act 1986* (SA), Part 4; *Workplace Health and Safety Act 1995* (Tas), s 35; *Occupational Health and Safety Act 2004* (Vic), Part 7 Div 4; *Occupational Safety and Health Act 1984* (WA), ss 29-35.)

Joint staff-management committees

[11.55] Joint staff-management health and safety committees are required in all jurisdictions (except the Australian Capital Territory), with powers to act in an advisory, consultative and investigatory capacity. Special powers of investigation, inspection and access to information are given to members in some cases. Such committees should be representative of the workforce and in larger workplaces there should be committees representing different sections or locations. Requirements vary between jurisdictions but such matters as the size and composition of the workforce, the operation of different shifts, departments and sub-units, different occupations and types of hazards are features that variously determine the number and size of committees.

The function of these committees is to review general measures taken to promote health and safety, investigate problems with the same, formulate procedures, make recommendations, and otherwise become concerned with representing the health and safety issues of workers, by creating and maintaining health and safety in the workplace. Protocols and education programmes should be drawn up by the committees to prevent recognised potential risks (such as needle-stick and back injuries), as well as the study of incident reports of other accidents and unexpected occurrences. The filing of incident reports to report potential accidents as well as actual mishaps should be encouraged.

(See *Occupational Health and Safety (Commonwealth Employment) Act 1991* (Cth), Part 3, Div 2; *Occupational Health and Safety Act 2000* (NSW), ss 17-18; *Work Health Act* (NT), Part IV Div 4A; *Workplace Health and Safety Act 1995* (Qld), Part 7 Div 4; *Occupational Health, Safety and Welfare Act 1986* (SA), Part 4; *Workplace Health and Safety Act 1995* (Tas), Part 5; *Occupational Health and Safety Act 2004* (Vic), s 72; *Occupational Safety and Health Act 1984* (WA), ss 36-41.)

Immediate threat to health and safety

[11.60] Where there is an immediate threat to health and safety, it follows from the worker's duty to take reasonable steps for self protection and protection of others that he or she may take reasonable measures to render the situation safe or to stop work if such a move is warranted. In some jurisdictions, legislation provides that in the face of an immediate threat to safety, an employee may cease work or a health and safety representative may direct employee to cease work. (See for example *Work Health Act* (NT), s 32; *Occupational Health and Safety Act 2004* (Vic), s 74; *Occupational Health and Safety Act 1989* (ACT), Part 5 Div 5.3.)

Default notices

[11.65] Under Commonwealth, Australian Capital Territory, South Australian and Victorian legislation, a health and safety representative can issue a Provisional Improvement Notice or Default Notice. Such a notice states that the health and safety legislation has been breached and requires action to be taken. The notice must be displayed in designated (relevant) places in the workplace, and the person is to take reasonable steps to remedy the breach. An inspector may be summoned and may verify or cancel the notice. Where it remains in place, failure to comply with it is an offence. (See *Occupational Health and Safety Act 2004* (Vic), ss 60-66; *Occupational Health and Safety Act 1989* (ACT), Part 5 Div 5.2; *Occupational Health, Safety and Welfare Act 1986* (SA), s 35; *Occupational Health and Safety (Commonwealth Employment) Act 1991* (Cth), s 29.)

Protection of employees, representatives and committee members

[11.70] All jurisdictions, except Queensland, protect to some extent employees, health and safety representatives and members of health and safety committees from victimisation such as demotion, changing working conditions, or dismissal, because of their activities related to health and safety issues (*Occupational Health and Safety (Commonwealth Employment) Act 1991* (Cth), s 76; *Workplace Health and Safety Regulations 1998* (Tas), Reg 35; *Occupational Health and Safety Act 1989* (ACT), s 210; *Occupational Health and Safety Act 2000* (NSW), s 23; *Work Health Act* (NT), s 45; *Occupational Health, Safety and Welfare Act 1986* (SA), s 56; *Occupational Health and Safety Act 2004* (Vic), Part 7 Div 9; *Occupational Safety and Health Act 1984* (WA), s 56).

Inspectorate

[11.75] All jurisdictions establish "inspectors" or "investigators" authorised to do such things as enter and inspect premises and documents, take photographs, conduct tests, take items of equipment, question people and issue notices to improve premises or cease specified activities. They are appointed by the responsible authority. Their role is to ensure that the requirements of the legislation are observed, and to identify and make recommendations concerning the causes of accidents, illnesses or dangerous occurrences in the workplace. Inspectors may be called in where issues of health and safety cannot be resolved within the workplace. (See *Occupational Health and Safety (Commonwealth Employment) Act 1991* (Cth), Part 4; *Occupational Health and Safety Act 1989* (ACT), Part 6 Div 6.2; *Occupational Health and Safety Act 2000* (NSW), Part 5; *Work Health Act* (NT), Part IV Div 2; *Workplace Health and Safety Act 1995* (Qld), Part 9; *Workplace Health and Safety Act 1995* (Tas), s 34; *Occupational Health and Safety Act 2004* (Vic), Part 9; *Occupational Safety and Health Act 1984* (WA), s 42.)

Prosecution

[11.80] A breach of the provisions of the occupational health and safety statutes may constitute an offence. The establishment of an offence differs between jurisdictions. In most jurisdictions, proceedings may be instituted where an offence has occurred. The persons or bodies that are able to institute such proceedings varies with each jurisdiction. The penalty for a breach of occupational health and safety legislative provisions is generally a fine, although in some jurisdictions individuals can face imprisonment (See, for example, *Occupational Health and Safety Act 2000* (NSW), s 12).

Criminal law statute provisions relating to manslaughter in general may also be relevant to acts or omissions causing the death of a person in the course of employment, and the penalty associated with such offences may involve imprisonment. In the Australian Capital Territory, Part 2A of the *Crimes Act 1900* creates the offence of "industrial manslaughter" which provides that where an employer or senior officer of an employer causes the death of an employee through recklessness or negligence, they are guilty of an offence punishable by imprisonment for up to 20 years.

[11.85] Case: *Australian Services Union of NSW v Mercy Centre, Lavington Ltd*, Unreported, NSW Chief Magistrates Court, 2005

The defendant was a non-profit organisation providing residential care facilities for intellectually impaired persons with behavioural difficulties. One of its workers was attacked twice by residents of the facility. On the first occasion the worker was stabbed with a syringe that the resident had acquired from a public toilet block whilst unsupervised on an earlier community excursion. The second incident involved the worker being struck with a lamp, verbally threatened and assaulted when she tried to restrain a violent resident.

The Australian Services Union brought a prosecution in relation to each incident alleging:
1. failure to provide sufficient supervision to residents on excursions; and
2. failure to ensure workers received adequate training (in this

case in self defence) and failure to provide adequate staffing levels to protect workers from physically violent residents. Chief Industrial Magistrate (CIM) Hart found that:

- Insufficient supervision during the excursion allowed the resident to obtain the syringe;
- The defendant had not put in place appropriate planning for such excursions to prevent residents finding and keeping dangerous items;
- The worker was given very little training in self-defence
- In the absence of such training, staffing levels should have been such that staff were not exposed to violent residents one-on-one.

The defendant was fined $27,300.

Workers' Compensation

[11.90] The social cost of workplace injury and the associated loss of income has led to the requirement, through legislation, that employers insure their employees against "personal injury arising out of or in the course of employment". Similar in some respects to compulsory third party insurance of drivers, it provides for all employers to insure employees with an insurance company so that payment for medical treatment, loss of income and rehabilitation will not be a burden on the employee or the public purse.

Workers' compensation is covered by legislation in each Australian jurisdiction (see [11.25], there are diverse approaches and these have been changing rapidly in recent years. Whilst the basic features (outlined below) are common throughout Australia, readers are cautioned against relying on what is read here to determine just what their entitlements are, and are advised to find out details of provisions in their jurisdiction. Information can be obtained from the Workers' Compensation Boards, Commissions or Courts, Departments of Industrial Relations, legal aid offices or unions. Employers should have claim forms and information for those who wish to lodge them.

No fault

[11.95] The basic principle of workers' compensation schemes is that they apply regardless of fault. The fact that the harm can be classified as an injury arising out of, or in the course of, employment, and the person harmed is a worker according to the legislation, is enough to create eligibility for compensation. The only exception to this may be where the worker is guilty of serious and wilful misconduct (interpreted by the courts as involving such activities as drunkenness, dangerous driving and practical jokes). There is no requirement to prove duty of care, breach of duty or direct causation, which makes it a much simpler means of getting compensation for harm at work.

Some jurisdictions have abolished the right of injured workers to sue their employers in negligence, and only allow them to claim under workers' compensation (the Northern Territory and South Australia). Others limit the right to sue an employer at common law (the Commonwealth, New South Wales, Queensland, Victoria, and Western Australia). The remainder do not limit claims under both common law and workers' compensation, however if one is successful in a negligence action, workers' compensation entitlements are lost. (See *Safety Rehabilitation and Compensation Act 1988* (Cth), Part 4; *Workers' Compensation Act 1951* (ACT), Ch 9; *Workers' Compensation Act 1987* (NSW), Part 5; *Work Health Act* (NT), s 52; *Workers' Compensation and Rehabilitation Act 2003* (Qld), Ch 5; *Workers' Rehabilitation and Compensation Act 1986* (SA), s 54; *Workers Rehabilitation and Compensation Act 1988* (Tas), Part X; *Accident Compensation Act 1985* (Vic), Part 4 Div 8A; *Workers' Compensation and Rehabilitation Act 1981* (WA), Part IV Div 2.)

A positive aspect of workers' compensation is the emphasis that has developed on rehabilitation, so that instead of paying (and laying) off workers who are injured, employers are required to provide means for workers to either return to their previous employment, or find satisfactory employment doing other work where this is reasonably available (*Safety Rehabilitation and Compensation Act 1988* (Cth), Part 3; *Workers' Compensation Act 1951* (ACT), Ch 5; *Workplace Injury Management and Workers Compensation Act 1998* (NSW), Ch 3; *Work Health Act* (NT), Part V Div 4; *Workers' Compensation and Rehabilitation Act 2003* (Qld), Ch 1 Div 7 and Ch 4 Part 3; *Workers' Rehabilitation and Compensation Act 1986* (SA), Part 3; *Workers Rehabilitation and Compensation Act 1988* (Tas), Part XI; *Accident Compensation Act 1985* (Vic), Part 6; *Workers' Compensation and Rehabilitation Act 1981* (WA), Part IX).

Who is covered by workers' compensation?

[11.100] Any employee who suffers injury through an accident caused by or in the course of employment; or a disease arising out of or significantly contributed to by employment, may be entitled to apply for workers' compensation. In the case of death, the employee's dependants may be able to claim. Usually, there are some exclusions and added categories to this rule, which differ across the Australian jurisdictions. For example, all Australian jurisdictions except Tasmania cover accidents "arising out of or in the course of employment". Tasmania covers accidents "arising out *and* in the course of employment". That is, in Tasmania the accident has to be both caused by the employment *and* occur during the course of the employment. In other jurisdictions only one of these criteria need be proved, thus the accident may be caused by the employment but occur out of work hours or even after the person is no longer employed. Entitlement to compensation for disease is generally more restrictive. (See *Safety Rehabilitation and Compensation Act 1988* (Cth), s 4(1); *Workers' Compensation Act 1951* (ACT), s 30(1); *Workers' Compensation Act 1987* (NSW), s 4 and *Workplace Injury Management and Workers Compensation Act 1998* (NSW), s 4; *Work Health Act* (NT), s 4; *Workers' Compensation and Rehabilitation Act 2003* (Qld), s 32; *Workers' Rehabilitation and Compensation Act 1986* (SA), s 30; *Workers Rehabilitation and Compensation Act 1988* (Tas), s 25(1); *Accident Compensation Act 1985* (Vic), s 82(1); *Workers' Compensation and Rehabilitation Act 1981* (WA), s 5(1).)

Courts have held that interpretation of workers' compensation should be liberal, so that where two or more meanings can be given to the legislation, the meaning most favourable to the worker should be used (*Wilson v Wilson's Tile Works Pty Ltd* (1960) 104 CLR 328; [1960] HCA 63, per Fullagar J; *Heath v Commonwealth* (1982) 151 CLR 76; [1982] HCA 61 per Murphy J). As the legislation in all jurisdictions is aimed at rehabilitation of injured workers, consideration should be given to the circumstances of individuals (*Workers Rehabilitation and Compensation Corp v James* (1992) 57 SASR 365 at 393-394 per Zelling J). The interpretation should also take account of contemporary industrial practices and social attitudes (*Hatzimanolis v ANI Corp Ltd* (1992) 173 CLR 473; [1992] HCA 21 per Mason CJ, Deane, Dawson and McHugh JJ).

Who is a "worker"?

[11.105] First one must establish that one is a "worker" according to the applicable legislation.

There are definitions in the workers' compensation legislation as to who is considered a worker. Generally, that will be anyone who has entered into or works under a contract of service or apprenticeship with an employer, whether the contract is written, oral or implied (see, for example, *Workplace Injury Management and Workers Compensation Act 1998* (NSW), s 4(1)). Some specific categories of workers are included where their situation may not otherwise clearly fit into the general definition, giving those persons the right to claim under the legislation. For example, salespersons, canvassers, collectors, or those paid by commission in the Australian Capital Territory, New South Wales, Queensland, and Tasmania (*Workers' Compensation Act 1951* (ACT), s 8; *Workplace Injury Management and Workers' Compensation Act 1998* (NSW), Ch 3; *Workers' Compensation and Rehabilitation Act 2003* (Qld), Sch 2, cl 4; *Workers' Rehabilitation and Compensation Act 1988* (Tas), s 4C). Contractors under some circumstances are to be included in some jurisdictions, as are police officers (see, for example, *Workers' Compensation and Rehabilitation Act 1981* (WA), s 5(1)) and volunteer firefighters (see, for example, *Workplace Injury Management and Workers' Compensation Act 1998* (NSW), Sch 1). Other categories of worker are specifically excluded in some jurisdictions, removing compensation rights from them (for example, members of Parliament are excluded under the *Safety, Rehabilitation and Compensation Act 1988* (Cth), s 5(8), as are professional sportspersons under the *Workers' Compensation and Rehabilitation Act 2003* (Qld), Sch 2). There may be separate compensation schemes for some categories of excluded workers.

Where there is doubt as to whether a person is actually a party to a contract of service, the courts consider the common law tests to establish whether the person is an employee (see Chapter 9). The totality of the relationship between alleged employer and worker must be considered. (See *Hollis v Vabu Pty Ltd* (2001) 207 CLR 21; [2001] HCA 44.)

Health carers are employees under a State or Commonwealth Act where they have entered into a contract of service with the Commonwealth (for example, in repatriation hospitals), with a State health care facility, or for a private employer. They are not covered by the legislation if they are private practitioners or independent contractors, that is, for example, under a contract for specific services as a visiting health care professional, or privately engaged by a patient as an agency nurse or homebirth midwife. In that case they have to arrange their own insurance.

What is an "injury"?

[11.108] The definition of "injury" varies, but in most jurisdictions means physical or mental injury or the aggravation, acceleration, or recurrence of a pre-existing injury arising out of, or suffered in the course of work, and generally includes also the contraction, exacerbation or acceleration of a disease where work is a contributing factor (which may have to have been "significantly substantial", material or major, according to jurisdiction) and death (see for example, *Workers Compensation Act 1958* (Vic), s 3). An autogenous disease (for example, subarachnoid haemorrhage), was held not to fall within the definition of "injury" under New South Wales and Queensland law in *Hockey v Yelland and Ors* (1984) AWCCD ¶73-555. The courts have established that the word "injury" should be given its ordinary meaning, which has generally meant the adverse impact of any external agent on the body.

> **[11.110] Case:** *Favelle Mort Ltd v Murray* (1976) 133 CLR 580; [1976] HCA 13 (High Court)
>
> A worker contracted viral meningeal encephalitis and claimed workers' compensation. The Court had to decide if the worker had suffered an "injury" within the ordinary meaning of the word.

[11.115] The Court decided that the disease was an injury because it was caused by an external factor. Sir Garfield Barwick CJ decided that the meningeal encephalitis was neither idiopathic nor autogenous: it was the result of the introduction into the employee's body of a foreign body, the virus. The morbid condition was not itself the relevant injury but merely the consequence of introduction of the virus into the body from without. The attack by, or reception of, the virus was the injury. He went on to say that a disease was a morbid condition of the body which may be initiated by either an outside cause or be idiopathic or autogenic: "Quite clearly when such a condition is idiopathic or autogenous, it will not qualify as an injury in the normal use of language."

There are particular diseases that are recognised as being associated with particular work. These are labelled "industrial diseases", and include such illnesses as silicosis in miners, or anthrax in those in the meat industry. The benefit of associating these diseases with an industry which tends to cause them is that in most jurisdictions legislation provides that when a worker in that industry contracts an industrial disease designated to that industry, the burden of proof is on the employer to prove that the disease was *not* caused by the person's work, rather than being on the employee to prove the causal connection. (See *Safety Rehabilitation and Compensation Act 1988* (Cth), s 7; *Workers' Compensation Act 1951* (ACT), s 28 and *Workers' Compensation Regulation 2002* (ACT), Sch 1; *Workers' Compensation Act 1987* (NSW), s 19 and *Workers' Compensation Regulation 2003* (NSW), Part 2, Sch 2; *Workers' Rehabilitation And Compensation Act 1988* (Tas), s 26, Sch 4; *Work Health Act* (NT), s 4(6), Sch 1; *Workers' Rehabilitation and Compensation Act 1986* (SA), s 31(2), Sch 2; *Workers' Compensation Act 1958* (Vic), Part 1, Div 3; *Workers' Compensation and Rehabilitation Act 1981* (WA), s 44, Sch 3.)

> "'Injury' could also be considered to include the 'injuries' health carers may be more likely to suffer than most workers, such as back and needle-stick injuries, attacks, infections and psychological trauma."

What events are covered?

[11.120] A connection must be established between the harm and employment. The central wording of the legislation describing the type of injury it covers is the same in all jurisdictions other than Tasmania, as mentioned at **[11.100]**. This wording covers all injuries "arising out of or in the course of" employment. This phrase has been interpreted widely by the courts.

[11.125] Case: *Kavanagh v Commonwealth* (1960) 103 CLR 547; [1960] HCA 25 (High Court)

K was employed packing stationery. During work he stopped and went to the washroom. He returned, telling his workmates he felt ill and had diarrhoea. He subsequently began vomiting, and was taken to hospital where he died. The cause of death was apparently a ruptured oesophagus resulting from the violent vomiting. The question before the High Court was whether he had died from an injury "arising out of or in the course of" his work, as it was argued that because the injury was not caused by K's work, he should not be eligible for workers' compensation.

[11.130] The Court decided that the ruptured oesophagus was an injury, so the issue was the meaning of the phrase "arising out of or in the course of employment". In so doing, it considered the fact that legislation had been changed. Originally the phrase had been "arising out of, and in the course of employment". The first three words require a causal connection with work, and so the phrase overall required that the connection be made. However, the change of the preposition "and" to "or" indicated a purpose,

> "to eliminate the necessity of finding such a causal connection. If there was such a causal connection, the injury was to be compensable even though it did not occur while the worker was engaged in his employment or anything incidental to his employment. [The meaning of 'arising out of' employment.] If, on the other hand, the injury occurred in the course of the employment, it

was to be compensable even though no causal connection could be found between it and the employment ... I think, that the words 'arising in the course of his employment' ought not to be regarded as meaning anything more or less than 'arising while the worker is engaged in his employment'" [per Fullagar J].

Dixon J held that it included the situation where the worker was "momentarily standing by considering his capacity to resume his duties". The distinction between the two elements in the words "arising of or in the course of" employment is now well established.

Activities incidental to employment

[11.135] The requirement that the accident or injury must arise in the course of employment is not limited to the required service, but extends to all activity incidental to that service. Thus cleaning or procuring equipment for use in employment may be incidental to it, including journeys to and from places for this to be done.

Activities during breaks

[11.140] Workers may be covered by workers' compensation for injury occasioned through activities during normal breaks whilst at work or in circumstances considered incidental to the particular employment situation. One is covered during morning tea, lunch and other normal breaks, if on the employer's premises, whatever one is doing. Sport and other activities engaged in during breaks are generally accepted as being part of work. In one case the playing of sport during the lunch hour was the subject of a workers' compensation claim. The employer had prohibited the playing of sport but had never bothered to enforce the ban. The High Court said an employee may do that which may be required, expected or authorised, which it held could include "taking a walk, dozing in the sun, or playing a game of table tennis or cricket" (*Commonwealth v Oliver* (1962) 107 CLR 353; [1962] HCA 38).

It would seem that one may also leave the employer's premises during a break (for example, to buy lunch, or collect clothes from the dry cleaner's), as long as one's activities are incidental to work, and one does not subject oneself to abnormal risk of injury. However not all excursions for lunch will qualify. The High Court in *Humphrey Earl Ltd v Speechley* (1951) 84 CLR 126; [1951] HCA 75 rejected the claim of an employee who was injured returning from a lunch consumed some distance away from the workplace. Dixon J made the following point:

> "The eating of lunch is not in itself a thing which is done for the purpose of (the employee's) duties. It is the satisfaction of a recurrent human want. But the conditions of the employment may be such as to make the obtaining and consumption of a meal something reasonably incidental to the performance of the actual duties. The point in such a case as this is not whether it is reasonable to eat lunch or reasonable to want fish for lunch. The question is whether the course adopted by the employee was reasonably

incidental to the performance on that occasion of his duties. This cannot be stretched to make everything he chooses to do during the interval he takes for lunch incidental to his employment ... There is a great difference between, on the one hand, the worker's taking advantage of an allowable interval for lunch in order to make it the occasion for an excursion for his own purposes and on the other hand his acting in a way which is reasonably calculated to fulfil the purposes of his employment and at the same time provide for his own reasonable wants."

Legislation in some jurisdictions deems a worker's temporary absence from the workplace on a work day to be within the course of their employment, but may exclude situations where the injury occurs as a result of the worker's voluntarily subjection to abnormal risk (see *Safety, Rehabilitation and Compensation Act 1988* (Cth), s 6(1)(b)(i); *Workers Compensation Act 1987* (NSW), s 11; *Work Health Act* (NT), s 4; *Workers Compensation and Rehabilitation Act 2003* (Qld), s 34; *Accident Compensation Act 1985* (Vic), s 83(1)(a)).

[11.145] Case: *Thompson v Lewisham Hospital* [1978] WCR 113 (Workers' Compensation Commission New South Wales)

A worker in the ward had a mechanical problem with her car, rang the National Roads and Motorists Association and asked them to send a representative to the hospital at about 3 pm that day. The representative arrived, and the car was towed, with the worker in attendance, to a nearby garage from which she began walking back to the hospital, stopping off for a few minutes at her home. On the way from her home to the hospital she was injured by a truck. She would have been absent from her workplace about 26 minutes if she had not been injured. The period of her absence was between 3 pm and 4 pm, a time, she argued, which was a "normal break" for those assisting in the ward. She gave evidence that instead of only spending the nominated time of 15 minutes from 3.45 pm until 4 pm for afternoon tea, non-nursing staff regularly spent the visiting hour from 3 pm to 4 pm in the day-room, because the "sister on duty doesn't like the girls to be going into the room and collecting flowers, or interrupting because we are not nurses".

[11.150] The Commission decided that the evidence could support a finding that the normal break allowed at the hospital was one of no less than 15 minutes but could be up to one hour: the break ordinarily began at 3 pm and concluded at 4 pm. Absence from work taken with the permission of the employer, and incidental to work, may not remove one from the course of employment.

[11.155] Case: *Kyriakidas v Rondo Building Services Pty Ltd* [1974] WCR 62 (Workers' Compensation Commission NSW)

A worker used to drive home each day for lunch as the employer did not provide facilities and his home was nearby. On the day in question he detoured from his route home to give his brother and friends a lift to a hotel. He was exceeding the speed limit, and collided with a telegraph pole, resulting in his injury. The Commission accepted that he was absent during a normal break, but had to determine whether he had subjected himself to an abnormal risk of injury.

[11.160] The Commission accepted earlier case law which defined "abnormal risk" as meaning one which is no more than unusual, and that a risk is abnormal when, in the particular circumstances, an act is accompanied by an unusual degree of risk, or is incidental to an act which in itself is inherently dangerous. It found that the employee had subjected himself to an abnormal risk of injury by speeding. Lack of qualifications, and inexperience, may be considered in determining whether one subjects oneself to an abnormal risk; so something done by a learner may be considered more risky than the same thing done by an experienced person. The legislation generally requires that the abnormal risk be voluntarily undertaken, thus requiring that the person undertakes it by freely exercised choice.

An employee who is injured while remaining at home or elsewhere for the purpose of being on call or working from home may be eligible for compensation if injured while carrying out activities incidental thereto (see, for example, at home while on call, *Commonwealth Bank of Australia v Wark* (1995) 22 AAR 181 (Fed Ct) and *Rowe v Flinders Medical Centre* (1979) 45 SAIR (Pt 2) 285 (FC); working from home, *Van Oosterom v Australian Metropolitan Life Assurance Co Ltd* [1960] VR 507 (FC)).

Journeys

[11.165] Travel to or from home and work is generally included in the activities covered, as is travel for the purposes of work. Wording of the statutes differs, and a guide to the different approaches of the jurisdictions is set out in Figure 11.1. Generally travel must be by the most reasonably direct route, without substantial deviation or voluntary interruptions. One is generally considered on one's journey when one leaves the boundary of one's residential property. In some jurisdictions, coverage extends to an injury received during or after a non-employment related interruption, or deviation from, an otherwise employment related journey if the risk of injury was not materially increased because of the interruption or deviation (see for example, *Workers' Compensation Act 1951* (ACT), s 36).

Figure 11.1: Journeys considered part of work for workers' compensation

Note that these categories are generalisations and subject to jurisdictional conditions and qualifications. They should not be relied on without checking the precise terms of the legislation.

Purpose of Travel	Cth	ACT	NSW	NT	QLD	SA	TAS	VIC	WA##
Home to/from work	✓	✓	✓	✓	✓	✓**			
Home to place of pickup*		✓							
Home to/from work residence	✓	✓							
Between places of work	✓			✓	✓				
For purpose of employment		✓					✓	✓#	✓###
To obtain medical certificate for compensation claim	✓	✓	✓	✓	✓	✓			
To receive medical treatment for injury	✓	✓	✓	✓	✓	✓			
For rehabilitation for workers' compensation	✓	✓	✓	✓	✓	✓			
For assessment for workers' compensation	✓		✓	✓	✓	✓			
To collect pay	✓	✓							
To place for work-related/approved education training	✓	✓	✓	✓	✓	✓			

Safety Rehabilitation and Compensation Act 1988 (Cth), s 6; *Workers' Compensation Act 1951* (ACT), s 36; *Workers' Compensation Act 1987* (NSW), s 10; *Work Health Act* (NT), s 4; *Workers' Compensation and Rehabilitation Act 2003* (Qld), s 35; *Workers' Rehabilitation and Compensation Act 1986* (SA), s 30; *Workers Rehabilitation and Compensation Act 1988* (Tas), s 25; *Accident Compensation Act 1993* (Vic), s 83; *Workers' Compensation and Rehabilitation Act 1981* (WA), s 19.

* Travel must be by the shortest convenient route, without substantial deviations or voluntary interruptions. One is generally considered on one's journey when one leaves the boundary of one's residential property.

** Only where on the specific request of employer or if journey is work-related.

\# Victoria specifically **excludes** journeys to and from the place of employment, places at which the worker receives training, medical certificate, medical advice or treatment, personal and household services, rehabilitation or payment of compensation.

\#\# Western Australia specifically **excludes** journeys between home and work, journeys between home and education, places for treatment or to receive compensation, and journeys between places of residence.

\#\#\# Except where injury is incurred during, or after, any substantial interruption, or substantial deviation from, the journey, made for any reason unconnected with the worker's employment.

A worker is also generally covered whilst at the places to which he or she has made a work-related journey (for example, undergoing education or training, receiving medical care etc).

[11.170] Case: *Buckman v Electricity Commission of New South Wales* [1975] WCR 128 (Workers' Compensation Commission NSW)

A worker travelling home in Sydney stopped for two and a half hours at a nightclub where he consumed a substantial amount of alcohol. After falling asleep on a suburban train he awoke just as the train was about to leave a station and wished to alight. He tried to jump from the train as it began to move and as a result fell between the train and the platform resulting in an injury.

[11.175] The Workers' Compensation Commission had to determine whether the time spent at the nightclub was a substantial deviation from his journey home, and if it was, whether he had materially increased the risk of injury to himself. It found that the two and a half hours spent at the club was a substantial interruption, and the amount of alcohol drunk materially affected his judgment to the extent of materially increasing the risk of him suffering harm on the way home.

The *Workers' Compensation Act 1987* (NSW), s 10(1A) now expressly states that injury received by a worker is taken to be attributable to serious and wilful misconduct of the worker (disentitling the worker to compensation) if the worker was at the time under the influence of alcohol or other drug unless the alcohol or drug did not contribute in any way to the injury or was not consumed or taken voluntarily.

Statutory extensions of the course of employment

[11.180] Legislation in some jurisdictions has extended the activities that are covered by workers' compensation. They are set out in Figure 12.2.

Sporting and other activities

[11.185] Under some circumstances, participation in sports as part of a workplace team, or in work-generated leisure activities which are authorised by the employer are covered (see, for example, *Black v Boolaroo Co-operative Society Ltd* (1958) 76 WN (NSW) 586 (FC) where the drowning of an employee at a picnic day was held to arise out of employment). Where more formal organised sporting matches are undertaken by workers in off-duty time or on weekends, especially where they are authorised, encouraged or otherwise supported by the employer, workers' compensation may apply to any accidents occurring (see for example, *R v Insurance Commissioner; Ex parte Michael* [1977] 1 WLR 109 where the worker was injured during an annual industry football game where the team and their clothing carried the employer's name).

Figure 11.2: Statutory extensions of the course of employment

(Originally adapted from *Halsbury's Law of Australia*, [450-210]-[450-300].) Note that these categories are generalisations, and should not be relied on without checking the precise terms of the legislation.

Activity	Cth	ACT	NSW	NT	QLD	SA	TAS	VIC	WA
Violence arising as a result of employment	✓								
Attendance at educational facility for work-related/approved activity	✓			✓	✓	✓		✓	✓
Attendance at place for workers' compensation purposes	✓			✓	✓			✓	✓
Activity as accredited trade union or employee organisation representative with employer's consent or authorised by an agreement or award			✓						

Safety Rehabilitation and Compensation Act 1988 (Cth), s 6; *Workers' Compensation Act 1987* (NSW), s 12; *Work Health Act* (NT), s 4; *Workers' Compensation and Rehabilitation Act 2003* (Qld), s 35; *Workers' Rehabilitation and Compensation Act 1986* (SA), s 30; *Accident Compensation Act 1985* (Vic), s 83; *Workers' Compensation and Rehabilitation Act 1981* (WA), s 19.

Where attendance is expected by the employer, or where payment or promotion is dependent upon attendance, the workers' compensation provisions are more likely to apply.

A worker's participation in sporting and social activity is expressly excluded from coverage under the workers' compensation scheme in South Australia and Tasmania, unless the involvement forms part of the worker's employment or is undertaken at the direction or request of the employer (see *Workers' Rehabilitation and Compensation Act 1986* (SA), s 30(4); *Workers' Rehabilitation and Compensation Act 1988* (Tas), s 25(6)(d)).

[11.190] Case: *Wolmar v Travelodge Australia Ltd* (1975) 8 ACTR 11 (Supreme Court)

A worker was injured at a Christmas party on the employer's premises, held by the management, to which workers were invited and expected to attend.

[11.195] In this case the Court adopted the following test when asked if attendance at a particular event was part of one's job:

"Here we have the situation where, on the one hand, the employer, for the purposes of improving relationships all round, offers hospitality to an employee and her spouse in the form of a gathering on the employer's premises attended solely by the manager and his wife and by other employees and their spouses. On the other hand the employee co-operates by bringing along herself, her spouse and her plate and thereby helps to make the occasion a success. It seems to me that this whole enterprise is so closely associated with the employment as to be incidental to it. I think the average office worker in Australia ... if asked about the matter, would express what I have said ... by saying that, these days, attendance at the annual Christmas staff party is part of the job" [at 16 per Dixon J].

Other cases have since established that the party need not be at work and the employee need not be obliged to attend.

It would seem, by the reference to contemporary expectations, that the approach taken above was meant to provide for flexibility over time, and that events other than Christmas parties, such as farewells to staff, celebrations and "team building" events could be included where these are considered part of the job. It is also arguable that events that are organised for the wellbeing of the hospitalised or institutionalised, which involve staff, such as trips away or to sporting events, even on a voluntary basis, could be considered incidental to work (see, for example, *Clancy v Department of Public Health* (1961) 78 WN (NSW) 1069; [[1962] NSWR 2] (FC) where the participation of an off-duty psychiatric nurse in a football game within the hospital grounds was encouraged for the benefit of patients, was considered to be in the course of employment).

Accommodation

[11.200] Workers may be compensated for injuries occuring while off duty if they are required to live in certain premises.

[11.205] Case: *Regan v Gladesville Hospital* [1977] WCR 107 (Workers' Compensation Commission NSW)

A nurse was injured when he fell on the stairwell in the nurses' residence of his place of employment while engaged in his own private affairs. He was not required by his employer to reside in the quarters, and was living there to benefit from the cheap and convenient accommodation it provided.

[11.210] If the nurse could show that his residence in the nurses' home was required as a condition of his employment, he could be eligible for workers' compensation. The Workers' Compensation Commission considered earlier cases which dealt with employees living on or near their place of employment rather than at their permanent home. It decided that in these cases there were two kinds of accommodation according to the facts: those situations where employees have no real choice of where they live, and those where they choose to live in premises purely for the sake of convenience, after exercising a real choice. In deciding this case the following questions were considered:

- Does the applicant's job require frequent movement from place to place, with or without short periods in any one place, making accommodation difficult thus requiring workplace accommodation?
- Is the applicant on call, or in any other way does he or she have restrictions on their activities at the time?
- Is it somehow disadvantageous or unreasonably impractical for the worker, in discharging her or his responsibilities, to live elsewhere?

If any of the above questions could have been answered in the affirmative, the Commission may have held that living in the nurses' home was incidental to the employment of the nurse in this case. However, the questions were answered in the negative by the Commission, therefore compensation was not available.

Travel

[11.215] Travel to, and attendance at, classes, conferences or for other purposes approved by the employer and considered part of one's development as an employee are generally considered to be part of one's employment for the purposes of workers' compensation law (see Figure 11.1).

Assault at work

[11.220] It is not unknown for health carers to be the subject of attack from patients, and under most circumstances, these situations are covered by workers' compensation legislation. Where the assault is the result of a private quarrel (which is not part of one's work) it would most likely not be accepted. Compare the case of *McCleod v Cockatoo Docks* [1971] WCR 313 where an assault after a jocular remark made while workers were waiting for a union meeting (which was being held during a lunchtime break) was held to be in the course of employment, with the case of *Bill Williams Pty Ltd v Williams* [1972] HCA 23, where Williams, having punched another man, O'Neill, over an argument about his alleged affair with O'Neill's wife, was threatened with a gun by O'Neill. Williams ran out of the premises and was shot in the back. The Court held that the argument was unrelated to the employment and interrupted the "course of employment".

Application for workers' compensation

[11.225] As noted above, workers' compensation is bound by rules and procedures. There are time limits for making claims, and it should also be remembered that the longer after an accident before a claim is made, the more difficult it may be to substantiate the claim. A worker wishing to make a claim does so by first notifying the employer, and is advised to do so as soon as possible after the injury. Then a claim must be made. Larger employers have specially designated personnel for dealing with compensation claims. All jurisdictions, except Western Australia (where the time limit is 12 months), the Australian Capital Territory (where a claim for permanent injury may not generally be made earlier than 2 years after the injury), and Victoria (where different time limits apply for different types of claims) require that the claim be made within six months of the injury. The Commonwealth legislation does not impose a time restriction on the bringing of a claim. Most Australian jurisdictions allow special leave for the court to grant an extension, but this may be difficult to obtain. The claim is to be made in writing and is lodged by the employer with the insurer. To challenge the claim the insurer must go to the appropriate board or tribunal.

The usual way to initiate a claim is to obtain a form from the employer when reporting the accident or illness. The report is then lodged with the relevant workers' compensation authority.

Importance of reporting all injuries

[11.230] Legislation in most jurisdictions requires that notice of an injury be given as soon as practicable after the worker becomes aware of the injury or, where the worker dies without having become so aware, as soon as practicable after the worker's death (*Safety, Rehabilitation and Compensation Act 1988* (Cth), s 53; *Workers' Compensation Act 1951* (ACT), s 93; *Workplace Injury Management and Workers' Compensation Act 1988* (NSW), ss 61, 254; *Work Health Act* (NT), s 80; *Workers' Rehabilitation and Compensation Act 1986* (SA), s 51; *Workers' Rehabilitation and Compensation Act 1988* (Tas), s 32; *Accident Compensation Act 1985* (Vic), s 102). Failure to give notice of an injury may preclude a person from entitlement to compensation. It is important that workers recognise the need to report all injuries, even minor ones for which they do not need treatment or time off. This particularly relates to back injuries that are considered minor and not deserving of any attention. After a series of these, an injury may occur which is exacerbated by the already existing weakness caused by the earlier minor injuries and requires more treatment or leave than it would, in isolation, require. Unless there is a record of the previous injuries, there may be no way of proving that the full extent of the harm is work-related. It is also important:

- not to treat minor injuries oneself, for if anything goes wrong or one has not realised the full extent of the harm, one's interference in the course of treatment may adversely affect one's claim to compensation;
- to consider whether sick leave should more appropriately be claimed under workers' compensation where the reason for leave is work-related "injury" or disease;
- that employers have provisions for recording incidents of injury, illness or pain even if there is doubt as to whether they are work-related or not. Workers should ensure that such incidents are recorded; and
- to produce to the employer any certificate stating that the worker is able to undertake light duties, even where there is no work of such nature available. Where light duties are not available, the worker may be deemed under the law to be totally incapacitated, and entitled to appropriate compensation

(see for example, *Workers Compensation Act 1951* (ACT), s 35). However the opportunity to offer such work must be made available to the employer.

Compensation

Death

[11.235] Where a worker dies as a result of an industrial injury, payment of compensation may be made to dependants, under all legislation (*Safety, Rehabilitation and Compensation Act 1988* (Cth), s 17; *Workers Compensation Act 1951* (ACT), s 77; *Workers Compensation Act 1987* (NSW), s 25; *Work Health Act* (NT), s 62; *Workers' Compensation and Rehabilitation Act 2003* (Qld), Chapter 11; *Workers Rehabilitation and Compensation Act 1986* (SA), s 44; *Workers Rehabilitation and Compensation Act 1988* (Tas), s 67; *Accident Compensation Act 1985* (Vic), ss 92, 92A; *Workers' Compensation and Rehabilitation Act 1981* (WA), Sch 1 cl 1). The definition of "dependant" varies, but spouses, legal or de facto, children, step-children, children in the care of the worker or those in a close family relationship who can show dependency on the worker at the time of death may generally apply. Compensation may be apportioned between dependants.

Incapacity

[11.240] Where a worker is rendered unable to work, compensation for medical treatment and loss of wages is awarded according to amounts established in the legislation. Where the worker is fully incapacitated the amount payable for loss of wages is generally based on the previous pay rate of the worker, with either the full amount or a percentage thereof applying for an initial period, 26 weeks in New South Wales, Australian Capital Territory, Northern Territory and Queensland, one year in South Australia and 13 weeks in Victoria. Thereafter the various Australian jurisdictions differ markedly in their provision of compensation. Some jurisdictions continue to compute the amount payable on the average weekly wages of the particular worker, and no special provision is made for dependants. Others compute the amount on different permutations of the average weekly wage and add an amount for each dependent person. If incapacity is partial, as well as medical and rehabilitation expenses, the amount payable will generally be the difference between the amount the worker can now earn and the amount which would have been earned if the injury had not occurred. In some Australian jurisdictions the employer is obliged to provide alternative work for an employee partially incapacitated by injury or disease.

Normally, compensation payments are in the form of regular payments, but under some circumstances a lump sum may be paid.

Common law claim for compensation

[11.245] As noted above, eligibility for workers' compensation does not rule out the right of the worker to sue the employer if negligence can be proved, however, one's right to sue in negligence is severely limited under workers' compensation legislation. Generally, a successful negligence action will provide substantially more compensation, although it is, of course, much harder to prove. A worker who has been receiving workers' compensation and who later brings a successful action against the employer in negligence will have the amount of workers' compensation already received taken into account in the amount of damages awarded. Again, there are time limits for such actions varying between jurisdictions.

Liability of Occupiers for Accidents on Their Property

[11.250] The common law establishes liability of an occupier of premises for harm to those who come onto those premises. This was once seen as having special features, but over time the courts have assimilated "occupier's liability" within the general duty owed in a negligence action (see discussion in McGlone and Stickley at para 10.15, *Australian Safeway Stores Pty Limited v Zaluzna* (1987) 162 CLR 479; [1987] HCA 7 discussed below at [11.60] and *Turnbull v Alm* [2004] NSWCA 173). There is also legislation in some jurisdictions covering occupiers' liability.

Who is an occupier?

[11.255] Occupiers are those who have the control of premises: they may or may not be the owner.

> "Wherever a person has a sufficient degree of control over premises that he ought to realise that any failure on his part to use care may result in injury to a person coming lawfully there, then he is an 'occupier' and the person coming lawfully there is his 'visitor': and the 'occupier' is under a duty to his 'visitor' to use reasonable care ... [an occupier need not] have entire control over the premises. He need not have exclusive occupation. Suffice it that he has some degree of control [*Wheat v E Lacon & Co Ltd* [1966] AC 552 at 578 per Lord Denning]."

Management of health care facilities would normally be the occupiers of the premises. Health carers would not be liable as occupiers simply because they are employees working on the premises (*Stone v Taffe* [1974] 1 WLR 1575). However, employees have a duty of care to the employer (as occupier) to take reasonable steps to further the employer's interests, including the interest in maintaining safe premises. Thus the employee should do what is reasonable to remove hazards and remedy any unsafe conditions (for example, wet, slippery floors or exposed dangerous equipment) either themselves, or through notifying the appropriate responsible person.

An occupier does not have to be in physical occupation of the premises, but may be an absent landlord or owner (*Thompson v Commonwealth* (1969) 70 SR (NSW) 398). Several people may be liable, to a different extent (depending on, for example, contractual agreements) (*Wheat v E Lacon & Co Ltd* [1966] AC 552).

Standard of care of an occupier

[11.260] In the past the standard of care an occupier owed to those entering premises depended on the category of the entrant. An entrant may be:

* An **invitee** or one with whom the occupier has a special relationship based on pecuniary, material or business interests.
* A **licensee**, who enters with the permission, express or implied, of the occupier, including visitors for social reasons or reasons unrelated to the occupier's business.
* An **entrant under contract**, such as a visiting medical officer or maintenance worker, who is engaged to enter the premises for certain specified purposes.
* An **entrant as of right**, or one who enters under some statutory power, not requiring the occupier's permission to do so.
* **Trespassers**, or those who enter premises without the consent, express or implied, of the occupier.

The categories above carried different duties of care in the past. However, the High Court has now stated categorically that *all* entrants, regardless of their purpose, are owed a similar duty of care according to the rules of the law of negligence. *Australian Safeway Stores Pty Ltd v Zaluzna Pty Ltd* (1987) 162 CLR 479; [1987] HCA 7, quoting from *Hackshaw v Shaw* (1984) 155 CLR 614; [1984] HCA 84 adopted the principle that all that is necessary for a duty of care for an occupier is a reasonable foreseeability of a real risk of injury to a visitor, and the standard of care is "What a reasonable person would do by way of response to the foreseeable risk?" This calls for an assessment of the magnitude of the risk, the degree of probability of its occurrence, the expense, difficulty and inconvenience of removing the risk (see, for example, *Smith v Littlewoods Organisation Ltd* [1987] AC 241). Following the *Review of the Law of Negligence*, those factors have to varying extents in each jurisdiction been repeated in civil liability legislation. For example, in the *Civil Liability Act 2002* (NSW), s 5B and s 5C provide:

"Section 5B
(1) A person is not negligent in failing to take precautions against a risk of harm unless:
(a) the risk was foreseeable (that is, it is a risk of which the person knew or ought to have known), and
(b) the risk was not insignificant, and
(c) in the circumstances, a reasonable person in the person's position would have taken those precautions.
(2) In determining whether a reasonable person would have taken precautions against a risk of harm, the court is to consider the following (amongst other relevant things):

(a) the probability that the harm would occur if care were not taken,
(b) the likely seriousness of the harm,
(c) the burden of taking precautions to avoid the risk of harm,
(d) the social utility of the activity that creates the risk of harm.

Section 5C

In proceedings relating to liability for negligence:

(a) the burden of taking precautions to avoid a risk of harm includes the burden of taking precautions to avoid similar risks of harm for which the person may be responsible, and

(b) the fact that a risk of harm could have been avoided by doing something in a different way does not of itself give rise to or affect liability for the way in which the thing was done, and

(c) the subsequent taking of action that would (had the action been taken earlier) have avoided a risk of harm does not of itself give rise to or affect liability in respect of the risk and does not of itself constitute an admission of liability in connection with the risk."

Legislation in Victoria, South Australia, the Australian Capital Territory and Western Australia establishes a single standard of reasonable care towards lawful entrants and specifies the matters a court should consider in determining whether that duty has been breached (*Wrongs Act 1958* (Vic), Part IIA; *Civil Liability Act 1936* (SA), Part 4; *Civil Law (Wrongs) Act 2002* (ACT), Ch 12 Part 12.1; *Occupiers Liability Act 1985* (WA)).

The categories described above are no longer relevant to the fact that a duty of care may exist to the entrant upon premises, but they may remain important in determining the foreseeability of harm and the reasonability of prevention from harm. Trespassers, for example, are not likely to be foreseeable or easily planned for in prevention of harm, so one would not be expected to take the same care to prevent harm to them as one would in the case of invitees, who one knows will be entering. If an occupier is aware of the likelihood of trespassers (for example, children who play in the grounds of a hospital), the occupier's duty is more likely to be extended to include those persons (see for example *Edson v Roads & Traffic Authority* [2006] NSWCA 68, where the RTA was held liable to a child trespasser who crossed a freeway in circumstances where not long beforehand the RTA estimated that roughly 25,000 people per year crossed the freeway at the location where the accident occurred). In South Australia, legislation provides that an occupier owes no duty of care to a trespasser unless the presence of trespassers on the premises and their consequent exposure to danger was reasonably foreseeable and the nature and extent of the danger was such that measures should have been taken to alleviate the risk (*Civil Liability Act 1936* (SA), s 20(6)). In the Northern Territory an occupier of premises owes no duty of care to a person who enters the premises with the intention to commit an offence punishable by imprisonment (*Personal Injuries (Liability and Damages) Act* (NT), s 9). In Western Australia, the duty to a person entering premises with the intention of committing an offence is limited to a duty not to intentionally create a risk or act with reckless disregard (*Occupier's Liability Act 1985* (WA), s 5(3)).

The categories also help to determine who is an occupier for the purposes of the law (for example, if one invites a person on to premises for one's benefit, it would seem one becomes an occupier for the purposes of that person's visit).

An occupier does not have to warn of obvious risks (*Romeo v Conservation Commission of the Northern Territory* (1998) 192 CLR 431; [1998] HCA 5. This common law principle is now reinforced in civil liability legislation such as *Civil Liability Act 2002* (NSW), s 5G which provides:

> "(1) In determining liability for negligence, a person who suffers harm is presumed to have been aware of the risk of harm if it was an obvious risk, unless the person proves on the balance of probabilities that he or she was not aware of the risk.
>
> (2) For the purposes of this section, a person is aware of a risk if the person is aware of the type or kind of risk, even if the person is not aware of the precise nature, extent or manner of occurrence of the risk."

Community health carers and occupiers' rights

[11.265] The legal principles described above affect everyone, but are most relevant to community workers. The owner or anyone in legal occupation of premises (for example, a tenant or a friend using someone's home) has the right to control who is allowed on those premises. This means that anyone may be excluded from premises for any reason, unless they have a statutory right to enter, such as a police officer with a warrant. That is, the owner or occupier of property is entitled to enjoyment of that property to the exclusion of all others, unless permission is granted to others to enjoy its use as well (see for example *Goslin v Goslin* [1965] QWN 45 (SC Qld)). Health carers may be confronted by refusal of entry by an occupier where someone on the premises (for example, a sick or abused child) needs care. If the carer were asked to leave a premises by the occupier, then even though someone, be they the occupier or another person, needs care, he or she should consider doing so. Where there is concern that people may suffer as a result of such a request, and the health carer has no statutory right to remain, he or she should leave, seeking appropriate legal assistance for the provision of care for the person needing it.

Special factors for health facilities

[11.270] In considering occupier's liability where the premises are a health facility, the courts may take into account the special circumstances of patients. For example, a facility offering aged care may need to take special precautions against slip and trip accidents. A mental health facility may need to take special care to avoid opportunities for self-harm. A facility offering day procedures may need to exercise care to avoid discharging a patient in circumstances where they may not have recovered fully from sedation and may, therefore, be at greater risk of injury. (See however *Cole v South Tweed Rugby League Football Club Limited* (2004) 217 CLR 469; [2004] HCA 29.) In such circumstances there may of course be some overlap between occupier's liability per se, and professional negligence as described in Chapter 6 (see for example *John James Memorial Hospital Ltd v Keys* [1999] FCA 678).

References and Further Reading

Australian Health and Medical Law Reporter (CCH, Sydney, 1991, Looseleaf Service)

Castile, P, "Alternative Dispute Resolution in Workers' Compensation and People of Non-English Speaking Background in New South Wales" (1993) 1(2) *Torts Law Journal* 184-193

Comment, "Changes to Workers' Compensation" *Queensland Police Union Journal* March 1997, p 27

Halsbury's Laws of Australia (Butterworths, Sydney, Looseleaf Service)

Ison, T, "Promoting Excellence: National Consistency in Australian Workers' Compensation, 1996, Interim Report of the Heads of Workers' Compensation Authorities to the Labour Minister's Council" (1996) 4(3) *Torts Law Journal* 286-294

The Laws of Australia (Lawbook Co, Sydney, 1993, Looseleaf Service, and online service – 26. Labour Law and 33.3 Occupiers Liability)

Li, J, "OHS Lessons" *Health and Aged Care Law Update* April 2006 (Blake Dawson and Waldron Lawyers)

McGlone, F and Stickley, A, *Australian Torts Law* (Lexis Nexis Butterworths 2005)

Michael, R and Jenkins, H, "Work-Related Trauma: The Experience of Perioperative Nurses" (2001) 8(1) *Collegian* 19

Purse, K, "Common Law and Workers' Compensation in Australia", (2000) 13(3) *Australian Journal of Labour Law* 260-277

Staunton, P and Whyburn, R, *Nursing and the Law* (4th ed, Saunders, Sydney, 1997), ch 6

Trindad, F and Cane, P, *The Law of Torts in Australia* (OUP, 1999), ch 17

12

12 Registration & Practice

Registration overview

Disciplinary action

Unprofessional conduct & misconduct

chapter 12

Registration and Practice

Registration Overview

[12.05] As a citizen of the State, the health carer is, of course, subject to the laws of the land. However, the special occupation of health carer gives rise to legal considerations peculiar to that occupation. As with all major professions, such as law, medicine, and accountancy, the State establishes a mostly self-regulatory system which gives health care professions respectability in the eyes of the public, autonomy in establishing the standards and procedures they recognise as necessary for such respectability, and a means of disciplining members of the profession if they fall short of that standard. The State itself will step in and take over these functions where activities are considered to be a breach of the criminal law (see below, Chapter 14) or are challenged in court by an aggrieved individual as, for example, battery (Chapter 4) or negligence (Chapter 6).

The health professional and registration boards

[12.10] Each jurisdiction has legislation and facilities for registration and regulation of health workers (see Figure 12.1).

Figure 12.1: Registrable health professions

Health profession	Governing Acts	Jurisdictions in which registration is required
Medical practitioners	Health Professionals Act 2004 (ACT) and Health Professionals Regulation 2004 Sch 2 (ACT)# Medical Practice Act 1992 (NSW) Health Practitioners Act (NT)* Medical Practitioners Registration Act (Qld) 2001 Medical Practice Act 2004 (SA)	All

Health profession	Governing Acts	Jurisdictions in which registration is required
	Medical Practitioners Registration Act 1996 (Tas) Medical Practice Act 1994 (Vic) Medical Act 1894 (WA)	
Nurses	Health Professionals Act 2004 (ACT) and Health Professionals Regulation 2004 Sch 3 (ACT) # Nurses and Midwives Act 1991 (NSW) Health Professionals Act (NT) Nursing Act 1992 (Qld) Nurses Act 1999 (SA) Nursing Act 1995 (Tas) Nurses Act 1993 (Vic) Nurses Act 1992 (WA)	All
Chiropractors	Chiropractors and Osteopaths Act 1983 (ACT) Chiropractors Act 2001 (NSW) Health Practitioners Act (NT) Chiropractors Registration Act 2001 (Qld) Chiropractors Act 1991 (SA) ## Chiropractors and Osteopaths Registration Act 1997 (Tas) Chiropractors Registration Act 1996 (Vic) Chiropractors Act 1964 (WA)	All
Physiotherapists	Physiotherapists Registration Act 1977 (ACT) Physiotherapists Act 2001 (NSW) Physiotherapy Act 1964 (Qld) Health Practitioners Act (NT) Physiotherapists Act 1991 (SA)** Physiotherapists Registration Act 1999 (Tas) Physiotherapists Registration Act 1998 (Vic) Physiotherapists Act 1950 (WA)	All
Optometrists	Optometrists Act 1956 (ACT) Optometrists Act 2002 (NSW) Health Practitioners Act (NT) Optometrists Registration Act 2001 (Qld) Optometrists Act 1920 (SA) Optometrists Registration Act 1994 (Tas) Optometrists Registration Act 1996 (Vic) Optometrists Act 1940 (WA)	All
Psychologists	Psychologists Act 1994 (ACT) Psychologists Act 2001 (NSW) Health Practitioners Act (NT) Psychologists Registration Act 2001 (Qld) Psychological Practices Act 1973 (SA) Psychologists Registration Act 2000 (Tas) Psychologists Registration Act 2000 (Vic) Psychologists Registration Act 1976 (WA)	All

Health profession	Governing Acts	Jurisdictions in which registration is required
Pharmacists	Pharmacy Act 1931 (ACT) Pharmacy Act 1964 (NSW) Health Practitioners Act (NT) Pharmacists Registration Act 2001 (Qld) Pharmacists Act 1991 (SA) Pharmacists Registration Act 2001 (Tas) Pharmacy Practice Act 2004 (Vic) Pharmacy Act 1964 (WA)	All
Dentists	Dentists Act 1931 (ACT) Dental Practice Act 2001 (NSW) Health Practitioners Act (NT) Dental Practitioners Registration Act 2001 (Qld) Dental Practice Act 2001 (SA) Dental Practitioners Registration Act 2001 (Tas) Dental Practice Act 1999 (Vic) Dental Act 1939 (WA)	All
Aboriginal Health Workers	Health Practitioners Act (NT)	NT
Occupational Therapists	Health Practitioners Act (NT) Occupational Therapists Registration Act 2001 (Qld) Occupational Therapists Act 1974 (SA) ### Occupational Therapists Registration Act 1980 (WA)	NT Qld SA WA
Opticians	Optical Dispensers Act 1963 (NSW) Optometrists Act 1920 (SA) Optical Dispensers Act 1966 (WA)	NSW SA WA
Osteopaths	Chiropractors and Osteopaths Act 1983 (ACT) Osteopaths Act 2001 (NSW) Health Practitioners Act (NT) Osteopaths Registration Act 2001 (Qld) Chiropractors and Osteopaths Registration Act 1997 (Tas) Osteopaths Registration Act 1996 (Vic) Osteopaths Act 1997 (WA)	All except SA
Podiatrists	Podiatrists Act 1994 (ACT) Podiatrists Act 2003 (NSW) Podiatrists Registration Act 2001 (Qld) Chiropodists Act 1950 (SA) Podiatrists Registration Act 1995 (Tas) Podiatrists Registration Act 1997 (Vic) Podiatrists Registration Act 1984 (WA)	All except NT
Radiographers	Radiographers Act (NT) Medical Radiation Technologists Registration Act 2001 (Qld)	NT Qld

Health profession	Governing Acts	Jurisdictions in which registration is required
	Medical Radiation Science Professionals Registration Act 2000 (Tas)	Tas
	Health Act 1958 (Vic) and Health (Medical Radiation Technologists) Regulations 1997 (Vic)	Vic
Speech Pathologists	Speech Pathologists Regulation Act 2001 (Qld)	Qld

\#   At the time of writing, the *Health Professionals Act 2004* (ACT) is partially commenced. Schedule 1, items 2-11, and Schedules 5-12 of the accompanying *Health Professionals Regulation 2004* are awaiting commencement. Thus, the Act currently covers medical practitioners, nurses and midwives. Once the remaining provisions of the Regulations commence the Act will also cover: pharmacists; dentists, dental hygienists and dental therapists; psychologists; dental technicians and dental prosthetists; podiatrists; physiotherapists; optometrists; and veterinary surgeons.

\#\#   *Chiropractic and Osteopathy Practice Act* 2005 was assented to on 14 July 2005. At the time of writing, new Election Regulations were awaiting finalisation to allow for the appointment of a new Board and the formulation of General Regulations. Once this process is complete the Act will be proclaimed.

\#\#\# *Occupational Therapy Practice Act 2005* was assented to on 27 October 2005. At the time of writing, new Election Regulations were awaiting finalisation to allow for the appointment of a new Board and the formulation of General Regulations. Once this process is complete the Act will be proclaimed.

*   The *Health Practitioners Act* (NT) came into force on 23 February 2005, providing for the regulation of many health care professions under the one legislative instrument.

**   When proclaimed the *Physiotherapy Practice Act 2005* (SA) will replace the current *Physiotherapists Act 1991* (SA).

The legislation provides for registration of practitioners by an established statutory Registration Board or Council. Each Australian jurisdiction has its own standards, and although they are similar, one must meet the requirements of the jurisdiction before one is eligible to practice in it. In this chapter the term "Registration Board" or "Board" will be used to refer to the appropriate body.

Mutual recognition

[12.15] Until 1993 any registered health care professional intending to practise in another Australian jurisdiction had to apply to the appropriate body in the second jurisdiction in advance for registration. Registration was not automatic, and each case was treated on its merits, so application had to be made some time before the applicant could practise in the new jurisdiction. As the respective governments recognised the inefficiency of this approach, it was agreed to pass legislation providing for mutual recognition of registration between jurisdictions. The Commonwealth and all Australian jurisdictions have passed legislation giving effect to this principle (*Mutual Recognition Act 1992* (Cth); *Mutual Recognition (Australian Capital Territory) Act 1992* (ACT); *Mutual Recognition (New South Wales) Act 1992* (NSW); *Mutual Recognition (Northern Territory) Act* (NT); *Mutual Recognition (Queensland) Act 1992* (Qld); *Mutual Recognition (South Australia) Act 1993* (SA); *Mutual Recognition (Tasmania)*

Act 1993 (Tas); *Mutual Recognition (Victoria) Act 1998* (Vic); *Mutual Recognition (Western Australia) Act 2001* (WA) and *Medical Act 1894* (WA)). The *Mutual Recognition Act* in each jurisdiction allows health professionals registered in one jurisdiction to practise in another simply by giving notice, including evidence of registration, and paying the prescribed fee to the relevant authority. This, however, does not affect:

- the application of laws in the new jurisdiction to the health professional and her or his practice in that jurisdiction; or
- the powers of the relevant Board in the new jurisdiction to regulate the conduct of the health care professional in respect of her or his practice in that jurisdiction.

Cancellation of a practising certificate in the first jurisdiction will have the effect of cancelling the certificate in the subsequent jurisdiction (see *Mutual Recognition Act 1992* (Cth), s 33(1)).

All jurisdictions except Western Australia also have legislation (called *Trans-Tasman Mutual Recognition Acts)* that provide for inter-country recognition of registration between Australia and New Zealand.

Function and powers of registration boards

[12.20] Although legislation varies throughout the country, there is much similarity in the general model of registration legislation. The Registration Boards generally have the following features and powers.

Composition

[12.25] Registration Boards are composed of members appointed by government and representative bodies, as well as members elected by the profession. This is to achieve an experienced and balanced body which can adequately deal with the many interests, functions and concerns of the health care profession. Some jurisdictions require at least one medical practitioner on the Registration Boards of some professions, such as those for nurses, which could be considered to be a cautious approach to self-regulation by that profession, but perhaps encourages inter-disciplinary consistency and exchange.

Education and research

[12.30] Registration Boards set the standard of education and practice (for example, the amount of clinical practice, prescription of exams, minimum age for acceptance), for the different classes of practitioners. They may set and recognise curricula, approve teaching programmes by granting recognition to universities, hospitals and/or other teaching institutions offering courses in health care, and the awards and qualifications they grant. The Registration Board may grant exemptions in some cases from requirements or conditions otherwise applying.

Registration Boards may have additional powers to carry out research into their particular profession and aspects of practice, to consult with bodies concerned with the use and employment of practitioners, to advise the government on matters relevant to the profession, to establish different branches of the profession, to develop a code of practice, and to authorise reports on, or disseminate information to, the profession.

Registration

[12.35] The Registration Boards maintain a register of those who have qualified for registration, with different registers for different branches of practice; for example, different specialties, such as "general", "mental health" and "enrolled" nurses. It may also register membership of specialist colleges; for example, fellows of Medical Colleges of paediatrics, psychology or gynaecology. The Boards maintain these registers, and practitioners must renew their registration regularly, mostly annually. One can only practise in an Australian jurisdiction in which one is registered or enrolled.

In theory there is no law specifically prohibiting a person from carrying out the functions of some health carers, for example, those of a qualified nurse or enrolled nurse, without registration. The law does contain some prohibitions, for example, it prohibits practising as a registered nurse or holding oneself out to be a registered nurse without registration. The purpose of registration is to maintain an acceptable standard within the profession, and patients must not be misled as to whether their health carer has met the requirements of the jurisdiction.

Each Registration Board determines the mode of application and requirements for registration, and all jurisdictions require regular renewal of registration by payment of a fee. A function not required but generally carried out by the Registration Board is the gathering of information through statistical data with regard to the number and characteristics of those registered.

Applicant must be of good health and character

[12.40] As well as educational qualifications, one of the requirements for registration as a registered health care practitioner is that the registrant be of good health and character. This is usually established by requiring certification from appropriate persons as to the applicant's state of health or character, such as a doctor's certificate, a reference from an employer or teacher, etc. This sets an additional personal (as opposed to a professional) standard for those entrusted with the care of the sick.

Temporary and "special events" registration

[12.45] Temporary or provisional registration may be available for exceptional cases, such as those from overseas jurisdictions who are visiting for purposes of research or teaching, or where the Registration Board determines that provisions should attach to registration. The details will differ between Australian jurisdictions.

In all jurisdictions except the Northern Territory there are procedures for authorising visiting health professionals to provide health care services to visitors for special events, such as sporting events (for example, the Olympics and Paralympics) or conferences (*Health Professionals (Special Events Exemptions) Act 2000* (ACT); *Health Professionals (Special Events Exemptions) Act 1997* (NSW); *Health Professionals (Special Events Exemptions) Act 1998* (Qld); *Health Professionals (Special Events Exemptions) Act 2000* (SA); *Health Professionals (Special Events Exemptions) Act 1998* (Tas); *Health Practitioners (Special Events Exemptions) Act 1999* (Vic); *Health Professionals (Special Events Exemptions) Act 2000* (WA)). The authorisation can include issuing prescriptions and processing or supplying certain drugs and substances. The Minister responsible may make a declaration that an event or class of events is a "special event" for the purposes of the legislation and set the period for which the authorisation is to have effect. Visiting health professionals are required to notify the stipulated authorities of their intention to provide the services and to comply with the law of the visited jurisdiction, along with any conditions placed on the authorisation.

Conditional registration

[12.50] Registration may be conditional where the applicant belongs to a particular group (for example, graduate medical practitioners who are undertaking postgraduate training approved by the Board) or where the applicant is suffering from impairment, requiring the imposition of a condition in the interests of professional integrity and patient safety.

Registration of nurse practitioners

[12.55] In recent years there has been recognition of the expansion of nursing practice through the registration of nurse practitioners. Most Australian juris-dictions are moving towards provision for expanded responsibilities and practices of nurses. New South Wales and Victoria were the first States to pass legislation to bring this into effect. A brief outline of the relevant provisions in those two States follows. The Australian Capital Territory (*Health Act 1993* (ACT), s 37B and *Health Regulation 2004*) and Western Australia (*Nurses Act 1992*) now also recognise and register nurse practitioners.

New South Wales

[12.60] The *Nurses and Midwives Act 1991* (NSW) was amended by the *Nurses Amendment (Nurse Practitioners) Act 1998* to do several things, including:

1) **Providing for the Nurses Registration Board to authorise registered nurses to practise as nurse practitioners.** Such authorisation is to be given only if the Board is satisfied that the person has sufficient qualifica-tions and experience to practise as a nurse practitioner (s 19A). A certificate of authorisation is to be issued to the nurse practitioner (s 17). Provision is also made for the issue of temporary authorisations (s 24). If an application for authorisation to practise as a nurse practitioner is refused, the applicant will be able to appeal against the determination (s 32(1)).

2) **Authorising the Board to carry out functions in relation to nurse practitioners,** such as setting requirements or conditions relating to authorisation to practise as a nurse practitioner (s 10). These are similar to the functions of the Board in relation to authorised midwives. Section 10 of the Act also allows the Board to recognise different areas of practice as a nurse practitioner.

3) **Allowing the Director-General of the Department of Health to approve guidelines relating to such functions of nurse practitioners as considered appropriate** (s 78A). These guidelines may make provision for the possession, use, supply and prescription of certain substances by nurse practitioners (note that a poison or restricted substance is a substance specified in the Poisons List under the *Poisons and Therapeutic Goods Act 1966* (NSW), but does not include a drug of addiction). The guidelines may specify the types of substances and the circumstances in which they may be possessed, used, supplied or prescribed. Contravention of these guidelines is not an offence but may constitute professional misconduct or unsatisfactory professional conduct.

Similar provisions to those applying to nursing practice in general apply in relation to nurse practitioners regarding such matters as:

- offences such as falsely claiming to be, or indicating that one is, a nurse practitioner, false statements in applying for registration as a nurse practitioner, etc; and
- suspension and cancellation of authorisation to practise as a nurse practitioner.

The *Poisons and Therapeutic Goods Act 1966* (NSW) allows the Director-General of the Department of Health to authorise a nurse practitioner, or class of nurse practitioners, to possess, use, supply or prescribe any poison or restricted substance (other than a drug of addiction) in accordance with the guidelines approved by the Director-General. A *poison* is a substance specified in Schedules 1, 2, 3, 5, 6 or 7 of the Poisons List. A *restricted substance* is a substance specified in Schedule 4 of the Poisons List.

A nurse practitioner who is authorised by the Director-General to possess, use, supply or prescribe a substance is not guilty of offences under the *Poisons and Therapeutic Goods Act 1966* (NSW) that relate to the authorised activities. Also, those who supply or possess, a poison or restricted substance in accordance with the prescription of a nurse practitioner, are exempted from the relevant offences under the Act (ss 10, 16).

Victoria

[12.65] The impetus for provision for nurse practitioners in Victoria came in July 1998, when the Victorian Nurse Practitioners Task Force issued a report on the provision for nurse practitioners. Amendments to the *Nurses Act 1993* were effected by the *Nurses Amendment Act 2000*. The amendments:

1) **Give authority to the Nurses Board of Victoria to establish categories of nurse practitioner for endorsement of registration certificates.** The

Board can then endorse already registered nurses to practise as nurse practitioners in nominated categories where they have satisfactorily completed a course of study and clinical experience that qualifies them to use the title "nurse practitioner" (s 8B). Different categories of nurse practitioner are established, and the Board may impose restrictions or conditions of the licence. Refusal to endorse a licence may be appealed to the Victorian Civil and Administrative Tribunal (VCAT) (s 58).

2) **Give authority to the Board to accredit courses of study and define clinical skills and experience required for each category of nurse practitioner (s 66).** These guidelines relate to the clinical assessment, management, evaluation and the obtaining, possessing, using, selling or supplying of drugs applicable to the category of practice.

3) **Give authority to the Board to authorise nurse practitioners to possess, use, supply and prescribe any Schedule 2, 3, 4 or 8 drug (s 8B(2)).** (See further **[13.15]**). This also involves amendments to the *Drugs, Poisons and Controlled Substances Act 1981*. The authorisation in relation to the possession, use, supply and prescription of these drugs is dependent upon the Board's approval of guidelines relating to the particular category of nurse practitioner. Those practitioners are subject to legislation prohibiting prescribing or administering a Schedule 8 poison to a person who is a drug dependent person.

4) **Require the board to establish a nurse practitioner advisory committee (s 79).** The Board is to have regard to the advice given by this committee in relation to all the functions the Board possesses in relation to the role of the nurse practitioner.

In respect of offences, cancellation and suspension, discipline etc, the provisions applying to nurses in general apply to nurse practitioners.

Appeals

[12.70] Those who are refused registration may appeal in all jurisdictions for review of the Registration Board's decision. Generally, however, the Registration Board may hold its own hearing into the matter, giving applicants an opportunity to put their case to it. If it still refuses to register the applicant or provide the type of registration sought, it must provide a written explanation of its reasons, and the applicant has the right to appeal to a court or an independent tribunal. For example, nurses may appeal as follows:

- **Australian Capital Territory:** To the Tribunal within 28 days of refusal (ss 46 and 47).
- **New South Wales:** To the Tribunal within 28 days of refusal (s 32).
- **Northern Territory:** To the Supreme Court within fourteen days of refusal (s 99).
- **Queensland:** To the District Court within 28 days of refusal (s 137).
- **South Australia:** To the Supreme Court within two months of refusal (s 49).
- **Tasmania:** To the Supreme Court within 14 days of refusal (s 72).

- **Victoria:** To the Victorian Civil and Administrative Tribunal (VCAT) within 28 days of the refusal (s 58).
- **Western Australia:** To a magistrate of the Local Court within one month of refusal (s 78).

In each case the court or tribunal may re-hear the case and, with the exception of South Australia (where it may remit the matter to the Registration Board for reconsideration), make a decision which upholds the Registration Board's decision, reverses it, or in some cases varies the Registration Board's decision. This decision is binding on the relevant Registration Board. The precise powers of the court or tribunal and the type of order it can make differ between the jurisdictions. Advice on how to appeal, such as which documents to file, should be sought from the appeal body involved, from a lawyer (or legal aid office) or one's union.

Disciplinary Action

Suspension or cancellation of registration

[12.75] All jurisdictions empower Registration Boards to carry out inquiries into complaints against practitioners for behaviour or practice which falls below standards generally established for professional practice. For medical practitioners and others, the Board may liaise with the Health Care Complaints Commission (or equivalent) on the best way to deal with the matter. The Board may be empowered to establish a special committee or tribunal to consider cases of alleged misconduct. The precise nature of the proceedings varies, with the Board setting its own methods of inquiry. However, in some circumstances there may be a power to summon witnesses and subpoena documents. Any investigation by the Board or its committee must not deprive the applicant of natural justice, that is, proper notice of the nature of the complaint, and the opportunity to present an adequate defence (see *Howden v City of Wittlesea* at **[10.125]**).

It is important to note that the primary intention of disciplinary proceedings carried out under registration legislation is neither to punish those involved (the function of criminal law), nor to compensate those harmed (the function of civil law). The primary intention of disciplinary procedures is the protection of the public, and the maintenance of standards within the profession.

Grounds for suspension or cancellation of registration

[12.80] The wording of the legislation varies between jurisdictions, but the following is a guide to those activities which will attract disciplinary action and may result in cancellation or suspension of registration:

- mental or physical incapacity;
- professional misconduct;
- alcohol or drug addiction;

- ceasing to hold or having qualifications withdrawn;
- conviction for a criminal offence;
- committing an offence against the registration legislation;
- making a false statement for registration;
- failing to comply with a lawful requirement of the Board.

Lack of mental or physical fitness

[12.85] A Board may inquire into the mental or physical fitness of a person to practise. He or she may be suffering from impaired mental or physical health which is considered likely to detrimentally affect his or her ability to practise competently. A case that considered an applicant's level of fitness, and the requirements for natural justice follows.

[12.90] **Case:** *R v Medical Council of Tasmania; Ex parte Blackburn* (26 February 1998, SC Tas, No M66/1997) (*Australian Health and Medical Law Reporter* ¶3-920)

The applicant was a 78-year-old doctor who was denied renewal of his practising certificate on the ground of lack of mental fitness to practise. It was alleged that, among other things, he was responsible for inappropriately prescribing anorectic stimulants, benzodiazepines and drugs of abuse. The Medical Council of Tasmania interviewed the applicant, who appeared unrepresented, and asked him a series of questions about medical practice, providing him with the appropriate answers if he was wrong. He was then asked if he had any questions and he said he did not. The Council produced a report that was unfavourable to him. This report, as well as other documentation was not made available to the applicant, and he was denied an opportunity to make further submissions to the Council. He was sent a letter stating that he was not permitted to renew his registration due to lack of mental capacity and skill, and told he could appeal to the Supreme Court.

[12.95] The Court held that the applicant was entitled to the exercise of the principles of natural justice. This was denied to him by the Council having the documents in their possession without the contents being disclosed to him, and without his being allowed the opportunity to respond or make submissions in relation to them. This resulted in a real risk of prejudice to the applicant. The Court ordered that the Council's decision to refuse renewal of the certificate be quashed.

Addiction to, dependence on, or overuse of drugs or alcohol can be a manifestation of lack of capacity to practise.

Unprofessional conduct or misconduct

[12.100] These concepts have been named and interpreted in different ways in most jurisdictions. They range from including an unsatisfactory standard of care to culpable behaviour, and are quite extensive in some jurisdictions. To give an idea of the different approaches, an outline of the main features of each jurisdiction for medical practitioners and nurses follows:

New South Wales

[12.105] For medical practitioners, "unsatisfactory professional conduct" includes:

- any conduct that demonstrates that the skill, knowledge, judgment or care of the practitioner is significantly below the standard reasonably expected of a practitioner of an equivalent level of training or experience;
- contravention of the Act or regulations;
- contravention of a condition of registration
- conviction under specified statutory provisions;
- failure to provide records to the Commission in accordance with the *Health Care Complaints Act 1993*;
- accepting or offering benefits in relation to referring patients or recommending products, and failing to disclose any pecuniary interests in referring a patient or recommending a product;
- over-servicing (providing a service that is "unnecessary, not reasonably required, or excessive");
- being involved in practice by unregistered persons;
- refusal or failure, without reasonable excuse, to render professional services within a reasonable time to someone requiring urgent attention, or to ensure someone else provides such services; or
- other "improper or unethical conduct" (*Medical Practice Act 1992* (NSW), s 36).

"Professional misconduct" is defined as unsatisfactory professional conduct which is of a sufficiently serious nature to justify suspension of the practitioner from practising medicine or the removal of the doctor's name from the register (*Medical Practice Act 1992* (NSW), s 37).

For nurses, "unsatisfactory professional conduct" is defined as:

- any conduct that demonstrates the knowledge, experience, skill, judgment or care of a nurse is significantly below the standard reasonably expected of a nurse of equivalent level of training and experience;
- contravention of a provision of the Act or its regulations, or a condition of registration;
- failure without reasonable excuse to comply with a direction of the Board to provide information with respect to a complaint under the Act;
- failure to provide the Commission with records pursuant to the *Health Care Complaints Act*;
- any other improper or unethical conduct relating to the practice of nursing (*Nurses and Midwives Act 1991* (NSW), s 4).

"Professional misconduct" is defined as unsatisfactory professional conduct which is of a sufficiently serious nature to justify the removal of the nurse's name from the register (*Nurses and Midwives Act 1991* (NSW), s 4).

Queensland

[12.110] The *Health Practitioners (Professional Standards) Act 1999*, which applies to both nurses and doctors, defines "unsatisfactory professional conduct". This includes:

- professional conduct of a lesser standard than might reasonably be expected by the public or the person's peers
- incompetence, lack of knowledge, judgment, care or skill;
- infamous conduct in a professional respect
- misconduct in a professional respect;
- conduct discreditable to the medical/nursing profession;
- over-servicing;
- influencing or attempting to influence another medical practitioner/nurse in a way that might compromise patient care;
- fraudulent or dishonest behaviour in the registrant's practice.

South Australia

[12.115] For medical practitioners the law provides that "unprofessional conduct" includes:

- improper or unethical conduct;
- incompetence or negligence in the provision of medical treatment;
- contravention of the registration legislation or a code of conduct or professional standard endorsed by the Board; and
- conduct that constitutes an offence punishable by imprisonment of one year or more.
- Unprofessional conduct committed before the commencement of the Act or within or outside South Australia or the Commonwealth is included (*Medical Practice Act 2004* (SA), s 3).

The definition is largely the same for nurses with two differences: a contravention or failure to comply with a condition imposed on registration or enrolment is included as unsatisfactory professional misconduct, however conduct that constitutes an offence punishable by imprisonment for one year or more is not included in the definition (*Nurses Act 1999* (SA), s 3).

Tasmania

[12.120] For medical practitioners "professional misconduct" will include:

- contravening the registration legislation, a condition of registration, or a foreign medical law;
- failure to comply with a requirement of the Board;
- failure to pay on time a fine, costs or expenses imposed by the Act;

- incompetence;
- deceptive or misleading conduct;
- conduct capable of bringing the profession into disrepute;
- fraud;
- practising while suspended; and
- trying by means of threat or inducement to prevent a complaint against them (*Medical Practitioners Registration Act 1996* (Tas), s 45).

A nurse will be guilty of "professional misconduct" where they:

- contravene the registration legislation, a foreign nursing law, a provision of the Nursing Code, an authorisation, or a condition of registration or enrolment;
- fail to pay a fine imposed on them under the Act;
- fail to honour an undertaking given to the Board or tribunal;
- are negligent or incompetent in nursing practice; or
- behave in a fraudulent or dishonest manner in nursing practice (*Nursing Act 1995* (Tas), s 56).

Victoria

[12.125] The definition for medical practitioners and nurses of "unprofessional conduct" is substantially the same and includes:

- professional conduct of a lesser standard than would reasonably be expected of a practitioner, or by one's peers or the public;
- influencing or attempting to influence the conduct of a medical practice in such a way that patient care may be compromised;
- failure to act when required to do so under an Act or regulation;
- a finding of guilt of an indictable offence, other specified offences, an offence which is likely to affect ability to practice, or an offence under the Act;
- contravention or failure to comply with a condition of registration;
- breach of an agreement with the Board;
- professional misconduct or infamous conduct in a professional respect;
- over-servicing, that is, providing a service that is "unnecessary, not reasonably required, or excessive";
- "unsatisfactory professional performance" (that is, professional performance which is of a lesser standard than that which the person's professional peers might reasonably expect) (doctors only) (*Medical Practice Act 1994* (Vic), s 3; *Nurses Act 1993* (Vic), s 3).

Western Australia and Australian Capital Territory

[12.130] The legislation in Western Australia and the Australian Capital Territory contains no definition for professional misconduct or unsatisfactory professional misconduct (*Medical Act 1894* (WA); *Nurses Act 1992* (WA); *Health Professionals Act 2004* (ACT)).

Northern Territory

[12.135] A health practitioner is guilty of professional misconduct if the health practitioner:

- contravenes the Act, a foreign health care policy, a code of practice authorised by the person's category of registration or enrolment, a condition or registration or enrolment, or a condition of authorisation;
- practises without a practising certificate;
- practises in a restricted area without authorisation;
- fails to pay on time a fine imposed by the Act;
- fails to honour an undertaking made to the board or tribunal;
- is negligent or incompetent;
- behaves fraudulently or dishonestly in health care practice (*Health Practitioners Act* (NT), s 56.

Other health care professions

[12.140] Specific provisions of legislation covering other health care professions are not considered in detail here. They are similar in principle and effect to the above, but health carers are encouraged to review the legislation that covers their profession in their jurisdiction.

Unprofessional Conduct or Misconduct in a Professional Sense

[12.145] The following cases and discussion explores types of behaviour the various courts and tribunals have considered unprofessional misconduct or misconduct in a professional sense.

Provision of drugs of addiction

[12.150] Case: *Re the Medical Practice Act 1992 and Dr Ghalib Mohammad Talib HAMAD* [2004] NSWMT 4

The Health Care Complaints Commission ("HCCC") alleged Dr H was guilty of unsatisfactory professional conduct or professional misconduct and requested that he be reprimanded. The particulars of the complaint were that he had, between 1997 and 1998:

(i) prescribed drugs of addiction (pethidine and morphine) to a number of patients in quantities in excess of recognised therapeutic standards as to what was appropriate in the circumstances;

(ii) in contravention of the *Poisons and Therapeutic Goods Act 1966*, he failed to:

a) apply for and obtain an authorisation to prescribe pethidine for continuous use for periods exceeding two months;
b) keep a drugs register;
c) ensure that the quantities of pethidine and morphine in his possession were stored in a sufficiently secure and safe receptacle.

[12.155] H conceded the factual basis for the complaint with the exception that he prescribed pethidine for "continuous therapeutic use ... for a period exceeding two months".

The Tribunal considered that H's prescribing and recording of drugs he administered and kept was, during the period which the complaint referred to, well below the standard of conduct of a competent medical practitioner and constituted professional misconduct. H was reprimanded and ordered to undergo a course operated by the Pharmaceutical Services Branch of the New South Wales Department of Health. The Tribunal did not consider suspension from practice was warranted as considerable time had elapsed between the events in question and the hearing and in the interim H had taken significant steps to prevent repetition of the causes of the complaint.

Surgery carried out in non-orthodox fashion

[12.160] Surgery carried out in non-orthodox fashion has had different reactions according to its acceptance by the medical profession.

[12.165] Case: *Ex parte Meehan; Re Medical Practitioners Act* [1965] NSWR 30 (SC)

A doctor carried out major elective surgery without the presence of another practitioner to assist with surgical procedures or to administer anaesthetics. No harm occurred to the patients, but his behaviour was found to be misconduct and he was suspended for 12 months. He appealed to the New South Wales Court of Appeal.

[12.170] The Court of Appeal decided that the doctor had been ill-advised but neither reckless nor indifferent to the patient's welfare. The Court reduced the suspension to a reprimand, because it was convinced the doctor would not repeat the conduct. It agreed that this behaviour was, however, misconduct:

"the only generalisation as to the meaning ... of 'infamous conduct in any professional respect' [the wording of the relevant legislation] which can be attempted as capable of application to the varying situations which may arise, is that it refers to conduct which, being sufficiently related to the pursuit of the profession, is such as would reasonably incur the strong reprobation of professional brethren of good repute and competence" [at 35, per Sugarman J].

However, a later case held that a doctor who carried out a non-urgent appendicectomy in a day surgery where there was no proper operating table, no operating theatre lights or recovery room was not guilty of professional misconduct, as there was a small but respectable minority view that such operations are acceptable (*Qidwai v Brown* [1984] 1 NSWLR 100).

In *Medical Board of Queensland v Bayliss* (6 & 8 February 1995, Queensland Medical Assessment Tribunal, No 10 of 1995), a doctor was found guilty of misconduct in a professional respect for failing to provide oxygen and a pulse oximeter and proper monitoring (including no recovery staff) in a clinic where general anaesthetics were administered. It was found that a patient fell into a coma and subsequent persistent vegetative state as a result of this.

Intimate relations with patients or past patients

[12.175] The following cases deal with intimate relations between practitioners and patients or ex-patients.

[12.180] Case: *Childs v Walton* (13 November 1990, CA NSW)

A psychiatrist engaged in sexual relationships with two former patients. She also disclosed confidential information to one of them. Her name was removed from the register by the New South Wales Medical Board and she appealed to the Court of Appeal, arguing that as the men were former patients, there was no misconduct "in the practice of medicine" as required by the legislation.

[12.185] The Court of Appeal held that the words "in the practice of medicine" do not describe the time at which the conduct occurs, but rather the nature of the conduct.

[12.190] Case: *Jacobsen v Nurses Tribunal and Anor* (3 October 1997, SC NSW, No BC9705032)

J, a registered mental health nurse and member of the Hunter Area Health Service's Rehabilitation Scheme, became the case manager of ZD, a woman variously diagnosed as schizophrenic and manic depressive, and a patient of the Residential Rehabilitation Team with which he worked. ZD's marriage had broken down and her five children were living with their father. She was anxious to have them move back with her, and, as J had space in his house, it was decided that ZD and two of her children would move into it as boarders, and he would cease to be her case manager. At this time it was found that J had no intention of having a personal relationship with her, but rather that he had a financial interest in her moving in and paying reasonable rent. It was also considered of benefit to her to have her children with her. ZD moved in about three weeks after another person was appointed case manager. J arranged for a new case manager without explanation and no reference was made to the fact that ZD's address was to be the same as J's. Some time afterwards, J's superiors in the Area Health Service expressed their opinion that it was inappropriate that ZD remain in the premises, and several months after moving in ZD, who was no longer a patient of the Residential Rehabilitation Team, left the house. Three months later, after frequent contact, J and ZD commenced a sexual relationship which lasted seven months.

The Tribunal found the plaintiff guilty of unsatisfactory professional conduct because:

- he invited or permitted ZD to reside in his home and subsequently engaged in an intimate relationship with her without adequate termination of the professional relationship between them; and
- he ended a formal professional relationship with a patient when about to be engaged in a personal relationship, demonstrating a lack of adequate knowledge in the practice of nursing.

The Tribunal held that forming a close personal, emotional and later sexual relationship with a patient against the advice of his colleagues and superiors was of a particularly serious nature, offended against the foundations of the nurse/patient relationship and amounted to professional misconduct.

J appealed to the Supreme Court on procedural matters, on the basis that no, or inadequate, reasons were given for the finding and that the penalty was excessive.

[12.195] The Court found J was aware that ZD was suffering various mental disorders which rendered her vulnerable and liable to be exploited and hurt. J fostered the relationship, and the transfer of her case to another case manager did not effectively terminate his power and influence over her. He still had all the confidential information he had gained about her case, and it was implicit that he would still assist in and be at least partly involved in her care and rehabilitation. The Court found it immaterial that ZD was no longer a patient of the Health Service: if she became ill again, she could again become a patient. The Court concluded that the conduct was of a particularly serious nature and "offended against the foundations of the nurse/patient relationship". This was of itself enough to take it out of the category of "unsatisfactory professional conduct" into that of "professional misconduct". However, given J's excellent record, his lack of intent to do harm, and lack of adequate advice and supervision, the Court reduced the period of removal of his name from the Register to 6 rather than 12 months.

The Court several times emphasised that the Tribunal's role is primarily protection of the public, not one of punishment. It also confirmed the principle that, whilst the practitioner is entitled to have allegations against him or her specifically identified in dealing with professional conduct, individual charges do not have to be made out specifically in the same way as they do in criminal law: a person may be charged with a course of conduct in the carrying out of a course of practice, so long as the separate allegations on which the charge against him or her is based are specifically identified.

Failure to properly assess and treat injuries to child

[12.200] Case: *Medical Board of South Australia v Christpoulos* (2000) SADC 47 (*Australian Health and Medical Law Reporter* ¶4-020.41)

A mother called the locum doctor when she noticed her child had red and bruised penis when changing his nappy, thinking he may have been bitten by a spider or some other creature. The defendant attended at her residence, and the mother alleged he looked at the naked child, said that his penis was bruised, said it looked as if the child had been hit, pinched or punched, prescribed panadol and left a few minutes later. Several days later the child was admitted to hospital unconscious, with bruises to the head, bilateral corneal abrasions and bruises around and to the penis. He died of cerebral anoxia. A man was later convicted of manslaughter in relation to the death.

In later investigations, the doctor told police the child was naked at the time of examination, and had a small bruise of one centimetre to the thigh only. He also stated that he could not find his consultation notes, which were normally stored in the boot of his car, or removed to his parents' garage.

When the Board was dealing with his matter 12 months later, the doctor "corrected" his initial statement, saying that the child was wearing a nappy at the time of examination and he did not remove it, or examine the child's groin or testicles, and that nothing would have warranted suspecting child abuse (however he later admitted he could not dispute the mother's account of events).

The doctor was charged with:
1) knowingly making inconsistent, false and misleading statements;
2) failing to carry out a proper examination of the child;
3) failing to keep proper notes;

4) failing to consider non-accidental injury and make further inquiries; and

5) failing to report suspected child abuse to authorities, as required by South Australian legislation (see Chapter 16).

[12.205] The Medical Practitioners Professional Conduct Tribunal found that, in respect of (1), the practitioner did not intentionally mislead the Tribunal in his revised statement. As he did not have his notes when he gave his statement to the police or later when he revised it, he rationalised the situation when he found out about the severity of the later injuries, and constructed a reason as to why he missed seeing the gross injuries to the child's penile area. However, his approach to presenting as unqualified fact what was in reality supposition was careless, and he should have been more sure of the accuracy of what he was reporting. His actions were improper and unethical.

As to the charges (2) to (5), the doctor was also guilty of unprofessional conduct. His examination of the child was perfunctory and below the standard expected of a medical practitioner. Given that, according to the mother, he recognised that the child had been assaulted, he should have made further inquiries and considered reporting the matter to authorities as required by law.

All circumstances must be taken into account

[12.210] In determining whether conduct warrants disciplinary action, all the circumstances of the case must be taken into account.

[12.215] Case: *Heathcote v New South Wales Nurses Board* (unreported, 12 April 1991, Dist Ct NSW)

On the night of 24 June 1987, at 2.10 am, a patient was brought to Wilcannia Hospital by his relatives. He was described as being "in the dings", a colloquial term meaning suffering from alcohol withdrawal. He was hallucinating, but as he had no signs of tremor, vomiting, or sweating, or feeling hot or cold, nor was he complaining of any head or chest pain, the charge nurse, H, decided he was not seriously ill. She checked his history and found he had previously been admitted for alcohol withdrawal.

The patient, confused and vague, wandered around the premises and disappeared temporarily, returning with wood to boil the billy for tea. Nurse Heathcote had rung the police because she feared for the patient's well being when he disappeared. He disappeared a second time, and so H rang the Director of Nursing at her home and told her about her concerns for the patient's safety. The Director of Nursing agreed with her contacting the police.

The police arrived soon after with the patient in their "paddy wagon", and in their presence H rang the medical officer of the

Royal Flying Doctor Service at Broken Hill and discussed the situation with him. She stated her concern that she could not ensure the safety of the patient in his present condition, as she had no adequate means of restraining him. She explained his condition and suggested he remain in police custody overnight. The doctor agreed, saying that the only other thing she should do "before he heads off to the police station is just do his sugar ... And wish him well as he goes away".

After a blood sugar test, which was normal, was carried out, H arranged with the police that they should let her know how the patient settled at the Police Station. She undertook to call in at 8.30 am to take his blood pressure. At 3 am the police reported that the patient was "sleeping", but at 8.30 am when she called at the Station, they informed her that he was dead, having hanged himself.

Subsequently, a complaint was made to the New South Wales Nurses Registration Board under s 19 of the *Nurses Registration Act 1953* (NSW) which was then in force. H was found guilty of misconduct by the Board, which suspended her registration for one year. Specifically, it alleged that she had:

1) failed to follow the Hospital Manual, which required staff to "obtain all relevant facts about a patient before calling the doctor";
2) failed to take and record basic observations;
3) failed to consult the patient's history and inform the doctor of it;
4) failed to obtain a proper history from the patient and his friends;
5) failed to tell the doctor her diagnosis or the results of her observations;
6) given the patient over to police, and failed to consider alternative action;
7) failed to consider the suitability of police custody and to advise them of necessary precautions and observations; and
8) failed to ask police to stay at the hospital for carrying out of (1), (2) and (3).

She appealed to the District Court as provided by the former Act, arguing that under the circumstances she had acted ethically and with all due care.

[12.220] The District Court overturned the finding of the Board, thus exonerating H's care of the patient. Ward J in his judgment stated that conduct cannot always be assessed in abstract terms and by consideration of text book or teaching utterances. It must be considered in the light of the circumstances existing at the time, including available facilities, misunderstandings, and "aberrant human behaviour". He went on to say that the question to which the Board must address itself is, "does the conduct of the nurse incur the strong reprobation of professional peers of good repute and competence?"

The Court held that H did make a proper systematic assessment within the limits of what was available to her in terms of co-operation by the patient, the amount of time available to her, and within the scale of priorities she faced at the time. She was trying, by observation, to find the cause of the patient's condition and was faced with some difficulty as he was "wandering uncontrollably". She did make and record adequate observations under the circumstances. She was faced with a novel situation, did not know what to do, and sought assistance from the Director of Nursing and the doctor.

The Court further held that H did read the history and inform the doctor of it. No further information had been sought by the doctor. Also there was strong argument before the Court that medical diagnosis is not part of a nurses' practice. H did state her opinion that the patient was "in the dings", and the doctor did not indicate that he did not understand that expression. However the doctor was not entitled to rely on her diagnosis. One witness did suggest that H should have insisted on either the doctor coming to see the patient or his being sent to another hospital with better facilities. The Court nevertheless decided that "It is not sufficient for some peers merely to express criticisms of judgments when other judgments are properly open in the circumstances" and relied on the fact that "there was a strong body of opinion that none of her conduct was such as to incur the strong reprobation of her professional peers of good repute and competence".

Ward J went on to say H did not have a duty to determine the suitability of the police custody and noted that she did ask the police to report to her, and arranged to check on the patient in the morning. Finally, he held that there was no obligation to consider alternative treatment, as the doctor had directed she "only" test the patient's blood and "wish him well as he goes away".

Ward J pointed out (at 21) of the decision, it is also necessary to take into account the fact that:

> "conduct cannot be always assessed in the abstract. It must be evaluated in the light of the exigencies existing due to factors which so often include aberrant human behaviour, insufficient facilities and misunderstandings due to language use. It is important the Board directs its attention in relation to consideration of professional misconduct to the question—does the conduct of the nurse incur the strong reprobation of professional peers of good repute and competence?—and that it recognises that what may appear initially to be misconduct will not necessarily be deemed so, if it is considered to be acceptable by a reputable minority view. The test is not met by merely finding contentious areas of criticism, often founded on abstract conceptions without consideration of existing unusual circumstances."

Meaning of "in the practice of medicine, nursing", etc

[12.225]   Sometimes the question arises as to whether the actions complained of took place in the practice of the professional's practice.

[12.230] Case: *Kahler v Nurses Registration Board and Anor* (21 February 1995, SC NSW, BC9504318)

K was a registered nurse administrator and supervisor of a hostel complex for ex-service personnel. A resident of the hostel, Mr G, who suffered from dementia, had been authorised for transfer from the hostel to a nursing home in the complex after his condition deteriorated and he was recognised as requiring the more specialised and intensive nursing care available at the nursing home. K failed to arrange for the transfer for several months. As a result Mr G did not receive necessary care, and on admission to the home was found to be in a serious condition, suffering from dehydration and multiple bedsores and lesions resulting from lack of proper care and treatment. The Nurses Tribunal directed that K's name be removed from the Register, finding that she failed to arrange for Mr G to be transferred to the nursing home after approval had been granted, and when Mr G's condition deteriorated over a period of over two months, she failed to ensure that he receive proper nursing care. These failures, the Tribunal said, were serious and fundamental in nature and deprived Mr G of a reasonable quality of life during the last months of his life. K appealed from this finding to the Supreme Court, arguing, among other things, that her actions were not part of the practice of nursing, but rather as an administrator of the hostel.

[12.235] The Court considered the phrase "in the practice of nursing" as it appears in the legislation. It considered and approved of the ruling in the case of *Childs v Walton* (see [12.180]), which determined the meaning of "in the practice of medicine" and held that the phrase does not have a temporal meaning but rather a qualitative or descriptive character. It does not limit the period during which the questionable conduct must occur if it is to be capable of satisfying the description, but rather describes its nature. Thus it need not occur while the relationship of health care practitioner and patient exists. It may occur at any time, and need not be conduct which occurs in the course of treating a patient. Further, the court held, the actions of a registered nurse performing only the narrow functions of an administrator of a combined hostel and nursing home complex could fall within the meaning of the term. However, in this case such considerations were not necessary, as K was directly involved in the day-to-day nursing care of Mr G, which removed her from the category of being only an administrator at the relevant times.

The following case is dealt with in some detail, because it deals with the nexus between activities that are related to professional practice and those that are not. It is also relevant to all professional health carers subject to similar legislative provisions, which apply in the majority of jurisdictions.

[12.240] Case: *Yelds v Nurses Tribunal & Ors* (2000) 49 NSWLR 491; NSWSC 755 (2 August 2000) (SC NSW)

The Health Care Complaints Commission lodged a complaint with the Nurses Tribunal that over a period of about six months a male nurse, N engaged in conduct that demonstrated a lack of adequate judgment and care in the practice of nursing and/or engaged in improper or unethical conduct relating to the practice of nursing. N was employed as a counsellor at a drug and alcohol counselling centre, having no nursing duties to perform there. The relevant complaints were that:

1) He falsely informed a patient, Ms MF, that he was a psychologist during a professional consultation.
2) He conducted counselling sessions at the centre with Ms MF in an inappropriate intimate manner and inappropriately suggested that she engage in conduct of a sexual nature with him.
3) He engaged in social contact with Ms MF outside of formal counselling such as conversing on personal and sexual matters, providing her with personal contact details and attending her home.
4) He maintained a sexual relationship with Ms MF for a period of approximately three months.
5) He invited Ms MF to Network 21 meetings and encouraged and permitted her to purchase an Amway business pack with himself and his wife as her sponsor.

The Tribunal found that the complaint was established to its "comfortable satisfaction" (see *Bannister v Walton* (1993) 30 NSWLR 699). The Tribunal made findings adversely to N to the effect of complaints 1, 4 and 5 and the general opening words of paragraphs 2 and 3 of the complaints. It held that whilst the behaviour of N did not occur "in the course of nursing" itself, it demonstrated inadequate knowledge and judgment that reflected on his ability to practise nursing, and involved conduct related to the practice of nursing. It held that N was guilty of unsatisfactory professional practise in relation to counts 1 to 4, and of professional misconduct in relation to count 5. N appealed, arguing that even if the alleged behaviour was proven and reprehensible, it did not reflect or reveal a specified defect so far as his ability to practice as a nurse is concerned, for the simple reason that he had not been employed and was not working as a nurse, but as a counsellor with very limited functions.

[12.245] The court found that N "certainly was not acting as a nurse, let alone a mental health nurse" (at 498). It upheld the appeal, not on the basis that the behaviour was not unethical or unprofessional, but because the Tribunal did not adequately consider whether N's actions fulfilled the requirements of the *Nurses and Midwives Act 1991* (NSW) to constitute professional misconduct or unsatisfactory professional conduct. Under s 4(2)(a) this includes conduct demonstrating a lack of adequate knowledge, experience, skill, judgment or care *in the practice of nursing*, and under s 4(2)(e) of the Act, "any other improper or unethical conduct *relating to the practice of nursing*" (emphasis added).

Section 4(2)(a): Conduct demonstrating inadequate knowledge, etc

[12.250] Adams J held that under the Act, "professional misconduct" necessarily adopts as its starting point a finding of "unsatisfactory professional conduct". It is essential to a finding of professional misconduct or unsatisfactory conduct that the conduct occur in, or be related to, nursing. It must demonstrate a lack or insufficiency of the specified qualities of the kind necessary for the practice of nursing in a real and significant way. However, the conduct need not occur in the *course* of nursing to satisfy the requirements of s 4(2)(a): it is both necessary and sufficient if it demonstrates a lack or insufficiency of the specified qualities of a kind necessary for the practice of nursing.

Adams J referred to *Childs v Walton* (above, see **[12.180]**) in holding that the phrase "in the practice of medicine" does not have a temporal meaning, but rather a qualitative or descriptive character, and *Jacobsen v Nurses Tribunal & Anor* (above, see **[12.185]**), in deciding that the nurse's position was one of power and influence that promoted his personal, private and economic interests.

Conduct, for the purposes of s 4(2)(a) need not be conduct as a nurse: the provision refers to "*any* conduct" (emphasis added). The issue is whether it demonstrates any of the specified defects relevant to his being a nurse. The fact that impugned conduct occurs when a nurse is undertaking nursing care of a patient strengthens the link between the conduct and the practice of nursing.

Adams J found that the alleged exploitation of the centre's patient in this case might reasonably have been regarded by the Tribunal as betraying such an attitude to appropriate professional responsibilities and was itself so inappropriate as to demonstrate, at least, a lack of adequate judgment or care within the meaning of s 4(2)(a)(iv) or (v) of the Act.

> "It was the fact that the N's alleged conduct concerned a relationship with a patient or patient of his, rather than the particular responsibilities of a counsellor compared with those of a nurse ... allowing "power and influence" over her, which was capable of providing a sufficient nexus between what he did at the Centre and the practice of nursing to satisfy the requirements of s 4(2)(a) of the Act. However, this line of reasoning, which required an analysis of both the requirements of general nursing and the duties actually performed by the appellant to demonstrate this nexus, was not adopted by the Tribunal" [at 500].

Section 4(2)(e): Improper or unethical conduct

[12.255] The alleged sexual conduct was improper or unethical only because of the relationship between the appellant and the patient through his employment at the centre as a counsellor. It was, therefore, capable of falling within s 4(2)(e) of the Act, providing the character of the employment and his professional relationship with the patient showed that this sort of conduct, in the circumstances, was related to his ability as a nurse.

The alleged pretence by the appellant that he was a psychologist was found to be both unethical and improper, and in the circumstances could relate to nursing.

The basis of the alleged misconduct in respect of the patient's involvement with Amway was that N would benefit financially from it. The judge found that taking financial advantage of the patient which involved no deceit or dishonesty does not necessarily demonstrate any of the specified defects in s 4(2)(a), nor would it, considered in isolation and provided there was no abuse of trust, constitute improper or unethical conduct relating to the practice of nursing. The necessary relationship between the alleged misconduct and the practice of nursing for the purposes of s 4(2)(e) is demonstrated "where the misconduct shows attitudes or characteristics inconsistent with the moral qualities fairly required of a person undertaking the responsibilities of nursing" [at 501].

Adams J concluded that the conduct taken as a whole was unethical and reflected on N's suitability to be entrusted with the work of a nurse. If it amounted to unsatisfactory professional conduct depended on the "aptness of the analogy between the responsibilities of a counsellor and those of a nurse". This essential link was not discussed at all in the Tribunal's reasons, though it referred extensively to the incidents of mental health nursing. Instead, the case was conducted on the basis that the questioned behaviour, if established of itself, amounted to unsatisfactory professional conduct.

Meaning of "infamous conduct in a professional respect"

[12.260] The meaning of "infamous conduct in a professional respect" was considered in the following case.

[12.265] **Case:** *Jemielita v Medical Board of Western Australia* (Supreme Court of Western Australia No 1106 of 1992) (*Australian Health and Medical Law Reporter* ¶77-063)

A total of 16 matters formed the basis of a complaint to the Medical Board of Western Australia in relation to a rural general practitioner. The Board found the doctor, J, had been careless, incompetent or guilty of misconduct on six occasions, and removed his name from the register. On these occasions J had:

1) severed the left lateral popliteal nerve during an operation to strip and ligate varicose veins. This resulted in the patient suffering foot drop. J had carried out an inadequate neurological examination of the patient, noting the foot drop, but failing to associate it with nerve damage;

2) inappropriately applied a vacuum extractor to a baby's left buttock during its delivery;

3) applied sponge-holding forceps to the scalp of another baby during its delivery, causing abrasions and injury;

4) failed to use sufficient anaesthetic when suturing cervical lacerations following delivery of a child and in so doing exhibited indifference to the patient's pain and suffering; and

5) & 6) falsely claimed medical benefits for carrying out a modified radical mastectomy on two patients (which would have major surgery under general anaesthetic) when he had in fact carried out a modified simple mastectomy in both cases (which required local anaesthetic), thus making him eligible for a lower rate of payment than that for which he claimed.

J appealed to the Supreme Court of Western Australia, claiming that the Board's decision to remove his name from the register was a grossly excessive penalty not warranted on the evidence. He argued that as he was a rural general practitioner, the Medical Board had erred in requiring a standard to be expected of a specialist and/or highly skilled medical practitioner who practised in the city. He claimed that as he had in fact provided a service to the mastectomy patients, and the difference in the fee for the service was small, he should not be held to be guilty of professional misconduct in respect of those cases.

[12.270] The Court considered the case of *Bolam v Friern Hospital Management Committee* [1957] 1 WLR 582 (see **[6.275]**ff) in coming to its decision that:

- urban and rural medical practitioners owe the same standard of care to their patients;
- a general practitioner does not owe the same standard of care as a specialist, as a general practitioner is not required to possess the same level of skill as a specialist; and
- thus J, as a rural general practitioner who at times carries out surgical and obstetric procedures, is required to have the same level of skill required of all general practitioners who also occasionally carry out surgical procedures and obstetrics.

The Court agreed that the actions of J did not warrant the removal of his name from the register, but ordered that he be suspended from practice or reprimanded, according to the nature of each incident. It found, in relation to (1), that the severance of the nerve was grossly careless and demonstrated incompetence, but that the failure to diagnose the patient's permanent nerve damage could not be said to amount to serious neglect of the patient's welfare. The failure of J to acknowledge that the nerve had been severed despite the evidence of three surgeons who identified the divided nerves during a later operation caused the Court concern. It ordered suspension for nine months for this incident. In relation to incidents (2) and (3)—the use of the vacuum extractor and the forceps on the babies—the Court found that the former action was inappropriate and the latter unwise. No one had suffered serious or permanent harm, but the incidents showed impatience and poor judgment in J's management of labour, and thus brought his competency in this area of practice into doubt. He was suspended for nine months for these incidents. In relation to incident (4), the Court acknowledged that the situation was a medical emergency, and J was motivated by the need to stop the cervical bleeding. Whilst not ignoring the patient's pain and suffering, the Court held that a reprimand was an adequate response to this incident. The Court held that the false claims of incidents (5) and (6) amounted to infamous conduct in a professional respect, despite the fact that the sums involved were small. It suspended his registration for 12 months for each of these incidents.

Once the period of suspension expired, the doctor would be required to adhere to conditions of practice set down by the Board.

Meaning of "incompetence" and "recklessness"

[12.275] Whilst the different jurisdictions use terms differently, a helpful approach to determining what constitutes incompetence and recklessness was offered in the following case.

[12.280] Case: *Boerema v Medical Board of Western Australia* (10, 19 June 1998, SC WA, BC9802646)

B was struck from the register for his treatment (or lack of it) of two patients.

Mr D: The first incident was his post-operative care of a Mr D, who had a reversal of a colostomy, after complications. Shortly after surgery, poor fluid output was noted, and considered of concern. The next morning nursing notes showed that B was paged because Mr D's abdomen was "grossly distended from pubis to sternum". B withdrew the naso-gastric tube six inches (fifteen centimetres), ordered physiotherapy and for the distension to be observed. Meantime, fluid flowed freely into the Yates inter-peritoneal drain. On the evening of the second post-surgery day B was contacted by nursing staff and informed that Mr D had a hard and distended abdomen, fluid sounds in the abdomen and dark green fluid and air passing into the Yates drain bag. B said he would visit the following day. The Board was told in a specialist report that these facts, plus eight recorded incidents of vomiting, a nasogastric drainage of 3,439 mls during the day, a raised white blood cell count and albuminuria presented an indication of intestinal fistula and a life-threatening condition within 48 hours of surgery. At this stage he required urgent corrective surgery. Instead no management plan was put in place for Mr D. On the fifth day after surgery, B saw Mr D and noted that he was "better". He ordered free fluids by mouth and removal of the Yates drain (considered at the coroner's inquest to be the two worst procedures that could have been taken). Seven days after surgery, a nurse questioned B on the possibility of septic shock and the need for more active treatment, and was told that if operated on, Mr D would not survive. A second opinion was sought on Mr D's treatment on the eighth day post surgery. Removal to Royal Perth Hospital for observation and possible laparotomy was recommended by a consulting surgeon who provided the opinion. This was agreed to and Mr D arrived at Perth Hospital in a state of shock. He underwent an emergency laparotomy, at which copious faecal stained peritoneal fluid was found throughout the abdominal cavity, leaking from a portion of the bowel re-anastomosis. Mr D's condition deteriorated and he died five days later from multi-organ failure and peritonitis.

Mrs W: Mrs W underwent surgery for the removal of varicose veins in her leg. Instead of removing the long saphenous vein, as intended, the femoral artery was removed, resulting in serious injury to the leg, with the prospect of amputation. Expert evidence to the Board was that recognition of the femoral artery is an integral step in the performance of such surgery and there is a clear difference between the pulsating artery and a saphenous vein. The error was not noticed either during or at the end of the operation. It concluded that a competent surgeon exercising reasonable skill and diligence would not have made this mistake.

The Board's finding: The Board considered B's long and distinguished surgical practice. It also took into account the fact that he conceded that his actions demonstrated incompetent and negligent professional conduct, and that he had elected to cease practising surgery. He did wish to continue limited non-surgical practice and consultancy. He demonstrated that circumstances at the time placed him under extraordinary stress and that this may have been the cause of his less than acceptable care. However, the Board held that its primary consideration is the public interest, and not to punish those before it (see *Jemielita v Medical Board of Western Australia* at [12.265]). It found B guilty of both gross carelessness and incompetence. Instead of deregistration, it ordered that he be of good behaviour for five years, refrain from surgical, procedural or medicolegal practice, and only carry out professional activities permitted by the Board. B appealed to the Supreme Court, arguing that the restrictions were excessive.

[12.285] The Supreme Court upheld the Board's ruling. It considered *Jemielita's* case and confirmed that incompetence involves unfitness to practise the particular field of medicine which is under examination, or an ability to perform the techniques or reach the judgments required for proper practice in that field. On the other hand, gross carelessness involves unacceptable conduct without any intentional wrongdoing on the part of the practitioner, suggesting also that the practitioner is unable to give the care required or is indifferent to the need for such care despite having the intellectual and technical ability to supply the care required (which may not be present in relation to incompetence).

The Court concluded that although there was no lack of care towards Mr D, there were elements of gross carelessness or incompetence on the part of B. In respect of Mrs W, there was no doubt that his conduct was grossly careless or incompetent. Merely ceasing to operate would not protect the public from any error of judgment he might make in some subsequent mode of practice if he were to be again subject to stress. If such practice were to be limited to such an extent that it is of minimal financial benefit to B, that is a "necessary incident of his name remaining on the Register of medical practitioners".

Readers might like to consider the situation of nurses in this case. There was evidence that on several occasions concern was expressed in relation to Mr D's treatment. Should they have taken further action to have his treatment reviewed? In what circumstances could they be held liable for not doing so?

Unsatisfactory behaviour must be related to professional practice

[12.290] One must also distinguish between conduct which may be improper and reprehensible in a general sense, and that which is improper and reprehensible in a professional sense.

> **[12.295] Case:** *Hoile v Medical Board of South Australia* (1960) 104 CLR 157; [1960] HCA 30 (High Court of Australia)
>
> A doctor had formed and pursued a sexual relationship with a nurse in the hospital. He was the medical superintendent of the hospital, and sexual activity occurred on hospital premises while the woman was on duty and on at least one occasion she was the only nurse on duty. This was held by the Medical Board to be misconduct. The doctor appealed to the High Court.

[12.300] The Court held:

"[not all] departures on the part of a medical practitioner from the standards of moral conduct amount to misconduct in a professional respect. But if his professional relationships are the occasion or source of the misconduct and it is sufficiently serious it may be deemed by the Medical Board to be infamous conduct in a professional respect" [at 163].

In this case the activity was held to be professional misconduct for:

"However much the general moral aspect of the matter may be emphasised as going to the relationship between man and woman, it remains true that the place was the hospital, the woman was a nurse, the man a doctor and moreover superintendent of the hospital" [at 163].

A case which set out some general guidelines regarding the nature of misconduct is *Pillai v Messiter (No 2)* (1989) 16 NSWLR 197, the facts of which are set out at **[13.170]**. In that case the Court (per Kirby P) made the following points:

- The purpose of discipline is protection of the public from not only "delinquents and wrong-doers within professions" but also "seriously incompetent professional people" who are "ignorant of basic rules or indifferent as to rudimentary professional requirements" (at 201).
- Something more than professional incompetence or deficiencies in practice is required:

> "It includes a deliberate departure from accepted standards or such serious negligence as, although not deliberate, to portray indifference and an abuse of the privileges which accompany registration as a medical practitioner" [at 200].

The Court also considered the effect of the removal of the appellant from the register, considering whether this would achieve the objective of protecting the public. It decided it would not where, as in that case, the event was an isolated, unintended error. Also, in that case, others had failed to notice the mistake, making the punishment of one person inappropriate.

[12.305] Case: *Versteegh v Nurses Board of South Australia* (4 December 1992, SC SA) (*Australian Health and Medical Law Reporter* ¶77-064)

The nurse, V, who worked at a nursing home faced charges in relation to:

1) *drugs* (failing to give residents drugs as prescribed, failing to check, count and record as required by law, discarding a bottle that contained methadone tablets, and failing to record administration of drugs);
2) *breach of confidentiality* (requesting a medical practitioner other than the resident's own practitioner to review the resident's leg ulcer without seeking the resident's consent or authority from her doctor); and
3) *unsatisfactory nursing care* (not permitting a patient with multiple sclerosis to be seated when being washed, causing pain and suffering).

V was found guilty of professional misconduct under s 41 of the *Nurses Act 1984* (SA). She was reprimanded by the Registration Board, and certain conditions were placed on her right to provide nursing care. The Board had referred to its own guidelines, the policy of the nursing home where she worked, legislation on drugs and the International Council of Nursing Code of Ethics.

V appealed to the Supreme Court arguing, among other things, that she had not fallen short of the required standard. She argued that in respect of (1), she had rather made a simple mistake in some circumstances, and in others had failed to make necessary entries because she had been very busy. In respect of (2), she argued that she had only been trying to act in the patient's best interests, and in respect of (3), she had acted in the most suitable way in the circumstances.

[12.310] The Court held that the failure to give drugs when they were prescribed and to make accurate records of drug administration was likely to compromise the care of the residents significantly. It noted the importance of checking drugs to ensure none are missing (see Chapter 13 on legislative provisions relating to the administration of drugs). It also found that V had breached confidentiality by calling in another doctor. She could not say she was acting in the resident's interest, it concluded, for if she was, she would have discussed the matter with the resident's practitioner (and one might add, the resident) first. Finally, her conduct with the resident suffering from multiple sclerosis could not be excused on the basis that she had acted according to her own judgment (as presumably her judgment should have led her to treat the resident differently). The Court held that "unprofessional conduct" has a broader meaning than common law negligence and is not limited to "disgraceful or dishonourable" conduct. Rather it is conduct which falls short of that followed and approved of by other members of the nursing profession.

Intention of practitioner

[12.312] Two cases which involved what was considered serious misconduct, but which attracted different responses by the respective Medical Boards give insight into the legal approach to the intention of the practitioner involved.

[12.315] Case: *Ex parte Fitzgerald; Re New South Wales Medical Board* (1945) 46 SR (NSW) 111 (SC)

A practitioner ("F") issued a certificate under the *Lunacy Act 1898* (NSW) in circumstances the Board found to be "gravely and inexcusably wrong". He had not examined the person for whom the certificate was written. F was suspended for 12 months. He appealed to the Supreme Court.

[12.318] The Court, while accepting the gravity of the behaviour, nevertheless allowed F to retain his practising certificate. Jordan CJ said that this case was exceptional, and indicated that the Court would consider:

- the general depravity or lack of scruple on the part of the doctor; or
- the likelihood of repetition of the behaviour.

[12.320] **Case:** *Stevenson v Medical Board of Victoria* (unreported, 27 June 1986, SC Vic) (cited in Dix et al (1988), p 40)

A doctor, S, dealing with home births diagnosed pre-eclampsia but "deliberately prescribed a course of treatment which he knew was unorthodox and contrary to long-accepted medical opinion and practice, and he thereby, and knowingly, put at serious risk both the mother and the foetus".

[12.325] The court found against S because he acted on beliefs which had no reasonable scientific foundation, which had been given no scientific credence and which, the court held, he must have known were likely to endanger the mother and child irrespective of the correctness of his beliefs. One should not act on beliefs that:

- have no established scientific foundation;
- are not accepted by one's profession; *and*
- would put another person in danger,

even if one believes one is right.

Readers may wish to note the different dates of these cases, and to consider whether:

1) the facts in the case of *Fitzgerald* fit into the criteria mentioned above; and
2) *Fitzgerald* would be decided differently today.

[12.330] **Case:** *Cranley v Medical Board of Western Australia* (21 December 1990, SC WA) (*Australian Health and Medical Law Reporter* (1991) ¶77.036)

A doctor, C, had been charged with infamous behaviour in a professional respect under the *Medical Act 1894* (WA). He had adopted the "harm reduction" approach to drug addiction. This involved prescribing for known drug addicts doses of intravenous Valium for self-administration, oral Doloxene and Valium, and oral Rohypnol and Valium. C prescribed these drugs because, under the circumstances the physical and social harm resulting from this approach to treatment of the patients justified the risk of abuse. He argued that the addicts were "needle-fixated", that Schedule 4 drugs were less harmful than Schedule 8 drugs, and that the substitution of these drugs could lead to a cure. The Board rejected this approach and opted instead to rule that on the basis that:

1) the treatment was not orthodox treatment; and
2) by regulation the prescription of the drugs should have been authorised by the Health Department, C was guilty of the charge. C appealed to the Supreme Court.

[12.333] The Supreme Court, in relation to (1), accepted evidence that although C's treatment was unorthodox, there was a "respectable" body of medical opinion which recognised the potential therapeutic value of the "harm reduction" approach. It would not be appropriate to find someone who did not follow the orthodox approach guilty of misconduct on that basis alone. There might be a fine line between harm reduction strategy and misconduct, but it would be unsafe to find misconduct on the basis of particular doctors disagreeing with his judgment. In relation to (2) the Court held that although C should have notified the Health Department, his failure to do so did not in the circumstances constitute misconduct. Whilst the Court did not specifically apply the test in *Stevenson* (at **[12.320]**), this finding appears consistent with it. This case is also relevant to the discussion on drugs in Chapter 13.

Criminal offences

[12.335] In most Australian jurisdictions conviction for a serious criminal offence can render a person subject to disciplinary procedures. The seriousness of the offence in some cases is defined by the penalty it attracts; there being no specific definition in others. Criminal conviction itself need not lead to disqualification from practising: see the outline of legislation relating to disciplinary action above at **[12.75]**.

[12.340] Case: *Skinner v Beaumont* [1974] 2 NSWLR 106 (CA NSW)

The doctor, S, had been convicted of conspiring to unlawfully procure two miscarriages. He had referred them to an unregistered practitioner. He was duly removed from the medical register. He appealed against that removal on the grounds that it was not in the public interest for disqualification for this type of offence.

[12.345] Hutley J of the Supreme Court held (at 109):

"The deliberate defiance, even with good motives, of a legal and professional responsibility, cannot in my opinion be excused, otherwise the distribution of drugs to alleviate the cravings of addicts would be an exculpatory circumstance."

However, he considered S's good reputation and the fact that the occasion would not arise again (due to change in the law which made abortion more widely available). This fact, the judge said, was critical to his decision. He also considered the welfare of the public, declaring that it would be deprived of a good practitioner.

Contrast this case with the following one.

[12.350] Case: *Basser v Medical Board of Victoria* [1981] VR 953 (SC)

A doctor, B, provided prescriptions to patients for toxic drugs improperly and unreasonably, without proper medical grounds and in greater than reasonable doses. He neither examined the patients adequately nor supervised their use of the medication. His name was removed from the register. He appealed from this decision to the Supreme Court.

[12.355] The Court treated his behaviour as very serious, here invoking such descriptions as "reckless indifference" and "gross negligence", although they did not consider the criminality or otherwise of his actions. The Court said:

"It should not be accepted that the concept of moral turpitude was an additional ingredient in every charge of infamous conduct. If a sense of reckless indifference or gross negligence were proven against a medical practitioner in any respect right-thinking colleagues of the person charged would inevitably regard such conduct as reprehensible, disgraceful, shameful or dishonourable."

[12.360] Case: *Chan and The Nurses Board of Western Australia* [2005] WASAT 115

In 2004, C applied to the Nurses Board to be registered as a nurse. She had previously been registered although that registration had elapsed some years earlier. C had been convicted of stealing and fraud in 2000 and was sentenced to a 9 years imprisonment. At the time of her application she was on parole. However, that information was not revealed in her application to the Board. The Board refused her application on the grounds that she had been convicted of an offence the nature of which rendered her unfit to practise as a nurse. C sought review of the decision of the Board refusing her application for registration as a nurse.

[12.365] The Tribunal held that the convictions fundamentally undermined C's entitlement to claim she was of trustworthy and honest character or that she was a person of integrity. Furthermore, the time that had elapsed since her convictions was insufficient to claim that her integrity had been restored. A nurse must be capable of establishing relationships of trust with employers, colleagues and patients and it could not be said that C would enjoy such trust. As a result, the decision of the Board was affirmed.

The fact that reprehensible and even illegal behaviour may not lead to disqualification was demonstrated in the case of a lawyer who was convicted of culpable homicide through negligent driving. It was held that his behaviour did not render him any less able a lawyer, and so any disciplinary action should take account of this. He was suspended from practice only while serving his prison sentence. (*Ziems v Prothonotary of Supreme Court of New South Wales* (1957) 97 CLR 279; [1957] HCA 46.) However, this case may be decided differently if heard today. Lawyers misappropriating trust funds, however, will find little sympathy or mercy, for such activity reflects on their ability to act competently and in the interests of the patient. Similarly, abuse of drugs could be considered as going to the very heart of health care practice, while a criminal conviction for an unrelated offence may not render one unable to competently carry out health care.

Fitness to practise

[12.370] Registration Boards may undertake an investigation into the mental or physical fitness of a person to practise (see, for example, *Medical Practitioners Registration Act 2001* (Qld), s 45). Such matters as drug addiction or misuse may come under this heading if there is no specific provision for disciplinary action for those conditions in the legislation of a particular jurisdiction. Where a person has been found unable to cope with stress, or has some other emotional, psychological or physical difficulty in providing care of a proper standard, the Board may take action. In reviewing a person's fitness to practise, the Board may require the person to undergo a medical examination before it will allow her or him to practise (see, for example, *Medical Act 1894* (WA), s 13(6)(f)).

Disciplinary action or removal or suspension from registration

[12.375] On receiving notice of a potential ground for such an action, the Registration Boards have various powers to carry out inquiries, and to require evidence to be brought, and witnesses to appear, before them. A health carer who is subject to an inquiry has the right to appear before the Board either in person or, in some jurisdictions by counsel, to present a defence to the charges. Health carers should be aware of the provisions of any Registration Board that governs them. Information should be sought from the Board itself, or the relevant union. Legislation can be obtained from the internet at www.austlii.edu.au.

Whatever the legal procedure of an inquiry by a Board, any health carer who is being dealt with under disciplinary provisions should seek legal advice.

In the interest of maintaining a high quality profession, the Registration Boards are provided with the power to take the following measures against someone found guilty of behaviour which may attract disciplinary action:

- reprimand;
- suspended from practice for a period of time;

- cancel registration;
- impose restrictions or conditions on practice;
- fine; or
- require an undertaking to refrain from similar behaviour in the future.

A Board may also remove from its register anyone who is shown to be ineligible to remain on it. This includes those whose registration has lapsed, or those who no longer fulfil the technical requirements for registration (see, for example, *Medical Practice Act 1992* (NSW), Pt 3).

Appeal from the Board's decision

[12.380] A person against whom a decision has been made by a Board may appeal to a court or tribunal nominated in the legislation, see **[12.70]**. The appeal may be by way of rehearing (a reconsideration of the facts) and the appeal court may uphold, reverse or substitute the Board's decision or vary the Board's orders.

Checklist

TYPICAL STEPS OF DISCIPLINARY PROCEDURES FOR HEALTH CARERS

✓ Complaint or information brought to Board's notice, health carer notified.

✓ Board decides to hear matter. If Board finds sufficient evidence on initial inquiry, it will decide to hold a formal hearing.

✓ Health carer supplied with written complaint, required to respond.

✓ The Board reviews the evidence, calls witnesses, considers the person's defence.

✓ If the health carer is found guilty Board takes disciplinary action:
 - reprimand;
 - place on probation;
 - suspend registration;
 - refuse to renew practising certificate;
 - suspend practising certificate; or
 - cancel practising certificate and remove health carer's name from register.

✓ Health carer may appeal Board's decision in court or tribunal nominated by the relevant legislation.

✓ Appeal will result in:
 - upholding of Board's decision;
 - reversal of Board's decision; or
 - substitution of Board's decision with another.

✓ Health carer or Board may appeal this decision in higher court.

References and Further Reading

Australian Health and Medical Law Reporter (CCH, Sydney, 1991, Looseleaf Service)
Bryant, R, "Nursing Culpability: A Proposal for Changes in Nursing Regulation" *Australian Health Law Bulletin* 11 (3)
Chiarella, M, "Nurse Practitioner Stage 3 Report" (1996) 4 *Health Law Bulletin* 85
Chiarella, M, "Nurse Practitioners" (1996) 3 *Collegian* 6 at 25
Dix, et al, *Law for the Medical Profession* (Butterworths, Sydney, 1988)
Edwards, S, "Appeal Against Medical Board's Decision Upheld (*Jemielita v Medical Board of WA*)" (1993) 1 *Health Law Bulletin* 2 at 61
Halsbury's Laws of Australia (Butterworths, Sydney, Looseleaf Service)
Joint Committee on the Health Care Complaints Commission *Unregistered Health Practitioners: The Adequacy and Appropriateness of Current Mechanisms for Resolving Complaints: Discussion Paper*, Sydney, Joint Committee on the Health Care Complaints Commission, 1998
Ottley, R, "Sexual Misconduct—To What Extent Are Doctors Accountable?" (1996) 4 *Health Law Bulletin* 49
Shinn, M, "Guidelines for Misconduct Hearings" (1993) 2 *Health Law Bulletin* 49
Staunton, P and Whyburn, R, *Nursing and the Law* (4th ed, Saunders, Sydney, 1997)
The Laws of Australia (Law Book Co, Sydney, Looseleaf Service)
Wynne, A, "Nursing Practitioner Services in Victoria" (2001) 9 *Health Law Bulletin* 13 at 47

IV

Regulatory

13 Drugs

Statutory law regarding drugs

Regulation of drug prescription

Common law concerning drugs

chapter 13

Drugs

Introduction

[13.05] This chapter focuses on the law related to the regulation of the medicinal use of drugs in humans. There are two main areas of possible legal liability for health carers handling and giving drugs: breach of the statutory provisions (Acts and regulations), and breach of the duty of care owed to the patient (negligence). There is also legislation applying generally in relation to drugs, from testing and manufacture to possession and use.

Health carers are also in a position to wrongfully possess, administer and use drugs, knowingly or inadvertently.

Drug induced injuries may occur from practices related to the manufacture and sale of drugs, as well as research with drugs (for example, see Brazier (1992), ch 8).

Statutory Law Regarding Drugs

[13.10] Federal legislation deals with such matters as the quality, testing, manufacture and labelling of drugs, as well as the licensing of manufacturers. There are numerous State and Territory statutes and regulations on drugs, consisting primarily of the following:

Commonwealth	Therapeutic Goods Act 1989
	Therapeutic Goods Regulations 1990
	Narcotic Drugs Act 1967
Australian Capital Territory	Poisons Act 1933
	Poisons Regulations 1933
	Poisons and Drugs Act 1978
	Poisons and Drugs Regulation 1993
	Drugs of Dependence Act 1989
	Poisons (Public Institutions) Order 2000

New South Wales	Poisons and Therapeutic Goods Act 1966
	Poisons and Therapeutic Goods Regulation 2002
	Drugs Misuse and Trafficking Act 1985
	Poisons Act 1966
Northern Territory	Poisons and Dangerous Drugs Act
	Poisons and Dangerous Drugs Regulations
Queensland	Health Act 1937
	Health (Drugs and Poisons) Regulations 1996
South Australia	Controlled Substances Act 1984
	Controlled Substances (Poisons) Regulations 1996
	Controlled Substances (Prohibited Substances) Regulations 2000
	Controlled Substances (Volatile Solvents) Regulations 1996
	Controlled Substances (Exemptions) Regulations 2004
	Controlled Substances (Pesticides) Regulations 2003
	Controlled Substances (Expiation of Simple Cannabis Offences) Regulations 2002
	Drugs Act 1908
	Food Act 2001
Tasmania	Poisons Act 1971
	Poisons Regulations 2002
Victoria	Drugs, Poisons and Controlled Substances Act 1981
	Drugs, Poisons and Controlled Substances Regulations 1995
	Drugs, Poisons and Controlled Substances (Commonwealth Standard) Regulations 2001
	Drugs, Poisons and Controlled Substances (Confiscation) Regulations 2004
	Drugs, Poisons and Controlled Substances (Industrial Hemp) Regulations 1998
	Drugs, Poisons and Controlled Substances (Volatile Substances) Regulations 2004
	Therapeutic Goods (Victoria) Act 1994
Western Australia	Poisons Act 1964
	Poisons Regulations 1965

Such legislation covers all aspects of possession, sale, dispensing and administration, including criminal offences relating to those drugs classed as illicit. The legislation categorises drugs into nine different Schedules (S1–S9), according to their nature and effect. These are found either at the end of the relevant legislation, or in a separate poisons list or as regulations. Each Australian jurisdiction lists those drugs to be included in the classifications which are set out at [13.15].

The *Therapeutic Goods Act 1989* (Cth) provides for the manufacture, importing, testing and registration or listing of drugs that meet the standards required for recognition of their safety. Drugs considered potentially more dangerous must pass the stringent testing required for registration. Those drugs, which are less hazardous, are placed on a separate listing.

Drug schedules

[13.15] The National Drugs and Poisons Schedule Committee (NDPSC) was established under the *Therapeutic Goods Act 1989* (Cth), s 52B, to facilitate the uniform classification and scheduling of drugs. The decisions of the NDPSC in relation to the *Standard for the Uniform Scheduling of Drugs and Poisons*, are recommended for inclusion in State and Territory legislation, but have no force in Commonwealth law. The various Australian jurisdictions have adopted the Schedules to the Standard which contain classifications for drugs according to their nature. The classifications are as follows:

Schedule 1	Substances or preparations of such danger to life as to warrant supply only by medical practitioners, pharmacists, dentists, veterinary surgeons, and authorised nurses or midwifery practitioners. There are no longer any Schedule 1 poisons.
Schedule 2: Pharmacy Medicine	Substances or preparations for therapeutic use, the safe use of which may require advice from a pharmacist but which should be available to the public from pharmacies or licensed persons only.
Schedule 3: Pharmacist Only Medicine	Substances and preparations for therapeutic use which require pharmacist advice for safe use, but should be available to the public without prescription.
Schedule 4: Prescription Only Medicine	Substances and preparations, the use of which requires professional management and monitoring and thus require a prescription, and (i) substances intended for therapeutic use the safety and efficacy of which require further evaluation, and (ii) new therapeutic substances.
Schedule 5: Caution	Substances and preparations which have a low to moderate potential to cause harm and require careful handling, storage and use. The potential for harm of these products can be reduced through the use of packaging containing warnings and directions for use.
Schedule 6: Poison	Substances and preparations of a similar nature to, but more dangerous than, those in Schedule 5. The potential for harm of these products may be reduced by distinctive packaging containing strong warnings.
Schedule 7: Dangerous Poison	Substances and preparations with a high potential for causing harm which thus require particular precautions in their manufacture, handling, storage or use, or requiring special regulations regarding labelling, storage, possession or availability.
Schedule 8: Controlled Drug	Substances and preparations commonly called "drugs of addiction", "dangerous drugs" or "narcotics". There are severe restrictions on the dispensing and possession of these drugs in an attempt to prevent misuse or abuse.
Schedule 9: Prohibited Substance	Substances and preparations which are drugs of abuse, the manufacture, possession, sale or use of which should be prohibited by law except for amounts which may be necessary for medical or scientific research conducted with the approval of Commonwealth and/or State or Territory authorities.

The order of the Schedules of greatest to least restriction would appear to be 9, 7, 8, 4, 1, 3, 2, 6, 5. The most important categories for health carers are those listed as Schedule 4 drugs (available only on prescription by a doctor, dentist or veterinary surgeon) and Schedule 8 drugs (drugs of addiction). They may change from time to time, at which stage those involved in administering drugs should be notified.

Regulation of Drug Prescription, Administration etc

[13.20] Every jurisdiction has detailed legislation governing the possession, prescription, administration and recording of the use of restricted drugs and drugs of addition. There is no short way around the matter: health carers should be familiar with the legislation (including regulations outlining the procedures required in administering drugs) in their State. Most hospitals and health care institutions have drawn up procedural directions, which are written to ensure that legal dictates are followed. Employees are both entitled to, and should, have access to such procedural directions. Compliance with the legislation is the responsibility of the individual health carer, as vicarious liability (see **[6.765]**) may not be available for breaches. Senior administrative staff should also be particularly aware of the law regarding dispensing, storage and handling of drugs.

A comprehensive account of all of the legislative provisions throughout the country is not practicable here. The following is an outline of the main provisions that apply. A more detailed summary of the *Drugs of Dependence Act 1989* (ACT) is set out in Appendix 4 to demonstrate the complexity and comprehensiveness of drug legislation, as well as the legal restrictions on such matters as prescribing, storing ansd administering drugs. The following outline provides a more detailed summary of legislative provisions that are similar across jurisdictions.

Prohibition and controls over drugs

[13.25]
Illegal or illicit drugs: This term is given to scheduled drugs used for non-therapeutic reasons, that are not legally prescribed or are otherwise illegally obtained.

Restricted substance: Drugs only obtainable on a doctor's prescription, for therapeutic purposes. They are generally those listed in Schedules 4 and 8. Note the difference from those drugs (Schedules 1 to 3), which may only be supplied by certain people.

Dispensing drugs

[13.30] Dispensing a drug means making a drug available from a central supply for individual use in accordance with a prescription for that drug, a process generally carried out by a pharmacist. There may, however, be provision in the legislation for other licensed persons to dispense where no pharmacist is available. Those allowed to dispense drugs are specifically designated by legislation, and the process and recording of both storing and dispensing of drugs is set out in some detail.

Supplying drugs

[13.35] At law, this means making a drug available to another person. Those who supply drugs must be licensed, and the conditions of supply are restricted. It is worth noting that legislation has established that where one has more than a stipulated amount of nominated drugs (mainly, those known as "illicit" drugs) in one's possession, the drug may be deemed to be intended for supply, no matter what the actual intention may be (see for example *Drugs Misuse and Trafficking Act 1985* (NSW), s 29). Possession for supply is a more serious offence than mere possession for personal use of a prohibited drug.

Possession of drugs

[13.40] In law this involves having a substance in one's physical control (not necessarily on one's person). Certain drugs may only be in the possession of specified persons, which can include doctors, veterinary surgeons, emergency services personnel, appropriate nursing staff in a health care institution, rural community and industrial nurses under appropriate circumstances. In some cases, health carers can apply to have restricted drugs or narcotics in their possession (for example, nurses in Tasmania under the *Poisons Regulations 2002* (Tas), Reg 9 and indigenous health workers in Queensland under the *Health (Drug and Poisons) Regulation 1996* (Qld)). Wrongful possession of prohibited drugs will attract penalties at law.

Prescription of drugs

[13.45] This is the granting of the right to a particular person to prescribe a drug for the use of another person. "Restricted drugs" (a term here used to refer to drugs requiring prescription which are listed in Schedule 4 or Schedule 8) must be prescribed in writing by a medical practitioner, except in emergencies. In that case the drug may be ordered by word of mouth, in which case most States require that the prescription be written up and signed within a prescribed time, usually 24 hours. Provision for the form of prescriptions, those who can prescribe drugs and the drugs which require prescription are established by the legislation. Generally, a prescription must be written or printed in ink, signed, contain the name of the recipient, the drug, the dosage, the route, adequate instructions for use and the number of times the drug may be dispensed, or, for certain substances, the time between repeated administration. Not all legislation is this detailed, but in those States where it is not, practice directives and hospital protocols will establish the requirements. The legislation generally allows only doctors, dentists or veterinary surgeons to prescribe those drugs in the specially designated schedules, and lays down specific rules for the prescription of drugs of dependence. However, nurses are increasingly being permitted to prescribe some scheduled drugs (that is, to decide to administer a drug without a doctor's order) in certain circumstances. These include emergencies in remote areas where a doctor's prescription is not practicable (for example, *Poisons Regulations 2002* (Tas), Reg 60) and midwifery (for example, in Victoria a midwife may give a single dose of morphine or pethidine in an emergency, if such practice is in accordance with the written instructions of the doctor and is approved practice in that hospital).

It is an offence to write a prescription unless one is authorised to do so. It is also an offence to alter a prescription or obtain one by false pretences.

Administration of drugs

[13.50] This means the actual giving of the drug, orally, by injection, per rectum or other route. Health carers are permitted to administer prohibited drugs where they are required to do so as a part of their duties. Drugs for which detailed instruction regarding administration is given in legislation are:

Schedule 8 drugs. These generally require that in health institutions a register be kept and the following be recorded:

* patient's name;
* prescribed drug and dose;
* prescribing doctor's name;
* date and time of administration;
* balance of ampoules or capsules, tablets etc in supply;
* signature of two nurses (or a nurse and a doctor) who checked the preparation and administration of the drug (at least one of the nurses should be registered); and
* any error is to be ruled through in ink with the entry still legible, with the correction entered, dated and initialled on the same page

(see *Drugs of Dependence Act 1989* (ACT); *Poisons and Therapeutic Goods Regulation 2002* (NSW); *Poisons and Dangerous Drugs Act* (NT); *Health (Drugs and Poisons) Regulations 1996* (Qld); *Controlled Substances (Poisons) Regulations 1996* (SA); *Poisons Regulations 2002* (Tas); *Drugs, Poisons and Controlled Substances Regulations 1995* (Vic); *Poisons Regulations 1965* (WA). Other requirements apply to first aid services).

[13.55] Case: *McIntosh & Western Sydney Area Health Service* [1999] NSWIRComm 557

This was an application made by the New South Wales Nurses' Association on behalf of M seeking reinstatement, re-employment, or monetary compensation in lieu thereof, following her alleged harsh, unreasonable or unjust dismissal. M was a registered nurse. She was dismissed for having falsified the signature of a witness to four entries in the drug register and having breached the hospital's policies on the administration of drugs.

The alleged falsification of the register was the forging of a witness' signature against four entries and the alleged breach of policy was the administration of those drugs without witness. M denied the allegations. The nurse whose signature was allegedly forged gave evidence that the signature in the register was not hers and she did not witness the administration of the drugs. The four patients who were to receive the drugs all gave statements alleging they did not receive the drugs as indicated in the register.

The Commissioner preferred the evidence of the other nurse on duty over that of M. He also commented on M's continued inability to acknowledge her shortcomings or errors. In those circumstances, he concluded that the termination of Ms McIntosh's employment was not harsh, unreasonable or unjust.

Storage and recording of drugs

[13.65] Schedule 8 drugs must be kept under lock and key, separate from other drugs, with especially nominated persons having control of the key. Some jurisdictions stipulate the nature of the cupboard in which they must be kept (for example, fixed to the wall or floor, and resistant to attack by hand tool for 30 minutes, power tools for 5 minutes). Where there is a pharmacist he or she is responsible for storage and recording of all restricted substances. Otherwise the medical superintendent or director of nursing of a health care facility is held responsible. Scheduled drugs other than Schedule 8 drugs must be stored in a place where the public does not have access, in varying degrees of security (*Drugs of Dependence Act* 1989 (ACT), ss 114, 115; *Poisons and Therapeutic Goods Regulation 2002* (NSW), regs 72-75; *Code of Practice for the Storage and Transport of Schedule 8 Substances* (NT) authorised under *Poisons and Dangerous Drugs Regulations* (NT), reg 10; *Health (Drugs and Poisons) Regulation 1996* (Qld), regs 118, 119; *Code of Practice for the Storage and Transport of Drugs of Dependence authorised under Controlled Substances (Poisons) Regulations 1996* (SA), reg 20; *Poisons Regulations 2002* (Tas), Part 3, Div 7; *Drugs, Poisons and Controlled Substances Regulations 1985* (Vic), reg 33; *Poisons Regulations 1965* (WA), reg 56). The storage of drugs and recording of their use in a ward is the responsibility of the charge nurse, who must maintain the prescribed security by ensuring that the drug cupboard is locked when not in use. The key is always to be in the possession of the most senior nurse on the ward at any time and must not be left where others have access to it. A regular inventory of Schedule 8 drugs must be kept. In health care facilities in most jurisdictions, drugs are to be transported in a locked container.

[13.70]   Case: *NSW Nurses' Association (o/b of Jane Rawlinson) v Hunter Area Health Service* [2003] NSWIRComm 411

The applicant was a registered nurse employed by the respondent. Her employment was terminated following an incident described by the applicant in her affidavit as follows:

"6. I was working on the evening shift . . . helping a fellow registered nurse check out some Panadeine Forte for a patient . . .

7. When I took the two tablets out of the box that made the box empty. I said to the other staff member "what can we put in this box to see how long it takes for someone to notice there is a Panadeine Forte Box sitting on the bench with something in it".

8. I suggested Panadol, my colleague suggested Metformin tablets (Diabex) because they look a lot like Panadeine Forte so I put them in the box and closed the lid and put the box up on the bench next to the Dangerous Drugs cupboard.

9. The next day . . . was my day off. I became aware that overnight a registered nurse on duty found the box and put the box in the Dangerous Drugs cupboard. The morning staff registered nurse found the "extra box"of Panadeine Forte and called the pharmacist.

10. My colleague who was with me on the [previous] night . . . arrived at work the next afternoon she inquired about the "practical joke".

11. My colleague telephoned the pharmacy and asked the pharmacist to take a closer look at the tablets and would find that the tablets were Metformin not Panadeine Forte. The pharmacist notified the Director of Nursing who then notified the General Manager who notified Human Resources who suspended me until further notice."

An inquiry by hospital management determined that the applicant had resealed the Panadeine Forte box, replacing the tamper proof seal. The applicant denied this. The resident pharmacist and a registered nurse who inspected the packet the day after the "practical joke" both failed to notice that the contents were not as described on the box.

Whilst Harrison DP noted that there was a case for compassion toward the applicant he ultimately concluded that "the gravity of the offence is of sufficient magnitude that termination of employment could not be found to be harsh, unreasonable or unjust". The applicant's continued employment in nursing was to be determined by the NSW Nurses' Registration Board.

[13.75] Every ward must keep a drug register of specified drugs (usually Schedules 4, 8 and 9–"restricted" drugs). The Australian Capital Territory, the Northern Territory and South Australia provide that administration of a narcotic drug must be witnessed by another person. Both the nurse preparing and administering and at least one other witness (nurse or doctor) should sign the register. Any error must be corrected and witnessed, with the erroneous material carefully ruled through and not obliterated, and a marginal note with the correct details and the signatures of both parties legibly entered with the date (and preferably time) of the correction, and initialled by the witnesses. It is recommended that if it is possible to do so clearly and legibly, the names of the signatories should be printed as well.

Most jurisdictions require that the balance of restricted drugs should be checked regularly by two people, any unusable drugs destroyed as discussed below. Any discrepancies should be immediately notified to the head pharmacist of a hospital and person in charge of nursing, so that an investigation can be carried out. Where drugs are lost or stolen, the police and the Health Department should be notified.

Destruction of drugs

[13.80] Where a Schedule 8 drug is unusable it must be destroyed and accounted for by at least two people, who record such destruction in the register. Loss must be recorded, and where a drug is only part used, the remainder of the drug must be destroyed, again witnessed by two people and recorded in the register. Exact details differ: carers should be aware of the precise requirements in their jurisdiction and workplace.

Where less than a full ampoule, tablet or unit of a scheduled medication is used, the remainder should be destroyed, with the destruction witnessed and signed for by both the person who destroys the drug and the witness. Any unusable or out-of-date drugs should be returned to the pharmacist and duly recorded and witnessed in the record. Signatures of "witnesses" should not be sought after the drug has been destroyed, to satisfy requirements, and one should make sure that the ampoules, tablets, etc which remain are really the drug prescribed and not a substitute. Where there is no pharmacist, the director of nursing or medical superintendent is responsible for these procedures.

Health carers in remote areas, paramedics, ambulance officers and doctors in private practice who are authorised to possess restricted drugs and drugs of addiction are also required to keep drugs secure, keep proper records, and record the use and destruction of drugs in a similar manner. The possession and conveyance of restricted drugs and narcotics has expanded (and can be expected to expand more) with the increased development of "hospital in the home" programs, home-based palliative care, community nursing and nurse practitioners in private practice. Those providing care in these areas should be aware of the detailed requirements for handling drugs in their jurisdiction. These health carers have responsibility for overseeing the proper adherence to legislative and administrative requirements, and of ensuring regular and thorough inventory of the drugs in their possession; immediately reporting any discrepancy in numbers to the appropriate authority. They should ensure they are authorised to possess, prescribe and administer drugs that they are expected to use, and the circumstances under which they can do so. The only way one can find out the detailed extent of these responsibilities is to have access to the legislative requirements and administrative procedures manuals, both of which should be made available through an employer. It is incumbent on health authorities to ensure that adequate legislative provisions, and detailed guidelines which conform with the law are available in this rapidly changing area of health care.

Prescription of drugs of addiction

[13.85] New South Wales, the Northern Territory, Queensland and Victorian doctors may not prescribe drugs of addiction for drug-dependent people other than under specified circumstances. In addition, there may be special requirements for the prescribing of such drugs for a period of more than several weeks in other cases. Special circumstances are recognised, and permission may be sought to extend the time limit for therapeutic reasons. Victoria restricts the prescription of amphetamines, dexamphetamine, methadone, dextromoramide, methylamphetamine and methylphenidate and requires doctors to be licensed to prescribe them except in specified circumstances (*Drugs, Poisons and Controlled Substances Regulations 1985* (Vic), reg 18). In the Australian Capital Territory, a doctor cannot prescribe a drug of dependence for a drug-dependent person without the approval of the chief health officer, unless the person is an inpatient and will require the drug for less than 14 days (*Drugs of Dependence Act 1989* (ACT), s 58). Health carers should be wary about the extended administration of Schedule 8 drugs and inquire into the authorisation of their administration, as in most cases notification and permission of the chief health officer (or equivalent) is required for prescription other than short-term therapeutic use. In Western Australia the Supreme Court found that a doctor who treated heroin-addicted patients with combinations of valium, doloxene and rohypnol as part of a harm-reduction policy to get them to desist from the use of heroin was not guilty of "infamous conduct in a professional respect" under the *Medical Act 1894* (WA) (see **[12.330]**).

Drug order forms

[13.90] Health carers should insist on the correct prescribing of drugs by physicians. This means they should be able to clearly read the name of the drug, the dosage, route, frequency and any special instructions, as drugs should not be administered unless properly prescribed.

A patient's drug order form is recognised by some as a prescription form for the purposes of drug legislation, and it is suggested that nurses and other health carers should not use this form except where hospital policy establishes the use of drug order forms for verbal orders. In that case it is suggested staff should be very careful that a verbal order is clearly marked as such. It is suggested that a more satisfactory approach is the one set out in the Checklist at **[13.160]**. If they wish to record a (temporary) oral order by a physician it is suggested that to enter the administration of the drug in the drug administration form, the heath carer clearly indicates that the drug was given subject to a verbal order, thus preventing any mistake as to their record purporting to be a prescription as such, or the impression that the order was written by a doctor, and no further action required. It is also suggested that some clear and distinguishing marker (such as a sticker) be applied to the patient's notes with a clear notation on it of the fact that the order is to be written up, and the time by which this must be done.

Emergencies

[13.95] In emergencies, all jurisdictions provide that oral orders for administration of restricted drugs may be given to authorised health carers such as nurses and paramedics, with the requirement that the doctor giving the order must write the prescription up, for example, in the patient's notes, either as soon as practicable or within 24 hours. Because of legal limitations on the prescribing of drugs, oral orders should only be accepted in emergencies or where the doctor cannot reasonably attend to write the prescription, and should not be based on the convenience of those involved. In all cases the checklist on telephone orders (below, **[13.160]**) should be followed as closely as possible.

Jurisdictions differ in provisions for the administration of opiates and other restricted drugs on a verbal order in an emergency. The details of the patient, the drug, time and route of administration, amount given and further doses ordered, as well as the name of the prescribing doctor and signature of authorised person administering it must be noted.

Recording and witnessing emergency oral orders and administration of drugs should follow the above rules as closely as is practicable under the circumstances. Temporary recording (for example, on the patient's skin, plaster cast) may be the only practical way of doing this, with proper records made as soon as possible afterwards. The use of witnesses is also an important consideration.

Non-scheduled drugs and complementary medicines

[13.100] Health carers have access to non-restricted drugs, such as panadol, kaomagma, laxatives and many different creams and lotions, which they may administer and apply on their own initiative. It should be remembered that although the handling and administering of these drugs may not be the subject of legislation, carers should carefully follow any hospital procedure requirements, or they may be subject to a negligence action (see **[13.130]**ff), disciplinary action (see **[13.115]**), or health care complaints (see Chapter 18).

Under the *Therapeutic Goods Act 1989* (Cth), the Commonwealth Government has established a Complementary Medicines Evaluation Committee to provide scientific and policy advice relating to controls on the supply and use of complementary medicines. These can include vitamin, mineral, naturopathic, homoeopathic or herbal preparations, which become regulated medicines under the Act.

This means that those involved in using complementary therapies should also be aware of the legislative requirements as to the use of these therapies, and any restrictions on them. The recent publication of the Therapeutic Goods Administration entitled *"The Regulation of Complementary Medicines in Australia—An Overview"* (April 2006) is a useful resource for further information on legislative requirements associated with complementary medicines and can be accessed at www.tga.gov.au/cm/cmreg-aust.htm.

Re-packaging drugs

[13.105] An important point to bear in mind is that, ideally, drugs should never be changed from the container in which they are dispensed. Provision for labelling of drugs by the dispensing pharmacist, giving their category (such as "POISON" or "CAUTION"), or warnings and use (for example, "Not for internal use"), is made in the legislation, and this should not be altered.

Where drugs are left with patients for their own administration in special containers, with, for example, compartments for different days, this should be seen as administration of, rather than dispensing of, the drugs. The patient should be well instructed (preferably in writing in addition to verbal instructions), as to taking the drugs. Information as to the name of the drug, its identification (colour, size etc), any information regarding the taking of it, side-effects and contra-indications that are relevant should be provided in writing elsewhere, as well as orally. This gives both the patient and others who may need to deal with her or him in an emergency, necessary information.

Drugs and criminal law

[13.110] There are criminal sanctions in the legislation for the unauthorised possession, supply, administration and self-administration of restricted drugs, with some specifically named drugs of dependence having more severe penalties than others. There are also penalties for the forging or fraudulent obtaining of, or wrongful giving of, prescriptions for restricted substances or drugs of dependence. Health carers have access to restricted and non-restricted drugs and drugs of dependence. They should be very careful that not only do they not misuse this privilege, but that they never cut corners and compromise the clear guidelines for handling of drugs. Misuse of drugs by health workers is considered such a serious matter by the community, that one should not give cause for doubt as to one's integrity in handling them.

Disciplinary action

[13.115] Health professionals who are found guilty of a criminal offence in relation to drugs, or who misuse or are addicted to drugs may lose their practising certificate, even where the law has technically not been broken but the health professional has been careless or negligent (see Chapters 6, 12; *Cranley v Medical Board of Western Australia*, see **[12.330]**). In the period July 1997 to June 1998, the Nurses and Midwives Board of New South Wales

Professional Standards Committee found a nurse guilty of professional misconduct and cautioned him or her for failing to appropriately consult as required and administering medication without authorisation. From July 1998 to June 1999 four drug-related matters were referred to the New South Wales Nurses and Midwives Tribunal for inquiry. Conditions were placed on the registration/enrolment of two of those nurses. One accredited nurse was suspended from the roll and two others were deregistered.

[13.120] Case: *Re the Medical Practice Act 1992 and Dr Gerritt Reimers, Case note, HCCC Annual Report 2003-2004, p 30*

Dr R was prosecuted by the HCCC before the New South Wales Medical Tribunal on complaints of professional misconduct and impairment. The complaints related, amongst other things, to the wrongful handling and misappropriation of anaesthetic drugs, self-administration of drugs of addiction whilst on duty, and admitted addiction to narcotics. The complaints spanned the period of 1996 to 2000. Dr R gave evidence that he diverted supplies of drugs from patient controlled anaesthesia for his own use.

Dr R admitted the habitual use of narcotics during the time that he cared for a patient at Hornsby Hospital. Following a routine operation for bowel cancer, the recovery room nurse noted that the patient was in poor condition and repeatedly drew Dr R's attention to this. Dr R's attempts to resuscitate the patient were ineffective. The nurse summoned other medical officers to assist. The patient was found to have suffered serious brain damage as a result of hypoxia and died a few days later.

A police investigation followed and Dr R was charged with manslaughter. Ultimately, he was found not guilty of those charges. Following admissions to colleagues of his drug dependency, the Medical Board suspended Dr R from practice until the case could be prosecuted before the Medical Tribunal.

The Tribunal noted:

"Dr Reimers has exhibited extremely significant deficiencies both of character and of skill in the practice of medicine. He was shown to be willing on many occasions to put his own interest above those of patients, probably, in the case of SB, at least contributing to her tragic death."

The Tribunal considered the only appropriate order was deregistration for a period of at least 10 years.

Dr R was also the defendant in civil proceedings arising out of the same incidents.

[13.123] Investigation: *HCCC Report on an investigation of incidents in the Operating Theatre at Canterbury Hospital* 8 February-7 June 1999

The incident under investigation involved the injection of a substance containing a caustic agent, phenol, into the biliary tree and/or pancreatic duct of patients who underwent Endoscopic Retrograde Cholangio Pancreatography (ERCP) procedures at Canterbury Hospital during the period 4 February to 7 June 1999. The error was discovered by a scout nurse on 7 June 1999. The solution used as contrast medium for the procedures was Phenol 10% in 60% Conray 280; the contrast medium intended for the procedures was Conray 280, 20ml. It became apparent that supplies of Conray 280, 20ml had been replaced with 5ml bottles of a diluted form of Conray 280 containing 10% phenol. 24 patients were exposed to the incorrect solution.

[13.125] The investigation looked at the standard of care provided by the medical practitioner, Dr D, who performed the procedures and the nursing staff in the operating suite and made recommendations to the relevant professional bodies. The report addressed only problems raised at Canterbury Hospital, not aspects of the complaint concerning individual practitioners.

The two questions central to the investigation were:

- how was the correct solution replaced by an incorrect solution; and
- how did the incorrect solution come to be used.

The Commission concluded that the Phenol 10% in 60% Conray was incorrectly requisitioned and supplied to the operating theatre. All health professionals who checked the substance after receipt into the operating theatre failed to adequately check the label before the substance was used during a procedure. Despite the fact that a number of health professionals noticed that the label of the incorrect substance bore the warning "Use Under Strict Medical Supervision – Caustic Substance", none of them recognised the significance of the warning.

Dr D was suspended from service as a visiting medical officer by the Area Health Service and subsequently faced disciplinary proceedings. Dr D faced charges of professional misconduct before the Medical Tribunal. The Tribunal found Dr D guilty of the lesser charge of unsatisfactory professional conduct only and he was reprimanded.

The nurse who was the instrument nurse for almost all of the procedures concerned, N, was dismissed from her employment and also subsequently faced disciplinary proceedings. N subsequently unsuccessfully challenged her dismissal in the Industrial Relations Commission, where Deputy President Sams stated "[it] ill behoves a nurse of twenty-three years experience whose role in the incident was so central and whose actions were so manifestly careless, to lay blame at everyone else and assume not a skerrick of responsibility" (*Nicholls and Central Sydney Area Health Service* [2000] NSWIRComm 161 (25 August

2000)). The Nurses Tribunal also found the charges of professional misconduct against N proven and she was suspended from practice and conditions were placed on her registration.

Civil actions were also brought by many of the affected patients against the hospital and Dr D.

Common Law Concerning Drugs (Negligence)

[13.130] Apart from statutory law, health carers should be aware of the need to take reasonable care to prevent harm to patients from negligent handling and administration of drugs. The reader is referred to the discussion of negligence in Chapter 6, however, here we will consider cases specifically dealing with the giving of drugs.

Where patient agreement to treatment has been given, health carers should give consideration to the following matters.

Consent

- What is the purpose of the medication—therapeutic, research, behaviour modification? Has this been discussed with the patient, or person responsible?
- Has information about the medication's effects, side-effects and risks been given to the patient or person responsible?
- Has a choice of treatment been offered where this is available?

Reasonable Care

- Are there less drastic, effective alternatives?
- Has the patient been checked for adverse reaction to the drug?
- Have appropriate precautions been taken where relevant (for example, patient safety)?
- Is there an adequate agreed means of monitoring the effects of treatment, so that patient feedback is heard and acted upon?
- Is there an adequate means of long-term supervision of drugs (for example, proper history, prevention of addiction, etc)?

Unclear order

[13.135] An order may be unclear because it is illegible, or does not fully specify requirements.

[13.140] Case: *Prendergast v Sam and Dee Ltd, Kozary and Miller, The Times,* London, 14 March 1989

Dr M wrote a prescription for Mr P, who was suffering from asthma. The prescription was for ventolin inhaler, phyllocontin and amoxil. The pharmacist, Mr K, read "amoxil" as "daonil" which is a drug for treating diabetes, which P did not have. As a result of taking the daonil, P suffered irreversible brain damage. He sued the doctor pharmacist, and the pharmacy in negligence, on the basis that the doctor's writing was negligently illegible, and the pharmacist was negligent in providing the wrong drug. Dr M argued that, despite the illegible prescription, the chain of causation was broken because the pharmacist should have realised the drug prescribed was not daonil, because, among other things:

- K should have got in touch with the doctor when he found the prescription hard to read;
- the dosage strength ordered was not appropriate for daonil, but was for amoxil;
- that the other drugs ordered were for treating asthma, and daonil was not;
- that the prescription was for 21 tablets only—a short course appropriate for amoxil but not for daonil; and
- daonil is taken only once a day, whereas the prescription was provided for three tablets a day.

[13.145] The Court rejected Dr M's argument, stating that the chain of causation had not been broken. It said that it was not outside the realms of reasonable foreseeablity that the doctor could have ordered daonil. It said that the doctor could not rely on the pharmacist to second-guess the doctor's order, or to get in touch with him if he had difficulty reading it.

However, this does not excuse the person who has trouble reading a doctor's order from investigating further. The person prescribing a drug should be questioned if an order is not clear, or if the order seems an unreasonable one, and health carers are required to use reasonable knowledge and care in so doing.

[13.150] Case: *Norton v Argonaut Insurance Co,*
144 So 2d 249 (1962) (CA Los Angeles United States)

A three-month-old baby was treated with lanoxin elixir, the original order being "2.5cc (0.125 mg) q6h x 3 then once daily". After the child was digitalised, the mother was instructed in administration and maintenance of the dose and the child was treated at home. On second admission the admitting doctor noted that the mother was giving medication, but did not specify what it was. He increased the dose, telling the mother, and wrote "Give 3.0cc lanoxin today for 1 dose only", neglecting to specify the form of the drug, the route, and the fact that the mother was giving the medication. Later that day the assistant director of nursing volunteered to assist in the ward due to its lack of staff, and began by checking the medications. On reading this order, and being unfamiliar with the fact that there was a paediatric suspension of lanoxin, she questioned other doctors and nurses about a written order for lanoxin which did not specify route, and appeared excessive. Due to their not fully understanding the nurse's lack of knowledge about the drug, and the circumstances of its proposed administration (the mother had already given the day's dose), the nurse was advised by these people to give the drug in the dosage written down. Wrongly believing that there is a presumption that unless specified, drugs are to be given intramuscularly, the nurse gave the child 3cc lanoxin intramuscularly. The child died.

[13.155] The Court found the hospital, doctor and nurse jointly liable for the child's death. First, the doctor did not properly record the specific drug (paediatric suspension), and omitted the route by which it was to be given. Two specific and important points regarding the administration of drugs was made by the Court, as follows:

1   Where a drug order is not clear, nurses should make absolutely certain what the doctor intended. This should be done by consulting the doctor who wrote the order, for, as this case shows, consulting others may lead to errors.
    Only in emergencies, where the prescribing doctor is not available and the drug must be given, should another doctor be consulted. One must be very careful, as we learn from this case, to procure a freshly written and full order, clearly giving the name of the drug, the dosage, route and frequency, and ensuring the patient's name and history are clearly identified with the order. Do not make any presumptions.
2   Although nurses may not be expected to have the same depth of knowledge about drugs as that expected of doctors, they should at least have some familiarity with any drug they administer.

Health carers should be familiar with the standard dosage, effects, side-effects and contra-indications of the drugs they give. One should consult the label on the drug itself, and a reference (a pharmacopoeia should be available). If there is a discrepancy in the information on the label and the drug order (such as an ordered dosage in excess of the recommended dose in the reference) this should be questioned.

The further point could be made that the nurse in *Norton's* case (see [13.150] above) helped out in an area of specialty in which she was not competent. Although this is covered to some extent in the second point made by the Court, one could add that inexperienced carers should be cautious of undertaking specialist activities, even where attempting to help overworked colleagues. In this case it could be argued that the nurse should have undertaken only those basic nursing activities that did not require a knowledge of paediatric nursing. See the discussion of what one should do when asked to work in an area in which one does not feel competent (see [6.445]ff).

Telephone orders

[13.160] Some comments were made regarding telephone orders at **[13.90]**-
[13.95]. Most health care institutions have established procedures for the
taking of telephone drug orders. The following is suggested as an advisable
procedure in providing for reasonably careful taking of such orders.

Checklist
HOW TO TAKE A TELEPHONE DRUG ORDER: RECOMMENDED
PRACTICE
✓ Write the order as it is being given.
✓ Read it back to the prescribing doctor.
✓ Get a colleague to hear the order from the doctor, write it down, and
repeat it to the doctor.
✓ Resolve any discrepancy or difficulty in hearing the order before the
telephone conversation is completed.
✓ The order should be written, preferably on the drug administration
form (*not* on the drug order form), and clearly marked as an *administration of a drug pursuant to telephone order* (preventing it being
considered a written order by the prescribing doctor, or the
erroneous reading of the actual written doctor's order as a fresh
order for repeat administration).
✓ Ensure the drug and its administration is checked and witnessed as
required when entered on the drug administration form.
✓ Record on that patient's notes that special action is required, namely
the writing up of the order by the doctor. Take any further action to
ensure follow up, such as flagging for action, contacting doctor to
secure written order, etc, that is required.

The reader is referred to the case of *Collins v Hertfordshire County Council* (see
[6.410]) where a telephone order was misheard, with fatal results. The difficulties of identifying those situations where a telephone drug order may be
misheard suggests that this form of ordering should only be used in
emergencies or where a written order would be extremely difficult to obtain,
and should not be used as a tool of convenience. Some States require that
telephone orders are restricted to use in emergencies, but the legislation does
not define these instances.

Transcribing of drug orders

[13.165] To prevent drug errors, it is suggested that one should not
transcribe orders and administration of drugs from the drug order or administration forms to other records. Where a drug has been ordered by a doctor, one
may write in the patient's notes something like: "Seen by Dr Smith. Analgesia
prescribed as per drug order form" not—"Seen by Dr Smith. Pethidine 75 mgm
imi 4th hourly prn ordered." Mistakes can be made in the transcription, and

someone may be tempted to rely on the secondary source rather than the original, and may end up giving the wrong medication. Conversely, nurses should not give prescribed medication on the basis of any written source (such as the nurses' notes or doctor's consultation form) other than the original drug order on the drug order form.

[13.170] Case: *Pillai v Messiter (No 2)* (1989) 16 NSWLR 197 (Court of Appeal, NSW)

A patient died from an overdose of phenytoin. The order for the drug had been transcribed from an out-of-date prescription sheet on to a new one. The patient had been ordered phenytoin 230 mg daily, and tegretol 1,400 mg daily. In transcribing, the doctor wrote the new order as phenytoin 1,400 mg to be given three times daily. A number of other doctors and nurses had also not noticed the error in transcription. The transcribing doctor was struck off the register for misconduct in a professional respect and appealed to the Court of Appeal.

[13.175] Although the Court of Appeal held that the doctor's error was an "unfortunate mistake", it held that it was not enough to constitute misconduct to the extent of attracting the penalty of being struck off the register. Certainly such a mistake could lead to liability in negligence on the doctor's part, possibly also on the part of the other nurses and doctors who failed to detect the mistake.

(This case is also discussed at **[12.300]**.)

Giving the wrong drug

[13.180] There may be several reasons for a patient receiving the wrong drug, for example:

- the drug order is unclear (dealt with above);
- a verbal order is misheard; and
- failure to check the label on the drug.

Mistake in verbal orders

[13.185] There is a responsibility on the part of health care staff to carefully check at the time of receiving it, a verbal order for treatment with which they are not familiar.

[13.190] Case: *Henson v Board of Management of Perth Hospital* (1939) 41 WALR 15 (SC)

A resident doctor instructed a student nurse to administer glycerine and carbol ear drops to a patient. The nurse understood him to have ordered undiluted acid carbol, but when she went to question the doctor he was gone. She checked with a staff nurse, who was also unsure, but poured some carbolic acid into a bottle to give to the patient, instructing him to pour some of it into his ear. When he did so damage was caused to his ear drum and he sustained some permanent hearing loss.

[13.195] The Court found both nurses and the doctor liable in negligence. It held that the student nurse, while not being expected to know as much as a staff nurse, should have exercised due care in ascertaining whether she had obtained the correct medication. The staff nurse, it seems, had even less chance of escaping liability, especially as it was shown that she burnt her fingers when pouring out the carbolic acid! The doctor was also negligent, the Court said, because he failed to give adequate instructions when a student nurse was involved, and failed to record the order in writing.

Failure to check drugs

[13.200] Failing to check drugs is, of course, a serious failure in the eyes of the law.

[13.205] **Case:** *Bugden v Harbour View Hospital* [1947] DLR 338 (SC Canada) (initial hearing)

The plaintiff was treated at the defendant hospital for an injury to his thumb. The doctor decided to set it and asked nurse B, an experienced graduate nurse, for some novocaine. Nurse B asked nurse S to get the novocaine. Nurse S handed nurse B a phial which was labelled, and, without looking at the label nurse B handed it to the doctor, who, also without checking the label, injected it into Bugden. The drug injected was in fact adrenalin, and Bugden died within an hour.

[13.210] Nurse S argued that nurse B's failure to read the label was an intervening factor and nurse B in turn pointed to the doctor's failure to read it as an intervening factor (see **[6.890]**). The Court did not accept either argument, holding that the foreseeablity of harm to the patient was enough to require all involved to take care, and found the nurses liable, while exonerating the doctor. In the English case of *Collins v Hertfordshire County Council* (see **[6.410]**) the Court stated (at 606) that:

"every surgeon takes responsibility for what he injects into a patient as local anaesthetic and that he should take some step reasonably to make sure, before he injects it, that he is injecting that which he ordered."

It is suggested that, based on the principles of negligence, this statement can be extended to cover all drugs given by all health care personnel.

Giving the wrong dosage

[13.215] There are cases where the wrong dosage has been given for various reasons, such as not reading or not hearing the order correctly. This may be because of illegibility or carelessness on the part of the doctor ordering it, or carelessness on the part of those receiving the order.

This has been discussed to some extent earlier in this chapter. A case occurred in Victoria where a 19-month-old girl was given 500 milligrams of aminophylline for asthma instead of 50 milligrams. The doctor ordering the drug had been on duty for many hours and had failed to write the order clearly. The two registered nurses on duty had failed to question the excessive dosage (described in O'Sullivan (1983), p 192). Such unfortunate events lead to accountability at law. Nurses should check the label on the bottle or ampoule carefully, and the mode of administration should be clearly written down. Nurses must also check when the last dose was given.

> **[13.220] Case: *Smith v Brighton and Lewes Hospital*,**
> ***The Times*, 2 May 1958 (England)**
>
> The patient was ordered 30 injections of streptomycin at eight-hour intervals for a severe case of boils. She received 34 doses, and as a result suffered damage to the eighth cranial nerve, causing loss of balance. On investigation of the facts it was found that there had not been an adequate record of the number of injections, and no cut-off date had been established. This was the responsibility of the ward sister.

[13.225] As a result the nurses who administered the extra injections were held not liable. An added feature of this case was that the ward sister, believing the nurses were the ones who would be held responsible, had attempted to shield the nurses by concealing from the doctor the fact that the extra doses had been given. This, the trial judge held, was an "ugly and unfortunate feature" of the case, and may have prevented the woman from receiving the benefit of the doctor's knowledge of the circumstances. The hospital was found liable for a large sum of money based on the ward sister's negligence.

Giving the drug to the wrong patient

[13.230] Even where it is thought that a patient's name is known, their identity should be carefully checked. Patients may say "yes" when asked "Are you Mrs So-and-So?" just to be polite or helpful, when they did not hear the question correctly. Positive identification should be made by having the patient state their name and date of birth. Special care should be taken where it is known or suspected that there are two or more patients with the same surname. This care should be taken even where the health carer feels familiar with the patient's name.

Giving the drug in the wrong site

[13.235] Special requirements for the administration of drugs must be known by, and/or communicated to, those administering drugs or patients taking them. Injections may cause harm if given subcutaneously rather than intramuscularly.

[13.240]   Case: *From Medical Protection Society Report 1974* (described in Langslow (1981), p 23)

A general practice doctor prescribed kenalog (triamcinolene acetonide) for a patient. The nurse administering it was not aware of the manufacturer's warning that the drug should be given by deep intramuscular injection to avoid subcutaneous fat atrophy. As the result of the subcutaneous injection of the drug and resulting fat atrophy, the woman sued the doctor. The Medical Protection Society settled on behalf of the doctor.

[13.245] The nurse was not sued in this case, but it is quite feasible that in a similar situation she could be. Nurses, in particular, may also be interested in the following cases.

[13.250]   Case: *Cavan v Wilcox* [1975] SCR 663 (SC Canada)

A nurse administered an injection of bicillin into a patient's deltoid muscle. Despite the fact that she had pulled back the plunger to check that no blood vessel had been pierced, the substance entered the circumflex artery, and as a result the patient developed gangrene of part of his hand.

[13.255] The Court found the nurse not liable in negligence, as she had checked that she had not penetrated any blood vessel, which was satisfactory precaution under the circumstances. The Court also decided that knowledge of the proximity of the artery to the injection site was not part of nurse training, and therefore not part of the body of knowledge that should be possessed by the reasonable nurse. Readers may decide that today a court in Australia would come to a different conclusion. Hitting of the sciatic nerve is, of course, a danger of which nurses should be aware. This was the conclusion of the following United States case.

[13.260]   Case: *Honeywell v Rogers*, 251 F Supp 841 (1966) (District Court Pennsylvania United States)

A student nurse gave an injection of iron dextran to an 11-month-old child. The mother gave evidence that it was given towards the centre of the buttock and not the outer and upper quadrant.

[13.265] There the Court took into account the training, supervision and knowledge of student nurses in the giving of injections, and determined that the injection was negligently given by the student nurse in question.

Failure to check for adverse effects

[13.270] It should be evident by what has been said that health carers should be aware of the likely adverse effects of the drugs that they give. This may be information:

* learned from lectures or in textbooks current and relevant to the profession;
* set out on the drug label or accompanying brochure;
* established by a circular distributed by the employer; or
* recorded in a patient's notes by the prescribing physician.

> **[13.275] Case:** *Chin Keow v Government of Malaysia*
> [1967] 1 WLR 813 (Privy Council England)
>
> A doctor ordered penicillin for a patient, whom he knew had been given penicillin previously. The doctor was aware of the possibility of an adverse reaction to penicillin. However he had given many doses (as many as 100 per day) without any such reaction. In this case he went ahead and gave the injection. It was only after the death of the patient from an adverse reaction that his outpatient card was consulted and found to be marked "Allergic to penicillin".

[13.280]   The Court found the doctor liable. It said that it would take into account the probability of adverse reactions, and what the reasonable practitioner should know about them when considering what, if any, liability to impose. The doctor should have made further inquiries; the fact that reactions are rare was not justification for his failure to do so. Drugs requiring specific attention from health carers, such as digoxin and insulin, are the most obvious drugs about which they should take care, but as pointed out above, not the only ones.

Other cases involving the failure to take proper precautions to prevent adverse reactions are *Battersby v Tottman* (1985) 37 SASR 524 (see above, **[5.245]**), where the serious condition of the patient was held to warrant excessively large doses of the drug Melleril, despite the danger of adverse effects. *Robinson v Post Office* [1974] 1 WLR 1176 established the accepted medical precaution of giving a test dose of anti-tetanus serum as a legal requirement. The likelihood of adverse effects of a drug must be reasonably probable and reasonably part of the knowledge of the profession for it to be necessary to be taken into account.

Standing orders

[13.285] Protocols or standing orders may establish procedures to be followed in the administration of some restricted drugs, which may allow for them to be given by health carers such as nurses and paramedics in certain situations, such as emergencies, or as routine treatment for the patients of particular practitioners (most often occurring in obstetric practice). They generally take the form of general prescriptions. The legality of these is far from certain, except in cases where they have been recognised by legislation (see **[13.45]** above). The fact that they are written orders to be followed in relation to particular patients (those in intensive care, or patients of a particular obstetrician, for example) in specific circumstances is generally considered acceptable as proper prescriptions. It is of concern that there is no clear legislative provision establishing their status at law, and setting out the requirements that must be met in order for a standing order to be legally recognised. They have not been legally challenged at this stage, to the authors' knowledge. In the meantime, there is a risk that they will be considered unlawful. Standing orders are often used as an administrative convenience rather than a way of dealing with emergencies. So long as they are used in cases of emergency, the following checklist should ameliorate any liability.

Checklist
PROTOCOLS AND STANDING ORDERS
✓ Is the order clearly written, with the name of the drug, dosage, route and frequency unambiguous?
✓ Does it identify precisely which patients are to receive the medication?
✓ Does it clearly state under which circumstances those patients are to be given the drug, and the conditions which are to preclude its administration?
✓ Does it note any special observations or care which may be required prior to, or subsequent to, administration?
✓ Is the order not only signed, but the name of the prescribing doctor quite clear?
✓ Is the order clearly dated?
✓ Has the administration set a period for review of this type of order where there is no legal time limit?
✓ Is the order current (within that date)?

Outdated drug orders

[13.290] Drug orders should be periodically reviewed, and in any case nurses should check when the orders were written. Sometimes a law or institutional practice may mean that an order is out-of-date. Other situations might arise where a certain number of administrations of a particular drug are ordered and a proper check on those given is not kept (the case of *Smith v Brighton and Lewes Hospital* **[13.220]** is also relevant here).

References and Further Reading

Looseleaf references such as *The Laws of Australia* (Lawbook Co.); *Halsbury's Laws of Australia* (Sydney, Butterworths) are useful as are the following:

Australian Health and Medical Law Reporter (CCH, Sydney, 1991)

Brazier, M, *Medicine, Patients and the Law* (Penguin, 1992), ch 8

Dix, et al, *Law for the Medical Profession* (Butterworths, Sydney, 1988)

Forrester, K, "Use of Standing Orders—It Depends on Where You Stand" (1999) 7 *Journal of Law and Medicine* 17

Health Care Complaints Commission, *Annual Report 2000-2001*, accessed at www.hccc.nsw.gov.au/downloads/ar00-01.pdf in March 2006

Health Care Complaints Commission, *Annual Report 2001-2002*, accessed at www.hccc.nsw.gov.au/downloads/ar01-02.pdf in March 2006

Health Care Complaints Commission, *Annual Report 2003-2004*, accessed at www.hccc.nsw.gov.au/downloads/ar_03-04.pdf in March 2006

Health Care Complaints Commission, *Report on an investigation of incidents in the Operating Theatre at Canterbury Hospital 8 February – 7 June 1999*, 3 September 1999, accessed at www.hccc.nsw.gov.au/downloads/canterbu.pdf in March 2006

Langslow, A, "Drugs Draw Judicial Fire" (1981) 10(10) *Australian Nurses Journal* 23

Murchison, I A and Nichols, T, *Legal Foundations of Nursing Practice* (Macmillan, London, 1970)

O'Sullivan, J, *Law for Nurses* (Law Book Co, Sydney, 1983)

Review of Professional Indemnity Arrangements for Health Care Professionals, *Compensation and Professional Indemnity in Health Care: A Discussion Paper* (Department of Health Housing and Community Services, 1992)

Skene, L, *Law & Medical Practice—Rights, Duties, Claims & Defences* (Lexis Nexis Butterworths 2004) at [9.57]

Staunton, P and Whyburn, R, *Nursing and the Law* (4th ed, Saunders, Sydney, 1997), ch 7

Therapeutic Goods Administration website at www.tga.gov.au including information regarding the National Drug and Poisons Schedule Committee at www.tga.gov.au/ndpsc.

14 Criminal law & health care

Principles of criminal law

Defences to a criminal charge

Substantive offences relevant to health care

End of life decision making

Criminal negligence

Abortion

Victims of crime

Crime by patients

chapter 14

Criminal Law and Health Care

Introduction

[14.05] Criminal law deals with the prosecution of offenders by the State, as a result of their conduct against people or property, whether someone is directly harmed by that conduct or not. The interest of criminal law is in the punishment of the perpetrator, not in the fate of the victim, who must pursue remedies in civil actions. This lack of interest has been mitigated somewhat by the development of criminal injuries compensation mechanisms in each Australian jurisdiction.

The basic outline of a criminal action and the proof required for a conviction is dealt with in Chapter 3. It is important to have this in mind when considering specific actions under criminal law.

Criminal law can encompass a number of issues of particular interest to the health care professions. These include:

- murder (see **[14.210]**);
- manslaughter (see **[14.215]**);
- euthanasia (see **[14.220]**ff);
- abortion (see **[14.445]**);
- surrogacy agreements (see **[9.290]**);
- dealing with victims and perpetrators of crime (see **[14.555]**ff);
- domestic violence and child abuse (see **[16.120]**ff);
- offences related to infectious diseases (see **[16.10]**ff); and
- drug offences (see **[13.25]**ff).

Over the centuries, English common law developed a series of principles that underlie criminal law. Before specific criminal offences are dealt with, the most important principles will be considered.

Principles of Criminal Law

Principle 1: Criminal offences must be established by law prior to a charge

[14.10] Criminal laws cannot be retrospective—that is, if certain conduct is not an offence when committed, the later enactment of a law making the conduct an offence will not enable prosecution for the conduct which predated the creation of the offence.

Each Australian jurisdiction, as well as the Commonwealth, has legislation establishing criminal offences and penalties. However, as we inherited the common law from England, we also inherited our initial set of criminal offences from there. In New South Wales, South Australia and Victoria, as well as the Australian Capital Territory, common law has continued to be a source of criminal offences, modified over time by statute.

Technically, criminal law covers all statutory provisions that authorise the prosecution for, and set penalties for, a nominated activity. Offences are scattered throughout various pieces of legislation, but each Australian jurisdiction has a major statute covering the more serious offences (The main ones are: *Crimes Act 1914* (Cth); *Crimes Act 1900* (ACT); *Crimes Act 1900* (NSW); *Criminal Law Consolidation Act 1935* (SA); *Crimes Act 1958* (Vic)). The Northern Territory, Queensland, Tasmania, Western Australia and the Commonwealth have Criminal Codes (*Criminal Code Act* (NT); *Criminal Code 1899* (Qld); *Criminal Code Act 1924* (Tas); *Criminal Code* (WA); *Criminal Code Act 1995* (Cth)), which are intended to be independent of the common law (although it may be used as an aid for interpreting the provisions; Colvin et al, (1998), p 8). Again, the Criminal Codes are not the sole source of criminal offences—other legislation, such as that on drugs, also sets out prohibitions and penalties.

Criminal law comes from the establishment of two kinds of offences. First, there are the general catalogues of criminal offences, in the Crimes Acts or Criminal Codes. These are dealt with in this chapter. Secondly, there is a body of offences created in the multitude of statutes, regulations and by-laws, which are not part of the Crimes Acts or Criminal Codes, but do attract penalties. These offences are an adjunct to the main thrust of the legislation in which they appear and the penalties may be quite severe. They may cover anything from using a hose at prohibited times to drug importation.

Generally, a crime must involve:

- *capacity* to commit a criminal offence
- *action* which is recognised at law as being criminal (*actus reus*)
- *intention* to carry out the action (*mens rea*)
- *absence* of any defence.

Principle 2: There must be an act

[14.15] Generally it has been held that a crime cannot be committed by omission, that is, by failing to act, stemming from the basic idea that one shouldn't be punished for something one didn't do.

Omission

[14.20] This is not always the case, however, for failure to act may make a person open to conviction, for example, for failing to fulfil a duty of care (see **[14.30]**, **[14.430]**ff).

> **[14.25] Case:** *R v Coney* (1882) 8 QBD 534 (Court for
> Crown Cases Reserved England)
>
> C was in a crowd watching an illegal prize-fight. He took no part in it, or in the management or encouragement of it. He said and did nothing. He was convicted of assault as a principal in the second degree, although the jury found that he did not aid or abet the fight.

[14.30] Hawkins J stated (at 557-558):

> "It is no criminal offence to stand by, a mere passive spectator of a crime, even of a murder. Non-interference to prevent a crime is not itself a crime. But the fact that a person was voluntarily and purposefully present witnessing the commission of a crime, and offered no opposition to it, though he might reasonably be expected to prevent and had the power so to do, or at least to express his dissent, might [provide prima facie evidence] ... that he wilfully encouraged and so aided and abetted."

In the case of *R v Russell* [1933] VLR 59 (SC Vic), Russell, who after an argument with his wife, stood by and watched her drown herself and their two young children in a swimming pool, was convicted of being a principal in the second degree, because the jury was entitled to find that his mere voluntary presence indicated that he assented to and was willing to abet the crime.

The position with regard to homicide is special, and will be dealt with more specifically below.

There was another element in the case of *Russell*: so far as the children were concerned, his failure to prevent them from drowning resulted in his being found guilty of manslaughter. If a person has a particular relationship of care to another, or has put them in danger, and intentionally refuses to give reasonable aid to them, that person may be guilty of a crime. This is similar to the duty of care and its breach, in a negligence action, which in this case must be such as to attract criminal sanction (see the discussion of criminal negligence below **[14.430]**ff). This could apply to health workers who fail to resuscitate or otherwise aid a person in their care who requires life-saving attention.

Principle 3: There must be an intention to commit the act

[14.35] The accused must have intended to carry out the prohibited act. Intention may include three states of mind:

1) having the *aim of doing the prohibited act or causing the prohibited event* (for example, the death of a person); or
2) being *reckless* that certain consequences may result from one's act that are not the primary aim; or
3) being *criminally negligent* in one's actions. This is sometimes referred to as "gross negligence". It requires a much more serious degree of negligence than the civil action, and is dealt with in more detail below.

The level of culpability may be less in the event of (2) recklessness or (3) criminal negligence.

The Code jurisdictions build in the element of intention required in the legislative provision for each offence listed. Where there may be some ambiguity, the above principle will inform the court in its interpretation.

Continuation of an act which is accidental, and to which one then applies criminal intent, becomes a criminal act.

[14.40] Case: *Fagan v Metropolitan Police Commissioner* [1969] 1 QB 439; [1968] 3 All ER 422 (Divisional Court England)

F accidentally drove his car onto the foot of a policeman who was directing him how to park it. The policeman said several times "Get off, you are on my foot". F indicated that he could wait, and after the policeman repeated his order several times slowly turned on the ignition and moved the car. The Court was undecided as to whether the initial driving onto the officer's foot was a deliberate act, but F argued that he had not intended any assault when he actually drove onto the officer's foot. Therefore, he argued, *mens rea* (criminal intent) was absent at this time. Later when he had mens rea, he continued, he did not carry out any act, and thus he could not be convicted of assault. He was convicted and appealed.

[14.45] The Court decided that where an act was a continuing one, there did not need to be mens rea at the inception of that act, so long as at some stage while it was ongoing, the accused formed the mens rea. He was convicted. This principle was followed by the English Court of Appeal in *R v Miller* [1982] 3 All ER 386. The defendant in that case fell asleep in another person's house while smoking. He awoke to find the mattress alight, and left without doing anything, allowing the house to catch fire. In determining whether *actus reus* (guilty act) and the mens rea concurred in time, the Court said the whole course of events should be considered. The judges held that the innocent setting in train of events culminating in criminal harm imposes on the defendant a duty of intervention sufficient to make them guilty in law if they have a guilty mind at the time of inactivity.

This approach was endorsed in principle by the High Court in the case of *Royall v The Queen* (1991) 172 CLR 378; [1991] HCA 27, although the issue was approached in a different way. In that case the defendant had engaged in a course of violent conduct towards his victim, causing her to fall (either because she was pushed or she fell or jumped in trying to escape him). The question was what was the correct time for assessing whether the accused had the relevant mens rea for murder. The Court allowed the consideration of the overall sequence of events, even though it may have been difficult for the jury to be confident precisely when the defendant's mens rea crystallised.

A person may be held criminally liable for unintended consequences when a planned offence "goes wrong". This can include, for example, a bank robbery where someone is hurt, contrary to initial intentions, or where a victim unreasonably attempts escape by opening a car door when it is in motion and jumping out (*R v Roberts* (1971) 56 Cr App R 95).

Principle 4: Any act must be voluntary

[14.50] One cannot be found guilty of an act over which one does not have physical control. As well as accidents, there is the defence of automatism (see **[14.165]**ff). Where an accidental occurrence cannot be isolated from other actions constituting an intention to commit a crime, one cannot plead that it was involuntary.

[14.55] Case: *Ryan v The Queen* (1967) 121 CLR 205; [1967] HCA 2

R took a loaded and cocked rifle into a service station and pointed it at an employee, T, demanding money, which he was given. When R was about to tie T up, he was startled by a sudden movement by T. R's finger involuntarily squeezed the trigger and T was killed. R argued that he should not be found guilty of murder because the squeezing of the trigger was involuntary. He was found guilty by the Supreme Court of New South Wales, appealed unsuccessfully to the Court of Appeal, and applied for leave to appeal to the High Court.

[14.60] The High Court said that the death was caused by a combination of events which were carried out with the intention to rob. All actions, including the loading and cocking of the gun were as much a part of causing death as was the actual pulling of the trigger. This final act could not be isolated from the earlier ones, and so it could not be held to have been purely accidental and unforeseen.

This ruling is in keeping with the felony–murder rule, which in some Australian jurisdictions provides for the treatment of an unintended death during the commission of some of the serious offences, such as murder (see, for example, *Crimes Act 1958* (Vic), s 3A).

Strict liability

[handwritten: guilty act]

[handwritten: Criminal notes]

[14.65] There is a general requirement that all offences require both actus reus and mens rea; however, in some cases one may be found guilty of an offence even where one did not have mens rea. Such offences require only that one has committed the act prohibited, state of mind being irrelevant. The removal of the requirement of mens rea must be clear from the wording of a statute, either explicitly or by necessary implication. Necessary implication occurs when the act prohibited is a grave social evil, the legislation is known to the public at large, and the activity can reasonably easily be avoided.

Proudman v Dayman (1941) 67 CLR 536; [1941] HCA 28 established that where the imposition of strict liability would result in the punishment of a class of people whose conduct could not in any way affect the observance of the law, strict liability should not be applied. If one does have control then one may be held liable for not taking proper care. Strict liability usually applies to:

* traffic offences (for example, parking);
* preparation and selling of food (for example, content of sausages); and
* activity on licensed premises.

Principle 5: One cannot normally be vicariously guilty in criminal law

[14.70] Generally, guilt must be personal, as mens rea is normally required.

[14.75] Case: *R v Huggins* (1730) 2 Ld Raym 1574; 92 ER 518 (all the judges of King's Bench, Exchequer and Common Pleas England)

In 1730 a prison superintendent, H, was convicted of murder. His underling, B, had placed a prisoner in a cell in conditions which eventually caused his death. H was not fully aware of the conditions of the deceased's incarceration.

[14.80] On appeal the Court held that H could not be found guilty because only the one who immediately does the act is guilty. If it is the act of an employee, unless it is done by the command or direction of the employer or superior, or he or she is an accomplice to the crime, the latter is not guilty.

Exceptions to this principle are:

* liability through others;
* liability through incitement;
* delegation; and
* accomplices to crime.

Liability through others

[14.85] One may carry out a crime through another who has not the appropriate mens rea: for example, the woman who, wishing with her lover to kill her husband, gives her children poison in the guise of good medicine to put in his drink, may, with the lover, be found guilty of murder. The children, who unknowingly carried out the act, would not be guilty (*Female Poisoner's Case* (1634) Kelyng 53; 84 ER 1079). This very ancient principle has been adapted into legislation regarding, for example, murder.

Liability through incitement

[14.90] When a person incites another to commit a crime, that person will, in most circumstances, be guilty of the completed crime as an accomplice. The means for doing this are not important, rather the court is interested in determining whether the accused sought to reach and influence the mind of the other person towards commission of a crime. It is not essential that the person who incites the other is successful in so doing: where the inciter does not reach the mind of the prospective incitee (for example, a letter goes astray), the offence will be one of attempted incitement. Where the incitee's mind is reached, but not influenced enough to commit the offence, the incitement has still occurred. The intentions and actions of the person inciting are vital to the proof of the offence, regardless of any action or otherwise of the prospective perpetrator.

Delegation

[14.95] The case of *Huggins*, above, dealt with this situation, but there the court held that delegation did not exist. However, a corporation may be criminally liable for the offences of employees where the crime can be shown to be the act of the corporation (for example, where the employee is instructed to carry it out). Corporations may be liable for certain statutory offences, such as the serving of liquor to underage drinkers, or occupational health and safety breaches. It is suggested that the reasoning of the courts is as follows; where one delegates a function, and that function is bound by a licence, one cannot complain about being unaware of the delegate knowingly carrying on the enterprise in contravention of the licence.

Accomplices to crime

[14.100] A man may be principal in an offence in two degrees. As a principal in the first degree he is the actor, or absolute perpetrator of the crime; and, in the second degree, he who is present, aiding and abetting the fact to be done. Which presence need not always be an actual immediate standing by, within sight or hearing of the fact; but there may also be a constructive presence, as when one commits a robbery or murder, and another keeps watch or guard at some convenient distance (Williams et al (1983), p 443). An accomplice to a crime assists in the event, and may be either a principal in the second degree, who is present during the act, or an accessory who is not present during the act, but has been of assistance before or after the act. The distinction is of little comfort to the accomplice, however, because principals in the second degree and accomplices before the act are liable to the same punishment as a principal in the first degree (See, for example, *Crimes Act 1900* (NSW), ss 345, 346; *Criminal Code* (NT), s 12; *Criminal Code* (Qld), ss 7, 8, 9; *Crimes Act 1958* (Vic), ss 323, 324; *Criminal Code* (WA), ss 7, 8, 9).

Principle 6: The precise act for which one is charged must have been committed

[14.105] A person cannot be found guilty of an offence unless the act specified in the charge has been committed. Even where one believes one is committing a crime, and intends to do so, if the act has not been established by law to be criminal there is no crime. The following case raised much discussion on the practical and philosophical aspects of when an attempt to commit a crime, where the commission is factually or legally impossible, should be punished (see, for example, Brett, Waller and Williams (1997), p 450ff).

[14.110] Case: *Haughton v Smith* [1975] AC 476; [1973] 3 All ER 1109 (House of Lords England)

S was convicted of attempting to handle stolen goods. In fact the goods had been seized by the police and were in their custody in a van. S, ignorant of the police involvement, met the van and arranged for disposal of the goods. The Crown conceded that the goods were, while in the custody of police, no longer "stolen goods" in the strict sense of that term, when the alleged offence was committed. S appealed on the ground that as the goods were no longer stolen, he could not be convicted of attempting to handle stolen goods.

[14.115] The House of Lords agreed. Lord Morris said (at 1122): "the presence of a guilty mind does not transform what a man actually does into something that he has not done".

Viscount Dilhorne added (at 1126):

"A man cannot attempt to handle goods which are not stolen. A man taking an umbrella from a club thinking it the property of someone else [when it is in fact his own] does not steal. His belief does not convert his conduct into an offence if his conduct cannot constitute a crime."

This was a case involving *legal impossibility*, that is, the attempted act is not a crime, contrary to the accused's belief. Other cases may involve *factual impossibility* where the act would be an offence, but (unbeknownst to the accused in most cases) it is impossible to complete.

This principle also includes the rule that criminal law cannot be [...]
tive: that is, any offence for which a person is charged must have be[...]
established by legislation as an offence *before* the commission of the a[...]

Principle 7: Ignorance of the law is no excuse

[14.120] This principle has been held as a basic rule in criminal law. The accused cannot say that he or she did not know that the conduct constituted an offence. However, a mistake as to what the law is may mean that the requirement for *mens rea* has not been met (simply put, one can't have a guilty mind if one doesn't know the action is wrong). This, of course, does not mean that one can remain blissfully deliberately ignorant of the law, everyone has a responsibility to take reasonable steps to know what is wrong, and it appears that the principle applies unless the accused can show that it was not reasonably possible for them to have known the law (for example, the legislation had not been published). Even then, it would most likely be a mitigating factor in determining penalty rather than culpability. Many problems have arisen in determining whether the accused's confusion stemmed from a mistake of fact (which may be an excuse) or a mistake of law (see, for example, Brett, Waller and Williams (1997), ch 13).

guilty
criminal
blame
worthy

Principle 8: Presumption of innocence

[14.125] All readers are probably familiar with the aphorism that one is "innocent until proven guilty". This is one of the fundamental principles of criminal law, and leads to the rule that the prosecution must prove the guilt of the accused, and that the accused does not have to prove anything.

In the courtroom the accused attempts to throw doubt on the prosecution case, in adducing evidence, but at no stage, with the exceptions below (see **[14.150]**ff), does the accused have to present proof of *not* having committed the offence, except in a handful of statutory exceptions. Thus if nurse Jane Doe is accused of murder, it is not her lawyer's task to prove that she did not commit the offence: it is up to the prosecution to prove that she did, the proof being strong enough to convince a jury beyond a reasonable doubt that she was the person who caused the death and that she had the intention to do so. Her lawyer's task is to produce evidence which will cause the jury to have reasonable doubt as to her guilt and, unless they are convinced beyond a reasonable doubt that she committed the murder, even where they think she probably did, they must enter a "not guilty" verdict.

[14.130] Case: *Woolmington v Director of Public Prosecutions* [1935] AC 462 (House of Lords England)

W had an argument with his wife. He told the Court that he threatened to kill himself, and produced a loaded gun. Somehow in the ensuing activity it went off, killing her. The jury convicted

him of murder, the judge having told them that if they were
satisfied that he killed his wife, the killing was to be considered
murder unless he convinced them that it was something less, for
example manslaughter or excusable homicide. W appealed,
basing his argument on error in the judge's instructions. The
Appeal Court upheld the conviction, but the case went to the
House of Lords, where the conviction was quashed.

The House of Lords, in one of the most quoted statements of criminal law,
stated that:

> "Throughout the web of English Criminal law one golden thread is always to
> be seen, that it is the duty of the prosecution to prove the prisoner's guilt
> subject to ... the defence of insanity and subject also to any statutory
> exception. If, at the end of and on the whole of the case, there is a
> reasonable doubt ... whether the prisoner killed the deceased with a
> malicious intention, the prosecution has not made out the case and the
> prisoner is entitled to an acquittal."

Exceptions

[14.135] Exceptions to this principle, situations where the accused has the
onus of proof, occur where he or she offers the defences of insanity or
diminished responsibility (see below).

Defences to a Criminal Charge

[14.140] A defence to a criminal charge may be an absolute or a partial (or
qualified) defence. An absolute defence is one which, if successful, leads to a
finding of "not guilty" (for example, self-defence). A partial defence results in
one being found guilty of a lesser offence than that charged (for example,
diminished responsibility).

   While insanity may be pleaded as a defence to any alleged crime (although
it is usually reserved for more serious offences), diminished responsibility is a
specific statutory defence to a charge of murder. If the jury finds the defendant
did carry out the act for which he or she is being tried, but was suffering from
diminished responsibility at the time, they are to return a verdict of manslaughter. Insanity and diminished responsibility are exceptions to the rule that the
accused does not have to prove innocence.

Insanity

[14.145] The defence of insanity, as stated, is always an absolute defence, in
that those who successfully plead insanity are not guilty of the offence on the
grounds of insanity. This does not mean that they are allowed to go free. Instead
of being convicted and punished for a crime, they are dealt with according to

their illness. The defence has the onus of proving insanity, and must positively adduce evidence to convince the jury of this. In practice insanity is mainly used as a defence to a charge of homicide, and the general result is that the accused will be kept in a psychiatric institution. In most jurisdictions the term "insanity" has been replaced by expressions such as "mental impairment" (see, for example, *Crimes Act 1900* (ACT)) and "unsoundness of mind" (see, for example, *Criminal Code* (WA)).

McNaghten Rules

[14.150] The rules relating to common law establishment of insanity were formulated in 1843 by the House of Lords, who had to decide how to establish whether one Daniel McNaghten, charged with murder, was insane according to law. He had attempted to shoot the Prime Minister, Sir John Peel, but mistakenly shot his secretary. McNaghten was allegedly suffering delusions of persecution. The Lords decided that jurors should be instructed that every person is to be presumed sane, and to possess normal responsibility for her or his crimes, unless the contrary is proved to the jury's satisfaction. To establish a ground of insanity the accused must show that, at the time of committing the act, he or she was labouring under such a defect of reason, from disease of the mind, as not to know the nature and quality of the act (that is, not to know what they were doing) or, if they did know, that they did not know that what they were doing was wrong (for example, knowing that they were killing someone but wrongly believing it was in self-defence, or that the person was a wartime enemy).

The application of the McNaghten Rules in each Australian jurisdiction must be considered in light of the relevant Act or Code.

Diminished responsibility

[14.155] Available as a defence to a charge of murder in some jurisdictions (see for example *Criminal Code 1899* (Qld), s 304A), diminished responsibility generally requires proof of an abnormality of the mind (whether arising from a condition of arrested or retarded development of mind, or any inherent illness, or induced by disease or injury) which had substantially impaired the accused's mental responsibility at the time of the offence. Again, it must be proved by the accused.

Other defences to a criminal charge

[14.160] Other defences include automatism, duress, self-defence, necessity and provocation. The Crown bears the burden of proving beyond reasonable doubt that the accused's defence has not been made out.

Automatism

[14.165] This defence is used where physical conduct has occurred which was involuntary because all bodily movements were wholly uncontrolled and uninitiated by any function of the conscious will.

Automatism is a temporary condition of mind, it may have one of many causes, and results in a person carrying out acts of which he or she is totally unconscious. It may be drug-induced, or the result of disease (for example, post-epileptic automatism or hypoglycaemic episodes), or of injury (for example, concussion).

A defence of automatism is essentially a denial of voluntariness. In *Ryan v The Queen* (1967) 121 CLR 205; [1967] HCA 2, Barwick CJ stated that automatism was simply an expression for the absence of voluntary conduct.

[14.170] Case: *R v Ross Gillett*, NSW District Court, Berman DCJ 25 November 2004, No 03/11/1112

G was driving his car on 2 May 2003 when his vehicle came into collision with three other vehicles. One of those vehicles, containing a young couple and their daughter was pushed into the path of an oncoming vehicle, which was unable to avoid collision. All three members of the family were killed. The incident had striking similarities with an accident that had occurred ten years earlier where G was involved and was observed slumped over the steering wheel. G was prosecuted on three charges that he had driven his vehicle in a manner dangerous to other persons. G's case was that shortly before the collision on 2 May 2003 he suffered a fit or seizure which meant his actions were involuntary.

In order to succeed the prosecution needed to prove, beyond reasonable doubt, that G's actions were voluntary. The case was thus framed in three ways:

(i)   G did not suffer a fit or seizure on the afternoon in question; alternatively,

(ii) given G's awareness of what he was doing and ability to control his motor vehicle, his actions should still be considered voluntary; alternatively,

(iii) at a time shortly before the accident, when G was driving voluntarily, he was nonetheless driving dangerously because of the risk that he would suffer a fit or seizure causing him to lose control of his car. To succeed on this ground, the prosecution needed also to prove that G did not believe on reasonable grounds that it was safe for him to drive that afternoon.

Berman DCJ was not convinced beyond reasonable doubt that G did not suffer a complex partial seizure on the afternoon in question and accepted expert evidence in concluding that G also had a complex partial seizure immediately before the 1993 accident. After consideration of the eyewitness and medical evidence, Berman DCJ was not satisfied beyond reasonable doubt that G was acting voluntarily when his vehicle collided with that of the young family.

This left for consideration the third manner in which the prosecution had stated its case. Berman DCJ was satisfied beyond reasonable doubt that in the time leading up to the accident, G was driving voluntarily until he had the seizure. He stated the test of whether G was driving dangerously as he approached the scene of the accident as follows:

"whether at the relevant time, as a result of his condition, the mere fact of him driving in that condition constituted driving in a manner dangerous to another person or persons because driving in that condition subjected them to a real, substantial and significant risk of injury or death over and above that ordinarily associated with the driving of a motor vehicle, including driving by persons who may, on occasions, drive with less than due care and attention" (at [155]).

Berman DCJ was satisfied that because of G's epilepsy and the risk that he would suffer a seizure whilst driving, his driving on the day in question was a real danger to other people, satisfying the test stated above. With regard to the question of whether G believed that it was not dangerous for him to drive, Berman DCJ, considering the facts surrounding the 1993 accident and G's medical history, concluded that G did not believe it was safe for him to drive. G was found guilty on each of the three counts and subsequently sentenced to seven years imprisonment.

[14.175] The question of responsibility for crime committed while under the self-induced influence of alcohol or drugs was considered in the following case.

[14.180] Case: *R v O'Connor* (1980) 146 CLR 64; [1960] HCA 17 (High Court)

O was charged with wounding with intent to resist arrest. He had consumed an hallucinogenic drug and alcohol when he stole items from a policeman's car. The policeman, happening upon the scene, arrested him for larceny. O stabbed the policeman with a knife. It was accepted by the Court that at the time O "could have been rendered incapable of reasoning and of forming an intent to steal or wound". He was convicted, failed on appeal to the Court of Appeal, and went to the High Court.

[14.185] The Court held that the fact that intoxication was self-induced does not mean that the person had the intention (mens rea) for the commission of an offence, which may have been done involuntarily. Barwick CJ stated (at 465) that:

"It seems to me to be completely inconsistent with the principles of the common law that a man should be conclusively presumed to have an intent which, in fact, he does not have, or to have done an act which, in truth, he did not do."

The onus of proof of intention lies upon the Crown. A later case, *R v Coleman* (1990) 19 NSWLR 467, applied this case, holding that the only question the jury has to determine in relation to the requisite states of mind was whether the accused had in fact formed them.

This approach may be modified by statute. For example, in Queensland, the *Criminal Code 1899*, ss 27 and 28, provide that a person who intentionally causes herself or himself to become intoxicated or stupefied is unable to claim they are not criminally responsible for an act or omission on the grounds that at the relevant time they were of such a state of mental disease or mental infirmity as to deprive them of the capacity to understand or control their actions.

Duress

[14.190] The definition of duress espoused by Smith J in *R v Hurley* [1967] VR 526 (FC) (at 543) and substantially followed in *R v Lawrence* [1980] NSWLR 122, involves the following elements:

- the accused carried out the offence under threat of death or grievous bodily harm being unlawfully inflicted on someone if the offence were not carried out;
- under the circumstances a person of ordinary strength would have capitulated;
- the threat was present at the time of offence, was continuing, was imminent and impending;
- the accused reasonably believed that the threat would be carried out;
- the crime was not murder or some other offence so heinous it should be excepted;
- the accused had not exposed herself or himself to the application of duress; or
- the accused had no way of safely preventing the application of the threat.

Self-defence

[14.195] Self-defence is the commission of an offence undertaken to protect oneself or certain classes of other people from threatened harm by another and may constitute a defence to a criminal charge in some circumstances.

In order for self-defence to apply the force used must be necessary to avert the danger and reasonable in light of the danger posed (see *Zecevic v Director of Public Prosecutions (Vic)* (1987) 162 CLR 645; [1987] HCA 26). The use of excessive force may negative the defence.

Checklist
WHEN SELF-DEFENCE IS A VALID DEFENCE TO A CHARGE OF ASSAULT
✓ Did the accused have a reasonable and honest belief of actual or imminent attack likely to harm? If no, self-defence is ruled out. If yes, continue.
✓ Was the force used more than required for the accused's protection? If no, self-defence is established. If yes, continue.
✓ Did the accused realise that the force was more than required? If no, self-defence is established. If yes, consider assault or manslaughter, depending on the circumstances.

The checklist above can be applied to charges of murder, manslaughter or assault. Generally, no alternative finding to a charge of assault is available, as there is with murder (see **[14.200]**ff) so the finding will either be "guilty" or "not guilty". However there are grades of assault, such as "assault with intent to cause grievous bodily harm", "assault causing actual bodily harm", and simply "assault". Each has progressively diminishing penalties.

The Criminal Codes and Acts of each jurisdiction vary slightly in their application of the common law test of self-defence and the acceptable level of force to be used. Readers may also wish to note the self-defence protections to civil claims, such as in the *Civil Liability Act 2002* (NSW), s 52, as follows:

"52 No civil liability for acts in self-defence
(1) A person does not incur a liability to which this Part applies arising from any conduct of the person carried out in self-defence, but only if the conduct to which the person was responding:
  (a) was unlawful, or
  (b) would have been unlawful if the other person carrying out the conduct to which the person responds had not been suffering from a mental illness at the time of the conduct.
(2) A person carries out conduct in self-defence if and only if the person believes the conduct is necessary:
  (a) to defend himself or herself or another person, or
  (b) to prevent or terminate the unlawful deprivation of his or her liberty or the liberty of another person, or
  (c) to protect property from unlawful taking, destruction, damage or interference, or
  (d) to prevent criminal trespass to any land or premises or to remove a person committing any such criminal trespass,
and the conduct is a reasonable response in the circumstances as he or she perceives them.
(3) This section does not apply if the person uses force that involves the intentional or reckless infliction of death only:
  (a) to protect property, or
  (b) to prevent criminal trespass or to remove a person committing criminal trespass."

Provocation

[14.200] Provocation is available to reduce a charge of murder to one of manslaughter and may have application in some jurisdictions to a limited number of other offences. In *Masciantonio v The Queen* (1991) 183 CLR 58 the majority stated:

> "Homicide, which would otherwise be murder, is reduced to manslaughter if the accused causes death whilst acting under provocation. The provocation must be such that it is capable of causing an ordinary person to lose self-control and to act in the way in which the accused did. The provocation must actually cause the accused to lose self-control and the accused must act whilst deprived of self-control before he has had the opportunity to regain his composure."

The elements of provocation are not consistent across the Australian jurisdictions, however, in *Stingel v The Queen* (1990) 171 CLR 312; [1990] HCA 61 the court noted that:

> "One finds in the authorities ... a perception that, in this particular field of criminal law, the common law, the Codes and other statutory provisions, and judicial decisions about them, have tended to interact and to reflect a degree of unity of underlying notions."

One area on which the various Australian jurisdictions differ in their definition of murder is in relation to the traditional requirement of "sudden and temporary loss of control". Some jurisdictions require that any response to provocation be sudden and in the heat of passion, as an immediate reaction to the provocation. In other jurisdictions provocation can apply where murder is not necessarily immediate to the provocation, which allows a jury to consider, for example, the killing of a spouse who has been abusive or violent for a long time, but doing it when that person is not an actual threat, when the retaliation is more likely to be effective, for example, when they are asleep.

In *Green v The Queen* (1997) 191 CLR 334; [1997] HCA 50, McHugh J commented regarding the "ordinary person" or objective element of the offence, stating:

> "In my opinion, the phrase 'an ordinary person in the position of the accused' means an ordinary person who suffered the provocation which the accused suffered as the result of the conduct of the deceased. The standard against which the loss of self-control is judged is that of a hypothetical ordinary person. That person is unaffected by the accused's idiosyncrasies, personal attributes or past history, save and except that the words 'in the position of the accused' require that the hypothetical person be an ordinary person who has been provoked to the same degree of severity and for the same reasons as the accused. In the present case, this translates to a person with the minimum powers of self-control of an ordinary person who is subjected to a sexual advance that is aggravated because of the accused's special sensitivity to a history of violence and sexual assault within his family."

Substantive Offences Relevant to Health Care

The unlawful causing of death (homicide)

[14.205] Homicide is the unlawful killing of another person. It may be either murder or manslaughter.

Murder

[14.210] Murder is causing the death of a person by another who intended the death, and where the killer had no legal justification for bringing about that death. One example of where deliberate killing may be justified is in war. Where the killing of another is lawful it is known as justifiable homicide. All Australian jurisdictions prohibit unjustifiable, intentional killing.

Manslaughter

[14.215] Manslaughter is the unlawful causing of the death of another, but with lack of intention to kill, so that death results from an unlawful act, or one which is grossly negligent. It is in these circumstances called involuntary manslaughter. A verdict of voluntary manslaughter, however, may result where a person has intended to kill, but the charge is reduced because of mitigating circumstances such as provocation or diminished responsibility.

The victim of homicide must be a human being, generally defined at common law as any being having been born by being completely extruded from the body of its mother and having an independent existence in the sense that it does not derive its power of living from its mother (*R v Hutty* [1953] VLR 338 per Barry J at 339).

Definitions to the same effect are contained in the Codes of Queensland (s 292), Tasmania (s 153) and Western Australia (s 269). Where, as the result of criminal injuries before birth, a child who is born alive subsequently dies, this will also be homicide.

In some jurisdictions legislation states that any person who causes the death of child *in utero* in such a manner that he or she would have been guilty of murder if the child had been born alive is guilty of a crime (see, for example, *Criminal Code* (Tas), s 165).

The killing of a foetus (abortion) (see **[14.445]**), or of a child in the process of birth (child destruction) (see **[14.550]**) may be subject to different considerations. There is also provision in some jurisdictions (for example, New South Wales (s 22A), Tasmania (s 165A) and Victoria (s 6)) for separate consideration for the killing of a child by its mother, who is suffering from the consequences of its birth or lactation subsequent upon it, within 12 months (or two years in Victoria) of its birth (infanticide). This is really a form of the diminished responsibility defence, reducing the offence from murder to manslaughter.

Euthanasia

[14.220] Euthanasia (a Greek word meaning "good death") is the deliberate bringing about of the death of a person to end what is considered to be an intolerable existence. Euthanasia is defined here as either an active measure to cause death (called "active euthanasia") or the withholding of treatment which causes, or hastens death (called "passive euthanasia"). The former may be the criminal offence of homicide, the latter is more problematic. Some commentators say it cannot be homicide as there is no act to cause the harm, but it has been quite clearly established that, where there is a duty of care, an omission can amount to criminal negligence at least (see **[14.430]**ff). It could also, of course, constitute civil negligence.

Technically, whether active or passive, euthanasia can amount to homicide. The courts, however, have provided relief from the harshness of such provisions by developing principles, which nevertheless are vague and difficult to apply satisfactorily to the advancement of modern technology. This has resulted in intense legal debate and calls by law reform bodies for change.

The principle of "sanctity of life"

[14.225] The sanctity of life is a principle established by law, that is, the prohibition of murder applies for all human beings (see Lipman (1986)). It states that life has an absolute value, and one cannot dispense with a life even when it is considered an inferior one, as at law there is no such thing as an "inferior" life, or a life that is not worth living. However, there is also a right to be free from unwanted or harmful actions. This right is protected by criminal sanctions against assault and battery (see, for example, Brett, Waller and Williams (1997), ch 3) and civil actions available for assault and battery (see above Chapter 4). Active killing is forbidden, but so are omissions adversely affecting someone whose welfare is one's responsibility. A recent departure from the sanctity of life principle was the recognition that sometimes a life may be so awful that it is recognised, at least morally, that one may be justified in not extending what amounts to a painful and unbearable existence by extraordinary means (Templeman J of the English Court of Appeal in *Re B (A Minor)* [1981] 1 WLR 1421; see **[14.380]**). In *Airedale NHS Trust v Bland* [1993] AC 789 (see **[14.295]**) Lord Keith of Kinkel spoke for the majority (at 859) when he clarified the well-established legal principle:

> "The principle [of the sanctity of life] is not an absolute one. It does not compel a medical practitioner on pain of criminal sanctions to treat a patient, who will die if he does not, contrary to the express wishes of the patient. It does not compel the temporary keeping alive of patients who are terminally ill where to do so would merely prolong their suffering [see also the extensive coverage of the sanctity of life in *A (Children)* at **[14.390]**]."

As has been stated earlier (see above, Chapter 4), an adult who understands the implications of such a decision can refuse treatment necessary for the continuation of life. Where a person ends their own life, medical personnel are not implicated, unless they assist them to do so. Making available the means to suicide, such as drugs or instruments, or giving information with the specific intention of assisting the suicide may be an offence (*AG v Able* [1984] 1 All ER 277).

It was emphasised in *Bland's case* (see **[14.295]**, **[14.275]**) that where treatment has been refused there is no question of health carers who accede to the refusal having aided or abetted suicide unless that is the health carer's clear and positive intention. It is simply that the patient has, as he or she is entitled to do, declined to consent to treatment which might otherwise have the effect of prolonging life, and the doctor has, in accordance with the law, complied with the patient's wishes. The person must be fully aware of the decision he or she is making, and of the consequences of it. It would seem that so long as staff have made reasonable attempts to ensure this understanding, and voluntary refusal on the part of the person, the provision only of care and comfort should not amount to criminal behaviour.

[14.230] Case: *Re B (an adult: refusal of medical treatment)* [2002] 2 All ER 449

B, aged 43 years, suffered a devastating illness rendering her tetraplegic. She expressed her desire verbally and in a written advance directive not to be kept alive by the use of a ventilator. Following surgery, she was able to move her head and speak and repeated her request for the ventilator to be withdrawn. Her mental capacity was assessed and she was found to be competent to refuse treatment. However, her treating doctors were not prepared to remove the ventilator. B applied to the court for a declaration that she had the mental capacity to refuse treatment and as such the continued utilisation of artificial ventilation was a trespass to her person.

[14.235] The case was heard at her bedside. In upholding Ms B's competence and thus her right to refuse treatment and require the ventilator to be withdrawn, Dame Elizabeth Butler-Sloss stated:

> "The doctors must not allow their emotional reaction to or strong disagreement with the decision of the patient to cloud their judgment in answering the primary question whether the patient has the mental capacity to make the decision."

☑ Checklist
WHEN A PATIENT REFUSES TREATMENT
- ✓ Is the patient competent and aware of the decision?
- ✓ Has the patient had the opportunity to discuss the decision with family (or others he or she may wish to consult) and staff?
- ✓ Have the consequences and effects to the patient, family (and staff) been discussed?
- ✓ Have the reasons for rejecting the treatment and alternative action or treatment—including that offered by other doctors or facilities—been canvassed?

    ✓ Has the patient been offered general care and comfort if the decision to refuse treatment is maintained?

    ✓ Have all staff who are and will be involved in the patient's care been included in any staff decision-making discussions?

This checklist may assist those concerned in such a situation feeling that they are doing something that is wrong, that they do not believe in, or about which they have not been fully informed. It cannot guarantee the legality of any decision made. While recognising that there are some situations where a person makes a genuine decision to refuse treatment, health carers should act on any reasonable doubt as to their ability to do so.

End-of-Life Decision-Making

[14.240] Where a person is terminally ill, and death is imminent, the law remains the same: one should not kill (and that means to actively hasten death), no matter how unbearable the person's situation and no matter how much he or she may wish to die.

[14.245] Case: *R v Cox, The Age*, 15 May 1992 (Queen's Bench Division)

Dr C treated B, an elderly patient who was terminally ill with rheumatoid arthritis complicated by internal bleeding, gangrene, anaemia, gastric ulcers and bedsores. She was in constant and unbearable pain, to the extent that she howled with pain "like a wounded animal" when her son touched her hand. Massive doses of heroin did not help her, and she decided she wanted to die. Having informed her family of this, and stating that she would refuse all treatment except analgesics, she begged Dr C to "cut short her agony". Dr C gave her two ampoules of potassium cyanide, a lethal dose. The injection was given at the request of the patient and in full knowledge that it would cause her death. Charges were brought against Dr C after a nurse who was aware of his action reported him to the police. As B had been cremated before the investigation began (thus preventing the prosecution proving the drug caused the death), Dr C was charged with attempted murder. Dr C did not deny giving the drug in the full knowledge that it would cause death, but argued that a doctor is entitled to do all that is proper and necessary to relieve pain and suffering even if the measures taken might incidentally shorten life (see *R v Adams*, [14.275]).

[14.250] Dr C was found guilty, the judge directing the jury that it is never lawful to use drugs for the sole purpose of hastening death.

Aiding and abetting suicide

[14.255] Suicide is no longer a crime in any Australian jurisdiction. However, aiding and abetting suicide remains so in many jurisdictions (*Crimes Act 1900* (ACT), s 17; *Crimes Act 1900* (NSW), s 31C; *Criminal Law Consolidation Act 1935* (SA), s 13A(5); *Crimes Act 1958* (Vic) s 6B(2)(b); *Criminal Code Act* (NT), s 168; *Criminal Code 1899* (Qld), s 311; *Criminal Code Act 1924* (Tas), s 163; *Criminal Code* (WA), s 288). Under the *Criminal Code Act 1995* (Cth), s 474.29A a person is guilty of an offence if they use a carriage service to access, transmit, make, publish or distribute material that directly or indirectly counsels or incites suicide if that is the person's intention in so doing.

[14.260] Case: *R v Maxwell* [2003] VSC 278

M's wife suffered from advance breast cancer and metastases. She told a friend of her decision to end her life by ceasing to eat and drink. M was able to persuade her from this process of starvation but did so on the promise that he would help her end her life if her health did not improve. Soon afterwards her condition was described as terminal. M cared for her and continued to seek medical assistance for her. The wife's friends had provided her with a book entitled "*Final Exit. The Practicalities of Self-Deliverance and Assisted Suicide for the Dying*" following earlier discussions concerning euthanasia. She chose a technique for ending her life from the book and when it became apparent she could not perform the necessary acts alone, she asked M to help her. M agreed, purchasing the necessary equipment for his wife and completing the steps detailed in the book, leading to his wife's death. M pleaded guilty to aiding and abetting his wife to commit suicide.

[14.265] In sentencing M Coldrey J stated:

"Since the law continues to regard what you did as an offence, the denunciation of it and the deterrence of others remain elements of any sentence to be imposed. However, I do not believe that thoughtful members of the community, knowing all the facts relating to you personally and the unique circumstances of this tragic case, would regard your immediate imprisonment as necessary. In my view, this is a case where justice may be tempered with mercy."

M was sentenced to eighteen months imprisonment with the period being wholly suspended.

Legislation allowing voluntary euthanasia

[14.270] The Northern Territory made news when the Legislative Assembly there passed the *Rights of the Terminally Ill Act* (NT), which provided that where:

- a patient was terminally ill and subject to unbearable suffering, with no prospect of relief from alternative treatment, and persistently requested assistance to die; and
- a comprehensive list of requirements, such as further medical opinions including a psychiatric report, informed consent and waiting periods, and counselling had been met;

any action by a doctor in assisting that person to die through active measures would not be homicide.

This was the first legislation of its kind in the world (the Dutch Government did, after decades of official tolerance of assisted termination of life under strict guidelines, pass similar legislation in 2000). Contrary to the name of the Northern Territory Act, it did not in fact bestow an enforceable right: no one was obliged to assist the person, and assistance was dependent upon medical assessment. However it did provide a means of assisted death for those who found their suffering unbearable, with no alternative treatment. Four people were assisted to die under the Act, until the Federal Government, using its powers under s 122 of the Constitution (which permits it to make laws for the Northern Territory, the Australian Capital Territory and Norfolk Island) passed the *Euthanasia Laws Act 1997* (Cth), prohibiting those Territories from enacting laws that would allow "the form of intentional killing of another called euthanasia, (which includes mercy killing) or the assisting of a person to terminate his or her life". This legislation took effect by altering the self-government legislation of the territories and is reflected in: *Northern Territory (Self-Government) Act 1997*, s 50A; *Australian Capital Territory (Self-Government) Act 1998*, ss 23(1A) and 23(1B); *Norfolk Island Act 1979*, s 19(2)(d) and 19(2A).

There are two principles at law that provide guidance in dealing with this difficult issue.

Principle 1: "Double effect"

[14.275] Despite the fact that the administration of drugs, when it is anticipated that they will hasten death, would normally be unlawful homicide, judges at common law have held that where a patient has no prospect of recovery and is in severe pain, someone may administer increasingly potent doses of a drug necessary to relieve that pain, even if it is known that the drug will, in all likelihood, hasten the patient's death. It is argued that the intention is to relieve pain, not to cause death, and therefore not wrong. This means of pain relief must be the only reasonable choice in the circumstances, and death must be imminent, that is, any shortening of life which can be anticipated must be insubstantial. What is "insubstantial" is a matter of judgment for the doctor.

This principle was enunciated by Lord Devlin in the case of *R v Adams*, *The Times*, 9 April 1957, where he was directing the jury as to the administration of drugs to a patient who was terminally ill and in pain. He stated that no doctor has the right in the case of the dying (nor in the case of the healthy), to "cut the thread of life". If the purpose of medicine, the restoration of health, is no longer possible for someone however, the administration of adequate pain relief should not be considered the cause of death:

"[T]here is still much for a doctor to do, and he is entitled to do all that is proper and necessary to relieve pain and suffering, even if the measures he takes may incidentally shorten life. That is not because there is any special defence for medical men. ... The law is the same for all ... no act is murder which does not cause death. 'Cause' means nothing philosophical or technical or scientific. ... If, for example, because a doctor has done something or has omitted to do something death occurs ... at 11 o'clock instead of 12 o'clock or even on Monday instead of Tuesday, no people of common sense would say: 'Oh the doctor caused her death.' They would say the cause of death was the illness or the injury which brought her into hospital."

This case was endorsed in *Bland's case* (see **[14.295]**) where Lord Goff of Chieveley stated:

"The doctor who is caring for a [terminally ill patient] cannot, in my opinion, be under an absolute obligation to prolong his life by any means available to him, regardless of the quality of the patient's life. Common humanity requires otherwise, as do medical ethics and good medical practice accepted in this country and overseas. As I see it, the doctor's decision whether or not to take any such step must (subject to his patient's ability to give or withhold his consent) be made in the best interest of the patient. It is this principle too which, in my opinion, underlies the established rule that a doctor may, when caring for a patient who is, for example dying of cancer, lawfully administer pain killing drugs despite the fact that he knows that an incidental effect of that application will be to abbreviate the patient's life. Such a decision may properly be made as part of the care of the living patient, in his best interests; and on this basis, the treatment will be lawful. Moreover, where the doctor's treatment of his patient is lawful, the patient's death will be regarded in law as exclusively caused by the injury or disease to which his condition is attributable."

The foundation of the principle of double effect is not clearly defined and has varied between cases; it may be premised on a number of different considerations in isolation or in combination. In some cases, (see, for example *R v Arthur*, *The Times*, 6 October 1981, pp 1, 12; *Bland's case*) it has been suggested that the doctor is not guilty of homicide because the cause of death was not the administration of the drugs but rather the underlying disease process. In other cases it has been suggested that the doctor lacked the necessary intention to kill. The argument being that the giving of medication, ostensibly with the intention of giving comfort and relief from pain, but in doses which it is recognised will most probably result in side effects causing death, is to give the medication devoid of any intention to cause death.

The High Court decision in *R v Douglas John Edwin Crabbe* (1985) 156 CLR 464; [1985] HCA 22 may help determine how the issue may be approached by Australian courts. In that case, the Court stated (at [9]):

"In should now be regarded as settled law in Australia, if no statutory provision affects the position, that a person who, without lawful justification or excuse, does an act knowing that it is probable that death or grievous bodily harm will result, is guilty of murder if death in fact results."

And went on to say:

"Of course, not every fatal act done with the knowledge that death or grievous bodily harm will probably result is murder. The act may be lawful, that is, justified or excused by law. A surgeon who competently performs a hazardous but necessary operation is not criminally liable if the patient dies, even if the surgeon foresaw that his death was probable" (at [10]).

South Australia: Legislative provision of "double effect"

[14.280] Section 17 of the *Consent to Medical Treatment and Palliative Care Act 1995* (SA) has provided protection for health carers who administer drugs to those who are terminally ill for the purpose of pain relief, despite the fact that it may shorten their life expectancy.

"17(1) A medical practitioner responsible for the treatment or care of a patient in the terminal phase of a terminal illness, or a person participating in the treatment or care of the patient under the medical practitioner's supervision, incurs no civil or criminal liability by administering medical treatment with the intention of relieving pain or distress—

    (a) with the consent of the patient or the patient's representative; and

    (b) in good faith and without negligence; and

    (c) in accordance with proper professional standards of palliative care,

even though an incidental effect of the treatment is to hasten the death of the patient;

(2) A medical practitioner responsible for the treatment or care of a patient in the terminal phase of a terminal illness, or a person participating in the treatment or care of the patient under the medical practitioner's supervision, is, in the absence of an express direction by the patient or the patient's representative to the contrary, under no duty to use, or to continue to use, life sustaining measures in treating the patient if the effect of doing so would be merely to prolong life in a moribund state without any real prospect of recovery or in a persistent vegetative state.

(3) For the purposes of the law of the State—

    (a) the administration of medical treatment for the relief of pain or distress in accordance with subsection (1) does not constitute an intervening cause of death; and

    (b) the non-application or discontinuance of life sustaining measures in accordance with subsection (2) does not constitute an intervening cause of death."

Principle 2: "Extraordinary measures"

[14.285] Another means of avoiding the intransigence of the "sanctity of life" principle is the *dictum* that no one is required, morally or legally, to prolong life by extraordinary means under certain circumstances. Of course the question then arising is what is meant by extraordinary means, and there is uncertainty in both medical and legal circles on this point.

This approach has been developed by moral theologians to distinguish those attempts at preserving life which are morally required of any person (for example, Pope Pius XII (1957)). But note the change of approach to that of treatment being "disproportionately burdensome" (Skegg (1984), p 146).

In a medical context [writers] regard "ordinary" means as "all medicines, treatments, and operations, which offer a reasonable hope of benefit for the patient and which can be obtained and used without excessive expense, pain, or other inconvenience", whereas "extraordinary" means are ... "medicines, treatments and operations which cannot be obtained without excessive expense, pain or other inconvenience, or which, if used, would not offer a reasonable hope of relief" (Skegg (1984), p 144).

Obviously the definition is not only vague, but covers classifications which will differ over time. This, Skegg argues, is not a reason for abandoning it, but he gives two other reasons for doing so. First, he points out that courts should not adopt the moralists' distinction because it is quite different from that used by the medical profession, which considers "extraordinary" more in the light of "heroic" or "unusual", and distinctions are blurred. Secondly, he argues that the moralists' distinction is based on Roman Catholic theology, and so based on presumptions not all would accept. Courts have adopted the ordinary/extraordinary means approach, and have accepted that some treatment, such as naso-gastric feeding and intravenous fluids are ordinary treatment, whereas intra-gastric feeding and mechanical means of respiration have been considered extraordinary treatment. (See discussion in *Bland's Case* at **[14.295]**). The President's Commission has suggested that the more appropriate test would be that of proportionate or disproportionate benefit ((1983), p 88).

In South Australia, s 17 of the *Consent to Medical Treatment and Palliative Care Act 1995* (set out at **[14.280]**) provides that for the purposes of the law in that State, the administration of medical treatment for the relief of pain or distress in accordance with subs 17(1) of that Act, or non-application or discontinuance of life sustaining measures in accordance with subs 17(2) of that Act "does not constitute an intervening cause of death", although a medical practitioner is not relieved from the consequences of negligence in deciding whether a person is terminally ill. Life sustaining measures are defined as those that "supplant or maintain the operation of vital bodily functions that are temporarily or permanently incapable of independent operation, and include assisted ventilation, artificial nutrition and hydration and cardio-pulmonary resuscitation".

Persistent vegetative state

[14.290] A person diagnosed as being in a persistent vegetative state is in a particularly difficult legal category. The person has overwhelming damage or dysfunction of the cerebral hemispheres, which removes the capacity for self-aware mental activity, where the diencephalon and brainstem functions remain, preserving autonomic and motor reflexes such as respiration, swallowing, blinking, and spontaneous unco-ordinated movement, and sleep-awake cycles. The person thus has no cognitive functions, such as awareness or sensory perception. Whilst very much alive according to law, and with a possibly indefinite life expectancy, the question of whether the person has any "interests" in continued health care is problematic. For a discussion of the issues surrounding the decision to withdraw treatment from those in a persistent vegetative state, see Freckelton (1993) and Kerridge (2005); ch 22.

[14.295] Case: *Airedale NHS Trust v Bland (Bland's Case)* [1993] 1 All ER 821 (House of Lords)

Anthony Bland, a 21-year-old patient in the care of the applicant health authority had been in a persistent vegetative state for three and a half years after suffering a severe crushed chest injury which caused catastrophic and irreversible damage to the higher functions of the brain. He was being fed artificially and mechanically by a nasogastric tube. The unanimous opinion of all doctors was that there was no hope whatsoever of recovery or improvement of any kind, or expectation that Bland would ever recover from his persistent vegetative state.

The consultant specialist reached the conclusion that it would be appropriate to cease treatment, including the withdrawal of the nasogastric tube and thus nutrition, as well as such treatment as antibiotic therapy. This view was supported by others, and the health authority applied to the court for declarations that it and the responsible physicians could lawfully discontinue all life-sustaining treatment and support measures designed to keep Bland alive including ventilation, nutrition and other medical treatment. This was to be for the sole purpose of enabling him to end his life and die peacefully with the greatest dignity and the least pain. The plaintiff's action was supported by Bland's parents and family.

The Official Solicitor appealed to the Court of Appeals which affirmed the judge's decision. The Official Solicitor then appealed to the House of Lords. The argument was that the withdrawal of life support was both a breach of the doctor's duty to care for Bland indefinitely if need be, and a criminal act.

[14.300] The House of Lords held that where a patient is incapable of deciding whether or not to consent to treatment, health carers are under no absolute obligation to prolong the patient's life regardless of the circumstances. Medical treatment, including artificial feeding and the administration of antibiotic drugs, could lawfully be withheld from an insensate patient who had no hope of recovery when it was known that the patient would shortly thereafter die, provided reasonable and competent medical opinion was of the view that it would be in the patient's best interests not to prolong her or his life by continuing that form of treatment and that such treatment was futile and would not confer any benefit on the patient.

This was a landmark case in that it established that a person can have life-preserving measures removed with the sole intent that they should die. The judges broke with common law precedents by rejecting the formerly accepted notion that only extraordinary measures can be withdrawn from a person by allowing the discontinuance of life support by removal of hydration and nutrition. In doing this they accepted the argument of expert witnesses that nutrition and hydration were treatment just like any other, as it substitutes a function that has naturally failed. The removal of the feeding tube, they said, did not amount to a criminal act because if the continuance of an intrusive life support system was not in the patient's interests the doctor was no longer under a duty to maintain the patient's life but was simply allowing the patient to die of the pre-existing condition and the death would be regarded in law as exclusively caused by the injury or disease to which the condition was attributable. Throughout the extensive consideration of the law by the Law Lords is expressed their dissatisfaction with the common law as it stood. They recognised its inappropriateness in many cases, and its inability to cope with modern medical knowledge and technology, as well as changing social attitudes.

As a result some of the judges made the following points:

- The taking of active steps to end a patient's life is unlawful;
- Doctors should, from time to time seek the guidance of the court in all cases before withholding life-prolonging treatment from a patient in a persistent vegetative state. This should be by way of declaratory relief. In time a body of expertise would develop, and only those cases which are exceptional would need to be brought to court.
- Lords Browne-Wilkinson and Mustill declared that it is imperative that the moral, social and legal issues raised by the withholding of treatment from an insensate patient with no hope of recovery should be considered by Parliament (that is, that legislation clarifying the law be passed).

The following Australian case, whilst primarily concerned with the terminology utilised in the Victorian legislation, is consistent with the finding in *Bland's case*. The decision of the Victorian Civil and Administrative Tribunal that treatment is futile if it is not fulfilling a medical purpose and there is no obligation to maintain life where treatment is futile, was upheld by the Supreme Court.

[14.305] Case: *Gardner, re BWV* [2003] VSC 173

BWV was a 68 year-old woman in a persistent vegetative state (PVS). Before she had progressed to a PVS, and was still ambulatory but incompetent, her husband had consented to the insertion of a percutaneous endoscopic gastrostomy (PEG). The husband requested the feeding be ceased. The Public Advocate had been appointed as guardian to BWV and sought clarification from the court as to whether PEG feeding could lawfully be ceased. The evidence of BWV's family was that she would not wish her life to be sustained in such a manner and had in fact expressed a desire not to be kept alive in that manner to her husband some years earlier.

The primary issue to be determined was whether the use of a PEG for artificial nutrition and hydration should be classified as "medical treatment" or "palliative care". The *Medical Treatment Act 1988* (Vic) precludes palliative care from the type of treatment that can be refused under the Act by a patient's guardian.

Morris J held that PEG feeding was a medical procedure as it involves "protocols, skills and care which draw from, and depend upon, medical knowledge". He likened it to ventilation and administration of drugs. He interpreted the statutory definition of palliative care as including "reasonable provision of food and water" to mean "ordinary feeding by mouth". Thus, the Public Advocate, as BWV' guardian was entitled to refuse PEG feeding on her behalf. (See also *MC, Re* [2003] QGAAT 13; *TM, Re* [2002] QGAAT 1.)

[14.310] Diagnosis of persistent vegetative state, as opposed to other forms of brain function deficit, should be very carefully undertaken. In the case of *Northridge v Central Sydney Area Health Service* (discussed at **[5.165]**), O'Keefe J pointed to evidence that the Royal College of Physicians in the UK recognises:

1 a transient vegetative state,
2 a chronic vegetative state, which should only be made after a period in excess of four weeks of being continually in a vegetative state, and
3 persistent vegetative state, which should only be made after a patient has been in a chronic vegetative state for more than 12 months following a head injury or more than six months following other causes of brain damage.

Scans of the brain and other tests may be used to determine whether there are signs of cerebral activity in assisting diagnosis. The National Health and Medical Research Council has since released an advisory document on diagnosing PVS entitled *Post-coma Unresponsiveness (Vegetative State): A Clinical Framework for Diagnosis* (available at www.nhmrc.gov.au/publications/synopses/hpr23syn. htm).

In the following case, the notion of futile treatment was considered, however, the patient was not in a PVS but in a coma.

[14.315] Case: *Isaac Messiha (by his tutor Magdy Messiha) v South East Health* [2004] NSWSC 1061

M, a 75 year-old male, suffered an asystolic cardiac arrest at his home. He was without oxygen for at least 25 minutes before ambulance officers arrived. He was taken to hospital where he was unconscious and in a deep coma from the time of his admission. M was under the care of Dr J, the head of the ICU. Dr J was of the opinion that M had suffered severe hypoxic brain damage and the regime of treatment being employed should be ceased and M placed under palliative care. The family were opposed to this course and obtained the opinion of another doctor, Dr P. Dr P was of the opinion that there was "no realistic possibility of meaningful recovery of cerebral function" and saw no useful therapeutic measures as being indicated. The family continued their opposition to the change in treatment and sought the opinion of an independent neurologist, Prof L. Prof L examined M and expressed an opinion consistent with that of Dr L and Dr J. Dr J determined that M's treatment regime should cease, he should be removed from ICU and provided with comfort care. The family brought an application before the Court to restrain Dr J and other hospital staff from this course of action, believing, contrary to medical opinion, that if the current treatment regime were continued, thus prolonging life by even a short period of time, M's condition might improve.

[14.320] Howie J was of the opinion that treatment can be burdensome upon a patient notwithstanding that their comatose state prevents their awareness of the effects of treatment upon the body. He stated:

"The evidence is that, apart from preserving the life of the patient for a relatively brief period, the current treatment is futile in that there is no real prospect of significant recovery by the patient" (at [26]).

In dismissing the application, Howie J went on to opine:

"The withdrawal of treatment may put his life in jeopardy but only to the extent of bringing forward what I believe to be the inevitable in the short term. I am not satisfied that the withdrawal of his present treatment is not in the patient's best interest and welfare" (at [28]).

"Locked-in" state

[14.325] Case: *Auckland Hospital v Attorney General* [1993] 1 NZLR 235 (High Court of New Zealand)

"L" was suffering from Guillian-Barre syndrome. He was unable to communicate or respond in any way to his environment. He was not brain-dead but the extent of denervation meant that his brain was not connected with any part of his body, except perhaps with the visual pathways. He required ventilatory support in order to exist. The Hospital Board and L's doctor sought a declaration from the New Zealand High Court that disconnecting the ventilator would not be a criminal act.

[14.330] This case, as the *Bland* case, above, caused the judges some concern that the legal principles which have been developed are not suitable to modern medical technology and knowledge. Strict adherence to the principle that removal of so-called "life-preservation" is a crime poses problems. Thomas J expressed his concern by stating that the issues before the Court could not be resolved by legal logic, but required rather the application of the common principles of humanity. The Court stated that while it could make a declaration to this effect, it would have to do so very carefully. It said that the question to answer was whether the doctor had a legal duty to continue life support, or whether there was justification in removing it. Justification in ceasing treatment is its futility. The Court declared that a doctor who removes life support for a patient who is effectively lifeless should not be held responsible for the person's death. In this case the ventilation was deferring death rather than preserving life. The court held that removing it would not be a criminal offence.

[14.332] Case: *Re HG* [2006] QGAAT 26

HG was a 58 year old male who suffered a brain stem stroke rendering him completely paralysed except for the ability to blink and to move his eyes up and down. Loss of his swallow reflex left him unable to receive food or hydration orally or via nasogastric tube. It was determined that his pre-stroke condition likely remained intact, however, he was left with no ability to communicate. Prior to the stroke, HG was suffering from Wernicke's encephalopathy and Korsakoff's psychosis and had been previously appointed a financial trustee and Adult Guardian to consider his future accommodation needs.

HG had no contact with family or friends. As HG's statutory health attorney, the Adult Guardian, was asked to make decisions regarding his health care. In particular, the Adult Guardian was asked to decide whether a PEG should be inserted or whether the artificial hydration being provided should be ceased, allowing HG to die. The Adult Guardian consented to the cessation of artificial hydration, however, in-home carers who had previously worked with HG sought review of this decision on the basis that HG could make his own health care decisions. The Adult Guardian thus consented to the reinstatement of artificial hydration and sought advice, directions and recommendations from the GAAT pursuant to s 82 of the *Guardianship and Administration Act 2000*.

[14.334] The essential issues for the Tribunal's consideration were whether:

(1) withholding artificial nutrition and withdrawing artificial hydration constituted "health care" pursuant to the *Guardianship and Administration Act 2000*;
(2) continuing artificial hydration and commencing artificial nutrition would be inconsistent with good medical practice.

The Tribunal found HG did not have the capacity to make decisions regarding the withholding of artificial nutrition. The Tribunal noted the definition of health care in the legislation was broad and under Schedule 2, s 5B "includes withholding or withdrawal of a life-sustaining measure for the adult if the commencement or the continuation of the measure for the adult would be inconsistent with good medical practice". The Tribunal stated (at 64-65):

"Before a decision to withhold or withdraw a life-sustaining measure will be a 'health matter' for which consent can be given, the commencement or continuation of the measure must be inconsistent with good medical practice. This test will not be satisfied just because the withholding or withdrawal of the measure is consistent with good medical practice. More must be demonstrated. There must be evidence that the provision of the measure is inconsistent with good medical practice. Therefore, if there was evidence that there were two medically and ethically acceptable treatment options, one being the provision of the measure, the test in the legislation is not satisfied and consent could not be given to the withholding or withdrawal of the measure.

On the medical evidence before it, however, the Tribunal is satisfied that the commencement of artificial nutrition and continuing of artificial hydration is inconsistent with good medical practice. The Tribunal makes this finding notwithstanding the fact that an individual health professional may, on the facts of this case, be prepared to commence or continue artificial nutrition and hydration for a limited time in order to persuade those close to the adult of the reasons that it is appropriate to withhold or withdraw the measure."

The Tribunal went on to declare that the commencement and/or continuation of artificial nutrition and hydration to HG would be inconsistent with good medical practice and thus the Tribunal consented to the withholding of artificial nutrition and the cessation of artificial hydration.

Discussion

[14.335] It is argued that the principles of double effect and extraordinary measures are in fact "intellectually deceitful devices" (to use McLean's words, see **[14.350]**), adopted to maintain the semblance of the "sanctity of life" principle, as an absolute principle, rather than to accept that both the medical profession and society in general acknowledge that in some cases there should be an exception to the "sanctity of life" principle for those whose lives are "so awful" as to be a burden too cruel for them (or their families or society) to bear. The real issue, says the President's Commission (p 82, n 13),

> "is whether decision makers have considered the full range of foreseeable effects, have knowingly accepted whatever risk of death is entailed, and hold the risk to be justified in light of the paucity and undesirability of their options."

The criminal law arrives at a similar resolution of the problem but unfortunately via a more obtuse and distorted path through the fictions of double effect and extraordinary means. Where death is imminent, one can give medication for relief of pain even if it would otherwise be contra-indicated, and can withhold treatment which is extraordinary in the circumstances.

The logic behind the principle that omissions to act (for example, the withholding of treatment) cannot be held to be the cause of death and thus culpable, whereas actions (such as the giving of a lethal injection to end unbearable suffering) can be held to be the cause of death and thus culpable, is questioned by Skene (1998, p 229).

Legislation and guidelines

[14.340] The Australian Capital Territory, the Northern Territory, South Australia and Victoria have enacted legislation, and New South Wales has issued guidelines giving effect to advance directives. The provisions of this legislation were considered at **[5.270]**. In the following case no advance directive had been made.

[14.345] Case: *Re Kinney* (unreported, 23 December 1988, SC Vic, No M2/1989) (CCH ¶22-340)

A man who suffered from leukaemia, and was on bail facing a charge of murder, attempted suicide and was being treated in hospital. His wife sought an injunction to prevent doctors carrying out exploratory surgery to stop bleeding and/or other active measures to prolong or save her husband's life. She based her claim on the severe pain he was suffering, the fact that he had expressed a wish to die, and her belief that he would rather die than return to gaol. She argued that he could thus be considered to have refused treatment.

[14.350] The Supreme Court of Victoria held that as no refusal of treatment certificate had been signed by the patient in accordance with the *Medical Treatment Act 1988* (Vic) and there was no other documentary evidence that he did not wish to receive treatment, either for the leukaemia or the overdose, it could not issue the injunction. Compassion and sympathy alone were not enough to allow the court to issue the injunction, it said, and to do so would be to assist suicide. Very powerful consideration would be required to prevent doctors from saving a person's life. This is in accordance with the general principle that despite the fact that suicide is not an offence, the state has an interest in preventing suicide.

In 1993 the New South Wales Health Department issued guidelines on the treatment of the terminally ill. The guidelines were subsequently revised and superseded by the *End-of-Life Care and Decision-Making Guidelines* released in 2005 (available at www.health.nsw.gov.au/policies/gl/2005/GL2005_057.html). These guidelines are aimed at generating a respect for human life, the patient's autonomy, consultation with relatives, access to medical care and a professional approach to the issues involved. They stress that a management plan should be developed in consultation with the patient, establishing goals and lengths of treatment, as well as circumstances in which it may be foregone. Where the patient cannot participate in decision-making, the family should be consulted to establish the patient's wishes and expectations in as much as they can be identified. Full assessment and documentation of the patient's condition and the decision-making process should be made, and where life support (except for palliative care) is considered burdensome and futile it may be removed. Cardio-pulmonary resuscitation should not be carried out if the patient does not want it, or it would be "clearly futile" or "prolong suffering". In all cases records should be made which are clear and unambiguous, which detail discussions and set out the patient's wishes, clearly identifying what treatment is to be given and what treatment is to be forgone.

Quality of life

[14.355] Given that there is a legal obligation on the part of doctors to provide reasonable care to their patients, it has been argued that the quality of the life they are preserving is of no concern to the law at all. Thus, a person must be kept alive even where the quality of their life is very poor. Indeed this was stated by Vincent J in the Supreme Court of Victoria when he ordered the Queen Victoria Hospital to take all necessary and reasonable measures consistent with proper medical practice to preserve the life of a baby born with spina bifida in that hospital (*Re F: F v F* (unreported, 2 July 1986, SC Vic) (quoted from *The Age*, Melbourne, 3 July 1986, p 1, see also *Re 'A' Children*, [14.395]). The judge said:

> "The law does not permit decisions to be made concerning the quality of life nor any assessment of the value of any human life."

It is important to note that this decision was made as the result of an urgent hearing in which the hospital was not represented and did not provide evidence of the child's condition. Vincent J stated that his decision was limited to the facts before him and was not intended to cover all cases of failure to treat. The decision has not been followed in other cases.

[14.360] Case: *Re Quinlan*, 348 A 2d 807 (reversed on Appeal 355 A 2d 647 (1976)) (Court of Appeal New Jersey United States)

In this landmark case, Q, a 22-year-old, was in a permanent comatose state, which was diagnosed as being irreversible. Her unfortunate position was that she was not "brain dead", but was also not "sapient". In the Court hearing, Dr P described her condition as follows:

> We have an internal vegetative regulation which controls breathing, which controls to a considerable degree blood pressure, which controls to some degree heart rate, which controls chewing, swallowing, and which controls sleeping and waking. We have a more highly developed brain, which is uniquely human, which controls our relation to the outside world, our capacity to talk, to see, to feel, to sing, to think. Brain death necessarily must mean the death of both of these functions of the brain, vegetative and sapient (137 NJ Sup Ct at 238; 348 A 2d 807; see also on this point Hunsaker (1984)).

[14.365] In the words of the Court, she was in a "permanent vegetative state". When her father requested that all extraordinary life-sustaining treatment be discontinued, the New Jersey Superior Court disagreed, stating that the decision to discontinue the treatment would be making a decision based on giving an evaluation to the quality of a particular sort of life.

This approach, "if life can be substantially maintained, no matter in what condition, there is an obligation to sustain it", is also known as the "medical feasibility model" developed by Macmillan (1978). She argues that the only grounds for withholding treatment should be that of medical unfeasibility, which must be diagnosed with a "high degree of certainty" (p 624) and only occurs in two situations:

1) death is imminent (it will occur within six months to a year); or
2) the person is irreversibly unconscious.

There was in *Re Quinlan,* however, reliance in the last analysis, on the opinion of the physician attending: so long as he felt compelled to maintain life, it should be maintained. This decision contains a fundamental logical flaw in its adoption of two potentially conflicting principles: the need to maintain life if it can be maintained, but the reliance on the physician's opinion as to whether it should be maintained. The point should not be laboured, however, at this stage, because the case was taken on appeal to the New Jersey Court of Appeal which overturned the lower court's decision (*Re Quinlan,* 355 A 2d 647 (1976)).

That Court held that there is a constitutionally guaranteed right (in the United States), of privacy, which includes a right to permit one's existence to terminate by natural forces. This right could be enforced in this case by Q's guardian on her behalf, and could be exercised where the family and physicians were of the opinion that her condition was irreversible, and they had consulted with an ethics committee of the hospital and received the committee's concurrence (at p 671). Hunsaker (1984), points out (at p 23) that basing its decision on the prognosis of the reasonable impossibility of return to cognitive and sapient life, rather than on the fact of brain death, shifted the cessation of treatment to the prediction rather than the post-diction of brain death. The problem with this, he points out, is that the prediction can be wrong. This is quite clearly a permission by the Court to make a decision based on the predicted quality of life of the patient. The approach was followed in the following case.

[14.370] Case: *The Superintendent of Belchertown State; School et al v Saikewicz*, Mass 370 NE 2d 417 (1977) (Court of Appeal United States)

This case involved a profoundly retarded adult, resident of the school, who contracted acute myeloblastic monocytic leukaemia. The applicant requested a guardian *ad litem* be appointed to decide whether chemotherapy should be given. The guardian was appointed, and recommended no treatment, on the grounds that the benefits would be outweighed by the discomfort, increased by the patient's inability to appreciate its purpose and the temporary relief it would give. The judge of the Probate Court ruled accordingly, and the matter was taken to the Appeal Court to consider, *inter alia*, whether the decision was correct.

[14.375] That Court recognised the ambiguity in the term "quality of life". It can refer to a value placed upon a particular person's life, or the actual interests and values of the person herself or himself. The Court (at 432) preferred the latter approach:

"Rather than reading the judge's formulation in a manner that demeans the value of the life of one who is mentally retarded, the vague, and perhaps ill-chosen, term 'quality of life' should be understood as a reference to the continuing state of pain and disorientation precipitated by the chemo-therapy treatment. Viewing the term in this manner, together with the other factors properly considered by the judge, we are satisfied that the decision to withhold treatment from Saikewicz was based on a regard for his actual interests and preferences, and that the facts supported this decision."

In *A (Children)* (see [14.395]), the English Court of Appeal held that it was not a matter of determining whether a person's life is worth living or not, based on what is seen as that person's quality of life, but the interests and preferences of that person in continuing life, giving the quality of experience it provides.

The following case considered whether the Public Guardian in New South Wales is impowered to determine what health care and major and minor medical and dental treatment a person may receive, has the power to consent to "end-of-life" decisions and to the making of "do not resuscitate" orders.

[14.377] Case: *WK v Public Guardian (No 2)* [2006]
NSWADT 121 (20 April 2006)

Mr X had been a hospital inpatient for approximately six months
when this matter came before the NSW Guardianship Tribunal.
Mr X was 73 years old and suffered from end stage kidney disease
and dementia. Some time before the application was brought
Mr X's treating doctor, sister-in-law and nephew discussed Mr X's
condition and the decision was consequently made to cease
dialysis. Shortly thereafter the nephew's business partner
contacted the treating doctor and expressed his concern at that
decision. As a result, the doctor decided not to stop dialysis and
applied to the Guardianship tribunal for the appointment of a
guardian for Mr X.

The Guardianship Tribunal appointed the Public Guardian as
Mr X's guardian and in so doing gave him powers to determine
what health care and major and minor medical and dental
treatment Mr X may receive. The Public Guardian subsequently
consented to a palliative care regime for Mr X which included the
termination of haemodialysis (which would inevitably lead to
death) and a "do not resuscitate" order.

Before the decision was to take effect, an application was
lodged with the Administrate Decisions Tribunal for a review and
stay of that decision. The Tribunal heard the application the
following day and granted a stay of the decision. A hearing of the
substantive application took place approximately two weeks later.

The Tribunal reasserted that the Public Guardian can only
make decisions that relate to the functions specified in the
Guardianship order and noted (at 9-11):

> "The first function the Guardianship Tribunal gave to the Public
> Guardian was the health care function which allows the Public
> Guardian to determine what health care and major and minor
> medical and dental treatment Mr X may receive. The decision to
> consent to the withdrawal of dialysis treatment is not a decision
> about what major or minor medical treatment he may receive. The
> term 'health care' is a general term. While it is possible that it
> could include consenting to 'end-of-life' decisions, I am reluctant
> to give it such a broad interpretation in the absence of some clear
> indication that that is what the Guardianship Tribunal intended...
>
> By virtue of the 'consent to medical treatment' function given
> to it by the Guardianship Tribunal, the Public Guardian has power
> to consent, or not to consent, to the proposed medical treatment.
> The term 'medical treatment' is relevantly defined in s 33 to mean
> (a) medical treatment (including any medical or surgical
>   procedure, operation or examination and any prophylactic,
>   palliative or rehabilitative care) normally carried out by or
>   under the supervision of a medical practitioner...

The definition of 'medical treatment' includes 'palliative care'. However, the ordinary meaning of the words in s 33 defining 'medical treatment', are not sufficiently broad to encompass the withdrawal of life sustaining treatment...

A decision to withdraw life sustaining medical treatment is not a decision carried out for the purpose of promoting and maintaining the health and well-being of a person. These objects and the definition of 'medical treatment' in s 33 lead to the conclusion that while the Public Guardian may consent to treatment which will prolong the life of a person, there is no power to consent to the withdrawal of treatment that will result in a person's death."

As a result the Tribunal remitted the decisions of the Public Guardian to the Guardianship Tribunal for review.

It is worth noting, that given the importance and potential impact of this decision, the Public Guardian might be expected to take the matter on appeal.

Withdrawing treatment from newborn infants

[14.380] When a baby is born with serious handicaps or of very low birth weight, the prognosis and expected quality of life (in any meaning of the term) of the child may be a critical issue in determining whether to institute treatment. As it is not always possible to make a rapid assessment of the baby's condition and the extent of her or his disabilities, health carers must sometimes make quick decisions relating to resuscitation and commencing or continuing treatment based on incomplete information. Different policies have been adopted to deal with this problem, some facilities insist on full care for all babies over, say, 23 weeks gestation, others withhold treatment from all babies under a nominated weight or with specified ailments, yet others adopt a case-by-case decision-making approach, in consultation with parents. The English Court of Appeal attempted to clarify the term "quality of life" where handicapped neonates are concerned.

[14.385] **Case:** *Re B (A Minor)* [1981] 1 WLR 1421 (Court of Appeal England)

An infant was born with Down's Syndrome, intestinal blockage and with severe mental and physical handicaps, though it was probable she would have some sapient functions in the sense used in *Quinlan,* above. The court saw the question as being whether it was in the best interests of the child for her to be allowed to die within the next week, or to have the operation required to correct the bowel problem. If she did have the operation it was not certain whether she would suffer any handicap or whether she would have any quality of life.

[14.390] The court ruled (at 1424):

> "at the end of the day it devolves on this court to decide whether the life of the child is demonstrably going to be so awful that in effect the child must be condemned to die, or whether the life of this child is still so imponderable that it would be wrong for her to be condemned to die."

Lord Templeman went on to say that there may be other instances where damage is so certain and the child's life bound to be so full of pain and suffering that the court might be moved to rule that treatment be withdrawn; but he found too little certainty of such a future for the child in this particular case. The Court ordered that the required treatment be given. The novel point here, for English law, is the possibility that the certainty of a very poor quality of life, in the meaning accepted as a ground for withholding treatment in the United States *Saikewicz* case, may be accepted by the English courts.

Since then, the English courts have recognised consideration of the quality of life of moribund infants, and the lawfulness of managing some neonates "towards their deaths", giving them treatment to make them comfortable rather than to extend their lives (*Re C (a Minor) (wardship: medical treatment)* [1989] 2 All ER 782; *Re J (a Minor)* [1990] 3 All ER 930, [1992] 4 All ER 614; *Re C (a Minor) Lloyd's Law Reports (Medical)* [1998] FamD 1; and see *A (Children)* (22 September 2000, Court of Appeal, No B1/2000/2969) below at **[14.395]**.

The question of quality of life for infants came painfully into focus in the following case.

[14.395] Case: *A (Children)* (22 September 2000, Court of Appeal, No B1/2000/2969)

Two girls, Mary and Jodie, were born joined at the ischium. Each had four limbs, but the lower part of the spines were fused, and the spinal cords conjoined. Each twin had her own brain, heart lungs, liver and kidneys, with a shared bladder. Jodie's aorta fed into Mary's aorta, and the arterial circulation ran from Jodie to Mary. Jodie was alert, responsive and fed well. Evidence was that if she were to be separated from Mary she would have the opportunity of a separate good quality life and to participate in activities appropriate to her age and development. If she were not separated, it was predicted that her heart, which was supporting both twins, would fail in three to six months. She would be restricted in movement and development by the increasingly deteriorating body of Mary.

Mary was in a very poor state. Mary had a poorly developed brain not compatible with normal development, and her heart and lungs were incapable of sustaining life. She shared Jodie's circulatory system and depended on it. If not separated from Jodie, she would be dependent upon her vital organs until they gave out, and this time would be spent in pain and discomfort.

> She would not develop physically or mentally. Separating her from Jodie would inevitably cause her instant death.
>
> Both twins were condemned to a very short and poor quality of life unless surgery was carried out to save Jodie that would result in the effective intentional termination of Mary's life.

[14.400] In a long and obviously difficult and sad consideration of the circumstances, the Court of Appeal authorised the surgery. It endorsed the following principles in coming to that decision:

- intention;
- necessity and self-defence;
- application in Australia; and
- legislation.

Intention

Mary had a right to life. Every human being is of equal value, and one life cannot be considered less valuable than another, however Jodie also has a right to life.

All persons are entitled to bodily integrity and autonomy, and to have their bodies whole and intact. Mary and Jodie do not have this integrity and autonomy. There is thus a strong presumption that an operation would be in their interests.

The object of an operation would be to provide this integrity, and Jodie would benefit accordingly. The death of Mary would not be intended, although it would be an inevitable consequence. She would gain bodily integrity as a human being, and she would die, not because she was intentionally killed, but because her body could not sustain that integrity. Continued life would hold nothing for her except pain and discomfort, if indeed she could feel anything at all.

The operation would therefore be in the best interests of each of the twins, and the court does not have to value one life over another.

Necessity and self-defence

[14.405] Ward LJ (with whom Brooke LJ agreed) considered that there was also an argument based on the principle of self-defence. He likened the circumstances of the twins to one where the life of a person is threatened by another, and stated at paragraph 7.7:

> "I can see no difference in essence between [the] resort to legitimate self-defence and the doctors coming to Jodie's defence and removing the threat of fatal harm to her presented by Mary's draining of her life-blood. The availability of such a plea of quasi self-defence, modified to meet the quite exceptional circumstances nature has inflicted on the twins, makes intervention by the doctors lawful."

The judges gave much attention to the principle of necessity in the criminal law (see also **[4.240]**). The judges, in discussing it, considered other situations where one is faced with the choice between two evils, both threatening loss of life: one involving the loss of more lives than the other, but both requiring an action which will end life. An example is the order by a ship's commander to seal the engine room of his warship where there was a fire and flood it with inert gas, knowing that if anyone was inside they would be killed, to save the rest of the crew. They concluded that the least harmful option must be taken, and that to do so is a defence to a charge of murder in criminal law. The act must be taken to avoid inevitable and irreparable evil, no more must be done than is reasonably necessary to avoid the evil, and the harm done must not be disproportionate to the harm inflicted. All judges urged caution in using the defence of necessity, emphasising the need to act in proportion to the harm to be avoided. They agreed that this was a case in which the surgery was justified, as it was the less harmful option.

Application in Australia

[14.410] The English and United States principles on quality of life must be recognised as not necessarily applying in Australia. However, there is little reason to believe that the case law mentioned above would not be followed here, and legislation in some Australian jurisdictions indicates a willingness by society to move in that direction.

Legislation

[14.415] The right to reject a personally unacceptable quality of life by rejection of treatment is recognised at law. Legislation in several Australian jurisdictions allows a person to make an advance directive to reject treatment if they become incompetent (see **[5.270]**). Judges in *Airedale* and *A (Children)* expressed regret that there is little legislative clarification of the law in relation to withholding or withdrawing treatment where the person is not competent. Readers might like to consider whether it is possible or feasible to develop such legislation. What situations would be covered? How would principles apply? How would "extraordinary treatment" or "quality of life" be defined? What defences would be available?

Life support

[14.420] The principles set out above also apply to the withholding or withdrawing of life support. In all jurisdictions, except South Australia and Western Australia, death has been defined as the irreversible cessation of circulation of the blood, or irreversible cessation of all function of the brain. Queensland has this definition only for the purposes of the *Transplantation and Anatomy Act 1979* (Qld). South Australia and Western Australia require irreversible cessation of all brain function. Thus, in most States, the patient is already dead and the life support machinery may be switched off. In South Australia and Western Australia one would have to rely on the principle of extraordinary care, which makes the decision much more difficult.

The difference between coma, brain death, permanent vegetative state, and "locked-in syndrome" must be clearly established in the minds of those who are caring for those suffering from these conditions. Before any decision to with-hold or withdraw treatment is made, all health carers should be clear on the distinctions, and diagnosis as to which condition is present should be made as carefully as is medically possible, all of those involved being satisfied that the diagnosis is correct.

Do not resuscitate orders

[14.425] Since the development of cardio-pulmonary resuscitation for patients with particular heart conditions, this procedure has been adopted in most situations of sudden cardiac failure in hospitals and elsewhere. The result may be the prolongation of life, which is of a quality so poor that the resuscitation is recognised as not being in the patient's interest.

The legal issues for medical personnel involve those discussed throughout this chapter. Is the failure to resuscitate a criminal act? Are there some circumstances which make it a criminal act? As can be seen, the answers are not certain. Health carers should take into account the patient's wishes, their prognosis, and what they can reasonably expect to be the outcome of cardio-pulmonary resuscitation on this particular person in the circumstances.

Considerations in initiating CPR might include the following:

- Has the patient left instructions not to resuscitate? If so, these should be respected unless there is reason to believe that circumstances have changed since the instructions were given, or that the patient would for some reason have changed her or his mind. Legislation should ensure this right. If no, then CPR is an option.

- Can CPR be expected to work in this case? If not, or it confers no real benefit, or simply prolongs the dying process, then it is legitimate to consider not using it on the basis that no person is required to give futile medical treatment.

- Given we can expect life to be prolonged, are there indications that the quality of life will be substantially reduced? If yes, then has prior consultation with the patient, or relatives if this is not possible (who may give advice on the patient's preferred lifestyle and wishes), determined that CPR is not in the person's interests.

- Where either the outcome of CPR, or the patient's wishes in relation to its administration are uncertain, it is suggested that CPR should be attempted until the outcome can reasonably be predicted.

There should not be a policy of disguising "Do not resuscitate" orders, for example by using codes or stickers. This creates distrust, not only on the part of the patient, but also on the part of those who must consider the legal implications of such an instruction. Where a code or unspoken instruction has been issued, it may be open to a court to find that the reasons for the order may not have been properly considered, or could be malicious or reckless, whereas the full recording of reasons, with the result of consultation with the patient and/or family if this has occurred, indicates an intention to abide by ethical and legal principles. Commentators consider this an important part of the medical relationship with those who are considered in danger of cardiac arrest (see, for example, Brazier (1997), p 458). Hospitals are increasingly developing policies including involvement of patient and family in "Do not resuscitate" decisions.

Figure 14.1: Summary of the law relating to withholding or withdrawing treatment from people in different circumstances

Palliative Care: Includes nursing care such as provision of comfort, prevention of pressure sores, warmth, proper hydration and nutrition, and pain relief.	Refusal to give palliative care by someone who owes a duty to care for another who has not competently refused it is neglect and might lead to conviction for homicide if the person dies as a result.
Extraordinary Care: Generally, care other than palliative care. Depends on the specific circumstances of the case.	Withholding extraordinary care from a patient who cannot decide on treatment has been accepted at law where it is considered futile or not in the interests of the patient, when weighed with the life expectancy of the patient and pain and distress it might cause (see *Saikewicz* at [14.370]; *Bland* at [14.295]).
Those who are competent	These people may refuse all treatment. Necessary and/or reasonable treatment may not be withheld or withdrawn from them against their will as this may constitute negligence, however they cannot demand futile treatment. Active measures cannot be taken to end their lives, nor can they be assisted to take their own lives. Suicide is not an offence, but it is not assault or battery to prevent someone from committing suicide. Common law indicates that those who are terminally ill may be given adequate pain relief, even though it is recognised that this may shorten their life (see [14.275]ff).
Coma: Coma, as distinct from vegetative state or "locked-in syndrome", is a state of unconsciousness, from which the person may be reasonably expected to recover, even if it lasts for months.	Where a person is in a coma, only critical treatment which is clinically futile can be withheld or withdrawn from them. The person may have made an advance directive, stating their wish to have treatment withheld or withdrawn under certain circumstances. The only jurisdiction where failure to obey an advance directive is an offence is Victoria, where the *Medical Treatment Act 1988* (Vic) creates the offence of medical trespass for so doing.
Vegetative-State: The cerebral cortex is no longer functioning, but the brain stem is (see description in *Quinlan*). The person has no perception or cognition, breathes spontan-eously, has no hope of recovery but may live for many years. Diagnosis is currently based on CAT and PET scans to detect brain function. To be differentiated from long-term coma.	In Australia, the courts have allowed the removal of basic nutrition from persons in a PVS state (see [14.300]). In the United States courts have allowed that removal of both extraordinary care and basic nutrition (see *Saikewicz* at [14.370]).

"Locked-in Syndrome": This condition is different from PVS: the cerebral cortex may be operative, but the brain stem is not. It may, for example result from Guillain-Barre syndrome or cerebro-vascular accident. The patient is conscious but unable to respond to their environment, and requires ventilation and other artificial life-preserving measures.	As with the patient with coma or PVS, this patient is legally alive, and technically critical treatment cannot be withdrawn or withheld unless it is futile. As artificial life-preservation cannot be considered futile in a strict sense, it would seem that removal of this would be homicide. See however, for an exceptional case, *Auckland Hospital v Attorney-General* at **[14.325]**.
Brain-death: Total absence of brain activity, with artificial ventilation required to maintain circulation.	Legally the person is dead, and no further treatment of any kind need be given. Logically, "treatment" of a brain-dead person is covered by the laws relating to organ transplants from cadavers and handling of dead bodies.

Criminal Negligence

[14.430] It is rare for a charge of criminal negligence to be laid against a health worker. It may, however, occur where something has gone horribly wrong, with unintended results, and it is established that the health carer in question either intended some degree of harm to occur, or was so reckless with regard to human life or safety that a jury finds their actions serious enough to amount to a criminal act. There is no definition of "criminal negligence" in the legislation. Where it involves an unintended death it may be termed involuntary manslaughter. The Court has held that the core of manslaughter by criminal negligence is "a great falling short of the standard of care" which a reasonable person would have exercised and "involving such a high risk that death or grievous bodily harm would follow that the doing of the act merited criminal punishment" (*Nydam v The Queen* [1977] VR 430 at 445).

[14.435] Case: *R v Bateman* (1925) 19 Cr App R 8
(Court of Criminal Appeal England)

A doctor unintentionally caused severe internal injury to a patient during delivery of a child, and then neglected to send her elsewhere for necessary treatment, resulting in the patient's death. The patient's bladder was ruptured, her colon crushed against the sacral promontory, the rectum ruptured and the uterus almost entirely missing. This led to charges of manslaughter as a result of criminal negligence.

[14.440] The Court said that, contrary to civil negligence, criminal negligence is based on the degree of culpability involved, rather than the amount of harm caused. The defendant must have shown a disregard for the life and safety of another, so reckless as to amount to a crime against the state and conduct deserving of punishment. Based on these considerations, Bateman's conviction in the lower court was quashed at the appeal hearing.

Findings of criminal negligence have involved, for example, an anaesthetist addicted to anaesthetic drugs who removed the anaesthetic tube from a child during an operation and put it to his own mouth, causing the child to die from oxygen deprivation (*The Lancet*, 28 February 1959). In that case the doctor received a sentence of 12 months' imprisonment. A physician who had given prescriptions for an inordinately and irresponsibly large number and high dosage of drugs to a patient who subsequently died from the effects of drug induced depression of the gag reflex was also held to be criminally negligent (*Pennsylvania v Youngkin* 427 A 2d 1356 (1981)).

The level of culpability or degree of negligence required to be proved is much higher in criminal negligence that in a civil claim. The Privy Council pointed out in the case of *Akerele v The King* [1943] AC 255, where many children died as the result of too strong a solution being injected into them, that once an action has taken place, its consequences no matter how horrible cannot add to its criminality. Although it is usually a jury which decides whether the negligence of a person is criminal, the judge decides in the first place whether it has been gross enough to go to the jury. In the case of *R v Adomako* [1994] 2 All ER 79 the House of Lords reviewed the law of criminal negligence at length. In that case an anaesthetist was found guilty of criminal negligence where a patient undergoing surgery died as the result of disconnection of a tube from the anaesthetic machine, depriving him of oxygen. Despite an alarm and the falling of the patient's heart rate and blood pressure, the anaesthetist did not check the integrity of the machine. The House of Lords said that the ordinary principles of criminal negligence apply to establish breach of duty, and causation. If these are proved, the next question for the jury is whether the breach was one of gross negligence, and therefore a crime.

Abortion

[14.445] The law regarding abortion is contained in the crime legislation of each Australian jurisdiction, with the exception of the Australian Capital Territory (see *Crimes Act 1900* (NSW), Pt 3, Div 12; *Criminal Code 1899* (Qld), ss 224-226; *Criminal Code Act* (NT), ss 172-174; *Criminal Law Consolidation Act 1935* (SA), Pt 3, Div 17; *Crimes Act 1958* (Vic), ss 65-66; *Criminal Code* (WA), s 199; *Criminal Code* (Tas), ss 134-135). Generally, there are six main elements to the law:

- the woman need not actually be pregnant (the intention to abort is the crucial factor);
- the prohibition is against the *unlawful* procuring of miscarriage;
- a woman must not unlawfully bring about her own miscarriage;

- a person must not aid another in unlawfully procuring a miscarriage;
- an attempt by any person to procure an unlawful miscarriage is just as serious an offence as if it were successful; and
- a person must not supply the means for procuring an unlawful miscarriage; the means may be "any drug or noxious thing, or any instrument or thing whatsoever".

It is important to note that each jurisdiction may have complementary legislation setting out further requirements for induced miscarriage, such as the location for the procedure, the number of practitioners certifying its necessity, etc. Some of these are set out below. Health carers should be familiar with the law in their jurisdiction, so that they are not inadvertently involved in unlawful procedures.

The meaning of "unlawful"

[14.450] The crucial element in the legal definition is the unlawfulness of the abortion. What constitutes unlawfulness varies with each jurisdiction. At common law, the only accepted ground for inducing an abortion was imminent danger to the life of the mother.

Early English precedent

[14.455] In the 1930s the courts began to clarify the term "imminent danger to the life of the mother".

[14.460] Case: *R v Bourne* [1938] 3 All ER 615 (Criminal Court England)

Dr B was approached by a young woman who was pregnant as a result of a particularly vicious multiple rape. He formed the view that she was likely to suffer severe psychological detriment from continuation of the pregnancy and therefore agreed to carry out an abortion. Dr B then handed himself over to the police and was charged. The subsequent trial resulted in his acquittal, the judge instructing the jury that "danger to the life of the mother" included danger of psychological harm where the doctor has an honest belief that the woman would become a "physical or mental wreck".

Victoria

[14.465] Judicial interpretation of the term "unlawful" remains relevant. The principle in the case of *R v Bourne* was expressed more practically in a Victorian case in the Supreme Court, *R v Davidson* [1969] VR 667, where it was held that the prosecution must establish that the person carrying out the abortion (the accused):

- the accused did not honestly believe on reasonable grounds that the woman would suffer serious danger to life or physical or mental health "not being the normal dangers of pregnancy or childbirth"; and
- the accused did not honestly believe that nothing less than abortion was required to avert the danger.

New South Wales

[14.470] A later case in the District Court of New South Wales, *R v Wald* (1971) 3 NSWDCR 25 adopted the approach of *Davidson*, but extended the considerations the person carrying out the abortion may take into account to include any

> "economic, social or medical ground or reason which in their view could constitute reasonable grounds upon which an accused could honestly and reasonably believe there would result a serious danger to her physical or mental health."

Both *Davidson* and *Wald* recognised the defence of necessity to a charge of unlawful abortion, that defence involving the above two requirements of need and proportion.

The accused need not be correct in her or his belief in the necessity of abortion, only to have a reasonable and honest belief in it. This would require that some consideration of alternatives would have been made by the accused, and rejected on reasonable and honest grounds.

These two cases were heard at relatively low levels of the court hierarchy, where binding precedent is not really established, but they have been accepted as the law on abortion so far. It is suggested that the law is more likely to favour those who ensure that the operating doctor discusses the issues with the woman, and canvasses alternatives with her, recording both this and the belief (or otherwise) in the necessity of the abortion.

[14.475] Case: *CES & Anor v Superclinics Australia Pty Ltd & Ors* (1995) 38 NSWLR 47 (CA NSW)

A woman who believed she was pregnant visited the defendant's surgery on five different occasions, on all of which she was told she was not pregnant. Her purpose for seeking a determination of pregnancy was so that if she was pregnant she could have an abortion. She was in fact pregnant, but by the time this was established it was too late to have the abortion. She sued the defendant for the resulting physical and emotional harm which she endured in bearing and caring for the child.

The trial judge found in favour of the defendants, on the ground that although the doctors should have recognised the plaintiff's pregnancy, she could not claim damages because for her to have had an abortion would have been illegal, as she had not established that she would have suffered serious harm to her physical or mental health. He determined that for this reason, had she found out earlier and had had an abortion, it would have been a crime. The law does not allow damages to be paid to a person who had lost the chance to perform an illegal act. Despite the doctor's negligence, she had no avenue to recover damages. The case was appealed.

[14.480] The Court of Appeal reversed this finding, ruling that the defendants had been negligent in not diagnosing the pregnancy, resulting in mental, physical and economic harm associated with carrying a child to term and giving birth when the pregnancy was unexpected and unwanted. Even if an abortion were to have been illegal, the defendants would not have been complicit in any illegal activity in giving the woman the correct results of the tests. Even so, Kirby P found that the danger to the mother's health need not be restricted to the period of the pregnancy: it could crystallise at the birth, or even after it. Given the increased recognition of such conditions as post-natal depression and serious economic and social pressures on women with children, the gravity of the dangers posed by a pregnancy have to be balanced and evaluated in each case. In this case there was sufficient evidence to suggest that a medical practitioner could form the opinion that the woman was facing a serious danger to her mental health by having to continue with the pregnancy.

Australian legislation

[14.485] Other Australian jurisdictions have set out in their legislation when an abortion may be lawful.

South Australia

[14.490] In South Australia, s 82A of the *Criminal Law Consolidation Act 1935* (SA) (amended in 1969) permits a doctor to carry out an abortion in the following circumstances:

- *Non-emergency:* the operation is to be carried out in a hospital and two doctors (one of which is the operating doctor) must be of the opinion that the woman faces a greater risk to her life or mental or physical health if the pregnancy were continued or the child would suffer such physical or mental abnormalities as to be seriously handicapped.
- *Emergency:* a medical practitioner may carry out a termination of pregnancy where it is immediately necessary to save the woman's life or prevent grave injury to her mental or physical health.

Section 81 of that Act provides for a maximum sentence of life imprisonment for an unlawful attempt to procure an abortion.

Northern Territory

[14.495] The Northern Territory has similar provisions to South Australia in its *Criminal Code Act* (NT), except that non-urgent terminations are restricted to a gynaecologist or obstetrician and the woman must have been pregnant for no more than 14 weeks (see s 174). There are three time-frames established under the Act:

- *Non-emergency where the pregnancy is less than 14 weeks:* a gynaecologist, with the concurrence of another medical practitioner, may carry out a termination of pregnancy where both doctors are of the belief that the woman would suffer greater physical or mental harm if the pregnancy were to continue, or the child would be seriously handicapped.
- *Emergency where such harm is immediately imminent and pregnancy not more than 23 weeks:* a medical practitioner may terminate such a pregnancy.
- *Emergency where the woman's life is in immediate danger:* a medical practitioner may terminate the pregnancy. There is no time restriction.

Where the woman is under 16 years of age or otherwise unable to give consent, the consent of each person who has the right to give consent on her behalf is required (the Act fails to make any stipulation about emergencies, but presumably all the common law defences would apply; see **[4.170]**ff, **[5.20]**).

Queensland

[14.500] The *Criminal Code 1899* (Qld) makes it an offence for a person to unlawfully terminate a pregnancy, the exception for this being an abortion carried out "for the preservation of the mother's life". This has, however been interpreted to include preservation of her physical or mental health, along the lines of *Attorney-General (Qld) (Ex rel Kerr) v T* [1983] 1 Qd R 404; *R v Bayliss and Cullen* (unreported, 31 January 1986, District Court Brisbane); *Vievers & Anor v Connelly* (1994) Aust Torts Reports ¶81-309.

Western Australia

[14.505] The *Criminal Code* (WA), s 199 together with s 334 of the *Health Act 1911* (WA) provides that carrying out an illegal abortion is an offence. It is not an offence to perform an abortion if it is carried out by a medical practitioner in good faith, with reasonable care and skill in circumstances where:

1) the woman has given informed consent; or
2) the woman will suffer serious personal, family or social consequences if the abortion is not performed; or
3) the woman will suffer from serious physical or mental health problems if the abortion is not performed; or
4) the pregnancy is causing serious danger to her physical or mental health.

In all cases the woman must give informed consent unless, in the case of (3) and (4), it is impractical for her to do so. If the pregnancy is over 20 weeks, two medical practitioners who are members of a panel appointed by the Minister must agree that the termination is justified on the basis of the health of the woman or the foetus. The abortion must also be carried out in a ministerially-approved health facility.

Informed consent is defined as freely given consent where a medical practitioner (other than the practitioner carrying out the abortion) has properly, appropriately and adequately provided counselling about medical risks of both termination and continuation of the pregnancy, and advised the woman of the availability of further counselling and advice, whatever her decision.

A woman under 16 who is supported by a custodial parent or guardian cannot give informed consent unless a parent or guardian has been informed and has had the opportunity to be involved in the counselling process and consultation with the doctor as to whether the abortion should be performed.

Tasmania

[14.510] Section 164 of the *Criminal Code* in Tasmania provides that a person is not guilty of a crime if an abortion is legally justified. An abortion will be legally justified where:

a) two medical practitioners have certified that continuation of the pregnancy would involve greater risk of injury of physical or mental injury to the woman; and
b) where practicable to do so, the woman has given informed consent.

Australian Capital Territory

[14.515] The Australian Capital Territory decriminalised abortion with the introduction of the *Crimes (Abolition of Abortion) Act 2002* (ACT) which deleted the sections dealing with abortion from the *Crimes Act 1900* (ACT). The *Health Act 1993* (ACT), Pt 5A provides that only a doctor may carry out an abortion and it must be done in an approved medical facility.

Who may carry out an abortion?

[14.520] Any person may offer the defence that they carried out a procedure in an emergency, and it was intended to prevent a real and imminent danger of death or serious harm, so long as it is done in a responsible way, and there is no better medical help available. At common law this constitutes the defence of necessity. Section 282 of the *Criminal Code* (Qld) provides:

> "A person is not criminally responsible for performing in good faith and with reasonable care and skill a surgical operation upon any person for the patient's benefit, or upon an unborn child for the preservation of the mother's life, if the performance of the operation is reasonable, having regard to the patient's state at the time and to all the circumstances of the case."

The person must weigh the dangers and not aggravate the existing condition. Where there is no emergency it is advised that a nurse or other health carer should not carry out an abortion unless supervised by a doctor, as it is considered a medical procedure although there may be no criminal sanction against this. Note, however, the provisions in South Australia and the Northern Territory above. Also, in the Australian Capital Territory only a medical practitioner may carry out a termination of pregnancy.

Other jurisdictions may have legislation determining who may or may not carry out a termination of pregnancy. Hospitals may have procedural requirements. For example, a hospital board may require certain procedures, such as certification of the need for the termination by two doctors, and permission by the superintendent.

Some Nurses Registration Acts prohibit the carrying out of terminations by nurses.

At what stage of pregnancy can an abortion be carried out?

[14.525] Where there is no emergency, and a foetus is capable of independent life, it is possible that termination of pregnancy could be murder or child destruction. Unless there are specific requirements for late-term abortions, the law is generally unclear as to where the line is drawn. Specific guidance for emergencies, such as where the woman is in immediate danger of severe mental or physical harm, exists in some jurisdictions (see above), and it would seem illogical to set a time limit in such situations. The Northern Territory and South Australia specifically state that, in emergencies, one doctor is required to be of the opinion that the termination is required.

Does the foetus have any rights?

[14.530] The short answer to this question would appear to be: no. The foetus is not a person until it has lived independently outside the mother's body (see also **[6.210]**). The courts have considered the question of whether the foetus has a right to live in several cases.

[14.535] Case: *F v F* (1989) FLC ¶92-031

A husband applied to the Family Court for an injunction to prevent his estranged and pregnant wife from terminating the pregnancy of their prospective child. He argued, among other things, that the foetus had a right to protection against abortion, and that he could enforce that right on its behalf.

[14.540] The court considered precedent, and made the following important points:

- A court cannot make ethical judgments—it is concerned with legal rights. Its task is to interpret and apply the law, not particular moral or ethical precepts (readers may like to compare this approach with the use by many courts of public policy).

- "The foetus has no right of its own until it is born and has a separate existence from its mother." This was held by the English case of *Paton v British Pregnancy Advisory Service* [1979] 1 QB 276. Note also the case of *K v Minister for Youth and Community Services*, where an application was sought to be brought in the name of a foetus to prevent an abortion, Street CJ (with whom the other judges agreed) said:

  "I am not, as at present advised, satisfied that the unborn child or foetus has the requisite status to participate as a party in proceedings of a character of those before the equity division or in those such as are sought to be brought before this court."

Note also the law on reporting stillbirths at Chapter 15.

Do others have any rights?

[14.545] In the case of *F v F*, the court also addressed the right of third parties to determine whether a termination will be undertaken. The court followed those cases mentioned in determining that a father has no right to stop the mother having a legal abortion (at 77-438):

  "To grant the injunction would be to compel the wife to do something in relation to her own body which she does not wish to do. That would be an interference with her freedom to decide her own destiny."

Child destruction

[14.550] There is a period when a child may, for the purposes of criminal law, be neither a foetus whose destruction is abortion, nor a legal person whose destruction is murder. Some may consider this the period from when the child is capable of being born alive, others require that the child be in the process of being born. In some Australian jurisdictions a special offence of child destruction covers the intentional killing of such a being (see *Crimes Act 1958* (Vic), s 10; *Criminal Law Consolidation Act 1935* (SA), s 82A(7)-(8); *Crimes Act 1900* (ACT), s 42). The Northern Territory, Western Australia and Queensland have an offence of "killing unborn child" which carries a maximum penalty of life imprisonment for preventing a child being born alive where a person is about to be delivered of a child (*Criminal Code Act* (NT), s 170; *Criminal Code 1899* (Qld), s 313; *Criminal Code* (WA), s 290). In Tasmania the offence is stated as "causing the death of a child before birth" (*Criminal Code Act 1924* (Tas), s 165). In New South Wales it is referred to as injury to a child at time of birth (*Crimes Act 1900* (NSW), s 42).

Midwives, especially, should be aware of the law relating to abortion and child destruction in their jurisdiction. This book cannot deal with the detail of particular regulations and administrative procedures in each Australian jurisdiction, which can change relatively quickly. These may establish further restrictions on the carrying out of terminations, and should be consulted.

Victims of Crime

[14.555] Where the patient is apparently a victim of a criminal offence (for example, assault, rape) the health carers should be aware that evidence of the offence might be required (for example, vaginal smears, samples of clothing, photographs and descriptions of wounds). Police, or other investigators appointed by them, will want to collect such evidence, so for this purpose it is important that the patient be undisturbed as much as possible, after any urgent treatment has been given. However, it must be remembered that the physical examination is subject to the consent of the person, and police have no right as such to require such an examination. Special training in forensic health care, which includes the mental, physical and emotional care of the victim, the gathering of evidence, presentation in court and principles of giving testimony is recognised as essential for proper dealing with victims of crime.

A victim of sexual assault should ideally not have a bath or shower no matter how desirable this may be, until examination has been carried out and evidence collected. It should be borne in mind, however, that the person must not be forced against their will in this matter, but the victim should be reminded that prosecution by the police will be much more difficult without this evidence. Reassurance and comforting will therefore be an essential part of the health professional's caring for victims of violence, as they will be distressed and uncomfortable.

Collection of forensic evidence

[14.560] Those working in emergency and other receiving wards should be familiar with the hospital's procedures for dealing with such patients and should be aware of any special personnel for handling the collection of evidence or liaison with police. Where someone believes a crime has been committed there is also an obligation to inform appropriate authorities in the public interest. Failure to report serious crime may amount to complicity in it under circumstances, where is assists the perpetrator.

Because of their close relationship with the victims of crime, health professionals may find that they possess information, witness events and facts which may make them useful witnesses in later court cases. They may have received a dying statement which can later be admitted in evidence. It is suggested that while health carers should not shirk their civic duty to assist in the process of justice, they should not actively involve themselves in potential criminal cases by undertaking activities for the patient (such as, getting or giving information, contacting people, discussing the case with others, or intervening in private disputes) which are not part of their normal professional duties.

It is equally important for health workers to remember the requirements of confidentiality, no matter how much one might be tempted to discuss exciting details of criminal events with others. Potential witnesses in a case are warned by lawyers involved in the case against discussing certain matters with other witnesses or the press. Spreading allegations about the guilt of specific or identifiable persons may amount to defamation.

Patients Allegedly the Perpetrators of Crime

Care, examination and forensic evidence

[14.565] Similar advice applies to those caring for people who are charged with, or accused of, crime, with several further important points. There are many rules relating to the collection of forensic evidence. In most jurisdictions these are set out in their respective *Crimes Acts* or *Criminal Codes* (see **[14.10]**). South Australia enacted the *Criminal Law (Forensic Procedures) Act* in 1998. The Australian Capital Territory and New South Wales have also enacted legislation, *Crimes (Forensic Procedures) Act 2000*. The Commonwealth enhanced its legislation governing forensic procedures under the *Crimes Act 1914* via the *Crimes Amendment (Forensic Procedures) Act 2001*. The various legislative instruments generally establish the following rules with some variations. Forensic procedures are divided into two categories. Intimate procedures (including photography and taking of casts) involving the external anal and genital regions and buttocks, the breasts of women, the taking of blood samples, dental impressions and pubic hair. Non-intimate procedures involve other parts of the body and the taking of fingerprints, buccal swabs and other hair. A medical practitioner or nurse may carry out forensic procedures at the request of police, who are responsible for ensuring there is proper authority to carry out the procedure. The person must be given the opportunity to consent to a forensic procedure, and informed of the legal implications of its being carried out. If the person does not consent, a senior police officer can generally order the carrying out of a non-intimate procedure. Intimate forensic procedures can only be carried out in certain circumstances, and must have the consent of the suspect or a magistrate's order. In addition, the person may be entitled to request the presence of a medical practitioner. Special rules may apply regarding forensic procedures involving a child or incompetent person. In the case of intimate procedures, a person of the same sex as the subject of the procedure should carry it out where this is reasonably possible, or such a person may be present.

Health carers called on to carry out a forensic procedure are responsible for informing the person of the medical aspects of the procedure (in line with the law generally) where consent is requested.

A person is not guilty at law until they have been convicted by a court. It is for a court to determine guilt, not health care staff. Even where the patient has been convicted of a crime, it is not for health care workers to determine and carry out their punishment. That is the task of law enforcement agencies. These principles are established by the *Human Rights and Equal Opportunity Commission Act 1986* (Cth), which prohibits discrimination against anyone for the reasons given (Ch 18). Health carers should give the same standard of treatment to every person they care for, although the degree of friendliness they exhibit may vary. Failure to give this standard could be considered unethical and may result in a complaint to the Human Rights and Equal Opportunity Commission.

References and Further Reading

Ashby, M and Mendelson, D, "*Gardner: re BWV*: Victorian Supreme Court Makes Landmark Australian Ruling on Tube Feeding" (2004) 8 *Medical Journal of Australia* 181 at 442-445

Battin, M, "Voluntary Euthanasia and the Risk of Abuse: Can we Learn Anything from the Netherlands?" (1992) 20 *Law Medicine and Health Care* 133

Bennett, G and Hogan, B, "Criminal Law, Criminal Procedure and Sentencing" [1989] *All ER Annual Review* 94

Book, M, "Withholding or Withdrawing Life Sustaining Treatment: New Legislation in WA" *Australian Health Law Bulletin* 13 (9)

Bowen, T, and Saxton, A, "New developments in the Law—Withholding and Withdrawal of Medical Treatment" *Australian Health Law Bulletin* 14 (5)

Brazier, M, *Medicine, Patient and the Law* (Penguin, 1992)

Brody, H, *Ethical Decisions in Medicine* (Little Brown, Boston, 1981)

Brown, D, Farrier, D, and Wesibrot, D, *Criminal Laws: Materials and Commentary on Criminal Law and Process of NSW* (Federation Press, Sydney, 1996)

Buchanan, J, "Euthanasia: the Medical and Psychological Issues" (1995) 3 *Journal of Law and Medicine* 136-145

Dearden, I, and Tronc, K, *Criminal Precedents* (LBC Information Services, Sydney, 1996)

Corns, C, "Withdrawal of Life-Support: Some Criminal Prosecution Aspects" in Freckelton, I and Petersen P, *Controversies in Health Law* (The Federation Press, Sydney, 1999), p 44

Dix, et al, *Law for the Medical Profession* (Butterworths, Sydney, 1988), p 296

Freckelton, I, "Withdrawal of Life Support: The `Persistent Vegetative State'" (1993) 1 *Journal of Law and Medicine* 34

Geraghty, E, "What Price Uncertainty? The Persistent Vegetative State in New South Wales" [2002] *Macquarie Law Journal* 9

Gillett, G, "Ethical Aspects of the Northern Territory Euthanasia Legislation" (1995) 3 *Journal of Law and Medicine* 145-152

Gillies, P, *Criminal Law* (4th ed, Law Book Co, Sydney, 1993)

Gillon, R, Editorial (1981) 7 *Journal of Medical Ethics* 56

Halsbury's Laws of England (4th ed, Butterworths, London), Vol 30

Hunsaker, D, "Unnatural Life vs Natural Death: Some Legal and Ethical Considerations" (1978) 7 (1) GMUL Review

Kerridge I, Lowe, M and McPhee, J, *Ethics and Law for the Health Professions* (2nd ed, Federation Press, Sydney, 2005), particularly chapter 21 "Euthanasia" and chapter 22 "Post Coma Unresponsiveness and Brainstem Death".

Kuhse, H and Singer, P, "Active Voluntary Euthanasia, Morality and the Law" (1995) 3 *Journal of Law and Medicine* 129-135

Kuhse, H, *Caring: Nurses, Women and Ethics* (Blackweel Publishers, Oxford UK, 1997)

Kuhse, H, (ed), *Willing to Listen, Wanting to Die* (Penguin, Sydney, 1994)

Kuhse, H, "Quality of Life and the Death of `Baby M'" (1992) 6 *Bioethics* 233-250

Lanham, D, *Taming Death by Law* (Longman Professional Publishing, Melbourne, 1993)

Lipman, Z, "The Criminal Liability of Medical Practitioners for Withholding Treatment from Severely Defective Newborn Infants" (1986) 60 *Australian Law Journal* 286

Macmillan, E, "Birth Defective Infants: a Standard for Non-Treatment Decisions" (1978) 30 *Stanford Law Review* 595

McLean, S, and Maher, G, *Medicine, Morals and the Law* (Gower Publishing, Hampshire, 1985)

Mendelson, D, "The Northern Territory's Euthanasia Legislation in Historical Perspective" (1995) 3 *Journal of Law and Medicine* 136-145

Mendelson, D, "End of Life—Legal Framework" in Freckelton, I and Petersen P, *Controversies in Health Law* (Federation Press, Sydney, 1999), p 59

Meyers, D, *Medico-Legal Implications of Death and Dying* (Lawyers Co-operative Publishing, San Francisco, 1981)

Miller, F and Brody, H, "Professional Integrity and Physician-Assisted Death" (1996) 26 *Monash Bioethics Review* 41

Morgan, D and Veitch, K, "Being Ms B: B, Autonomy and the Nature of Legal Regulation" (2004) 26 *Sydney Law Review* 107

O'Connor, D and Fairall, P, *Criminal Defences* (Butterworths, Sydney, 1996)

Ormrod, L J, "A Lawyer Looks at Medical Ethics" (1977) 45 (Pt 4) *Medico-Legal Journal* 104

Otlowski, M, *Active Voluntary Euthanasia—A Timely Reappraisal* (University of Tasmania Law School Occasional Paper, University of Tasmania Hobart, 1992)

Paris, J and Reardon, F, "Court Responses to Withholding or Withdrawing Artificial Nutrition and Fluids" (1988) 253 (No 15) *Journal of the American Medical Association* 2243

Petersen, K, "Criminal Abortion Laws: An Impediment to Reproductive Health" in Freckelton, I and Petersen P, *Controversies in Health Law* (Federation Press, Sydney, 1999), p 28

Pope Pius XII, "Address of 24 November 1957 to Doctors" (1957) 49 *Acta Apostolicae Sedis* 1027-33

President's Commission for the Study of Ethical Problems in Medical, Biological and Behavioural Research, *Deciding to Forgo Life-Sustaining Treatment* (Government Printer, Washington, 1983)

Robertson, J, "Organ Donations by Incompetents and the Substituted Judgment Doctrine" (1976) 76 *Columbia Law Review* 48

Roulston, R, *Introduction to Criminal Law in New South Wales* (2nd ed, Butterworths, Sydney, 1980)

Royal College of Nursing 1994, Memorandum, *House of Lords Select Committee on Medical Ethics, Volume II- Oral Evidence* (HMSO, London), p 70

Schurr, B, *Criminal Procedure NSW* (LBC Information Services, Sydney, 1996)

Skegg, P, *Law Ethics and Medicine* (Clarendon Press, London, 1984)

Skene, L, *Law & Medical Practice: Rights, Duties, Claims and Defences* (2nd ed, Butterworths, Sydney 2004)

Skene, L, "The Schiavo and Korp cases: Conceptualising End of Life Decision Making" *Australian Health Law Bulletin* 13 (2)

Starke, J, "Current Topics: The Problem of the Legal Status of the Foetus in Utero" (1990) 63 *Australian Law Journal* 719

Thompson, P, "The Law and Active Euthanasia: Whose Life is it Anyway?" (1995) 2 *Journal of Law and Medicine*, 233-246

United Kingdom Central Council for Nursing, Midwifery and Health Visiting ("UKCC") 1994, Memorandum, *House of Lords Select Committee on Medical Ethics, Volume II- Oral Evidence* (HMSO, London), p 139

Waller, L and Williams C R, *Brett, Waller and Williams Criminal Law* (8th ed, Butterworths, Australia, 1997)

Wallace, M, "Euthanasia and the Law: Some Implications for Nurses" *The Politics of Euthanasia* (Royal College of Nursing Australia, Sydney, 1995)

White, B, and Willmott, L, "Futility, Finances and Families: Decisions to Withdraw Life-Sustaining Medical Treatment" *Australian Health Law Bulletin* 13 (4)

White, B, and Willmott, L, "Charting a Course Through Difficult Legislative Waters: Tribunal Decisions on Life Sustaining Measures" *Australian Health Law Bulletin* 12 (4)

Williams, C R, *Brett and Waller's Criminal Law* (Butterworths, Australia, 1983)

Williams, G, "Euthanasia" (1973) 41 *Medico-Legal Journal* 14

15

15 State involvement in birth & death: Registration & coronial inquiries

Notification of births

Notification of death

Coroners' inquests

chapter 15

State Involvement in Birth and Death: Registration and Coronial Inquiries

Introduction

[15.05] There are times when matters concerning individuals must be reported to the State. These include births, deaths, child abuse and neglect, and the knowledge that someone has a certain infectious or sexually transmitted disease. There are also deaths, which, because of their unusual or unexplained nature, or other circumstances defined by statute, should be brought to the notice of the coroner (usually via the police). Health carers may believe that they will probably not be concerned with reporting these events very often, if at all. However, child abuse and domestic violence in particular are matters of growing public concern. Also, those in remote regions, or practising in aspects of health care which have high mortality rates, may be involved in reporting to the authorities concerned. The notification of births and deaths, as well as coroner's inquests, will be dealt with in this chapter, the reporting of infectious diseases and child abuse in Chapter 16.

Notification of Births

[15.10] In each Australian jurisdiction there is legislation that establishes a register of births deaths and marriages, maintained by a body known as the "Registrar of Births, Deaths and Marriages" (*Births, Deaths and Marriages Registration Act 1997* (ACT); *Births, Deaths and Marriages Registration Act 1995* (NSW); *Births, Deaths and Marriages Registration Act 1996* (NT); *Births, Deaths and Marriages Registration Act 2003* (Qld); *Births, Deaths and Marriages Registration Act 1996* (SA); *Births, Deaths and Marriages Registration Act 1999* (Tas); *Births Deaths and Marriages Registration Act 1996* (Vic); *Births, Deaths and Marriages Registration Act 1998* (WA)). All births, including stillbirths (defined below **[15.30]**) must be recorded in the register. The furnishing of details of a birth to the Registrar is generally the joint responsibility of the parents of that child.

Who is responsible for notification to Registrar-General

[15.15] In all Australian jurisdictions the chief executive officer of the hospital or institution where a child is born is required to ensure that the birth is notified to the Registrar. A doctor or midwife who is present at the birth may also have responsibility for ensuring notification, particularly where the child is born outside of a hospital. Queensland, Tasmania, Victoria and Western Australia also require a person present at the birth to ensure notification. Failure to notify is an offence, however, in most jurisdictions, reasonable grounds for believing that notice has already been given will provide a defence.

Time limit for notice

[15.20] The time limits for notifying are:

Jurisdiction	Time Limit
Australian Capital Territory	7 days
New South Wales	21 days
Northern Territory	10 days
South Australia	7 days
Queensland	2 working days
Tasmania	21 days
Victoria	21 days
Western Australia	1 month

Additional requirements

Victoria

[15.25] In Victoria, the *Health Act 1958* imposes additional notification requirements on all births. The Act requires notification of a birth within 48 hours to the chief executive officer of the council of the municipal district in which the mother of the child usually resides, or if unknown, the municipal district where the birth takes place. Notification is required as follows:

- where the birth is in a hospital or other institution, by the Director of Nursing or person in charge of the institution;
- where the birth occurs elsewhere, by the midwife or other attendant at the birth, within 24 hours;
- where there is no attendant, by the father, or if he is not resident in the house where the birth occurs, the occupier of the house.

The form of notification is contained in the Schedule of the Act. This additional reporting requirement is intended to ensure that the local Maternal and Child Health Centre can be notified.

Victoria also requires that the birth be reported to the consultative body which has been set up to study obstetric and paediatric conditions under the *Health Act*

1958 (Vic), the *Consultative Council on Obstetric and Paediatric Mortality and Morbidity* (CCOPMM*).* Information provided to the CCOPMM is privileged by legislation and, unless released by CCOPMM, is not accessible by any third party including the Courts. Persons responsible for reporting to this body are:

- where the birth is in a hospital, the proprietor of the hospital;
- where the birth occurs elsewhere, the midwife or where there is no midwife present, the registered medical practitioner attendant at the birth;
- in other cases, the proprietor of a hospital to which mother and child are admitted as a result of the birth, or any other medical practitioner who undertakes care and treatment of the mother and child.

The recent amendments to the *Health Act* amend the functions of CCOPMM to enable consideration of mortality and morbidity of 15, 16 and 17 year olds (s 162F(1)(a)), to clarify the authority of health service providers to provide information to CCOPMM (s 162FA) and to provide for CCOPMM to disclose information to specified bodies in special circumstances (s 162FB). The CCOPMM consists of a twelve member Council and four committees: Maternal Mortality Committee, Stillbirth Committee, Neonatal Mortality Committee, and Infant and Child Mortality Committee. For more information, see the website at: www.health.vic.gov.au/perinatal/ccopmm/.

Stillbirths (child not born alive)

[15.30] In all Australian jurisdictions a stillborn child is defined as a child of at least 20 weeks' gestation, or if the period of gestation cannot readily be established with a body mass of at least 400 grams, that exhibits no signs of respiration or heartbeat, or other signs of life, after delivery .

Stillbirths must be registered in the same way as births, with the same people being responsible. The Australian Capital Territory, New South Wales, South Australia, Tasmania and Victoria all require notification of a stillbirth to be made within 48 hours. Note the different definitions of what is a "child" according to the requirements for registration of stillbirth, and the definition of "person" for the purposes of criminal law (see **[14.215]**ff) and civil law (see **[6.210]**ff).

All jurisdictions make it an offence to fail to give notice of a birth or stillbirth, or to give false information.

  Checklist
WHEN HEALTH CARERS HAVE A RESPONSIBILITY TO REGISTER THE BIRTH OF A CHILD
To determine a birth for the purposes of notification:
✓ Is the foetus of at least 20 weeks' gestation?
✓ Does it weigh at least 400 grams?
If yes to either, it is a "child" for the purposes of notification, and is a live birth or stillbirth.
Determination of live or stillbirth:
✓ Has the child exhibited signs of respiration, heartbeat or other signs of life?
If yes, it is a live birth.

Notification of Death

[15.35] All deaths must be notified to the relevant Registrar in each jurisdiction. Stillbirths may be dealt with differently (see below). New South Wales has a *Child Death Review Team*, which records details of the deaths of children for review in monitoring trends in child deaths. For more information, research reports and fact sheets that aim to increase public awareness about ways to reduce the number of preventable child deaths, see the website at: www.kids. nsw.gov.au/publications/cdrt2000.html.

All sudden, suspicious or unexpected deaths should be reported to the police and the coroner (see below **[15.65]**).

Who is to report the death?

[15.40] In all jurisdictions, except Queensland and Western Australia, the medical practitioner attending the person must be the notifier of the death. In Queensland a spouse or relative of the deceased, and in Western Australia the funeral director or other person who arranges for the disposal of the remains, must report it to the Registrar.

In the Australian Capital Territory, New South Wales, Northern Territory, South Australia, Tasmania and Victoria a medical practitioner must notify the Registrar of a death within 48 hours of examining the body or being present at the death. In Queensland and Western Australia, the time limit for notification is 14 days.

Certification by a doctor, and/or a coroner's certificate, if an inquest has been held, must accompany registration of a death.

There is a penalty for failure to notify a death to the Registrar, but in most jurisdictions there is also the defence that the person reasonably believed the death had already been reported by some other person.

Perinatal deaths

[15.45] In Queensland and Western Australia notification of a perinatal death is the same as for all other deaths; a stillborn child is thus registered on both birth and death registers. Stillbirths are not required to be registered as deaths in the Australian Capital Territory, New South Wales, Northern Territory, South Australia, Victoria and Tasmania. In Tasmania special provision is made for notification of perinatal deaths to the *Council of Obstetric and Paediatric Mortality and Morbidity* under the *Perinatal Registry Act 1994* (Tas).

Coroner's Inquests

[15.50] Coroners have a long history. The role of coroner was created as a means of accounting for suspicious deaths and disappearances in the days when there was not the same efficiency in keeping track of persons through the records that we have today. However, the role has continued to ensure that sudden or unexpected deaths are accounted for, and foul play ruled out. It is a way of contributing to an orderly means of accounting for the death of every person in our society, unearthing criminal and negligent activity, and identifying otherwise unrecognised harmful practices.

Generally speaking, the Coroner's Court investigates deaths that:

* are sudden and of unknown cause;
* occur under suspicious circumstances;
* occur during or shortly after surgery or other invasive procedure; or
* occur in custody.

The coroner is a magistrate appointed for the purpose of a particular inquiry, or as a permanent coroner. The Coroner's Court is at the level of the Magistrates' or Local Court. Health carers, especially doctors and nurses, stand a good chance of being witnesses in such an inquiry. Coroners are also given jurisdiction to investigate the cause of fires. The legal terminology used is "inquest" for a determination of the cause of death, and "inquiry" for a determination into the cause of a fire.

All Australian jurisdictions have legislation providing for a coroner and Coroner's Court (*Coroners Act 1997* (ACT); *Coroners Act 1980* (NSW); *Coroners Act* (NT); *Coroners Act 2003* (Qld); *Coroners Act 2003* (SA); *Coroners Act 1995* (Tas); *Coroners Act 1985* (Vic); *Coroners Act 1996* (WA)).

Role of the coroner

[15.55] The purpose of a coroner's inquest is to determine the manner and cause of a person's death, or to identify the deceased where identity has not been established. Additionally, the coroner in some jurisdictions is empowered to investigate the cause of fires (exceptions are Northern Territory, South Australia, Western Australia and Queensland). In the Australian Capital Territory and the Northern Territory, coroners are also given power to investigate disasters. It is important to note that the coroner does not make a finding as to guilt or innocence and is generally required to refrain from framing a finding in such a way as to appear to determine criminal or civil liability. In the Australian Capital Territory, New South Wales, and Queensland, where a coroner makes a *prima facie* finding that the death has resulted from an indictable offence, he or she will refer the matter to the Director of Public Prosecutions. The Director of Public Prosecutions will decide whether to lay charges. Where the coroner's finding suggests that there may have been negligence on the part of any person, it is up to relatives of the deceased who may be entitled to sue to take any appropriate action.

The coroner may go further than a simple finding of cause and may also make recommendations and comments regarding public health and safety and the administration of justice.

An incidental utility of the coroner's office is the publicity which may be given to unsafe practices or products, and the resultant educative effect on the public. Waller ((1982), pp 6-7) points out for example, the publicity and agitation for protective laws and education of the public as a result of the deaths of infants in backyard pools in Sydney in the 1970s. Not only were the coronial inquiries a source of information and education, but the coroner's office lent support to the moves to reduce the number of deaths. Staunton and Whyburn ((1997), p 224) mention also the adoption by hospitals in New South Wales of thermostatically controlled hot water systems to prevent patient burns, after a coroner recommended this preventative measure after investigating a death by burning from hot water in a shower.

When a coroner's report is presented to a government department with recommendations, some jurisdictions require that the department is required to respond within a certain time stating what action will be taken in respect of the recommendations (see for example, *Coroners Act* (NT), ss 27, 35, 46A and 46B). Where the death occurred in custody there are generally strict requirements as to investigation and accountability.

The coroner may find that the standard of health care was not the cause of the death, and exonerate, and even praise, health carers involved in the deceased's treatment. Where he or she finds a health professional's actions may cause a professional body to inquire into or take steps in relation to that conduct, the coroner may give information to the relevant disciplinary body for investigation and possible disciplinary action (see for example, *Coroners Act 2003* (Qld), s 48).

When is a coroner's inquest held?

[15.60] Coroner's inquests are subject to legislation, varying amongst the Australian jurisdictions, but generally coroners have discretion to initiate an inquest except where the legislation requires an inquest to be held. For example, an inquest is mandatory where a person dies under, or as a result of, anaesthesia.

More specifically, an inquest is mandatory or discretionary under the circumstances listed in Figure 15.1.

Figure 15.1: Grounds for holding an inquest

("M" = Mandatory, "D" = Discretionary)

Because of the vagueness and/or differences in wording of the categories, the wording is approximate in some cases, for the sake of generalisation, and it should be noted that literal reliance on them could lead to error. Legislation should be checked if a more precise listing for a particular jurisdiction is required.

	ACT	NSW	NT	Qld	SA	Tas	Vic	WA
Suspected homicide/ suspicious circumstances	D	M	D	D			M	M	
Identity of deceased not known		M	M	D		M	M	D
Sudden death of unknown cause	D	D				D	D	
Fact, time or place of death not known		M			D			
Violent, sudden or unnatural death of unknown cause	D	D	D	D	D	D	D	D
Person found drowned	D							

	ACT	NSW	NT	Qld	SA	Tas	Vic	WA
Death occurred in the process of detaining a person or person escaping from custody		M		M		M		M
Death occurred while person in custody	M	M	M	M	M	M	D	
Death within 24 hrs of being discharged from hospital					D			
Death occurred at place of work (not natural)						M		
Death caused as a result of injuries sustained whilst in custody			M					
Place or circumstances of death require inquest						M		
Deceased was in care or temporarily absent from a psychiatric institution		D		D	D	M	M	M
Death while held in care				D	D	M	M	M
Death while under, or as a result of, or within 24 hrs of administration of an anaesthetic	M	M	D		D	D	D	D
Death during, or within a specified timeframe, or as a result of, an operation or a medical, surgical, dental, diagnostic or like nature	D	D		D	D			
Inquest prescribed by regulation							M	M
The Minister, Attorney-General, State Coroner or Chief Magistrate requires investigation	D	M		M	M	M	M	M
Inquest requested by relative					D		D	
Death may have been caused or contributed to by police, or care								M
No certificate as to cause	D	D	D	D	D		D	D
Not seen by a medical practitioner within 3 months before death	D	D						
Death appears to be attributable to accident	D	D	D		D	D	D	

Where a coroner is of the understanding that another inquiry is being undertaken into a death (for example, a trial or a royal commission) he or she may dispense with an inquest.

All jurisdictions, except South Australia, make provision for certain persons to request that the coroner carry out an inquiry.

In the Australian Capital Territory, a coroner may hold a hearing into whether an inquest, or review of prior findings in relation to a death, should be carried out where requested to do so by a person with sufficient interest in the death (*Coroners Act 1997* (ACT)).

In New South Wales, the *Coroners Act 1980* (NSW) provides that a spouse, parent, child, sibling or person having a sufficient interest, may request an inquest within 28 days of the death of a person who died within 24 hours of receiving an anaesthetic. The coroner must hold an inquest or provide reasons for declining to do so. An appeal against the coroner's decision not to hold an inquest may be made to the Supreme Court; that court may order the coroner to conduct an inquest.

In the Northern Territory, there is no specific provision for relatives to apply for an inquest, but the legislation requires that the coroner notify the "senior next of kin" or "any person" if he or she decides not to carry out an inquest where one is authorised under the Act. Any person receiving notification of the coroner's decision may appeal that decision to the Supreme Court (*Coroners Act* (NT)).

In Queensland, a person may request an inquest; no time limit is imposed, and reasons must be given for refusal (*Coroners Act 2003* (Qld)).

In Tasmania a person with "sufficient interest" may seek an inquest. The coroner has discretion to determine if a person has a sufficient interest and whether the inquest is warranted. A refusal must be accompanied by reasons and may be appealed against to the Tasmanian Supreme Court within 14 days of receiving the decision (*Coroners Act 1995* (Tas)).

In Victoria, any person may request an inquest that is authorised under the legislation. There is no limit on the circumstances of the death, and no time limit is given. The coroner must give reasons for refusal. An appeal against the coroner's decision not to hold an inquest may be made to the Supreme Court. That court may order the coroner to conduct an inquest (*Coroners Act 1985* (Vic)).

In Western Australia, any person may ask a coroner to hold an inquest into a death where such an inquest is authorised by the legislation. Again written reasons for a refusal must be given and an appeal against the refusal may be made to the Supreme Court (*Coroners Act 1996* (WA)).

Health carers should ascertain the precise circumstances which apply in their jurisdiction; there will probably be established practices and procedures which they need to know. Also it should be noted that the catch-all categories for reporting used in some jurisdictions, such as "sudden death from unknown cause" or "circumstances requiring investigation", may include many of the more detailed circumstances listed by other jurisdictions. It is safe to say that a death under or as the result of an anaesthetic, or any sudden, unexplained or unexpected death where a person is receiving health care or in a health care or welfare institution would be one which could be considered to require investigation. This could include the involvement in an inquest of the health carer(s) of such person, even if the death had no apparent connection with the health care. In these cases health carers should be prepared for possible appearance at an inquest.

Reporting of deaths

[15.65] As set out above, there is legislation in all Australian jurisdictions for the reporting of deaths and signing and lodging of death certificates with the government. Where a death may be the subject of a coronial inquiry the coroner or police must be notified.

In all jurisdictions except the Australian Capital Territory, legislation provides that a person must report a death that is or may be reportable to a police officer or coroner immediately after he or she becomes aware of the death, unless the person has reasonable grounds to believe that the death has already been reported (*Coroners Act 1996* (WA), s 17; *Coroners Act 1985* (Vic), s 13; *Coroners Act 2003* (SA), s 28; *Coroners Act 2003* (Qld), s 7; *Coroners Act 1995* (Tas), s 19; *Coroners Act 1980* (NSW), s 12A; *Coroners Act* (NT), s 12). In practice this would, in most cases, cover unexpected deaths occurring in health care facilities or in custody, as well as other sudden, unnatural suspicious or unexpected deaths. However the extent of compliance with such legislation has been the subject of debate and investigation; see for example the *Inquiry into the Review of the Coroners Act 1985 Victoria*, details of which appear at the website: www. parliament.vic.gov.au/lawreform/.

Tasmanian legislation specifically provides that the death of a person who was held in custody or care immediately before death, or which occurred during an escape or detainment attempt, must be reported to a coroner as soon as possible by the person in whose custody or care the person was held or by the police officer, correctional officer, authorised officer or prescribed person attempting to detain that person. (See *Coroners Act 1995* (Tas), s 19(4)).

In New South Wales a medical practitioner must not give a certificate as to cause of death for the purposes of registering a death where the death has occurred in circumstances that make the death reportable to a coroner (see *Coroners Act 1980* (NSW), s 12B).

In the Northern Territory, a medical practitioner present at or after the death of a person is required to report the death as soon as possible to a coroner if the death is a reportable death, he or she does not view the body, or he or she is unable to ascertain the cause of death. In addition, the death of a person held in care or custody immediately prior to death must be reported as soon as possible by the person whose care or in whose custody the deceased was held (see *Coroners Act* (NT), s 12).

Victoria requires that a doctor present at, or after a death, must report the death as soon as possible to the coroner if: it is a reportable death; or the doctor does not view the body; or he or she is unable to determine the cause of death; or no doctor attended the person within fourteen days before death and the doctor who is present is unable to determine the cause of death from the deceased's immediate medical history. Tasmanian legislation also specifically provides that where a person was held in care immediately before death, the person under whose care the deceased person was held at the time of death must report the death to the coroner immediately (see *Coroners Act 1985* (Vic), s 13).

Western Australia places a specific obligation on medical practitioners to notify a coroner where the medical practitioner was present at the time of a death that is or may be reportable or shortly after; or he or she is unable to ascertain the cause of death; or in his or her opinion, the death occurred under suspicious circumstances. It also specifically provides that where a person was a person held in care immediately before death, the person under whose care the deceased person was held at the time of death is responsible for reporting the death to a coroner immediately (see *Coroners Act 1996* (WA), s 17).

Health carers should be aware of the reporting requirements they are expected to fulfil in their jurisdiction and those of their employer, and the allocation of responsibility for the preparation of requisite forms.

Post mortem and other examination of the body

Post mortem

[15.70] A coroner can order a post mortem examination of the deceased, either as part of a preliminary investigation to determine if an inquest is required, or as part of the inquest itself (*Coroners Act 1997* (ACT), s 21; *Coroners Act 1980* (NSW), s 48; *Coroners Act* (NT), s 20; *Coroners Act 2003* (Qld), s 19; *Coroners Act 2003* (SA), s 22(i); *Coroners Act 1995* (Tas), s 36; *Coroners Act 1985* (Vic), s 27; *Coroners Act 1996* (WA), s 34). In the Northern Territory (*Coroners Act* (NT), s 21), Tasmania (*Coroners Act 1995* (Tas), s 37: restricted to persons with sufficient interest), Victoria (*Coroners Act 1985* (Vic), s 28) and Western Australia (*Coroners Act 1996* (WA), s 36), any person can request the carrying out of a post mortem, and if the coroner declines to order one he or she must furnish reasons for so doing. An appeal may be brought to the Supreme Court. In New South Wales, where the coroner is of the opinion that some suspicion of having negligently caused or contributed to death falls on a particular medical practitioner, the practitioner must be advised of this by the coroner, who shall not take part in the post mortem examination, although he or she may be present at the examination (*Coroners Act 1980* (NSW), ss 48(2) and 48(3)).

In recognition of sensitivities and cultural beliefs that may cause serious distress to relatives and family of the deceased, all jurisdictions except South Australia provide for coroners to allow for an objection to the holding of a post mortem by next of kin (*Coroners Act 1997* (ACT), s 20; *Coroners Act 1980* (NSW), s 48A; *Coroners Act* (NT), s 23; *Coroners Act 2003* (Qld), s 19(5); *Coroners Act 1995* (Tas), s 38; *Coroners Act 1985* (Vic), s 29; *Coroners Act 1996* (WA), s 37). Whilst not obliged to accede to the objection, coroners in all jurisdictions must give reasons for not doing so, and time must be given for an appeal to the Supreme Court regarding the decision made. In Queensland, the coroner is required to provide a copy of the order only to the family (*Coroners Act 2003* (Qld), 19(6)). In the Australian Capital Territory, whilst there is no provision for appeal, the coroner is required to consider cultural beliefs and religious beliefs before directing that a post mortem be carried out (*Coroners Act 1997* (ACT), s 28).

[15.75] Case: *Abernethy v Deitz* (1996) 39 NSWLR

A man died after a road traffic accident. The coroner ordered a post mortem which was objected to by his widow, as the family were strong adherents to the Jewish faith and believed that a post mortem was a desecration of the deceased. The coroner refused to accede to the objection. This decision was appealed.

[15.80] The Court held that the causes of death, including septicaemia, pneumonia, renal failure and multiple trauma were not questioned, and there was no indication of any other cause. Medical evidence was accepted that a post mortem would reveal nothing in relation to the cause of death that was not already known. The cause of death was clearly known, and there was no evidence that the interests of society would be served if there were a post mortem. In these circumstances, the wishes of the deceased's legal personal representative and family should be the determining factor in deciding whether to carry out a post mortem.

[15.85] Case: *Simon Unchango (Jnr), Ex Parte Simon Unchango (Snr)* (19 August 1997, Supreme Court of Western Australia in Chambers, CIV 1891 of 1997) (from *Australian Health and Medical Law Reporter* ¶34-220.41)

A 12-day-old Aboriginal baby died suddenly. The most likely cause of death was considered to be Sudden Infant Death Syndrome (SIDS), however the coroner held that without a post mortem other causes could not be ruled out and that it was in the interests of the health of the Aboriginal community to determine more accurately the cause of death. Concern was expressed that the age of the child was low for SIDS and that SIDS is related to respiratory disease which may have a public health significance. It was also suggested that, as the baby had been in shared accommodation, there was the possibility that intoxication in co-sleepers could have led to "overlay" of the baby, a matter that should be inquired into by police. Finally, concern at the high Aboriginal mortality rate and a consequent desirability to make proper medical inquiries into deaths was cited as a reason for the post mortem. The child's father testified to the traditional belief of his people that if subjected to a post mortem, the child's spirit would roam and not be able to enter dreamtime, affecting both the child's spirit and the community.

[15.90] The Court overruled the coroner's order for a post mortem for the following reasons:

- the evidence indicated that death occurred as a result of natural causes, and intervening factors such as "overlay" were excluded by police;

- the court's intervention would not prevent the coroner from definitively establishing the cause of death;
- the finding that there was a cause of death other than SIDS would not advance the situation; and
- it is necessary to consider the strong cultural beliefs of relatives and the community, and the traumatic effect of a post mortem.

Exhumation

[15.93] A coroner may issue a warrant for the exhumation of a body, where necessary, to investigate a death and this may include removal of a body to a designated place (*Coroners Act 1997* (ACT), s 27; *Coroners Act 1980* (NSW), s 53; *Coroners Act* (NT), s 24; *Coroners Act 2003* (Qld), s 20; *Coroners Act 2003* (SA), s 22(h); *Coroners Act 1995* (Tas), s 39; *Coroners Act 1985* (Vic), s 30; *Coroners Act 1996* (WA), s 38). The Northern Territory, Tasmania, Victoria and Western Australia allow a short period for next of kin to object and appeal the matter to the Supreme Court if the objection is not acceded to.

Preparation for inquest

Disposition of the body

[15.95] Inquiries into death are generally made by the police on behalf of the coroner. In some jurisdictions, the coroner may appoint investigators to assist in the process (see for example, *Coroners Act 1996* (WA), s 14; *Coroners Act 1997* (ACT), s 59). The investigators need to gather information and interview those concerned. If an inquest is likely and this is known at the time of death, the body should be left as it was at that time. Drainage, nasogastric tubes, catheters and the like should remain in or on the body, disconnected and capped where required. Staff should be aware of the procedures established by their employer in this regard.

Keeping an account of the events

[15.100] As soon as health carers are aware that an inquest may be held, it is in their interest to write personal statements as to what happened, date them and keep them. These may later be used to aid their memories, when they give evidence (sometimes much later).

Preparation of statement

[15.105] If their evidence is considered of interest, health carers may be asked questions, and to make a formal statement, by police. They should assist police in their inquiries. Legal advice may be sought if there is concern about what to say. Even if not approached by police, a person may decide to consult a lawyer if they are in any way concerned that they may be implicated in the death of a person, and in this case should consider legal advice before making any statement to police.

The inquest

Juries

[15.110] The Australian Capital Territory (*Coroners Act 1997* (ACT), s 41) and Tasmania (*Coroners Act 1995* (Tas), s 55) specifically provide that a coroner sits without a jury. The Northern Territory, Queensland, South Australia, Victoria and Western Australia do not make any provision for having a jury. In New South Wales an inquest is generally held without a jury unless the Minister or State Coroner directs that the inquest be held with a jury or a relative so requests.

Giving of evidence to the coroner

[15.115] Coroners have wide powers for the directing of evidence to be placed before them. This includes the testimony of witnesses, records and exhibits. As an inquest is an inquisitorial process, there are no parties as exist in a civil case. Those who appear before the coroner do so at his or her discretion, as witnesses. Anyone considered to have a sufficient interest may appear in person, or be represented by a lawyer. They may examine and cross-examine other witnesses (*Coroners Act 1997* (ACT), s 42; *Coroners Act 1980* (NSW), s 32; *Coroners Act* (NT), s 40(3); *Coroners Act 2003* (Qld), s 36; *Coroners Act 2003* (SA), s 20(i); *Coroners Act 1995* (Tas), s 52(4); *Coroners Act 1985* (Vic), s 45(3); *Coroners Act 1996* (WA), s 44). In some jurisdictions the Attorney-General may appear or be represented, call and examine witnesses and make submissions (*Coroners Act* (NT), s 40(1); *Coroners Act 2003* (Qld), s 36; *Coroners Act 2003* (SA), s 20(i); *Coroners Act 1995* (Tas), s 52(3); *Coroners Act 1985* (Vic), s 45(2); *Coroners Act 1996* (WA), s 43).

The coroner has the discretion to decide who has sufficient interest. Where, for example, a hospital's practices may be in question, or a union or other body believes its reputation has been damaged or legal liability may result from the findings, or a party has some financial interest in the outcome, for example an insurer, they will most likely be allowed to have their counsel appear, produce documents or witnesses, and examine and cross-examine other witnesses at the inquest.

Summons to appear

[15.120] Health carers may agree to give evidence at an inquest, in which case they will answer questions under oath if so required. They will usually be approached by the police and asked for information regarding the incident, and if their evidence is considered of potential use, asked to attend the inquest so as to give evidence formally.

If relatives of a deceased person believe that staff or the hospital are at fault regarding a death, they may insist on an inquest in the hope of obtaining information to assist a possible civil case, to decide whether there is enough evidence to proceed with a negligence action. They can be represented by lawyers who will cross-examine those involved.

Where it seems likely that a person who is required to give evidence will not appear voluntarily, the coroner may compel that person's appearance by summons or subpoena (*Coroners Act 1997* (ACT), s 43; *Coroners Act 1980* (NSW), s 35; *Coroners Act* (NT), s 41(1); *Coroners Act 2003* (Qld), s 37(4); *Coroners Act 2003* (SA), s 23(i)(a); *Coroners Act 1995* (Tas), s 53(1); *Coroners Act 1985* (Vic), s 46(1); *Coroners Act 1996* (WA), s 46(1)(a)). A notice of summons or subpoena is generally required to be served personally on the specified witness, or by leaving it with a responsible adult at their last or usual place of residence (*Coroners Act 1997* (ACT), s 44; *Coroners Act 1980* (NSW), s 37(1); *Coroners Act 2003* (Qld), s 37(5); *Coroners Act 2003* (SA), s 41). If a summons is not obeyed, a warrant for the arrest of the person may be issued (*Coroners Act 1997* (ACT), s 45; *Coroners Act 1980* (NSW), s 39; *Coroners Act* (NT), s 41(4); *Coroners Act 2003* (Qld), s 37(7); *Coroners Act 2003* (SA), s 23(2); *Coroners Act 1995* (Tas), s 53(5); *Coroners Act 1985* (Vic), s 46(4); *Coroners Act 1996* (WA), s 46(4)). The person can be forcibly brought before the coroner by the police, and kept in custody or released on recognisance (a promise with or without a monetary surety) to ensure their presence at the hearing. Failure to turn up or refusal to give evidence when required to is an offence, with severe penalties (*Coroners Act 1997* (ACT), s 88; *Coroners Act 1980* (NSW), ss 42 and 45; *Coroners Act* (NT), s 40(3); *Coroners Act 2003* (Qld), s 37(6); *Coroners Act 2003* (SA), s 36; *Coroners Act 1995* (Tas), s 53(4); *Coroners Act 1985* (Vic), s 46(3); *Coroners Act 1996* (WA), s 46A). These powers can also apply to the production of documents in the witness's possession or over which he or she has power.

Health care records, or any other documents, may be required by the coroner, usually with the person who wrote them being present to testify to their having written the documents and to explain them where this is required. However, records can be admitted without the writer being there to testify to them.

Depositions (statements on oath) of witnesses, medical reports and other documents produced during the inquiry or inquest are usually made available to those who can demonstrate a sufficient interest (*Coroners Act 1997* (ACT), s 51; *Coroners Act 1980* (NSW), s 34; *Coroners Act* (NT), s 40(2); *Coroners Act 2003* (Qld), s 54; *Coroners Act 2003* (SA), s 37; *Coroners Act 1995* (Tas), s 52(1); *Coroners Act 1985* (Vic), s 45; *Coroners Act 1996* (WA), s 42). These will generally be the other witnesses in the case, and may be the relatives of the deceased and those who were involved in his or her care.

Procedure during an inquest

[15.125] The coroner is required to examine witnesses on oath or affirmation. This means that any false testimony is perjury and subject to punitive action. Evidence of witnesses is generally given by way of an affidavit (a sworn written statement) which the person is asked to read out in court, and given the opportunity to amend or expand if they wish.

Answering questions

[15.130] When giving evidence in any hearing, witnesses should keep in mind that questioning is often designed to test the accuracy and truth of their answers. Some general rules to follow are:

- Speak slowly and clearly.
- Consider answers carefully. It is better to pause and collect one's thoughts than to rush into answers. Back-tracking, correcting oneself (or worse, being corrected by others), and stumbling through the answer gives a bad impression. If it is difficult to remember precisely how something happened, one should say so.
- It is no disgrace to forget. The best approach is to be honest and say that one can't remember something, or cannot recall precisely how it happened, than to answer untruthfully or to fabricate an answer. One is not in the witness box to please the person asking the questions, nor to appear efficient and helpful, but to answer questions to the best of one's ability.
- Remain calm, despite attempts to test one's self control.

Witnesses may be required to answer all questions (except those where the answer might incriminate them, see **[15.140]**). It is an offence to refuse to answer other questions. It is also an offence to refuse to take the oath or affirmation, to refuse to produce documents, or to impede or disrupt the proceedings. Such actions may be contempt of court, attracting fines or imprisonment.

Coroner's inquiries are generally held in open court. However, the coroner may order that:

- the court be closed to the public;
- witnesses be excluded from the court; and
- reporting of evidence given, or of the proceedings, be prohibited.

The law is different across jurisdictions, but grounds for carrying out the above include the belief that witnesses may be exposed to retaliation, that juveniles require protection, or that it is in the public interest to suppress reporting of the hearing (*Coroners Act 1997* (ACT), s 40; *Coroners Act 1980* (NSW), s 44; *Coroners Act* (NT), s 42; *Coroners Act 2003* (Qld), ss 43 and 41; *Coroners Act 2003* (SA), s 19; *Coroners Act 1995* (Tas), s 56; *Coroners Act 1985* (Vic), s 47; *Coroners Act 1996* (WA), ss 45 and 49).

Rules of evidence

[15.135] The coroner is not bound by the rules of evidence and has a broad discretion to conduct the proceedings as he or she sees fit and appropriate for the particular case (*Coroners Act 1997* (ACT), s 47; *Coroners Act 1980* (NSW), s 33; *Coroners Act* (NT), s 39; *Coroners Act 2003* (Qld), s 37; *Coroners Act 2003* (SA), s 24; *Coroners Act 1995* (Tas), s 51; *Coroners Act 1985* (Vic), s 44; *Coroners Act 1996* (WA), s 41). However, he or she is bound by the rules of natural justice:

> "It can now be taken as settled that, when a statute confers power upon a public official to destroy, defeat or prejudice a person's rights, interests or legitimate expectations, the rules of natural justice regulate the exercise of that power unless they are excluded by plain words of necessary intendment" (*Annetts v McCann* (1990) 170 CLR 506 ; [1990] HCA 57 at [2]).

(See also discussion regarding natural justice at **[1.115]**.) In practice there is, therefore, a degree of formality, inasmuch as it assists the provision of fairness to all concerned.

Coronial hearing practice has resembled fairly closely the adversarial procedure of trials. Thus, after reading out her or his statement, the witness, if necessary, is led through the statement by her or his counsel to clarify it and emphasise important points. Counsel for other parties may then cross-examine and the witness's counsel may re-examine the witness to clarify matters that may have become confused in the cross-examination.

Because the coroner is aware of the need for fairness he or she will generally keep the rules of evidence in mind, and will disallow irrelevant evidence and opinion other than expert opinion. Hearsay evidence may, however, be admitted. It is within the coroner's jurisdiction to allow evidence according to the perceived justice of so doing.

An example of the use of hearsay evidence occurred in an inquest that was held in Canberra into the death of a baby who died after undergoing an operation to correct a skull abnormality (*Canberra Times*, 27 February 1993). A nurse who assisted anaesthetists during the operation gave evidence that she had thought there had been an emergency during the surgery, and gave details of anaesthetists asking the surgeons to stop the operation because of concern for the baby's condition. She had herself accompanied the baby to the intensive care unit and stayed there for half an hour because of her own concern. The coroner was critical of the care the baby received.

Must witnesses give incriminating evidence?

[15.140] When under oath or affirmation, one is obliged to tell the truth. This puts one in an awkward position where to answer a question may concede that one has committed, or was otherwise party to, a criminal act or civil wrong (incriminating oneself). Witnesses are not compelled to answer a question that may incriminate them in South Australia (*Coroners Act 2003* (SA), s 23(5)). In the Australian Capital Territory a person is not excused from producing a document or thing on the grounds of self-incrimination, but such evidence cannot be used against them in other proceedings against them (with the exception of proceedings for an offence against the *Coroners Act* itself) (*Coroners Act 1997* (ACT), s 43). In Western Australia a person need not answer a question that may incriminate him or her unless the coroner rules that the answer is necessary for the ends of justice, but if the question is answered to the satisfaction of the coroner, a certificate must be given to the witness, which makes the evidence inadmissible against the person in any criminal proceedings (*Coroners Act 1996* (WA), s 47). Similar provisions also apply in the Northern Territory (*Coroners Act* (NT), s 38) and New South Wales (*Coroners Act 1980* (NSW), s 33AA) where the protection is extended to civil proceedings. In Tasmania evidence of a witness that is against their interests may not be used against them in other proceedings, except in relation to perjury (*Coroners Act 1995* (Tas), s 54). In Queensland a witness must answer if required to do so by the coroner, however, evidence that they give is not admissible against them in subsequent proceedings other than for perjury (*Coroners Act 2003* (Qld), s 39).

When may a statement be incriminating?

[15.145] This occurs in two ways:

- a person may be asked a question, such as "Did you give the wrong information to the doctor?" The answer may directly indicate that he or she committed a crime by concealing information and thus deliberately risking the patient's death. In these circumstances, to answer yes to this question would incriminate the person;
- a question may be asked that the witness perceives is part of a pattern of questioning which, if continued, might lead to the inference that he or she committed a crime. For example, the person may be asked a question when, if the answer is yes, it is anticipated that this will invite further questioning that will show that the person deliberately and recklessly jeopardised the deceased's life, determining a course of action which resulted in the person's death. This perceived trend may only be a suspicion, but the witness may nevertheless claim the privilege. It may be that the coroner requires an investigation into why the question is not being answered.

> **[15.150] Case: *Ex parte P; Re Hamilton* (1957) 74 WN (NSW) 397 (Supreme Court)**
>
> This involved a criminal case, not a coroner's inquest. In a criminal case the accused has no immunity from answering incriminating questions, but any other person has. In this case a woman, P, was called as a witness in the prosecution of R for illegally procuring abortions. P had turned up at the door when police were arresting and questioning R. When asked at the committal, "On 29 March, did you go somewhere at about 9 am?" P refused to answer this question on the ground that her answer might incriminate her. The magistrate ruled that she was in contempt of court. P appealed to the Supreme Court.

[15.153] The Supreme Court held that to ask P where she went on 29 March was, in the light of the evidence of the police, to seek to forge a link in a chain of evidence which, if completed, would support a finding that P had conspired to procure the commission of a crime, that is, unlawful abortion, and that as long as she was neither acting in bad faith nor attempting to obstruct the course of justice, her refusal to answer was not contempt.

This case is extracted from the *Australian Digest* (2nd ed), Vol 12, col 289. In *Redfern v Redfern* [1891] P 139, Bowen LJ stated at 147:

> "[A] party cannot be compelled to discover that which, if answered would tend to subject him to any punishment, penalty, forfeiture or ecclesiastical censure."

This formulation was cited as "well settled" in *Pyneboard Pty Ltd v Trade Practices Commission* (1983) 152 CLR 328; [1983] HCA 9. The extension of the privilege to coronial cases was confirmed in the same case.

Findings of the coroner

[15.155] The coroner (or jury in a Coroner's Court) cannot make a finding of guilt, or otherwise, regarding the death of a person. The result of the inquest will be the establishment of:

* the identity of the deceased;
* the time and place of death; and
* the manner and cause of death.

In all jurisdictions except South Australia the coroner may make observations on other matters, such as public health or safety and the administration of justice (*Coroners Act 1997* (ACT), s 52; *Coroners Act 1980* (NSW), s 22A; *Coroners Act* (NT), s 34; *Coroners Act 2003* (Qld), s 46; *Coroners Act 1995* (Tas), s 28; *Coroners Act 1985* (Vic), s 19; *Coroners Act 1996* (WA), s 25). It has been held that the findings (limited to those facts mentioned above) can be challenged, but that insofar as the coroner may consider it appropriate to make additional observations with respect to such findings, it is not appropriate for a court to overturn those observations (*Kahn v West* [1999] VSC 530 paragraph 37, per Warren J). In Western Australia where the death is of a person held in care, a coroner must comment on the quality of the supervision, treatment and care of that person while in that care (*Coroners Act 1996* (WA), s 25). The coroner cannot find that a person is guilty of an offence, and in most jurisdictions this extends to his or her comments on those findings. If the coroner is satisfied that there is sufficient evidence against a person to put them on trial for an indictable offence, the Director of Public Prosecutions, Commissioner of Police or Attorney-General as nominated must be notified, and the coronial inquiry may be discontinued for the pursuit of the criminal proceedings. There are also limits on findings and comments on civil liability so as not to appear to determine liability.

In some jurisdictions the Supreme Court may order an inquiry or inquest be quashed or void and a new inquiry or inquest held. Reasons for such action might include the presence of fraud, the discovery of new facts or evidence, irregularity in proceedings and insufficient evidence to support the coroner's findings (see *Coroners Act 1980* (NSW), s 47; *Coroners Act 1997* (ACT), s 93; *Coroners Act 1995* (Tas), s 58A. In South Australia there is also a right of appeal to the Supreme Court (*Coroners Act 2003* (SA), s 27).

Examples of findings of coroners include the following cases.

[15.160] Case: Melbourne, 1991: Death of woman after giving birth: "Doctor 'contributed' to woman patient's death" *Canberra Times*, 9 October 1991

Ms Cox died after suffering shock from post-natal haemorrhage.

The coroner concluded that the doctor attending her contributed to her death, and:

- the doctor, (Dr Barnett) had failed to take sufficient steps to stop her condition deteriorating, in that he left the hospital having given her drugs to minimise bleeding after the birth, believing staff were monitoring her condition, and that he made "no enquiries of her condition during the morning and did not know of her condition until he was paged";
- there was uncertainty as to who had clear responsibility for the patient's condition, as her regular obstetrician, Dr Lucas, was replaced by Dr Barnett during his absence, and that Dr Lucas failed to appreciate her condition, failing to consult fully with Dr Barnett;
- both doctors and an anaesthetist did not act properly in agreeing that her condition was stable after a blood transfusion, even though she was unwell;
- Ms Cox should have been transferred to a hospital with an intensive care unit, or at least had a doctor remain with her; and
- the hospital staff did not act properly in not informing the doctors that they had an emergency supply of blood for transfusion.

[15.165] Case: *In the death of Taylor Ainalidis* State Coroner of Victoria (Case No 1908/00) 1 February 2003

Master Ainalidis was admitted to the Royal Children's Hospital at three weeks of age following several episodes of hypoxaemia and hypertension. He was diagnosed with Tetralogy of Fallout, a congenital heart condition, and surgery was undertaken to correct the problem. The resuscitation process involved the use of a Rebreathe Bag and circuit. A problem developed and Master Ainalidis was unable to be resuscitated. Inability to achieve chest movement was initially interpreted as a blocked endotracheal tube and as such the tube was removed and replaced. However, the original tube was not blocked and further inquiries indicated that the stickiness of the bag may have been the cause.

The autopsy report indicated that there was no anatomical cause for the failure of resuscitation and that it would appear the most likely cause of collapse was failure of adequate ventilation.

The product manufacturer's information sheet indicated that the product should only be used whilst the rubber showed no signs of stickiness. In addition, autoclaving was not advised.

The TGA tested the bag and reported degradation of the rubber causing stickiness which prevented the bag from inflating.

The coroner concluded:

- the death of Master Ainalidis was principally as a result of the failure of the rebreathe bag immediately following surgery;

- there was a problem with the bag causing the folds to stick together and compromising oxygen delivery;
- the bag was reusable with recommended cleaning procedures; these procedures were not followed by the hospital.

The bag was subsequently recalled and is no longer used by the hospital.

[15.170] Case: *In the death of Cheryl Hoggins* State Coroner of Victoria (Case No 2116/00) 18 March 2003

Mrs Hoggins, 48 years old, was admitted to the Austin Hospital following about six weeks of suffering "flu like symptoms". She was diagnosed with acute liver failure and underwent a liver transplant approximately one week after admission. She had a complicated post-operative course with shock, thrombocytopenia, renal failure and fluctuating encephalopathy. This series of problems was thought by the clinicians to be suggestive of sepsis and she was treated with antibiotics whilst investigative procedures were undertaken to determine the source. As part of the search for the source of the sepsis, the right subclavian vascular access line was replaced by the ICU registrar. On the advice of the supervising clinician a chest x-ray was not taken after the procedure to confirm the positioning of the catheter. Expert evidence suggested that within four hours of the procedure Mrs Hoggins exhibited signs of hypotension with elevated central venous pressure. A routine chest x-ray was taken approximately seven hours after the catheter exchange, however, that x-ray was not reviewed. A second chest x-ray was taken approximately twenty-one hours after the exchange which showed that the catheter was in the right atrium. The clinician ordered the catheter to be pulled back and it was during this process, approximately 27 hours after the initial procedure, that Mrs Hoggins went into respiratory distress and died.

The provisional hospital autopsy findings were of two perforations in the interior wall of the right atrium and blood clot in the pericardial space. No evidence of septic focus was found in the abdomen, thorax or pelvis.

The coroner concluded:

- Mrs Hoggins died as a result of penetration of the heart by a guide wire following central venous catheterisation;
- there was no chest x-ray following the exchange of the catheter to check positioning;
- there was a failure by the clinicians to follow hospital (unwritten) and manufacturer's procedures, which required a check x-ray be taken;

- the two chest x-rays that were taken following the procedure showed the catheter tip in a position that should have raised the concern of cardiac wall perforation;

had procedure been followed and a chest x-ray taken to check the positioning of the catheter after it was placed, there is a distinct possibility that Mrs Hoggins may have survived.

[15.175] In each of the preceding cases it would be open to those concerned to consider bringing a civil action in negligence, but the coroner's criticism does not mean that they would necessarily succeed.

A case where the coroner's findings were challenged follows.

[15.180] Case: *In the matter of an application pursuant to s 28a of the Coroner's Act 1975: Ex parte Crowe* (20 February 1992, SC SA, No 2223 of 1989)

A woman died three days after minor gynaecological surgery. She developed pleural effusion requiring an underwater-sealed drain of the plural cavity. The forensic pathologist produced a report that in his opinion the patient was in renal failure in the days before her death. However he repeatedly stressed that it would be advisable to obtain the opinion of specialists in the area. Indeed there was evidence put to the deputy coroner by experts in renal medicine and intensive care.

An expert in renal medicine testified that the deceased was not suffering from renal failure, but from a physiological response to hypovolaemia induced by low serum albumin caused by loss of albumin into the pleural cavity. However the renal expert did express the view that more careful monitoring of fluid balance should have taken place in view of the deceased's condition at the time.

One expert in intensive care opined that the deceased suffered from pulmonary embolus resulting in pulmonary infarction, and the deceased had developed a disorder of "capillary leakage", with the intravenous fluids leaking into the pleural cavity. He did not believe the cause of death was excessive intravenous fluid, but also stated that central venous monitoring or a regular fluid balance should have been undertaken. Another intensive care expert could not determine the cause of the deceased's illness but believed she had pneumonia and septicaemia. He was also critical of the non-availability of fluid balance charts.

The deputy coroner nevertheless relied on this evidence and made adverse comments on the treating doctor's care of the patient, finding that she died of cardiac failure consequent on acute pulmonary oedema caused by too much intravenous fluid.

The applicant doctor appealed to the Supreme Court, arguing that the Deputy Coroner's findings were against the evidence, and inadequate.

[15.185] The Court concluded that excessive amounts of fluid were not given, but rather the deceased had developed escape of fluid due to endotoxic shock. There was pulmonary oedema, but its cause had not been demonstrated.

Disappearances

[15.190] Where the coroner investigates the disappearance of a person he or she can determine:

- the circumstances of the disappearance;
- whether the person is alive or dead; and
- if alive, where the person is believed to be.

References and Further Reading

Australian Health and Medical Law Reporter (CCH, Sydney, 1991)

Chivell, W, "Coronial Investigation" (1996) 165 *Medical Journal of Australia* 396

Freckelton, I, "Causation in Coronial Law" (1997) 4 *Journal of Law and Medicine* 289

Lynch, M, "Forensic Pathology: Redefining Medico-Legal Death Investigation" (1999) 7 *Journal of Law and Medicine* 67

Lynch, M, "The Coroner, the Forensic Pathologist and the Unborn Child" (1999) 7 *Journal of Law and Medicine* 415

O'Sullivan, J, *Law for Nurses* (Law Book Co, Sydney, 1983), ch 18

Selby, H, *The Aftermath of Death* (Federation Press, Sydney, 1992)

Selby, H, *The Inquest Handbook* (Federation Press, Sydney, 1998)

Staunton, P and Whyburn, R, *Nursing and the Law* (4th ed, Saunders, Sydney, 1997), ch 9

Waller, K M, *Coronial Law and Practice in New South Wales* (2nd ed, Law Book Co, Sydney, 1982)

16

16 State involvement in threats to health or welfare

Notifiable disease

Sexually transmitted diseases

AIDS

Child abuse

Spouse abuse

chapter 16

State Involvement in Threats to Health or Welfare

Introduction

[16.05] The state has an interest in the affairs of its citizens when their illness or activities pose a threat to the health of others in society. This may require the reporting of those who have a notifiable disease or who engage in child abuse.

Notifiable Disease

[16.10] A person may have a contagious disease, which requires isolation and special treatment, or be engaged in activity which is potentially or actually dangerous to the health of others. The state role therefore involves prevention as well as cure.

There are many ways in which the state acts to maintain public health. This is mainly by activities such as:

- regulating standards, such as the care of public baths;
- licensing and regulating the preparation and serving of food;
- developing community public education programmes; and
- encouraging regular health checkups and providing specialised clinics and information centres.

The state goes further, however, when dealing with notifiable infectious and sexually transmitted diseases. It reserves the right to intervene in the private lives of the citizens involved, and where necessary quarantine them and subject them to compulsory treatment.

This raises the issue of the relative weight to be given to the freedom of the individual and the protection of others. As with mental health there may be conflict between the "medical" centred approach and the "rights" centred approach. However, there is much less conflict regarding the nature, cause and treatment of diseases in the public health area. The case of a New South Wales woman who was detained involuntarily because she was HIV-positive and had announced that she would continue to act as a prostitute, raised questions as to the manner in which the state regulates public health, and under what circumstances, if at all, a person should be detained and treated against their will on the basis of a doctor's diagnosis.

There is legislation in each jurisdiction that lists those diseases that must be reported to the state, and the powers given to relevant authorities to ensure the containment of any threat to public health (*Public Health Act 1997* (ACT), *Public Health Regulation 2000* (ACT), Public Health Notifiable Conditions Determination 2005 (ACT); *Public Health Act 1991* (NSW), *Public Health (General) Regulation 2002* (NSW); *Cancer Registration Act* (NT), *Notifiable Diseases Act* (NT); *Public Health Act 2005* (Qld), *Public Health Regulations 2005* (Qld); *Public and Environmental Health Act 1987* (SA), *Public and Environmental Health (Notifiable Diseases) Regulations 2004* (SA), *South Australian Health Commission (Cancer) Regulations 1991* (SA); *Public Health Act 1997* (Tas), *HIV/AIDS Preventative Measures Act 1993* (Tas); *Health Act 1958* (Vic), *Health (Infectious Diseases) Regulations 2001* (Vic), *Cancer Act 1958* (Vic), *Cancer (Reporting) Regulations 2002* (Vic); *Health Act 1911* (WA), *Health (Notification of Cancer) Regulations 1981* (WA), *Health (Cervical Cytology Register) Regulations 1991* (WA), *Health (Notification of Adverse Event after Immunisation) Regulations 1995* (WA)). In some circumstance this may involve the detention and treatment of individuals, seizure of goods and property for de-contamination and the closure of premises and enterprises. The diseases involved are described variously by such terms as "infectious", "scheduled" and "notifiable" in the different legislation of the various Australian jurisdictions dealing with public health. In this chapter, all diseases that must be reported are called "notifiable diseases".

Jurisdictions differ in their classification of reportable diseases and the consequent obligations and powers applying to each classification. The list of diseases that must be reported also changes over time. The list is published in a Government Gazette (the official publication of Government notices in each jurisdiction) when changes are made.

Some jurisdictions retain a distinction between sexually transmitted, infectious and notifiable diseases. Those suffering from infectious diseases may be subject to more stringent controls than those with diseases categorised as notifiable; those with sexually transmitted diseases coming under powers more specifically related to the nature of such disease.

Examples of notifiable diseases

Infectious and transmissible diseases

[16.15] Diseases notifiable across jurisdictions are:

AIDS (except Tasmania) considered in some jurisdictions to be a sexually transmitted disease (see below)	Avian influenza (except Northern Territory and South Australia)(influenza generally in New South Wales, Tasmania, Victoria and Western Australia)
Anthrax (except South Australia)	
Arbovirus infection (including dengue fever)	Brucellosis

Campylobacteriosis (except New South Wales)	Plague
	Poliomyelitis
Chlamydia trachomatis	Q Fever
Cholera	Rabies (except Australian Capital
Diphtheria	Territory and Queensland)
Haemophilus influenzae serotype B (HiB)	Rubella
	Salmonella infections
Hepatitis (mostly all forms)	Shigellosis
Human immunodeficiency virus	Syphilis
Legionellosis or Legionnaire's Disease	Tetanus (except New South Wales)
Leptospirosis	Tuberculosis (except South Australia)
Listeriosis	Typhus or Typhoid Fever (except
Malaria	South Australia)
Measles	Viral haemorrhagic fever
Meningococcal infections	Yellow Fever
Mumps	Yersiniosis (except New South Wales
Pertussis (whooping cough)	and Victoria)

Cancer

[16.20] All Australian jurisdictions require the reporting and registering of cancer, with some jurisdictions having special legislation for this purpose. (*Public Health Regulations 2000* (ACT), Pt 4; *Public Health Act 1991* (NSW), s 14; *Cancer Registration Act* (NT); *Public Health Act 2005* (Qld), Ch 6 Pt 2; *South Australian Health Commission (Cancer) Regulations 1991* (SA), *Public and Environmental Health (Cervical Cancer Screening) Regulations 1993* (SA); *Cancer Act 1958* (Vic), Pt 3, *Cancer (BreastScreen Victoria Registry) Regulations 2003* (Vic), *Cancer (Reporting) Regulations 2002* (Vic); *Health Act 1911* (WA), s 289C, *Health (Notification of Cancer) Regulations 1981* (WA), *Health (Cervical Cytology Register) Regulations 1991* (WA)). The legislation generally requires reporting of cases of cancer in similar terms to the reporting of other notifiable diseases. Cancer is generally defined as:

"a malignant growth of human tissue which if unchecked is likely to spread to adjacent tissue or beyond its place of origin and which has the propensity to recur."

Some jurisdictions go on to include carcinoma, sarcoma, any mixed-tumour, leukaemia, any type of lymphoma, melanoma and non-invasive *in situ* carcinoma. Western Australia adds all neoplasms of the brain, spinal cord and cranial nerves, and any other intracranial neoplasms, whether benign or malignant.

Most jurisdictions now have special cervical cytology registers and breast screening services that register instances of cancer. Registers have been established for epidemiological purposes as well as for the early detection and prevention of cancer. (For example see, *Public Health Regulation 2000* (ACT), Pt 3 (establishes a cervical cytology register); *Public Health Act 1991* (NSW), Pt 3B (establishes the New South Wales Pap Test Register); *Public Health Act 2005*

(Qld), Ch 6, Part 3 (establishes a Pap Smear Register); *Public Health (Cervical Cytology Register) Regulations* (NT); *Public Health Act 1997* (Tas), Pt 7 (establishes a Cervical Cytology Register); *Public and Environmental Health (Cervical Cancer Screening) Regulations 1993* (SA); *Cancer (BreastScreen Victoria Registry) Regulations 2003* (Vic); *Health (Cervical Cytology Register) Regulations 1991* (WA)). Identifying information on the registers is confidential except with the consent of the person involved.

There are many more diseases listed as notifiable diseases, and procedures for reporting them, in different jurisdictions. The account which follows is general only.

Who must report notifiable diseases?

[16.25] In New South Wales notifiable diseases (termed "scheduled medical conditions") are listed and categorised in Sch 1 of the *Public Health Act 1991* (NSW). The Act requires that:

- any medical practitioner who has attends a person and has reason to believe that person is suffering from a scheduled medical condition, or as a result of any postmortem examination believes that a person has died from such a condition (s 14); or
- in some cases a pathologist who certifies that a person is suffering from a scheduled medical condition (s 16), must notify the Director-General of the Health Department.

A person who provides care for someone in a hospital or other health care facility who has reasonable grounds for believing that a person is suffering from a notifiable disease must notify the chief executive officer of the facility, who in turn must notify the Director-General. Whilst identities of those who are HIV-positive are to be strictly confidential, the Director-General can apply to the District Court for an order requiring a medical practitioner to disclose the name and address of a person suffering from HIV or AIDS where identification of that person is necessary in order to safeguard public health (s 18).

In Queensland, Schedule 1 of the *Public Health Regulation 2005* (Qld) lists notifiable diseases. The *Public Health Act 2005* (Qld) requires a medical practitioner who examines a patient and believes the person has or had a notifiable condition must notify the chief executive (s 70). A person in charge of a hospital must notify the chief executive if an examination by a doctor in the hospital indicates the person has or had a notifiable condition (s 71). The director of a pathology laboratory must notify the chief executive if they receive a request for a pathological examination of a specimen in relation to a notifiable condition or if examination of a specimen indicates that the person from whom the specimen was taken has a notifiable condition (ss 72 and 73).

In South Australia, notifiable diseases are listed under Schedule 1 of the *Public and Environmental Health Act 1987* (SA). Notification is to be made to the South Australian Health Department, and is required where a medical practitioner suspects that a person suffers from or has died from a notifiable disease (s 30). South Australia also provides that local councils must be notified by the

Health Department of any occurrence of notifiable disease in their jurisdiction (s 35).

In Victoria, a list of notifiable diseases is in Sch 3 of the *Health (Infectious Diseases) Regulations 2001* (Vic). Medical practitioners must notify the Department of Human Services where they become aware that a person shows evidence of, has died of, or is a carrier of a notifiable disease (reg 8). Pathologists are required to report detection of notifiable diseases to the Department of Human Services (reg 7).

In Western Australia the occupier of premises (including a hospital or other health facility) in which a person is found to be suffering from or suspected to be suffering from an infectious disease must give notice to the local government. The parent or guardian of a child, or head teacher at a school attended by a child is similarly obliged. A medical practitioner who examines a person who has or is suspected of having a notifiable disease must inform the occupier, local government, and the Executive Director of Public Health (*Health Act 1911* (WA), s 276).

In Tasmania (Part 3 of the *Public Health Act 1997* (Tas)), the Northern Territory (s 8, Part II of the *Notifiable Diseases Act 1981* (NT)) and the Australian Capital Territory (Part 6 of the *Public Health Act 1997* (ACT)) the relevant legislation has similar requirements to other jurisdictions regarding notification by medical practitioners, chief executives of health care facilities and pathologists. The Australian Capital Territory extends the responsibility to report to authorised nurse practitioners (s 102).

The role of health carers

[16.30] Health carers should all be aware in general of the legal requirements regarding notifiable diseases. Notification by medical practitioners is required, and in some cases the health facility involved, but employees should make sure that suspected notifiable disease is brought to the notice of the management.

What information must be given?

[16.35] Personal information, as well as the details of any contacts must be supplied in circumstances where there is a danger to public health (for example, caused by a person's actions). Relevant facts may include such matters as the school attended, in the case of a child, and details of contacts there if the disease is very infectious. However, the general principle is that the notification of identifying information is strictly limited, and privacy preserved wherever possible. Most jurisdictions have a prescribed form for reporting.

What can authorities do?

[16.40] There are powers provided by legislation that the designated person (usually the chief medical officer or other similarly designated medical officer within the Health Department), may cause the inspection of premises where the person is residing or elsewhere. In some cases property may be seized and/or dealt with (for example, disposed of, fumigated) according to the orders of that officer, and the nominated person and any other person may be required to undergo tests, and/or be removed, by force if necessary, to a specified institution. There may be distinctions drawn between powers available where different diseases are concerned.

Sexually Transmitted Diseases (Other Than AIDS)

[16.45] Such diseases include gonorrhoea, syphilis, chancroid, lymphogranu-loma venereum and granuloma inguinale. However, as these diseases are no longer the threat to community health that they once were, in some jurisdictions they are no longer reportable, or if they are, they are categorised along with other notifiable diseases. Thus the above provisions, as well as powers to examine and detain the person apply generally to sexually transmitted diseases, but there are some specific requirements which apply to this type of disease.

In New South Wales, a medical practitioner must provide the person with information including ways of preventing transmission of the disease to others. A person who knows that he or she suffers from a sexually transmissible medical condition is guilty of an offence if he or she has sexual intercourse with another person unless the other person has been informed of the risk and voluntarily accepted the risk, before intercourse takes place. (Public Health Act 1991 (NSW), ss 12-13; Public Health Regulations 1991 (NSW), Reg 5).

In Western Australia, venereal disease may only be treated by a medical prac-titioner and that practitioner must notify the executive Director of Public Health. It is an offence for a person suffering from venereal disease not to place themselves under treatment by a medical practitioner and in the case of gonorrhoea, soft chancre and syphilis the legislation proscribes the frequency with which they must attend for treatment and advice until they receive a certificate of cure. Medical practitioners are obligated to inform patients in writing of the contagious nature of the disease and the legal consequences of infecting others. Any person who knowingly infects another person with a venereal disease commits an offence (Health Act 1911 (WA), ss 297-300, 302, 310).

Victoria requires that a person with an infectious disease must not knowingly or recklessly infect another person with an infectious disease (this is not restricted to sexually transmitted infectious diseases) (Health Act 1958 (Vic), s 120).

It is also an offence in most jurisdictions to knowingly or recklessly place others at risk of contracting a notifiable disease (see for example Public and Environmental Health Act 1987 (SA), s 37; Public Health Act 1997 (Tas), s 51).

Confidentiality must be maintained

[16.50] In some jurisdictions the name of the patient and contacts need not be disclosed. Identity may only be required if the person refuses treatment and then may be subject to other requirements of confidentiality; for example, names must be kept confidential by authorities.

Acquired Immunodeficiency Syndrome (AIDS)

[16.55] Legislation regarding the reporting of AIDS is similar to other notifiable diseases with some differences and exceptions.

As with other notifiable diseases, any medical practitioner who is aware, or has reasonable grounds to believe, that a person is suffering from, or died of HIV/AIDS, must report this to the prescribed authority. Also, those carrying out pathology tests are generally required to notify the Health Department of the results if they show that a person is suffering from HIV/AIDS.

In contrast to most other notifiable diseases (with the exception in some jurisdictions of other sexually transmittable diseases), where a person is diagnosed or suspected of having HIV/AIDS their identifying information is not disclosed on notification forms, and this information remains confidential unless specific circumstances require such information to be supplied, such as the need to trace contacts, or notify partners, where the behaviour of the person involved necessitates this. It is only where the behaviour of a person becomes a public health issue that such information would be disclosed to a state authority. (See, for example, *Public Health Act 1991* (NSW), s 17).

Testing

[16.60] Testing for HIV is generally not compulsory, however jurisdictions may provide that testing is required for some purposes (for example, all jurisdictions require testing of blood for transfusion), or immunity from legal action if precautions have been taken by testing of tissue (for example, where donor sperm is to be used). Tasmania has introduced the *HIV/AIDS Preventative Measures Act 1993* (Tas) which provides that confidential testing is available for those who request it, or for those required by statute to undergo testing. Also, a magistrate can order that the person be detained for up to 28 days to prevent the spread of infection, and that period may be renewed for a further period of 28 days. Legislation in most jurisdictions requires that counselling and information be given to those who are to be tested for HIV (see, for example, *Health Act 1958* (Vic), s 127). In recent years there has been much discussion regarding the merits of making HIV testing compulsory for pregnant women.

Blood transfusion, tissue donation and blood-borne disease

[16.65] Legislation in all Australian jurisdictions requires that a declaration may be required by blood donors to the effect that they are not, to their knowledge, infected with the HIV virus, and have not been involved in activities which place them at risk of being so infected. This prevents action against those collecting blood, unless they lacked reasonable care in so doing (see further **[17.20]** and **[17.40]**). Falsification of this form is an offence, either specifically established, or under provisions in the crimes legislation regarding false representations (for example, it is specifically made an offence under the following legislation: *Human Tissue Act 1983* (NSW), s 20E; *Transplantation and Anatomy*

Act 1979 (Qld), s 48A; *Human Tissue Act 1985* (Tas), s 30(3); *Health Act 1958* (Vic), s 136).

Sexual intercourse, prohibited behaviour and disease

[16.70] In New South Wales, it is an offence to have sexual intercourse with another person knowing one has a sexually transmissible condition, where the other person has not knowingly consented. In South Australia the Health Commission may give directions to a person as to their conduct (which presumably includes sexual conduct). (Examples of specific legislation are: *Public Health Act 1991* (NSW), s 13, *Crimes Act 1900* (NSW), s 36 (causing grievous bodily disease); *Crimes Act 1958* (Vic), s 19A).

In 2005 there were two notable convictions for transmission of HIV. Kanengele-Yongo was convicted before the NSW District Court for maliciously inflicting grievous bodily harm and sentenced to twelve years imprisonment. Kanengele-Yongo was HIV positive and infected two women following brief relationships with each where he denied he had any sexually transmissible diseases and refused to wear a condom. He was originally charged with maliciously causing a grievous bodily disease, pursuant to s 36 of the *Crimes Act 1900* (NSW), which carries a much more severe penalty, however, difficulties proving intent as required for that offence led to those charges being dropped and the lesser charges being pursued. In Queensland, Reid was convicted of committing a malicious act with intent and sentenced to 10 years' imprisonment. Reid repeatedly reassured his partner that he was not HIV-positive and engaged in unprotected sex, transmitted the disease to his partner. The prosecutor alleged that Reid deliberately infected his partner as a means to securing their relationship.

In the New Zealand case of *Police v Dalley* [2005] NZAR 682 the Court held that a HIV positive man was not obligated to inform his sexual partner of his HIV status where he took reasonable precautions to avoid the risk of transmission. Dalley, who was HIV positive, had oral sex and vaginal intercourse with a woman without disclosing that he was HIV positive. A condom was used for the vaginal intercourse. Thomas J found that the risk of transmission of HIV as a result of oral sex was so low that it did not register as a risk and as Dalley did not ejaculate, he had taken reasonable care to avoid danger to his partner. With regard to the vaginal intercourse, Thomas J held that the use of a condom was sufficient to constitute taking reasonable care and precautions to prevent transmission. Dalley was therefore found not guilty of the charge of criminal nuisance.

Whether having sexual relations under such conditions could also be considered homicide or attempted homicide has been mooted but not decided by the courts. Webb and Howie (1985) argue that it is possible that a person who infected another intentionally or recklessly could be guilty of murder or attempted murder if the illness is fatal. They, nevertheless, point to problems of proof, particularly causation. Factors such as the degree of risk involved, the likelihood of contracting the disease, and the intention to infect the other person must be established (*R v Nuri* [1990] VR 641). Where a single act of intercourse held a one in 200 chance of HIV transmission, a court held that the defendant was not guilty of placing another in danger of death or serious injury as it did not amount to the necessary "appreciable danger" of death or injury required to make out the criminal offence (it could nevertheless amount to an offence under public health legislation) (*R v B* (unreported SC Vic 1995)).

Concern about the use, or threat of the use, of syringes filled with HIV-infected blood to intentionally infect others, either out of malice or during the commission of offences, has led some Australian jurisdictions to make specific provision and heavy penalties for such offences. For example, New South Wales (*Crimes Act 1900* (NSW), s 36) and Victoria (*Crimes Act 1958* (Vic), s 19A) provide that the malicious infliction or attempted infliction of a serious disease is an offence carrying a penalty of up to 25 years' imprisonment. In Queensland, intentional transmission of a serious disease is a crime liable to punishment for life (*Criminal Code 1899* (Qld), s 317(e). In the absence of such specific provisions, such offences would be covered by general provisions related to actions, ranging from reckless endangerment and attempted murder, to assault and threatening harm to another. As a person may be potentially liable for the death, many years later, of someone from a disease with which they have been maliciously infected, the offence could possibly amount to murder. This would also apply to the malicious actual or threatened injection of a person with HIV-positive blood, or other attempts to infect a person.

It is more likely that public health legislation would be invoked where a person has not taken reasonable steps to prevent the transmission of a notifiable disease to others. All jurisdictions have established offences for such behaviour. (See, for example, *Public Health Regulation 2000* (ACT), reg 21; *Public Health Act 1991* (NSW), ss 11, 13; *Notifiable Diseases Act* (NT), s 7; *Public and Environmental Health Act 1987* (SA), s 37; *Public Health Act 1962* (Tas), s 51; *Health Act 1911* (WA), ss 264, 310; *Public Health Act 2005* (Qld), s 143). Victoria has created the offence of knowingly or recklessly infecting another (*Health Act 1958* (Vic), s 120).

Disclosure of the identity of a person with a notifiable disease

[16.73] Whilst legislation is generally framed to avoid the recording of identifying information where possible, particular attention has been paid to the protection of identities in the reporting of HIV-positive status, coded information being sufficient. (See, for example, Public Health (Reporting of Notifiable Conditions) Code of Practice 2006 (ACT), 2.5-2.7; *Public Health Act 1991* (NSW), s 17; Guidelines for Notification of Notifiable Diseases, Human Pathogenic Organisms and Contaminants 2006 (Tas), 13.2; *Health (Infectious Diseases) Regulations 2001* (Vic), Sch 4.) In most jurisdictions it is an offence to disclose the identity of a person with a notifiable disease, subject, of course, to reporting requirements. See **[7.215]**ff on disclosure to third persons.

State control of those who are HIV-positive
Compulsory examination

[16.75] Like all those who have a notifiable disease, a person with HIV/AIDS must undergo medical examination if required by the chief medical officer (see **[16.85]**). The *HIV/AIDS Preventative Measures Act 1993* (Tas), s 10 provides that the Secretary *may* require a person to undergo compulsory HIV testing where:

   (i) the person is charged with a crime of a sexual nature under Chapter 19 or Chapter 20 of the Criminal Code; or

   (ii) it is necessary to determine the medical treatment of another person who may be at risk of becoming infected with HIV and whose condition is caused by the person required to undergo the test.

In addition, the Secretary *must* require a person to undergo HIV testing where they reasonably believe that the person:

   a) is HIV positive; and

   b) behaves in such a way as to place other persons at risk; and

   c) is likely to continue to behave in such a way.

Compulsory blood testing on admission to facilities

[16.80] No jurisdiction has legislation providing for compulsory blood testing of patients on admission to hospital or other health facilities, although there have recently been calls to pass such legislation. A person may be required by a health services provider to undergo HIV testing before elective medical or dental procedures are carried out. If he or she refuses, the health provider can either carry out the procedure according to the Infection Control Guidelines of the National Health and Medical Research Council, or refer the person to someone else. There are many arguments for and against such measures. Health care providers should very carefully consider the legal implications of whatever policy they adopt.

State control of those with infectious diseases
Powers to detain and treat

[16.85] Under public health legislation, all jurisdictions provide the power for those with certain notifiable diseases to undergo compulsory medical tests and treatment, and, if necessary (usually meaning if the person refuses to undergo treatment or behaves in a way that poses a danger to others) to be removed to a hospital or other health facility and be detained there until they are no longer infectious (see *Public Health Act 1997* (ACT), s 113; *Public Health Act 1991* (NSW), Pt 3 Div 6, *Notifiable Diseases Act* (NT), ss 11, 13; *Public Health Act 2005* (Qld), Ch 3 Pt 4 Div 2; *Public and Environmental Health Act 1987* (SA) 1987, Pt 4 Div 2; *Public Health Act 1997* (Tas), ss 41-47; *Health Act 1958* (Vic), s 121; *Health Act 1911* (WA), s 263). An example of how this legislation works occurred in New South Wales when a prostitute who was HIV-positive refused to refrain from plying her trade. She was detained under the order of the chief medical officer of health under s 500A(1) of the *Public Health Act 1991* (NSW) (as it was at that time).

The *HIV/AIDS Preventive Measures Act 1993* (Tas) provides that those who are infected with the HIV virus will be required to take all reasonable steps to prevent transmission of the disease to others (s 20). A magistrate can impose restrictions for a period of 28 days on the movements of a person who knowingly or recklessly places another person at risk of contracting HIV. The person may also be required to undergo medical and psychological assessment (s 21).

There is concern that these provisions allow for detention of citizens without proper legal process. In New South Wales, South Australia, Tasmania and Victoria there are specific provisions for periodic review of the orders, and appeals to the court against them (*Public Health Act 1991* (NSW), ss 25, 31, 41; *Public and Environmental Health Act 1987* (SA), ss 32, 34; *Public Health Act 1997* (Tas), ss 44-46; *Health Act 1958* (Vic), ss 121,122). The Australian Capital Territory, the Northern Territory, and Western Australia do not have specific provision for time limits on detention. In the Australian Capital Territory a person may apply in writing for a public health direction to be revoked (*Public Health Act 1997* (ACT), s 117). In addition, a right of appeal lies to the Supreme Court where a Magistrate has made an order at the chief medical officers request requiring a person to comply with a public health direction (*Pubic Health Act 1997* (ACT), s 132). In the Northern Territory provision is made for appeal to the Local Court against a notice requiring them to carry out specified measures (*Notifiable Diseases Act* (NT), s 11). In those jurisdictions without specific provisions one would have to rely on common law and/or administrative law rights to appeal a decision to detain.

Victoria provides emergency powers, which may be utilised if an emergency is proclaimed by the Governor in Council for the purpose of stopping or preventing the spread of an infectious disease. These powers permit the Secretary of the Department of Human Services to specify proclaimed areas, prevent entering or leaving these areas by any person, cause the arrest without warrant and detention of persons within the area, and the seizing, disinfecting or destroying of property (*Health Act 1958* (Vic), Pt 6 Div 4). Tasmania, Queensland, the Australian Capital Territory and New South Wales have similar emergency provisions (*Public Health Act 1997* (Tas), Pt 2 Div 2; *Public Health Act 2005* (Qld), Chapter 8; *Public Health Act 1997* (ACT), Pt 7; *Public Health Act 1991* (NSW), s 4).

Needle exchange

[16.90] Needle exchange is a positive measure for infection control. There are laws in some jurisdictions specifying the method and facilities for disposing of needles and syringes. As the possession or supply of equipment for administering illicit drugs is a criminal offence, development of needle exchange/supply programs has required the introduction of provisions exempting workers in the programs from criminal liability for their activities. The following is generally the rule:

- it is illegal to possess specific ("illicit") drugs except for trace amounts such as that left in syringes and needles;
- it is illegal to possess equipment for the administration of illicit drugs, except for the possession of needles and syringes;
- it is an offence to self-administer illicit drugs.

(See *Drugs of Dependence Act 1989* (ACT), *Crimes Act 1900* (ACT); *Drugs Misuse and Trafficking Act 1985* (NSW); *Misuse of Drugs Act* (NT); *Drugs Misuse Act 1986* (Qld); *Controlled Substances Act 1984* (SA); *Poisons Act 1971* (Tas); *Drugs Poisons and Controlled Substances Act 1981* (Vic); *Poisons Act 1964* (WA)).

The Australian Capital Territory *Drugs of Dependence Act 1989* (ACT), Part 7 provides that medical practitioners, nurses, pharmacists and health workers can apply to the Chief Medical Officer for authorisation to distribute syringes and needles, and protects them from prosecution under the *Crimes Act 1900* (ACT).

In New South Wales the *Drugs Misuse and Trafficking Act 1985* (NSW), s 11 and the *Drugs Misuse and Trafficking Regulation 2000* (NSW), regs 5 and 7 provide that possession of implements for the administration of prohibited drugs except syringes and needles is an offence. Authorised persons are exempt from these provisions to the extent that it is necessary to facilitate an authorised needle exchange program. A general exemption exists for pharmacists.

The Northern Territory *Misuse of Drugs Act* (NT), s 12 provides that medical practitioners, pharmacists or other authorised people are exempt from the offence of supplying needles and syringes.

In Queensland, medical practitioners, pharmacists and authorised persons may supply syringes and needles (*Drugs Misuse Act 1986* (Qld), s 10(3)). The *Drugs Misuse Regulations 1986* (Qld), regs 3 and 4 set out requirements for safe disposal of needles, syringes and dangerous drugs.

In South Australia, it is an offence to possess any piece of equipment used in the administration of drugs, however, injecting equipment is exempted from those provisions. See the *Controlled Substances (Exemptions) Regulations 2004* (SA), reg 4.

In Tasmania permits are issued for a specified period to medical practitioners, pharmacists, nurses and needle exchange officers to supply needles and syringes, who may authorise their employees to supply them (*HIV/AIDS Preventive Measures Act 1993* (Tas), Part 3).

In Victoria, those who sell or supply needles and syringes as part of a needle exchange program are also exempt from criminal liability. A list of those authorised to sell or supply needles and syringes is kept by the Secretary of the Health Department, and places authorised to act as needle exchange centres are specified in regulations (*Drugs, Poisons and Controlled Substances Act 1981* (Vic), s 80(5), *Drugs, Poisons and Controlled Substance Regulations 1995* (Vic)).

In Western Australia, the possession of needles and syringes is not an offence, whilst the possession of other utensils for smoking or manufacturing illicit drugs is (*Misuse of Drugs Act 1981* (WA), ss 5 and 6). Pharmacists and needle exchange workers are exempt from criminal sanctions for aiding and abetting offences (*Poisons Act 1964* (WA), s 36A).

Other infection control measures

Immunisation

[16.95] The Commonwealth provides vaccines for such diseases as polio-myelitis, mumps, measles, rubella, diphtheria, influenza, hepatitis B, pertussis and tetanus. It requires children to be vaccinated under certain circumstances, for example, for eligibility for Family Assistance (*see A New Tax System (Family Assistance) Act 1999*, Part 2 Div 2). The National Health and Medical Research Council recommends that children be immunised according to its schedule of child immunisation. The Australian Capital Territory, New South Wales, Tasmania, Western Australia and Victoria have legislated to require the provision of an immunisation history on enrolment to school (*Public Health Regulation 2000* (ACT), Pt 2; *Public Health Act 1991* (NSW), Pt 3A, *Public Health (General) Regulation 2002* (NSW), Pt 4; *Public Health Act 1997* (Tas), Pt 3 Div 2; *School Education Act 1999* (WA), s 16; *Health Act 1958* (Vic), Pt 7, *Health (Immunisation) Regulations 1999* (Vic)).

Other measures

[16.100] Public health legislation provides wide powers to health authorities to search, quarantine and sanitise premises, and seize property where there is an actual or suspected danger to another person or the community. Control of hazardous materials and practices are other authorised means of infection control. Authorised inspectors can enter premises and inspect them for compliance with health standards (for example, inspection of air-conditioning units, food preparation areas). Health care facilities such as hospitals, hostels and nursing homes may carry out other activities that are covered by public health legislation and are also subject to infection control standards required for licensing and accreditation (for example, under Hospitals, Private Hospitals, Nursing Homes and Supported Accommodation legislation, that provide for sanitary conditions, clean and dirty utility rooms, sterilising and autoclaving equipment, and infection-control procedures).

Discrimination against those with a notifiable disease

[16.105] There is federal legislation and legislation in all jurisdictions prohibiting discrimination against those with mental or physical handicap or impairment. Most jurisdictions include as handicap or impairment the "presence in the body of organisms capable of causing disease". Commonwealth legislation also provides that some international human rights instruments are to be followed in Australia. New South Wales has also prohibited discrimination on the ground of a person's sexual preference, and this ground has also been included in the grounds covered by the *Human Rights and Equal Opportunity Commission Act 1986* (Cth).

Anti-discrimination legislation appears to establish that health carers cannot refuse a patient treatment, or give inferior treatment simply because a person has a notifiable disease. A health carer could be in breach of anti-discrimination legislation if he or she gives a patient less favourable care or treatment than would be given to another patient who does not have the illness.

[16.110] Case: *Taikato & Nakhle v Western Sydney Area Health Service* [1999] NSWADT 52

T and N were not married but had been living in a de facto relationship for a number of years. They were unable to conceive a child and sought medical assessment and assistance accordingly. T was infected with both Hepatitis B and C. The couple were offered treatment on the Gamete Intra Fallopian Transfer (GIFT) Program. In the normal course of GIFT, excess oocytes are cryogenically preserved. However, because of T's Hepatitis infection, the treating doctor, Dr S, decided not to provide cryopreservation to T. This decision was based on two concerns. Firstly, that there was a risk of the spread of Hepatitis B and C to other embryos if genetic material was infected with either disease and cryo preserved as a result of the fact that the plastic vesssels in which gametes were frozen sometimes leaked or shattered. Secondly, that there was a risk of transmission of Hepatitis C to the laboratory staff through the practice of mouth pipetting. T and N were not advised at the time of the treatment centre's decision not to preserve excess oocytes.

[16.115] Following one failed attempt to achieve pregnancy through the GIFT program, Dr S advised T and N that, because of the risk of transmission of Hepatitis C, the clinic was postponing assistance to the couple until blood testing demonstrated the absence of the virus from T's blood, but requested that they contact the clinic again in six months to determine whether there was any update on the situation. T and N lodged complaints with the Anti-Discrimination Board alleging unlawful discrimination. The matter was referred to the Administrative Decisions Tribunal. The Tribunal felt that the complaints of T and N should be considered as separate complaints. Only the complaint of T is discussed here.

The Tribunal noted that the scientific knowledge with regard to the transmission of Hepatitis C at the relevant time was not clear and that there remains uncertainty as to the ways in which people can potentially contract the disease. The majority held:

- T's hepatitis was a physical impairment under the *Anti-Discrimination Act 1977* (NSW);
- the less favourable treatment T had received from the clinic was on the grounds of her physical impairment;
- the clinic did not do all that was reasonably practicable to assist T to have the full services provided to her.

The Tribunal concluded that T was subjected to unlawful discrimination and awarded $15,000 in damages.

Domestic Violence: Child Abuse

[16.120] The basic legal principle applying to the welfare of children is that parents have the responsibility of the care, protection and upbringing of their children. The parenting of a child is a private matter, with any disputes or disagreements within the family being dealt with under the *Family Law Act 1975* (Cth). Parties are encouraged to work out differences through mediation and conciliation, or, failing that, through a parenting order of the Family Court. However where a child is charged with an offence, abused or in need of care, State child welfare authorities are authorised to act, and the Family Court is precluded from jurisdiction. All Australian jurisdictions provide for the reporting of suspected child abuse except Western Australia, and this is outlined below. Although they are not required to report domestic violence that does not involve children to the state, health carers are often the first to learn of it in many cases, and can assist the victims in preventing it from happening again.

Child in need of care or maltreated

[16.125] Jurisdictions differ widely in their definitions of maltreatment of children or children in need of care *(Children And Young People Act 1999* (ACT); *Children (Care and Protection) Act 1987* (NSW), *Crimes Act 1900* (NSW), ss 43-44; *Community Welfare Act* (NT); *Child Protection Act 1999* (Qld); *Children's Protection Act 1993* (SA); *Children, Young Persons and Their Families Act 1997* (Tas); *Children and Young Persons Act 1989* (Vic); *Child Welfare Act 1947* (WA)). Similar patterns occur, however, in the multiple descriptions of those children. They include:

- neglect;
- maltreatment and abuse;
- adverse environment; and
- a child's behaviour.

Neglect

[16.130] Under the category of "neglect—lack of care" children are included:

- who have no parents or guardian, or are neglected or abandoned by them, or whose parents or guardians are unwilling or unable to care for them;
- who are not being provided with a necessity of life (such as food, shelter, clothing or medical care) and that is likely to cause harm to their wellbeing;
- who have no fixed address, have no visible means of support, or are persistently absent from school without satisfactory reason; and
- where there is an irretrievable breakdown between the child and parents.

Maltreatment and abuse

[16.135] Children who have been maltreated and abused include those:

- who are, have been or are in danger of being, physically, mentally or emotionally harmed;
- who have been exposed to domestic violence and that exposure has caused or is likely to cause significant harm to their wellbeing;
- who have been threatened with death, abuse or neglect by the person with whom they reside;
- who have been sexually abused or exploited or involved in child prostitution; and
- being under the age of 14 years and employed or engaged in any circus, travelling show, acrobatic entertainment or exhibition by which his health and welfare are likely to be lost, prejudiced or endangered.

Adverse environment

[16.140] Children falling under the category of "adverse environment" include? children exposed to moral danger, in "bad" company, whose physical, mental or emotional development is in danger because of the company they are in or circumstances in which they live.

Child's behaviour

[16.143] Those falling under this category may include:

- children who commit an offence while under the age of criminal responsibility, are involved in illegal activity, likely to fall into a life of crime, or are uncontrollable;
- children whose person with parental responsibility is unable to or unwilling to prevent them from engaging in self-damaging behaviour.

Reporting of child abuse

Voluntary reporting

[16.145] Five jurisdictions provide for the voluntary reporting to the authorities that a child is maltreated or in need of care. In South Australia and Western Australia, where there is no provisions for voluntary reporting, there is nonetheless protection from legal action such as defamation.

In the Australian Capital Territory a person who believes or suspects that a child or young person (between 12 and 18 years) is in need of care and protection may report the circumstances to the chief executive of the Department of Health, Housing and Community Care (*Children and Young People Act 1999* (ACT), s 158).

In New South Wales, s 24 of the *Children and Young Persons (Care and Protection) Act 1998* (NSW) provides that any person believing on reasonable grounds that a child is at risk of harm may notify the Director-General of the Department of Community Services.

In Queensland a person can notify the Chief Executive if that person suspects that a child is being or is likely to be harmed (*Child Protection Act 1999* (Qld), s 22).

In Tasmania an adult who knows, believes or suspects on reasonable grounds that a child is suffering, has suffered or is likely to suffer abuse or neglect has a responsibility to take action to prevent that abuse or neglect. One step they may take to prevent the abuse is to inform the Secretary of their knowledge, belief or suspicion (*Children, Young Persons and Their Families Act 1997* (Tas), s 13).

In Victoria where a child is believed to be in need of protection any person may notify a protective intervener (Director-General of Community Services or police officer) (*Children and Young Persons Act 1989* (Vic), s 64).

In these jurisdictions, where a person acts in good faith in reporting suspected child abuse, it is not considered to breach privacy laws, and the person cannot be sued in defamation. In Western Australia, s 146 of the *Child Welfare Act 1947* provides that a person who on reasonable grounds and in good faith makes a report as to the circumstances of a child for the purpose of enforcing the provisions of the Act is not liable to any action for damage or any other legal proceedings in respect of that report. In South Australia, s 12 of the *Children's Protection Act 1993* affords persons who voluntarily notify the Department of a suspicion of child abuse or neglect with the same protection from civil or criminal liability as those who report pursuant to the Act's mandatory reporting provisions.

Mandatory reporting

[16.147] All jurisdictions, except Western Australia, make it an offence for nominated professionals to fail to report suspected child abuse to the authorities. Again, reporting in good faith and to the right authorities is not a breach of confidentiality, and the professional cannot be sued for this, or for defamation.

In the Australian Capital Territory, s 159 of the *Children and Young People Act 1999* (ACT) contains a list of people including doctors, dentists, enrolled or registered nurses, teachers, police officers, public servants providing children's services, school counsellors and child-care centre workers who must report if they reasonably suspect that a child or young person is suffering or has suffered sexual abuse or non-accidental physical injury. The report must state the name or description of the child or young person and the grounds for the person's suspicion.

In New South Wales, s 27 of the *Children and Young Persons (Care and Protection) Act 1998* (NSW) imposes a duty on those who, in the course of their professional work deliver health care, welfare, education, children's services residential services or law enforcement wholly or partly to children, or hold a management position in an organisation that carries out these activities. The duty is to inform the Director General of Community Services, as soon as practicable, if they have reasonable grounds to suspect a child is at risk of harm.

Under the *Ombudsman Act 1974* (NSW) the head of a government agency must notify the Ombudsman of details of child abuse allegations or convictions against any employee, and must arrange for employees to notify him or her of such matters that come to their attention. Disclosure under these Acts does not breach obligations of confidentiality.

In the Northern Territory, s 14 of the *Community Welfare Act* (NT) provides that *any person* who suspects maltreatment shall report this to the police or Minister for Community Welfare. Where a report has been made to the police, it may be investigated by them and action taken for the protection of the child.

In Queensland, ss 76KC and 76L of the *Health Act 1937* (Qld) provide that a medical practitioner or registered nurse must immediately report where they suspect a child has been, is being or is likely to be harmed. The notice must include the child's name, where the child lives, the names of the parents, where the parents can be contacted, details of the harm, and the person reporting's name, address and telephone number. A child who is being, or is likely to be harmed, may be detained by a hospital for treatment for up to 96 hours before further action is required to keep the child in care. The person to be notified is an officer authorised by the chief health officer.

In South Australia, s 11 of the *Children's Protection Act 1993* (SA) provides for mandatory reporting by doctors, pharmacists, dentists, registered or enrolled nurses, psychologists, social workers, police officers, teachers, community corrections officers, day care providers, those who hold management positions in organisations that supervise children and employees or volunteers in a government agency providing services for children of suspected abuse or neglect. Notification is to be made to the Department for Community and Family Services and must be accompanied by a statement of the observations, information and opinions on which the suspicion is based.

In Tasmania, s 14 of the *Children, Young Persons and Their Families Act 1997* (Tas) requires a wide category of prescribed persons, including medical practitioners, nurses, dentists, psychologists, school principals and teachers, and probation officers, who suspect a child is being abused or neglected must report this to the Secretary. The report must be accompanied by a statement of the observations, information and opinions on which the suspicion is based.

In Victoria, s 64 of the *Children and Young Persons Act 1989* (Vic) requires doctors, psychologists, registered or enrolled nurses, teachers, principals, welfare workers, child care workers, probation and parole officers and police officers to report their belief on reasonable grounds that a child is in need of protection because he or she has suffered or is likely to suffer significant harm as a result of either physical injury or sexual abuse and parents are unlikely to protect the child from this harm. The report must be made to the Secretary to the Department of Health and Community Services.

Care of an abused child

[16.150] All jurisdictions provide for the appropriate authority to remove children from immediate danger and provide for their protection and welfare.

Generally, authorised officers or police officers can enter premises and take children to a place where they can be assessed and treated. All jurisdictions provide that welfare officers, police officers or a medical officer may, if necessary, direct that a child be detained in a hospital or elsewhere for examination and immediate treatment. The child may only be detained for a specified period before an application must be made for an order for further care if required (*Children and Young People Act 1999* (ACT) (may be kept up to 2 working days); *Children and Young Persons (Care and Protection) Act 1998* (NSW), s 45 (the Director-General of the Department of Youth and Community Services must make an application to the Children's Court at the first available opportunity and no later than the next sitting day of the Court for further orders); *Community Welfare Act* (NT), s 15 (may be kept up to 48 hours); *Health Act 1937* (Qld), s 76L (may be kept up to 96 hours); *Children's Protection Act 1993* (SA), s 16 (may be kept until the end of the working day following the day on which the child was removed); *Children, Young Persons and Their Families Act 1997* (Tas), s 21 (may be kept up to 120 hours); *Children and Young Persons Act 1989* (Vic), s 69 (may be kept up to 24 hours); *Child Welfare Act 1972* (WA), s 29 (may be kept up to 48 hours if under six years of age; otherwise the matter must be brought before the Court as soon as possible)). This may be done against the parents' will. Depending on the situation, the child may be made a ward of the court, or alternative action may be taken to ensure the child's welfare. Magistrates' Courts and Supreme Courts of the various Australian jurisdictions also have jurisdiction to deal with children who are in need of care, as have community advocates and guardianship tribunals (see Chapter 5).

Domestic Violence: Spouse Abuse

Domestic violence as criminal activity

[16.155] Abuse of an adult family member is, like child abuse, a crime. There is no excuse for violence against or maltreatment of another, except self-defence or perhaps necessity or, less likely, duress. Provocation will not exonerate a person from being answerable to the law for their actions (although it may mitigate the punishment they may face) (see **[14.200]**ff). As well as being the subject of general assault and violence provisions in each jurisdiction's Crimes Acts, there are special laws relating to domestic violence (*Domestic Violence and Protection Orders Act 2001* (ACT); *Crimes Act 1900* (NSW), Pt 15A, ss 43-44; *Domestic Violence Act* (NT); *Domestic and Family Violence Protection Act 1989* (Qld); *Domestic Violence Act 1994* (SA); *Justices Act 1959* (Tas), *Family Violence Act 2004* (Tas); *Crimes (Family Violence) Act 1987* (Vic); *Justices Act 1902* (WA), *Restraining Orders Act 1997* (WA)).

Health carers may be confronted by cases of domestic violence. There is no legal obligation, however, for health carers to report suspected domestic violence that does not involve children.

Domestic violence includes spouse abuse (including de facto partners) and increasing recognition of violence by any person against another in their domestic environment (for example, relatives who assault and abuse elderly parents). Despite common conceptions, spouse and child abuse occur across the social spectrum (Scutt (1985)). As the problem has been increasingly recognised, governments have attempted to give the victims of domestic violence more appropriate protection through the law. Health carers who come across situations of domestic violence can help by being aware of the possibility of victims obtaining legal and other assistance, and by pointing this out, helping victims to take control of the situation, whilst themselves remaining objective. General practice surgeries and hospital emergency rooms should have information available about victims' assistance programs and services, as well as legal aid offices. Often domestic violence may involve sexual assault: patients may not be aware that unwanted sexual activity may constitute an assault, even where the parties are married or living in a de facto relationship.

Dealing with domestic violence

Immediate assistance

[16.160] In the Northern Territory, Queensland, Tasmania and Victoria domestic violence legislation allows police varying enhanced powers of entry into homes, search, seizure of weapons and detention without a warrant where they believe domestic violence has taken place, is taking place or is threatened (*Police Administration Act* (NT), s 126(2A); *Police Powers and Responsibilities Act 2000* (Qld), s 372; *Family Violence Act 2004* (Tas), s 10; *Crimes (Family Violence) Act 1987* (Vic), s 18AB). In the Australian Capital Territory and New South Wales, the powers of entry legislation is of general application and allows a police officer to enter premises where the officer believes on reasonable grounds that an offence or a breach of the peace is likely to be committed, or a person has suffered physical injury or there is imminent danger of injury (*Crimes Act 1900* (ACT), s 190; *Enforcement (Powers and Responsibilities) Act 2002* (NSW), s 9). There are also units of specially trained police officers to deal with domestic violence and child abuse. Victims and those fearing domestic violence should consider making use of domestic violence services existing in the larger cities (whether run by the police or not) to assist them in deciding the best course to take for their protection and that of their children. The Legal Aid Office or Magistrates Court Registry can also give advice. Emergency accommodation can be arranged in some circumstances.

Prosecution

[16.165] Assault is a crime, which invokes the possibility of prosecution. The victim of spouse abuse may understandably not wish to pursue criminal action, as this often makes matters worse.

However, in all jurisdictions if police believe, and have evidence to show, that there has been domestic violence, they can apply for a protection order (see **[16.175]**ff below) for a person, or arrest them and take them to the police station to be charged. Any person who has committed, or is in the process of committing, an offence may be arrested by the police and charged, and a court can release such a person on bail. Strict conditions can be imposed to ensure violence is not undertaken or repeated. If the conditions are breached the person can be arrested and detained.

The power to arrest and prosecute independently of the alleged victim's wish to do so can relieve him or her from this task, and may prevent exacerbation of the actual or potential offender's wrath against the victim (as they can be seen to have no choice in the matter). Once a protection order is in existence, a breach of the order allows police to arrest and charge the person: they are not required to prove an assault or likely assault. This makes it much easier for the police to arrest a person who creates a potential threat to another. Police can generally only arrest in response to:

- offences already committed;
- complaints of threatened violence (in some jurisdictions); or
- an order or injunction issued by a court.

Protection from future domestic violence

Commonwealth legislation

[16.170] Under s 114 of the *Family Law Act 1975* (Cth) the Family Court may issue an "injunction" restraining the movements and actions of a person who it is believed poses a threat to the welfare of their spouse or children. The injunction may prohibit the person at whom it is directed from contacting the applicant or person on whose behalf the injunction is issued, or from entering premises or areas where that person lives, works, or goes to school. The legislation does not cover de facto relationships.

State and Territory legislation

[16.175] In all Australian jurisdictions, where a person fears violence from another, either towards them or a child, that person can apply to a magistrate's court for an injunction to restrain the person (variously called a "domestic violence", "intervention", "restraining", "apprehended violence" or "protection" order). Some jurisdictions have enacted legislation to cover domestic violence specifically, with special procedures and orders available (*Domestic Violence and Protection Orders Act 2001* (ACT); *Crimes Act 1900* (NSW), Pt 15A; *Domestic Violence Act* (NT); *Domestic and Family Violence Protection Act 1989* Qld); *Domestic Violence Act 1994* (SA), *Summary Procedure Act 1921* (SA); *Restraining Orders Act 1997* (WA); *Family Violence Act 2004* (Tas); *Crimes (Family Violence) Act 1987* (Vic)).

In New South Wales police are obliged to apply for a protection order where domestic violence has occurred or is threatened, unless the victim/intended victim does so, or there is good reason not to apply (*Crimes Act 1900* (NSW), s 562C(3)).

Legislation differs across jurisdictions, but the following gives a general list of those who can apply for protection orders and those who may be protected by them.

Figure 16.1: Protection orders under domestic violence legislation

Those who may seek a protection order	Those who may be protected by a protection order
Person for whom protection is sought	Domestic partner of alleged perpetrator
Police officer	Child of domestic partner of alleged perpetrator
For a child: parent, guardian, person acting on behalf of child, in some cases the child themselves	Relative of an alleged perpetrator
	Spouse of an alleged perpetrator
For an adult: someone given authority to do so by the person, court or legislation	Person living / has lived in same household as alleged perpetrator
For a workplace order: employer	Person having intimate personal relationship (past or present) with alleged perpetrator
For a person with a legal disability: public advocate	
	Biological parent of alleged perpetrator
	Child who regularly resides with the target of the violence
	Child of whom the target is or has been a guardian
	Child of whom the target is or has custody

"Spouse" includes de facto spouse and ex-spouse. "Domestic partner" includes former domestic partner.

A lawyer is not required, and the police, the court, or a domestic crisis centre may assist in the application. In some jurisdictions the respondent may be remanded in custody pending the hearing where this is considered necessary (see, for example, *Bail Act 1978* (NSW), s 32; *Domestic Violence Act* (NT), s 7; *Domestic and Family Violence Protection Act 1989* (Qld), s 69(2); *Family Violence Act 2004* (Tas), s 12).

In granting an injunction the court must be satisfied, on the balance of probabilities, that:

- the respondent has engaged in domestic violence or has threatened such conduct (and is likely to do so again); or
- the applicant has reasonable grounds to fear, and in fact fears, violence or harrassment.

When considering an application, courts will also take into account the need for protection of those threatened, the welfare of any child affected, the accommodation needs of the applicant, and hardship that would be caused to the respondent by an injunction. Normally a court will not impose restrictions on someone unless they have been heard in their own defence, but where the matter is serious and urgent enough, an order may be made *ex parte*, that is, in the absence of representation by the respondent (*Crimes Act 1900* (NSW), s 562BB(2); *Domestic Violence Act* (NT), s 4(3); *Domestic and Family Violence)*

Protection Act 1989 (Qld), s 39A; *Domestic Violence Act 1994* (SA), s 9 and *Summary Procedure Act 1921* (SA), s 99C; *Family Violence Act 2004* (Tas), s 23; *Crimes (Family Violence) Act 1987* (Vic), s 8; *Restraining Orders Act 1997* (WA), ss 26, 27). In some jurisdictions a member of the police force may apply to a magistrate for an order by telephone. This is available only where it would not be practicable to apply more formal means (for example, *Crimes Act 1900* (NSW), s 562H; *Domestic Violence Act* (NT), s 6; *Domestic Violence Act 1994* (SA), s 8 and *Summary Procedure Act 1921* (SA), s 99B; *Crimes (Family Violence) Act 1987* (Vic), s 8(4)). In Western Australia, telephone applications are not restricted to members of the police force (*Restraining Orders Act 1997* (WA), s 20). Such orders may be interim, that is, pending a full hearing where both parties put their case (*Domestic Violence and Protection Orders Act 2001* (ACT), Pt 6; *Crimes Act 1900* (NSW), s 562BB(4); *Domestic and Family Violence Protection Act 1989* (Qld), s 34B; *Family Violence Act 2004* (Tas), s 23; *Crimes (Family Violence) Act 1987* (Vic), s 8). A full hearing is the ideal legal model, but the circumstances may be such that the magistrate or judge decides such an order may be a final one.

Effect of a domestic violence order

[16.180] Where an order has been made whether the respondent was present at the time, or not, if after receiving a copy of the order the respondent contravenes the order in any respect, he or she is guilty of an offence and liable for punishment *Domestic Violence and Protection Orders Act 2001* (ACT), s 34; *Crimes Act 1900* (NSW), s 562; *Domestic Violence Act* (NT), s 10; *Domestic and Family Violence Protection Act 1989* (Qld), s 80; *Domestic Violence Act 1994* (SA), s 15 and *Summary Procedure Act 1921* (SA), s 99I; *Family Violence Act 2004* (Tas), s 35; *Crimes (Family Violence) Act 1987* (Vic), s 22; *Restraining Orders Act 1997* (WA), s 81).

If an order is made, it must be served on the respondent, and has effect from the time he or she receives it. Breach of the order will lead to arrest and detention. The applicant should keep their copy of the order and show it to the police.

Caring for those with an order

[16.185] If a patient has a protection order restricting access to them by another person, those attending the patient may lawfully refuse to assist that person in access. Hospital authorities may deny such a person entry on to premises, on the ground that they have a duty of care to the patient involved, which involves protecting the patient from those who may cause them harm. However, health carers are advised that the law is not theirs to administer, and, if the person insists on access, they should contact the police (through administrative channels where appropriate) on the patient's behalf. While not getting directly involved in others' domestic concerns, health carers should assist in the lawful protection of their patients.

References and Further Reading

Australian Health and Medical Law Reporter (CCH, Sydney, 1991) ¶39-210ff

Breckenridge, B and Laing, L, *Challenging Silence: Innovative Responses to Sexual and Domestic Violence* (Allen & Unwin, Sydney, 1999)

Byard, R, Donald, I and Chivell, W, "Non-lethal and Subtle Injury and Unexpected Infant Death" (1999) 7 *Journal of Law and Medicine* 47

Campbell, M, "Infectious Diseases and Discrimination" *Australian Health Law Bulletin* 13 (8)

Department of Human Services, South Australia, *Reporting Child Abuse and Neglect: Mandated Notification* (Department of Human Services Adelaide)

Flaskerud, J, *AIDS/HIV Infection: A Reference Guide for Nursing Professionals* (WB Saunders Co, Philadelphia, 1989)

Intergovernmental Committee on AIDS Legal Working Party, *Final Report* (Department of Health, Housing and Community Services, Canberra, 1992)

Kelsall, H, Robinson, P, and Howse, G, "Public Health Law and Quarantine in a Federal System" (1999) 7 *Journal of Law and Medicine* 87

Laws of Australia Vol 17. Family Law/17.5 Domestic Violence

McPhee, J, and Stewart, C, "Recent Developments in Law" *Journal of Bioethical Inquiry* 2 (3)

Reeson, L, "The NSW Pap Test Register and its Significance to GPs" (1997) 6 *Health Law Bulletin* 15

Reynolds, C, *Public Health Law in Australia* (Federation Press, Sydney, 1995)

Scutt, J, *Women and the Law* (Law Book Co, Sydney, 1990), ch 9 (this book has an extensive bibliography)

Scutt, J, *Even in the Best of Homes* (Penguin, 1985)

Scutt, J, "Nursing, Law and AIDS" (1989) 18 (No 9) *Australian Nurses Journal*

Stewart, C, "HIV, Non-Disclosure and Infection in Australia" 2 (3) *Journal of Bioethical Enquiry* 123

The Community Law Reform Committee of the Australian Capital Territory, Research Paper No 1, *Domestic Violence* (Australian Institute of Criminology, Canberra, 1993)

V

Ethical/Legal Issues

17 Human tissue transplants & reproductive technology

Human tissue transplant

Blood transfusions & donations

Donation of tissue by a living person

Donation of tissue after death

Assisted conception & reproductive technology

Surrogacy agreements

Posthumous parenthood

Genetic testing

chapter 17

Human Tissue Transplants and Reproductive Technology

Human Tissue Transplant

[17.05] Legislation exists in all Australian jurisdictions regarding the transplantation of human tissue from both live and dead donors (*Transplantation and Anatomy Act 1978* (ACT); *Human Tissue Act 1983* (NSW); *Human Tissue Transplant Act* (NT); *Transplantation and Anatomy Act 1979* (Qld); *Transplantation and Anatomy Act 1983* (SA); *Human Tissue Act 1985* (Tas); *Human Tissue Act 1982* (Vic); *Human Tissue and Transplantation Act 1982* (WA)). All jurisdictions prohibit "trading in tissue", that is, an arrangement whereby tissue is supplied in exchange for money. This does not include the necessary expense in the removal of tissue, or sale of tissue that has been treated or processed for therapeutic, medical or scientific purposes (*Transplantation and Anatomy Act 1978* (ACT), Pt 7; *Human Tissue Act 1983* (NSW), Pt 6; *Human Tissue Transplant Act* (NT), Pt 5; *Transplantation and Anatomy Act 1979* (Qld), Pt 7; *Transplantation and Anatomy Act 1983* (SA), Pt 7; *Human Tissue Act 1985* (Tas), Pt 4; *Human Tissue Act 1982* (Vic), Pt 8; *Human Tissue and Transplantation Act 1982* (WA), Pt 5).

What is "tissue"?

[17.10] "Tissue" is broadly defined in transplantation legislation as an organ, or part of an organ of a human body, as well as a substance extracted from an organ or from part of a human body. For the purposes of donations of tissue by living persons, foetal tissue, spermatozoa and ova are excluded from the definition of tissue. The transfer of foetal tissue, spermatozoa and ova is covered in some jurisdictions by separate legislation (see **[17.95]**ff). Tissue may be:

- regenerative, that which is replaced in the body by natural process after it is removed (for example, blood or bone marrow); or
- non-regenerative, that is all other tissue.

(See *Transplantation and Anatomy Act 1978* (ACT), ss 4 and 6; *Human Tissue Act 1983* (NSW), ss 4 and 6; *Human Tissue Transplant Act* (NT), ss 4 and 6; *Transplantation and Anatomy Act 1979* (Qld), ss 4 and 8; *Transplantation and Anatomy Act 1983* (SA), ss 5 and 7; *Human Tissue Act 1985* (Tas), ss 3 and 5; *Human Tissue Act 1982* (Vic), ss 3 and 5; *Human Tissue and Transplantation Act 1982* (WA), ss 3 and 6.)

Transplantation legislation is mainly concerned with establishing the requirements for valid consent to removal of the tissue: who may consent and under what circumstances they may do so. It also prescribes some of the conditions which apply to the removal of the tissue. Legislation dealing with donations from live donors usually covers:

- blood transfusions;
- other regenerative tissue;
- non-regenerative tissue; and
- conditions under which consent must be given.

In dealing with donations after death, the legislation usually covers:

- a definition of death;
- postmortems; and
- a determination as to who may give permission for removal of tissue.

Non-therapeutic nature of tissue removal

[17.15] The first point to note regarding tissue transplantation is that under the common law it has never been lawful to remove a body part where that removal was not therapeutic for the donor. It constituted the criminal offence of maiming, and as one cannot consent to the commission of a crime against oneself, there was no legal way one could donate parts of one's body (Devlin, *Samples of Lawmaking* (Oxford University Press, London, 1962), pp 83-103; Lord Justice Edmund Davies, "A Legal Look at Transplants" (1969), 62 *Proceedings of the Royal Society of Medicine* 633; Australian Law Reform Commission, *Human Tissue Transplants* (ALRC 7, 1977), pp 22ff).

Once tissue donation became acceptable in Australia there has been strict controls over the conditions under which it is done, including the prohibition of any profit making from the donation of tissue (by the donor or anyone else). Australia has adopted the approach of "opting in", that is, requiring a person to positively indicate when competent that he or she is willing to donate tissue after death. Thus a person is presumed not to consent unless positive consent has been given. The alternative approach, adopted by some other countries is a system of "opting out", that is, a person is presumed to consent to donation unless there is a clear indication that he or she does not wish to do so. In Western Australian the *Human Tissue and Transplant Act 1982* (WA), s 32A provides that the Executive Director may, with the approval of the Minister, issue codes of practice in relation to tissue donation and transplantation.

Blood Donations and Transfusions

Giving of blood

Adults

[17.20] The statutes provide that any adult of sound mind may consent to the removal of blood from his or her body for the purpose of use in transfusion of another person or any other therapeutic, medical or scientific purpose (*Transplantation and Anatomy Act 1978* (ACT), s 20; *Human Tissue Act 1983* (NSW), s 19; *Human Tissue Transplant Act* (NT), s 14; *Transplantation and Anatomy Act 1979* (Qld), s 17; *Transplantation and Anatomy Act 1983* (SA), s 18; *Human Tissue Act 1985* (Tas), s 18; *Human Tissue Act 1982* (Vic), s 21; *Human Tissue and Transplantation Act 1982* (WA), s 18). There is no requirement that the consent be written (except in New South Wales), nor special procedures or requirements regarding what information is given for consent, so the law follows the general law of consent.

Some jurisdictions require that blood is donated in a particular place, such as a Red Cross Centre (Australian Capital Territory, Northern Territory and Tasmania) or hospital (Australian Capital Territory, Northern Territory and Tasmania) (see *Transplantation and Anatomy Act 1978* (ACT), s 22; *Human Tissue Transplant Act* (NT), s 15; *Human Tissue Act 1985* (Tas), s 20).

Some legislation contains provisions that may be considered special requirements for the protection of the community. New South Wales requires that those supplying blood, blood products or semen must have an authorisation to do so (*Human Tissue Act 1983* (NSW), Part 3A). Some jurisdictions require donors to provide a statutory declaration regarding their medical suitability as a donor (see *Human Tissue Act 1983* (NSW), s 20D and *Human Tissue Regulation 2005* (NSW), Form 1 of Schedule 1; *Blood Donation (Transmittable Diseases) Act 1985* (ACT), s 5; *Notifiable Diseases Act* (NT), s 26A(2); *Blood Contaminants Act 1985* (SA), s 4; *Blood Transfusion (Limitation of Liability) Act 1986* (Tas), s 4; *Health Act 1958* (Vic), s 132 and *Health (Infectious Diseases) Regulations 2001* (Vic), Reg 18; *Blood Donation (Limitation of Liability) Act 1985* (WA), s 11). Legislation in each jurisdiction also protects donors from liability for the transmission of certain blood-borne diseases resulting from donation in specified circumstances (see further **[17.40]**).

Children

[17.25] Parents or guardians may give their consent in writing to the donation of blood by children, but most jurisdictions require not only that it be for therapeutic or scientific purposes, but that there be medical assurance that the child is unlikely be harmed by the donation, and that the child has also consented (*Transplantation and Anatomy Act 1978* (ACT), 21; *Human Tissue Act 1983* (NSW), ss 20 and 20A; *Transplantation and Anatomy Act 1979* (Qld), s 18; *Transplantation and Anatomy Act 1983* (SA), s 19; *Human Tissue Act 1985* (Tas), s 19; *Human Tissue Act 1982* (Vic), s 22; *Human Tissue and Transplantation Act 1982* (WA), s 19). The *Human Tissue Transplant Act*

(NT) has no express provisions in relation to the issue of children as blood donors.

Blood transfusions

Adults

[17.30] Adults may, of course, agree to the administration of a blood transfusion to themselves. Similarly, an adult may refuse a blood transfusion, even if that refusal puts her or his life in jeopardy. (See *Malette v Shulman* (1991) 2 Med LR 162 (CA Ontario) at **[4.190].**) The law in this respect is the same as that applying to all medical treatment to adults (see Chapter 4).

Children

[17.35] Normally parents, as guardians, can give or refuse consent for medical treatment of their children. However, where parents refuse to allow for emergency or life-saving treatment medical staff can act against their wishes (see above, Chapter 5). Specific legislation in most Australian jurisdictions provides for the giving of a blood transfusion to a child where its life is in danger and parents either cannot be reasonably contacted or refuse the transfusion. This occurs either through provisions permitting blood transfusions specifically, or permitting emergency treatment generally (see *Human Tissue & Transplant Act 1982* (WA), s 21; *Transplantation and Anatomy Act 1979* (Qld) s 20; *Human Tissue Act 1985* (Tas), s 21; *Human Tissue Act 1982* (Vic), s 24; *Transplantation & Anatomy Act 1978* (ACT), s 23; *Emergency Medical Operations Act* (NT), ss 2 and 3; *Consent to Medical Treatment and Palliative Care Act 1995* (SA), s 13). Most Australian jurisdictions provide that a practitioner can only proceed with giving the transfusion when consent is not reasonably obtainable; corroboration of the need is supplied by another doctor; and the transfusion is necessary for the saving of the life of the child and is both necessary and proper.

Blood transfusions and blood-borne disease

[17.40] Most Australian jurisdictions have legislation exempting medical bodies, health workers and donors from liability if someone contracts certain transmittable disease such as Hepatitis B, C, or HIV as a result of a blood transfusion where statutory requirements have been complied with. This immunity does not extend to situations involving negligence or where those collecting or administering the blood had reason to believe that the blood may be contaminated and have not taken all reasonable steps to prevent its administration. All jurisdictions have legislation to this effect except Queensland (*Blood Donation (Transmittable Diseases) Act 1985* (ACT); *Human Tissue Act 1983* (NSW), s 20F and *Human Tissue Regulation 2005* (NSW), Reg 14; *Notifiable Diseases Act* (NT), Part 3A; *Blood Contaminants Act 1985* (SA); *Blood Transfusion (Limitation of Liability) Act 1986* (Tas); *Health Act 1958* (Vic), Part 6 Div 7; *Blood Donation (Limitation of Liability) Act 1985* (WA)).

Testing blood for the purpose of diagnosis involves more than just simply testing blood. Where it is likely that the results may indicate serious disease, especially one like HIV, those who are giving the blood should be counselled as to this possibility, and care should be taken in informing them if the results are positive. Of course those donating blood who have testified to being suitable donors are indicating that they are extremely unlikely to be HIV-positive.

Donation of Tissue by a Living Person

Regenerative tissue

Adults

[17.45] An adult may give written consent to the removal of regenerative tissue from their body for the purpose of transplantation to another person or other therapeutic, scientific or medical purposes. There are, however, provisions in the legislation for all States except South Australia and Western Australia for a further certificate, signed by a medical practitioner other than the surgeon who is to carry out the transplant, stating:

- the terms of consent;
- that the consent was freely given in the presence of the doctor who is signing;
- that proper medical advice and information was given; and
- that the person consenting is an adult of "sound mind".

Where this certificate is provided, the legislation states that it is sufficient authority for a medical practitioner (other than the doctor signing the certificate) to remove the regenerative tissue, as long as he or she is not aware of any revocation of the consent (*Transplantation and Anatomy Act 1978* (ACT), ss 8, 10, 15, 19; *Human Tissue Act 1983* (NSW), ss 7, 9, 12, 15; *Human Tissue Transplant Act* (NT), ss 8, 10, 11, 13; *Transplantation and Anatomy Act 1979* (Qld), ss 10, 12, 13, 15; *Transplantation and Anatomy Act 1983* (SA), ss 9, 15; *Human Tissue Act 1985* (Tas), ss 7, 9, 14, 17; *Human Tissue Act 1982* (Vic), ss 7, 9, 10, 12; *Human Tissue and Transplant Act 1982* (WA), ss 8, 15). South Australia and Western Australia require that family members and friends must be absent when the consent is signed.

Children

[17.50] All jurisdictions except the Northern Territory provide for donation of regenerative tissue from children. This invokes more restrictions than apply to adults. Parents (and in some jurisdictions, guardians) may give consent for a child to donate regenerative tissue but this usually must be in writing with further restrictions. The recipient may be restricted to other members of the family (*Transplantation and Anatomy Act 1978* (ACT), s 13; *Human Tissue Act 1983* (NSW), s 10; *Transplantation and Anatomy Act 1979* (Qld), s 12B; *Human*

Tissue Act 1985 (Tas), s 12; *Human Tissue Act 1982* (Vic), s 15; *Human Tissue and Transplant Act 1982* (WA), s 13).

There are special requirements regarding consent. This must be accompanied by a certificate stating that information was given, consent was obtained from the child as well as the parents, and the child both understood and agreed to the removal of the tissue. In Queensland, consent must be obtained in the presence of a designated officer. In Queensland and Victoria, a child who is incapable, by reason of age, of understanding the procedure may nevertheless be a donor of tissue where the recipient family member is in danger of death. In Queensland, three medical practitioners are required to certify accordingly. In New South Wales, a child who is incapable of giving consent by reason of his or her age may be a donor where additional preconditions are met. Those preconditions require that two medical practitioners certify that the transplantation is to a sibling who is likely to die or suffer serious irreversible damage without the transplant and any risk to the donor is minimal. In South Australia, approval must also be obtained from a three member Ministerial Committee consisting of a judge, a medical practitioner and a social worker or psychologist (*Transplantation and Anatomy Act 1978* (ACT), s 13; *Human Tissue Act 1983* (NSW), ss 11, 11A; *Transplantation and Anatomy Act 1979* (Qld), ss 12C, 12D, 12E *Transplantation and Anatomy Act 1983* (SA), s 13; *Human Tissue Act 1985* (Tas), s 13; *Human Tissue Act 1982* (Vic), s 15; *Human Tissue and Transplant Act 1982* (WA), ss 11, 13.

Figure 17.1: Summary of provisions for consent and use of regenerative tissue from children

Jurisdiction and Act	Parent may consent	Guardian may consent	Tissue for sibling or parent	Tissue for relative
Transplantation and Anatomy Act 1978 (ACT)	Yes	No	Yes	Yes
Human Tissue Act 1983 (NSW)	Yes	No	Yes	No
Human Tissue Transplant Act (NT)	No	No	No	No
Transplantation and Anatomy Act 1979 (Qld)	Yes	No	Yes	No
Transplantation and Anatomy Act 1983 (SA)	Yes	Yes	Yes	Yes
Human Tissue Act 1985 (Tas)	Yes	No	Yes	Yes
Human Tissue and Transplant Act 1982 (WA)	Yes	No	Yes	Yes
Human Tissue Act 1982 (Vic)	Yes	No	Yes	No

Non-regenerative tissue

Adults

[17.55] Non-regenerative tissue can be taken from an adult under the same conditions as for regenerative tissue, with the added requirement that the removal occur no less than 24 hours after consent is given, to provide a cooling-off period. The tissue may be removed only for transplantation into another living person (*Transplantation and Anatomy Act 1978* (ACT), ss 9, 10, 16, 19; *Human Tissue Act 1983* (NSW), ss 8, 9, 13, 15; *Human Tissue Transplant Act* (NT), ss 9, 10, 12, 13; *Transplantation and Anatomy Act 1979* (Qld), ss 11, 12, 14, 15; *Transplantation and Anatomy Act 1983* (SA), ss 10, 16; *Human Tissue Act 1985* (Tas), ss 8, 9, 15, 17; *Human Tissue Act 1982* (Vic), ss 8, 9, 11, 12; *Human Tissue and Transplant Act 1982* (WA), ss 9, 16). At the time of writing, the Western Australian Parliament had approved amendments to the *Human Tissue and Transplant Act 1982* (WA) which would bring Western Australia into conformity with the rest of Australia by removing restrictions on paired kidney exchanges, a process whereby donors with incompatible recipients swap places to allow for compatible transplants.

Children

[17.60] Donation of non-regenerative tissue by children is specifically banned in South Australia, Victoria and Western Australia (*Transplantation and Anatomy Act 1983* (SA), s 12; *Human Tissue Act 1982* (Vic), s 14; *Human Tissue and Transplant Act 1982* (WA), s 12). In other jurisdictions it is impliedly prohibited. In the Australian Capital Territory similar certification to that prescribed for removal of regenerative tissue from children is required. The tissue to be removed must be for use in transplantation to another family member. Along with the consent of the child, consent of both parents of the child is sought, where that is possible. The matter is then referred to a Ministerial Committee comprising a judge, medical practitioner and social worker or psychologist for authorisation (*Transplantation and Anatomy Act 1978* (ACT), s 14).

Person other than operating surgeon must take consent

[17.65] To prevent vested interests in securing consent, the person who gives information about transplantation of tissue must not be the person or persons who removes the tissue. Consent permits a third party to carry out the operation (*Transplantation and Anatomy Act 1978* (ACT), ss 15-18; *Human Tissue Act 1983* (NSW), ss 12-14; *Human Tissue Transplant Act* (NT), ss 11, 12; *Transplantation and Anatomy Act 1979* (Qld), ss 13-14A; *Transplantation and Anatomy Act 1983* (SA), ss 15-17; *Human Tissue Act 1985* (Tas), ss 14-16; *Human Tissue Act 1982* (Vic), ss 10, 11, 16; *Human Tissue and Transplant Act 1982* (WA), ss 15-17).

Revocation of consent

[17.70] All donors may revoke their consent at any time, which is reinforced by legislation in most jurisdictions, and this revocation is absolute in its effect (*Transplantation and Anatomy Act 1978* (ACT), ss 24, 25; *Human Tissue Act 1983* (NSW), s 16, 17; *Human Tissue Transplant Act* (NT), s 16; *Transplantation and Anatomy Act 1979* (Qld), s 21; *Transplantation and Anatomy Act 1983* (SA), s 14 (in relation to children only); *Human Tissue Act 1985* (Tas), s 22; *Human Tissue Act 1982* (Vic), ss 18, 19; *Human Tissue and Transplant Act 1982* (WA), s 14 (in relation to children only). In some jurisdictions the law specifically requires that health care workers to whom the donor indicated her or his revocation must inform the designated officer or equivalent, who is authorised under the legislation, for example, a senior administrative medical practitioner in a hospital, who must then inform the operating surgeon (*Human Tissue Act 1983* (NSW), s 16; *Human Tissue Transplant Act* (NT), s 16; *Transplantation and Anatomy Act 1979* (Qld), s 21; *Human Tissue Act 1982* (Vic), ss 18, 19; *Transplantation and Anatomy Act 1978* (ACT), s 25 (for children only); *Human Tissue Act 1985* (Tas), s 22). It has already been stated at **[4.75]**, that revocation of consent to any treatment may take place at any time, and is absolute, so it would seem a legally sound argument that a carer who is aware of a patient revoking consent to any treatment should promptly inform those who propose to carry it out. Except in South Australia and Western Australia, where a designated officer becomes aware of a revocation of consent, he or she must determine if any person is intending to rely on the consent, and inform them of the revocation. He or she must also return the certificate of consent to the person who made it. Those who are caring for donors should know who the designated officer is.

Donation of Tissue after Death

[17.75] Perhaps one of the most challenging situations for medical staff is to deal with the family of those who have died suddenly and violently and who are on artificial respiration to preserve tissues for donation. To their family, these people may seem to be alive. The important thing for all to remember is that a person must be legally dead before any action can be taken to remove tissue from that person. The family may be consulted, and consent gained prior to death, however, this should not affect the treatment of the patient.

Definition of "death"

[17.80] All jurisdictions except Western Australia and South Australia have a statutory definition of "death", which states that it involves irreversible cessation of all brain function, or irreversible cessation of blood circulation (*Transplantation and Anatomy Act 1978* (ACT), s 45; *Human Tissue Act 1983* (NSW), s 33; *Human Tissue Transplant Act* (NT), s 23; *Transplantation and Anatomy Act 1979* (Qld), s 45; *Human Tissue Act 1985* (Tas), s 27A; *Human*

Tissue Act 1982 (Vic), s 41). Western Australia and South Australia provide that where respiration and circulation are being maintained by artificial means tissue shall not be removed unless two doctors have certified to irreversible cessation of all brain function (*Human Tissue and Transplant Act 1982* (WA), s 24(2); *Transplantation and Anatomy Act 1983* (SA), s 24(2). In all jurisdictions except Queensland the definition of "death" applies for all purposes. Queensland's definition is restricted to removal of tissue for purposes of the *Transplantation and Anatomy Act 1979* (Qld).

Most jurisdictions require that where a prospective donor is on life support there are certain requirements regarding both the number and seniority of the medical personnel who declare the person dead, and the specific certification that is required of them as to the cessation of circulation or brain function (*Transplantation and Anatomy Act 1978* (ACT), s 30; *Human Tissue Act 1983* (NSW), s 26; *Human Tissue Transplant Act* (NT), s 21; *Transplantation and Anatomy Act 1979* (Qld), s 45; *Human Tissue Act 1985* (Tas), s 25A).

Consent for donation of tissue

[17.85] Where the deceased died at a hospital, or where the person is on life support, the medical or designated officer authorised under the legislation may inquire whether the person has specifically expressed their consent to the use of any organ after death, and there has been no change of mind. Some jurisdictions require that consent be in writing, others that, if oral, it be before witnesses. Such consent is considered to be conclusive at law. Where the person has expressed unwillingness to donate, that too is conclusive. The difficult situation is where no opinion either way has been expressed. The next of kin may be asked for their consent or otherwise to the removal of tissue.

For the purposes of the legislation, with minor variations, "senior available next of kin" are defined in a list in hierarchical order, so that where permission is required from next of kin, those in the category closest to the patient should be sought. The categories are generally in the following order:

For a deceased child:
- parent;
- brother or sister 18 years of age or older;
- person who was a guardian of a deceased child immediately before death.

For a deceased adult:
- current spouse;
- son or daughter 18 or over;
- parent;
- brother or sister 18 or over.

(See *Transplantation and Anatomy Act 1978* (ACT), s 4; *Human Tissue Act 1983* (NSW), s 4; *Human Tissue Transplant Act* (NT), s 4; *Transplantation and Anatomy Act 1979* (Qld), s 4; *Transplantation and Anatomy Act 1983* (SA), s 5; *Human Tissue Act 1985* (Tas), s 3; *Human Tissue Act 1982* (Vic), s 3; *Human Tissue and Transplantation Act 1982* (WA), s 3).

The law requires that where the wishes of the deceased are not known, permission be sought from the senior available next of kin where practicable, seniority being established according to the above list. Withdrawal of consent by the relevant relative must be honoured, and the law may also provide that where there are two or more senior next of kin an objection by one of those persons shall be effective. (See *Transplantation and Anatomy Act 1978* (ACT), s 27; *Human Tissue Act 1983* (NSW), s 23; *Human Tissue Transplant Act* (NT), s 18; *Transplantation and Anatomy Act 1979* (Qld), s 22; *Transplantation and Anatomy Act 1983* (SA), s 21; *Human Tissue Act 1985* (Tas), s 23; *Human Tissue Act 1982* (Vic), s 26; *Human Tissue and Transplantation Act 1982* (WA), s 22.) This places the duty on health carers to report withdrawal of consent by the next of kin, and in this situation such report would obviously have to be rapid and unequivocal.

Where there is no indication of the person's wishes and there is no available eligible next of kin, the designated office may give permission for the transplant, except for New South Wales, Queensland Tasmania and Western Australia which are silent on this point (*Transplantation and Anatomy Act 1978* (ACT), s 27(3); *Human Tissue Transplant Act* (NT), s 18(3); *Transplantation and Anatomy Act 1983* (SA), s 21(3); *Human Tissue Act 1982* (Vic), s 26(1)).

Before considering removal of tissue from a deceased person, one must first rule out any situation where the coroner will have jurisdiction over the body (as established in Chapter 15). Even where this is the case, the coroner may, if satisfied it will not prejudice the coronial inquiry, permit removal of tissue from the body, and may stipulate conditions under which the removal is to take place (*Transplantation and Anatomy Act 1978* (ACT), s 29; *Human Tissue Act 1983* (NSW), s 25; *Human Tissue Transplant Act* (NT), s 20; *Transplantation and Anatomy Act 1979* (Qld), s 24; *Transplantation and Anatomy Act 1983* (SA), s 23; *Human Tissue Act 1985* (Tas), s 25; *Human Tissue Act 1982* (Vic), s 27; *Human Tissue and Transplantation Act 1982* (WA), s 22).

Postmortems and anatomical examinations

[17.90] In most jurisdictions consent for the postmortem examination of a body, or its use for scientific or teaching purposes, is subject to similar requirements to those outlined above for the donation of tissue after death. This means that a postmortem may be carried out, other than at the direction of a coroner:

- where the deceased expressed a wish or consent;
- where no wish or consent was expressed and senior next of kin consents; or
- where no wish or consent has been expressed and senior next of kin have not disagreed or their wishes are unable to be ascertained.

(See *Transplantation and Anatomy Act 1978* (ACT), s 32; *Human Tissue Act 1983* (NSW), s 28; *Transplantation and Anatomy Act 1979* (Qld), s 26; *Transplantation and Anatomy Act 1983* (SA), s 25; *Human Tissue Act 1982* (Vic), s 28; *Human Tissue and Transplant Act 1982* (WA), s 25.)

It is the responsibility of the designated officer of the health facility involved to establish the situation in each case.

Assisted Conception and Reproductive Technology

[17.95] Despite the fact that assisted conception and reproductive technology raises many very difficult social and legal questions which touch on such issues as the conceptualisation of the body as property, motherhood, parenthood and the less fundamental questions of succession and inheritance (for example, Bates and Turner (1985), especially pp 451ff) legislation affecting assisted conception and reproductive technology exists only in South Australia, Victoria and Western Australia (*Reproductive Technology (Clinical Practices) Act 1988* (SA); *Infertility Treatment Act 1995* (Vic); *Human Reproductive Technology Act 1991* (WA)). There are, however, many Commonwealth and State reports which make ethical and legal recommendations. Where there is no law, various ethical guidelines form the basis of medical practice. The main ethical statement is that of the National Health and Medical Research Council (see **[17.130]**).

The term "assisted conception" is here used to include the various means of transplanting material from one person to another for the purposes of bearing a child. It is included in this chapter because it is a form of transplantation.

For the purposes of this discussion the approach to classification of procedures reflects that used by the New South Wales Law Reform Commission, *Report on Artificial Conception-In Vitro Fertilisation*, Report No 58 (NSW Government Printer, 1988). This report described conception as the fertilisation of an ovum by a sperm. This would differentiate some procedures to which modern technology is applied and, strictly speaking, bring about fertilisation itself (including artificial insemination and in vitro fertilisation) from those through which an already fertilised egg is transferred into another woman for the duration of the pregnancy. Procedures such as ZIFT (zygote intra fallopian transfer), PROST (pro-nuclear stage ovum transfer), TET (tubal embryo transfer), are included in the report's definition of in vitro fertilisation. Other procedures which have been developed, including the direct fertilisation of an egg by injection of sperm, would also be covered by the legislation.

Who are the parents?

[17.100] All jurisdictions, including the Commonwealth, have established quite clearly that where a woman gives birth to a child as the result of assisted conception the child is the child of that woman and her spouse (including de facto husband), if he has given his consent to the procedure. Conversely, the law states that a person donating gametes has no legal connection whatsoever with any resulting child. This means that where the spouse does not consent to the procedure, or there is no spouse, the genetic father does not become the legal father of the child: there is, it seems, a gap created in the parental relationships of the child (that is, there is an automatic assignment of maternity but there is no system for automatic assignment of paternity). (See *Family Law Act 1975* (Cth), s 60H; *Parentage Act 2004* (ACT), s 11; *Status of Children Act 1996* (NSW), s 14; *Status of Children Act* (NT), ss 5D, 5E and 5F; *Status of Children Act*

1978 (Qld), ss 15-18; *Family Relationships* Act *1975* (SA), s 10c-10e; *Status of Children Act 1974* (Tas), s 10C; *Status of Children Act 1974* (Vic), ss 10C-10F; *Artificial Conception Act 1985* (WA), ss 5, 6, 7.

The result of the legislation is that a donor of gametes has no legal claim whatsoever on a child born as the result of an assisted conception procedure, and the child also has no right to the parentage of that person. This applies even where donors are known.

Artificial insemination

[17.105] Artificial insemination, or implantation of seminal fluid into the vagina or uterus through means other than natural physical copulation has been used for many years as a means of promoting conception where the sexual act is not desired. This is not illegal, although some jurisdictions require licensing of those carrying out the procedure. One growing concern of the state is for more accurate recording of genetic origins of children, as a result of the recognition of:

- the psychological need for such information on the part of those born as a result of assisted conception procedures; and
- the need for proper medical histories, where these may have significant effects for children.

Common law

[17.110] Artificial insemination can be legally carried out by any person. At common law there is a presumption that a woman giving birth to a child is its mother, because no other possibility was considered. There is also a presumption that if that woman was married at the time of conception, her husband is the father. This presumption is rebuttable, however, where paternity is known to be otherwise. The common law presumption has been supplanted by legislation (see **[17.100]**).

Legislation

[17.115] The only jurisdictions to have legislated regarding artificial insemination are Victoria, South Australia and Western Australia.

In South Australia, under the *Reproductive Technology (Clinical Practices) Act 1988* (SA), a licence is not required in respect of artificial insemination if it is carried out by a medical practitioner who has submitted his or her name for registration with the Minister and has made an undertaking to observe the code of ethical practice.

In Victoria, s 7 of the *Infertility Treatment Act 1995* (Vic) specifically identifies the process of donor insemination, that is, artificial insemination of a woman using sperm from a man who is not her husband. Such a procedure must be carried out only:

- at a hospital or licensed centre by, or under the supervision of, a doctor approved by the Infertility Treatment Authority, and the requirements of the *Infertility Treatment Act* have been followed; or

- elsewhere, by a doctor approved by the Infertility Treatment Authority, and the requirements of the *Infertility Treatment Act* have been followed.

In Western Australia the *Human Reproductive Technology Act 1991* (WA) provides that a licence from the Commissioner of Health on the advice of the Reproductive Technology Council is required to carry out artificial insemination, unless the person is a medical practitioner to whom an exemption has been granted, and who has agreed in writing to comply with the Code of Practice which has been established by the Council.

Elsewhere, it seems that the practice is self-regulated or unregulated. This is of some concern with regard to:

- records of genetic origin;
- maintenance of medical history;
- control of the spread of disease;
- liability for negligent practice; and
- issues of consent.

Consequently there have been recommendations from some Australian jurisdictions that artificial insemination should be regulated, at least when it is not a private act, and not a regular part of one's practice. The New South Wales Law Reform Commission, for example, draws a distinction between artificial insemination as a practice and as an act (New South Wales Law Reform Commission, *Human Artificial Insemination*, Report No 49 (NSW Government Printer, Sydney, 1986); available online at www.lawlink.nsw.gov.au/lrc.nsf/pages/R49TOC). It recommends that the former, defined as carrying out the procedure for a fee or reward, or advertising or holding oneself out as being prepared to carry out the procedure, should be performed by or under the supervision of a medical practitioner. The latter, according to the Commission (p 26), is a private act, and one which should not be regulated:

> "neither the law nor parliament should presume to regulate the private sexual behaviour of mature, competent persons ... the principles of personal freedom and autonomy should apply so far as possible, and that if a woman chooses or a man and woman choose, to achieve pregnancy by artificial insemination that is no concern of the State."

In those jurisdictions where there is no legislation regarding artificial insemination, it is generally carried out as a practice in fertility clinics where sperm is screened and ethical codes of practice followed. However, no qualifications or specific conditions are legally required. Health professionals carrying out the procedure elsewhere should consider the potential legal implications of doing so. As with any other medical procedure, a duty of care is owed to the woman who is the subject of artificial insemination. As well as the responsibility not to harm her through general medical procedures, there is a duty to her to ensure all reasonable measures are taken to prevent infection by sexually transmitted disease and AIDS; and to prevent harm to the future child.

Cloning

[17.120] One area of reproductive technology in which the Commonwealth has legislated is in relation to cloning with the introduction of the *Prohibition of Human Cloning Act 2002* (Cth). Through COAG, each of the States has since enacted complementary legislation (*Research Involving Human Embryos and Prohibition of Human Cloning Act 2003* (Qld); *Human Cloning and Embryo Research Act 2004* (ACT); *Human Cloning and Other Prohibited Practices Act 2003* (NSW); *Human Cloning and Other Prohibited Practices Act 2003* (Tas); *Prohibition of Human Cloning Act 2003* (SA); *Infertility Treatment Act 1995* (Vic), Part 4a, Div 1; *Human Reproductive Technology Act 1991* (WA), s 7). Kerridge (at p 443) suggests that the prohibition approach taken in Australia is consistent with the view of the international community; however the United Nations has failed to pass a treaty regarding human cloning. In 2005, however, the United Nations General Assembly did adopt a Declaration on Human Cloning, by which Member States were called on to adopt all measures necessary to prohibit all forms of human cloning inasmuch as they are incompatible with human dignity and the protection of human life (see United Nations Fifty-Ninth General Assembly Plenary 82nd Meeting (AM)).

Other reproductive technology procedures

[17.125] Clinics carrying out reproductive technology procedures in jurisdictions other than South Australia, Victoria and Western Australia are subject to the general law. There are also requirements for accreditation by the federal government (see **[17.130]**).

Despite the inference in legislation and ethical guidelines that only some reproductive technology consists of experimentation or research, some commentators argue that the proceedings involved are all experimental, and the effects of treatments are recognised as being neither entirely predictable nor safe (Scutt (1990), p 189). For this reason health carers should take particular care to ensure that clients are adequately informed of the nature and risks, and of the sometimes low success rate of the technology. Indeed Victoria provides an extensive list of matters to be discussed with clients of infertility clinics by counsellors, such as the risks involved, the role and responsibility of the doctor, side effects and alternative treatments.

Regulating bodies

[17.130] In Victoria, the *Infertility Treatment Act 1995* (Vic) creates the Infertility Treatment Authority, a body that administers the Act by such means as issuing licences, approving facilities, administering the keeping of records and access to them, monitoring compliance with licences, administering the storage of gametes and embryos and promoting research. The Victorian Civil and Administrative Tribunal may review licensing decisions.

In South Australia, the *Reproductive Technology Act 1988* (SA) establishes the South Australian Council on Reproductive Technology, and in Western Australia, the *Human Reproductive Technology Act 1991* (WA) establishes the Western

Australian Reproductive Technology Council. These have such functions as advising the Minister on matters relating to reproductive technology, including conditions for licences, developing a code of practice, promoting research on the causes of infertility, and the social implications of reproductive technology. They promote debate on reproductive technology and collaborate with similar bodies. The Western Australian Council also has a monitoring role.

In other Australian jurisdictions fertility clinics are guided by the *Ethical Guidelines on the Use of Assisted Reproductive Technology in Clinical Practice and Research* 2004, issued by the National Health and Medical Research Council of Australia (NHMRC). The guidelines require that facilities offering reproductive technology be accredited by a recognised accreditation body. This is currently the Reproductive Technology Accreditation Committee established in 1987 by the Fertility Society of Australia (see www.fsa.au.com/), the peak body representing scientists, doctors, researchers, nurses, consumer groups, patients and counsellors in reproductive medicine in Australia and New Zealand. The Fertility Society of Australia has also developed a Code of Practice to set and maintain minimum standards for clinics or centres offering assisted reproductive technology, and to encourage continuous improvement in the quality of care offered to people accessing fertility treatment in Australia and New Zealand. Research must be approved by a Human Research Ethics Committee (HREC) established by the facility (or the Committee of another facility) in conformance with NHMRC requirements (*Statement on Human Experimentation and Supplementary Notes*). Innovations and major changes in treatment procedures require approval of a HREC.

Other requirements under the NHMRC Guidelines are:

- clinics must respect the privacy of participants and confidentiality of all records (see also Chapter 7 regarding privacy);
- donated gametes are not to be used unless the donor has consented to release of identifying information about him/herself to any children conceived using those gametes
- do not select sex of embryos for nonmedical purposes;
- ensure careful evaluation of any use of pre-implantation genetic diagnosis;
- do not undertake or facilitate commercial surrogacy;
- limit the number of embryos created to that number likely to be required by the participants in the course of their treatment;
- have clear policies that limit the duration of storage, as it is not desirable to leave gametes or embryos in storage indefinitely; and
- cloning of humans is unacceptable.

State and federal policy, as well as hospital or clinic policy, may also inform practice in those jurisdictions lacking specific legislation.

Regulation of procedures

[17.135] In Victoria, a fertilisation procedure, storage of reproductive material, or research involving gametes or embryos, must not be carried out except in accordance with the *Infertility Treatment Act 1995*.

Certain procedures are prohibited under Part 4A of the Victorian Act. These include:

- intentional hereditable alteration of the genome of a human cell;
- creating a human embryo for a purpose other than achieving pregnancy in a woman;
- cloning of human embryos;
- creating or developing a human embryo containing genetic material of more than two persons;
- developing a human embryo outside the body of a woman for more than 14 days;
- creating a chimeric or hybrid embryo;
- commercial trading in human eggs, sperm or embryos;
- placing the embryo of a human in an animal and vice versa;
- procedures aimed at selecting the sex of a child;
- procedures involving the gametes of people known to be dead;
- research on an embryo that is fit to transfer to a woman where:
  - the embryo would be damaged;
  - the likelihood of pregnancy resulting from the transfer of the embryo to a woman would be reduced;
  - the embryo was not formed for use in a treatment procedure and each person who produced a gamete which formed the embryo has not given consent;
  - the spouse of the donor has not consented; or
  - the couple have not received counselling, including counselling as required by the legislation.

Doctors, scientists and counsellors, as well as hospitals and research institutions must be approved by the Infertility Treatment Authority, a statutory body established by the Victorian Parliament to administer the regulation of infertility treatment (see www.ita.org.au/default.asp?siteaction=home). There is a detailed list of matters to be discussed by counsellors in the *Infertility Treatment Regulations 1997*.

The Act has separate provisions for procedures involving no donor, a sperm donor, an egg donor or both, and limits their practice to specific situations, where the above requirements are also satisfied. Detailed requirements as to by whom and how consent must be given are set out (for example, both the donor and the donor's spouse must provide consent to the donation of gametes and to the particular purpose of the donation).

There are further conditions placed on the use of more than one egg, and the control and disposition of gametes and embryos.

In South Australia, s 13 of the *Reproductive Technology (Clinical Practices) Act 1988* (SA) provides that a person must not carry out an artificial fertilisation procedure except in pursuance of a licence. The Minister must not grant a licence unless satisfied that the:

i. licence is necessary to fill a genuine and substantial social need that cannot be adequately met by existing licensees;

ii. applicant is a fit and proper person to hold a licence; and

iii. applicant has the appropriate staff and facilities for carrying out the procedures for which the licence is sought.

The Minister can authorise officers to inspect and monitor compliance with the Act. Procedures must be carried out in accordance with licence conditions and the codes of practice established under the Act. The code of ethical practice is set out in Schedule 3 of the *Reproductive Technology (Code of Ethical Clinical Practice) 1995* (SA). Part 2 of the Regulations lists prohibited practices including:

- culturing or maintaining an embryo outside a body;
- transfering more than three embryos or ova per cycle;
- mixing gametes or embryos from different sources;
- the use of gametes in certain cases, for example, where they are of close family members;
- implantation of embryos that have been used for research unless there is reasonable expectation of normal development; and
- the mixing of reproductive material from different sources.

In Western Australia, the *Human Reproductive Technology Act 1991* (WA) provides two types of licence can been issued by the Commissioner for Health: a practice licence and a storage licence (s 27). There are penalties for carrying out procedures in breach of a licence. Section 7 of the Act prohibits:

- unapproved research or diagnostic procedures;
- human cloning;
- embryo flushing or the production of a chimera;
- the replacement of the nucleus of a cell of an egg in the process of fertilisation or any embryo;
- placement of a human embryo in the body of an animal, or animal embryo in the body of a woman; and
- payment for supplying reproductive material.

Eligibility for treatment

[17.140] The legislation in South Australia, Victoria and Western Australia requires that to be eligible for treatment, a couple must be married or living in a de facto relationship, one or both must be infertile or there must appear to be a risk that a genetic defect would be transmitted to a child conceived naturally. The Western Australian legislation provides for single women to access treatment, however she would still need to be able to meet the medical infertility criteria (*Reproductive Technology Act (Clinical Practices) Act 1998* (SA), s 13(3)(b) and *Reproductive Technology (Code of Ethical Clinical Practice) 1995* (SA), Pt 3; *Infertility Treatment Act 1995* (Vic), s 8; *Human Reproductive Technology Act 1991* (WA), s 23).

The legislation has been challenged in South Australia as discriminating on the grounds of marital status under the *Sex Discrimination Act 1984* (Cth). Section 109 of the Australian Constitution provides that a provision of a

Commonwealth Act overrides a conflicting State provision. The court held that the requirement that the woman be married is indeed contrary to the *Sex Discrimination Act*, and is thus invalid (*Pearce v South Australian Health Commission* (1996) 66 SASR 486; see also Stuhmcke (1996)).

In Victoria, the *Infertility Treatment Act 1995* (Vic) provides, in s 8, that eligibility for infertility treatment is to be limited to women who are married or living in a de facto relationship. This provision was challenged in the Federal Court in *McBain v Victoria* (2000) 99 FCR 116. The court ruled that s 8 is inconsistent with the *Sex Discrimination Act 1984* (Cth), as it is discriminatory on the basis of marital status. The Australian Catholic Bishops Conference (who had appeared as amicus curiae) sought to challenge the decision in the High Court, however the High Court unanimously dismissed the application. Section 8(1) of the Act thus appears to be inoperative to the extent that it restricts the application of any treatment procedure to a woman who satisfies the marriage requirement. This has thrown some uncertainty on the law, as there are provisions in the Act that apply to the woman's husband. It would seem, however, that an unmarried woman who fulfils the requirement of infertility set out in the Act is not barred from treatment.

Access to infertility treatment to a woman who was living in a stable lesbian relationship was denied by a Queensland infertility clinic (*QFG & Anor v JM* (1997) EOC ¶92-902). In that case it was held that the clinic (which specialised in infertility) had not unlawfully discriminated against her, because the reason for refusing the treatment was that she did not fulfil the requirements of infertility applied to all applicants: that is, the inability, after 12 months of heterosexual intercourse, to fail to become pregnant. That decision was appealed to the Queensland Supreme Court and the Queensland Court of Appeal. After the Court of Appeal remitted the case to the Anti-Discrimination Tribunal, the clinic's refusal of treatment was allowed. The result in QFG is actually confirmed by later amendments, which allow IVF clinics to discriminate on the ground of sexuality and marital status. (See *QFG & GK v JM* [1997] QSC 206; *JM v QFG & GK* [1998] QCA 228. Leave to appeal to the High Court was refused: *JM V GK* B34/1998. See also Mortensen, QUT Law & Justice Journal.)

This raises the issue of what should be considered infertility in Australia. Legislation providing for assisted reproductive technology in South Australia, Victoria, and Western Australia, and accrediting bodies in some other jurisdictions (except, for example New South Wales) envisage it as meaning that between them, a couple cannot, through heterosexual activity, produce a child. If one is considering a woman alone, whether she engages in heterosexual activity or not, the "cause" of not being able to produce a child may be social rather than physical: she does not wish to engage in heterosexual activity for the purpose. This has been called "social infertility" making the question of infertility more than a simple question of physical condition.

Interestingly, legislation in both the Northern Territory and Western Australia provides that where a woman who is in a de facto relationship with another woman undergoes, with the consent of her de facto partner, an artificial fertilisation procedure as a consequence of which she becomes pregnant, then the de facto partner will be presumed to be a parent of the child born as a result (*Status of Children Act* (NT), s 5DA; *Artificial Conception Act 1985* (WA), s 6A).

Storage and use of gametes, zygotes and embryos

[17.145] In South Australia, there is no set time limit for storage of embryos. A person on whose behalf an embryo is stored has the right to review the storage every 12 months. Reproductive material is to be destroyed if consent for storage or use is revoked (*Reproductive Technology (Code of Ethical Clinical Practice) 1995* (SA), Pt 4 Div 3).

In Victoria, reproductive material must not be stored without the consent of the donor. Gametes may be stored for ten years and embryos for five years, or longer if the Authority approves. Embryos must not be removed from storage unless for use in a treatment procedure or approved research, or a donor has died, or consent to removal has been given in writing by both the persons who produced the gamete, or under authority of the Act (*Infertility Treatment Act 1995* (Vic), ss 51-55; *Infertility Treatment Regulations 1997* (Vic), reg 12).

In Western Australia, the time limit for storage is set by the Western Australian Reproductive Technology Council, and is generally ten years. The consent of those donating the material is essential, and all rights remain vested in the gamete donors. The right to decide on disposition of an embryo vests jointly in the couple producing it, and if one of them dies, in the remaining donor. In the case of a dispute between them, if one of them applies to the Commissioner of Health, he or she may direct the licensee to maintain storage (*Human Reproductive Technology Act 1991* (WA), ss 24-26).

The NHMRC *Ethical Guidelines for Clinical Practice of Assisted Reproductive Technology* 2004 contain provisions relating to the storage of gametes and embryos at Part 8. The guidelines include the following:

- Limit the duration of storage of gametes and embryos;
- Ensure the safety and identity of gametes and embryos;
- Explain options for use and disposal of stored gametes and embryos;
- Do not store gametes from deceased or dying persons or those in a postcoma unresponsive state;
- Dispose of embryos respectfully;
- Where the persons contributing to an embryo disagree as to whether or not to continue storage of an embryo, the embryo should be kept in storage until the dispute is resolved.

Records

[17.150] Another important issue regulated by the legislation is the keeping of records and the releasing (or confidentiality) of records. In Victoria, the legislation requires full records are to be kept of:

- all parties involved in assisted reproductive technology (ART) procedures;
- donors of gametes and origins of embryos;
- destruction of gametes, zygotes and embryos;

- all ART procedures carried out;
- consent and withdrawal of consent to storage and removal from storage of embryos;
- confirmed pregnancies resulting from a treatment procedure;
- all persons born as a result of treatment procedures including details of any physical abnormalities evident at birth;
- any treatment of a woman and her partner if relevant, and the outcome of treatment; and
- transfer of material to or from a centre.

(See *Infertility Treatment Act 1995* (Vic), ss 62-70; *Infertility Treatment Regulations 1997* (Vic), regs 13-18, Schs 1 and 2.)

The Act has detailed requirements in relation to the giving of information to donors (including who will receive the material and whether a pregnancy has resulted from the donation) and recipients of reproductive material (in relation to the donor). Identifying information may only be given with the consent of a person who stands to be identified (see *Infertility Treatment Act 1995* (Vic), ss 71-73.) Information may be given to a person born as a result of a fertilisation procedure about his or her parents under certain circumstances, with identifying information requiring the consent of anyone who stands to be identified. Extensive provision is made for counselling and confidentiality in relation to the strictly regulated giving of identifying information. See *Infertility Treatment Act 1995* (Vic), ss 74-82) *Infertility Treatment Regulations 1997* (Vic), Sch 3).

In South Australia, Part 5 of the *Reproductive Technology (Code of Ethical Clinical Practice) Regulations 1995* (SA) comprises record keeping and access to information. Similar detailed records to those required in Victoria are to be kept, including:

- records relating to the assessment of a donor's personality;
- collection, storage, use and disposal of reproductive material;
- clinical standards and procedures used by the licensee; and
- criteria for determining the suitability of use of research embryos in treatment.

Donors and those receiving treatment may have access to their records. Persons over 16 years of age, born as the result of a treatment, may have access to non-identifying information.

In Western Australia, details of records to be kept are set out in ss 44-50 of the *Human Reproductive Technology Act 1991* (WA). Details similar to those in other jurisdictions are to be kept, including the reasons why each participant was considered eligible for treatment. Records are to be available to the Commissioner for Health. Access to personal information is available to the person him or herself, and identifying information is protected, and only to be made available with the consent of the person to be identified

The NHMRC *Ethical Guidelines for Clinical Practice of Assisted Reproductive Technology* 2004 contain provisions relating to record keeping at Part 10. The guidelines include the following:

- Maintain integrity and privacy of personal information;
- Record details of participants, treatment procedures and outcomes; and
- Keep records of the number of people born using gametes or embryos provided by the same person, including the sex of the child and the number of families to which they have been born.

Research involving human embryos

[17.155] One area of concern surrounding ART that has received much attention from the media in recent years is the use of excess ART embryos in research. In recognition of these concerns, and the public concern over the use of embryos in research generally, the Federal government enacted the *Research Involving Human Embryos Act 2002*. The object of the Act is stated as being to "address concerns, including ethical concerns, about scientific developments in relation to human reproduction and the utilisation of human embryos by regulating activities that involve the use of certain human embryos created by assisted reproductive technology". The majority of Australian jurisdictions have since followed with like legislation (*Human Cloning and Embryo Research Act 2004* (ACT); *Research Involving Human Embryos (New South Wales) Act 2003*; *Research Involving Human Embryos and Prohibition of Cloning Act 2003* (Qld); *Research Involving Human Embryos Act 2003* (SA); *Human Embryonic Research Regulation Act 2003* (Tas); *Health Legislation (Research Involving Human Embryos and Prohibition of Human Cloning) Act 2003* (Vic)).

Surrogacy Agreements

[17.160] Whilst surrogacy agreements do not require medical technology to be carried out, they are included here because they are a form of assisted reproduction, and often do involve medical technology, either in the form of artificial insemination or in vitro fertilisation. In fact, the critical legal aspects of surrogacy agreements are:

- the agreement itself, which in some circumstances may be an offence (see **[9.290]**; and
- the changing of the legal parentage of the child.

Policy

[17.165] In 1991 Australian Health and Welfare Ministers produced a policy in relation to surrogacy agreements (see discussion paper, Australian Capital Territory Attorney-General's Department (1993)). The policy holds that:

- surrogacy should be discouraged;
- any surrogacy agreement should be unenforceable, thus totally ineffective, in law (although it need not be an offence);
- commercial surrogacy (that is, surrogacy involving payment except for necessary expenses) should be an offence; and
- advertising, procuring and paying for surrogacy should be illegal.

The policy envisaged uniform legislation across all Australian jurisdictions, however, no such legislation has emerged. Most Australian jurisdictions have issued reports declaring that these agreements are against public policy, and thus should at least be discouraged. (For a list of such reports see **[9.270]**.)

Legislation

[17.170] In Victoria the *Infertility Treatment Act 1995* (Vic) renders all surrogacy agreements void, makes commercial surrogacy (that is, surrogacy involving payment except for necessary expenses) illegal, and prohibits any publication:

- to the effect that a person is willing to enter into a surrogacy agreement;
- that advertises for someone to act as a surrogate mother;
- to the effect that a person is willing to arrange a surrogacy agreement;
- that facilitates a surrogacy agreement for money; or
- to the effect that a person acts or agrees to act as a surrogate mother for money (s 60).

In South Australia the *Family Relationships Act Amendment Act 1988* (SA) declares that all surrogacy agreements are illegal and void. Facilitating or entering surrogacy agreements for money is an offence, as is any publication that:

- advertises a person's willingness to enter into a surrogacy agreement;
- seeks such a person; and
- advertises a person's willingness to facilitate a surrogacy agreement.

Queensland passed the *Surrogate Parenthood Act* in 1988 (Qld). It is similar to those described above. However, it also simply prohibits entering into any surrogacy agreement, commercial or otherwise. It is thus the only State that makes a surrogacy agreement illegal per se.

In Tasmania, the *Surrogacy Contracts Act 1993* (Tas) makes surrogacy contracts void and unenforceable, and commercial surrogacy is an offence. Those:

- attempting to arrange surrogacy contracts (whether commercial or non-commercial) on behalf of others;
- offering or giving technical or professional services to achieve a pregnancy for the purposes of surrogacy; or
- advertising in relation to surrogacy,

are guilty of an offence.

Western Australia has no legislation specifically dealing with surrogacy agreements, however, it has produced reports which deal with surrogacy. The Select Committee Report (1999) on the *Human Reproductive Technology Act 1991* (WA) recommended that some non-commercial surrogacy arrangements be allowed.

In the Australian Capital Territory the *Parentage Act 2004* (ACT), Part 4, prohibits commercial substitute parent agreements. Other offences under the

Act include procuring someone to enter into a substitute parent agreement with a third party and advertising in relation to substitute parent agreements.

Other jurisdictions

[17.175] There are no prohibitions on surrogacy in other jurisdictions. However, where there is a dispute between birth and substitute parents (for example where the birth parents refuse to hand over the child) agreements are likely to be considered unenforceable as being against public policy. The birth parents would remain the legal parents for the purposes of the law, with the birth certificate in their name. A dispute as to who should have the child would be a matter for the Family Court, which would make a parenting order under the *Family Law Act 1975* (Cth), based on the welfare of the child being the paramount consideration.

Re Evelyn (1988) FLC ¶92-807 dealt with the enforcement of a surrogacy agreement. This case involved a child born as a result of a surrogacy agreement, where the birth parents did not want to give her up. The Family Court held that the agreement could not be enforced as where a case involves the custody of a child, the paramount consideration is the welfare of the child, thus considerations of immorality become irrelevant (see also *Matter of Baby M* at **[9.295]**ff.)

[17.180] Case: *Application of A and B* (2000) 26 Fam LR 317; NSWSC 640 (7 July 2000)

In this case the birth mother was the sister of W and was artificially inseminated with sperm donated by the sister's husband, H, as part of a surrogate parenthood arrangement. W and H brought the application for adoption of the resultant child and were fully supported by the birth mother. DOCS opposed the application.

The child was cared for by the prospective parents from the time she was discharged from hospital as an infant. No secrecy was observed towards the child and she had free and regular contact with the birth mother and her half-sister.

Bryson J pointed out (at para 14) that an adoption application involves the interests of parents (both birth and adoptive) as well as of infants, although the child's interests remain paramount. He opined that because of the rarity of surrogacy agreements there is a speculative element in all predictions as to how the emotional lives and happiness of people involved will be affected. Bryson J was of the opinion that:

> "the paramountcy of the welfare and interests of the child in this case altogether overwhelms public policy considerations, not expressed in any legal rule, about whether surrogate parenthood should occur or should be encouraged". (para 28)

Bryson J held that the matters supporting the conclusion that an adoption order should be made having regard to the interests and welfare of the child were overwhelming in favour of completing the adoption process. However, he went on to state:

"I repeat the statement of Windeyer J in *W: Re Adoption* (NSWSC 6 July 1998) '*It is important to state that in coming to this decision, the Court is not determining whether surrogate births are or are not to be encouraged*'. It would be incorrect to interpret this decision as expressing approval or endorsement of surrogate parenthood, or as expressing general readiness to ratify surrogacy arrangements with adoption orders. I share the disquiet which has been expressed elsewhere, including by the Law Reform Commission, about surrogate parenthood, and I share the Commission's disapproval of commercial arrangements and their view that surrogacy should not be encouraged and that it is appropriate for the legislature to consider regulating it. These general considerations cannot control my task of adjudication on the facts of the instant case and in conformity with the legal rules found in the *Adoption of Children Act 1965*, including the paramountcy rule. I do not regard surrogate parenthood as an ideal arrangement, but the circumstances of the present case appear to me to be as favourable as are ever likely to be encountered."

Posthumous Parenthood

[17.185]   One application of ART that has received considerable attention from the media and the academic arena recently is in relation to facilitating the conception or birth of a child after the death of one or both of the parents, that is, posthumous parenthood. There are a number of possible ways for posthumous parenthood to arise, namely where:

1.   a male dies leaving behind frozen spermatozoa or pre-embryos;
2.   a female dies leaving behind frozen pre-embryos;
3.   both the male and female die, having contributed to a pre-embryo;
4.   sperm is harvested from a male after death or whilst he is in a persistent vegetative state (PVS);
5.   ova are harvested from a female after death or whilst she is in a PVS;
6.   the life of a female in a PVS is maintained in order that a foetus may be supported to a viable age.

The legal issues associated with posthumous parenthood span a wide array of legal areas including family law, probate law, property law, health law, and procedural law. There are few legislative provisions regarding posthumous parenthood. The *Infertility Treatment Act 1995* (Vic), s 43 expressly prohibits the insemination of a woman with the sperm of a man known to be dead or the transfer to a woman of a gamete from a person known to be dead. The NHMRC Ethical Guidelines for the Clinical Practice of ART state (at 6.15):

"Clinics must not facilitate the use of gametes in such circumstances unless all of the following conditions are met:

• a deceased person has left clearly expressed and witnessed directions consenting to the use of his or her gametes; or

• a person in a postcoma unresponsive state ("vegetative state") prepared clearly expressed and witnessed directions, before he or she entered the coma, consenting to the use of his or her gametes; or

• a dying person prepares clearly expressed and witnessed directions consenting to the use, after death, of his or her gametes; and

• the prospective parent received counselling about the consequences of such use; and

• the use does not diminish the fulfilment of the right of any child who may be born to knowledge of his or her biological parents".

The guidelines also state that an appropriate period of time should have elapsed before conception is attempted.

A number of cases concerning various aspects of posthumous parenthood have come before the courts in the United Kingdom, United States of America and Australia. Perhaps the most well known case is the case of Diane Blood, which led to the introduction of new legislation in the United Kingdom, the *Human Fertilisation and Embryology (Deceased Fathers) Act 2003*. In Australia, the cases of *AB v The Attorney-General for the State of Victoria* [2005] VSC 180 (27 May 2005) and *YZ v Infertility Treatment Authority (General)* [2005] VCAT 2655 (20 December 2005), two cases involving the same plaintiff, provide the most recent consideration of the issue.

In *AB* the plaintiff sought a declaration as to the legality of using her dead husband's sperm together with her ovum to form an embryo and to transfer that embryo to her body in the hope of achieving pregnancy. Hargrave J held that the terms of s 43 of the *Infertility Treatment Act 1995* prohibited only insemination with sperm of a man known to be dead and the transfer of an oocyte of a woman known to be dead, and thus the procedure sought by the plaintiff fell outside the legislative provisions of s 43. However, s 12(3), requiring the consent of the donor, prohibited the proposed procedure being carried out in Victoria. In *YZ* the plaintiff sought to have the sperm exported to another State, following refusal of the Authority to allow such export. The Tribunal approved the export of the sperm. In doing so, the Tribunal paid regard to the guiding principles set out in s 5 of the *Infertility Treatment Act* and commented that the plaintiff should not be prejudiced by the fact that the State in which her husband died (Victoria) had different legislative provisions to that in which they lived (Australian Capital Territory).

See also *MAW v WAHS* (2000) 49 NSWLR 231, where the Court found that its *parens patriae* jurisdiction did not extend to enabling the Court to consent to the removal of sperm from a man in a comatose state. *In the matter of Gray* [2000] QSC 390, the Court held that its *parens patriae* jurisdiction did not extend to enabling the court to consent to the removal of sperm from a deceased male.

Genetic Testing

[17.190] In the reproductive context, genetic testing primarily concerns prenatal testing (PT) and pre-implantation genetic diagnosis (PGD), but may also extend to kinship testing.

Traditionally, PT and PGD have been used to allow for termination of a pregnancy where a genetic abnormality is apparent. However, with the rapid expansion of our understanding of genetic bases, the possibility of using these techniques to detect a wide range of traits beyond disease and abnormality arises (see Green (1997)). Such rapid expansion and increased utilisation of genetic technologies prompts the consideration of to what extent, if any, PT and PGD should be regulated in Australia.

A thorough consideration of the legal and ethical aspects of this controversial topic is beyond the scope of this book but is mentioned to highlight the particularly sensitive nature of this area of health care and the potential for rapid technological developments to impact on the provision of health care services and their regulation.

A brief consideration of some of these issues follows.

As discussed earlier, the current legal framework in relation to ART is limited (see [17.95]). In Victoria, Western Australia and South Australia, legislation restricts the use of ART to those who are infertile or at risk of passing on a genetic condition to a naturally conceived child (see [17.140]). Hence, PGD is available only in limited circumstances. In addition, Victoria expressly prohibits the use of sex-selection techniques unless the indication for sex selection is the avoidance of a sex-linked genetic abnormality (*Infertility Treatment Act 1995* (Vic), s 50). In Western Australia it is an offence to carry out a diagnostic procedure on an embryo unless it is approved by the Code of Practice or the Reproductive Technology Council (*Human Reproductive Technology Act 1991* (WA), s 7). The South Australian legislation is silent on the issue of PGD.

Part B of the NHMRC Guidelines (referred to at [17.130]) contain provisions relating to sex selection and PGD. Section 11 provides that sex-selection must not be undertaken except to prevent the transmission of a serious genetic condition. Section 12 contains the following provisions regarding PGD:

- PGD must not be used for prevention of conditions that do not seriously harm the person to be born;
- PGD must not be used for selection in favour of a genetic defect or disability in the person to be born;
- When requested to select an embryo that is tissue compatible with a sibling, clinics must seek advice from an ethics committee; and
- Access to clinical geneticists and genetic counselling must be provided to those seeking PGD.

The Australian Law Reform Commission has undertaken a major inquiry into the ethical, legal and social implications of the new and emerging genetic technologies entitled, *Essentially Yours: The Protection of Human Genetic*

Information in Australia (ALRC 96, 2003) available on Austlii at www.austlii. edu.au/au/other/alrc/publications/reports/96/. The terms of reference of the inquiry were to consider how best to:

*   protect privacy (see **[7.355]**ff);
*   prevent unfair discrimination; and
*   ensure high ethical standards in research and practice,

with respect to human genetic information.

The report considered a wide range of issues surrounding the collection, use and storage of human genetic information. Perhaps the most immediately relevant section to this discussion is Part C: Genetic Testing. The report divides genetic testing into three categories: medical testing, identification testing and kinship testing, with the section on medical testing expressly including consideration of genetic carrier, pre-implantation and prenatal testing.

The report notes that to date the medical profession have been the primary "gatekeepers" to access to such testing and the information it produces. It recommends that additional accreditation standards be imposed on laboratories conducting such testing and additional legal protection should be introduced to ensure testing is consensual. The Inquiry also considered whether amendment to the legislation governing human tissue and organ transplants that each Australian jurisdiction has enacted (see **[17.05]**) may be a suitable means of protecting the privacy interests connected with the handling of genetic samples. The Inquiry ultimately concluded that the regulation of the handling of genetic samples should not be primarily reliant upon amendments to the Human Tissue Acts.

The complexity of the issues surrounding genetic information is highlighted in the following extract from the Executive Summary:

"The experience of the Inquiry, mirrored overseas, is that the rapid pace of change has produced two powerful, but conflicting, social reactions. On the one hand, there is very strong public support for breakthroughs promising better medical diagnosis and treatments, and for assisting with law enforcement (including identification of missing or deceased persons); on the other, there are anxieties about increased loss of privacy and the potential for genetic discrimination, as well as about capacity to regulate genetic science in the public interest.

The major challenge for the Inquiry was to find a sensible path that meets twin goals: to foster innovations in genetic research and practice that serve humanitarian ends, and to provide sufficient reassurance to the community that such innovations will be subject to proper ethical scrutiny and legal (and other) controls.

The current methods of regulation and conflict resolution involve a patchwork of federal, state and territory laws; official guidelines; personal and professional ethics; institutional restraints; peer review and pressure; oversight by public funding authorities and professional associations; supervision by public regulatory and complaints-handling authorities; private interest; and market pressures."

References and Further Reading

ACT Attorney-General's Department, *Surrogacy: Discussion Paper* (Canberra, ACT Government, 1993)

Australian Health and Medical Law Reporter (CCH, Sydney, 1991)

Australian and New Zealand Intensive Care Society Working Party on Brain Death and Organ Donation, *Recommendations Concerning Brain Death and Organ Donation* (Melbourne, Australian and New Zealand Intensive Care Society, 1998)

Australian Department of Community Services and Health National HIV/AIDS Strategy (AGPS, Canberra, 1989)

Bates, F and Turner, J, *The Family Law Casebook* (Law Book Co, Sydney, 1985), Ch 13

Bennett, B, "Prenatal Diagnosis, Genetics and Reproductive Decision-making", (2001) 9 *Journal of Law and Medicine* 28-40

Blackford, R, "Surrogate Motherhood and Public Policy" *Quadrant* (2003), Vol XLVII, No 3

Cooke, S, "Use of Sperm After Death in Victoria" *Australian Health Law Bulletin* 13 (10)

Dawson, K, *Reproductive Technology: The Science, the Ethics, the Law and the Social Issues* (Melbourne, VCTA Publishing, 1994)

Douglas, G, *Fertility and Reproduction* (Sweet and Maxwell, London, 1991)

Dower, T, "Redefining Family: Should Lesbians Have Access to Assisted Reproduction?" (2001) 25 MULR 466

Finlay, et al, *Family Law: Cases and Commentary* (Butterworths, Sydney, 1986), pp 259ff

Frame, T, "The Perils of Surrogate Motherhood" *Quadrant* (2003), Vol XLVII, No 6

Freedman, W, *Legal Issues in Biotechnology and Human Reproduction* (Quorum Books, New York, 1991)

Goold, I, "Tissue Donation: Ethical Guidance and Legal Enforceability" *Australian Health Law Bulletin* 11 (3)

Green, R, "Parental Autonomy and the Obligation Not to Harm One's Child Genetically" (1997) 25 *Journal of Law, Medicine & Ethics* 5

Health Department of Western Australia, *Directions Given by the Commissioner of Health to Set the Standards of Practice under the Human Reproductive Technology Act 1991 on the Advice of the WA Reproductive Technology Council* (Health Dept of WA, Perth, 1993)

Keeling, S, "Duty to Warn of Genetic Harm in Breach of Patient Confidentiality" *Australian Health Law Bulletin* 12 (2)

Kerridge, I, Lowe, M & McPhee, J, *Ethics and Law for the Health Professions* (Federation Press, Sydney 2005)

Lang, A, "What is the Body? Exploring the Law, Philosophy and Ethics of Commerce in Human Tissue" (1999) 7 *Journal of Law and Medicine* 53

Liu, A, *Artificial Reproduction and Reproductive Rights* (Gower Press, UK, 1991)

McLean, S (ed), *Legal Issues in Human Reproduction* (Gower Press, UK, 1989)

Magnusson, R, "The Use of Human Tissue Samples in Medical Research: Legal Issues for Human Research Ethics Committees" (1999) 7 *Journal of Law and Medicine* 390

Mortensen, R, "*A Reconstruction of Religious Freedom and Equality: Gay, Lesbian and De Facto Rights and the Religious School in Queensland*" [2003] QUTLJ 16

National Health and Medical Research Council (Australia), *An Australian Code of Practice for Transplantation of Cadaveric Organs and Tissues* (AGPS, Canberra, 1990)

National Health and Medical Research Council (Australia) *Ethical Guidelines on the use of Assisted Reproductive Technology in Clinical Practice and Research* (2004) accessed at www.nhmrc.gov.au/publications on 15/04/06

National Bioethics Consultative Committee (Australia), *Reproductive Technology: Record Keeping and Access to Information, Birth Certificates and Birth Records of Offspring Born as a Result of Gamete Donation* (Adelaide National Bioethics Consultative Committee, 1989)

New South Wales Health, *Review of the Human Tissue Act: Discussion Paper Assisted Reproductive Technologies NSW* (Health Department, October, 1997)

New South Wales Law Reform Commission, *Human Artificial Insemination*, Report No 49 (NSW Government Printer, Sydney, 1986)

Peterson, K, Baker, H, Pitts, M, & Thorpe, R, "Assisted Reproduction Technologies: Professional and Legal Restrictions in Australian Clinics" *Australian Health Law Bulletin* 12 (3)

Rodin, J, et al (eds), *Women and New Reproductive Technologies: Medical, Psychosocial and Ethical Dilemmas* (L Erlbaum, New Jersey, 1991)

Rowland, R, *Living Laboratories Women and Reproductive Technologies* (Sun Books, Australia, 1992)

Scutt, J, *Women and the Law* (Law Book Co, Sydney, 1990)

Stuhmcke, A, "Access to Reproductive Technology: *Pearce v SA Health Commission*" (1996) 5 AHLB 39

Sutherland, E and McCall Smith, A, *Family Law and Medical Advance* (Edinburgh University Press, Edinburgh, 1990)

Walker, K, "The Bishops, The Doctor, His Patient and the Attorney-General: The Conclusion of the *McBain* Litigation" [2002] *Federal Law Review* 18

18 Expanding recognition of human rights

Health consumers' rights

International law

Domestic law

Other approaches to health consumers' rights

Discrimination & the law

Implications for health care workers

chapter 18

Expanding Recognition of Human Rights

Human Rights—Health Consumers' Rights

[18.05] The law as outlined in the chapters so far has described what can be said to be patients' rights: the right to refuse treatment, to reasonable and prompt treatment, to confidentiality and privacy, to access to records, to legal advice, and so on. Health carers' rights, such as those relating to employment are also described. Every duty or requirement at law applying to health carers gives rise to a subsequent right on the part of those to whom the duty is owed. Some hospitals have developed a "Bill of Rights", which points out to patients their legal rights, sometimes adding further rights which are not legally enforceable, and which could more accurately be described as moral rights or aspirations than as legal rights.

What is a "right"?

[18.10] For the purposes of this discussion, it is presumed that a right which is recognised by society is access to some entitlement to a benefit which is acknowledged as belonging to a particular person, and which that person can demand of others. Those of whom the demand is made in turn have an obligation to provide that access. Rights are either legally enforceable, when the person can call on the state to enforce them, or simply a recognised acceptable form of behaviour. If the latter, they are arguably not "rights" in the traditional sense at all. The former attribute of legal enforceability is obviously more valuable than the latter. The main rights of health consumers can be summarised as follows:

Common law rights
- to reasonable care (Chapter 6 and 9);
- to refuse treatment (Chapter 4);
- to confidentiality (Chapter 7); and
- to correct information in relation to services (Chapters 4 and 5).

Statute-based rights
* to refuse treatment (in some Australian jurisdictions) (Chapter 4);
* to special consideration if they are suffering from a disability or are aged (see below and Chapter 5);
* to privacy in specified situations (Chapter 7); and
* to freedom from discrimination in the availability and quality of services.

Administratively established rights
These are "rights" set out in guidelines, protocols and administrative directives developed by an organisation, government department or health facility. These "rights" may vary between service providers, but examples are:

* confidentiality;
* access to records;
* the assistance of interpreters;
* knowledge of the costs involved in treatment; and
* knowledge of available services.

Administratively established rights generally do not have the force of law. However, breach of them could provide the basis for a civil action, or for disciplinary action for unprofessional conduct. This would depend on the circumstances, and whether there was a clearly established obligation on the part of the health care provider. An example of a document outlining patients' rights is the Victorian Public Hospital Patient Charter 2002; which can be found online at: www.nh.org.au/Header/Patient_Rights_and_Responsibilities/.

Patient rights can also be seen to arise from ethical codes such as the *Code of Professional Conduct* under s 99A of the *Medical Practice Act 1992* (NSW), which is reproduced in full at Appendix 5. An extract follows:

* Listen to patients and respect their views;
* Treat patients politely and considerately;
* Respect your patients' privacy and dignity;
* Observe professional boundaries with patients. This includes not engaging in personal relationships or sexual behaviour with patients (this principle is subject of a specific policy in relation to sexual misconduct issued by the New South Wales Medical Board), see also *Medical Board of Queensland v Hashim* [2006] QHPT 001) (see also Chapter 13);
* Treat information about patients as confidential;
* Give patients full information about their condition and treatment, outlining the risks and benefits, and prognosis;
* Give information to patients, parent, guardian or person responsible in a way they can understand;
* Wherever possible, check that the patient, parent, guardian or person responsible has understood the information given and the course of action proposed, and that they consent to it, before you provide treatment or investigate a patient's condition;
* Respect the right of patients to be fully involved in all decisions about their care;

- Respect the right of patients to decline treatment or decline to take part in teaching or research;
- Respect the right of patients to a second opinion;
- Be readily accessible to patients and colleagues when you are on duty;
- Recognise the fundamental role of the patient, parent, guardian or person responsible in decision-making about and treatment of the patient;
- Give priority to the investigation and treatment of patients on the basis of clinical need, bearing in mind the needs of other patients;
- Investigations or treatment should be based on clinical judgment of the patient's needs and the likely effectiveness—not prejudiced by views about a patient's lifestyle, culture, beliefs, race, colour, gender, sexuality, age, religion, social, economic or insurance status;
- If the medical practitioner believes that their beliefs might affect the treatment they provide, this should be explained to patients, along with their right to see another doctor;
- A medical practitioner should not refuse or delay treatment because they believe that a patient's actions have contributed to the patient's condition, or because they may be putting yourself at risk. If a patient poses a risk to a medical practitioner's health or safety, they may take protective steps before investigating the condition or providing treatment;
- A medical practitioner must act in their patient's best interests when making referrals and providing or arranging treatment or care; and not ask for or accept any inducement, gift or hospitality which may affect or be seen to affect their judgment.

Some of the rights outlined in this book apply to a person because he or she is the recipient of health care as a patient of health professionals. They are based on the emerging recognition in our society of the equality of all people and their claim to health care, and the upholding of the principle that the dignity, autonomy and integrity of all should be acknowledged and preserved. Other rights apply to those who are employees, based on the recognised need for equal access to work and a basic standard of conditions. Finally, some rights apply to all human beings regardless of personal circumstances. The specifics are based on the international articulation and development of human rights. It is this last group which is dealt with in this chapter.

Human Rights in International Law

[18.15] Alongside domestic (federal and State) law, there has grown a body of international law based on the recognition of human rights. Although the domestic legal application or enforceability of such rights may be problematic (see below), human rights notionally apply to any person and are based purely on their membership of the human race. They are said to be universal (applying to everyone) and immutable (they cannot be limited or qualified). The recognition of human rights at an international level takes the form of international declarations, conventions, and treaties. The documents are drawn up, and nations subscribe to the principles contained in them.

Drawn up by the United Nations in 1948, the Universal Declaration of Human Rights (see www.un.org/Overview/rights.html) initiated the recognition of human rights. By means of further conventions and agreements, nations have committed themselves to recognising the rights of all people to dignity, physical security, self-fulfilment, and equal access to justice. Australia was involved in the formulation of the Declaration and is a signatory to many of the subsequent more detailed conventions and agreements.

International law is complex, and in many ways different from domestic law. In the following discussion it will be outlined in very simple form only, with a view to giving an understanding of the obligations of health carers which have resulted from our federal government's involvement in the area of international human rights law.

The first and most important point to make about law between nations is that it does not consist of a set of rules which can be enforced by a court as is possible in national legal systems. Nations are all sovereign entities, able to do whatever they like within their own territory. Thus a head of state or government of a particular country cannot be forced to change their ways, however disagreeable others may consider them. One can negotiate, attempt to persuade, apply economic or political sanctions, as was the case for South Africa and Iraq, but only under certain closely defined circumstances take up arms against another nation. The United Nations General Assembly can condemn a country's activities, and serve as a forum for international moral and political disapprobation. There is also the International Court of Justice (see www.icj-cij.org/) to which nations can take their grievances for a ruling on the legality of a nation's activities. The jurisdiction of the court, however, rests on the consent of the parties. The United Nations may call on member nations to contribute to a peace-keeping armed force in its name.

International conventions

[18.20] A declaration or convention establishing human rights is, thus, not legally binding. Nations may sign a convention, signifying their agreement in principle with it. (Of course, a nation may choose not to sign or ratify a convention.) A nation may then ratify the convention (thus becoming a party to it), meaning acceptance of its provisions, and an undertaking to enact laws consistent with them within their own borders ("domestic law"). Nations may make reservations to specific clauses of the convention if they are not prepared or equipped to put these into effect. A convention may also set up an international committee to which parties to it undertake to make regular reports on measures taken to give effect to the convention within their territory. They may be asked by the Committee to explain apparent failure to act, or unsatisfactory progress in the recognition of the rights involved. Such failure can result in an adverse report to the United Nations General Assembly, and possible action by the member States as outlined above.

The *International Covenant on Civil and Political Rights* has an Optional Protocol, ratified by Australia, which provides that an individual can take a complaint to the United Nations Human Rights Committee (see www.ohchr.

org/english/about/index.htm). The complaint must relate to government action denying a human right to that person, and complainants must have exhausted the avenues of complaint in their own country. Several Tasmanians lodged a complaint with the Committee in relation to the provision in the *Criminal Code* (Tas) that prohibits homosexual acts between consenting adults. The Committee handed down the finding that the provision was in breach of human rights. When the Tasmanian government refused to repeal the provision, the federal government passed legislation based on the foreign affairs power in the Australian Constitution (see below), and its status as a party to the International Covenant, which provided a defence against a prosecution under the Tasmanian law (see **[18.75]** below regarding the *Human Rights (Sexual Conduct) Act 1994* (Cth)).

Foreign affairs power

[18.25] The Australian Constitution limits the Commonwealth Parliament's powers to legislate for the States, but s 51(xxix) (the "foreign affairs power") provides some power to legislate where the federal government has signed an international agreement (see **[1.60]**). As a result of this power the federal government has legislated for human rights. In fact, some States have also done this (see **[18.230]**ff).

The following are the main international instruments that establish rights which are relevant to health care workers:

* *International Covenant on Civil and Political Rights* (Article 7): prohibits medical or scientific experimentation without consent.
* *International Covenant on Social, Economic and Cultural Rights* (Article 12): establishes the right to the highest attainable standard of physical and mental health, to be attained by, among other measures, methods to reduce stillbirth, epidemics, endemic and occupational diseases.
* *Declaration of the Rights of the Child* (Principle 4) and United Nations *Convention on the Rights of the Child* (Article 24): bestows on children the right to special protection and access to medical care respectively.
* *Declaration on the Rights of Mentally Retarded Persons* (Article 2): bestows the right of proper medical care and physical therapy.
* *Declaration on the Rights of Disabled Persons* (Article 6): includes the right to medical, psychological and functional care, rehabilitation, counselling and vocational training.
* *Principles for the Protection of Persons with Mental Illness and for the Improvement of Mental Health Care*, is devoted to setting out the rights of those with a mental illness.

Human Rights in Domestic Law

[18.30] Australia is a party to, or has adopted, all the instruments nominated above, and is therefore obliged to promote legislation in Australia that advances these rights. All except the last one mentioned are attached to the *Human Rights and Equal Opportunity Commission Act 1986* (Cth) as Schedules to that Act, and a complaint can be made to the Human Rights and Equal Opportunity Commission that an alleged breach of a convention has occurred. The Commission has no judicial power in such cases but this is certainly a way of establishing that one has been denied one's rights, and of putting pressure on an offender to desist from such an activity and to compensate for the harm that has been caused. States and Territories also have anti-discrimination laws to give effect to the major human rights conventions. These matters are dealt with below.

Human rights and the Equal Opportunity Commission

[18.35] In 1981, the federal government inaugurated the Human Rights Commission. It consisted of seven part-time Commissioners, and one full-time Commissioner. That Commission became the Human Rights and Equal Opportunity Commission (the Commission) in 1986 (see www.hreoc.gov.au/). The Human Rights and Equal Opportunity Commission is a national independent statutory government body, and the federal Attorney-General is the Minister responsible in Parliament for the Commission. The Commission is administered by the President. He is assisted by the Human Rights, Race, Sex, Disability and Aboriginal and Torres Strait Islander Social Justice Commissioners. Under the legislation administered by the Commission, it is responsible for inquiring into alleged infringements under five Commonwealth anti-discrimi-nation laws—the *Racial Discrimination Act 1975*, the *Sex Discrimination Act 1984*, the *Disability Discrimination Act 1992* and the *Age Discrimination Act 2004* as well as inquiring into alleged infringements of human rights under the *Human Rights and Equal Opportunity Commission Act 1986*. The *Human Rights and Equal Opportunity Commission Act 1986* (Cth) empowers the Commission to inquire into, and deal with complaints about, alleged breaches of human rights listed in the Schedules attached. The Schedules contain the *International Convention Concerning Discrimination in Respect of Employment and Occupation*; the *International Covenant on Civil and Political Rights* (establishing rights of citizenship, political freedom, rights to hold public office, to vote, etc); the *Declaration of the Rights of the Child, Declaration on the Rights of Mentally Retarded Persons*, and *Declaration on the Rights of Disabled Persons*. The rights contained in these documents can be summarised as follows:

- The rights of all people to:
  - privacy;
  - marriage and family;
  - their own language, culture and religion;
  - participation in public affairs;
  - freedom of expression, movement, association and assembly;
  - protection of their inherent right to life;
  - liberty and security of person;

- freedom from degrading treatment or punishment; and
- equal treatment with others under the law.
- The rights of children to:
  - a name and nationality;
  - opportunities to develop fully in conditions of freedom and dignity;
  - adequate care, affection and security, including prenatal and postnatal care;
  - education;
  - special treatment and care of handicapped; and
  - protection against cruelty and neglect.
- The rights of mentally retarded or intellectually disadvantaged persons to:
  - proper medical care and therapy;
  - economic security;
  - education, training and work and trade union membership; and
  - a qualified guardian and a review of procedures which may deny them their rights.
- The rights of disabled persons to:
  - respect;
  - family and social life;
  - economic security;
  - protection from discriminatory treatment (Human Rights Commission, Annual *Report, 1981–82,* Vol 1, p 1, also set out in Tay (1986), p 26).

Section 3 of the *Human Rights and Equal Opportunity Act 1986* (Cth) defined "human rights" as the rights and freedoms recognised in the *International Covenant on Civil and Political Rights,* declared by the Declarations (Rights of the Child, Rights of Mentally Retarded Persons and Rights of Disabled Persons) or recognised or declared by any relevant international instrument (an international instrument in respect of which a declaration under s 47 of the Act is in force).

The Human Rights and Equal Opportunity Commission's powers include:

- Scrutiny of Commonwealth legislation referred to it for breaches or potential breaches of the above rights.
- the carrying out of inquiries into Commonwealth government acts and practices;
- the development of educational programmes for the public;
- the hearing of complaints of breaches of rights as set out in the Schedules by individuals or groups who allege such breaches, within the Commission's area of responsibility (for example, it does not have jurisdiction over State governments or instrumentalities, or some individuals); and
- hearing of complaints under the Commonwealth Racial, Sex and Disability Discrimination Acts (see below).

However the rights listed in the Schedule are not enforceable and are not made unlawful under the Act. The Commission's powers relating to all such rights except employment matters (see **[18.75]**ff) extend only to Commonwealth government authorities, or matters referred to it by the Commonwealth

Attorney-General (this would include health facilities run by the Commonwealth government).

The Act also establishes the Aboriginal and Torres Strait Islander Social Justice Commissioner, whose functions, in relation to Aboriginal and Torres Strait Islanders, include reporting to the Minister on human rights, promoting discussion and awareness of human rights, undertaking research and educational programmes and examining Commonwealth legislation.

Other Approaches to Health Consumers' Rights

[18.40] The Consumers Health Forum of Australia ((1990) Pt 3, esp pp 34-38) points out ways of determining and enforcing the rights of health consumers, which it considers are more effective than legislation:

*   licensing of facilities, manufacturers and health care personnel;
*   establishing codes of practice, adherence to which is necessary to gain a licence; and
*   establishment of outcome standards for facilities.

The Forum recommends that where a practitioner breaches the code of practice, tribunals with quasi-judicial power similar to the State equal opportunity tribunals (see below) could deal with complaints. It also points out (p 38) that not only are there many problems surrounding legal redress itself but that access to the law is often hindered by barriers such as lack of information about legal mechanisms, lack of financial resources, emotional, physical and intellectual cost, and the law's delay.

Trade practices legislation

[18.45] All Australian jurisdictions have trade practices legislation. (*Trade Practices Act 1974* (Cth); *Fair Trading Act 1992* (ACT); *Fair Trading Act 1987* (NSW); *Consumer Affairs and Fair Trading Act* (NT); *Fair Trading Act 1989* (Qld); *Fair Trading Act 1987* (SA); *Fair Trading Act 1990* (Tas); *Fair Trading Act 1999* (Vic); *Fair Trading Act 1987* (WA)). This legislation provides that it is an offence for a service provider to engage in conduct which does, or is likely to, mislead or deceive in relation to the service provided. The Commonwealth legislation, constrained as it is by the Constitution, applies to corporations only, however legislation in the States and Territories applies to individuals as well. This legislation also applies to the provision of health care, providing that false and misleading representations cannot be made about such matters as the need for the medical service, its nature, quality and efficacy, the quantity, nature, characteristics or suitability of the service. In considering whether someone has breached the provision, the court can take into account any undue influence, coercion or overzealous persuasion on the part of the health carer. The legislative provisions also apply to those offering complementary health care.

Health care complaints

[18.50] All Australian jurisdictions have established some form of statutory mechanism for dealing specifically with health care complaints. The websites for the various bodies are as follows:

State or Territory	Website
NSW	www.hccc.nsw.gov.au
Victoria	www.health.vic.gov.au/hsc/
Queensland	www.hqcc.qld.gov.au
South Australia	www.hcscc.sa.gov.au
Western Australia	www.healthreview.wa.gov.au
Tasmania	www.healthcomplaints.tas.gov.au
ACT	www.healthcomplaints.act.gov.au
Northern Territory	www.nt.gov.au/omb_hcscc/hcscc

In the past complaints about health care which were not the subject of legal action were received by Health Departments, which acted upon them where it was thought appropriate to do so. Over time, there has been an increased recognition of patients' rights, and the need for a mechanism for dealing with complaints about services and health providers independent of Health Departments. The trend has thus been to provide independent statutory units or Commissions to deal with complaints. Legislation sets up independent complaints units with power to receive and deal with complaints in relation to a very broad range of health services. These units are independent of the Health Departments, and facilitate voluntary conciliation of those complaints which are amenable to this process. Where conciliation is not appropriate, or serious allegations involving misconduct or negligence are involved, powers of investigation or referral to an appropriate disciplinary board or investigatory body are provided.

The legislation establishing these complaint units generally provides for the following functions and powers:

- investigation of complaints, including those that are not amenable to conciliation, are serious, or are referred by the Minister;
- publication of information and education concerning the operation of the legislation;
- inquiries into issues in relation to provision of health services and the causes of complaints;
- provision of advice to the Minister responsible on matters relating to health services;
- powers to examine witnesses; and
- powers to obtain warrants for search and seizure, for the production of information and documents and to impose penalties for non-compliance with directions relating to providing information, or for providing false information.

They also provide for:

- protection from reprisals against those involved in a complaint (for example, threats, bribery, refusal to provide services); and
- immunity from legal action for making a complaint, statement, or report or for the performance of a function under the Act.

In the Australian Capital Territory the *Health and Community Care Complaints Act 1998* (ACT) establishes the Health and Community Complaints Commission and Commissioner, along similar lines to those outlined for other jurisdictions. In the Northern Territory the *Health and Community Services Complaints Act* (NT) establishes the Health and Community Complaints Commission and Commissioner, who is to develop a Code of Health and Community Rights and Responsibilities. Consultation is to take place between the Commissioner and the relevant registration board if a registered health carer is involved in a complaint. Complaints that cannot be conciliated are investigated by the Commissioner, who can require attendance and examine witnesses and documents. A review process is available through the Health and Community Services Complaints Review Committee.

In New South Wales the Health Complaints Commission was established by the *Health Care Complaints Act 1993* (NSW). If more serious matters are investigated, and substantiated, the Commission can prosecute the matter before the relevant tribunal or professional disciplinary body. A Health Conciliation Registry deals with matters that can be conciliated. If conciliation fails, the complainant can institute legal proceedings.

In South Australia, the Health and Community Services Complaints Commission was established relatively recently by the *Health and Community Services Complaints Act 2004* (SA) proclaimed in October 2005.

In Queensland the *Health Rights Commission Act 1991* (Qld) established the Health Rights Commission. The Commissioner must investigate complaints, and may refer a matter to the health carer's registration board for disciplinary action. Conciliation is to be attempted.

In Tasmania the *Health Complaints Act 1995* (Tas) established the Health Complaints Commission. It provides for the Commissioner to establish and regularly review a Charter of Health Rights. Serious complaints can be investigated (with powers vested in the Commissioner to subpoena people and documents) and may result in criminal or disciplinary action in the appropriate forum. Conciliation is encouraged where appropriate.

In Victoria the *Health Services (Conciliation and Review) Act 1987* (Vic) established the Health Services Commissioner. More serious complaints are investigated, and disciplinary procedures may be brought against the respondent if these are substantiated. Conciliation of complaints is encouraged, including all possible attempts to resolve the issue between the parties before the matter is brought to the Commission.

In Western Australia, the *Health Services (Conciliation and Review) Act 1995* (WA) established the Office of Health Review, to which complaints may be made by consumers, representatives of consumers and health providers. Serious complaints may be investigated, and may be referred to the relevant registration board.

The complaints bodies are not intended to actively seek or obtain damages for negligent treatment or assault or battery. The services are largely free of cost to consumers with complaints. For smaller claims where the potential cost of legal advice and court action might be a major factor in discouraging patients with claims from seeking redress, conciliation enables their claims to be negotiated with little or no cost to the parties. It combines equity of access with limitation of cost, and may lead to agreement in many cases (Health Rights Commissioner, *Annual Report 1992/3* (Queensland Government Printer, Brisbane, 1993), p 9).

The first priority of these bodies is to provide a means whereby conciliation is possible. This means encouraging the parties themselves to come to an agreement, which may result in some compensation. Where conciliation is not a viable option, their function is to determine the facts of the situation complained about, and to bring about a more satisfactory standard of health care through influencing the establishment of more effective procedures and practices by the health provider involved. They are also a means for referral of matters to disciplinary bodies, the Ombudsman, the Director of Public Prosecutions, Tribunals or other appropriate bodies for further action where indicated. In addition, they may establish standards of practice generally. In this process, they are a means of:

* empowering complainants;
* providing them with the opportunity of acquiring necessary information which they may be otherwise unable to obtain;
* providing complainants with an opportunity to resolve the matter with the health provider; and
* providing complainants with the satisfaction of seeing that the practice complained of will cease in the future.

Discrimination and the Law

What is "discrimination"?

[18.55] For legal purposes, discrimination is an act which makes distinctions between individuals or groups with the result of disadvantaging some and advantaging others. The act does not have to be done with the conscious intent of harm. This is why legislation is not punitive—it is aimed at conciliation, compensation and education.

We discriminate all the time: some people we like and call our friends, with others we have more distant relationships. Seriously ill patients are given more care and attention than those whose illness is minor. Some discrimination, then, is good or at least acceptable by the standards of our society. Other discrimination—that of denying recognised basic human rights—is the subject of moral approbation and, in recent times, legal prohibition.

Direct discrimination

[18.60] All Australian anti-discrimination law prohibits direct discrimination— that is, discrimination which treats one person less favourably than another on the ground of a characteristic appertaining to the prescribed status (for example, colour) or a characteristic thought to appertain to that characteristic (for example, that all people of a particular race are lazy). The result is that on this ground, the person is treated less favourably than a person who is not of that status. They are discriminated against precisely because of their status. An example is the case of *Wardley v Ansett Transport Industries Pty Ltd* (1984) EOC ¶92-002. This case involved a complaint by Ms W, a pilot, who was denied a position with an airline because of its policy of not hiring women. She claimed that she was the victim of unlawful discrimination because of her sex. In evidence there was a letter from the general manager of the airline to the Women's Electoral Lobby stating that the policy of not hiring women does not mean that women cannot be good pilots, but "we feel that an all male pilot crew is safer than one in which the sexes are mixed". Ms W demonstrated her clear ability for the position, and the Anti-Discrimination Board ruled that she was the victim of unlawful discrimination.

Indirect discrimination

[18.65] Indirect discrimination is more subtle, and hence harder to detect and to remedy. It is often the result of "policies and practices which form the structures and patterns of an organisation in particular, and society as a whole" (Ronalds (1987), p 199).

Indirect discrimination is prohibited in all legislation and the elements necessary for it are basically the same. Indirect discrimination concentrates on the results of an act rather than the reasons for it. It occurs in the following way:

- S, a woman, wants a service or a job (for example, to be a police officer), but is told that a certain condition is required (for example, being a certain height);
- the requirement or condition is unreasonable and unnecessary (that is, a person could do the job just as well whether or not they fulfil this condition);
- S cannot fulfil this condition; and
- a substantially higher proportion of persons of a different status to S (for example, men, who are, on average, taller), can comply with the condition.

The unnecessary and seemingly neutral condition, although innocently and without consideration applied, indirectly discriminates against S and many women. It is the result of an erroneous belief that only people of a certain height can do a particular job, and no conscious discrimination against women is intended, but the effect is to discriminate. Another basis of indirect discrimi- nation, called "homosocial reproduction", is the employment of people who have similar backgrounds, education, or social status to those doing the employing, even though such attributes are irrelevant to the ability to carry out the work (recruitment in one's image) (see Wallace (1985), p 21).

Federal legislation

[18.70] As stated above (see **[18.35]**), the federal government has attempted to ensure the recognition of human rights generally in Australia under the *Human Rights and Equal Opportunity Commission Act 1986* (Cth). This Act established the Human Rights and Equal Opportunity Commission. The Commission also hears specific complaints of discrimination in employment under the *Human Rights and Equal Opportunity Commission Act 1986* (Cth), as well as under the *Sex Discrimination Act 1984* (Cth) and the *Racial Discrimination Act 1975* (Cth).

Employment discrimination

Human Rights and Equal Opportunity Commission Act 1986

[18.75] Because the federal government can legislate on complaints about breaches of the human rights conventions under its foreign affairs power, it can legislate on discrimination in employment, as it is a party to the International Labour Organisation Conventions. There are a large number of ILO conventions, not all of which have been ratified by Australia. (For more information on the ILO generally, see their website at www.ilo.org/). Thus the Act sets out provisions covering employers throughout Australia. The Human Rights Commissioner can inquire into any act by an employer that is alleged to discriminate on the grounds of race, colour, sex, religion, political opinion, national extraction or social origin, age, medical record, criminal record, impairment, marital status, mental, intellectual or psychiatric disability, nationality, physical disability, sexual preference or trade union activity. "Impairment" includes malfunction or total or partial loss of a part of the body, and the presence in the body of an organism causing disease, which includes HIV seropositivity. Discrimination means any distinction, exclusion, or preference made on the basis of one of the listed grounds that has the effect of nullifying or impairing the equality of opportunity or treatment in employment or occupation (s 3).

Discrimination on these grounds is not unlawful, but enables the Commissioner to attempt to effect a settlement of the matter through conciliation. Whereas in the past, the Commission could conduct a hearing and make a finding that could be enforced by the Federal Court, amendments to the Act which commenced in April 2000 meant that this is no longer to be the case. The Commission no longer conducts public hearings into complaints of unlawful discrimination under the *Disability Discrimination Act 1992* (Cth), *Racial Discrimination Act 1975* (Cth) and the *Sex Discrimination Act 1984* (Cth). These hearings are now conducted by the Federal Court and the Federal Magistrates Service. The Commission may, among other things, inquire into any practice that may constitute discrimination, examine legislation for discriminatory employment provisions, promote equal employment opportunity and undertake research and educational programmes on the issue. Exceptions to wrongful discrimination apply where the discrimination is in respect of the inherent requirements of the job, or where the employment is conducted in accordance with the tenets of a religion or creed and is made in good faith to avoid injury to the religious susceptibilities of adherents to that religion or creed.

It is of interest in passing to note the more recent *Human Rights (Sexual Conduct) Act 1994* (Cth), which provides that sexual conduct involving only consenting adults (a person who is 18 years old or more) acting in private is not to be subject, by or under any law of the Commonwealth, a State or a Territory, to any arbitrary interference with privacy within the meaning of Article 17 of the *International Covenant on Civil and Political Rights*. (See Schedule 2 to the *Human Rights and Equal Opportunity Commission Act 1986*; *Rodney Croome & Anor v The State of Tasmania* (1997) 191 CLR 119; [1997] HCA 5.)

The Federal Magistrates Court now provides links to significant decisions on its website (see www.fmc.gov.au/). For example, *Fenton v Hair & Beauty Gallery Pty Ltd & Anor* [2006] FMCA 3 deals with pregnancy and disability discrimination in employment. The following is an earlier example of discrimination on the basis of disability.

[18.80] Case: *Melvin v Northside Community Service Incorporated* [1996] HREOCA 20 (19 July 1996) (Human Rights & Equal Opportunity Commission No H 95/93, Hearing under previous provisions of the Act)

The complainant lodged a complaint with the Human Rights and Equal Opportunity Commission against Northside Community Services Inc ("NCS") alleging discrimination pursuant to the *Disability Discrimination Act 1992* (Cth).

After 10 years of service as a registered nurse with permanent part-time status in the employ of NCS in charge of the nursery, at its Civic Occasional Care Centre, ("the COCC"), the complainant was dismissed from that employment. The reason given for her dismissal was that that she was unable to perform some of the inherent requirements of her employment. It was claimed that because of her defective eyesight, she would pose an unacceptable risk to the safety of the children she was employed to care for, and to herself.

The complainant maintained that there was insufficient evidence to support these claims and that her dismissal amounted to direct discrimination within the meaning of Act. In the alternative, she claimed her employer's failure to provide her with necessary facilities to enable her to carry out her responsibilities, was indirect discrimination under the Act.

The complainant's duties included:

- first aid, programming and basic care of the babies;
- checking the nursery and playground equipment for broken toys and food scraps and to ensure cleanliness and safety;

- greeting parents and making notes in relation to the children;
- coping with children that were unwell and who had medical problems such as diabetes, epilepsy, and physical deformity;
- checking children for rashes, feeding them, observing their colour and their general health, looking for "sticky eyes", runny noses or coughs and other indications of illness; and
- observing the babies while they slept to make sure their breathing was normal and their colour good, and that they were neither over- nor under-dressed.

The complainant claimed that she never had difficulty performing such tasks and it was accepted that she had done so satisfactorily, having been employed at the COCC as a child carer for some 10 years. There was no evidence of her creating occasions of danger to herself or the children during all her years of employment and no evidence that her visual incapacity became critical by reason of changes occurring in the nature of child care professional services.

However, the complainant was embarrassed doing desk-work because of her myopia. In order to read documents, she had to hold them very close to her face. The complainant thought that she would appear unprofessional doing this. She asked to be relieved of such work. However, at no time did she refuse, or indicate that she was unable, to do such work.

The Executive Director of NCS consulted the COCC's insurer who advised her that she would be negligent not to address the question of the complainant's eyesight, having been put on notice that it was defective. The Director of Children's Day Care Services within the Australian Capital Territory government, advised that she request the complainant to obtain documentation from her doctor or specialist indicating whether she was physically fit to perform her specified duties. A report was obtained from an optometrist who the Commissioner found was an inappropriate source of advice, and which did not adequately address the question of the complainant's ability to carry out her employment.

[18.85] The Commissioner found that pressure for the complainant to do clerical work came from other employees, and that the ostensible reason for her dismissal included other employees unhappy at having to take on more clerical work. He dismissed the evidence of the optometrist and those expressing "concerns" about the complainant's capacities, relying rather on the combined effect of the fact of the complainant having done such work through many years during which there was little change in her eye condition, her own testimony that she was able to do the work, that of the eyewitnesses, and both a specialist ophthalmologist and the Royal Blind Society who gave evidence to the Commission.

The Commissioner held that to establish discrimination, the complainant would have to show that she was employed by NCS, she had a disability as defined by the Act, she was dismissed from her employment, and this dismissal resulted in her being treated less favourably than the employer treated employees without the disability referred to. These factors were proved in this case. However, even if discrimination has been proved by reference to those elements, she would also have to show that NCS was not justified in doing what it did in virtue of the provisions of subs 15(4) of the Act. That subsection effectively requires that, given the above elements are proved, the complainant, because of her disability, was unable to carry out the inherent requirements of the employment. This would involve taking into account her training, qualifications and experience relevant to the employment, her performance as an employee, and all other relevant factors that it is reasonable to take into account.

The complainant had performed the work for 10 years, her eyesight had not significantly changed in that time, and there was no acceptable evidence that she was or had become unable to perform the inherent requirements of her particular employment. She was discriminated against by reason of her visual impairment. As to the issue of whether the discrimination was not justified (ie, unlawful) by virtue of subs 15(4) of the Act, the evidence showed that the complainant was able to carry out the inherent requirements of her particular employment. At the very least her employer had not obtained evidence from a suitably qualified specialist that she was unable to adequately carry out her employment. She was in fact dismissed from her employment by reason of her disability and her complaint was substantiated.

In awarding damages, the judge took into account the age of the complainant, which militated against her finding further work, and her retraining in order to make herself more employable. Her compensation included past and anticipated future loss of capacity to earn. In addition, embarrassment and other psychological stresses since her dismissal were taken into account. The complainant was awarded a total of $56,692.80 in compensation.

The Federal Court considered what constitutes an inherent requirement of a job in the following case.

[18.90] Case: *Commonwealth v Human Rights and Equal Opportunity Commission* (1998) EOC ¶92-909

A soldier was discharged from the army when his HIV-positive status was established. He was in excellent health and symptom-free. He complained to the Human Rights and Equal Opportunity Commission that he had been unlawfully discriminated against because of his condition, as he could carry out his duties adequately. The Defence Force said that as he might suffer injury when he was deployed on training, and that this might result in the spillage of blood, he was a health risk to other soldiers. The Commission did not accept this argument, stating that the risk of exchange of bodily fluids was not confined to the army, and thus being able to "bleed safely" was not an inherent requirement of being a soldier, which it interpreted narrowly as meaning whether the complainant could perform the tasks of a soldier. The case was appealed to the Federal Court.

[18.95] The Federal Court reversed the decision of the Commission. The inherent requirements of a job include those relevant to all foreseeable activities that the job might require, and the physical and social environment in which the person must work. A soldier's life is not the same as most others—no one is seeking to kill other workers, nor do they train with lethal weapons in intrinsically dangerous situations. The Court also pointed out that any interpretation of the term "inherent requirements of a job" must be restricted by the duty of care owed by the employer to other workers to ensure a safe workplace within the nature of the enterprise. There is also a duty of care to fellow employees. The soldier's HIV status was thus relevant to the inherent requirements of the job and thus the need to "bleed safely".

Workplace Relations Act 1996 (Cth)

[18.100] This Act requires that the Industrial Relations Commission must refuse to certify any agreement that discriminates against an employee on similar grounds to those listed in the *Human Rights and Equal Opportunity Commission Act 1986* (Cth). Australian Workplace Agreements are deemed to contain anti-discrimination provisions if they are not specified in the agreement. However, these do not include youth wages, inherent requirement of a job, and employment by religious institutions in accordance with the doctrines of that religion.

Exceptions in federal laws

[18.105] There are some exceptions to the employment provisions of the federal anti-discrimination law. Such exceptions are where:

- the characteristic in question is a genuine occupational qualification (for example, a male actor for a male part in a play, or a wet-nurse);
- services offered are validly applicable to only one sex (for example, counselling for women victims of sexual assault);
- services are of an intimate nature, such as attendants at toilets, or where people are required or may wish to undress (for example, dressing rooms in clothing shops or for medical examination).

Religious bodies, sporting bodies, charities and voluntary bodies are excepted in some circumstances. Despite the fact that health carers provide services of an intimate nature, it is not generally considered a genuine occupational qualification that a carer is of a particular gender. Sensitive areas such as rape units in hospitals would be considered as exceptions.

Racial discrimination

[18.110] Having ratified the *International Convention on the Elimination of all Forms of Racial Discrimination* ("Racial Discrimination Convention"), the federal government enacted the *Racial Discrimination Act 1975* (Cth), prohibiting the discrimination, in certain areas of activity, against any person on the basis of race, national or ethnic origin or colour. Discrimination is defined by s 9 of the *Racial Discrimination Act* as the doing of any act:

> "involving a distinction, exclusion, restriction or preference based on race, colour, descent or national or ethnic origin which has the purpose or effect of nullifying or impairing the recognition, enjoyment or exercise, on an equal footing, of any human right or fundamental freedom in the political, economic, social, cultural or any other field of public life."

The areas of activity covered by the Act include employment, accommodation, delivery of goods, facilities and services, education, the disposal of land, and the administration of Commonwealth laws and programmes. The Racial Discrimination Convention is attached to the Act in the form of a Schedule, outlining rights and freedoms relating to people based on race. A case that shows how not only staff but management of health care facilities can be liable for racist discrimination follows.

[18.115] Case: *Daniels v Queensland Nursing Homes Pty Ltd* [1995] HREOCA 2 (24 January 1995)

The complainant, of Burmese origin, was trained as a registered nurse in her home country, but as her qualifications were not recognised in Australia, was employed as an assistant nurse by the respondent company. She complained of racist comments by another staff member, Nurse D (who was the senior nurse there, and a long-term acquaintance of the Director of Nursing) and that she was dismissed from her job because of her race. She was dismissed after a third alleged incident concerning a patient. Two earlier incidents had occurred, one in which she had swung the chair of a difficult patient (Patient "R") around "with all her strength". The second incident involved lifting the leg of a patient (Patient "G") contrary to established procedures. As Patient G had severe osteoporosis (unbeknownst to the complainant or other assistant nurses), the leg fractured. Evidence was given by the Director of Nursing that she warned the complainant on both occasions that this behaviour was unsatisfactory, and told her a third incident would result in her dismissal. A "Reprimand Book" was kept by the Director, with a record of the incidents and a notation that the complainant had received a warning beside each. A third incident did occur. Nurse D claimed that he witnessed the complainant lifting a patient (Patient "F") from a chair into bed, and that while another nurse (Nurse "G") lifted the top half of the patient, the complainant had lifted the patient by one foot, causing the patient distress.

The Director of Nursing dismissed the complainant testifying that she relied on the information about the third incident from Nurse D, as well as the incident with Patient G, and did not think the complainant should be given an opportunity to explain the incident because of the seriousness of the former incident. Whatever the complainant said would not change her mind. She also did not bother speaking to the nurse with whom the complainant was lifting Patient F (Nurse G), nor did the chief executive officer, whom she notified of her intention to dismiss the complainant. She also refused to allow the complainant to resign.

[18.120] The Commission held that having regard to the gravity of the matters alleged, the complainant must prove on the balance of probabilities, that she was a victim of unlawful racial discrimination or that her race, colour or national or ethnic origin was at least a reason for her dismissal or that there was conduct that discriminated against her. To do this, she would have to show that, dismissal of non-Australian staff was carried out in a way that was less favourable than dismissal of Australian staff. Non-white, non Anglo-Australian staff who contravened instructions or nursing standards, were for that reason dealt with more harshly than white-Australian staff, in not being afforded the opportunity to resign.

The Commission also concluded that some of the staff at the nursing home were subjected to racist comments and abuse by Nurse D, that neither the Director of Nursing nor the officers of the respondent company gave directions not to engage in racist abuse or racist jokes, and that the former had condoned Nurse D's behaviour, which was grounded in race. This had created a hostile working environment for the complainant and others of Asian origin and in this environment Nurse D was critical of the complainant. It held that the race or ethnic origin of the complainant was a reason for his report about Patient F, and he had been looking for an opportunity to report ill of her. He could not have seen what occurred when Patient F was being lifted into bed. His report was false.

Whilst no reports were made by staff about the racist abuse to the Director of Nursing, the Commission was critical of the fact that there was no system in place whereby non-white non Anglo-Australian staff were assured that such complaints would be taken seriously nor that a complainant would not be viewed adversely for so complaining. Neither the Director of Nursing nor any other officer of the respondent could have expected anybody to make such complaint to her about Nurse D, taking into account the regard in which she held him and the length of time she had known him.

The Commission determined that the turnover in staff of Asian origin was not the result of a racist policy, and the percentage of non Anglo-Australian staff employed at the nursing home had not decreased to such a significant respect since the current Director of Nursing had been appointed, that a racist attitude could be inferred from that. However, although there was a personality clash between the Director of Nursing and the complainant, that, or poor communication, were not the only reasons for the Director of Nursing deciding to act upon Nurse D's report of the Patient F incident. The Patient G incident caused her grave concern, but she did not in fact give the complainant a warning in respect of Patient R, and that the incidents concerning Patient R were written as they appeared in the Reprimand Book after the occurrence of the Patient G incident. The Director of Nursing, knowing of, and tolerating, Nurse D's attitude, and in reliance on his report, summarily dismissed the complainant without giving her or Nurse G an opportunity to deny that false report.

It was also determined that the chief executive officer of the respondent company acted on the advice of the Director of Nursing, and was not himself motivated by racist attitudes in agreeing to the termination. But the respondent company did not take all reasonable steps to prevent Nurse D's ill-will towards the complainant. Its decision to terminate her employment was thus in part actuated by the race or ethnic origin of the complainant, and unlawful conduct for which the respondent should be held liable.

Sex discrimination

[18.125] As a consequence of having signed the *International Convention on the Elimination of all Forms of Discrimination against Women* ("CEDAW"), the federal government passed the *Sex Discrimination Act 1984* (Cth). As with the *Racial Discrimination Act 1975* (Cth), CEDAW is attached as a Schedule to the *Sex Discrimination Act*. This Act prohibits discrimination on the ground of sex, marital status or pregnancy, in the same areas as those provided for in the *Racial Discrimination Act*. The definition of discrimination in ss 5, 6 and 9 of this Act is, however, different. It involves the discriminator treating:

> "the aggrieved person less favourably than, in circumstances that are the same or are not materially different, the discriminator treats or would treat a person [of different sex, marital status or who is not pregnant]."

The Act goes on to say that the grounds of discrimination include not only a characteristic that appertains generally to persons on the grounds of their sex, marital status, or those who are pregnant, but also characteristics which are "imputed to them" (for example, "all women complain too much"; "pregnant women are irrational").

[18.130] Case: *Bear v Norwood Private Nursing Home*
(1984) EOC ¶92-019 (Sex Discrimination Board SA)

The complainant worked as a nurse assistant at the hospital. She became pregnant. She was temporarily absent with a threatened miscarriage, but returned to work. She was dismissed, and complained that the dismissal was because of the pregnancy, and thus unlawful.

[18.135] The Board held that she was not unfairly dismissed. The basis for the action was not her pregnancy or temporary disability following the threatened miscarriage or tiredness. Rather it was because she was not doing her work satisfactorily. It would have been discrimination if:

- there had been a policy of dismissing pregnant nurses;
- her dismissal was the result of a belief that pregnant women in general should not be employed as nurses;
- her appearance had been considered undesirable; or
- the dismissal was to prevent a risk to herself or foetus.

A case where a veterinary surgeon was dismissed on the ground of pregnancy is *Kimler v Lort Smith Animal Hospital* [1995] HREOCA 20. In that case the complainant was held to be unlawfully dismissed, as the basis of the dismissal was a belief that as a pregnant woman she should not be working. She was told that one of the nurses was bitten on the breast by a dog a few weeks previously, and the employer was concerned that something like that could happen to her. See also *Fenton v Hair & Beauty Gallery Pty Ltd & Anor* [2006] FMCA 3.

[18.140] Case: *Jordan v North Coast Area Health Service (No 2)* [2005] NSWADT 258

J worked as a blood collector at Lismore Base Hospital. She became pregnant but initially continued performing her duties until she more than once asked the operations manager for what she called "light duties" because she was finding it difficult to perform her duties due to her late stage pregnancy. The operations manager attempted to locate a suitable position for her but was unable, and so by agreement J absented herself on a combination of annual leave and long service leave before commencing maternity leave. J alleged discrimination pointing to other, non-pregnant NRAHS employees whose requests for alternative duties were met, and argued that because the difference between their circumstances and hers was that she was pregnant, it should be inferred that her request, which was essentially to the same effect as theirs, was refused because of her pregnancy.

The tribunal held that the inference could not be drawn. It is not supported by the evidence. The non-pregnant employees who were doing alternative duties were usually doing so under a statutory entitlement arising from a work-related injury. On the issue of direct discrimination, at the time there were no positions available and no funds to create a position. These were held to be the real reasons why J's request was not met. Turning then to indirect discrimination, an alternative way in which NRAHS's conduct could have contravened the *Anti-Discrimination Act 1977* was if J had to, but could not, comply with an unreasonable requirement that substantially more men than women could comply with (s 24(1)(b)). The requirement was identified as being that in order to continue in active full-time employment with NRAHS, blood collection workers on wards must carry out their normal duties. The tribunal was satisfied that of those to whom the requirement was directed, the proportion of men able to comply with the requirement was substantially higher than that of women in the later stages of pregnancy. However, a finding of unlawful discrimination under s 24(1)(b) is possible only if a requirement is shown to be not reasonable. The tribunal noted the requirement that in order to continue in active paid employment a blood collection worker must carry out their normal duties, should be approached on the basis that it is, on its face, reasonable.

The tribunal held that whilst opportunities for NRAHS to provide alternative full-time duties for J were limited, it was possible for NRAHS to have made considerably greater efforts to accommodate her needs through alternatives that would have both enabled her to remain in full-time employment, and would have enabled blood collections to be done. Whether there was, or could have been available funds, was not the subject of inquiry or even reflection by NRAHS even though alternative duties were, in other circumstances, provided with a budgetary impact; whether swaps were possible between or among other employees was not the subject of inquiry by NRAHS; and whether the *Anti-Discrimination Act 1977* effectively imposed a legal requirement on NRAHS was never contemplated. As a result, the requirement imposed on J was, in the circumstances, not reasonable.

An award of compensation was made to J in the sum of $7,500.

Sexual preference, marital status

[18.145] Cases where women have been denied access to reproductive technology on the basis of their marital status (or lack of it), and sexual preference have been mentioned in Chapter 17.

Sexual harassment

[18.150] Health carers and patients should be free from sexual harassment in the workplace. The *Sex Discrimination Act*, as well as the legislation in the Australian Capital Territory, Queensland, South Australia, Tasmania, Victoria and Western Australia (outlined below), prohibits sexual harassment in the workplace and in educational facilities. Sexual harassment is defined in the *Sex Discrimination Act* as an unwelcome sexual advance, or "an unwelcome request for sexual favours ... or ... other unwelcome conduct of a sexual nature". Where the person being harassed has reasonable grounds for believing that rejecting the advance, refusing the request or objecting to the conduct disadvantaged or would disadvantage them in connection with their employment or their studies (*Sex Discrimination Act 1984* (Cth), s 28). Ronalds ((1987), p 119) points out:

"The concept of 'disadvantage' could incorporate factors such as a hostile work environment, mental anguish, lack of job opportunities or other matters which had a negative result on the person. ... In educational institutions it could involve a threat to fail a student or a failure or a deferment or a denial of access to a particular course or class, or the use of specialist equipment."

Where management does not take proper action to prevent or remedy sexual harassment in the workplace it may be found vicariously liable, as it is also for other acts of sexual discrimination. The Act provides, however, that if management has taken all reasonable steps to prevent the employee from offending it will not be found liable.

[18.155] Case: *Boyle v Ishan Ozden* (1986) EOC ¶92-165 (Human Rights Commission (as it was then called))

The complainant worked at a take-away shop. She brought a complaint against the manager of the shop who had allegedly unlawfully sexually harassed her. Because she rejected his advances he dismissed her the next day. The complaint also named the owners of the shop, who were overseas at the time, and who argued that they could not be responsible for actions taken in their absence.

[18.160] The Commission found (p 76,614) that the owners were vicariously responsible for the manager's sexual harassment, even though they did not know of it, for the purposes of this case:

"there was no evidence that any steps had been taken to prevent commission of the acts ... complained of ... In saying that I do not criticise them. It would be difficult to envisage a situation in which they would have given such instructions. But the fact is that s 106 attaches vicarious liability to them unless they have done something active to prevent the acts complained of."

Harassment may not have a sexual content, but may nevertheless occur, motivated by the sex of the person who is victimised (that is, "sexist" harassment).

[18.165] Case: *Hill v Water Resources Commission* (1985) EOC ¶92-127 (Equal Opportunity Commission NSW)

The complainant became the first female clerical officer to enter an almost completely male-dominated area. It was made quite clear to her that she was unwelcome, with many acts of harassment including withholding of mail she was expecting, goods being unloaded from a truck being thrown with unnecessary force to her, failure by employees to recognise her authority and carry out instructions, false information that the goldfish she kept in her office had been killed, and the fouling of toilets she had had re-allocated from males to females.

[18.170] The Tribunal held that this was discrimination, as a man would not have been harassed in this way. It accepted the complainant's argument that the harassment produced a hostile work environment and that it was sufficiently pervasive to affect adversely the terms and conditions of employment. Conditions of employment include the psychological and emotional work environment. The Water Resources Commission was found liable for acts of sexual harassment by its employees against the complainant, and damages of $34,827.34 were awarded for distress, loss of wages and promotion opportunities, and long-term psychological effects. This was because "either no action or very limited action was taken and often there was a lengthy delay before any action was taken" as a result of her complaints to management.

There is legal argument that the federal legislation against sexual discrimination cannot cover male employees who are discriminated against, as it is based on the convention which deals with discrimination against women. There is no question, however, that prohibition against sexual discrimination goes both ways under State legislation.

[18.175] Case: *Ahern v Burra Burra Hospital* (unreported, 22 March 1982, Sex Discrimination Board SA)

A male student nurse was refused accommodation in the nurses home attached to the hospital. This accommodation was available to female nurses and was better than alternatives. The hospital claimed that it was not obliged to provide accommodation to student nurses: that this was a benefit it could bestow at will. Ahern complained of sexual discrimination to the Board.

[18.180] The Board held that although the hospital was not obliged to provide accommodation it did so for female nurses as a matter of course. It was held that accommodation was a benefit applying to employment. The male nurse was thus denied a benefit enjoyed by other nurses, and this was a breach of the legislation.

Patients and staff who are victims of discrimination or sexual harassment should complain firstly to the employing authority where it occurs. If this is neither feasible (it may be the discriminator) nor successful, one may go to:

• the appropriate body where there is anti-discrimination legislation in their jurisdiction;
• the police where the act amounts to sexual or other assault;

- the appropriate professional disciplinary body governing the alleged offender; or
- (for patients), under the general complaints procedures regarding medical treatment (see **[18.35]**) and (for patients and employees) to the Human Rights and Equal Opportunity Commission.

Discrimination and disability

[18.185] The *Disability Discrimination Act 1992* (Cth) provides for complaints by those with a disability to complain of discrimination. They can also complain under complementary State legislation where it exists. The definition of disability is broad, including physical, sensory, intellectual or psychiatric impairment, as well as the presence in the body of organisms causing or capable of causing disease (thereby including HIV and AIDS). The legislation also prohibits discrimination because a person uses a wheelchair, cane, hearing or guide dog, permitting the presence of the dogs in places where they would be otherwise prohibited. The areas of activity covered are similar to those covered by the *Racial Discrimination Act* thus including the delivery of health care services.

[18.190] Case: *Purvis v New South Wales* (Department of Education and Training) [2003] HCA 62 (11 November 2003)

This important decision of the High Court concerned the suspension and subsequent exclusion from school of a pupil who repeatedly assaulted teachers and other pupils, where the pupil's behaviour was a consequence of brain damage.

The pupil was a ward of the State but had been in full time foster care for some time. He sustained severe brain injury when he was about 6 or 7 months old as the consequence of an encephalopathic illness. The injury resulted in damage to the parieto-occipital lobes and bilateral damage to the frontal lobes of his brain. As a result he suffered from an intellectual disability, visual difficulties, epilepsy and behavioural problems in the nature of disinhibited and uninhibited behaviour.

The High Court by majority noted that the Commissioner did not correctly apply s 5(1). The Commissioner's conclusion about the reason for Daniel's suspensions and exclusion (his disturbed behaviour) was seen as being determinative of the question of less favourable treatment. The circumstances which surrounded Daniel's treatment were not identified. There was no determination of how a person without the disability would have been treated in circumstances that were the same as, or not materially different from, the circumstances surrounding Daniel's treatment. Accordingly the High Court by majority dismissed the appeal and thereby overturned the initial finding that the State had discriminated against the pupil Daniel on the grounds of his disability.

> **[18.195]** Case: *Hollingdale v North Coast Area Health Service* [2006] FMCA 5
>
> This matter concerned the termination of employment of H, a clinical psychologist who suffered bi-polar disorder and keratoconus. The Court was required to consider H's behaviour leading to suspension and disciplinary action. H accepted that the Area Health Service was under an obligation to deal with complaints or concerns about the fitness or behaviour of its professional staff but asserted that the Area Health Service unjustifiably delayed the disciplinary process. The employer directed a change of duties to a project officer position which H refused to perform, allegedly due to vision problems. H refused direction to attend work due to her asserted medical condition and was then dismissed.
>
> The Court found for the employer, saying that H's behaviour justified action taken against her by the employer. There was no unlawful discrimination.

Discrimination and special consideration for the aged

[18.200] The *Aged Care Act 1997* (Cth) and the *National Health Act 1953* (Cth) establish rights for those in government nursing homes and hostels. The *Aged Care Act 1997* (Cth) authorises the Minister to make "quality care principles", dealing with the lifestyle and personal care of residents, and those receiving community care. "User rights principles" are also established, which require those providing residential care to ensure security of tenure, and a complaints mechanism.

The Department of Health and Ageing, as well as community visitors and patient advocates recognised by the Department can inspect nursing homes. Government funding will not be given to hostels unless there is general compliance with the legislation, and where there is doubt about the standard of care, a Hostel Standards Review Panel can be directed to review the matter to ensure standards are upheld.

Measures to achieve equality

[18.205] Perhaps the most important and controversial exception to discrimination in anti-discrimination legislation is the provision that measures intended to achieve equality are exempted from prohibition. It allows acts and special programmes to meet specific needs of a group, which are designed to result in furthering equality of that group within the rest of society. This provision for affirmative action gives recognition to the fact that socialisation, fewer educational opportunities and social attitudes which have been the result of, for example, racial or sexist discrimination in the past, have put some people at a disadvantage that no strictly equal treatment will remedy.

It is thus not unlawful to discriminate in favour of one of the mentioned classes of people if that discrimination is a means of bringing about equality of access to employment or conditions of employment, or access to goods and services, where those measures are to bring about the same degree of access as that enjoyed by others. Measures such as training programmes for particular groups of people, for instance English classes or nursing orientation classes for migrant employees are lawful. Exemption is also provided for discriminating where the service offered is such that it will not work effectively without it, for example, female nurses for treating rape victims, or gender-specific counselling, however, in most cases the employer or provider of services must apply for the exemption from the Human Rights and Equal Opportunity Commission.

[18.210] Case: *Proudfoot v ACT Board of Health* (1992) EOC ¶92-417

The complainant alleged that the provision of health services for women by the Australian Capital Territory Women's Health Service and the Canberra Women's Health Service, both funded by the Commonwealth and the Australian Capital Territory governments, were discriminatory, in that they provided services for medical problems not exclusive to women. This was despite the fact that men, on average, die several years earlier than women, and men also have specific health problems. The complaint was brought under the federal *Sex Discrimination Act*, was not resolved by conciliation, and went to the Human Rights Commission. It was argued there that the health services offered were based on a holistic approach to health care, and in the recognition that many health problems faced by women, although common to both sexes, cannot be dealt with in isolation to their social and psychological environment, and their discriminatory treatment in the mainstream of the medical system.

[18.215] The Human Rights Commission (as it then was) held that the services were prima facie discriminatory, however it accepted the argument that a person's health includes indivisible physical and mental elements, and that in addressing the health needs of women some problems which are faced by both sexes may be included in ancillary services. The Commission also recognised the disadvantages in gaining access to optimal health care which women in general may face because they have less financial resources, less influence in gaining services, and are more burdened by their child-bearing and child-rearing role in society, and in the widespread occurrence of domestic violence. On this basis, the Commission held that the provision of the health services was justifiable under s 33 of the *Sex Discrimination Act*, which provides an exemption if the purpose of the discrimination is to ensure that a person of a particular sex may have equal opportunities with the other sex.

Remedies under federal legislation

Conciliation

[18.220] The Racial, Sex and Disability Discrimination Acts provide a mechanism for dealing with complaints of discrimination where the legislation applies. There is a Race Discrimination Commissioner, a Sex Discrimination Commissioner and a Disability Discrimination Commissioner attached to the Human Rights and Equal Opportunity Commission (the Commission) to administer the respective Acts and who refer appropriate matters to the Commission. Complaints are directed to the Commission, which, after accepting that the complaint is actionable under the law, must attempt to resolve it through conciliation. This approach, which is very different from the usual legal adversarial method of seeking satisfaction for a wrong, has been adopted because it is believed to be a more satisfactory way of handling discrimination than making it a criminal offence, which may be difficult to prove and which may make the situation worse. It is also considered better than making the sole avenue of redress a civil action, with the need for the aggrieved person (complainant) to bring protracted and expensive legal action.

In order to bring about resolution by conciliation, a conference of the parties is to be called. The Commission may provide written notice to a person believed to be capable of doing so, to provide the Commission with relevant information or documents, and the Commission may require any person who can provide relevant information to attend a conference. A compulsory conference is confidential and must not disadvantage either the complainant or respondent. Failure to comply can result in a fine or result in adverse findings in the next possible step. Giving false or misleading information can lead to imprisonment for six months.

Litigation

[18.225] Where a complaint is "terminated" (for example, rejected as unfounded, or cannot be conciliated) the person may make an application to the Federal Court or the Federal Magistrates' Court. That Court, if it is satisfied that the discrimination has occurred, can make any order it thinks fit, such as re-instatement of employment, restitution, declarations, and compensation. In doing so it can take a report of the Commissioner into account.

State and Territory legislation

[18.230] All jurisdictions have legislation prohibiting defined acts of discrimination on specified grounds. They have similar exceptions and exemption provisions to the federal legislation. Each has adopted an agency for dealing with complaints, which respond in a similar way to the Commission. The powers of the agency and the enforceability of its findings differ according to jurisdiction, however, unlike the Human Rights and Equal Opportunity Commission, those bodies do have some powers of enforcement of decisions.

Australian Capital Territory

[18.235] The *Discrimination Act 1991* (ACT) prohibits discrimination on the grounds of:

- sex, sexuality, transsexuality, marital status, pregnancy, sexual harassment, status as parent or carer, breastfeeding;
- age;
- race;
- impairment;
- religious or political conviction;
- profession, trade, occupation or calling; and
- association with a person with any of the above characteristics,

in the areas of employment, provision of goods and services, and accommodation, among others. The Act also prohibits sexual harassment and racial vilification, unlawful advertising and victimisation of complainants. The agency involved is the Discrimination Commissioner, who investigates and conciliates complaints, and the Discrimination Tribunal. The Commissioner's role under s 112 of the *Discrimination Act* is to promote an understanding and acceptance of, and compliance with the Act; to undertake research and develop educational and other programs to promote the objects of the Act; to review the consistency of laws in the Australian Capital Territory with the Act and report to the Attorney-General; respond to requests by the Attorney-General to examine possible inconsistencies in proposed laws with the Act; and to advise the Attorney-General on any matter relevant to the Act's operation. In the context of an individual complaint, the Commissioner attempts to assist in a conciliation process; ultimately a matter may be brought before the Tribunal. For a more detailed explanation of the process, see the Commissioner's website at: www.hro.act.gov.au/handlingcomplaint.html. The Australian Capital Territory is the first jurisdiction in Australia to have an explicit statutory basis for respecting, protecting, fulfilling and promoting civil and political rights in the form of the *Human Rights Act 2004* which protects rights in the *International Covenant on Civil and Political Rights* summarised by the Australian Capital Territory Human Rights Commissioner (see www.hro.act.gov.au/publications.html) as follows:

- recognition and equality before the law;
- life from the time of birth;
- protection from torture and cruel, inhuman or degrading treatment;
- protection of the family and children;
- privacy and reputation;
- freedom of movement;
- freedom of thought, conscience, religion and belief;
- peaceful assembly and freedom of association;
- freedom of expression;
- take part in public life;
- liberty and security of person;

- humane treatment when deprived of liberty;
- children in the criminal process;
- a fair trial;
- criminal proceedings;
- compensation for wrongful conviction;
- not to be tried or punished more than once;
- not to be subject to retrospective criminal laws;
- freedom from forced work;
- ethnic, religious or linguistic minorities.

The *Human Rights Act* also recognises that people can have other rights under domestic or international law, for example, under other treaties to which Australia is a party (such as the *Convention on the Rights of the Child*). The Act introduced a new rule of statutory interpretation in s 30, which provides that in working out the meaning of a Territory law, an interpretation that is consistent with human rights is as far as possible to be preferred. Cases addressing that new rule can be found on the Australian Capital Territory Human Rights Commissioner's website; for example, *Robertson v Australian Capital Territory* [2005] ACTSC 35 which concerned the making of a psychiatric treatment order in relation to a mental health patient (see www.hro.act.gov.au/casesdecisions. html).

New South Wales

[18.240] The *Anti-Discrimination Act 1977* (NSW) prohibits discrimination on the grounds of:

- race, colour, nationality, descent and ethnic, ethno-religious or national origin;
- sex, pregnancy, marital status; sexual preference, transgender;
- physical and intellectual impairment; and
- age,

in the areas of employment, education, provision of goods and services, accommodation, industrial organisations, and registered clubs, among others. The Act also prohibits racial, homosexual, HIV/AIDS, and transgender vilification, sexual harassment and victimisation of complainants. The agencies involved are the Anti-Discrimination Board, which investigates and conciliates complaints, and the Administrative Decisions Tribunal, which hears and determines unconciliated matters. There is an appeal mechanism to the Supreme Court.

Northern Territory

[18.245] The *Anti-Discrimination Act* (NT) prohibits discrimination on the grounds of:

- sex, sexuality, marital status, pregnancy;
- parenthood, breastfeeding;
- age;
- race;

- impairment;
- religious belief, political opinion;
- irrelevant medical or criminal record;
- trade union or employer association activity; and
- association with a person with any of the above characteristics,

in the areas of education, work, facilities, clubs, provision of goods and services, and accommodation, among others. The agency involved is the Anti-Discrimination Commissioner, who investigates and conciliates complaints.

Queensland

[18.250] The *Anti-Discrimination Act 1991* (Qld) prohibits discrimination on the grounds of:

- sex, marital status, lawful sexual activity, pregnancy, parental status, breast-feeding;
- age;
- race;
- impairment;
- religion, political belief or activity;
- trade union activity; and
- association with a person with any of the above characteristics,

in the areas of employment, provision of goods and services, and accommodation, among others. The Act also prohibits sexual harassment, incitement to racial or religious hatred and victimisation of complainants. The agency involved is the Anti-Discrimination Commissioner, who investigates and conciliates complaints and where that is unsuccessful, the Anti-Discrimination Tribunal which hears and determines the matter.

The *Industrial Relations Act 1999* (Qld) also makes discrimination on a wide number of grounds unlawful. Matters are taken to the Queensland Industrial Relations Commission.

South Australia

[18.255] The *Equal Opportunity Act 1984* (SA) prohibits discrimination on the grounds of:

- race, nationality, colour, ancestry, or origin (either of the person or their associate(s));
- sex, sexuality, marital status, pregnancy;
- physical and intellectual impairment; and
- age,

in the areas of employment, provision of goods and services, and accommodation, amongst others. The Act also prohibits sexual harassment and victimisation of complainants. The agencies involved are the Commissioner for Equal Opportunity who investigates and conciliates complaints, and where it is unsuccessful, the Equal Opportunity Tribunal, which hears and determines the

624 Part V Ethical/Legal Issues

matter. There is an appeal to the Supreme Court. The *Racial Vilification Act 1996* (SA) prohibits racial vilification.

Tasmania

[18.260] The *Anti-Discrimination Act* 1998 (Tas) makes discrimination unlawful on the following grounds:

- race;
- age;
- sex, sexual orientation, lawful sexual activity, marital status, pregnancy, breastfeeding, parental status, family responsibilities;
- disability;
- industrial activity;
- political or religious belief or non-belief, affiliation or activity;
- irrelevant medical or criminal record; and
- association with a person with, or believed to have any of the above characteristics,

in most areas of public life. The Act also makes unlawful conduct that offends, humiliates, intimidates, insults or ridicules another person on the basis of one of the above grounds. It also renders unlawful publicly inciting hatred of a person because of their race, disability, sexual orientation or religious belief or non-belief. Complaints are made to the Anti-Discrimination Commissioner, who attempts conciliation. Unconciliated matters and appeals from the Commissioner's findings go to the Anti-Discrimination Tribunal.

Victoria

[18.265] Section 17 of the *Equal Opportunity Act 1995* (Vic) prohibits discrimination on the grounds of:

- race, colour, ethnic or national origin;
- sex, marital status, pregnancy, breastfeeding;
- lawful sexual activity, sexual orientation, gender identity;
- age, physical features;
- the state of being a parent, childless or de facto spouse;
- lawful political or religious belief or activity;
- physical impairment (including presence of organisms causing disease), mental illness or mental disability; and
- industrial activity,

in the areas of employment, education, provision of goods and services, and accommodation, disposal of land, community service organisations, municipal or shire councils, sport among others. The Act also prohibits sexual harassment and victimisation of complainants. The agencies involved are the Equal Opportunity Commission, which investigates and conciliates complaints, and the Civil and Administrative Tribunal, which hears and determines unconciliated matters.

Western Australia

[18.270] The *Equal Opportunity Act 1984* (WA) prohibits discrimination on the grounds of:

* race;
* sex, marital status, pregnancy, family responsibilities, and family status;
* religious or political conviction;
* physical or mental impairment; and
* age,

in most areas of public life. The agencies involved are the Commissioner for Equal Opportunity, which investigates and conciliates complaints, and where it is unsuccessful, the Equal Opportunity Tribunal, which hears and determines the matter.

Which Act should one use?

[18.275] In the various Australian jurisdictions which have anti-discrimination legislation, two pieces of legislation, federal and State, may cover a particular situation. The federal government has entered into an arrangement with some of those jurisdictions to enable them to act as its delegate. This means that it is possible to obtain advice on which jurisdiction is most appropriate when lodging the complaint with most State or Territory administrative bodies, and the complaint can be processed under both federal or State or Territory legislation.

The *Racial Discrimination Act*, the *Sex Discrimination Act*, the *Disability Discrimination Act* and the *Human Rights and Equal Opportunity Commission Act* are based on international instruments (documents creating legal rights and duties), are valid enactments, and apply throughout the country. Other areas of discrimination are covered by State or Territory legislation, but not specifically prohibited by Federal legislation (for example, homosexuality, status of being a parent etc). Different powers and functions held by the Human Rights and Equal Opportunity Commission and State or Territory anti-discrimination bodies may determine which Act to choose.

Exemptions

[18.280] Exemptions, which apply in the State or Territory legislation, are similar to those which apply in the federal legislation.

Measures to achieve equality

[18.285] All State and Territory legislation (except the *Anti-Discrimination Act 1977* (NSW)) has an exception to the prohibition of discrimination, where that discrimination is part of measures to achieve equality for a particular group of people: to put them on an equal footing with others. This allows for the taking of positive steps to overcome the effects of past discrimination. Examples include the provision of special medical services for particular groups of people, such as rural Aborigines, or the provision of special education facilities so that those who may have missed out in the past because of their race or their gender can catch up and have equal access to work. The Commonwealth government has also established the Equal Opportunity for Women in the Workplace Agency (see www.eowa.gov.au/) under the *Equal Opportunity for Women in the Workplace Act 1999* (Cth). EOWA is a statutory authority located within the portfolio of the Australian Commonwealth Department of Employment and Workplace Relations. The Act requires private sector companies, community organisations, non-government schools, unions, group training companies, and higher education institutions with 100 or more people to establish a workplace program to remove the barriers to women entering and advancing in their organisation. The Act sets out steps in implementing an equal opportunity program, and the Agency provides guidelines to assist compliance with the reporting. Failure to implement a program or submit a report can result in naming in Parliament and ineligibility for government contracts or specified forms of financial assistance. EOWA receives annual reports from approximately 3000 organisations covered by the Act on the progress of their workplace programs, and assists them in developing their programs to achieve greater outcomes for women and for business.

Implications for Health Care Workers

[18.290] The connection between international instruments on human rights and domestic law means that health carers in the relevant jurisdictions should not be discriminated against on the grounds discussed above, and also that they should not discriminate in their work against others on those grounds. They should not refuse to treat, or give any less than accepted treatment to, patients because of their age, marital status (or lack of it), sexual preference, or because they are mentally ill or suffering from a contagious disease, or a socially stigmatised one such as HIV/AIDS, or because they are suffering from a drug-related illness such as alcoholism or drug dependency.

Where the giving of treatment places the health carer in danger of harm, then reasonable discriminatory activity may be acceptable, for example, in nuclear medicine where special conditions may apply to pregnant women. Where carers find that the practice is to treat someone differently, they need to examine why this is so: it should be purely on the grounds of need (the patient's or their own).

Discrimination and the HIV-positive patient

[18.295] No legislation refers expressly to HIV infection or AIDS as a ground for discrimination (but see above at **[7.275]** regarding the *Public Health Act 1991* (NSW), under which such disclosure is prohibited in respect of AIDS and/or HIV infection), however, complaints may be made, according to circumstances and the legislation in the particular jurisdiction, of discrimination on the ground of impairment, sexuality, sexual preference, or homosexuality. The basis for discrimination may be that the complainant is assumed to fit the category, does fit the category, is a member of a high-risk group, or associates with such a person. Complaints of discrimination by HIV-positive patients under specific legislation can thus now be made in all jurisdictions.

Complaints of discrimination against patients on the basis of HIV/AIDS with differing outcomes can be compared by reviewing the cases below.

[18.300] Case: *Ferguson v Central Sydney Area Health Service & Anor* (1990) EOC ¶92-272

A patient who was homosexual and whose lifestyle was considered to be at "high risk" of being exposed to HIV complained to the New South Wales Equal Opportunity Tribunal that he was discriminated against on the grounds of his homosexuality by being refused elective surgery until his antibody status was obtained.

[18.305] The Tribunal found that it was the man's medical status and high-risk category that was the causal factor in his being treated as he was, and not the fact that he was homosexual. Any person in the high-risk category, male or female, homosexual or heterosexual, whose high-risk status was discovered would be treated in the same way at that time. Readers are referred to *Commonwealth of Australia v Human Rights and Equal Opportunity Commission* above (see **[18.90]**).

[18.310] Case: *G v L* (1995) EOC ¶92-712

A patient, a nurse, was told by his doctor he required surgery and would be referred to a specialist surgeon. The doctor then asked him if he was gay and when the patient confirmed this the doctor stated a test would be required to determine his HIV status before he could have the surgery. The complainant said he had had a test some months previously and had not participated in unsafe sex since then. He reminded the doctor he was a nurse, understood the nature of HIV/AIDS infection, and that every patient should be treated with due precautions. The doctor then reiterated his refusal to treat the complainant unless he had a test, and terminated future appointments.

[18.315] The doctor admitted that he had unlawfully discriminated against the complainant and settled with the complainant for $5,000 and $17,000 legal costs (indicating the cost of legal representation).

Those subjected to discrimination may have a remedy in tort action for negligence where the failure to treat them resulted in foreseeable harm, and there is no defence of self-protection by the defendant available. Hospitals should provide proper training and information regarding the treatment of HIV infections, and reasonable safeguards should be taken. See also **[16.70]**ff.

References and Further Reading

Anti-Discrimination Board of New South Wales, *Anti-Discrimination and Equal Employment Opportunity (EEO) Guidelines for Managers, Team Leaders and Supervisors* (Anti-Discrimination Board of New South Wales, Sydney, 1997)

Australian and New Zealand Equal Opportunity Law and Practice (CCH, Sydney, 1985)

Bunney, L, "Discrimination and Assisted Reproductive Technology" 5 *Health Law Bulletin* 57

CCH industrial law editors, *Countering Sexual Harassment: A Manual for Managers and Supervisors* (CCH, Sydney, 1992)

Department of Health and Family Services, *Standards and Guidelines for Residential Aged Care Services Manual*, Aged and Community Care Division, Commonwealth Department of Health (Department of Health and Family Services, Canberra ACT, 1998)

Jenkins, K and Lawrie, C, *Women in the Workplace: Sexual Harassment and Discrimination* (Prospect Media, Sydney, 2000)

Kinley, D, *Human Rights in Australian Law: Principles, Practice and Potential* (Federation Press, Sydney, 1998)

Larbalestier, J and Russell, D (ed), proceedings *Women and Law Conference: Working for Women? Anti-Discrimination, Affirmative Action, and Equal Opportunity*, 22nd September 1995 (Women's Studies Centre, University of Sydney, 1996)

McCullough, S (ed), *Older Residents' Legal Rights* (Federation Press, Sydney, 1992)

National Conference of Legal and Policy Officers from Human Rights/Equal Opportunity/Anti Discrimination Organisations, (1st) Darwin, 10-11 August 1995 (Anti-Discrimination Commission, Darwin, 1995)

Pettman, R, *Incitement to Racial Hatred: Issues and Analysis* (AGPS, Human Rights Commission Canberra, 1982)

Phillips, R and Merrilyn, J, *Older Residents and the Law* (Residential Care Rights, Melbourne, 1996)

Quinn, G, McDonagh, M and Kimber, C, *Disability Discrimination Law in the United States, Australia, and Canada* (Oak Tree Press, Dublin, 1993)

Redfern Legal Centre, *Questions of Rights: a Guide to the Law and Rights of People with an Intellectual Disability* (Redfern Legal Centre, Sydney, 1992)

Ronalds, C, *Residents' Rights in Nursing Homes and Hostels: Final Report* (AGPS, Canberra, 1989)

Ronalds, C, *Discrimination: Law and Practice* (Federation Press, Leichhardt, 1998)

Stuhmcke, A, "Access to Reproductive Technology: *Pearce v SA Health Commission*" (1995) 5 *Health Law Bulletin* 39

Tay, Alice Erh-Soon, *Human Rights for Australia*, Human Rights Commission Monograph Series No 1 (AGPS, Canberra, 1986)

Thornton, M, *The Liberal Promise: Anti-discrimination Legislation in Australia* (Oxford University Press, Melbourne, 1991)

Wallace, M, "The Legal Approach to Sex Discrimination", in Sawer, M, *Program for Change* (Allen & Unwin, Sydney, 1985)

West, D, *Older Residents and the Law: Training Manual* (Residential Care Rights, Older Persons Action Centre, Office of the Public Advocate, Melbourne, 1996)

Williams, G, *Human Rights under the Australian Constitution* (Oxford University Press, Melbourne, 1999)

The various State and Territory anti-discrimination bodies mentioned in this chapter have produced reports on discrimination on various grounds, as well as annual reports.

On AIDS specifically there are reports by the different bodies established to deal with it, such as NACAIDS. See also References and Further Reading for Chapter 16 for other references on AIDS.

19

19 Decision making, law & ethics

The ethical decision making process

Dealing with a dilemma

Towards ethical duty statements

chapter 19

Decision-Making, Law and Ethics: A Discussion

Introduction

[19.05] The purpose of this chapter is to apply the information given in previous chapters to decision-making, and to raise for contemplation the many dilemmas which may confront the health carer in everyday experience. Examples of the kinds of questions that arise are: what to do when a patient asks if they have cancer when other carers and/or family do not wish them to be told; whether to report a colleague who has acted negligently; and whether a patient should be informed that treatment under anaesthesia was negligent.

The previous chapters in this book have been concerned with the legal aspects of decision-making in health care. This chapter will address ethical principles (which sometimes have legal support) and their place in the decision-making process. The aim is to outline a proposed pattern of thinking: not to give a final answer as to how to act in any situation. A model for clarifying values will be offered, together with suggestions for reasoning so that one may reach an acceptable decision on how to proceed. As this is a book about law, it is not intended that this analysis be other than an outline of some of the main ethical issues, an indication of their relationship to the law, and a brief guide to ethical decision making developed from the authors' experiences.

The Ethical Decision-Making Process: One Approach

What is the issue?

[19.10] A health carer who is confronted with a difficult situation, and is unsure how to act, needs to answer certain questions. The first step, however, is to identify what kind of question to ask. This can be done in a logical fashion by determining what sort of issue one is dealing with:

Is it a factual issue?

[19.15] The question of what to do may be resolved by becoming better informed on the facts of the case, for example, what the diagnosis and prognosis are, and the likely medical and social outcome of proposed action. Establishing whether a patient is temporarily comatose, in a persistent vegetative state, or brain dead, for example, is crucial in deciding what care to give. Anguish to both health carers and relatives over whether, and how, to treat such a patient may be relieved by simply establishing the facts.

Is it a legal issue?

[19.20] Having clarified the facts, decisions as to how to act may become quite clear after determining what the law is in a particular situation, and being satisfied that fulfilling any legal requirements or obligations poses no ethical dilemma, that is, does not cause a conflict between one's moral values. One may not need to go any further.

Is it an ethical issue?

[19.25] Here one has determined the answers to the above questions, but is uncertain how to act, because any perceived solution poses some degree of conflict with one's sense of right and wrong. The law governing a particular activity may be contrary to what the health carer considers to be the right thing to do (for example, prohibiting disclosure of facts, such as a patient's likelihood to harm another person, recalling the HIV example given at **[7.275]**). It could permit alternative courses of action, each of which could in some way potentially conflict with an ethical principle to some degree (for example, the advantages and disadvantages of withholding of non-therapeutic but life-preserving treatment compared with those of the administering of such treatment). Health carers need to go further in this situation, and determine how they *ought* to act, either because of, or despite, the answers to the above questions. The issue is most likely an ethical one, because it requires the health carer to rank the values involved in each alternative in some order of merit.

What is ethics?

[19.30] First it may be instructive to consider what ethics is *not*.

Ethics is not simply the study of "right" conduct. It is not a set of guidelines that, if followed, will always lead to correct behaviour. It is not law or etiquette, although these matters may be considerations in determining ethical issues. Ethics is not merely the study of how people act in the face of difficult choices. It is not the following of orders, or doing what everyone else does. It is not a study of policy or public opinion, although, again, these may be relevant considerations. Ethics is definitely not a matter of "gut feelings", although these may be a starting point for canvassing the alternatives, and deciding what one ought to do.

Ethics, it is suggested, is the study of rational processes for determining the course of action in the face of conflicting choices. This study, of necessity, involves the identification, weighing and the choosing of values. This process must result in the development by a person of an initial moral (value) statement about a particular issue.

Such a statement may be, for example, that under no circumstance should one make an untrue statement. It is a basis for clarity in reasoning out the common problems that health carers face, such as being asked by a patient whether they are suffering from cancer.

One reason for considering the issue of ethics may be concern as to what prevents action in the face of immoral or ethically questionable activities carried out by, or condoned by, members of the health care profession in past and current practice. Examples are the frequent failure to object to lack of proper consent on the part of patients when participating in a medical procedure, and being party to the signing of consent forms which are clearly not understood; tolerating the use of anaesthetised women as anatomical exhibits (and in some cases vehicles for practising inserting and removing IUDs); and failing to tell the truth to patients. More serious examples are the activities that occurred over extended periods of time in Chelmsford Hospital in Sydney (see Royal Commission into Deep Sleep Therapy, *Report* (NSW Government Printer, Sydney, 1991). Inquiries carried out into the treatment of psychiatric patients considered the treatment not only to be grossly negligent but serious enough to raise the question of criminal charges. Many of the health carers involved, including nurses, were not the key health carers investigated by the inquiries, and no legal action could be taken against them. However, they played an important part in the suspect activities, often unquestioning, either as participants or witnesses to the events. Is the failure to act in circumstances like those outlined above because these health carers see law and ethics as a matter of etiquette, or doing what they are told, or what everyone else does, or something else which points to the acceptability of failure to act? It seems the concept of ethics is in need of clarification, for these events ought never to have happened.

Indeed there are some major questions where the law may well be involved. Chelmsford is an extreme example, and it might be hoped that health carers will never again fail to question such situations. In such extreme cases of course, health carers may not only have an ethical duty to prevent them, but a legal one as well.

In practice, health carers have only rarely been the subject of legal proceedings, even where their actions (or omissions) are legally culpable under criminal law (see Chapter 14) or civil law (see Chapter 6). The emerging recognition of patients' rights, and increasing understanding of the legal system by patients means that this may change (see, for example, *Darling's* case at **[6.450]**). The political sensitivity of failings in the health system perhaps goes some way towards explaining the increasing number of government enquiries regarding health system failures. (See for example, the *Queensland Public Hospitals Commission of Enquiry Report*, 30 November 2005, by G Davies, arising from matters at Bundaberg Hospital.)

As to the connection between law and ethics, this was outlined in the case of *Furniss v Fitchett* [1958] NZLR 396. (See discussion at **[7.205]**.) In that case a doctor disclosed details of a woman's mental condition for evidence in matrimonial proceedings in court, in circumstances in which he ought to have known she would be harmed. The court had to consider whether the ethical code was a relevant reference for determining a duty of care. The Chief Justice said (at 405):

> "The British Medical Association's Code of Ethics is evidence of the general professional standards to which a reasonably careful, skilled and informed practitioner would conform. I think, it was admissible for that purpose, and it, therefore, became necessary to decide whether the law, as distinct from the ethical code of the British Medical Association, permitted any departure from those standards."

Codes of ethics thus become not only ethical guides, but, for the purposes of the law, standards by which "reasonably careful, skilled and informed" practice will be judged by the courts, disciplinary bodies and complaints units.

Codes of ethics

[19.35] There are many codes of ethics for the different health care professions. Examples are the Hippocratic Oath for the medical profession, which has been replaced by the Declaration of Geneva and the International Code of Medical Ethics (prepared by the World Medical Association); codes of ethics of the Australian Dental Association and the Australian Physiotherapy Association. Sometimes these include etiquette and policy as well as ethical principles. In 2005, New South Wales introduced a *Code of Professional Conduct* under the *Medical Practice Act 1992* (NSW), which is reproduced on the New South Wales Medical Board website at www.nswmb.org.au/ (see Appendix 5). At the time of writing, medical boards in the Australian jurisdictions have adopted, or are in the process of adopting provisions in essentially the same terms as the New South Wales Code. The International Council for Nurses has issued a statement "A Code for Nurses: Ethical Concepts Applied to Nurses", which is considered here as an example of an ethical code. The most recent version, issued in 2005 and now simply called *The ICN Code of Ethics for Nurses*, is available online at www.icn.ch/icncode.pdf. It includes the following ethical statements:

- the fundamental responsibility of the nurse is to promote health, prevent illness, restore health, and alleviate suffering;
- inherent in nursing is respect for life, dignity and rights of citizens, unrestricted by considerations of age, colour, creed, disability, illness, gender, sexual orientation, nationality, politics, race or social status;
- nurses promote an environment in which the rights, values, customs and spiritual beliefs of the individual, family and community are recognised;
- nurses carry personal responsibility for nursing practice and maintaining competence by continual learning;

- nurses maintain the highest standard of practice and personal conduct, and use judgment in relating to individual competence when accepting and delegating responsibility;
- nurses take an active role in promoting nursing practice, as well as health and social needs of the public; and
- nurses co-operate with co-workers and protect patients from danger from co-workers or others.

Other principles which some, but not all, codes of ethics have in common are those which require carers to:

- maintain confidentiality;
- preserve the dignity of the patient;
- not abandon a patient;
- maintain accurate records;
- consult others where they lack competence;
- restrict advertising and refrain from touting for "business"; and
- maintain a high moral standard of living which does not bring the profession into disrepute.

While the codes provide a list of principles to be followed, the very length and variety of values and principles expressed can be bewildering. Codes of ethics may guide a person in establishing values, but moral dilemmas arise from the need to choose between more than one value or principle. What is more important—telling the truth or protecting someone from harm? This chapter is not concerned with establishing priorities among values: there are many books that will provide guidance for that. This chapter is about establishing a rational and consistent approach to weighing values that are accepted by the individual health carer.

As mentioned in Chapter 12, most jurisdictions provide (directly or indirectly) for disciplinary action for unethical conduct. In New South Wales for example, s 99A(4) of the *Medical Practice Act 1992* provides that the provisions of a code of professional conduct are a relevant consideration in determining for the purposes of the Act what constitutes proper and ethical conduct by a registered medical practitioner. Most registration boards have drawn up codes of ethics, as have, for example, the State nurses unions and many hospitals. Health carers should be familiar with the codes relevant to their area of practice.

Dealing with a Decision-Making Dilemma

[19.40] Ethical principles are not absolute rules: they guide one's actions rather than dictate them. They prescribe behaviour, setting out what one "ought" to do, and thus create duties. Ethical dilemmas arise from a conflict of duties (for example, where a patient discloses to his or her psychiatrist that he or she intends to harm a third person—the duty to maintain a patient's confidence and not disclose that information, and the duty to warn someone when we know they are in danger). This requires the weighing of values and determining to which one priority will be given. The following is a suggested guide only.

Step 1: Investigate and communicate facts and reasons for action

[19.45] The first step in resolving ethical dilemmas, such as those posed in **[19.05]**, is to make sure one has a firm grasp of all the facts. The nature of the diagnosis, the prognosis, and just what the patient has been told must be known. An example occurs where a patient is diagnosed as having cancer and the prognosis is poor, the doctor and family do not want the patient to be told, and a health carer caring for the patient believes both that this is wrong and that the patient should be informed. The health carer should be aware that there may be considerations of which he or she is ignorant, and which others have taken into account. Talking to doctor and family should establish the reasons for not telling the patient. Given that the patient's attitudes and likely reaction to the news, as well as the attitudes of her or his family have been investigated, the reasons for not telling the patient can be addressed. They may convince the carer that in fact not telling the patient is more in accord with their hierarchy of values than not, or, conversely, help the family to realise that it is not in the patient's interest not to know, and that it is their own need to come to grips with the situation that is the barrier to telling the patient. Realising this and discussing it may help them to deal with it. The situation should thus be discussed, and all who take care of the patient should be given the opportunity to air their concerns and opinions. This process may shape the nature of the final outcome of the decision-making and minimise stress, ill-feeling and anger, adversely affecting both patient and carers.

The importance of this initial step cannot be underestimated: what appears to be a serious ethical problem in the care of a patient may turn out to be a matter of lack of understanding of the facts, or of communication between those involved in the patient's care. Communication in this context not only informs, it can be a source of support, education and clarification of one's values and emotions.

Step 2: Ascertain legal obligations

[19.50] If, after considering the facts (and reasons for the course others are taking if this is relevant) the health carer is still unsure of the right course of action, the next thing to do is to consider the law. Are there any legal requirements attached to the situation in question? The answer may make the course of action clear. Good health care goes beyond considering whether one is covered by law, and in some cases, as described at **[19.10]**, the issue becomes an ethical one. Where the law clearly establishes a course of action it should be followed, but health carers might consider agitating for change in the law where it is contrary to their moral position.

An example: Disclosing information

[19.55] An example of a dilemma is the situation outlined above where the nurse is asked by a patient, "Do I have cancer?", when the doctor and family do not wish the person to know. The health carer has been instructed not to tell the patient, but feels that he or she should know, particularly as the person suspects something serious is wrong, and is anxious.

Is there a legal obligation to tell the truth?

[19.60] There is no legal obligation to tell someone the truth. However, one can be sued for failing to give information to a person to their detriment, and deliberate lack of full and frank disclosure can amount to this. Presumably no one is trying to harm the patient, and it has been decided not to tell because:

- telling the patient is too difficult for those involved; or
- their conviction that it is in the patient's interest to act in this way.

There is a third possible reason—to hide the facts from the patient and so prevent legal action. This is considered below at **[19.135]**ff.

Telling the truth is too difficult

[19.65] In this case the way to resolve the problem may be to engage someone else to tell the person, perhaps a counsellor or friend, or a colleague who is more experienced, or to seek assistance or support in facing this difficult task. In this case the problem is not an ethical one, but a practical one. Calling on the resources of others is a legitimate way of easing a difficult burden.

Conviction that not telling the truth is in patient's interest

[19.70] Where the concern is for the patient's wellbeing, it is a matter of considering whether withholding the truth is indeed in her or his interest—akin to the therapeutic privilege concept. This involves firstly establishing facts. Would the patient be likely to suffer harm if not told the truth? Does not telling the truth amount to deception (and does that matter, such as perhaps in the use of placebo medication)? It could be that the relationship between patient and health carer(s) (or indeed the patient–hospital relationship) could be destroyed if he or she also feels that health carers cannot be trusted.

Legal obligations to the patient

[19.75] From the legal point of view the probability of harm is also an important consideration, where failure to disclose results in detriment to the patient in terms of health or quality of life. (See discussion at **[6.435]** regarding *Wighton v Arnot* [2005] NSWSC 637.)

It seems that patients cannot sue the doctor or hospital simply because they were not told the truth, they would have to show that:

1) withholding the information was unreasonable; and

2) he or she actually suffered some physical or economic harm as the result of this.

If it is foreseeable that failure to disclose the truth would cause such harm, and there is no reasonable justification for so doing, then the person should be told, according to law. On the other hand, the health carer may be concerned that telling the patient may cause severe depression, or lead to other harm. In weighing up the relative potential for harm, the answer to the dilemma may be resolved by considering legal obligations to the patient.

Legal obligations to employer and colleagues

[19.80] Legal obligations are owed to the employer. Does the law require one to carry out the orders of a superior without question (see Chapter 6)?

One obligation owed to the employer, and indeed also to one's colleagues, is to maintain the patient's confidence in them. This is an ethical duty, and in some cases, also a legal one (see Chapter 10).

A consideration of the legal issues arising from this dilemma may determine what action should be taken, and resolve the issue, that is, the decision is a legal one. However, on balancing the harm that may result from either course of action, and the legal ramifications of that action (that is, looking at the *consequences* of either telling the patient or not doing so), it may be difficult to determine which is the best course to take. This leads to the need to weigh the relative *values* the health carer puts on the different outcomes that would result from either action. It is time to consider the third type of issue: the ethical decision.

Step 3: Determine the best ethical option

[19.85] Where there is no legal imperative to act in a particular way (that is, the options are all legally acceptable, the question becomes what option to adopt based on moral principles (see for example, Johnstone (1989), p 76—she would add care and compassion to these (Chapter 4)). These are:

* *beneficence*: the aim of health care should be to benefit the patient, and the benefit should be greater than any burdens placed on her or him by medical treatment;
* *autonomy*: medical care should promote the self-determination of patients, which means that all decision-making should ultimately be theirs;
* *non-maleficence*: the avoidance of harm to the patient. Some writers argue that it is important to distinguish the stricture not to harm others, from that of aiming to benefit, as the latter may require active measures to prevent them from foreseeable harm, and may mean taking risks to do this; and
* *justice*: can mean either giving a person their due, or ensuring equal access to the benefits available. Both of these meanings can apply to health care. In our society it is recognised that a person's due is reasonable, dignified

medical care, based on their need for it, and equal access to medical care means that no one is the subject of unreasonable discrimination.

There are other values which have been adopted, those considered "first order" principles (see above), others, such as truth telling, loyalty to employer and colleagues, serving as "lower order" principles or rules, providing the means for "first order" principles to be assembled in rank according to one's values. Writers distinguish between principles and rules (for example, Johnstone (1989), p 83). The model given in this chapter is based on a "rational" approach to ethics, relying as it does on a set of abstract rules and eschewing emotion. Even utilitarians, who recognise that people have desires and interests, work at rules of rational choice for maximising the satisfaction of these desires and interests, concentrate on which emotions to cultivate and on which desires to change, determining this by rational calculation rather than feelings. However, in formulating the model set out here, an attempt has been made to take into account the feminist-generated "ethic of care". Held ((1994), pp 169-170) says of this approach:

> "Some think it should supersede 'the ethic of justice' of traditional or standard moral theory. Others think it should be integrated with the theory of justice and rules ... Achieving and maintaining trusting, caring relationships is quite different from acting in accord with rational principles, or satisfying the individual desires of either self or other. Caring, empathy, feeling with others ... all may be better guides to what morality requires in actual contexts than abstract rules of reason, or rational calculation."

Given that these principles are adopted, they underlie an imperative:

* *If X is a desirable or necessary result of medical care, more than any other result, one ought to do those things targeted at achieving X.*

For example, if one believes that autonomy is a desirable or necessary value to exercise, one would be impelled to carry out acts fostering it, and be constrained from those inhibiting it.

* *If, however, in bringing about X one also causes Y, which is not desirable, and one wants to avoid Y, one is impelled to act in a way maximising X and minimising Y to the best of one's abilities.*

That is, for example, if to promote a person's autonomy will involve giving that person information which will cause them severe emotional harm, one may be impelled to modify the amount or type of information, always considering support and counselling to allow for as much autonomy that is compatible with achieving the desired or necessary outcome.

This imperative also applies where an undesirable outcome, is the result of any available option.

In practice, where a problem is an ethical one, the task is generally a choice between conflicting duties. These may be legal duties (for example, a duty to provide reasonable care for a patient, and a duty to carry out the directions of another). They may be duties dictated by moral values (for example, the duty to uphold the patient's autonomy, and the duty to prevent him or her from suffering harm from disclosure of information). It is most likely that the health carer will have to choose between favouring one accepted moral principle (such as always telling the truth) over another (such as never causing the patient harm or distress). The question becomes, which principle takes precedence. In the case of the hypothetical patient with cancer described above, the conflict is between beneficence (causing as little pain as possible by not telling her or him) and autonomy and justice (telling the truth). One could argue that other values mentioned above are also involved. The answer produced should be capable of being expressed as a moral statement, which is consistent with any other moral statement the health carer may develop, and applicable to all situations. Moral statements are explained further below.

Towards Ethical (Duty) Statements

[19.90] The following analysis is developed from Brody (1981), pp 18ff.

Moral values are expressed in the formula: "*In situation X, person P ought to do Y.*" This involves determining:

* the conditions under which the statement is applicable;
* what is to be done; and
* who is to do it.

Such statements should be clearly differentiated from other statements, such as:

* statements of fact: "*In situation X person P does Y*";
* aesthetic statements: "*Person P likes to do Y*"; and
* commands: "*Person P is to do Y*".

Expressive statement

[19.95] Often people consider they are making a moral statement, when in fact they are expressing a personal reaction to a particular situation. This is, rather, an *expressive statement* (or "gut reaction"), for example:

A. Expressive statement: "I feel that people should know if they have cancer."

This is a "should/ought" statement, but does it apply all the time?

Value statement

[19.100] To give validity to a moral statement one should be able to establish the reason which underlies it. This becomes a *value statement*:

B. Value statement: "People should know if they have cancer (because ...)."

A value statement sets out what is "good" or "bad", "right or wrong". In determining whether there is justification for the expressive statement, it may become apparent that there should be some qualifications to it. One should not be able to think of any situation which negates a proposed justification. For example, if the reason given in statement B was "because people always benefit from the truth", one should not be able to think of any circumstances where someone would not benefit from being told the truth. Philosophers commonly describe a hypothetical situation: A Jewish family is hiding in your house. The Gestapo knock on the door and ask if you are harbouring any Jews. It is unlikely that telling the truth in this case would benefit the Jews. This, they argue, throws doubt on the proposed justification, and the value statement must be qualified accordingly.

Prescriptive statement

[19.105] One can then turn the value statement into a *prescriptive statement*—one which qualifies the value statement (there are arguably few or perhaps even no value statements which can be applied absolutely):

C. **Prescriptive statement: "In situation X (or every) situation, person P (or every person) ought to tell someone if they have cancer."**

Duty statement

[19.110] A prescriptive statement turns the principle into an "ought" (duty) statement, relating the duty to a particular person or people.

D. **Duty statement: "The duty to tell a person if they have cancer is more (or less) important than any other duty (or X duty) to them or others."**
A duty statement also stipulates situations and conditions under which action ought to be carried out. Can you think of a situation in which a health carer may not have a duty to tell someone if they have cancer? Some have argued that there are different cultural approaches to telling a person they are going to die, which would place exceptions on medical staff directly giving this news to them. Should we be influenced by the belief that such information would make a person depressed? Is it more important to tell them anyway, so that they can prepare themselves and their affairs, and not find out in a way that makes them feel the truth has wrongly been withheld from them? (It may be instructive to consider other expressive statements such as "I feel that health carers should never disclose to a third person the fact that a person is HIV-positive".) In considering exceptions to the original statement, one can identify duties arising from prescriptive statements, and rank them in order of importance.

Another way of determining whether one can advance from an expressive statement to a prescriptive statement is by asking the question: What would happen if the proposed prescriptive statement were to be applied? Would all the consequences (for example, those suggested at [19.115]) be acceptable, given *other* moral values which one holds, and which also form the basis of prescriptive statements (such as "you should never harm another by your actions" or "you should treat all people equally")? One might modify the statement about telling a person they have cancer to take into consideration different situations so that it is compatible with other statements (or change the other statements, if the duty to tell the person they have cancer is considered to apply at all times in all situations).

One approach: Consider consequences

[19.115] One approach to deciding which is the best course of action to take, in line with one's values (expressed as either a prescriptive or duty statement), is to list the consequences of each possible course of action in a given situation, and consider whether they are consistent with those values. Figure 19.1 represents this process. This approach can, to some extent, incorporate principles from two different ethical theories, the "deontological" theories (based on keeping to binding moral rules) and "teleological" theories (based on the results of one's actions). Brody (1981) outlines a "consequentialist" model (at p 354), on which this outline is based. He describes the different ethical philosophies, as do Johnstone ((1989), Ch 3) and Singer (1994).

It is not a matter of acting intuitively and justifying the actions later: we ought to make our values explicit so that we can judge the consequences of acts by:

- stating values and consequences in plain language; and
- listing value statements and consequences in close juxtaposition, to make direct comparisons and decide the outcome most in line with those values.

Some inconsistencies in one's thinking may become apparent. For example, one may start with the ethical statement that abortion is wrong because all surgery for non-illness is wrong. This leads to a prescriptive statement, for example that "Where a person is not physically ill he or she should not have surgery". The consequence of this statement would lead to the rejection of plastic surgery where the patient is not "physically ill". If one believes that plastic surgery in some situations (for example, to restructure facial bone after injury which has resulted in disfigurement) is acceptable, it is necessary to revise the original statement: not all surgery for non-illness is wrong. It also means that one cannot reject abortion for this reason. Further reasons must be considered, and unless they can be applied to all possible situations must also be discarded as a ground for rejecting abortion. The process is thus repeated with each proposed ethical statement, considering all possible consequences of applying it, until consistency has been achieved.

Figure 19.1 sets out three possible outcomes of considering the consequences of a proposed action. The action will result in either:

1) one consequence, which is consistent with all one's value statements;
2) several consequences which are consistent with all one's value statements; or
3) any consequence which is consistent with one value statement conflicting with another value statement.

These are explained further below.

Figure 19.1: Steps in Ethical Decision–Making

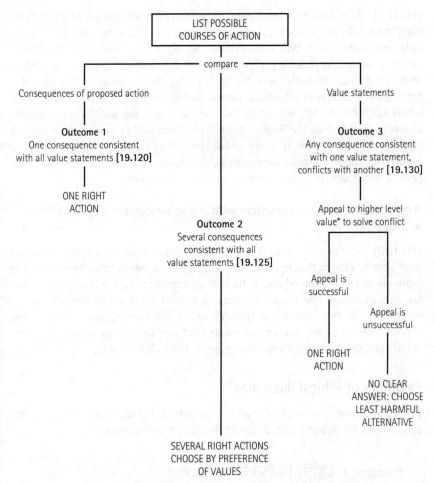

* A higher level value is one which is considered more important. For example, one might consider that all being equal, non-maleficence is more important than support of colleagues. For example, where a nurse is confronted by a conflict between protecting patients (such as reporting incompetent practices) and support of colleagues, he or she may invoke the higher value of non-maleficence to patients (consideration of the law might help to underscore this decision).

One consequence consistent with all value statements

[19.120] Here there is no real ethical problem. It is a situation where there is only one right way to act, and thus no question as to what one ought to do. Readers may be surprised, on attempting to list situations where this is the case, how few they can come up with.

Several consequences consistent with all value statements

[19.125] There may be several ways of dealing with a situation which may be consistent with one's moral values. In this case one is dealing with two "right" outcomes rather than two evils. Where this occurs it is necessary for health carers to weigh the relative preference of the different outcomes, according to their values (for example, whether it is preferable to preserve the life of a terminally ill person or allow the person to die more quickly and humanely— where both are morally acceptable outcomes). If one accepts that beneficence and non-maleficence are "higher order" principles, and preservation of life is a lesser order one, serving to bring about the higher order principles, one could argue that the dilemma is answered by choosing the "higher order" principle, beneficence, over the lower order one, preservation of life.

A consequence which is consistent with one value statement and conflicts with another

[19.130] Here one has to rank one's values, determining which have priorities over others. Where this leads to one consequence being consistent with the higher level value outlined above, there is a preferred action. As the other values are also desirable, one would consider action which gives as much scope to recognition of those values as possible under the circumstances. Where one cannot identify a clear preference for at least one value over others, all values being considered of equal importance, there is no clear answer.

Examples of ethical dilemmas

[19.135] Some examples of real life situations follow, to provide practical suggestions for dealing with different decision-making problems.

Example 1: LIGHT GETS IN THEIR EYES

X is concerned that the bright fluorescent lights in the intensive care ward, which are never turned off, are distressing to the patients there. However, they are considered necessary for proper care of the patients. X identifies a possible conflict between values: that of the comfort of the patients, and their proper medical treatment.

However, following the steps outlined above, he or she realises that several fallacies might be involved here: first the belief that the constant light is necessary all the time for the recovery of all the patients (a presumed scientific fact), and secondly, that it has to be so bright (limited, either-or solution). X determines to do some research and clarify the facts, and, if he or she determines that the accepted amount of light is not necessary, to investigate alternative lighting with the supervisor. The facts may indicate that constant bright lights are necessary for reasonable treatment.

Having determined just what the situation is with regard to that particular ward and the patients cared for there, X considers the consequences of different approaches to the problem according to Figure 19.1 and thus reaches a conclusion with regard to the legal and ethical obligations to her or his patients. Whatever the outcome X will at least have the satisfaction of knowing that he or she has attempted to maximise a very important value principle: beneficence (benefiting each patient), while giving all reasonable consideration to other values, such as non-maleficence (not causing undue harm or distress to any of them).

Example 2: THE ERRANT ANAESTHETIST

An anaesthetist leaves a patient under anaesthesia in the care of a nurse while he watches a sporting event on television. The nurse reports the incident, and the anaesthetist is admonished. He later begins to ask colleagues who it was who "dobbed him in", implying she will suffer for her actions. The nurse wonders if she did the right thing.

In this case the nurse, after considering the facts and referring to Figure 19.1, decides she has to weigh the consequences of patient care, responsibility to her employer and loyalty to a colleague. She can then review her expressive, value, prescriptive and duty statements to arrive at a decision that is consistent with these. Given that she concludes that the consequences of reporting the event are more acceptable than those of not doing so in this case, she can refine her duty statement to include such situations among those imposing a duty to report to the administration. The opposite result would occur if she decides the consequences of *not* reporting are acceptable.

The nurse's colleagues may also refuse to disclose who had reported the doctor when he sought this information. This action would be consistent with the values they held in relation to both beneficence (patient care) and justice (loyalty to a colleague).

Example 3: THE CARDIAC ARREST

A young woman has a cardiac arrest while under anaesthesia. Y (an intern) writing up her notes is told: "Do not put this in the report". After considering the facts involved and consulting Figure 19.1, Y concludes that the significant harmful consequences to A (the patient) (through lack of information) if it is not recorded in the patient's notes, and significant harm to others (through repeated similar action in the future) could result if the adverse reaction to anaesthesia is not reported, but that she may be victimised if the arrest is recorded. Y wants to do the right thing. Should the matter be recorded in the patient's notes? Should it be reported to the appropriate authority?

This problem is not only an ethical one, it also involves legal issues. There are strong legal reasons for recording the cardiac arrest. Y is not only protecting those concerned who are neglecting their responsibility for reasonable care through responsible recording, she is also acting negligently in not recording the event (see Chapters 6 and 7). There is also a duty to the employing hospital to take reasonable measures to ensure patient care and safety (see Chapter 10).

Ways of dealing with this sort of situation are to take the matter to the supervisor or the next uninvolved administrator (see below) from whom one should receive support, or, as a general measure, to relieve staff of the responsibility of having to deal with this sort of pressure, to institute the use of incident reports (see below).

Examples 4 and 5: THE UNFORTUNATE REMOVALS

A woman who has a lump in her breast undergoes surgery to determine if it is malignant. While she is anaesthetised a section is sent to pathology for testing, while the surgeon waits for a result, ready to remove the breast if it is malignant. The surgeon does not want to wait for the result of tests, and, convinced they would be positive anyhow, removes the breast. In fact the results are negative. Staff are concerned that if the woman is not told of the mistake she will believe she has cancer, and if she is told they are revealing information which is damaging to the hospital and surgeon.

A woman is having a caesarean haemorrhage and instead of giving her a drug to arrest the bleeding, the anaesthetist mistakenly injects her with a drug which has the opposite effect and she bleeds even more. As a result she has to have a hysterectomy. Those who witness the event are concerned as to whether they should inform her of the reason for the hysterectomy.

In this type of case, where health carers believe it is in the patient's interest to know, the issue involves legal considerations as well as ethical ones. See for example the NSW *Code of Professional Conduct* Standard 2.5, which provides:

"Act immediately to put matters right, if it is possible, if a patient under your care has suffered serious harm, through misadventure or for any other reason."

You should explain fully to the patient what has happened and the likely short- and long-term effects. When appropriate, you should offer an apology. If the patient lacks the maturity to understand what has happened, you should explain the situation honestly to those with parental responsibility for the child. If the patient is cognitively impaired you should provide explanation to the patient's parent, guardian, carer or person responsible. See also the NSW *Code of Professional Conduct* Standard 1.2 which provides:

"Keep clear, accurate and contemporaneous patient records."

The interplay between the ethical standards and the legal ones are recognised at NSW *Code of Professional Conduct* Standard 2.5 which provides:

"Co-operate fully with any formal inquiry into the treatment of a patient, subject to appropriate advice from your medical defence organisation. You should not withhold relevant information."

Given the analysis of the law regarding disclosure, health carers are reminded that documents are the property of the hospital, subject to freedom of information where it is a public hospital and other legislation such as the *Privacy Act 1988* (Cth) where it is a private institution.

Nurses may have a specific perspective in such a case. It is not the province of the nurse to discuss the doctor's treatment with her or his patient. The nurse could risk adverse action from the employer if the patient were told and there is thus a disincentive to disclose information. The nurse may therefore find there is a difference between her or his value statements and the law.

In this type of case some may argue that the harm done to the principles of loyalty to employer and colleagues would be serious, undermining trust in medical care in general, and resulting in defamation of innocent people.

If hospital administration does not provide assistance, health carers may decide to go higher up the chain of control, until satisfaction is achieved. These matters are of such a serious nature that they are also candidates for consideration by the relevant disciplinary tribunal.

What action is taken would depend on the result of comparison of the consequences of different alternatives with the nurse's personal value statements and priorities. It can be seen, however, that most serious ethical matters are also likely to be legal ones.

One result of not disclosing facts to patients is that health carers might be expected to live a lie, for example, where a patient wrongly believes he or she either does or does not have cancer. In this case they could, in the authors' view, be justified in expressing their concern at being asked to act contrary to their values, and attempt to change the situation.

A way of making health carers more accountable was adopted by the administrator of a theatre unit in a large hospital. This was the mandatory use of incident reports for every unusual or unanticipated occurrence which happened during surgery which were to include irregular consent procedures. The incident reports were to be signed by both the surgeon and the assisting nurse. There was no discretion in the matter. The result of doing this was twofold:

- the reporting of the event was required, so no personal blame could be placed for making a report and there could be no recriminations; and
- the number of unusual and unanticipated events was reduced considerably, as staff sought to avoid the need to resort to these forms.

Over recent years, throughout Australia, there has been increasing recognition and implementation of incident reporting and "open disclosure" of such adverse events to patients, in recognition of patient autonomy principles and as a means of reducing future adverse events. The authors note in particular the important and helpful work of the Australian Council for Safety and Quality in Health Care, leading ultimately to the recent establishment in New South Wales of the Clinical Excellence Commission (see www.ice.nsw.gov.au/) and of the national body the Australian Commission on Safety and Quality in Health Care (see www.safetyandquality.gov.au/).

Conclusion

[19.140] There are no perfect answers to these problems, and from the examples given above it can be seen that practicalities and politics may play a distorting role in decision-making and should be taken into account. Consequently one cannot have an ethical program that will solve all of the problems all of the time.

However, one can be confident that with the fertile grounds of genetics, assisted pregnancy, antenatal testing, termination of pregnancy, assisted suicide, withdrawal of treatment and end of life decisions generally, there will remain many more ethical questions than easy answers.

References and Further Reading

There are many books that outline ethical principles and their use in medicine. This list includes some titles added for the third edition.

Annas, G, *Judging Medicine* (Humana Press, New Jersey, 1988)

Brody, H, *Ethical Decisions in Medicine* (Little Brown, Boston, 1981)

Bromberger, B and Fife-Yeomans, J, *Deep Sleep* (Simon & Schuster, Sydney, 1991)

Campbell, A, et al, *Practical Medical Ethics* (Oxford University Press, Auckland, 1992)

Freckelton, I and Petersen, P, *Controversies in Health Law* (Federation Press, Sydney, 1999)

Held, V, "Reason, Gender and Moral Theory" in Singer, P, *Ethics* (Oxford University Press, Oxford, 1994)

Johnstone, M, *Bioethics: A Nursing Perspective* (WB Saunders/Bailliere Tindall, Sydney, 1989) (third edition (1999))

Kerridge I, Lowe, M and McPhee, J, *Ethics and Law for the Health Professions* (2nd ed, Federation Press, Sydney, 2005)

Kuhse, H, *Caring: Nurses, Women and Ethics* (Blackwell, Oxford, 1997)

Kuhse, H and Singer, P, *Bioethics: An Anthology* (Blackwell Publishers, Oxford, 1999)

McLean, S (ed), *Death, Dying and the Law* (Dartmouth Publishing Co, Aldershot, 1996)

Mason, J and McCall-Smith, R, *Law and Medical Ethics* (Butterworths, London, 1983)

McConnell, T, *Moral Issues in Health Care: An Introduction to Medical Ethics* (Wandsworth, California, 1982)

Melden, A, *Ethical Theories: A Book of Readings* (2nd ed, Prentice-Hall, NJ, 1967)

Purtill, R, *Thinking about Ethics* (Prentice-Hall, NJ, 1976)

Reamer, F, *Ethical Dilemmas in Social Service* (Columbia University Press, New York, 1982)

Singer, P, *Practical Ethics* (Cambridge University Press, London, 1979)

A Guide to Abbreviations used in Law Report Citations

Where a date and/or number is given for a case (for example, "27 June 1980, SC NSW, No 226/80") this means the case is "unreported" and not published in the volumes of reports for that court. It is kept in a volume of "Unreported Cases" for the court, held by some Law Libraries, or available through them. Some of the most recent cases may be published by the time this book is read, or at least should be available online via www.austlii.edu.au. Most unreported cases on health care referred to in this book are summarised in the Australian Health and Medical Law Reporter.

A	Atlantic Reporter first series: US commercial reporting service which covers State Supreme Court reports from the north-eastern States, 1885-1938
A 2d	Atlantic Reporter second series (from 1938)
AC	Law Reports Appeal Cases (England) 1891-present
A Crim R	Australian Criminal Reports
ACL	Australian Current Law (commercial service which provides monthly information and case digests)
ACTR	Australian Capital Territory Reports (bound with ALR)
ACTSC	ACT Supreme Court
ALD	Administrative Law Decisions, Australia (reports of the Administrative Appeals Tribunal)
ALR	Australian Law Reports
ALJR	Australian Law Journal Reports
All ER	All England Law Reports from 1936
All ER Rep	All England Law Reports Reprints 1558-1935

ALMD	Australian Legal Monthly Digest (commercial service which provides monthly information and case digests)
ALR	Australian Law Reports
Aust Torts Rep	Australian Torts Reports: Commercial reporting service
AWCCD	Australian Workers Compensation Case Digests
CA	Court of Appeal
Cal App 3d	Californian Appeal Cases, third series
Cal Reptr	Californian Reporter
CB(NS)	Common Bench Reports, New Series
Ch	English Reports, Chancery Division
CLR	Commonwealth Law Reports (Australia)
Cr App R	Criminal Appeal Reports
DCR(NSW)	District Court Reports (New South Wales)
DLR	Dominion Law Reports (Canada)
ER	English Reports
EOC	Equal Opportunity Cases (commercial reporting service, Australia)
ExD	Law Reports, Exchequer Division, UK (1875-1880)
F	Federal Reports, US (1880-1924)
F 2d	Federal Reports, US, second series (from 1924)
FCR	Federal Court Reports
FLC	Family Law Cases (commercial reporting service, Australia)
FLR	Federal Law Reports 1956-present (Australia); Family Law Reports (UK)
F Supp	Federal Supplement US (federal District Court cases)
Fam LR	Family Law Reports (commercial reporting service, Australia)
HCA	High Court of Australia
HL	House of Lords
KB	Kings Bench Division (England)

LR (NSW)	New South Wales Law Reports 1880-1900
LT	Law Times Reports (England)
Lloyd's Rep Med	Lloyd's Reports (Medical) Medical Case Reports (UK) from 1998
Med LR	Medical Law Reports (UK)
NE	North Eastern Reporter (US commercial reporting service which covers State Supreme Court reports from the north eastern region, 1881-1936)
NE 2d	North Eastern Reporter, 2nd Series (from 1936)
NJ	New Jersey Supreme Court Reports (US)
NSWDCR	New South Wales District Court Reports
NSWLR	New South Wales Law Reports
NTR	Northern Territory Reports (bound with ALR)
NW	North Western Reporter (US commercial reporting service which covers State Supreme Court reports from the north western region, 1879-1941)
NW 2d	North Western Reporter, 2nd Series (from 1941) New York Supplement, Second Series (US)
NZLR	New Zealand Law Reports
P	Law Reports, Probate, Divorce and Admiralty Division (England) 1891-1971 or Pacific Reporter (US commercial reporting service which covers US Supreme Court reports from the western seaboard, 1883-1931)
P 2d	Pacific Reporter, Second Series (from 1931)
PD	Law Reports, Probate, Divorce and Admiralty Division (England) 1876-1890
QB	Law Reports Queen's Bench, Division 1891-present
QBD	Law Reports, Queen's Bench Division 1875-1890
QdR	Queensland Reports 1958-present
QSCR	Supreme Court Reports (Queensland) 1860-1881
QSR	Queensland State Reports 1902-1957
SASR	South Australian State Reports from 1971
SCR	Supreme Court Reports (NSW) 1862-1876

SCR	(Canada) Supreme Court Reports, Canada
SE	South-Eastern Reporter (US commercial reporting service which covers State Supreme Court reports from the south-eastern region 1887-1939)
SW 2d	South-Eastern Reporter, Second Series (from 1939)
SR (NSW)	State Reports (NSW) to 1970
SR (WA)	State Reports, Western Australia, 1980-present
SW	South-Western Reporter (US commercial reporting service which covers State Supreme Court reports from the south-western region, 1886-1929)
SW 2d	South-Western Reporter, Second Series (from 1928)
So 2d	Solicitors' Reports, Second Series (US)—covering all States
Tas LR	Tasmanian Law Reports 1904-1940
Tas R	Tasmanian Reports
Tas SR	Tasmanian State Reports
TLR	Tasmanian Law Reports 1905-1940, or The Times Law Reports (UK) 1884-1952
VLR	Victorian Law Reports to 1956
VR	Victorian Reports from 1956
WALR	Western Australian Law Reports to 1959
WAR	Western Australian Law Reports from 1959
WCBD (Vic)	Workers Compensation Board Decisions (Vic)
WCBD (WA)	Workers Compensation Board Decisions (WA)
WCR (NSW)	Workers Compensation Reports (NSW)
WCR (Q)	Workers Compensation Reports (Queensland)
WLR	Weekly Law Reports (England)
WN (NSW)	Weekly Notes (New South Wales)
WWR	Western Weekly Reports (Canada)

Comparable Provisions of Civil Liability Legislation in Australian Jurisdictions

	NSW Civil Liability Act 2002	ACT Civil Law (Wrongs) Act 2002	NT Personal Injuries (Liabilities and Damages) Act 2003	QLD Civil Liability Act 2003	SA Civil Liability Act 1936	VIC Wrongs Act 1958	TAS Civil Liability Act 2002	WA Civil Liability Act 2002
Duty of care – general principles	5B	43	-	9	32	48	11	5B
Causation – general principles	5D	45	-	11	34	51	13	5C
Causation - plaintiff cannot give evidence of what they would have done if they had been told of the risk	5D(3)(b)	-	-	11(3)(b)	-	-	13(3)(b)	5C(3)(b)
Causation - plaintiff bears onus of proof	5E	46	-	12	35	52	14	5D
Injured persons presumed to be aware of obvious risks	5G	-	-	14	37	54	16	5N
Standard of care for professionals	50	-	-	22	41	59	22	-

	NSW Civil Liability Act 2002	ACT Civil Law (Wrongs) Act 2002	NT Personal Injuries (Liabilities and Damages) Act 2003	QLD Civil Liability Act 2003	SA Civil Liability Act 1936	VIC Wrongs Act 1958	TAS Civil Liability Act 2002	WA Civil Liability Act 2002
Standard of care for professionals does not apply to the duty to warn of a risk	5P	-	-	22(5)	41(5)	60	22(5)	-
Liability based on non-delegable duty	5Q	-	-	-	-	61	-	-
Limitation on exemplary, punitive and aggravated damages	21	-	19	52	-	-	-	-
Mental harm	27-33	32-36	-	-	-	67-78	29-35	5Q-5T
Principles concerning resources, responsibilities etc of public or other authorities	42	110	-	35	-	83	38	5W
Proceedings against public or other authorities based on breach of statutory duty	43	111	-	36	-	84	40	(5X-5Y)
No civil liability for acts in self-defence	52	-	-	-	-	-	-	-
Damages limitations if loss results from serious offence committed by mentally ill person	54A	-	-	-	-	-	-	-
Good Samaritans	55-58	5	8	-	74	31A-31D	-	5AD-5AE
Apologies	67-69	12-14	11-13	69-72	75	14I-14L	6A-7	5AF-5AH
Limitation of the award of damages for the birth of a child	71	-	-	49A-49B	67	-	-	-

appendix 3

The National Privacy Principles

Privacy Act 1988 (Cth): Extracted from the website of the Office of the Privacy Commissioner, Australian Government at www.privacy.gov.au/.

There are at the federal level, ten privacy principles:

Principle 1 - Collection
Principle 2 - Use and disclosure
Principle 3 - Data quality
Principle 4 - Data security
Principle 5 - Openness

Principle 6 - Access and correction
Principle 7 - Identifiers
Principle 8 - Anonymity
Principle 9 - Transborder data flows
Principle 10 - Sensitive information

1. Collection

1.1 An organisation must not collect personal information unless the information is necessary for one or more of its functions or activities.

1.2 An organisation must collect personal information only by lawful and fair means and not in an unreasonably intrusive way.

1.3 At or before the time (or, if that is not practicable, as soon as practicable after) an organisation collects personal information about an individual from the individual, the organisation must take reasonable steps to ensure that the individual is aware of:

(a) the identity of the organisation and how to contact it; and

(b) the fact that he or she is able to gain access to the information; and

(c) the purposes for which the information is collected; and

(d) the organisations (or the types of organisations) to which the organisation usually discloses information of that kind; and

(e) any law that requires the particular information to be collected; and

(f) the main consequences (if any) for the individual if all or part of the information is not provided.

1.4 If it is reasonable and practicable to do so, an organisation must collect personal information about an individual only from that individual.

Health Care & the Law

1.5 If an organisation collects personal information about an individual from someone else, it must take reasonable steps to ensure that the individual is or has been made aware of the matters listed in subclause 1.3 except to the extent that making the individual aware of the matters would pose a serious threat to the life or health of any individual.

2. Use and disclosure

2.1 An organisation must not use or disclose personal information about an individual for a purpose (the *secondary purpose*) other than the primary purpose of collection unless:

    (a)   both of the following apply:

        (i)   the secondary purpose is related to the primary purpose of collection and, if the personal information is sensitive information, directly related to the primary purpose of collection;

        (ii) the individual would reasonably expect the organisation to use or disclose the information for the secondary purpose; or

    (b)   the individual has consented to the use or disclosure; or

    (c)   if the information is not sensitive information and the use of the information is for the secondary purpose of direct marketing:

        (i)   it is impracticable for the organisation to seek the individual's consent before that particular use; and

        (ii) the organisation will not charge the individual for giving effect to a request by the individual to the organisation not to receive direct marketing communications; and

        (iii) the individual has not made a request to the organisation not to receive direct marketing communications; and

        (iv) in each direct marketing communication with the individual, the organisation draws to the individual's attention, or prominently displays a notice, that he or she may express a wish not to receive any further direct marketing communications; and

        (v) each written direct marketing communication by the organisation with the individual (up to and including the communication that involves the use) sets out the organisation's business address and telephone number and, if the communication with the individual is made by fax, telex or other electronic means, a number or address at which the organisation can be directly contacted electronically; or

    (d)   if the information is health information and the use or disclosure is necessary for research, or the compilation or analysis of statistics, relevant to public health or public safety:

    (i) it is impracticable for the organisation to seek the individual's consent before the use or disclosure; and

    (ii) the use or disclosure is conducted in accordance with guidelines approved by the Commissioner under section 95A for the purposes of this subparagraph; and

    (iii) in the case of disclosure—the organisation reasonably believes that the recipient of the health information will not disclose the health information, or personal information derived from the health information; or

(e) the organisation reasonably believes that the use or disclosure is necessary to lessen or prevent:

    (i) a serious and imminent threat to an individual's life, health or safety; or

    (ii) a serious threat to public health or public safety; or

(f) the organisation has reason to suspect that unlawful activity has been, is being or may be engaged in, and uses or discloses the personal information as a necessary part of its investigation of the matter or in reporting its concerns to relevant persons or authorities; or

(g) the use or disclosure is required or authorised by or under law; or

(h) the organisation reasonably believes that the use or disclosure is reasonably necessary for one or more of the following by or on behalf of an enforcement body:

    (i) the prevention, detection, investigation, prosecution or punishment of criminal offences, breaches of a law imposing a penalty or sanction or breaches of a prescribed law;

    (ii) the enforcement of laws relating to the confiscation of the proceeds of crime;

    (iii) the protection of the public revenue;

    (iv) the prevention, detection, investigation or remedying of seriously improper conduct or prescribed conduct;

    (v) the preparation for, or conduct of, proceedings before any court or tribunal, or implementation of the orders of a court or tribunal.

2.2 If an organisation uses or discloses personal information under paragraph 2.1(h), it must make a written note of the use or disclosure.

2.3 Subclause 2.1 operates in relation to personal information that an organisation that is a body corporate has collected from a related body corporate as if the organisations primary purpose of collection of the information were the primary purpose for which the related body corporate collected the information.

2.4 Despite subclause 2.1, an organisation that provides a health service to an individual may disclose health information about the individual to a person who is responsible for the individual if:

    (a) the individual:

        (i) is physically or legally incapable of giving consent to the disclosure; or

        (ii) physically cannot communicate consent to the disclosure; and

    (b) a natural person (the *carer*) providing the health service for the organisation is satisfied that either:

        (i) the disclosure is necessary to provide appropriate care or treatment of the individual; or

        (ii) the disclosure is made for compassionate reasons; and

    (c) the disclosure is not contrary to any wish:

        (i) expressed by the individual before the individual became unable to give or communicate consent; and

        (ii) of which the carer is aware, or of which the carer could reasonably be expected to be aware; and

    (d) the disclosure is limited to the extent reasonable and necessary for a purpose mentioned in paragraph (b).

2.5 For the purposes of subclause 2.4, a person is *responsible* for an individual if the person is:

    (a) a parent of the individual; or

    (b) a child or sibling of the individual and at least 18 years old; or

    (c) a spouse or de facto spouse of the individual; or

    (d) a relative of the individual, at least 18 years old and a member of the individual's household; or

    (e) a guardian of the individual; or

    (f) exercising an enduring power of attorney granted by the individual that is exercisable in relation to decisions about the individual's health; or

    (g) a person who has an intimate personal relationship with the individual; or

    (h) a person nominated by the individual to be contacted in case of emergency.

2.6 In subclause 2.5:

child of an individual includes an adopted child, a step-child and a foster-child, of the individual.

parent of an individual includes a step-parent, adoptive parent and a foster-parent, of the individual.

relative of an individual means a grandparent, grandchild, uncle, aunt, nephew or niece, of the individual.

sibling of an individual includes a half-brother, half-sister, adoptive brother, adoptive sister, step-brother, step-sister, foster-brother and foster-sister, of the individual.

3. Data quality

An organisation must take reasonable steps to make sure that the personal information it collects, uses or discloses is accurate, complete and up-to-date.

4. Data security

4.1 An organisation must take reasonable steps to protect the personal information it holds from misuse and loss and from unauthorised access, modification or disclosure.

4.2 An organisation must take reasonable steps to destroy or permanently de-identify personal information if it is no longer needed for any purpose for which the information may be used or disclosed under National Privacy Principle 2.

5. Openness

5.1 An organisation must set out in a document clearly expressed policies on its management of personal information. The organisation must make the document available to anyone who asks for it.

5.2 On request by a person, an organisation must take reasonable steps to let the person know, generally, what sort of personal information it holds, for what purposes, and how it collects, holds, uses and discloses that information.

6. Access and correction

6.1   If an organisation holds personal information about an individual, it must provide the individual with access to the information on request by the individual, except to the extent that:

(a) in the case of personal information other than health information—providing access would pose a serious and imminent threat to the life or health of any individual; or

(b) in the case of health information—providing access would pose a serious threat to the life or health of any individual; or

(c) providing access would have an unreasonable impact upon the privacy of other individuals; or

(d) the request for access is frivolous or vexatious; or

(e) the information relates to existing or anticipated legal proceedings between the organisation and the individual, and the information would not be accessible by the process of discovery in those proceedings; or

(f) providing access would reveal the intentions of the organisation in relation to negotiations with the individual in such a way as to prejudice those negotiations; or

(g) providing access would be unlawful; or

(h) denying access is required or authorised by or under law; or

(i) providing access would be likely to prejudice an investigation of possible unlawful activity; or

(j) providing access would be likely to prejudice:
   (i) the prevention, detection, investigation, prosecution or punishment of criminal offences, breaches of a law imposing a penalty or sanction or breaches of a prescribed law; or
   (ii) the enforcement of laws relating to the confiscation of the proceeds of crime; or
   (iii) the protection of the public revenue; or
   (iv) the prevention, detection, investigation or remedying of seriously improper conduct or prescribed conduct; or
   (v) the preparation for, or conduct of, proceedings before any court or tribunal, or implementation of its orders;
   by or on behalf of an enforcement body; or
(k) an enforcement body performing a lawful security function asks the organisation not to provide access to the information on the basis that providing access would be likely to cause damage to the security of Australia.

6.2 However, where providing access would reveal evaluative information generated within the organisation in connection with a commercially sensitive decision-making process, the organisation may give the individual an explanation for the commercially sensitive decision rather than direct access to the information.

6.3 If the organisation is not required to provide the individual with access to the information because of one or more of paragraphs 6.1(a) to (k) (inclusive), the organisation must, if reasonable, consider whether the use of mutually agreed intermediaries would allow sufficient access to meet the needs of both parties.

6.4 If an organisation charges for providing access to personal information, those charges:
(a) must not be excessive; and
(b) must not apply to lodging a request for access.

6.5 If an organisation holds personal information about an individual and the individual is able to establish that the information is not accurate, complete and up-to-date, the organisation must take reasonable steps to correct the information so that it is accurate, complete and up-to-date.

6.6 If the individual and the organisation disagree about whether the information is accurate, complete and up-to-date, and the individual asks the organisation to associate with the information a statement claiming that the information is not accurate, complete or up-to-date, the organisation must take reasonable steps to do so.

6.7 An organisation must provide reasons for denial of access or a refusal to correct personal information.

7. Identifiers

7.1 An organisation must not adopt as its own identifier of an individual an identifier of the individual that has been assigned by:

    (a)   an agency; or

    (b)   an agent of an agency acting in its capacity as agent; or

    (c)   a contracted service provider for a Commonwealth contract acting in its capacity as contracted service provider for that contract.

7.1A However, subclause 7.1 does not apply to the adoption by a prescribed organisation of a prescribed identifier in prescribed circumstances.

7.2 An organisation must not use or disclose an identifier assigned to an individual by an agency, or by an agent or contracted service provider mentioned in subclause 7.1, unless:

(a)   the use or disclosure is necessary for the organisation to fulfil its obligations to the agency; or

(b)   one or more of paragraphs 2.1(e) to 2.1(h) (inclusive) apply to the use or disclosure; or

(c)   the use or disclosure is by a prescribed organisation of a prescribed identifier in prescribed circumstances.

7.3 In this clause:

    identifier includes a number assigned by an organisation to an individual to identify uniquely the individual for the purposes of the organisation's operations. However, an individual's name or ABN (as defined in the *A New Tax System (Australian Business Number) Act 1999*) is not an *identifier*.

8. Anonymity

Wherever it is lawful and practicable, individuals must have the option of not identifying themselves when entering transactions with an organisation.

9. Transborder data flows

An organisation in Australia or an external Territory may transfer personal information about an individual to someone (other than the organisation or the individual) who is in a foreign country only if:

    (a)   the organisation reasonably believes that the recipient of the information is subject to a law, binding scheme or contract which effectively upholds principles for fair handling of the information that are substantially similar to the National Privacy Principles; or

    (b)   the individual consents to the transfer; or

    (c)   the transfer is necessary for the performance of a contract between the individual and the organisation, or for the implementation of pre-contractual measures taken in response to the individual's request; or

    (d)   the transfer is necessary for the conclusion or performance of a contract concluded in the interest of the individual between the organisation and a third party; or

662 Health Care & the Law

    (e) all of the following apply:
        (i)   the transfer is for the benefit of the individual;
        (ii) it is impracticable to obtain the consent of the individual to that transfer;
        (iii) if it were practicable to obtain such consent, the individual would be likely to give it; or
    (f) the organisation has taken reasonable steps to ensure that the information which it has transferred will not be held, used or disclosed by the recipient of the information inconsistently with the National Privacy Principles.

10. Sensitive information

10.1 An organisation must not collect sensitive information about an individual unless:
    (a) the individual has consented; or
    (b) the collection is required by law; or
    (c) the collection is necessary to prevent or lessen a serious and imminent threat to the life or health of any individual, where the individual whom the information concerns:
        (i)   is physically or legally incapable of giving consent to the collection; or
        (ii) physically cannot communicate consent to the collection; or
    (d) if the information is collected in the course of the activities of a non-profit organisation the following conditions are satisfied:
        (i)   the information relates solely to the members of the organisation or to individuals who have regular contact with it in connection with its activities;
        (ii) at or before the time of collecting the information, the organisation undertakes to the individual whom the information concerns that the organisation will not disclose the information without the individual's consent; or
    (e) the collection is necessary for the establishment, exercise or defence of a legal or equitable claim.

10.2 Despite subclause 10.1, an organisation may collect health information about an individual if:
    (a) the information is necessary to provide a health service to the individual; and
    (b) the information is collected:
        (i)   as required by law (other than this Act); or
        (ii) in accordance with rules established by competent health or medical bodies that deal with obligations of professional confidentiality which bind the organisation.

10.3 Despite subclause 10.1, an organisation may collect health information about an individual if:

(a) the collection is necessary for any of the following purposes:
  (i) research relevant to public health or public safety;
  (ii) the compilation or analysis of statistics relevant to public health or public safety;
  (iii) the management, funding or monitoring of a health service; and

(b) that purpose cannot be served by the collection of information that does not identify the individual or from which the individual's identity cannot reasonably be ascertained; and

(c) it is impracticable for the organisation to seek the individual's consent to the collection; and

(d) the information is collected:
  (i) as required by law (other than this Act); or
  (ii) in accordance with rules established by competent health or medical bodies that deal with obligations of professional confidentiality which bind the organisation; or
  (iii) in accordance with guidelines approved by the Commissioner under section 95A for the purposes of this subparagraph.

10.4 If an organisation collects health information about an individual in accordance with subclause 10.3, the organisation must take reasonable steps to permanently de-identify the information before the organisation discloses it.

10.5 In this clause:

non-profit organisation means a non-profit organisation that has only racial, ethnic, political, religious, philosophical, professional, trade, or trade union aims.

Summary of Selected Provisions of the Drugs of Dependence Act 1989 (ACT)

This is a summary of some of the provisions of the *Drugs of Dependence Act 1989* (ACT). The Act is comprehensive, and is one of three Acts covering drugs in the Australian Capital Territory. The other Acts are the *Poisons Act 1933* (ACT), which deals with marketing, sale and supply of poisons, and the *Poisons and Drugs Act 1978* (ACT), which deals with the supply, packaging storage of scheduled poisons and drugs, and the prescription of specifically designated poisons or drugs. Each Act has Regulations. Of these the most relevant to health carers is the Drugs of Dependence Act, and the summary below gives an indication of the many regulations applying to the handling of drugs by health carers. The provisions of these Acts and

Regulations are similar to those in other jurisdictions.

For the purposes of this summary, "Class I institution" means a hospital, nursing home or other institution that has a dispensary and is used for the accommodation, treatment and care of persons suffering from mental or physical conditions;

"Class II institution" means a nursing home or other institution that does not have a dispensary and is used for the accommodation, treatment and care of persons suffering from mental or physical conditions;

"Drugs of dependence" are listed in the Schedules to the Drugs of Dependence Regulations and include methadone;

"Intern" means a person who is conditionally registered as a medical practitioner under the *Health Professionals Act 2004* (ACT) because the person would be entitled to apply for unconditional registration if the person had completed a period of supervised training that the person has started.

Supply and Administration

Issue of Prescriptions: s 57

A person who is not a doctor or veterinary surgeon shall not prescribe a drug of dependence. An intern shall not prescribe a drug of dependence except in the course of treatment conducted at an institution where he or she is working as an intern. A veterinary surgeon shall not prescribe a drug of dependence otherwise than for the treatment of an animal. (Maximum penalty: 20 penalty units, imprisonment for 1 year, or both).

Prescribing Drugs of Dependence: s 58

A doctor must not prescribe a drug of dependence unless it is for the treatment of a person's physical or mental condition, with the exception of methadone or buprenorphine prescribed in accordance with s 59. If a doctor believes on reasonable grounds that a person is drug dependent or has used a drug of dependence either continuously for a period exceeding two months or periods taken together that exceed 2 months, the doctor must obtain the approval of the Chief Health Officer before prescribing any drug of dependence for them. An exception is where the person requires the drug as a hospital inpatient for not more than 14 days. A doctor may not prescribe an amphetamine without the approval of the chief health officer. An exception is created where a doctor believes on reasonable grounds that a person is not drug dependent or taken a drug of dependence for more than two months, and: (i) the person is suffering from narcolepsy or attention deficit hyperactivity disorder; and (ii) the prescription is for a period of use not exceeding 2 months. (Maximum penalty: 20 penalty units, imprisonment for 1 year, or both).

Methadone or Buprenorpine: s 59

Where a doctor believes on reasonable grounds that a person is drug dependent in relation to any drug if dependence or prohibited substance he or she may, with the approval of the Chief Health Officer, prescribe methadone or buprenorphine for the treatment of the person's drug dependence if he or she believes on reasonable grounds that methadone or buprenorphine would be suitable for the treatment, and the treatment is to be provided at an opioid dependency treatment centre.

Written Prescriptions: s 60

Except for oral prescriptions, provided for below, a prescription for the supply of a drug of dependence shall, in addition to the requirements of any law in force in the Territory:

- be in legible handwriting and written in terms and symbols used in ordinary professional practice;

- specify the name, address and qualification of the person writing the prescription;
- specify the date on which the prescription is issued;
- specify the name and address of the person for whose treatment the drug is prescribed;
- specify the drug, and the quantity, form and strength of the drug, to be supplied;
- specify the number of times the drug is to be dispensed and, if it is to be
- dispensed more than once, the interval or intervals that are to elapse between the dispensations;
- *if the prescription is for an unusual or dangerous dose—bear the initials of the person writing the prescription beside an underlined reference to the dose* (Italics added);
- if the prescription is for an amphetamine:
  - if the Chief Health Officer has approved the prescription, be endorsed APPROVED BY CHO and include any approval number allocated by the chief health officer; or
  - if the approval of the Chief Health Officer was not required under s 58— be endorsed "CHO APPROVAL NOT REQUIRED";
- be signed by the person writing the prescription.

A doctor shall not issue a written prescription for a drug of dependence that fails to comply with these requirements (Maximum penalty: 20 penalty units, imprisonment for 1 year, or both).

Prescriptions Issued Orally: s 61

A doctor may only issue an oral prescription for a drug of dependence if the doctor believes on reasonable grounds that the quantity of the drug to be supplied is necessary for the emergency treatment of the person. It may only be issued to a pharmacist, or in a Class I Institution, if no pharmacist is available at the time at which the drug is required—a nurse in that institution.

The doctor must:

1) inform the pharmacist or nurse to whom the prescription is issued of:
   - her or his name, address and qualification;
   - the name and address of the person for whose treatment the drug is prescribed;
   - the drug, and the quantity, form and strength of the drug, to be supplied;
   - the number of times the drug is to be dispensed and, if it is to be dispensed
   - more than once, the interval or intervals that are to elapse between the dispensations;
2) *if the prescription is for an unusual or dangerous dose—inform that pharmacist or nurse accordingly* (Italics added);
3) within 24 hours, furnish the pharmacist or nurse to whom it was issued with a written prescription corresponding to the orally issued prescription and complying with the requirements set out above for written prescriptions.

Where a pharmacist or nurse has supplied a drug of dependence in accordance with an orally issued prescription, and he or she does not, within 72 hours, receive a written prescription from the doctor who issued it, corresponding to the orally issued prescription and in the required form, the pharmacist or nurse must notify a drug inspector in writing accordingly (Maximum penalty: 20 penalty units, imprisonment for 1 year, or both).

Supply on Prescription: s 80

A person must not supply a drug of dependence on a prescription unless the person is a pharmacist, doctor, person under the personal supervision of a doctor or pharmacist or, where the drug is methadone or buprenorphine, a nurse employed at an opioid dependency treatment centre conducted by the Territory. A doctor, or a person under the personal supervision of a doctor, shall not supply a drug of dependence upon a prescription otherwise than for the treatment of a patient under the doctor's professional care. A person shall not supply a drug of dependence on a prescription otherwise than to a person the supplier believes on reasonable grounds to be the person for whom the drug has been supplied, their guardian or parent (if the person for whom it is prescribed is a child), or if there is no guardian or parent, the duly authorised agent of the person.

Where an intern prescribes a drug of dependence, a pharmacist in control of a dispensary in a community pharmacy (pharmacy with a dispensary other than at a Class I Institution), or a person under the personal supervision of such a pharmacist, shall not supply that drug to any person on that prescription .(Maximum penalty: 20 penalty units, imprisonment for 1 year, or both).

Restrictions on Supply: s 81

A person shall not supply a drug of dependence on an order, written requisition or written prescription if that document:

1) appears to have been forged, or altered in a material particular by someone other than the person who signed it;
2) bears the word "cancelled" or any other indication that it is cancelled; or
3) was written more than six months before it is presented for supply. (Maximum penalty: 20 penalty units, imprisonment for 1 year, or both).

Forged Prescriptions, Requisitions and Orders: s 82

Where a person believes on reasonable grounds that an order, requisition or prescription presented to them for the supply of a drug of dependence has been forged or altered in a material particular they must immediately notify a police officer and a drug inspector, and forward a written report to the Chief Health Officer setting out the grounds on which he or she believes it to have been forged or altered. (Maximum penalty: 20 penalty units, imprisonment for 1 year, or both).

Supplying Dextromoramide and Hydromorphone: s 83

A person shall not, upon a written prescription, supply dextromoramide or hydromorphone unless the person is familiar with the handwriting of the person issuing the prescription, or verifies with the person who apparently issued the prescription that they did indeed issue it, or knows the person for whom the drug was prescribed. (Maximum penalty: 50 penalty units, imprisonment for 2 years, or both).

Administration—Witnesses: s 84

A person shall not administer a drug of dependence to a patient at an opioid dependency treatment centre conducted by the Territory except, if they are an intern, in the presence of a medical practitioner, dentist or nurse, and in any other case, in the presence of a doctor, intern, dentist, pharmacist or nurse, or an enrolled nurse who has completed a course on the use of drugs of dependence approved for the purpose of this section by the Minister. (Maximum penalty: 20 penalty units, imprisonment for 1 year, or both).

Distribution of Syringes—Approval: s 86 et seq

A doctor, pharmacist, nurse or health worker may apply in prescribed form to the Chief Health Officer for, and be granted, approval to supply syringes. An approval granted to a health worker is renewable yearly, and may be made subject to the condition that the health worker attend a further course of instruction. An approved person shall not, without reasonable excuse, fail to produce the approval for inspection by the police officer (Maximum penalty: 10 penalty units).

Approval—No Liability for Ancillary Offences: s 93

An approved person who supplies a syringe to another person shall not, by reason only of that supply, be taken to commit any offence under the Criminal Code, part 2.4, if they do so in the course of their professional practice or occupational duties, and have reasonable grounds for believing that it is to be used for the administration of a drug of dependence or prohibited substance. They must also believe that the supply of the syringe might assist in preventing the spread of disease. A person who prints or publishes a notice, announcement or advertisement in any form about the supply by approved persons of syringes in the circumstances referred to above shall not, by reason only of that printing or publishing, be taken to have committed any offence under the Criminal Code, Part 2.4.

Records, Safe-Keeping and Disposal

Drug Registers: s 99 (see attached Form 1)

A "prescribed person" (including a pharmacist, doctor or a person in charge of an opioid dependency treatment centre) shall keep, or cause to be kept, at the place where any drugs of dependence are kept by that person, a register of drugs of dependence in prescribed form. (Maximum penalty: 20 penalty units, imprisonment for 1 year, or both).

Entries in Drug Registers: s 100

A prescribed person shall, within 24 hours of manufacturing or receiving a drug of dependence, enter specified details of the drug in the relevant drug register. Where a prescribed person sells, supplies or administers a drug of dependence he or she shall, within 24 hours, enter specified details of the drug in the relevant drug register. All entries in a drug register must be signed (maximum penalty: 20 penalty units).

Ward Registers: s 101 (see attached Forms 2 and 2A)

A person who, for the time being, is in charge of a ward, shall keep in the ward a ward drugs of dependence register in the prescribed form. They must also keep in respect of methadone administered at an opoid dependency treatment centre for the purpose of treating drug dependency—a ward methadone register in the prescribed form. They must also keep in respect of buprenorphine administered at an opioid dependency treatment centre for the purpose of treating drug dependency—a ward buprenorphine register in the prescribed form. This section does not apply to a specially designated opioid dependency treatment centre, as they are covered by s 99 (maximum penalty: 50 penalty units, imprisonment for 6 months, or both).

Entries in Ward Drugs of Dependence Registers: s 102

A person who keeps, or causes to be kept, a ward drugs of dependence register shall enter, or cause to be entered, in that register, specified details in respect of each drug, of dependence that is supplied for use in the ward, within 24 hours after the drug is supplied:

- the date on which the drug was supplied;
- the name, quantity, form and strength of the drug; and
- in the case of a Class II Institution the name and business address of the person who supplied the drug.

A person who is to administer a drug of dependence to a patient in a ward shall enter in the relevant ward drugs of dependence register when the drug is removed from a drug cabinet for that purpose:

- the anticipated date and time of the administration;
- the name, quantity, form, strength and dose of the drug;
- the number accorded to the relevant prescription pursuant to s 97 (which requires prescriptions to be numbered);
- the name of the doctor who prescribed the drug;
- the name of the patient to whom the drug is to be administered; and
- the quantity of the drug remaining in the ward.

The entry must be signed. Where necessary, any amendments to the register relating to date and time of administration must be made within 24 hours of the original entry being made. In addition, a person who supplies a drug of dependence to a ward, or witnesses the administration of a drug of dependence to a patient in the ward must countersign the relevant entry in the ward drugs of dependence register (maximum penalty: 10 penalty units).

Entries in Ward Methadone Registers: s 102A

A person who administers methadone during a shift at an opioid dependency treatment centre for the purpose of treating drug dependency shall enter in the ward methadone register:

1) at the beginning of the shift:
   - the name of the centre and its location;
   - the strength and form in which the methadone is to be administered; and
   - the amount of methadone removed from the dispensary or other place
   - where the methadone is stored;
2) immediately after each dose of methadone is administered:
   - the date and time of administration;
   - the name of the patient to whom the methadone was administered;
   - the quantity of methadone administered;
   - the name of the person who administered the methadone;
   - the name of the person who witnessed the administration; and
   - the name of the doctor who prescribed the methadone; and
3) at the end of the shift:
   - the reconciliation amount for each dose; and
   - the quantity of methadone returned to the dispensary or other place where
   - the methadone is stored.

The person who administered the methadone and the person who witnessed that administration during the shift shall, at the end of the shift, sign the ward methadone register.

Entries in Ward Buprenorphine Registers: s 102B

The provisions in this section are identical to those in relation to methadone under s 102A only with reference to buprenorphine.

First-Aid Registers: s 103 (see attached Form 3)

A person authorised to have control of a first-aid kit containing a drug of dependence shall keep or cause to be kept, in a locked receptacle or room to which that person has exclusive access, a first-aid drugs of dependence register in prescribed form (Maximum penalty: 20 penalty units, imprisonment for 1 year, or both).

Entries in First-Aid Registers: s 104

A person who keeps a first-aid register shall enter, or cause to be entered, in the register information specified in this section in respect of each drug of dependence contained in the kit, and sign each entry (Maximum penalty: 10 penalty units).

Record of Disposal: s 105

Where a drug of dependence in relation to which an entry has been made in a register has been disposed of or surrendered (in accordance with s 120), the person who is required to keep the register shall enter in it details of the drug, date and method of disposal, or if surrendered, details of to whom it was surrendered, details of the drug and date of surrender, and that person shall sign the entry. The person who disposed of the drug and the person who supervised that disposal must also sign the register (maximum penalty: 10 penalty units).

Registers—General Provisions: s 106

Alterations: A person shall not alter, or cause or permit to be altered, an entry made in a register (this would include "whiting-out" or obliteration).

Corrections: A correction is to be made by the addition of a notation signed by the person making the notation and by a witness.

Availability of Register: Subject to s 109, a person who keeps a register shall retain possession of it for two years after the date of the last entry made in the register, and make it available for inspection on request by a drug inspector or a police officer authorised in writing for the purpose by the Minister.

Loss: A person responsible for a register shall, immediately upon discovering the loss or destruction of the register or part of the register:

1) advise the Chief Health Officer in writing;
2) make an inventory in the prescribed form of each drug of dependence kept by her or him for the purpose of compiling a new register; and
3) from records, reconstruct, as far as possible, that part of the old register which was lost or destroyed or compile a new register.
   (Maximum penalty: 20 penalty units, imprisonment for 1 year, or both.)

False Entries in Registers: s 107

A person responsible for a register shall not make, or cause or permit to be made, in the register an entry that is, to the knowledge of that person, false or misleading in any particular (maximum penalty: 20 penalty units, imprisonment for 1 year, or both).

Patients' Records: s 108

A person who administers a drug of dependence to a patient at an institution, or an opioid dependency treatment centre that does not form part of an institution, shall enter a record of the date and time of administration and a notation that the drug was administered in accordance with the prescription, on the prescription for that drug which forms part of the patient's clinical records and that person shall initial the entry (maximum penalty: 10 penalty units).

Transfer of Control of Pharmacies: s 109 (see attached Form 4)

Where a pharmacist takes control of a community pharmacy for a continuous period of more than 14 days, he or she must check the inventory and if the inventory is correct, mark and sign the inventory. The inventory is to be prepared by the outgoing pharmacist. If there are any discrepancies the pharmacists shall mark the inventory and notify a drug inspector orally immediately and in writing within 24 hours.

Storage of Drugs

The Act prescribes specifications for drug cupboards, key safes, strong rooms and vaults. The specifications for drug cupboards include such matters as the material (black mild steel plate of not less than 10 millimetres thickness), the type of welding, door, and locking system (fixed locking bar, welded to the inside face of the door plus a five-lever key lock or locking mechanism providing at least the same degree of security). There must be a clearance around the door of not more than 1.5 millimetres. It must be securely attached to a wall or a floor (with requirements depending on the type of wall or floor).

A key safe must be designed to be opened by means of a combination lock, and is used for the purpose of keeping the key to a vault, strong room, safe or drug cabinet. A safe is to be constructed in such a manner as to prevent ready access to its contents by cutting, sawing or unbolting, and be freestanding and weigh not less than 350 kilograms or be securely affixed or anchored to, or embedded in, a concrete floor or a concrete or brick wall.

Strong rooms must be of brick or concrete while vaults are to be made of reinforced concrete, with both reasonably expected to resist attempts to gain entry by tools, torch or explosives for a period of not less than one hour.

Safekeeping (of Drugs) by Doctors, Dentists and Veterinary Surgeons: s 113

A doctor, dentist, or person authorised to carry drugs of dependence as part of a first aid kit must keep drugs of dependence locked in a receptacle fixed to the premises or a locked room, unless the drug is being carried, in which case it must be carried in a locked bag or container.

Safe-Keeping (of Drugs) by Other Persons: s 114

Where a drug of dependence is kept by:

1) a pharmacist in control of a dispensary, not being the central store of an institution or a dispensary under the direct control of the chief pharmacist of an institution;
2) a person in charge, for the time being, of a ward at an institution;
3) a person in charge, for the time being, of an opioid dependency treatment centre which is not a ward; or
4) a person in charge of a Class II Institution;

that person shall keep the drug, or cause it to be kept, in a drug cabinet, or in a safe securely embedded in a concrete floor (maximum penalty: 50 penalty units).

Where a drug of dependence is kept in a drug cabinet or safe at a Class II Institution, opioid dependency treatment centre which is not a ward, or community pharmacy, the person in charge for the time being shall ensure that the drug cabinet or safe and the key safe, if any, is fitted with such warning devices and detectors as are, or as are of a type, approved in writing by the Chief Health Officer (maximum penalty: 50 penalty units).

Safe-Keeping at Institutions: s 115

A person in charge of a Class II Institution shall not keep, or cause or permit to be kept, at the institution a quantity of a drug of dependence exceeding that prescribed by a doctor for the treatment of a patient at the institution. A person shall not remove any quantity of a drug of dependence that is to be administered to a patient in the institution from the receptacle or place in which the drug is stored, until that quantity of the drug is required for that purpose (maximum penalty: 50 penalty units).

Loss or Theft of a Drug of Dependence: s 116

Where a person keeping a drug of dependence becomes aware of the loss or theft of a quantity of the drug:

• and he or she believes on reasonable grounds that the drug was stolen, notify a drug inspector and a police officer orally immediately, and in writing within 24 hours;
• in the case of a loss—give a written report of the circumstances of the loss to a drug inspector; and

- record the loss or theft accordingly in the relevant register (maximum penalty: 20 penalty units).

On recovery of a quantity or part of a quantity of a drug of dependence which was lost or stolen, the person who originally held that quantity or part shall record its recovery accordingly in the relevant register (maximum penalty: 20 penalty units).

Access to Combinations and Keys of Drug Receptacles: s 117

Where a "responsible person" keeps a drug of dependence in a place or drug receptacle designed to be opened by means of a combination lock, that person shall maintain personal access to, and keep confidential, the combination of the lock. "Responsible person" includes a pharmacist in control of a dispensary; a doctor, a nurse in charge, for the time being, of a ward at an institution and a person in charge of a Class II Institution (maximum penalty: 20 penalty units, imprisonment for 1 year, or both). Where a person responsible keeps a drug of dependence in a drug receptacle designed to be opened with a key, that person shall retain personal custody of the key; or if the key is kept in a key safe— maintain personal access to, and keep confidential, the combination of the lock of the key safe (maximum penalty: 20 penalty units, imprisonment for 1 year, or both).

Safe-Keeping—General: s 118

A person keeping a drug of dependence must keep it in conditions which preserve the stability and quality of the drug and except where he or she is a doctor, veterinary surgeon, dentist, or a pharmacist in control of the dispensary at a community pharmacy, ensure that only drugs of dependence or other drugs or prohibited substances are kept in the receptacle where the drug is kept. The drug receptacle or place where the drug is kept, and the key safe (if any) used for keeping the key to it, must be kept locked at all times except when it is necessary to carry out essential operations in connection with the drugs of dependence, or to gain access to any other items kept in that receptacle or place (maximum penalty: 20 penalty units, imprisonment for 1 year, or both).

Procedure for Disposal: s 120

A drug of dependence shall be taken to be unfit for use if it is contaminated, kept later than the "use-by" date, or otherwise unfit for use.

Where a person holds a quantity of a drug of dependence that the person wishes to dispose of, or which has become unfit for use, that person shall keep the quantity stored as for all drugs of dependence until it is disposed of or surrendered and ensure that that quantity is disposed of or surrendered in accordance with this section (maximum penalty: 20 penalty units, imprisonment for 1 year, or both).

Disposal: The drug must be disposed of under the supervision of, and in accordance with the direction of, a drug inspector, or surrendered to a drug inspector to be disposed of as the Chief Health Officer directs. Where a drug of dependence is held at a Class I Institution, it shall be disposed of in the presence of a doctor, intern, dentist, pharmacist or nurse or an enrolled nurse who has completed an approved course on the use of drugs of dependence, the Chief Pharmacist of the institution.

Surrender to a drug inspector: This must be by personal delivery, registered mail or courier service. Where a drug of dependence is surrendered to a drug inspector for disposal, disposal must be carried out in the presence of a Chief Pharmacist of an institution or a doctor, intern, dentist, pharmacist or nurse or an enrolled nurse who has completed an approved course on the use of drugs of dependence.

A chief pharmacist of an institution shall not be taken to hold a drug of dependence unless it is kept in the central control of the chief pharmacist.

Penalties – Drugs of Dependence Regulations 2005 – Notes

The value of a penalty unit if the person charged is:

(a) an individual, is $100;
(b) a corporation, is $500.

FORM 1 (FOR SECTION 99)

DRUG REGISTER

Location ....

Drug[1] .... Strength[1] .... Form[1] ....

Date[2]	Name and address/location[3]	Dealing[4]	Name and Address of prescriber	No.[5]	In[6]	Out[6]	Balance[7]	Remarks[8]	Signature[9]

1. One drug, 1 strength, 1 form only per page of register.
2. Date of dealing.
3. Name and address of other party to the dealing (and that party's agent, where applicable), or location of ward or dispensary to which or from which the drug is supplied.
4. Nature of dealing—whether manufacture, receipt, supply, administration, disposal, surrender, loss or theft.
5. No. of prescription or requisition.
6. Quantity of the drug coming in or going out.
7. Quantity of the drug still held.
8. Including—
   - if the drug is supplied by a veterinary surgeon—species and identification details of the relevant animal; or
   - if the drug is disposed of—signature of the drug inspector or Chief Pharmacist who authorised the disposal.
9. Signature of the person making the entry in the register.

FORM 2 (FOR SECTION 101)

WARD REGISTER

Institution and location ....

Drug[1] ....Strength[1] ....Form[1] ....

Date[2]	Source of supply[3]/ Patient's name	Dealing[4]	Name of prescriber No.[5]	In[6]	Out[6]	Balance[7]	Dose	Time of administration	Disposal[7A]	Remarks	Counter signature[8]	Signature[9]

1. One drug, 1 strength, 1 form only per page of register.
2. Date of dealing.
3. Name and address of supplier, or location of dispensary in Class I Institution from which the drug is supplied.
4. Nature of dealing—whether receipt, supply, administration, disposal, surrender, loss or theft.
5. No. of prescription or requisition.
6. Quantity of the drug coming in or going out.
7. Quantity of the drug still held.
7A. Quantity (if any) disposed of.
8. • If the drug is received—countersignature of supplier;
   • If the drug is administered—countersignature of witness;
   • If the drug is disposed of—countersignature of the person who authorised or witnessed the disposal.
9. Signature of the person making the entry in the register.

FORM 2A (FOR SECTION 101)

METHADONE REGISTER

Institution and location[1] ....

Strength[2] ....Form[2] ....Reconciliation amount[3] ....

Quantity of methadone removed from dispensary[1] ....Quantity of methadone returned to dispensary[3] ....

Signature of administrator[3] ....Signature of witness[3] ....

Date[4]	Patient's name	Time of administration	Name of prescriber	Dose	Balance[5]	Name of administrator	Ns

1. Complete at beginning of shift.
2. One strength, 1 form only per page of register.
3. Complete at end of shift.
4. Date of administration.
5. Quantity of the drug still held.

FORM 3 (FOR SECTION 103)

FIRST-AID REGISTER

Institution and location ....

Drug[1]................................Strength[1]...............................Form[1]...............................

Date[2]	Name and Address[3]	Dealing[4]	In[5]	Out[5]	Balance[6]	Remarks	Counter signature[7]	Signature[8]

1.   One drug, 1 strength, 1 form only per page of register.
2.   Date of dealing.
3.   Name and address of supplier, or person to whom the drug is administered (if the latter is ascertainable).
4.   Nature of dealing—whether receipt, administration, surrender, loss or theft.
5.   Quantity of the drug coming in or going out.
6.   Quantity of the drug still held.
7.   If the drug is disposed of—countersignature of the drug inspector who authorised the disposal.
8.   Signature of the person making the entry in the register.

FORM 4 (FOR SECTION 109)

DRUGS OF DEPENDENCE INVENTORY

Pharmacy: Pharmacy Stamp

Address: ....

....

Name of outgoing pharmacist:...

Name of incoming pharmacist:...

Drug	Form	Strength	Quantity stated in register	Actual quantity held	Discrepancy

.... Date: . . . / . . . / . . .

(Signature of outgoing pharmacist conducting inventory)

Inventory *Correct/*Incorrect

* Chief Health Officer notified

.... Date: . . . / . . . / . . .

(Signature of incoming pharmacist checking inventory)

*Incoming pharmacist to delete where inapplicable

appendix 5

Code of Professional Conduct

Duties of a Doctor Registered with the New South Wales Medical Board

Medical Practice Act 1992, s 99A
(as amended) July 2005

EXECUTIVE SUMMARY

The aim of this Code of Professional Conduct is to set out general principles in relation to the practice of medicine. These principles complement the requirements of the *Medical Practice Act 1992* and the *Health Care Complaints Act 1992* and case law. However, they are not a substitute for the provisions of law and case law and in the event of any doubt, the legislative provisions take precedence. The Code applies to all practitioners in New South Wales.

This summary should be read in conjunction with the detailed Code.

Standard 1

You must possess and apply adequate knowledge and skill in the practice of medicine.

Standard 2

You must observe professional and ethical obligations. These include:

- Education, teaching and training responsibilities
- Providing honest assessment of the performance of colleagues
- Putting patients first while putting aside your own personal views

- Maintaining trust with patients through your interaction with patients
- Arranging appropriate alternative treatment when the doctor/patient relationship deteriorates
- Disclosure of adverse events to appropriate authorities
- Responding appropriately to situations in which a complaint is made about your treatment or where treatment is unsuccessful
- Co-operating fully with the investigating authorities such as the HCCC and the NSW Medical Board in respect of adverse events
- Dealing appropriately with the next of kin of deceased patients
- Ensuring your professional position is not abused or compromised through improper financial or personal dealings with patients
- Ensuring that your own health or that of another practitioner does not put patients at risk
- Ensuring other practitioners do not place patients at risk through their health, conduct or performance
- Providing factual information about your services

Standard 3
You must ensure that you enjoy a good relationship with all colleagues in health care teams;
- Through treating colleagues with respect regardless of your personal views
- By working constructively with health care teams
- By ensuring patient treatment is covered during your own absence or unavailability
- Ensuring that a patient's care is co-ordinated
- Ensuring appropriate delegation and referral of care of a patient

Standard 4
You must display probity in your professional practice in respect of:
- Financial and commercial dealings
- Financial interests in hospitals, nursing homes and other medical organisations
- Not accepting gifts or other inducements
- Not entering into financial agreements with patients which may compromise the therapeutic relationship
- Ensuring that any documents signed by you are not false or misleading
- Ensuring that research in which you are engaged is conducted ethically and according to protocol and that you report fraud or misconduct in research to the appropriate authority

A. Introduction
Section 99A of the Medical Practice Act, 1992 (as amended), provides that the Medical Board may establish a Code of Professional Conduct. The provisions of such a Code are a relevant consideration in

determining what constitutes proper and ethical conduct by a registered medical practitioner.

In August 2003, the Board determined to prepare a Code of Professional Conduct, based on guidelines adopted in February 2000 by the NSW Medical Board entitled "**The duties of a doctor registered with the NSW Medical Board—Good Medical Practice**".

The aim of this Code of Professional Conduct is to set down standards to be observed by medical practitioners in their treatment of patients, their dealings with other practitioners and health care workers and registration and other authorities.

This Code sets out general principles in relation to the practice of medicine. It is not exhaustive, and cannot cover all forms of professional practice or conduct which may bring a practitioner's registration into question.

The Code complements legislation, but is not a substitute for the legislative provisions and case law that have developed in the area and in the event of any doubt, the legislative provisions and case law take precedence.

Guidance on specific issues and areas of practice is contained in a number of policy statements and other documents displayed on the Board's website.

All medical practice requires medical competence and high standards of individual patient care, and adherence to this Code is not alone a guarantee of clinical competence in managing individual patients.

The reasons for a Code of Professional Conduct
Practitioners, patients, employers, medical administrators and other members of the public frequently seek guidance from the NSW Medical Board on issues of ethical conduct for medical practitioners. Each situation needs to be considered on its individual merits with reference to the standards set out in the Code of Professional Conduct—Good Medical Practice—Duties of a Doctor Registered with the NSW Medical Board.

Legislative requirements and the principles set out in case law must be followed when judging the obligations of a practitioner in any given situation.

Breaches of the Medical Practice Act or Regulations may also constitute unsatisfactory professional conduct or professional misconduct.

This Code of Professional Conduct has been developed to assist both practitioners and members of the public to understand the duties of a practitioner registered by the NSW Medical Board in respect of patients, their colleagues and medical authorities.

The Code is based on a set of guidelines adapted with permission from the General Medical Council's (UK) publication Good Medical Practice, in February 2000.

B. Background

The NSW Medical Board was established in 1838 to provide registration for medical practitioners in NSW to ensure only those who had the qualifications, skills and experience to work as medical practitioners in NSW, were registered to do so. It has always been the role of the Board to protect the public. The Medical Practice Act 1992 (as amended) requires that the Board exercise its functions under the Act consistently with the object of the Act to protect the health and safety of the public by providing mechanisms designed to ensure that:

(a) medical practitioners are fit to practise medicine; and (b) medical students are fit to undertake medical studies in clinical placements

Functions of the Board include:
- Promoting and maintaining high standards of medical practice in NSW;
- Advising the Minister on matters relating to the registration of medical practitioners and standards of medical practice;
- Publishing and distributing information concerning the Medical Practice Act to registered medical practitioners and other interested persons; and
- Providing counselling services for registered medical practitioners and medical students

The Board publishes policies and guidelines for practitioners to ensure that medical practice is carried on in NSW such that the public is protected. It does this in the context of NSW's cultural diversity.

The Board works in a system of co-regulation with the Health Care Complaints Commission in dealing with complaints against practitioners. The Board has developed this Code of Professional Code to set out its view regarding proper standards, and to provide clear principles for the determination of complaints against practitioners.

Section 99A of the Medical Practice Act provides that the provisions of this Code of Professional Conduct will be relevant considerations in determining what constitutes proper and ethical conduct by a registered medical practitioner. It is expected that the principles set out in this Code of Professional Conduct will therefore be relevant considerations for the determinations of the Medical Board, the Health Care Complaints Commission and any quasi judicial or judicial body such as the Medical Tribunal or a Professional Standards Committee in dealing with complaints against medical practitioners.

C. Code of Professional Conduct

Key components of ethical medical practice for practitioners are to:
- make the care of the patient your primary concern;
- treat every patient politely and considerately;
- respect patients' dignity and privacy;

- listen to patients and respect their views;
- give patients information in a way they can understand;
- respect the right of patients to be fully involved in decisions about their care;
- keep your professional knowledge and skills up to date;
- recognise the limits of your professional competence;
- respect and protect confidential information;
- make sure that personal beliefs do not prejudice your patients' care;
- act quickly to protect patients from risk if there is good reason to believe that you or a colleague may not be fit to practise;
- not abuse your position as a doctor;
- work with colleagues in ways that best serve patients' interests; and
- be honest and trustworthy.

Standard 1
Clinical Competence/Performance
You must possess and apply adequate knowledge and skill in the practice of medicine.

Clinical Competence / Performance?
1.1 Good clinical care includes:
- an adequate assessment of the patient's condition, based on the history and clinical signs and appropriate examination;
- communicating with patients respectfully and with the assistance of a skilled interpreter where necessary;
- where appropriate, providing or arranging investigations or treatment;
- when necessary, taking suitable and prompt action; and
- when indicated, referring the patient to another practitioner.

1.2 In providing care you should:
- recognise and work within the limits of your clinical competence or supervision when making diagnoses and when giving or arranging treatment;
- be willing to consult colleagues;
- keep clear, accurate and contemporaneous patient records in accordance with the requirements of the Medical Practice Act Regulations 2003, Schedule 2 which deal with the form and contents of medical records.
- keep colleagues well informed when sharing the care of patients;
- pay due regard to effectiveness of care and the use of resources;
- prescribe only the treatment, drugs, or appliances that serve the needs of patients; and
- do your best to provide appropriate treatment in an emergency

1.3 In order to maintain your competence (knowledge and skill) you must:

- participate in educational activities, relevant to your area of practice, which develop and maintain your competence and performance throughout your working life and keep records of the continuing professional development you have undertaken; and
- observe and keep up to date with the laws and codes which affect your work

1.4 In order to maintain your performance you should:

- ensure that you report to authorities where the premises or equipment are inadequate;
- ensure that you do not work excessive hours in order to work safely;
- work with colleagues to monitor and maintain your awareness of the quality of the care you provide;
- take part in regular and systematic medical and clinical audit, and record all data carefully and honestly;
- respond to the results of audit to improve your practice, for example, by undertaking further training; and
- respond constructively to assessments and appraisals of your professional competence and performance.

Standard 2
Professional/Ethical Obligations
You must observe professional and ethical obligations. These include:

- Undertaking education, teaching and training responsibilities;
- Providing honest assessment of the performance of colleagues;
- Maintaining trust with patients through your interaction with patients;
- Putting patients first while putting aside your own personal views;
- Responding appropriately to situations in which a complaint is made about treatment provided by you, or treatment that is unsuccessful;
- Dealing appropriately with the next of kin of deceased patients;
- Arranging appropriate alternative treatment when the doctor/ patient relationship deteriorates;
- Ensuring your professional position is not abused through improper dealings with patients;
- Ensuring that your health does not put patients at risk;
- Ensuring other practitioners do not place patients at risk through their health, behaviour, conduct or performance;
- Reporting adverse events relating to the professional performance or conduct of colleagues; and
- Providing factual information about your services

2.1 Education, Teaching and Training

- You should encourage members of the public to be aware of and understand health issues and contribute to the education and training of other doctors, medical students and colleagues.
- If you have special responsibilities for teaching you should develop the skills, attitudes and practices of a competent teacher.
- You should make sure that students and junior colleagues under your supervision are properly supervised.
- You should be honest and objective when assessing the performance of those you have supervised or trained. Patients may be put at risk if you confirm the competence of someone who has not reached or maintained a satisfactory standard of practice.

2.2 References

- When providing references for colleagues, your comments should be honest and include all relevant information which has a bearing on the colleague's competence, performance, reliability and conduct.

2.3 Maintaining trust with and providing information to patients

Successful relationships between doctors and patients depend on trust. To establish and maintain that trust you should:

- listen to patients and respect their views;
- treat patients politely and considerately;
- respect your patients' privacy and dignity;
- Observe professional boundaries with patients. This includes not engaging in personal relationships or sexual behaviour with patients. *This principle is subject of a specific policy in relation to Sexual Misconduct issued by the NSW Medical Board.*
- treat information about patients as confidential. (There may be circumstances where the public interest requires that confidentiality be breached. You should seek appropriate advice in these circumstances.)
- give patients full information about their condition and treatment, outlining the risks and benefits, and prognosis. You should provide this information to the parent, guardian or person responsible where patients lack the maturity or ability to understand etc.
- give information to patients, parent, guardian or person responsible in a way they can understand;
- wherever possible, check that the patient, parent, guardian or person responsible has understood the information given and the course of action proposed, and that they consent to it, before you provide treatment or investigate a patient's condition;
- respect the right of patients to be fully involved in all decisions about their care;

- respect the right of patients to decline treatment or decline to take part in teaching or research;
- respect the right of patients to a second opinion; and
- be readily accessible to patients and colleagues when you are on duty.

2.4 Putting Patients First

- You should recognise the fundamental role of the patient, parent, guardian or person responsible in decision making about and treatment of the patient
- You should give priority to the investigation and treatment of patients on the basis of clinical need, bearing in mind the needs of other patients.
- The investigations or treatment you provide or arrange should be based on your clinical judgment of the patient's needs and the likely effectiveness. You should not allow your views about a patient's lifestyle, culture, beliefs, race, colour, gender, sexuality, age, religion, social, economic or insurance status, to prejudice the treatment you provide or arrange.
- If you feel that your beliefs might affect the treatment you provide, you should explain this to patients, tell them of their right to see another doctor, and where appropriate, refer them to another doctor.
- You should not refuse or delay treatment because you believe that a patient's actions have contributed to the patient's condition, or because you may be putting yourself at risk. If a patient poses a risk to your health or safety, you may take reasonable steps to protect yourself before investigating their condition or providing treatment.
- You must act in your patient's best interests when making referrals and providing or arranging treatment or care. You must not ask for or accept any inducement, gift or hospitality which may affect or be seen to affect your judgment. You must not offer such inducements to colleagues.

2.5 If Things Go Wrong

Patients who complain about the care or treatment they have received have a right to expect a prompt and appropriate response. You have a professional responsibility to:

- deal with complaints constructively and honestly;
- co-operate with any complaints procedure which applies to your practice;
- ensure that a patient's complaint does not prejudice the care or treatment you provide or arrange for that patient—it may sometimes be wise to arrange an appropriate referral to another doctor;
- act immediately to put matters right, if it is possible, if a patient under your care has suffered serious harm, through misadventure or for any other reason. You should explain fully to the patient

what has happened and the likely short and long-term effects. When appropriate, you should offer an apology. If the patient lacks the maturity to understand what has happened, you should explain the situation honestly to those with parental responsibility for the child. If the patient is cognitively impaired you should provide explanation to the patient's parent, guardian, carer or person responsible;

- co-operate fully with any formal inquiry into the treatment of a patient, subject to appropriate advice from your medical defence organisation. You should not withhold relevant information. Similarly, you must assist the coroner when an inquest or inquiry is held into a patient's death; and
- maintain adequate insurance or professional indemnity cover. The Health Care Liability Act provides that you must not practise medicine unless you hold insurance or are exempt from doing so.

2.6 When a patient dies, you should;
- explain, to the best of your knowledge, the reasons for, and the circumstances of the death to those with parental responsibility, the guardian, carer, patient's partner or next of kin, unless you know that the patient would have objected.

2.7 When the doctor / patient relationship deteriorates, you should:
- do your best to establish and maintain a relationship of trust with your patient. Rarely, there may be circumstances in which you find it necessary to end a professional relationship with a patient and in such cases you should tell the patient why you have made the decision; and
- ensure that arrangements are made quickly for the continuing care of the patient, should you terminate the relationship. You should transfer records or other information to the patient's new doctor on request.

2.8 Abuse of your professional position
You must not abuse your patient's trust. You must not, for example:

- use your position to establish improper personal relationships with patients or their close relatives;
- put pressure on your patients to give or lend money or to provide other benefits to you or other people (this is also dealt with in a separate Guideline concerning financial matters on the Board's website at www.nswmb.org.au)
- improperly disclose or misuse confidential information about patients;
- give patients, or recommend to them, an investigation or treatment which you know is not in their best interests;
- deliberately withhold appropriate investigation, treatment or referral;

- put pressure on patients regarding their insurance status;
- allow anyone who is not a registered doctor to carry out tasks which require the knowledge and skills of a doctor.

You should disclose any pecuniary interest you may have in giving a referral or recommendation to a patient.

2.9 Your duty to protect all patients
In order to protect your patients and the public, you should:

- be vigilant in identifying doctors or other colleagues whose health, conduct, behaviour or performance may be a threat to the public;
- do your best to find out the facts, then, if necessary, notify an appropriate person such as the hospital chief executive or the Medical Board. Your comments about colleagues must be honest. If you are not sure what to do, ask an experienced colleague or contact the Medical Board or your defence organisation for advice. The safety of patients must come first at all times; and
- report adverse events which reflect on the professional performance or conduct of colleagues to a hospital Chief Executive or Medical Board.

2.10 If your own health may put patients at risk
If you have a serious condition which you could pass on to patients, or if your judgment or performance could be significantly affected by a condition or illness, you should:

- take and follow advice from an appropriate medical practitioner on whether, and in what ways, you should modify your practice. Do not rely on your own assessment of the risk to patients; and
- have all the necessary tests and act on the advice given to you by a suitably qualified medical practitioner about necessary treatment and/or modifications to your clinical practice.

If in doubt, you will find more advice on what to do if you believe that you or a colleague (including a medical practitioner for whom you are providing medical care) may be placing patients at risk in, by contacting the Medical Board.

2.11 Providing information about your services
If you publish or broadcast information about services you provide, you must:

- ensure that the information is factual and verifiable;
- provide information in a way that conforms with advertising Regulations under the Medical Practice Act, the Trade Practices Act, and Fair Trading requirements;
- ensure that the information is not false, misleading or deceptive and that it does not create an unjustified expectation of beneficial

treatment or promote the unnecessary or inappropriate use of medical services;
- avoid making claims about the quality of your services or compare your services with those your colleagues provide; and
- not offer guarantees of cures, nor exploit a patient's vulnerability or lack of medical knowledge.

Standard 3
You must ensure that you enjoy a good relationship with all colleagues in health care teams:
- through treating colleagues with respect regardless of your personal views;
- by working constructively with all health care professionals in health care teams;
- by ensuring patient treatment is covered during your own absence or unavailability;
- by ensuring that a patient's care is co-ordinated; and
- by ensuring appropriate delegation and referral of care of a patient.

3.1 Working with colleagues
- You must always treat your colleagues fairly, and in accordance with anti-discrimination laws. You should not allow your views of a colleague's lifestyle, culture, beliefs, race, colour, gender, sexuality, religion or age to prejudice your professional relationship with the colleague.
- You should ensure that students or practitioners under supervision are not abused or harassed.
- You should respect the views of other colleagues even if they differ from your own.
- You must not make any patient doubt the knowledge or skills of colleagues by making unnecessary or unsustainable comments about them.

3.2 Working in teams
Health care is increasingly provided by multi-disciplinary teams, although you remain accountable for your professional conduct and the care you provide. You should:

- work constructively and respect the skills and contributions of all team members;
- ensure optimal communication with other members of the health care team;
- endeavour to resolve disagreement within the team. If you believe that the decision would harm the patient, tell someone who can take action. If necessary, and as a last resort, take action yourself to protect the patient's safety or health. ?If you are a team leader, you should:

- take responsibility for ensuring that the team provides care which is safe, effective and efficient;
- do your best to make sure that the whole team understands the need to provide a polite, responsive and accessible service and to treat patient information as confidential;
- make sure that colleagues understand their role and responsibilities in the team;
- make sure that a cohesive approach is taken when there is an error; and
- work to improve your skills as a team leader.

3.3 Arranging cover
- You should be satisfied that when you are off duty, suitable arrangements are made for your patients' medical care. These arrangements should include effective handover procedures and clear communication between doctors.
- You should satisfy yourself that doctors who stand in for you have the qualifications, experience, knowledge and skills to perform the duties for which they will be responsible.

3.4 Coordinating a patient's care
It is in a patient's best interests for one doctor, usually a general practitioner, to be fully informed about, and responsible for maintaining continuity of a patient's medical care. You should:

- be aware of the range of specialist services available to your patients; and
- actively coordinate a patient's care, or assure yourself that this task is being undertaken by another medical practitioner.

3.5 Delegation and referral
Delegation involves asking a nurse, doctor, medical student or other health care worker to provide treatment or care on your behalf. When you delegate or refer care or treatment you should:
- be sure that the person to whom you delegate or refer is competent to carry out the procedure or provide the therapy involved. You should always pass on all relevant information about the patient's history and current condition; and
- unless the patient objects, tell the referring doctor the results of the investigations, the treatment provided, and any other information necessary for the continuing care of the patient.

Standard 4
You must display proper standards of probity in your professional practice

4.1 Financial and commercial dealings
You must be honest in financial and commercial matters relating to your work. In particular you should:

- tell patients which part of your fee is not covered by a Medicare rebate;
- avoid financial involvement such as loans and investment schemes with patients. There may be a detrimental effect on a therapeutic relationship with a patient if therapeutic and financial aspects in a relationship between a doctor and patient are combined (*see also Guideline concerning financial matters on the Board's website at www.nswmb.org.au*)

4.2 Financial interests in hospitals, nursing homes and other medical organisations
- If you have financial or commercial interests in organisations providing health care or in pharmaceutical or other biomedical companies, these must not affect the way you prescribe for, treat or refer patients.
- If you have a financial or commercial interest in an organisation or hospital to which you plan to refer a patient for treatment or investigation, you must tell the patient about such interest.

4.3 Accepting gifts or other inducements
- You must not ask for or accept any material gifts or loans from companies that sell or market drugs or appliances.
- You must not ask for or accept fees for agreeing to meet sales representatives.

4.4 Signing certificates and other documents
Registered medical practitioners have the authority to sign a variety of documents, such as death certificates and sickness certificates, on the assumption that they will only sign statements they believe to be true.

- You must take reasonable steps to verify any statement before you sign a document.
- You must not sign documents which you believe to be false or misleading.

4.5 Research
If you take part in clinical drug trials or other research involving patients or volunteers, you should:

- ensure that the research protocol has been approved by a properly constituted research ethics committee;
- conduct all research with honesty and integrity;
- ensure that the individual has given informed, written consent to take part in the trial;

- ensure that the research is not contrary to the individual's interests;
- seek advice where your research involves children or adults who are not able to make decisions for themselves;
- follow all aspects of the research protocol;
- accept only those payments approved by a research ethics committee; and
- report evidence of fraud or misconduct in research to an appropriate person or authority.

index

Abortion
  defence of necessity, [14.520]
  early English precedent, [14.455]
  foetus capable of independent life,
    [14.525]
  law regarding, [14.445]
  legislation, [14.485]
    Australian Capital Territory, [14.515]
    New South Wales, [14.470]
    Northern Territory, [14.495]
    Queensland, [14.500]
    South Australia, [14.490]
    Tasmania, [14.510]
    Victoria, [14.465]
  pregnancy, stage of, [14.525]
  rights of others, [14.545]
  special medical procedure, [5.220]
  spouse, consent of, [5.210]
  third parties, rights of, [14.545]
  unlawfulness, [14.450]
    New South Wales, [14.470]
    Victoria, [14.465]
  who may carry out, [14.520]

Accident
  patients, involving, [11.05]

Addiction
  drugs of
    prescription of, [13.85]
    provision of, [12.150]-[12.155]

Adjudicative tribunals, [2.110]

Adults
  incapacity *see* **Incapacity**
  special medical treatment, [5.445]

Advance directives
  access to, [5.290]

common law, [5.260]
difficulties arising in relation to, [5.285]
future incapacity, [5.255]
general, [5.265]
jurisdictions giving legislative effect to,
  [5.270], [14.340]
legislation, [5.270], [14.340], [14.415]
life-saving treatment, refusal of,
  [5.255], [5.285]
living will, as, [5.255]
no advance directive made, [14.345]
psychiatric treatment not covered by,
  [5.280]
recording of, [5.290]
refusal of treatment agreed to in,
  [5.275]
specific, [5.265]
triggering event, [5.265]
validity, [5.255]

Adverse events
  communication and, [6.25]
  honest expression of regret, [6.25]
  preventable, [6.15]

Affirmative action
  federal legislation, [18.205]
  State and Territory legislation, [18.285]

Aged persons
  nursing homes, inspection of, [18.200]
  quality care principles, [18.200]
  rights of, [18.200]
  special consideration for, [18.200]
  user rights principles, [18.200]

Agents, [6.800]
  principal and, [10.35]

AIDS *see* **HIV/AIDS**

Emergency wards — *continued*
reasonable care, [6.535]
triage nurses, [6.525]

Employees
carrying out orders with reasonable
care, [10.60]
directions of employer, obeying, [10.50]
discipline of, [10.120]
disclosure of information by
confidential information, [10.65]
employer, to, [10.75]
duties, range of, [10.50]
health and safety responsibilities,
[10.80], [11.40]
implied undertakings, [10.50]
independent contractors, distinguished,
[6.775], [6.780], [10.10]
property of employer, taking reasonable
care of, [10.70]
refusal to work, [10.55]
responsibilities of, [6.760]
safety, role in, [10.80], [11.40]
serving employer faithfully, [10.65]
who is, [6.775]

Employers
contribution, [6.810]
discipline of employees, [10.120]
disclosure of information to, by
employees, [10.75]
implied undertakings, [10.85]
indemnity, [6.810]
information requested by, [7.345]
legal obligations to, [19.80]
responsibilities of, [6.760]
safety of employees, [10.95]-[10.115],
[11.35]
standard of medical treatment,
employees denigrating, [10.65]
vicarious liability, [6.765]
wages, payment of, [10.90]

Employment
activities in the course of, [6.805]
basic conditions of, [10.135]
contract of service, [10.05]
conduct of parties changing nature
of, [10.145]
features, [10.10]
unfair, [10.145]
control test, [6.780], [10.10]

hospitals, by, [6.780]
implied terms, [10.45], [10.135]
indicia of, [10.10]
multi-facet test, [6.780]
organisation test, [6.780]
tests to determine, [6.780], [10.10]

Employment discrimination
exceptions in federal law, [18.105]
overview, [18.85]-[18.95]
Workplace Relations Act 1996 (Cth),
[18.100]

End-of-life decision-making, [14.240]

English courts, [2.130]

Enterprise agreements
terms and conditions in, [10.135]

Equity
equitable remedies, [1.80]
principles of, [1.80]

Ethics
autonomy, [19.85]
beneficence, [19.85]
best ethical option, determining,
[19.85]
choice between conflicting duties,
[19.85]
codes of ethics, [7.160], [19.30], [19.35]
consequences, considering, [19.115]-
[19.130]
decision-making dilemmas, dealing
with, [19.40]-[19.85], [19.115]
disclosing information, [19.55]-[19.70]
ethic of care, [19.85]
ethical decision-making process,
[19.10]
ethical dilemmas, [19.40]-[19.85]
ethical (duty) statements, [19.90]
duty statement, [19.110]
expressive statement, [19.95]
prescriptive statement, [19.105]
value statement, [19.100]
ethical principles, [4.05], [19.05]
ethically questionable activities, [19.30]
examples of ethical dilemmas, [19.135]
first-order principles, [19.85]
giving information, guidelines as to,
[4.280]

Negligence — *continued*
elements of action for, [6.30]
incidence of medical litigation, [6.20]
incompetence, distinguished, [6.10]
joint liability, [6.930]
lack of information as ground for,
    [4.275], [6.435]
    causation, [4.415]
legislative reform, [6.10]
limitation period, [6.825]
multiple tortfeasors, [6.930]
personal liability, [6.765]
professional, [6.10]
reporting colleague who has acted
    negligently, [19.05]
standard of care *see* **Standard of care**
tort, [6.10]
vicarious liability, [6.765]

Nervous shock *see* **Psychological harm**

Non-delegable duties, [6.770]

Non-maleficence, [19.85]

Noscitur a sociis, [3.85]

Not for resuscitation orders
law relating to, [5.170], [14.425]

Notifiable disease
authorities, powers of, [16.40]
discrimination against those with,
    [16.105]
examples of, [16.15]
freedom of individual and protection of
    others, [16.10]
health carers, role of, [16.30]
infectious diseases *see* **Infectious
    diseases**
information that must be given, [16.35]
legislation, [16.10]
sexually transmitted diseases *see*
    Sexually transmitted diseases
State, role of, [16.10]
who must report, [16.25]

Novus actus interveniens, [6.885]

Nurses
code of ethics for, [19.35]
expanded health care practice, [6.580]
more staff, requests for, [6.460]
primary care tasks, [6.580]
registration of nurse practitioners,
    [12.55]

appeals, [12.70]
New South Wales, [12.60]
Victoria, [12.65]
triage nurses, [6.525]
whistleblowers, [6.460]

Nursing homes
inspection of, [18.200]

Obiter dicta, [3.115]

Occupational health and safety
default notices, [11.65]
employers, duties of, [11.35]
health and safety representatives,
    [11.50]
    protection of, [11.70]
immediate threats to health and safety,
    [11.60]
inspectorate, [11.75]
joint staff-management committees,
    [11.55]
    protection of members, [11.70]
overview, [11.30]
prosecution, [11.80]
workers
    protection of, [11.70]
    responsibilities, [10.80], [11.40]

Occupier
community health carers, [11.265]
duty of care to those on property,
    [6.255]
health facilities, [11.270]
liability for accidents, [11.250]
standard of care, [11.260]
who is, [11.255]

Offences
indictable, [3.35]
summary, [3.30]

Original jurisdiction, [2.60]

Ova
transfer of, [17.10]

Palliative care, [14.425]

Parens patriae jurisdiction, [4.200],
    [5.100], [5.115]
incompetent adults, [5.165]
refusal of treatment by parents, [5.140]

Parenthood
posthumous, [17.185]